The Post-traumatic Theatre of Grotowski and Kantor

Advance Reviews

"A brilliant cross-disciplinary comparative analysis that joins a new path in theatre studies, revitalizing the artistic heritage of two great twentieth-century masters: Tadeusz Kantor and Jerzy Grotowski."

—*Professor Antonio Attisani, Department of Humanities, University of Turin*

"Among the landmarks of postwar avant-garde theatre, two Polish works stand out: Grotowski's *Akropolis* and Kantor's *Dead Class*. Magda Romanska scrupulously corrects misconceptions about these crucial works, bringing to light linguistic elements ignored by Anglophone critics and an intense engagement with the Holocaust very often overlooked by their Polish counterparts. This is vital and magnificently researched theatre scholarship, at once alert to history and to formal experiment. Romanska makes two pieces readers may think they know newly and urgently legible."

—*Martin Harries, author of "Forgetting Lot's Wife: On Destructive Spectatorship,"*
University of California, Irvine

"As someone who teaches and researches in the areas of Polish film and theatre – and European theatre/theatre practice/translation more broadly – I was riveted by the book. I couldn't put it down. There is no such extensive comparative study of the work of the two practitioners that offers a sustained and convincing argument for this. The book is 'leading edge.' Romanska has the linguistic and critical skills to develop the arguments in question and the political contexts are in general traced at an extremely sophisticated level. This is what lends the writing its dynamism."

—*Dr Teresa Murjas, Director of Postgraduate Research, Department of Film,*
Theatre and Television, University of Reading

"This is a lucidly and even beautifully written book that convincingly argues for a historically and culturally contextualized understanding of Grotowski's and Kantor's performances. It should be required reading in any introduction to performance and theater studies course. I am convinced that this will not only be the book on each of the two directors but also and especially the only one that manages to develop a framework allowing a discussion of both men and their performances together. In other words, this will be the book on the subject the author set out to explore. It's very rare that one can say that about any book!"

—*Dr Anne Rothe, Department of Classical and Modern Languages,*
Literatures, and Cultures, Wayne State University

"In this authoritative study of two masterworks of twentieth-century theatre, Magda Romanska does more than offer astute close readings. Prying open the suffocating embrace of universalism in which Grotowski and Kantor have long been held, she restores their literary, historical, national, and aesthetic contexts. Thanks to her, two of the world's most influential, important and celebrated theatre artists will no longer also be among the least understood."

—*Professor Alisa Solomon, Director, Arts and Culture MA Program,*
Graduate School of Journalism, Columbia University

"Every page speaks volumes to the breadth of Romanska's readings and the number of sources she has used to bring both works into their multiple contexts. From the perspective of its potential use as course material, the in-depth exploration of some of the links that have been missing in Western criticism and scholarship is particularly valuable."

—*Professor Tamara Trojanowska, Department of Slavic*
Languages and Literature, University of Toronto

The Post-traumatic Theatre of Grotowski and Kantor

History and Holocaust in *Akropolis* and *The Dead Class*

MAGDA ROMANSKA

ANTHEM PRESS
LONDON • NEW YORK • DELHI

Anthem Press
An imprint of Wimbledon Publishing Company
www.anthempress.com

This edition first published in UK and USA 2014
by ANTHEM PRESS
75–76 Blackfriars Road, London SE1 8HA, UK
or PO Box 9779, London SW19 7ZG, UK
and
244 Madison Ave. #116, New York, NY 10016, USA

First published in hardback by Anthem Press in 2012

Copyright © Magda Romanska 2014

The author asserts the moral right to be identified as the author of this work.
All rights reserved. Without limiting the rights under copyright reserved above,
no part of this publication may be reproduced, stored or introduced into
a retrieval system, or transmitted, in any form or by any means
(electronic, mechanical, photocopying, recording or otherwise),
without the prior written permission of both the copyright
owner and the above publisher of this book.

British Library Cataloguing-in-Publication Data
A catalogue record for this book is available from the British Library.

Library of Congress Cataloging-in-Publication Data
The Library of Congress has catalogued the hardcover edition as follows:
Romanska, Magda.
The post-traumatic theatre of Grotowski and Kantor : history and
Holocaust in Akropolis and The dead class / Magda Romanska.
pages cm
Includes bibliographical references and index.
ISBN 978-0-85728-516-4 (hardback : alk. paper)
1. Grotowski, Jerzy, 1933–1999–Criticism and interpretation. 2.
Kantor, Tadeusz, 1915–1990–Criticism and interpretation. 3.
Holocaust, Jewish (1939–1945), in art. 4.
Theater–Poland–History–20th century. 5. Experimental theater. I.
Title.
PN2859.P66R66 2012
792'.0233'092–dc23
2012041201

ISBN-13: 978 1 78308 321 3 (Pbk)
ISBN-10: 1 78308 321 2 (Pbk)

This title is also available as an ebook.

CONTENTS

Foreword by Kathleen Cioffi   vii
Preface   xi
Acknowledgments   xiii
List of Illustrations   xv

Introduction   1

Part I   Our Auschwitz: Grotowski's *Akropolis*

Chapter 1	Jerzy Grotowski: A Very Short Introduction	49
Chapter 2	Native Son: Grotowski in Poland	57
Chapter 3	Grotowski: The Polish Context	62
Chapter 4	Grotowski, the Messiah: Coming to America	73
Chapter 5	The Making of an Aura	82
Chapter 6	On Not Knowing Polish	86
Chapter 7	"In Poland: That is to Say, Nowhere"	90
Chapter 8	*Akropolis*/Necropolis	93
Chapter 9	The Vision and the Symbol	95
Chapter 10	"This Drama as Drama Cannot Be Staged"	104
Chapter 11	Two National Sacrums	107
Chapter 12	"Hollow Sneering Laughter": Mourning the Columbuses	111
Chapter 13	Against Heroics	119
Chapter 14	Representing the Unrepresentable	122
Chapter 15	Trip to the Museum	126
Chapter 16	Bearing the Unbearable	129
Chapter 17	The Living and the Dead	136
Chapter 18	Jacob's Burden	141
Chapter 19	The Final Descent	147
Chapter 20	Textual Transpositions	150
Chapter 21	*Akropolis* After Grotowski	152
Illustrations		157

Part II Our Memory: Kantor's *Dead Class*

Chapter 22	Tadeusz Kantor: A Very Short Introduction	185
Chapter 23	*Dead Class*: The Making of the Legend	193
Chapter 24	*Dead Class* in Poland	196
Chapter 25	The Polish History Lesson	199
Chapter 26	*Dead Class* Abroad	201
Chapter 27	On Not Knowing Polish, Again	204
Chapter 28	The Visual and the Puerile	209
Chapter 29	The National and the Transnational	212
Chapter 30	Witkiewicz's Tumor	215
Chapter 31	An Age of Genius: Bruno Schulz and the Return to Childhood	229
Chapter 32	Conversing with Gombrowicz: The Dead, the Funny, the Sacred and the Profane	238
Chapter 33	Panirony: "A pain with a smile and a shrug"	244
Chapter 34	Raising the Dead	252
Chapter 35	*Dead Class* as Kaddish…	256
Chapter 36	*Dead Class* as *Dybbuk*, or the Absence	260
Chapter 37	The Dead and the Marionettes	262
Chapter 38	Men and Objects	267
Chapter 39	*Dead Class* as *Forefathers' Eve*	274
Chapter 40	*Dead Class*: The Afterlife	280
Postscript		283
Appendix		
	Table 1. Chronology of Events	286
	Table 2. Comparison between Wyspiański's *Akropolis* and *Genesis*	289
	Table 3. Comparison between Grotowski and Kantor	291
Notes		293
Bibliography		363
Index		389

FOREWORD

Kathleen Cioffi

This book unpacks the multiple layers of meaning in two of the most acclaimed theatre productions of the twentieth century: Jerzy Grotowski's *Akropolis* and Tadeusz Kantor's *Umarła klasa* [*The Dead Class*]. We not only get an unusually informed close reading of Grotowski's and Kantor's masterworks, but also one that situates these productions and their creators firmly in their literary, historical and political contexts. Too often, non-Polish theatre historians and critics, as Romanska points out, ignore the Polish aspects of Grotowski's and Kantor's theatres and construct their own deracinated meanings, while declaring that their inability to understand Polish does not matter. Meanwhile, Polish theatre historians and critics have often ignored the Jewish aspects of these productions, in part because it was once politically dangerous not to do so. *The Post-traumatic Theatre of Grotowski and Kantor* reclaims both the Polishness and the Jewishness of Grotowski's and Kantor's *chefs-d'œuvre*.

In the case of Grotowski, his own compatriots rejected his work early on, in part because his adaptations of the much-loved classics of Polish Romantic and neo-Romantic dramatic literature often conflicted with what the texts were meant to say. As early as 1958, Grotowski approvingly quoted Vsevelod Meyerhold in program notes for an early production: "To choose a play doesn't necessarily mean that one needs to agree with its author."[1] This attitude when applied to Polish classics amounted to blasphemy – for Polish intellectuals a much worse blasphemy than the explicitly anti-Catholic mockery of Grotowski's productions. Still, one of the primary sources of Grotowski's artistry was what Romanska calls "the Polish national canon": that is, the Polish Romantics and the neo-Romantic Stanisław Wyspiański. Only someone who was deeply steeped in knowledge of these Polish classics (not to mention in knowledge of Catholic dogma) could blaspheme against them as thoroughly as Grotowski did. However, this led to a situation where for many years Grotowski's work was only esteemed by those who did not fully understand it.

With Kantor, things were just the opposite. Polish critics generally valued his aesthetic in a way that they did not value Grotowski's. In fact, Kantor was praised for being not self-consciously avant-garde, not pompous, and not incapable of laughing at himself – in other words, for not being Grotowski. Foreigners also lauded Kantor, but they were introduced to him much later in his career than they were to Grotowski: Kantor's troupe, Cricot 2, started appearing abroad only in the 1970s, over 20 years after they first started performing in Cracow, whereas Grotowski's Laboratory Theatre had already had their heyday both in Poland and in the West by the end of the 1960s. Moreover, where Grotowski has had a huge influence abroad, Kantor remains to this day much less known outside of Poland.

The difference in the Polish reception of the two directors' work can in part be chalked up to politics. In order to do the work that he wanted to do, Grotowski practiced what Seth Baumrin has called "ketmanship," meaning the art of paying lip service to the powerful while being secretly opposed to them.[2] For example, Grotowski joined the Communist Party, and he even insisted that his actors become members, so that if the powers-that-be wanted to liquidate the theatre, they would be dissolving a party cell. Although this tactic, and other skillful manipulations of the political apparatus, did indeed gain the Laboratory Theatre a measure of artistic freedom, Grotowski was perceived by many fellow Poles as someone who collaborated with the regime. Kantor, on the other hand, not only refused to collaborate, but he also managed to establish Cricot 2 completely independent of the system for state subsidies for theatre and art – not an easy task in communist Poland. Moreover, Kantor was respected as a member of the heroic generation who actually took part in underground activities during World War II, while Grotowski was still a child during the war.

Politics also influenced the Polish acknowledgment, or lack thereof, of Jewish content in the works of both Grotowski and Kantor. As Romanska amply illustrates, Polish critics and audiences found Kantor's evocation of the now lost, mixed Jewish and Catholic world of his childhood village in *The Dead Class* deeply moving, but did not mention the Jewish imagery that causes it to be affecting. In Grotowski's case, in his stagings of two Wyspiański plays, *Akropolis* (first version, 1962) and *Studium o Hamlecie* [A Study of Hamlet] (1964), both were given Jewish slants: Grotowski's *Akropolis* was set in Auschwitz, and his Hamlet was a Jew. Although *Studium o Hamlecie* never officially premiered, both Polish theatre historians and Laboratory Theatre actors have suggested that it would never have passed censorship because of its depiction of the royal court as communist authorities persecuting the Jewish Hamlet. And, although *Akropolis* had a better reception than most of Grotowski's productions, Grotowski was still considered to have blasphemed against both the Polish and Jewish "national sacrums" by portraying Auschwitz prisoners as non-heroes.[3]

The differing foreign and Polish responses to Grotowski and Kantor can also be attributed to the fact that, whereas Grotowski was always more interested in transmitting his working methods than he was in creating productions, Kantor's interests lay in expressing his own artistic vision. Theatre historian Andrzej Żurowski writes that Kantor's theatre "is a 'separate theatre,' a 'lonely theatre,' around which one can see no meaningful movement, school, or following."[4] Grotowski, on the other hand, generated a stream of followers, both in Poland and abroad. These followers, whom I have elsewhere characterized as inhabiting an artistic territory that I call "Grotland,"[5] are influenced by various stages of Grotowski's work, from the theatrical period that Romanska deals with here (the so-called Theatre of Productions phase) through the Paratheatre, Theatre of Sources, Objective Drama, and Art as Vehicle phases. They range from people who worked directly with Grotowski during one or another of these phases (e.g. Helena Guardia and Nicolás Núñez, of the Taller de Investigación Teatral UNAM in Mexico) to people who worked with collaborators of Grotowski's (e.g. Jarosław Fret of Teatr ZAR, and the Grotowski Institute in Poland). They emphasize various strands of Grotowski's work in their own productions, whether it be the physical exercises that Grotowski developed with the Laboratory Theatre actors, or the ancient songs that he explored with Thomas Richards and Mario Biagini at the Workcenter of Jerzy Grotowski in Italy. As director Richard Schechner writes, "Grotowski's influence and importance is deep, wide, abiding, and growing."[6] Through the work of Schechner, Richards, Biagini, Fret, and other Grotlanders all over the world, this Grotowski influence shows no sign of abating.

However, although Żurowski's point about Kantor's "separateness" is well taken, and he certainly cannot be said to have established any kind of movement or school, his influence – both on theatre practitioners and performance artists within and outside Poland – has not been negligible. For example, in a 2011 blog entry about the Warsaw production of Tadeusz Słobodzianek's play *Nasza klasa* [*Our Class*], director Blanka Zizka writes that she noticed "that the set [was] purposefully reminiscent of Tadeusz Kantor's famous production of *Dead Class*."[7] Moreover, in October 2011 at New York's Martin E. Segal Theatre Center, in a meeting with Krzysztof Garbaczewski and Marcin Cecko, two representatives of the newest generation of Polish theatre artists, the young men claimed Kantor as an inspiration, particularly for their productions *Odyssey* and *The Sexual Life of Savages*. And in an upcoming issue of *Polish Theatre Perspectives*, artists as diverse as the American Robert Wilson, the Italian Romeo Castellucci and the Belgian Jan Fabre, among others, write pieces about what Kantor has meant to them.[8] Although Michal Kobialka – in a session on Grotowski and Kantor that I attended at New York University – lamented that Kantor was unlikely to be celebrated during the anniversary of his death in 2010 with anything like the number of lectures, conferences, panel discussions and theatre festivals held in celebration of Grotowski during the Year of Grotowski in 2009, Kantor is perhaps no longer as lonely as he once seemed to be.

Since fascination with both Grotowski and Kantor continues to grow, this book is all the more welcome. Romanska shows that *Akropolis* and *Dead Class* are more than just impressive displays of Grotowski's "dialectics of apotheosis and derision" and Kantor's iconoclastic imagery. They are works rooted in and inspired by other works of Polish literature: the intertextuality between the source texts and Grotowski's and Kantor's uses of them in part shapes the meanings of *Akropolis* and *Dead Class*. Romanska's descriptions of the works of Wyspiański and Tadeusz Borowski that inspired *Akropolis*, and the works of Witold Gombrowicz and Bruno Schulz that inspired *Dead Class*, are therefore crucially important for us to be aware of. Similarly, Romanska demonstrates how various other historical, political, and personal factors played into the devising of these performances, as well their reception. Grotowski and Kantor are two of the most significant theatre artists of the twentieth century; this book untangles the strands of meaning in their work in a most impressive way, and thus helps us to fully understand their achievement.

PREFACE

One of the challenges of this project has been to combine all of the disciplinary discourses – from Slavic studies, history, critical theory, and theatre and performance studies. As each field has its own history and disciplinary vocabulary that evolved *vis-à-vis* its own social, cultural, political and historical circumstances, the challenge is to bridge their semantic fields, focusing on "historical norms of comprehension, about which we know so little, and to which interpretation owes so much."[9] The challenge was also to balance the varied levels of subject expertise that each discipline brings; for Slavic studies scholars, mentioning the production history of Mickiewicz's *Forefathers' Eve* might seem a nuisance, but for the general performance studies scholars, who teach Grotowski and Kantor in avant-garde directing courses, it might be the first time they hear Mickiewicz's name. At the same time, while discussing formal aspects of Grotowski's and Kantor's works might seem for performance studies scholars a useless exercise, Slavicists might not be familiar with the theoretical battles that transpired around the critical and scholarly reception of these two works. Such is also the case with the historical context; many theatre scholars are unfamiliar with the complexity of political maneuvers around Poland, particularly during and after World War II, which affect Polish–Jewish relations and the representation of Polish Jews. Likewise, it was a balancing act to create a dialogue between American and Polish scholars, native speakers and those who don't speak the language, as each group and subgroup develops its own discourse and its own history. The fourth challenge was to contextualize both works without reducing their universal appeal, mindful of Kantor's dictum that "theatre needs to be universal to be national."[10] In scholarship, the two are not, and should not be, mutually exclusive. Finally, the most difficult aspect of the project was navigating even-handedly the political controversies that surround both works, in Poland and abroad, as they channel past and concurrent political currents, both global and local, leaving behind them the equally dense legacy of their afterlives.

In the great battle between Kantor and Grotowski, like most Poles, I started at first in Kantor's camp. My interest in Grotowski evolved much later, as I became aware of his stature among American theatre practitioners and scholars. In a sense – and not surprisingly, considering Grotowski's own methodology – my research on Grotowski became a form of search into my own native context. It's always strange to find yourself in the position of both anthropologist and native informer. This book is dedicated to all my American colleagues, who have patiently tolerated my halting responses to their questions about Polish history and culture, which are so often convoluted, but who have also always sensed that there is something left unspoken in our casual conversations over coffee. I owe them all immense gratitude and debt.

ACKNOWLEDGMENTS

This project started modestly as a paper presented at a panel on Stanisław Wyspiański, organized by the Slavic studies group at the Modern Language Association Conference in Chicago in 2007. For that reason alone, I need to first thank John Merchant for inviting me to the panel, and my co-panelists, Jessie Labov and Colleen McQuillen, for their very first words of encouragement. The revised paper then was published in *Theatre Survey* 50, no. 2 (2009) winning the American Society for Theatre Research 2010 Gerald Kahan Scholar's prize for the "Best Essay Written and Published in English in a Refereed Scholarly Journal." I would like to thank Martin Puchner, Catherine Cole, Kate Babbitt and Jonathan Geffner of *Theatre Survey*, and the Gerald Kahan selection committee, Sarah Bay-Cheng, Vera Foster, Barry Witham and Mary Trotter, for their faith in the project. In 2011, the same essay won the Aquila Polonica from the Polish Studies Association, and I have Brian Porter-Szucs to thank for his encouragement and support.

I also express my special gratitude to the Emerson College, Linda Moore, Richard Zauft, the Faculty Advancement Fund Grant Committee, and Robert and Judy Huret, whose grant made my research travel possible. My deepest gratitude also goes to my mentors, Martin Puchner and Elinor Fuchs, whose feedback and support throughout the years have been essential for this project. I would also like to thank my mentors and colleagues: Jonathan Culler, David Krasner, David Bathrick, Laurence Senelick, Melia Bensussen, Martin Harries, Jeffrey Rusten, Maureen Shea, Larry Switzky, Tom Kingdon, Kris Salata, Kermit Dunkelberg, Joanna Nizynska, Tamara Trojanowska, Hanna Musiol, Sara Warner, Harvey Young, Matthew Smith, and Dassia Posner. Special thanks also are due to my colleagues from the writing workshop at the Mellon School of Theatre and Performance Research at Harvard University, especially Heidi Bean, Bertie Ferdman, John Muse, Holly Maples, Corey Frost, Nikki Cesare, and Sasha Colby for their insightful comments and suggestions.

I would also like to express my heartfelt gratitude to all the librarians and archivists for their thoughtfulness and generosity. I would like to especially thank the librarians Cynthia Hinds, Eugenia Dimant and Joanna Epstein from the Harvard Widener Library in Cambridge; Marty Seeger, Melissa Camaiore and Erica Schattle from the Emerson College Library in Boston; Anna Halczak, Paulina Strojnowska, Bogdan Renczynski, Malgorzata Paluch-Cybulska, and Natalia Zarzecka from the Cricoteka Centre for the Documentation of the Art of Tadeusz Kantor in Cracow; Adela Karsznia-Karpowicz, Aneta Kurek, Sylwia Fijalkiewicz, and Grzegorz Ziółkowski from The Grotowski Institute in Wrocław; Emilia Tomasik from the Literature Museum in Warsaw; Lukasz

Ossowski from the Literary Institute in Warsaw; Magdalena Świszczowska- Piegdoń from the National Museum in Cracow; Diana Poskuta from the Słowacki Theatre in Cracow; Tatiana Drzycimska from Teatr Współczesny in Wrocław; Wojciech Płosa from the Auschwitz-Birkenau Museum Archives; Rudolf A. Haunschmied from the Gusen Memorial Committee; Carroll Wandell from the United States Holocaust Museum; and David Goldfarb, Monika Fabijanska, and Agata Grenda of the Polish Cultural Institute in New York.

Last, but not least, I would also like to thank my assistants Andie Anderson and Emma Futhey and my editor Kristen Ebert-Wagner, whose help was always invaluable and deeply appreciated; our Emerson staff, Jason Allen and Siouxanna Ramirez-Cruz, whose presence alone has always been vital.

LIST OF ILLUSTRATIONS

Cover, left	The body of a Soviet prisoner of war who committed suicide on an electrified barbed-wire fence in Mauthausen concentration camp. Tuesday, 1 September 1942–Thursday, 1 October 1942, Mauthausen, [Upper Austria] Austria. Courtesy of National Archives and Records Administration, College Park, MD. Bildarchiv Preussischer Kulturbesitz Dokumentationsarchiv des Oesterreichischen Widerstandes Yad Vashem Photo Archives.
Cover, right	*Akropolis*, 1963, dir. Jerzy Grotowski, set design by Józef Szajna, PBL Episode 207: Polish Lab Theater (1969). Courtesy of WNET.
Figures 1, 3, 5, 6	*Akropolis*, 1963, dir. Jerzy Grotowski, set design by Józef Szajna – The prisoners building the crematorium. Courtesy of The Grotowski Institute.
Figures 2, 4	Auschwitz crematorium. 2010. Photo by Bill Huston. Courtesy of the photo author.
Figure 7	Characteristic dead face of the *Muselmann*, with expressive, shiny eyes. Photo reprinted from André Leroy and Maximilian Attila, *Le deportation* (Paris: Le Patriote Résistant, 1968), inside cover. Author of the photograph unknown.
Figures 8, 9	Actors' masks for *Akropolis*, 1963. *Akropolis*, dir. Jerzy Grotowski, set design by Józef Szajna. Courtesy of The Grotowski Institute.
Figures 10, 11	*Akropolis*, 1963, dir. Jerzy Grotowski, set design by Józef Szajna. PBL Episode 207: Polish Lab Theater (1969). Courtesy of WNET.
Figure 12	A cart laden with the bodies of prisoners. Saturday, 5 May 1945–Saturday, 12 May 1945. Gusen, [Upper Austria] Austria. Photo by Sam Gilbert. National Archives and Records Administration, College Park Time/Life Syndication United States Holocaust Memorial Museum. Courtesy of Bud Tullin, Harold Royall and Stephen Adalman.
Figure 13	Corpses are piled on a cart in the Gusen concentration camp. Saturday, 5 May 1945–Thursday, 10 May 1945. Gusen, [Upper Austria] Austria. United States Holocaust Memorial Museum. Courtesy of Eugene S. Cohen.

Figure 14	*Akropolis*, 1963, dir. Jerzy Grotowski, set design by Józef Szajna. PBL Episode 207: Polish Lab Theater (1969). Courtesy of WNET.
Figure 15	Corpses at Mauthausen concentration camp. Liberation scene at Mauthausen. 1945. Mauthausen, [Upper Austria] Austria. Photo by Donald Dean. Courtesy of Center for Holocaust and Genocide Studies, University of Minnesota.
Figure 16	*I Shall Never Return*, 1988, dir. Tadeusz Kantor. Photo by Tommaso Lepera. Courtesy of the photo author.
Figure 17	View of a cart laden with the bodies of prisoners who perished in the Gusen concentration camp. Saturday, 5 May 1945–Saturday, 12 May 1945. Gusen, [Upper Austria] Austria. United States Holocaust Memorial Museum. Courtesy of Benjamin Ferencz.
Figure 18	Corpses at Auschwitz concentration camp. Courtesy of the Holocaust Research Project. <www.holocaustresearchproject.org>
Figure 19	Survivors and piles of corpses in the Gusen concentration camp. Saturday, 5 May 1945–Saturday, 10 May 1945. Gusen, [Upper Austria] Austria. United States Holocaust Memorial Museum. Courtesy of Benjamin Ferencz.
Figure 20	*I Shall Never Return*, 1988, dir. Tadeusz Kantor. Photo by Tommaso Lepera. Courtesy of the photo author.
Figure 21	*Let the Artists Die*, 1984, dir. Tadeusz Kantor – Final Emballage. The Last Work of Master Veit Stoss: Barricade. Photo by Witold Górka. Courtesy of Dorota Krakowska and Cricoteka.
Figures 22, 24	Auschwitz, pile of suitcases left by the victims. Courtesy of Auschwitz-Birkenau Museum.

ARTIST WANDERER
EXTERNAL EXILE
having neither home nor a place of his own,
looking in vain for a heaven,
never parting with his luggage,
in which there rest
all his hopes, illusions,
their treasure
and fiction,
which he jealously guards
to the end against intolerance
and indifference

—Tadeusz Kantor, *Actor's Predicament*[1]

---

1 Tadeusz Kantor, "Actor's Predicament." In Andrzej Wełmiński "The Grand Emballage of the Late 20th Century: Reconstruction of the emballage from the spectacle by Tadeusz Kantor 'I Shall Never Return.'" Exhibition catalogue, trans. Marta Orczykowska (Cracow: Polish Institute, Drukarnia Narodowa 1972), 22.

LIST OF ILLUSTRATIONS xvii

Figure 23	Emballage, 1961, drawing by Tadeusz Kantor. Courtesy of Dorota Krakowska and Cricoteka, Centre for the Documentation of the Art of Tadeusz Kantor.
Figure 25	Jew Wanderer [Hajduk i Żyd]. Drawing from Kazimierz Władysław Wójcicki and Wincenty Smokowski, *Obrazy Starodawne* [Pictures from Olden Days] (Warsaw: G. Sennewald, 1843), 108.
Figure 26	Tadeusz Kantor's Artist Wanderer. Photo by Konrad Pollesch. Courtesy of the photo author.
Figures 27, 28	*Kurka wodna* (*The Water Hen*; 1967). Photo by Jacek Stoklosa. Courtesy of the photo author.
Figure 29	Costume design for *Kurka wodna* (*The Water Hen*; 1967), dir. Tadeusz Kantor. Courtesy of Dorota Krakowska, and Cricoteka, Centre for the Documentation of the Art of Tadeusz Kantor.
Figures 30–33	Prisoners arriving at Auschwitz concentration camp. Courtesy of Auschwitz-Birkenau Museum.
Figure 34	Costume for Absent Old Man. *Dead Class*, 1975. Photo by Piotr Oleś. Courtesy of the photo author.

> The Absent Old Man
> I call him THE MAIN IDEA
> The basis for the entire spectacle.
> —Tadeusz Kantor[2]

Figure 35	Design drawing for *The Country House*, 1961, dir. Tadeusz Kantor. Closet. People as Coats on the Hangers. Courtesy of Dorota Krakowska and Cricoteka, Centre for the Documentation of the Art of Tadeusz Kantor.
Figure 36	*Dainty Shapes and Hairy Apes*, 1973, dir. Tadeusz Kantor. Coatroom. Exhibit "Tadeusz Kantor od *Małego dworku* do *Umarłej klasy*" [Tadeusz Kantor: From *The Country House* to *Dead Class*], 2010. Photo by W. Rogowicz. Courtesy of the National Museum in Wrocław.
Figure 37	*Dainty Shapes and Hairy Apes*, 1973, dir. Tadeusz Kantor. Sketch. Coatroom and 40 Mendelbaums. Courtesy of Dorota Krakowska, and Cricoteka, Centre for the Documentation of the Art of Tadeusz Kantor.
Figure 38	Bruno Schulz, "The Old Age Pensioner [Self-Portrait] and the Boys." Dated before 1937. By permission of Marek Podstolski. Courtesy of the Museum of Literature, Warsaw.

---

2 Tadeusz Kantor, from director's notes, 1974, quoted in Lech Stangret, *Tadeusz Kantor. Fantomy Realności* [Tadeusz Kantor: Phantoms of Reality] (Cracow: Cricoteka, catalogue for the exhibit of Tadeusz Kantor's theatrical constumes, 1996), 73.

Figure 39	Bruno Schulz, "The Old Age Pensioner [Self-Portrait] and the Boys on the Bench." Dated before 1937. By permission of Marek Podstolski. Courtesy of the Museum of Literature, Warsaw.
Figure 40	Bruno Schulz, "Chassids by the Well, waiting for Messiah," 1934. By permission of Marek Podstolski. Courtesy of the Museum of Literature, Warsaw.
Figure 41	*Dead Class*, 1975, dir. Tadeusz Kantor. Photo by Andrzej Lojko. Courtesy of the photo author.
Figure 42	*Dead Class*, 1975, dir. Tadeusz Kantor. Wax Figures of Children, 1989. Photo by Janusz Podlecki. Courtesy of the photo author.
Figure 43	*Dead Class*, 1975. Exhibit "Tadeusz Kantor od *Małego dworku* do *Umarłej klasy*" [Tadeusz Kantor: From *The Country House* to *Dead Class*], 2010. Photo by W. Rogowicz. Courtesy of the National Museum in Wrocław.
Figure 44	*Dead Class*, 1975. Exhibit. Ośrodek Propagandy Sztuki in Park im. H. Sienkiewicz, Łódź, Festiwalu Dialogu Czterech Kultur, 2008. Photo by Grzegorz Michałowicz. Courtesy of Polska Agencja Prasowa (PAP).
Figure 45	Senator Alben W. Barkley of Kentucky, a member of a congressional committee investigating Nazi atrocities, views the evidence firsthand at Buchenwald concentration camp. Weimar, Germany, 24 April 1945. Department of Defense. Department of the Army. Fort Leavenworth, Kansas. 18 September 1947. (Online version available through Archival Research Catalog (NAIL Control Number: NRE-338-FTL(EF)-3134(2)) at <http://arcweb.archives.gov/>. Accessed 1 August 2011.)
Figures 46, 47	Objects left by the victims who died in the gas chambers. Auschwitz Museum exhibit. Photo by Bill Huston. Courtesy of the photo author.
Figure 48	*The Dybbuk*, 1922, dir. Yevgeny Vaktangov, Moscow. The Beggars' Dance at Leah's Wedding. In the middle, as the Bride: Shoshana Avivit, who preceded Hanna Rovina in the part. Reprinted with permission of IDCPA, Tel-Aviv University and Habima Theatre.
Figure 49	*Wielopole, Wielopole*, 1980, dir. Tadeusz Kantor. Photo by Andrzej Lojko. Courtesy of the photo author.

INTRODUCTION

Theatre and Meaning

> Applied to drama, the word "meaning" is ambiguous. It covers the metaphysical content that is represented objectively in the complexion of the artifact; the intention of the whole as a complex of meaning that is the inherent meaning of the drama; and finally the meaning of the words and sentences spoken by the characters and their meaning in sequence, the dialogic meaning. [...] Drama cannot simply take negative meaning, or the absence of meaning, as its content without everything peculiar to it being affected to the point of turning into its opposite. The essence of drama was constituted by that meaning.
>
> —Theodor Adorno (1958)[1]

As Adorno points out in this short passage from his essay on Beckett's *Endgame*, the issue of meaning in theatre is complex.[2] Standing at the crossroads between all other arts, theatre is an intricate web of semiotic fields, woven from literal and figurative language, from visual and linguistic references that stand both alone and in sequence, from the interplay of positive and negative meanings, their pairings and contrasts. Meaning in theatre is multilayered, intertwined between form and content, text and context, history and culture. Reading theatre is thus sophisticated detective work that consists of unraveling the subsequent layers, from superficial asymptomatic reading to complex engagement with the visual, linguistic, and performative language of the theatrical work.

Unfortunately, a number of developments in the field of theatre studies in the US during the last 40 years have led some scholars away from the deep, multilayered approach needed to grasp the complexity of theatrical work, and towards a culturally monolithic American perspective. In her 2011 review of Marvin Carlson's book on German theatre, which she ironically titles "Lost in Translation," Gitta Honegger, a theatre critic, dramaturg and translator of Austrian drama, describes the main reason behind the decline of scholarship on theatre and performance in the US: a lack of language skills coupled with a lack of rigor and a cavalier attitude toward the historical, cultural, social and political contexts of the analyzed foreign works.[3] To make her point, Honegger cites an anecdote about American professors' reaction to contemporary German theatre:

> Ignorance of the German language did not prevent Ivy League theater experts from instantly voicing their irritation (too many words, no exciting stage effects) about

[Peter Stein's] deliberately text-oriented, finely tuned if fastidious production of a complex historical trilogy that examines, in difficult poetic language, issues of European identity, religious strife, territorial wars, and claims to power that are of particular relevance to the united Germany and its position within the expanding European Union. (One professor, for example, wondered how she, like most Americans, hated the production, while Germans apparently found it quite meaningful.)[4]

Quoting Günther Rühle, one of the most influential German theatre scholars, Honegger reiterates Adorno's point: "theatre is a grand cultural system, where movements within society announce and express themselves, where they are mirrored and disperse again. It is a dominant part of all our cultural expression."[5] As such, theatre cannot be analyzed outside of its cultural context. It must be, to borrow Michel Foucault's terminology, "analyzed as a complex and variable function of discourse."[6]

In her famous essay "On Not Knowing Greek,"[7] Virginia Woolf provocatively precludes any possibility of understanding Greek theatre, mainly because of our inability to truly know the ancient Greek language and its context. Lacking the linguistic and cultural competency that provides context and cues, we don't know where to laugh or cry. Woolf writes:

> For it is vain and foolish to talk of knowing Greek, since in our ignorance we should be at the bottom of any class of schoolboys, since we do not know how the words sounded, or where precisely we ought to laugh, or how the actors acted, and between this foreign people and ourselves there is not only difference of race and tongue but a tremendous breach of tradition. [...]
>
> So to grasp the meaning of the play the chorus is of the utmost importance. One must be able to pass easily into those ecstasies, those wild and apparently irrelevant utterances, those sometimes obvious and commonplace statements, to decide their relevance or irrelevance, and give them their relation to the play as a whole. We must "be able to pass easily"; but that of course is exactly what we cannot do. [...]
>
> Further, in reckoning the doubts and difficulties there is this important problem – Where are we to laugh in reading Greek? [...] Thus humour is the first of the gifts to perish in a foreign tongue.[8]

The "difference of race, tongue and tradition," as Woolf puts it, or *la différance*, as Derrida would call it, is always lost in translation.[9] How much, if anything, can we reclaim from culture that is not our own, from which we are historically or geographically removed, or both? Derrida reminds us that "Essentially and lawfully, every concept is inscribed in a chain or in a system within which it refers to the other, to other concepts, by means of the systematic play of differences."[10] Like linguistic units referring to one another within the structure of language though their differences, artworks too refer to one another, through the "systematic play of differences." They are in dialogue with one another and with the world around them. Or, as Adorno puts it: "[art]works are also critics of one another."[11] Detached from their own cultural discourse, they become something else: found objects in another – different – world of semiotic codes.

The move away from historical interpretation towards affective interpretation has influenced a number of critical fields, particularly those that lacked a strong tradition of historical criticism. In his now classic 1996 book *Making Meaning*, David Bordwell, a leading film scholar, attempts to reclaim the integrity of film theory, which, he argues, has gone astray from an intellectual activity of decoding – of finding a meaning – to an impulsive gesture of making meaning from a medley of one's own subjective neuroses and cultural reference points. Bordwell traces the critical turn towards "reader-response" criticism to Susan Sontag's 1964 essay "Against Interpretation," in which, as Bordwell writes, "Sontag demands that we recover our senses and art's sensuousness. [She suggests that] [t]he critic can produce 'a really accurate, sharp, loving description of the appearance of a work of art'" without knowing anything about its historical or cultural context.[12] According to Sontag, "[I]nterpretation is the revenge of the intellect upon art. [...] To interpret is to impoverish, to deplete the world – in order to set up a shadow world of 'meanings.'"[13] The value of the artworks, Sontag writes, "lies elsewhere than in their 'meanings.'"[14] Instead, Sontag proposes that more attention be given to "form in art."[15] Thus, she proclaims, the goal of art criticism should be to focus on "our own experience," while showing "how it is what it is [...] rather than show[ing] what it means. In place of a hermeneutics we need an erotics of art."[16] Sontag's essay launched the descriptive trope of reader response art criticism, which eventually came to disregard the content and historical context of the artwork. Bordwell argues that following Sontag's essay, American "literary and art criticism consisted mostly of 'impressionistic' descriptions of the faults and beauties of works."[17] Interpreting works of art in "a particular historical context" became – for nearly three decades – unfashionable, a critical *faux pas*.[18] Bordwell continues: "Because cinema studies has lacked a strong tradition of historical scholarship, critics who know only how to read a film are discovering a terra incognita."[19] To accelerate the process, Bordwell proposes a kind of new poetics, what he calls "historical poetics."[20] Returning to Aristotle, he reminds his readers that "in some traditions, 'poetics' has referred only to the 'productive' side of the process; 'aesthetics' was often assumed to account for the work's effect. But Aristotle was at pains to include in the *Poetics* a discussion of the audience's response to tragedy."[21] Thus, a new *historical* poetics would be "a conceptual framework within which particular questions about film's composition and effect can be posed."[22] It would involve a multilayered approach to the film text that accounts for a work's historical and cultural framework; it would be a critical synchronic interpretation based on detailed historiographic research, including nearly scientific observations of all the conditions that surround the creation of a particular film, its reception, and its afterlife.

Perhaps nowhere has Sontag's ill-advised motto become more problematic than in the field of performance studies – as formulated in its origins by the Schechner-Turner duo – which, having evolved in the late sixties and early seventies, missed New Historicism, as well as Formalism and Structuralism, and hence developed a methodology based almost exclusively on surface readings, which Honegger so forcefully criticizes in her essay. Fashioning itself as a response to the postmodern "crisis of language," performance studies frames the battle as "one [that] pits language – the 'literature of theater' – against gesture and 'nonverbal communication,'"[23] thus abdicating spoken and written language as a failed system of performative exchange.[24] Moving away from the dramatic/literary text towards performance-based/nonverbal communication, the performance studies methodology dismissed both the ontology and the phenomenology of language – its intra- and extralinguistic aspects – while replacing it with the cursory interdisciplinarity of the performative über-umbrella.[25] However, as Adorno tells us: "Even where language tends to reduce itself to pure sound, it cannot divest itself of its semantic element, cannot become purely mimetic or gestural."[26] Whether they were or weren't previously written, whether they are pronounced, sung, or made into pure sounds, words carry meaning, even if they're detached from their original field of signification. Words don't have to be bound to text to mean something. Without words, theatre turns into dance or pantomime, but even then, the absence of words carries a meaning in itself.[27] Nonverbal gestures have their own meaning. To put it differently, whether verbal or nonverbal, theatre is a system of codes and significations that is invariably connected to the outside world. Or, as Patrice Pavis argues, "*everything*" in theatre "is called into question" (emphasis mine).[28] The words, nonverbal gestures, silences, images, utterances and groans form, what Patrice Pavis calls "the language of the stage," its theatricality, and, like any other language, it has meaning that can be traced back to its cultural and historical context, and thus can be decoded.[29] As Adorno notes, there is simply no theatre without meaning.[30] Most importantly, however, by dismissing the "literature of theater," the performance studies methodology dismisses theatre's complex cultural and historical framework, its field of signifiers, thus evolving into a dehistoricized, decontextualized "ethnography of performance," a method of critical inquiry consisting mostly – to quote Honegger again – of looking at "impressive production photographs without any awareness of the plays or their complex social, political, and cultural circumstances."[31] As Shannon Jackson notes in her book, *Professing Performance*, performance studies has suffered from what she calls the "hyper-contextuality of performance," which "makes it difficult to locate [it] as a research object at all." As a result, "[t]he production and reproduction of knowledge is, to some extent, a formalist operation in de-contextualization."[32]

Performance studies' origins, and its evolution towards "loving descriptions" in lieu of historiography, to no small degree, can be traced back to the "Polish invasion" of the late sixties and early seventies: the hoopla that surrounded Jerzy Grotowski (and, on a smaller scale, Tadeusz Kantor), who took the New York avant-garde theatre world by storm. The forbidden fruit delivered straight from behind the Iron Curtain, Grotowski brought with him performances wrapped in an obscure and hermetic historical and cultural tradition that no one understood, performed in a little-known and difficult language that no one spoke. Like Polanski – Hollywood's favorite *enfant terrible* – with his Gothic stories, tragic legacy of the Jewish Ghetto, and aura of socialist utopia, Grotowski too brought with him the inscrutable Eastern European mystique. How was one to approach such a research object, and was it even possible? One obvious answer was to dismiss the difficult context and funny-sounding language, replacing it with the fashionable emphasis on "gesture and 'nonverbal communication'" while focusing on the formal qualities of the object – and trying, by any means possible, to replicate the final effects.[33] Ironically, in the performance art of the 1960s and 1970s, under the influence of Grotowski's aesthetics, the playwright was "no longer the originator of a dramatic text" – which now only served as "the armature for the performance text."[34] Instead, the performer was. Likewise, in the dominant mode of performance studies analysis, the critic, with his or her own set of cultural biases and standards – not the performance text – became the primary generator of meaning.[35] The critical result, however, was a combination of latent formalism and a reader-response criticism: "sharp and loving descriptions" of gestures and images replacing their textual and contextual analysis.

In a way, this book attempts the impossible: to turn back the clock and redeliver both Grotowski and Kantor in all their obscure, difficult, multilayered, funny-sounding Polish glory, with all of the complex and convoluted contextual and textual details of their two seminal performance pieces, *Akropolis* and *Dead Class*. The objective of this project is to partake in the kind of new historical poetics, or perhaps new historiography, that Bordwell prescribed nearly fifteen years earlier for film theory, as applied, belatedly, to Polish performance and theatre scholarship.[36]

Theatre and Context

Poland has long enjoyed a reputation for innovation in theatre and the performing arts. Beginning in the interwar period, in 1919, Julius Osterwa and Mieczysław Limanowski, inspired by Stanislavsky's Moscow Art Theatre, founded the theatrical group Reduta. Based first in Warsaw and later in Wilno, Reduta operated for 20 years, actively touring the country, and laying the foundation for the future development of Polish theatre, particularly a uniquely Polish, intimate directing style, and rigorous actor training. Osterwa's method, which emphasized group work, the role of the director, and close actor–director relationships, eventually became a model replicated in the postwar period by a number of theatre groups, including Grotowski's Laboratory Theatre. The Laboratory Theatre adopted not only Reduta's emblem but, most importantly, Reduta's methodology and "ethical heritage."[37] Following World War II, the communist government drew on strong prewar theatrical tradition, privileging "the Polish theatre, never stinting it money or other means."[38] Investing a lot of money in theatre, however, the communists also customarily used it as a tool of political propaganda, "an export" product meant to enhance Poland's international reputation. As the two Polish theatre critics Jerzy Tymicki and Andrzej Niezgoda point out, during the first decades of communist rule, between the 1950s and the 1970s, "Polish theatres toured extensively, taking part in international festivals […]. But the 'internationalization' of Polish theatre had two faces. On the one hand, it promoted Polish culture abroad. On the other, it masked communist power by showing its 'human face.'"[39] Regardless of the motives, the fortuitous result of the communist approach allowed Polish theatre to flourish on both the national and international scenes. Since then, Polish directors and designers produced a groundbreaking body of work that has been as influential as it has been elusive. Theatre artists like Józef Szajna, Konrad Swinarski, Leszek Mądzik, Krystian Lupa, Jan Klata, Anna Augustynowicz, and Krystyna Skuszanka, and groups like Teatr Ósmego Dnia, Teatr Zar, and Gardzienice, have had a significant impact on the world's stages, often spearheading new trends and ideas.

Among the many prominent Polish theatre artists of the era, however, Jerzy Grotowski and Tadeusz Kantor are unquestionably two of the most influential figures of twentieth-century theatre. In fact, as another Polish critic, Wojciech Szulczynski, notes: "[…] the Polish theatre won world renown through Tadeusz Kantor's Teatr Cricot 2, and Jerzy Grotowski's Polish Laboratory Theatre."[40] Or, to quote Halina Filipowicz, one of the leading Polish studies scholars, "Grotowski's and Kantor's achievements have been validated by an international theatre community as major contributions to the 20th-century avant-garde."[41] One need not look far to see Grotowski's and Kantor's impact on the European and American avant-garde over the last 50 years. Jerzy Grotowski's theories and methods influenced directors such as Peter Brook, Richard Schechner, and Joseph Chaikin, and groups like the Living Theatre, the Wooster Group, the Performance Group, and the Open Theatre. Tadeusz Kantor's aesthetic has influenced Reza Abdoh, Robert Wilson, Richard Foreman, Moisés Kaufman, the Quay Brothers, and many others. Despite their international influence, however, Grotowski's and Kantor's works remain a mystery to many Westerners, mainly because so few scholars speak the language. This project fills gaps in English-language scholarship on the subject through contextual and textual analyses of Grotowski's and Kantor's most influential works: *Akropolis*[42] and *Dead Class*.[43] Each piece is a pivotal masterwork, the culmination of years of research and experimentation, and a key to understanding the oeuvre of its respective director. Each is available on video and widely taught in basic and advanced theatre courses, and thus widely referenced across the English-speaking theatre landscape. But while theatre scholars are now generally familiar with both works, there is little understanding of the complex web of cultural meanings and significations that went into their making. They remain broadly – but not deeply – known. Irving Wardle once humorously noted that, with Polish theatre, "Every work refers back to some previous work, to the despair of the non-Polish public."[44] Polish is an obscure language, and those who have even tried to scratch the surface of Polish drama or literature know it is notoriously hermetic; Grotowski's and Kantor's theatres are no exception. On the contrary, their work is particularly dense and layered, and hence easily prone to surface readings and "loving descriptions" in lieu of critical exegesis and cultural – and linguistic – competency. The fact that Grotowski and Kantor were imports from behind the Iron Curtain certainly didn't help open their theatre up to the critical scrutiny it might have otherwise received, but it is only one of many reasons why their work for so long eluded critical inquiry.

The English-language scholarship on Grotowski and Kantor has been, to use Shannon Jackson's phrasing again, "a formalist operation in de-contextualization."[45] Following the 1968 English-language publication of Grotowski's *Towards a Poor Theatre*, the initial critical reception of *Akropolis* (which was shown in New York the following year) by American critical and theatrical circles predominantly focused on Grotowski's *mise-en-scène* and his acting methodology: "the extreme discipline of his actors, their athleticism, and their incomparable vocal skills."[46] There was virtually no attempt to historicize or contextualize *Akropolis*, or to understand Stanisław Wyspiański's complex modernist drama, on which Grotowski's piece was based. Ludwik Flaszen's English-language essay "Wyspiański's '*Akropolis*,'" published in *TDR: The Drama Review* in 1965, attempted to anchor Grotowski's production in Wyspiański's text, but Flaszen's attempt fell short, as if the author was afraid that focusing too much on Wyspiański's obscure play could potentially alienate the English-language readers. Instead, Flaszen's essay concentrates primarily on the visual aspects of the production, merely alluding to Wyspiański in its opening paragraphs as a way to contextualize the historical framework of Grotowski's vision. Flaszen writes,

> They both [Wyspiański and Grotowski] want to represent the sum total of a civilization and test its values on the touchstone of contemporary experience. To Grotowski, contemporary means the second half of the twentieth century. Hence his experience is infinitely more cruel than Wyspiański's and the century-old values of European culture are put to a severe test.[47]

Flaszen circumvents in-depth analysis of the "century-old values of European culture" that Wyspiański's text refers to, but – as his early role as dramaturg in Grotowski's group carried the authority of the insider's view – his avoidance of a direct confrontation with Wyspiański's text set the tone for the English-language critical responses to Grotowski's production that were to follow in the next four decades. Yet, the text of Grotowski's production is over 57 pages long, and Grotowski himself never disowned his debt to Wyspiański; on the contrary, his production, at least in Poland, was always known and critically framed as *Akropolis According to Wyspiański*.

As Grotowski's *Akropolis* is "now considered to be one of the most important theatre productions of the twentieth century,"[48] the absence of research on the topic is puzzling. The first English-language textual analysis of Grotowski's *Akropolis* was proposed by Robert Findlay in the 1984 article "Grotowski's 'Akropolis': A Retrospective."[49] The article provided an excellent description of Grotowski's piece, along with an overview of Wyspiański's *Akropolis*. Findlay's interpretation of concrete scenes and images, however, for the most part fell victim to the prevailing surface readings that by then dominated the Grotowski scholarship. It is to Findlay's credit that he attempted such analysis at all. As Grotowski's himself moved in the direction of "paratheatrical" research, no longer mounting actual theatrical productions, the scholarship on Grotowski eventually abandoned critical engagement with his past productions.[50] The English translation of Zbigniew Osiński's 1985 *Grotowski and His Laboratory* provided the first in-depth English-language overview of the production, though it missed some of its most salient aspects. Jennifer Kumiega's *The Theatre of Grotowski* (1985), Lisa Wolford's *Grotowski's Objective Drama Research* (1996), and the long-awaited Eugenio Barba memoir, *Land of Ashes and Diamonds: My Apprenticeship in Poland* (1999), all focused on acting, the rehearsal process, or the history of Grotowski's Laboratory Theatre. In 1997, Flaszen's essay on Wyspiański was reprinted in *The Grotowski Sourcebook*, edited by Richard Schechner and Lisa Wolford. *The Sourcebook*, a collection of previously published essays and interviews on and with Grotowski, became an authoritative text on Grotowski, but besides Flaszen's short essay, the anthology lacked any actual analysis of Grotowski's *Akropolis* itself. The same year the *Sourcebook* was published, in 1997, Mark Fortier's *Theatre/Theatre* was released, providing a short deconstructive analysis of *Akropolis* as a work structured primarily around the binary opposition between life and death. Fortier writes that *Akropolis* "recreates death and alienation, deferring resurrection on resurrection's eve and presenting rebirth as incineration and absence."[51] Although perceptive, Fortier's analysis lacks the contextualization of the very binary he describes. Following the *Sourcebook*, all major publications on Grotowski were either anthologies of previously available texts, or memoirs of former students and collaborators, recalling either the rehearsal process or the author's personal journeys and epiphanies in his or her relationship with Grotowski. Such is also the case with the most recent publications. In *With Grotowski, Theatre Is Just a Form* (2009), edited by Georges Ban, Grzegorz Ziółkowski, and Paul Allain, for example, the authors reprint Peter Brook's foreword to the filmed version of *Akropolis*, but that is as far as they go. Ludwik Flaszen's book *Grotowski & Company* (2010) is another collection of Flaszen's dramaturgical writings from the Grotowski Institute Archives, and, again, it reprints his short dramaturgical commentary on *Akropolis*, which accompanied the original production. However, the book doesn't add anything new to Grotowski scholarship. Similarly, Paul Allain's 2009 anthology, *Grotowski's Empty Room: A Challenge to the Theatre*, is a collection of recycled essays, which do not bring anything new to the discourse. James Slowiak and Jairo Cuesta's 2007 monograph, *Jerzy Grotowski*, provides a summary of *Akropolis*; however, it relies mostly on Findlay's and Flaszen's essays as a way to contextualize it.[52] In *Theatre: A Way of Seeing* (2005), Milly Barranger provides a two-page summary of the production, also based on previously published research.[53] None of the English-language scholarship on Grotowski (with the exception of Findlay's essay) engages Stanisław Wyspiański's *Akropolis* beyond a brief mention that it provides the basis for Grotowski's performance text, and that it is set at Wawel. Similarly nobody besides Robert Findlay, Jennifer Kumiega and Raymonde Temkine – a French theatre critic who, in addition to Eugene Barba, became one of Grotowski's most ardent early supporters – even mentions the connection between Grotowski and Tadeusz Borowski, a Polish Holocaust writer, whose work greatly influenced not just *Akropolis* but Grotowski's entire understanding of theatrical language. Kumiega cites the epitaph from Borowski, which eventually became a motto of the production, but she does not explain the relationship between Borowski's writing and Grotowski's theatre.[54] Temkine's pivotal book on Grotowski, published in France in 1968, devotes one paragraph to Borowski. Borowski's two collections, *Kamienny Świat* [The World Made of Stone] and *Pożegnanie z Marią* [*Farewell to Maria*] were translated into French by Laurence Dyèvre and Eric Veaux, and published in France in 1964 – four years before Temkine's book was released.[55] Veaux visited Teatr 13 Rzędów (The Thirteen Row Theatre) in 1963, when Grotowski was working on *Akropolis*, and it was in fact this experience that inspired him to translate Borowski's stories. Temkine's book was published in English in 1972, four years after its French version. Four years later, in 1976, Borowski's stories were translated into English. There were many occasions for the American – and British – theatre scholars specializing in Grotowski to discuss the connection between Grotowski and Borowski, even if one spoke neither French nor Polish.

The case with Kantor's *Dead Class* is oddly similar. Despite the impact of *Dead Class* on the contemporary avant-garde (from Richard Foreman, to Robert Wilson, to Krystian Lupa), there is a surprising lack of in-depth scholarship about this work as well. While Michal Kobialka, America's leading Kantor expert, speaks Polish, his book *A Journey Through Other Spaces: Essays and Manifestos, 1944–1990* (1993) is not a critical work, but primarily a collection of Kantor's Polish-language archival writings and manuscripts found in Cracow's Cricoteka archives. In his most recent book, *Further on, Nothing: Tadeusz Kantor's Theatre*, published in 2009, Kobialka provides what has been the most comprehensive analysis of *Dead Class* to date. Kobialka's essay attempts to frame *Dead Class* in the context of the European canon (among Beckett, Maeterlinck, and even Shakespeare), and it does engage extensively Witkacy's *Tumor Mózgowicz* [*Tumor Brainiowicz*] (a play that Kantor used as a framework for *Dead Class*), but it steers away from more difficult aspects of Kantor's masterpiece; it fails to mention Schulz, Mickiewicz, Anski, or Gombrowicz (all essential figures for Kantor's aesthetics), and it entirely avoids discussing the Polish–Jewish context – never mentioning the issue of the Holocaust that is crucial for the understanding of Kantor's work. Jan Klossowicz's Polish-language book *Tadeusz Kantor – Teatr* [Tadeusz Kantor – Theatre] has never been translated into English, which might be a good thing, considering the fate of Miklaszewski's *Encounters with Tadeusz Kantor* (2002). Like Kobialka's *Journey*, Miklaszewski's *Encounters* is a collection of chronologically arranged conversations, reviews, script fragments, and critical commentaries. Unfortunately, rather than citing original English-language reviews of Kantor's work, *Encounters* translator George M. Hyde chose to translate Miklaszewski's Polish translation of English-language reviews from Polish back into English. Not surprisingly, the results are flawed and sloppy. Kobialka's *Journey Through Other Spaces* and Miklaszewski's *Encounters with Tadeusz Kantor* are the only sources of translated primary texts for English-speaking readers, although each steers away from any deeper historical, literary, or national contextualization that might appear too challenging for nonnatives. Another newly released book, Noel Witts' *Tadeusz Kantor* (2010), offers another loving – and quite detailed – description of *Dead Class*, without making any attempts to delve deeper into the work's cultural and historical framework. To Witts' credit, however, the book does provide biographical details that were previously unavailable to English-speaking readers.

Why such dearth in the English-language scholarship of two of the most unquestionably influential theatrical works of the twentieth century? How is it that, despite their impact, popularity and teachability for the last 40 years, neither *Akropolis* nor *Dead Class* were ever carefully scrutinized, though each work offers a wealth of textual and contextual material? The absence of in-depth scholarship on *Akropolis* and *Dead Class* reveals one of the most pressing issues surrounding the field of theatre criticism: the need to straddle the very fine line between transnational and contextual approaches. Too narrow a contextual focus risks the ghettoization of a work within the constrained framework of its own ethnic literary and cultural canon; too broad a focus precludes an in-depth understanding of the work's complex web of visual and literary ethnic baggage. This is particularly true for works like *Akropolis* and *Dead Class*, in which the visual, nonlinguistic aspect is implicitly influenced by their national literary and linguistic subtext.

Theatre and Difference

Grotowski and Kantor have reigned over Polish theatre for the last five decades. But while both are considered masters of their domains, they represent distinct and frequently antithetical poles of influence. Their mutual antipathy is well documented. Although Grotowski was, for the most part, diplomatic in his relationship with Kantor, Kantor never hid his belief that Grotowski was a charlatan or, worse, an impostor. Recalling his 1976 interview with Kantor, Neal Ascherson recounts Kantor's unabashed candor on the topic: "[Kantor] doesn't think much of his Polish colleague Grotowski, so much revered in the West. 'He is just an orthodoxy. He affects to run a school, so that the pupils are entirely deformed. When young people come to me in Cracow, I say: I don't run a school, I create.'"[56] In 1978, two years after his European triumph of *Dead Class*, Kantor again spoke about Grotowski in an Italian interview for *Sipario*:

> Please, don't talk to me about Grotowski because I am not interested in him at all. Mr. Grotowski is a thief. He is successful in countries with bad, bad theatre. Grotowski is a thief! […] Mr. Grotowski is nothing for me, he's a thief. Mr. Grotowski travels as "a professor and savior of theatre," while I am an artist, private and individual.[57]

A year later, in 1979, the same sentiment surfaced in an interview with William Harris, who didn't cite Kantor himself, but instead wrote poignantly: "The subject of Grotowski irritates Kantor, who describes his colleague – without malice but with the same self-assuredness which colors the entire conversation – as a charlatan."[58] For his part, Grotowski simply ignored Kantor, which might have been the cruelest insult of all. (Sporadic reports indicate that later in his life, Grotowski expressed subtle admiration for Kantor's work. According to Flaszen, when Grotowski first saw Kantor's *Dead Class*, he said jokingly, "Unfortunately, I have to admit this is a masterpiece."[59]) Kantor and Grotowski's antipathy, and the anecdotes to which it gave rise, became the stuff of legend, and incited a bifurcation between their respective camps that precluded the intermingling of actors, devotees and ideas. If you chose one, you had to ignore the other. Any attempt to discuss them side by side not only seemed impossible; it seemed like sacrilege in the holiest of all conceptual theatre wars. They spoke with such different vocabularies that it became nearly impossible to create any kind of discourse that could embrace them both. Nevertheless, the recent years have ushered in a thaw as Polish scholars such as Zbigniew Osiński, Leszek Kolankiewicz, Krzysztof Pleśniarewicz and Grzegorz Niziołek have aimed at a more inclusive theoretical approach in analyzing Grotowski's and Kantor's works side by side.[60] Following the year of Grotowski, for example, the Grotowski Institute started an online publication, *PERFORMER*, whose first two issues were almost exclusively devoted to the two Polish directors.[61] Likewise, in 2009, Jagiellonian University in Cracow, Kantor's hometown, hosted a conference, "*Via Negativa. Wobec Grotowskiego – krytyczne interpretacje*" [Via Negativa. Vis-à-vis Grotowski – Critical Interpretations]. In December 2010, the Grotowski Institute responded by organizing its own conference "*Tadeusz Kantor – Inne Spojrzenia*" [Tadeusz Kantor – Other Perspectives], which attempted to shed light on Kantor's work from a more comprehensive theoretical perspective than hitherto employed. As each camp, Grotowski's and Kantor's, had traditionally remained anchored in its own city, Wrocław and Cracow, the 'cultural' exchange of conference venues was significant in so far as it opened new critical opportunities. This book, however, is the first English-language project to bridge the gap between the two directors by developing a comparative critical language through which one could simultaneously engage both Kantor's and Grotowski's works in a way that makes their differences and their similarities evocative of a broader conversation about theatre and meaning.

Kantor and Grotowski's mutual animosity partially stemmed from the fact that each of them found and spoke to a very different audience. Ellen Stewart, who hosted Kantor's Cricot 2 at LaMaMa each time the group performed in New York, vividly recalled the polarized atmosphere surrounding the two directors:

> Grotowski is worshipped in the U.S. like Stanislavski, but almost nobody is interested in Kantor. When in 1969, Grotowski's Laboratory Theatre came to New York for the first time, the NYU directing department organized series of workshops with Grotowski, Ryszard Cieślak and Ludwik Flaszen. And that's how it stayed. Grotowski was teaching at the universities, raising himself a group of student followers, and Kantor didn't create any school, and never taught at any university. Either way, Kantor hated Grotowski and eventually, I had to choose. I chose Kantor.[62]

As Stewart points out, Grotowski was renowned abroad, especially in the USA, while Kantor, though widely admired, for some reason never inspired the same lasting international devotion. On the other hand, in Poland the situation was completely reversed. As Konstanty Puzyna, one of Poland's most esteemed theatre critics puts it: "[In Poland] Grotowski's work was received differently [from Kantor's. Grotowski's work] evoked passionate disagreements and scathing attacks, divided critics and audiences into two camps. But with Kantor, nothing. No disagreements. He's brilliant, that's it. […] Full national accord."[63] Kantor, even 20 years after his death, remains a Polish household name, continuously "commanding respect and, more importantly perhaps, tolerance in its native land,"[64] whereas "the name Grotowski often doesn't ring a bell," even for those in theatre circles.[65] The disparity in the directors' native and international reputations has been a long-standing topic of debate both in Polish critical circles and among the expats. In 1969, writing on the occasion of Grotowski's successful international tours, one puzzled Polish critic noted: "Very often, when I am abroad discussing Polish culture with those who are genuinely interested in it, I notice that their tastes are drastically different from ours."[66] The impetus for this project stems from questions raised by that observation: Why are "their [theatrical] tastes […] drastically different from ours"? How is theatrical meaning codified outside its cultural context? How is it codified in its cultural context? What affects the reception of a theatrical work? Or, to quote Robert King: "How and how effectively does the work [of theatre] earn its credibility and project its worth? […] [W]hat is deserving of an audience's attention, respect, consideration or reflection?"[67] In the space between performance and its reception, how is the credibility of the theatre piece affected by its context and its audience? In other words, how does theatre "make meaning"? And, to quote Paul de Man's reiteration of Derrida's famous question, what is the difference?[68] Is there one, and if so, is it worth discerning?

Ironically, as if to spite each director, Grotowski's term *teatr ubogi* and Kantor's concept of *teatr biedny* have both been translated into English as "poor theatre." Similarly, in both French and German the semantic difference, so marked in Polish, between *teatr ubogi* and *teatr biedny* has been erased. In French, both are called *un théâtre pauvre*, and in German, *das arme Theater*. Kantor and Grotowski vehemently denied their shared conceptual roots, and they flinched at having to share the same vocabulary to denote their two different worldviews, methodologies, and radically different aesthetics. For Grotowski, *teatr ubogi* meant theatre of poor means, as opposed to rich theatre, with its elaborate costumes and sets. The word "poor" denoted material poverty. It meant focusing on actors as a principal means of expression. Grotowski said: "We consider the personal and scenic technique of the actor as the core of theater art."[69] Theatre became "a vehicle, a means for self-study, self-exploration; a possibility of salvation."[70] Fittingly for a theatre with a "sacred aim,"[71] the concept came from an article by Jan Maria Święcicki, a Catholic who wrote about "poor" and "rich" methods in Catholic homiletic practice. Flaszen recalls that "We used those terms during rehearsals. We talked about 'poor' and 'rich' methods in the technical and aesthetic sense."[72]

For Kantor, *teatr biedny* meant poor theatre, made of *objets trouvés*, French for "found objects"; but it also meant "meager," "pitiable," "pathetic," and "desolate." The word *biedny* denotes both material poverty and a psychological condition of complete destitution, loneliness, and loss. As Tamara Karren correctly notes, Kantor's theatre "is not a 'poor theatre' like Grotowski's. It is rather a theatre of negation."[73] It is foremost a theatre of absence, the Theatre of Death,[74] or as Kantor put it, "a game with the void."[75] William Harris adds that Kantor's "poor theatre, this theater of destruction and emptiness, predated Grotowski's codification of these ideas."[76] (The suggestion that Kantor was the first to explore the same concepts as Grotowski would be seen as accurate by his partisans and as blasphemy by Grotowski's followers.) Kantor's "poor" sets, props and "bio-objects,"[77] were meant to create and evoke an atmosphere that placed actors on equal footing with objects, by exposing the actors' selves as "small, poor, defenseless."[78] To quote a Polish reviewer, Bogdan Gieraczyński: "Grotowski assumed a full identification of the viewers with the actors; Kantor does not permit such a possibility. Indifference versus engagement, death versus life, that's the difference."[79] If Grotowski followed in Stanislavsky's footsteps, Kantor remained a firm disciple of Meyerhold, offering "a virtual upending of Konstatin Stanislavski's ideas about theatre art. Stanislavski urged people, within limits, to 'live' their parts. Kantor is instead emphatic that actors have to come to terms with death before they can understand and or portray life."[80]

Developing their two different aesthetics, Grotowski and Kantor drew on two different strands that came to dominate Polish drama and literature. The first dates back directly to the Romantic tradition of grand, national themes, as exemplified by Poland's three greatest national poet-dramatists Juliusz Słowacki, Adam Mickiewicz, and Stanisław Wyspiański. A second trend, exemplified by the work of Poland's two most revered avant-gardists Ignacy Witkiewicz and Witold Gombrowicz, evolved between

World Wars I and II, as a persiflage dabbling with the grotesque, and a response to the Romantic tradition. In fact, Witkiewicz and Gombrowicz frequently mocked the "sacred" ideals epitomized by the grand, national poets. Gombrowicz's writings, as Kathleen Cioffi notes, even now "continue to provoke by poking fun at such Polish sacred cows as Catholicism and Romanticism."[81] This satirical, self-mocking trend came to dominate postwar Polish theatre, blending seamlessly with the subversively ironic attitudes of Polish society vis-à-vis the communist regime. As Cioffi notes: "Jerzy Grotowski brought the first tradition into the twentieth century by adapting the works of the Polish Romantics and making the theatre itself a place where something 'sacred' took place."[82] The second tradition – the grotesque, satiric, avant-garde strand – was adopted by Tadeusz Kantor.[83] While Grotowski's "holy" theatre of Romantic traditions was "a theatre of no-laughter […] no sense of humour, no irony,"[84] Kantor's theatre has always been "a frightening and disturbing mixture of comedy and horror."[85] If Grotowski, as Jan Kott suggests, "never laughed at himself,"[86] Kantor would always be considered one of Poland's greatest "panironists," skillfully balancing between "metaphysics and a spoof."[87]

Konstanty Puzyna points out that one of the great distinguishing characteristics of Polish Romantic drama is its "philosophical and theological divagations, blending social and political issues with questions of individual and national freedom. The Polish Romantic protagonist often challenges God to a duel over his nation and humanity in a messianic, martyrological vision, in which Poland becomes the Christ of nations, redeeming the world from tyranny with its grand sacrifice."[88] Andrzej Walicki, a Polish-American scholar, defines Polish national messianism as "a belief in a redeemer, individual or collective, mediating between the human and the divine in the soteriological process of history."[89] Grotowski follows this messianic tradition, entering into a discursive dialogue with the Polish Romantics, both deferring to and challenging their prerogatives. Jan Kott argues that "In Grotowski's theatre, liberation comes through the tortured body, subjugated spirit, and death. Suffering and humiliation are the supreme – and perhaps only – human experiences. I don't know" – Kott adds – "if you have to believe in God to accept Grotowski's Metaphysics, but I do know that you have to abandon all dissent and all hope."[90] Grotowski's ethical attitude towards national messianism involves a strain of Romantic martyrology, which asks for supreme self-sacrifice in the name of values one can no longer name or believe in. In Grotowski's work, there is no meaning in one's self-sacrificial demise. Kott suggests that Grotowski's position of utmost nihilism and despair is fundamentally impossible to accept in a nation consistently bulldozed by the totalitarian powers of the twentieth century. Such a nation simply cannot survive without some sense of hope – even if it is, as Kott calls it, a "hopeless hope."[91]

Kantor's theatre, on the other hand, with its irreverent mixture of horror and the grotesque, is a postmodern dance of death, performed in a postapocalyptic world in which "nothing is sacred, and there are no bonds, laws or dogmas […] in which everything is allowed and everything can be expected."[92] Tragedy in theatre, Kantor believed, "can be achieved only through its opposite – through comedy. Otherwise, all you get is pathos [of the kind embraced by Grotowski]."[93] Puzyna suggests that both the pathetic (followed by Grotowski) and the grotesque (followed by Kantor) traditions have common roots in nineteenth-century Romantic drama, characterized by "loose poetic form, multi-plots, and digressions."[94] "The poetic irony, grotesque and parody," as Puzyna observes, comes from that tradition as well. Kantor's laughter is a madman's laughter, hysterical and helpless in the face of the absurdity of the world, death, and survival. In Kantor's interpretation of Polish messianism, Christ is a Jewish king, laughing bitterly on the cross at the absurdity of his demise. Kantor's Theatre of Death is irreverent, but it evokes both laughter and despair for the same reason: because it still clings, against its better judgment, to hope.[95] It is funny because it is tragic; it is tragic because it is funny. In Kantor's gallows humor "we see a certain satisfaction at the absurdity of one's death."[96] "The existential reason for laughing at death" – to quote Tomasz Bocheński – is a type of magical thinking meant to ward off death and oblivion.[97] It is also invariably bound to survival, if not of the flesh, then at least of the spirit: "Black humor is the domain of nomads and loners laughing at their powerlessness in the face of death."[98] Black humor has its roots in oppression and is invariably bound to a historical and political context. As Kundera puts it, it "is the humor of people who are far from power, make no claim to power, and see history as a blind old witch whose moral verdicts make them laugh."[99] Kundera describes this humor as emblematic of the tragedy of Central European nations with their "disabused view of history that is the source of their culture, of their wisdom, of their 'nonserious spirit' that mocks grandeur and glory."[100] Kundera explains further: "Big nations consider themselves the masters of history and thus cannot but take history, and themselves, seriously. A small nation does not see history as its property and has the right not to take it seriously."[101] Kantor's humor comes from that very awareness of one's inconsequentiality in the face of overwhelming historical and political forces.[102] Thus, we have the fundamental difference between Grotowski and Kantor: their different approaches to history. But this first difference is only one way to account for the differences in native and foreign reception of their work.

Theatre and Literature

Akropolis and *Dead Class*s are fundamentally different, but they also share the same cultural baggage. In a 1976 letter to Grotowski, Zbigniew Osiński points out surprising similarities between *Akropolis* and *Dead Class*: "the similar relationship between audience and actors, between the living and the dead, the common eschatology and shared ruthless judgment of the contemporary world and our situation in it."[103] Though in different ways, both works are steeped in Polish national literature from the Romantic era. Although one comes from the Polish Romanticism, and the other from the avant-garde tradition that evolved as a reaction to Romantic ideals, both are rooted in, and draw on, the Polish Romantic tradition to question the Polish – and by extension European – values that form the basis of Western civilization. In his 1979 Milan lecture, "Grotowski and the Polish Romantic Drama," Konstanty Puzyna gently pleads for more in-depth scholarship of Grotowski's work in the context of the Polish Romantics:

> Polish Romantic tradition asserts itself with full force in Grotowski's work. [...] It's the first time [in the history of Polish theatre] that the romantic sensibility is expressed

so accurately, so emotionally by the actors. [...] Grotowski's actors work with their bodies and voices, with their pain and their whole being, to evoke something that's mad and irrational, but also total, full and whole. Perhaps because you don't speak Polish, you can't fully understand the price the Romantics have paid in Grotowski's interpretation of their work. In Grotowski's work, the textual values of Romantic texts are subsumed in psycho-physical, emotional, rhythmic and extra-lingual layers. But when we, as critics, dismiss the language and the poetry completely, we destroy something important: the multiplicity of meanings that Romantic texts evoke.[104]

Echoing Puzyna's observation, the Polish theatre scholar Michał Masłowski recently noted that virtually all contemporary Polish scholars studying Grotowski's work agree that it is rooted in the tradition of Polish Romanticism, particularly Adam Mickiewicz's dramatic poem, *Dziady* [*Forefathers' Eve*]. Written between 1820 and 1832, *Forefathers' Eve* has four structurally distinct parts, that seamlessly blend national, politico-historical, mystical, ludic, messianic, soteriological and martyrological themes. In pagan tradition, Forefathers' Eve is a ritual of conjuring up the dead forefathers, particularly those whose souls can't find rest, in order to help them reach heaven. In Christian liturgy, Forefathers' Eve has evolved into All Souls' Day. In Jewish mysticism, which predates both, the idea of conjuring up the spirits to gain their knowledge was a central concept of Kabbalah.[105] In fact, the adjuration of spirits was a requirement for mastering the Torah (though it was strictly forbidden to pray directly to the dead or to ask them for anything). Likewise, customarily, "if the dead want to appear to the living, they are given permission to do so."[106] Mickiewicz believed the ritual of "conjuring up the spirits of dead ancestors is one of 'the most important' of all Slavic ceremonies," one which connected all of its cultural traditions.[107] Adapting *Forefathers' Eve* in 1961, Grotowski discarded the historical–national aspect of Mickiewicz's dramatic poem, focusing almost exclusively on its ritualistic dimension.[108] In this adaptation, as Ludwik Flaszen said, Grotowski wanted to show "how theatre is born from the ritual."[109] With its own ritualistic framework, *Akropolis* evolved out of these early experiments with Mickiewicz's *Forefathers' Eve*. As Grotowski explained: "[In *Akropolis*] The viewers are living people who witness the raising of the dead, as in Mickiewicz's *Forefathers' Eve*."[110] The binary opposition between the living and the dead, the actors and the spectators, that is at the center of *Akropolis*, forms the basis of Grotowski's entire aesthetics.

Although he drew his inspiration predominantly from the Polish interwar, avant-garde tradition of the grotesque, Kantor too has remained indebted to the Polish Romantics. In fact, Mickiewicz's *Forefathers' Eve* is perhaps the only source to which Kantor openly admitted: "I took from *Dziady* one major lesson. I admit it, I acknowledge my roots. But all Polish literature has its roots in Mickiewicz."[111] Kantor directed *Forefathers' Eve* while still a student at a gymnasium in Wielopole, and the elements of Mickiewicz's drama reverberate prominently in *Dead Class*. Writing about the connection between *Dziady* and Kantor's *Dead Class*, Leszek Kolankiewicz, an esteemed Polish scholar, even suggests that "Kantor's séance should be called the Twentieth-Century *Forefathers' Eve* in that it reaches back into the archaic modes of pre-Poland: the obligation of the living toward the poor lost souls of their departed."[112] Kantor believed that by focusing on the ritual of bringing up the dead, Mickiewicz captured a universal myth that could translate across cultures.[113] Combining aspects of pagan rituals with Christian liturgy and Jewish Kabbalah, *Forefathers' Eve* reappears in Kantor's *Dead Class* in a new, postapocalyptic context. Although in different ways, both Grotowski's *Akropolis* and Kantor's *Dead Class* trace their common lineage to Mickiewicz and the Polish Romantic tradition, particularly to the sacred, ritualistic dimension of Mickiewicz's *Forefathers' Eve*, with its emphasis on theatre as a meeting space between the living and the dead.

Indeed, it is difficult to imagine contemporary Polish theatre and literature without its Romantic roots. Yet, despite its importance, Polish Romantic literature is virtually unknown beyond Polish borders (with the conspicuous exception of Slavic departments). Jozef Witlin, a modern Polish writer, has joked that "To the world at large Polish literature is known as an unknown literature."[114] Helen Fagin argues that this erasure has to do with its "seemingly excessive [...] nationalism," as Polish poets had a "more immediate source for their romantic idealism [than their French or German counterparts] – the loss of their own political independence."[115] For that very reason, however, as Kundera suggests, Mickiewicz's Romantic poetry and drama can also be considered foundational for Poland's sense of national identity.[116] There is a great irony in that fact, as Halina Filipowicz points out; the Polish national literature "came to flower in the looming shadow of a phantom state that had been erased from the map of Europe."[117] Following three partitions, in 1772, 1773 and 1795, Poland existed only as an idea, divided among the Russian Empire, the Kingdom of Prussia and Habsburg Austria. It was a country that was not: the ultimate political and national embodiment of a Derridean ontological riddle. Or, as Benedict Anderson would put it, a perfect "imagined community": a national identity that rested solely on shared language and historical memory.[118] Polish literature, particularly Polish Romantic drama, became a primary signifier of national identity. As the Polish scholar Jerzy Ziomek notes: "with the loss of independence, Polish literature became a proxy for non-existent state institutions."[119] Romantic literature united people under the common liberatory, messianic narrative, with the Polish language (officially disallowed in the Russian part) as a stand-in for the nonexistent state and nationhood. In place of absent geographic and administrative ties, language and literature played an essential role in national survival.

Milan Kundera once described Poland's central location as a site of perpetual geo-schizophrenia. Central Europe, he argued, is a pit of contradictions. Located in the geographic heart of Europe and caught between "two halves which evolved separately: one tied to ancient Rome and the Catholic Church, the other anchored in Byzantium and the Orthodox Church,"[120] Central Europe has historically evolved a kind of double split consciousness (one perhaps unified only by its deep Judaic subconscious).[121] At the crossroads between East and West, and North and South, Poland's position was always politically precarious. In 2010, in a *New York Times* column written to commemorate the Katyń tragedy, Roger Cohen aptly summarizes the Polish state of mind:

> For scarcely any nation has suffered since 1939 as Poland, carved up by the Hitler–Stalin nonaggression pact, transformed by the Nazis into the epicenter of their program to

annihilate European Jewry, land of Auschwitz and Majdanek, killing field for millions of Christian Poles and millions of Polish Jews, brave home to the Warsaw Uprising, Soviet pawn, lonely Solidarity-led leader of post-Yalta Europe's fight for freedom, a place where, as one of its great poets, Wisława Szymborska, wrote, "History counts its skeletons in round numbers."[122]

Poland did not regain its independence until 1918, but even then it had not returned to its pre-partition borders.[123] Fittingly, for many centuries, it was viewed "as if it were 'a home on wheels to be pushed eastward or westward as may suit the imperial aims of either of its mighty neighbors.'"[124] In his *Struggles for Poland*, Neal Ascherson cites an anecdote about Poland's uneasy geographic predicament: "When a visitor commented that Poland was an abnormal country, [Kazimierz Brandys, a contemporary Polish novelist] retorted: 'It is a perfectly normal country between two abnormal ones.'"[125] Brandys was referring to Germany and Russia, the latter at that time undergoing its experiment with communism, the former just recovering from its experiment with fascism. Using a similar critical lens, Norman Davis, in what is now considered an authoritative English-language tome on Polish history, is less nuanced, arguing that Poland's geographic location creates a state of perpetual psycho-political emergency.[126] To drive his point home, Davis titles his book *God's Playground*. The view of Poland as a bundle of contradictions shaped by serendipitous historical forces and fickle geopolitical circumstances is by no means a recent, post–World War II assessment. It evolved subtly and became set in European consciousness throughout many centuries, particularly – perhaps curiously so – within the European dramatic tradition.

In 1636, Pedro Calderón de la Barca set the plot of his drama *Life Is a Dream* in Poland.[127] At that time, Poland was an empire, the Polish–Lithuanian Commonwealth, which spread from the Baltic Sea to the Black Sea and bordered both Sweden and Turkey. Culturally and politically, Poland's seventeenth-century northern and southern borders were at odds with each other, and Calderón's philosophical *tractatus* on the mutually exclusive natures of democracy and despotism, and predetermination and self-determination, seemed to fit naturally with the country's complex social, political and cultural makeup. Following in Calderón's footsteps more than two and a half centuries later, Alfred Jarry set his 1896 absurdist play *Ubu Roi* in Poland, "*c'est nulle part*" – that is to say, nowhere.[128] Jarry's choice reflected a similar sense of political and national aporia, though the historical context was drastically different; "In Jarry's play, Poland is a country that seems to be somewhat deranged, primitive, and strange, whose saving grace is that 'if there were no Poland, there would be no Poles!'"[129] For Jarry, Poland is an embodiment of the absurd, a country that was to be found nowhere.

Polish Romantic national drama grew out of particular historical circumstances, becoming, in turn, a source of inspiration for modern Polish theatre. As Harold B. Segel notes, "The importance of the Romantic drama for later Polish drama as well as theatre far exceeds that of Büchner in the German-speaking countries."[130] Daniel Gerould suggests that if it were known beyond Polish borders, the Polish Romantic drama would gain its rightful recognition in world theatre. According to Gerould, Polish Romantic drama is

> a strange and fascinating combination for anyone nurtured on the Anglo-American tradition where neither romanticism nor modernism in its symbolist phase produced anything of lasting theatrical value [...] In contrast to the imaginative sweep and breadth of perspective shown by Mickiewicz, the fuss about Hernani and Hugo's writings on the subject seem parochial, formalistic and no longer of much importance.[131]

However, as an object of study outside of Poland, Polish Romantic drama has been classified as "literature," and as such it has remained predominantly a domain of Slavic studies departments often subjected to the same modes of criticism as lyric poetry.[132] Likewise, Polish history has remained confined to the history department, often as a footnote to the battles of the twentieth-century empires. If Grotowski and Kantor, with their rich system of visual codes, have become part of the theatre and performance studies canon, the literary and historical context of their work has been left out of the discourse and generally disowned by theatre and performance studies departments. This disciplinary disconnect was partially prompted by the conceptual shift initiated by the field of performance studies that inadvertently, as Honneger points out, also affected theatre studies, that is, the rejection of dramatic/literary tradition in favor of "non-verbal communication." In her 1999 essay "Performing Bodies, Performing Mickiewicz: Drama as Problem in Performance Studies," Halina Filipowicz points out that "Twenty years later, the shift away from the 'writtenness' of dramatic texts has led to the relative neglect of drama as a field of investigation in both literature departments and theatre programs. In this sense, drama has become an orphaned 'genre.'"[133] As such, while remaining a sole domain of Slavic studies departments, Polish Romantic drama has remained on the margins, plagued by scarce and outdated critical and theoretical research, and the virtual absence of English-language translations of the actual plays. For a long time, the only anthology of Polish Romantic drama was Harold Segel's 1977 collection of three plays: Mickiewicz's *Forefathers' Eve*, Part III only, Krasiński's *The Un-Divine Comedy*, and Słowacki's *Fantazy*.[134] The collection is a conglomeration of translations from 1924, 1944 and 1967, published marginally by various Polish organizations abroad. Segel's hope had been that, since "most modern Polish drama and theatre are rooted in the Romantic tradition, and especially because Polish drama and theatre are being ever more widely disseminated abroad," the collection would become "an indispensable frame of reference for fuller understanding of later developments."[135] It didn't happen; at the Harvard library, the collection has been checked out twice since the time of its first publication (though Segel's anthology was reprinted in 1997).[136] Most recently, Słowacki's anthology was published under the title *Poland's Angry Romantic: Two Poems and a Play by Juliusz Słowacki* (2009).[137] To date, these two books remain the only English-language translations of Polish Romantic drama.

Likewise, there has been a scarcity of research on Polish Romantic drama available and accessible to English-speaking readers. For a long time, Manfred Kridl's anthologies *The Democratic Heritage of Poland* (1944),[138] *An Anthology of Polish Literature* (1957)[139] and his 1956 *A Survey of Polish Literature and Culture* (reprinted in 1967)[140] served as the main sources of scholarship on Polish drama and its context. Czeslaw Milosz's 1969 *The History of Polish Literature*[141] (reprinted in 1983, following Milosz's winning of the Nobel Prize in 1980) followed, along with Tymon Terlecki's 1983 monograph on Wyspiański[142] and Roman Koropeckyj's 2008 biography of Mickiewicz.[143] In 1996, Kazimierz Braun's *A History of Polish Theatre, 1939–1989: Spheres of Captivity and Freedom*,[144] which provides a brief background on Polish Romantic drama, joined the sparse collection.[145] Such a dearth of research has contributed to the exclusion of Polish Romantic drama from the canon of theatre and performance studies. None of the English-language canonical anthologies of world drama, theatre history or theory include any essays or translations of Polish Romantic drama. There is one lecture by Mickiewicz on "Slavic Drama" in Daniel Gerould's anthology *Theatre/Theory/Theatre*.[146] There is nothing in the all-important *Wadsworth Anthology of Drama*,[147] just as there is nothing in *The Longman Anthology of Drama and Theater: A Global Perspective*.[148] There is nothing in the classic Dukore anthology (the title of which is *Dramatic Theory and Criticism: Greeks to Grotowski*,[149] so it is quite ironic that Grotowski's essay on poor theatre is there, but there is nothing from the Polish Romantics). In Brockett's *History of Theatre*,[150] often called the "Bible" of theatre scholars, there is one chapter on theatre in Poland and Czechoslovakia after 1968 – nothing before then.

Two aspects of Polish Romantic drama – the influence of Jewish mysticism on the content of the drama, and the structural anticipation of Wagner's idea of total theatre – became essential to the development of Grotowski and Kantor's aesthetic. In Polish history, the entire nineteenth century was consistently marked by bouts of conspiracy, resistance, revolutionary uprising, failure, persecution and exile. During the partitions, Poles mobilized a number of times in various uprisings, including two failed major insurrections in the Russian-occupied part of the country: the so-called November Insurrection in November 1830 and the January Insurrection in January 1863. Following the November Insurrection, the Polish intelligentsia and political leadership emigrated, with many of them settling down in Paris, which eventually became the center of Polish cultural and political life. The Great Emigration, as it came to be known, had a lasting impact on Polish literature, as nearly all the Polish writers of the era, including Poland's two national poets, Adam Mickiewicz and Juliusz Słowacki, were part of that wave. As they spent most of their adult lives in exile for political reasons, the experience of exile shadowed their poetry. For example, Słowacki's "Hymn at Sunset," with its refrain "How Sad Am I, My God," captures feelings of loss, longing and loneliness. Likewise, Mickiewicz's "*Pan Tadeusz* was a eulogy written in exile. The sense of longing for home is stated unequivocally in the opening lines and is imparted throughout the poem, explaining its long-held resonance with émigrés."[151] While living abroad, "the Polish émigrés quickly discovered how closely their own situation resembled the Diaspora of the Jews."[152] Thus, the image of the Wandering Jew, a man without a land who is always a stranger and who can never find peace, became embedded in the poetic imagination of Polish literature and culture. For example, the Eternal Wanderer, a man without a home, who carries with him all that he owns, became a primary trope of Kantor's aesthetic, and a model for all other Kantorian bio-objects. It was fitting that the Polish Romantic poets identified with the Jewish diasporic experience. Both Juliusz Słowacki and Adam Mickiewicz – who is believed to have had a Jewish mother – attended the University of Wilno, a city in Lithuania, which used to belong to pre-partitioned Poland, and which at that time was a center of Orthodox Jewish culture. Both Mickiewicz and Słowacki were drawn to Jewish mysticism and Kabbalah. Since "to a great extent it was 'underground' activity frowned on by the ecclesiastic hierarchy of the Jewish community, it enjoyed the aura of the forbidden."[153] Jewish tropes thus appear in the poetry of both poets; however, they are most prominent in Mickiewicz's *Forefathers' Eve*. Abraham Duker argues that Mickiewicz "followed, at least at times, a course of mystical belief and actions closer to cabbalism than to normative Catholicism."[154] In addition to the Kabbalah motif of conjuring up the spirits, another important theme of *Forefathers' Eve* is Polish national messianism, "the suffering and redemption of Poland," which "is clearly a Christ parallel."[155] However, Duker suggests, in addition to obvious Christian metaphor, we also have "to consider the parallel of the two nations in exile, Poland and Jewish people, that suggested itself to the 'Great Emigration.'"[156] Mickiewicz's messianism, Duker argues, was taken directly from Jewish mysticism, and it draws on the Frankist concept of Poland as the chosen land of chosen people, "a basis for Polish Israel theory."[157] Frankism was a Jewish religious movement popular in the eighteenth and nineteenth centuries led by Jacob Frank, a self-proclaimed Jewish Messiah (1726–91). The Frankist movement had roughly 50,000 followers, most of them Polish Jews. *Forefathers' Eve*'s main character, Konrad, visits heaven to find a source of inspiration and an answer to his moral dilemmas. As Duker notes, the theme of the "ascension of the mystic's soul (*aliyat he-neshama*) during his sleep is prominent in Jewish mystical literature, in the *markabah* (chariot) visions, and *hekhaloth* (palaces) mysticism. The visit to heaven by the soul of the Hasidic Rebbe (Wonder Rabbi) is common in Hasidic lore."[158] Thus, Konrad's story is surrounded by a Kabbalistic framework, and the core of Mickiewicz's dramatic poem draws on Jewish mysticism. For a long time in Poland, however, Mickiewicz's masterpiece was viewed and interpreted solely through the prism of Christian and pagan liturgy, with emphasis placed on the Christian messianic, martyrological trope as the thematic core of the drama that was seen as defining Poland's national character. Discussion of the Jewish motifs has not been a part of the Polish educational discourse (though *Forefathers' Eve* is taught in every Polish high school).[159] Yet the Jewish motif in *Forefathers' Eve* is woven into the storytelling through both the symbolic and the linguistic structure of the drama. It is never obvious, always just under the surface, visible only to those who can recognize it, while remaining crucial to the Polish national dramatic poem. Likewise, in both *Akropolis* and *Dead Class*, the "Jewish motive is not stable. It appears and disappears like an echo, like the 'historical apparitions.'"[160] It is embedded in the ritualistic structure of each piece, stitched together from pieces of myths, symbols, references to the Old Testament, and Jewish literature. Mickiewicz's veiled representation of Jewish mysticism has been a model for both Grotowski and Kantor, who address the issue of Polish–Jewish history and relations in a similarly veiled, nondirect manner, while relying on Mickiewicz's messianic trope (Grotowski) and diasporic trope (Kantor) to structure their own aesthetics.

A second, equally important aspect of Mickiewicz's *Forefathers' Eve* that influenced both Grotowski and Kantor is its multithematic, polyvocal and polyformal structure. In a lecture on Slavic drama delivered in Paris in 1843, years after he wrote *Forefathers' Eve*, Mickiewicz, to quote Daniel Gerould, "addressed all classes of society, seeking a unity of spectators conceived as the 'nation' that he hoped to awaken to political action on a vast scale."[161] Some Polish critics, among them Andrzej Walicki, suggest, that the traditional interpretation of Mickiewicz's messianism through the prism of Polish nationalism is not accurate, as Mickiewicz "subordinated national cause to the cause of a universal regeneration of mankind, [believing] that universal tasks should be realized by means of chosen nations and chosen individuals."[162] According to Mickiewicz, dramatic form was superior to all other arts in being able to achieve such *en masse* mobilization. However, to spur the masses, drama had to unite all arts – music, opera, dance, religious and folk rituals and songs, popular melodrama, panoramas, architecture – to create a total theatre of the future that – as many critics pointed out – anticipated Wagner's later concept of *Gesamtkunstwerk*. Mickiewicz writes:

> The *drama* is the most powerful artistic realization of poetry. It almost always announces the end of one era and the beginning of another. […] The drama, in the highest and broadest sense of the word, should unite all the elements of a truly national poetry, just as the political institution of a nation should express all its political tendencies. […] Such a drama should be lyrical, and it should remind us of the admirable melodies of popular folk songs. […] It should also transport us into the supernatural world.[163]

Mickiewicz argues that, while Greek dramas as well as early Christian mystery plays connected all different theatrical elements, rites and rituals with elements of the marvelous and the sacred, presenting "the entire universe […] as Christianity conceived it," the contemporary drama abandoned such a model.[164] It is time, Mickiewicz argues, to reclaim the archaic theatrical tradition of drama as a point of juncture for all other arts and everyday rituals. The Parisian lecture crystallized Mickiewicz's ideas which, years earlier, he had implemented in *Forefathers' Eve*. Combining supernatural elements, the pagan and Kabbalic rituals of bringing up the dead, as well as elements of passion plays and the Christian liturgy with the "classical Greek tragedy, the Christian drama and theatre of the Middle Ages, the Catholic rites of confession, repentance, and sacrifice, and folklore," *Forefathers' Eve* is an ideal example of Mickiewicz's concept of total theatre.[165] Indeed, Mickiewicz's masterpiece is monumental; it would take over nine hours to stage the whole dramatic poem. Dariusz Kosiński jokes that *"Forefathers' Eve* is an ideal text for theatre, precisely because there is no theatre that could stage it."[166] It can't be staged "as written" because every directorial decision goes against the playwright's intention. Each director needs to choose which structural or thematic logic he or she wants to follow. It is theatre of metaphysics, transformation, ritual, death and music; it is rhapsodic, religious and political theatre.[167]

A structural and thematic hybrid, *Forefathers' Eve* influenced Wyspiański's concept of drama, particularly his own monumental work, *Akropolis*. The Polish-American scholar Tymon Terlecki argues that if it were not for Mickiewicz's concept of total theatre,

Wyspiański "would never have become a dramatic writer – at least not the one he is today."[168] Wyspiański was one of the earliest supporters of the Great Reform, which advocated scenographic grandeur.[169] In fact, in 1901, Wyspiański directed his own grandiose version of Mickiewicz's *Forefathers' Eve*. Like *Forefathers' Eve*, *Akropolis*, with its opulence and syncretic structure (part drama, part opera, part poem, with themes that stretch across cultures and epochs), "might appear to be a culmination or an extension of Wagnerian concepts," or *Gesamtkunstwerk*.[170] In *Akropolis*, Wyspiański fuses antique myths with those of the Bible and Old Testament, and folk tales and folk rituals into what can be called "a stratified or a syncretic myth, a myth embodying the entire culture": Cracow's Wawel blends seamlessly with Homer's Troy and the biblical story of Jacob and Esau; the river Vistula is both Jordan and Homer's Skamander; Christ is also Apollo.[171]

For Grotowski and Kantor, the Romantic notion of total theatre is important for a number of reasons; first, the theatrical work can potentially be a symbolic condensing of Polish and, by extension, European, civilization – as embodied by its artworks – into a syncretic and unified representation of all its traditions: the Hellenic, Judaic and Christian. Adapting Wyspiański's *Akropolis*, and combining syncretically Wawel with Akropolis and Auschwitz, into one place of national and European martyrdom, Grotowski is thus indebted to both Wyspiański and Mickiewicz. The work of theatre is to channel the "spirit of the nation" and, thus, also the crisis of its values, as both *Akropolis* and *Dead Class* do, while attempting to come to terms with the crisis of Western culture and identity following the trauma of the Holocaust. Second, the combination of theatre and ritual, of the sacred and secular worlds, in the dramatic work creates potential for challenge of the very notion of the sacred. *Forefathers' Eve* takes place in a liminal space between the sacred and the secular, between the world of the living and the world of the dead. Its time and space is always on the threshold between binary modes of being. Many Polish theatre scholars have argued that *Forefathers' Eve* is the foundational drama for modern Polish theatre precisely because it blurs the line between theatre and ritual, creating a model of sacred *mysterium* from which all subsequent Polish drama evolved, including Wyspiański's.[172] Both Grotowski and Kantor considered *Forefathers' Eve* the model for modern theatre;[173] and, likewise, both *Akropolis* and *Dead Class* blur the line between theatre and ritual. However, they also represent two different positionings towards the sacred, with two different ethical, teleological and ontological attitudes. Osiński argues that Kantor's theatre is a theatre of sacrilege, while Grotowski's theatre is a theatre of blasphemy. In Polish, *świętokradztwo* (sacrilege), and *bluźnierstwo* (blasphemy) differ in that one is a deed and another a speech act. Osiński suggests that, for Kantor, *świętokradztwo* (sacrilege) is essential to any art, but especially the avant-garde, which should always be a form of rebellion against God, almost a satanic gesture, since "pure unwavering goodness is sentimental."[174] The Theatre of Death uses the form of the ritual, but there is no ritualistic pathos in it. That's why *Dead Class* can combine laughter and solemnity, circus and metaphysics, "peculiar *commedia dell'arte* and eschatology, cabaret revue and dance macabre."[175] For Grotowski, on the contrary, there is no theatre without the pathos of the ritual. Osiński notes that Grotowski draws a further distinction, between *bluźnierstwo* (blasphemy) and *profanacja* (profanation). He who profanes does not value or acknowledge the sacred nature of the object he desecrates, but he who blasphemes is very well aware of the sacred; he is afraid and trembles before the divine. Thus, blasphemy reasserts, even re-establishes, the very sacred it challenges; it is a path to redemption.[176] As many critics have pointed out: "The interplay between, on the one hand, Polish and Christian traditions and, on the other, the blasphemy and degradation of those traditions" follows "'the dialectics of mockery and apotheosis' that dominated Polish Romantic dramas."[177] The Romantic heroes often challenge God in a self-sacrificial gesture, evoking fear, pity and tragic pathos. In that sense, Osiński suggests that in Grotowski's poetic imagination, Auschwitz/Akropolis becomes an embodiment of a modern Golgotha and a Greek sacrificial altar, a *thymele*.[178] Such a reading, however, has ethical implications. Kosiński, for example, offers a different interpretation, arguing that in *Akropolis* there are no sacrificial victims, there are only murderers and murdered; death is deprived of the sacred. Clurman offers the same assessment, writing "there is no redemption here and except for the closing moment – the march to the Holocaust – very little pathos."[179] Grotowski, however, believed that in *Akropolis*, the final descent into the oven embodies such an act of sacrifice; it's an absolute act of self-sacrificial redemption on the part of his actors.[180] According to Leszek Kolankiewicz, the last scene of Grotowski's *Akropolis* is transitional. His particular scene, Kolankiewicz stipulates, eventually led Grotowski to believe that words such as theatre, spectator, spectacle or actor were no longer relevant. They were to be replaced by words such as ritual, celebration and ceremony.[181] Operating within the framework of religious terminology and proposing that theatre in general should offer a "possibility of salvation," Grotowski in fact follows the national messianic tradition of Polish Romantic drama, particularly its "quest for total, imminent, ultimate, this worldly, collective salvation."[182] However, since in Grotowski's work, salvation comes through redemptive blasphemy and self-sacrifice, it is never really removed from the Romantic trope of soteriological messianic pathos. Agnieszka Wójtowicz suggests that Grotowski wants to "cure a romantic attitude with romantic attitude," replacing one sacred with another and never really escaping the national myths that he so vigorously wants to destroy. That is why Grotowski's theatre could never enter into Kantor's irreverent realm of the grotesque.[183] Osiński notes that in *Akropolis*, Grotowski's actors pronounce Wyspiański's text with piety, in whispers and undertones.[184] In that sense, we can argue that if *Akropolis* is a somber ritual, a "Black Mass"[185] as Peter Brook calls it, or "theatrical oratory," as Osiński calls it,[186] full of pathos and solemnity, Kantor's *Dead Class* is a combination of the *Forefathers' Eve* and the Kaddish, the Jewish prayer for the dead, but also of the Jewish holiday of Purim, a carnivalesque celebration of survival and revenge. As Ahuva Belkin notes, Purim "commemorates Haman's plan to annihilate the Jews, and their miraculous rescue. [...] [It] has remained an occasion for collective catharsis over a people's deliverance from its enemies; [...] a saturnalian and carnivalesque [...] mimesis of vengeance against evil."[187] Thus, while Grotowski remains within the realm of the sacred, Kantor disturbs it with a complex, multilayered structure of tragic grotesque that combines both an ironic solemnity and a mad abyss of carnivalesque laughter. Although in different ways, both Grotowski and Kantor draw on Romantic Polish drama, finding in *Forefathers' Eve* a source of inspiration and model for modern theatre.

Both *Akropolis* and *Dead Class* share *Forefathers' Eve*'s liminal dialectic of the world of the living meeting with the world of the dead, the sacred meeting with the secular, while simultaneously reassessing and challenging the foundational values of Polish and, by extension, European civilization.

Theatre and Politics

Outside of their native context, the subtle differences between Grotowski and Kantor, as well as their common cultural and literary background, gets lost in translation, or rather in the lack of it. Framed by the Cold War dynamics and the internal politics of the USA during the period from the late 1960s to the late 1970s, reception of both Grotowski and Kantor by American academic and theatre circles was marred by two contradictory impulses: an illicit fascination with the abstruse imports from behind the Iron Curtain, on the one hand, and the dismissive, even lackadaisical, exegesis of the actual object, on the other. As a result, the meaning of both *Akropolis* and *Dead Class* was construed through a culturally unspecific hybrid of global associations, digested and processed by the imperializing sensibility of Western academic and critical circles. In a 1971 essay, Jan Klossowicz, a prominent Polish theatre scholar, declares bluntly: "Certain statements made by foreign theatrical critics and [practitioners] who came to know the Polish theatre only on the occasion of Grotowski's foreign tours contain formulations which seem ridiculous to a Pole."[188] Klossowicz is not alone in this harsh assessment. Juliusz Tyszka, a Polish theatre scholar who visited the USA as a Fulbright Scholar from 1992–1993, cites an anecdote from a Grotowski seminar organized by New York University's (NYU) Performance Studies Department, in which he participated while in the USA. Following the screening of *Akropolis*, the discussion turned towards "the universal, supra-national, 'intercultural' aspects of *Akropolis*." When the discussion began, Tyszka notes, he and his Polish wife observed with some consternation that almost all American participants immediately proclaimed "the intercultural universalism" of Grotowski's production, arguing that "all layers of meaning are completely clear and understood to them as *Akropolis* is a product of global, not merely Polish culture."[189] As a Polish speaker, Tyszka was asked to confirm the validity of such a critical approach, which he couldn't do, citing numerous Polish-specific references which could not be understood by viewers unfamiliar with their cultural context. As a result, Tyszka was implicitly accused – as he put it – of being a "Polish-Catholic chauvinist, who sees signs of Polish culture everywhere, even when it's not there, since the absolute universalism of *Akropolis* is obvious for everyone to see."[190] The tone of the accusations suggested that "Poland, with its own culture, cannot produce anything of value, whether in theatre or anywhere else."[191] One performance studies student, Tyszka writes, passionately proclaimed that "she is glad, proud even that she doesn't speak Polish because she can see and interpret Grotowski's spectacle in much more comprehensive light, unencumbered by narrow values of the Polish national culture."[192] The discussion suggested that "American culture is more universal, richer than Polish culture, therefore American scholars can interpret the products of Polish culture better than Poles can." The irony was, Tyszka points out, that despite their "healthy" contempt for Polish culture, NYU performance studies students genuinely believed in the "universalism" of their own interpretations.[193] The discussion described by Tyszka, and the frustrations that he and Jan Klossowicz express, are recognized by Polish speakers who have attended performance studies panels or seminars. Likewise, they are also familiar to other foreign scholars whose own cultures have been "universalized" by such a discourse.

In her essay "Can the Subaltern Speak?" Gayatri Spivak eloquently argues that the mechanism that guides the discourse between superior powers and the oppressed is complex: "When we come to the concomitant question of the consciousness of the subaltern, the notion of what the work *cannot* say becomes important."[194] For years, Poles have spoken about their own culture from the subaltern position, a subaltern that has been historically forced to negotiate between a number of imperial powers and historical forces, often veiling and modulating the discourse. First, in the context of the Soviet regime, both Grotowski and Kantor were forced to veil and skirt the taboo subject of Polish–Jewish relations. Then, *vis-à-vis* the American left-leaning art circles, each of them – though for different reasons – was once again forced to navigate another set of unmentionables: the totalitarian character of socialist regimes, the complexity of Polish cultural and literary tradition, the convoluted history of Poland's three partitions and two World Wars, and, finally, the long, tragic and multifarious history of Polish–Jewish relations. As no one in American academe or the American theatre communities was particularly interested in any of these topics beyond the standard clichéd and politically expedient narratives, eventually both Grotowski and Kantor learned to speak between the lines, avoiding the topics that would bore and alienate their foreign critics and allies. In one of his interviews, Kantor once poignantly noted that "Theatre can be impossible to understand by the world, by foreigners. It can be closed in its own ethnic borders."[195] Kantor continued, "That is what's unfortunately happening with Polish Theatre because our greatest theatre – our greatest Romantic Theatre – is impossible for foreigners to understand."[196] Well aware that he was in no political position to expect foreigners to try to understand "our theatre,"[197] no matter how great, Kantor resigned himself to not speaking of his own theatre's cultural framework.

As both Grotowski and Kantor stressed the extralingual aspects of their work, the foreign critics readily discarded the need for textual or contextual analysis in favor of "loving descriptions," at worst, and formal critique, at best. Some – as Richard Schechner or Robert Kanters did in their treatment of Grotowski's work – went so far as to suggest that *not* knowing a work's language or cultural context has a liberating effect that enables one to more fully grasp its meaning. As a result of such self-reflective epistemology – "imperialist object constitution," as Spivak would call it – knowledge becomes displaced from the object of study to the subject who studies; the subject's imperial self-perception becomes a sole source of meaning.[198] However, neither Kantor nor Grotowski ever fully condoned such an approach. Grotowski, like Kantor, aware of his inferior political position, resigned himself to that acquiescent position simply because a demand for full intellectual engagement and commitment from his foreign colleagues and supporters would risk estrangement from the discourse altogether. In an interview with Raymonde Temkine, for example, Grotowski diplomatically states: "Whether one understands Polish or not is unimportant. But I do not share Robert Kanters' opinion that one's inability to understand the language is 'an asset in a theatre which values much more the myth as it is shown in the play than the text of the play itself.'"[199] Reading between Grotowski's lines, Temkine admits philosophically: "The Poles, because of their language and culture, must experience the effects of the play more strongly than we do."[200]

The glorification of cultural incompetency as a way of knowing theatrical works meant the proliferation of dehistoricized operations in de-contextualization, asymptomatic surface readings, and misreadings – of both the linguistic and the visual layers of *Akropolis* and *Dead Class*. One particular example: in his analysis of *Akropolis*, Robert Findlay interprets one of the most evocative visual images – the actor fluttering his hands over the ropes stretched across the stage – as a symbol of nature's indifference towards human suffering (trembling trees), with the actor's "fluttering hands and fingers remarkably imitative of birds in flight."[201] Findlay's interpretation follows the trope of "nature's indifference" towards human life, its joys and sufferings, that prevailed in nineteenth-century Anglo-Saxon poetry.[202] The image, however, is more literal, and it has nothing to do with poetry or nature; it illustrates the desperate act of suicide – "going on the wires" – committed by Auschwitz (and other concentration camp) prisoners who routinely threw themselves onto the electric barbed wire. Electrocuted, their bodies would tremble and shake before freezing limply on the fence in the final pose. The image functions as a sign for those who understand it, but it lacks signification for those who are not familiar with its context. In that sense, Grotowski's *Akropolis* enters into a dialogue with the cultural initiates, but leaves out those unfamiliar with the cultural markers.[203] Understanding the reality of Auschwitz is part of the cultural competency and historical context essential to understanding the symbolic and visual language of *Akropolis*. That knowledge was part of everyday life in Polish postwar culture, yet it was unavailable to foreigners who have not researched this aspect of Holocaust experience.

The linguistic aspect of each production is as important as the visual aspect, as it brings forth layers of meanings and a breadth of reference that would otherwise go unnoticed. Most foreign critics readily echoed Schechner and Kanters' recommendation that the language of both *Akropolis* and *Dead Class* is no more than "gibberish."[204] "The words don't mean anything," wrote Martin Gottfried confidently on account of *Akropolis*, but "are purposely garbled and rechanneled into incantation, ritualized expression, repetition and finally word-destruction."[205] A British critic asserted that in *Dead Class*, the words are merely "guttural and sonorous sounds [that] express mood rather than meaning."[206] The postmodern crisis of language, that for theatre meant moving away from textual towards performance-based language, resulted in the dismissal of text; critical dismissal was revalorized as formal gesture. However – as Adorno reminds us – in drama, even negative meaning becomes meaningful; the words have meaning by way of what they negate. The words, even if they appear as gibberish, have both sequential and nonsequential meaning; each word functions in relation to other words, but is also its own nexus of cultural signposts. For example, in Kantor's *Dead Class*, Old Men and Women randomly exclaim names from Greek mythology and Roman history, the two paramount subjects of pre–World War I

Polish secondary education. Dislodged from their context, dredged up from the long-forgotten corners of memory and shouted out at random, these bits and pieces of the European literary canon can appear as "gibberish" to those unfamiliar with Polish, but they do have meaning. They symbolize the fragmentation and dissociation of European identity at the turn of the century; the literary bedrocks of European culture no longer signify the power of history, nor the cultural heritage that guards centuries of European domination. Decontextualized, stripped of dignity, they become "small and defenseless," ridiculously discarded in the despised domain of mundane childhood Sunday-school lessons. These small linguistic flashes represent the crisis of Western civilization, its values and its history. In addition to the broader context, however, each reference also carries its own distinct set of meanings. For example, "Cleopatra's nose" specifically alludes to Blaise Pascal's remark from *Pensées*, that if "Cleopatra's nose had […] been shorter, the whole face of the world would have been changed" (as neither Caesar nor Marc Antony would have fallen in love with her).[207] Mentioning Cleopatra's nose in a stream of other ancients, Kantor thus performs a sleight of hand, while also making a profoundly ironic comment about the arbitrary nature of history; the life and death of millions of people depends on chance, on a roll of the dice – or a woman's nose. There is no difference. Pascal's remark in fact, is part of the Polish vocabulary, often cited as a proverb.

In another example, the Old Men and Women repeat a statement: *Idy Marcowe* (Ides of March). Celebrated on the fifteenth day of March, the Ides of March was a festival in ancient Rome dedicated to the god of war, Mars, celebrating military might and the victory of the empire. The Ides of March is also known as the date that Julius Caesar was murdered, betrayed by Brutus, his beloved stepson. In *Julius Caesar*, Shakespeare dramatizes the famous exchange between Caesar and the Soothsayer, who warns Caesar to "beware the Ides of March." Thornton Wilder's 1948 novel, *The Ides of March*,[208] also narrates these events. (The Polish Television Theatre showed the filmed version of Wilder's book in 1962.)[209] In the West, the Ides of March came to symbolize betrayal and brute military violence. In the Polish culture of the 1970s, the Ides of March also became a code word for the events of March 1968, when most of the country's remaining Jews were forced by the communist government to immigrate to Israel. (There is even a 1989 Polish movie, *Marcowe Migdały* [The Almonds of March],[210] which poignantly tells the story of the 1968 events from the point of view of Polish and Polish-Jewish students who were suddenly forced to part ways and make difficult moral choices. The title of the movie is a play on words: *The Almonds of March/ The Ides of March* [*Marcowe Migdały / Idy Marcowe*].) Thus, by shouting "Ides of March," Kantor's characters bring forth a complex nexus of meaning: the lingering sense of betrayal that for a long time pervaded Polish society; shame at the betrayal of the Jewish community during the war and in 1968; bitterness at the betrayal of Poland by the Allies in 1939 and 1945.[211] Although the random outbursts may seem to be "gibberish" to those who don't understand the words, those who do understand them can see the multilayered, multidimensional levels of significations that address not only broader European, but also specifically Polish, history and culture. Without the cultural competency that includes visual, linguistic and historical knowledge, the meanings of *Akropolis* and *Dead*

Class are dismantled in the critical selfsame. Stripped of their origins, both productions become *tabulae rasae* onto which foreign scholars project their own thoughts, desires and cultural references. Images are misread and words turned into "gibberish."

Theatre and History

In *Aesthetic Theory*, Adorno argues that "art is a product of history."[212] Most importantly, however, Adorno suggests that form in art is a function of historical circumstances. He writes, "The basic levels of experience that motivate art are related to those of the objective world from which they recoil. The unresolved antagonisms of reality return in artworks as immanent problems of form."[213] Such is the case with both Grotowski and Kantor. Both became influential foremost for their formal innovations; however, each aesthetic theory, Grotowski's theory of *teatr ubogi* and Kantor's theory of *teatr biedny*, grew out of a particular historical moment, a "sedimentation of a historical process," as Adorno would put it.[214] Both works have been transformational for Polish theatre; internationally, they're considered quintessential milestones in the development of theatre insofar as they articulate, incomparably, the dilemma of the twentieth century. Martin Harries notes that "the twentieth century had a particular investment in a formal logic that placed the spectator in a spot where that spectator had to contemplate her own destruction. [...] [I]t obliges the spectator to think about mass death."[215] Following Adorno's *Dialectic of Enlightenment*, Harries further suggests that the most pertinent question for twentieth-century art and aesthetic is the question of representation post-Auschwitz. On the level of both form and content, twentieth-century art has been dominated by the attempts to find a way to understand, redefine and perhaps even reclaim and rescue the failed project of the European Enlightenment, its ethical, social, political and historical objectives.[216] Auschwitz, as a symbol of a failure of Western thought, is a foundational trauma for postwar art and politics as they have tried to grapple with the issues of Western identity and memory. Poland, "periodically invaded, partitioned, dismembered, oppressed, and brutalized, and itself guilty of oppression and backwardness, [...] has embodied the modern tragedy in a world dominated by great powers."[217] Understanding Polish theatre – particularly Grotowski's and Kantor's works, precisely because they have influenced Western theatre so profoundly – can help us understand the relationship between form and history, politics and representation, and trauma and post-memory, as they become articulated and concealed within the layers of post-traumatic performative language. As Osiński points out, both *Akropolis* and *Dead Class* are artworks made "after the catastrophe of humanism, destruction of the subject and rational thought. In both, we see confrontation of the dead/actors and the living/spectators."[218] The tension between the viewers and actors, the living and the dead, is also a tension between history and present; it is an articulation of modernity on trial as judged by its dead. It is also – in different ways – a reevaluation of the Polish literary canon, and of Polish national identity. Analyzing both *Akropolis* and *Dead Class* can help us reveal the ways in which trauma, when translated through the prism of performance, can significantly alter and deflect the interpretation of pre-traumatic artworks. This book was partially inspired by Maurice Halbwachs' premise that "present concerns determine what of the past we remember and how we remember it."[219] For both *Akropolis* and *Dead Class*, as Barba puts it: "the context is socialist Poland, during a period in its history which was marked by the dreariness of a police regime and by the fervor of an intellectual and artistic life that was at the same time a liberating cry and a tireless fashioning of liberty."[220] Both *Akropolis* and *Dead Class* are also works of memory. But what and how do they remember? What and how do they forget?

Both *Akropolis* and *Dead Class* engage the issues of Polish–Jewish relations and the Holocaust in a nondirect, veiled manner. Both works also address Auschwitz (though Kantor never mentions it in any context). To understand why and how important this framing was, however, we need to understand the long history of Polish–Jewish relations. For many years following World War II, the near-extermination of a Jewish community whose numbers once constituted a third of Poland's population was a taboo subject. Although Polish literature and cinema were almost solely devoted to the experience of the war, particularly the Holocaust, often the narrative was co-opted by the communist regime for its own purposes. Auschwitz, as an idea, was useful to Poland's communist propagandists insofar as its memory created national unity by underscoring Polish and universal human – rather than Polish-Jewish – suffering: "Auschwitz was presented and groomed as a site of Polish national martyrdom."[221] This line of propaganda was in turn used to forge myths of commonality with – and debt to – the Soviet Union by linking that mythology to the sacrifices of the Soviet army that "liberated" Poland from German rule. Auschwitz thus acquired an aura of Polish ownership that elevated the primacy of Polish suffering (as well as that of the Soviet guarantors of its political apparatus) as a means of forging a national identity. The primacy of the Jewish story remained mostly unaddressed in both public debate and most scholarship. Moreover, for the communist government it was expedient to avoid the subject of Jewish suffering insofar as Poland's few remaining Jews provided the communists with useful scapegoats for the nation's chronic shortages, economic malaise and deplorable living conditions. They were characteristically denounced as "American imperialists."[222]

This strategy reached its nadir in the 1968 expulsion of the country's remaining Polish Jews to Israel. The purges had already begun in 1965 in the army and party. Writing in 1966, Joseph Lichten, an American scholar, summarized the events: "The present enemy is more formidable than one from the past. For a Jew today, Poland is a more hostile place than Germany. But it is the Polish Communist Party which has imposed itself on the Polish people – and not Poland itself – that is responsible for vindictive acts against the Jews."[223] In 1968, the scale and tone of the government's anti-Semitic propaganda grew more ominous.[224] In March 1968, students protested in Warsaw to protest the censorship and totalitarian educational policies of the PZPR (the Polish United Workers Party – the Communist Party), which stifled any kind of intellectual engagement and freedom of speech. The protests were quickly and violently suppressed by the government of Władysław Gomułka. The violent response strengthened the position of Gomułka's rival, the fiercely anti-Semitic Mieczysław Moczar, the emissary of Moscow and the chief of the Polish Communist Secret Police.

As a result, the country's Jews were expelled from the government, the **PZPR** and the universities. The anti-Semitic purges and rhetoric were essentially orchestrated by the Soviets in response to the emerging conflict in the Middle East. Culminating in the 1967 Six Day Arab–Israeli War, which delineated the Cold War's political spheres of influence (with the USA supporting Israel, and the Soviet Union supporting the Arab states), the tensions in the Middle East indirectly influenced the situation of Jews in Eastern Europe. In Poland, under pressure from the Soviet Union, the combination of events ultimately precipitated a government-organized Jewish exodus to Israel, amidst the protests, instigations, shame, regret and resentment of different social and political groups, concluding a disastrous chapter of Polish–Jewish history, "a crisis of conscience in Polish society whose aftershocks can still be felt."[225] It is a supremely ironic fact that, as Allen Kuharski notes, "As Ida Kaminska, the distinguished artistic director of Warsaw's Jewish Theater, was packing her bags to emigrate to the U.S., the Polish Laboratory was riding the wave of the international success of *Akropolis* and *The Constant Prince*."[226] To this day, Poles are grappling with the question of what exactly happened in 1968 and why thousands of Polish citizens were suddenly forced to leave their own country.

The subtle layers of meanings – political, historical and literary – that both Grotowski and Kantor construct are lost for most American theatre scholars, for whom Polish history remains on the far margins of European history. Likewise, for the average educated American, as well as for many American scholars of humanities not specializing in this issue, the image of Poles has been that of "raging anti-Semites."[227] For theatre scholars, this image has defined and limited most American interpretations of both *Akropolis* and *Dead Class*. The memory of the Holocaust, which took place on Polish soil, combined with the events of 1968, contribute to such a view of Poles, shadowing many American pop culture movies set during World War II, as well as other American mass media. This image was cemented by Lanzmann's 1985 documentary *Shoah*, a syllabus staple taught in many graduate and undergraduate-level courses across the USA, particularly in film, theatre and performance studies departments, where it is often used as an artifact of trauma studies discourse. Travelling the villages around Auschwitz, Lanzmann interviews local Polish peasants about what they remember from the time of war. They narrate their stories, perhaps for the first time in their lives, with Lanzmann implicitly suggesting that they are somehow implicated in the Nazis' master plan. Lanzmann's anger and bitterness are palpable and understandable, but they are directed at impoverished, traumatized and often illiterate peasants who have themselves been brutalized by German and Russian armies more times than they can or care to remember. They are trying to be helpful, awkwardly confirming Lanzmann's ironic statements, often disoriented and surprised that he is making them, yet incapable of detecting his irony.[228] (It also doesn't help that most of the dialogue has been badly mistranslated in subtitles. Parts of the text have been cut, as the translator either doesn't translate some sentences or adds something.)[229] The film represents a sliver of Polish society without acknowledging its own class, economic, educational and social stratifications, nor addressing the historical background and colonial context of Polish–Jewish relations. Like every society, Polish society has always been stratified, and different groups during different time periods and for different reasons responded differently to their Jewish fellow countrymen. As Czerniaków, the

Polish-Jewish writer, wrote: "I often ask myself whether Poland means Mickiewicz and Słowacki, or the street gang. The truth lies somewhere between."[230] Nonetheless, the unambiguous vision of Polish society as unilaterally anti-Semitic often comes as a shock to many Polish scholars coming to the USA, but it is a vision that sooner or later they have to confront. The situation is even more complicated for Polish-Jewish intellectuals living in the USA who are naturally torn by contrary impulses and loyalties, yet are habitually forced into a corner to make oversimplified statements about a complex, nuanced and multilayered issue of Polish–Jewish relations and identity.[231]

Most recently, the *New York Times*, for the first time ever, published a more nuanced assessment of Polish–Jewish relations, acknowledging that subtleties often got lost in foreign perception:

> Shifting political power struggles during and after the war, among other complications of Polish Jewish history, led some Polish Jews at certain points to side with Soviets against Nazis and Polish partisans [who fought both Soviets and Nazis]. The whole moral morass, essential to Polish identity, tends to be lost on outsiders, many of whom unthinkingly regard the country, throughout most of the last century at least, as just a Jewish killing field.[232]

For years, given their own weak political and economic position, Polish immigrants had little power to address the negative mainstream cultural representations, and these images filtered down to many academic fields, including theatre and performance studies. Lacking the nuanced approach of careful historicism, the theatre and performance studies Holocaust discourse has been fundamentally structured around the American pop cultural representation of the Holocaust. A case in point is Gene Plunka's *Holocaust Drama* (2009), published by Cambridge University Press, in which the author contextualizes the historical framework of the Holocaust through the prism of American movies and TV series, the NBC miniseries *Holocaust*, Spielberg's *Schindler's List*, and Lanzmann's *Shoah*, among others. Not one Polish, or Polish-Jewish, play or movie is mentioned in the entire book, though the word Auschwitz is central to the book's very premise. In fact, despite the wealth of Polish language literature on the subject, Plunka's bibliography doesn't include a single Polish writer or critic (with the sole exception of the Austrian-Jewish writer Martin Buber, who was also fluent in Polish). Tellingly, Plunka does not forget to include plenty of German playwrights, writers and philosophers. Such a narrow imperial definition of what constitutes, as Plunka calls it, an "effective piece of Holocaust literature"[233] is obviously a problem, particularly since Poland was the Holocaust epicenter. Unfortunately, as the example of Plunka's book indicates, the decontextualization and dehistorization of the Holocaust in the field of theatre and performance studies has created a vacuum; discourse around Auschwitz and its representation in theatre scholarship in the USA has developed without input from, or acknowledgment of, Polish or Polish-Jewish traumatic and post-traumatic experiences. Likewise, the American interpretations of both *Akropolis* and *Dead Class* have left out the complex history with which both works engage, often replacing it with a limited, pop cultural understanding of Polish–Jewish relations.

As Susan A. Glenn and Naomi B. Sokoloff point out in their book, *Boundaries of Jewish Identity*, between the ethnic, racial, religious, national and cultural definitions, there is no such thing as a stable, "essential Jewish self."[234] As such, it would be equally difficult, if not impossible, to define the essential Polish self or the essential Polish-Jewish self. But it may perhaps be possible to delineate the historic and geographic boundaries of the Polish-Jewish experience, as it developed through centuries of upheavals, partitions, wars, calamities, catastrophes and renewal. This experience is "unique to the Western world. Poles and Jews lived together for centuries, sharing the same land."[235] The history of Polish–Jewish relations is complex and long, reaching back to the Middle Ages. Writing about the status of Jews in Old Poland, Artur Sandauer, an esteemed Polish-Jewish writer, essayist and theatre critic, points out that during medieval times, while Jews were persecuted everywhere else in Europe, Poland was "an exception to the rule." The Polish King "Kazimierz the Great brought Jews to Poland in 1334 and gave them special privileges." Sandauer writes:

> There is a typical fact which attests to the friendly reception of the Jews. The Jews would give each new habitat a Hebrew name, usually drawn from the Old Testament. [...] They called Poland, "Polin" and supplied for the word a fictional etymology by breaking it up into "po" (here) and "lin" (rest). For three centuries [...] Poland was truly a country in which the Jews could rest. Contemporary Poland did not discriminate against Jews on the scale of Western Europe. [...] On the whole the Jews lived in peace and developed their culture in ceremonial Hebrew and in a German dialect employed for everyday use. The latter soaked up Hebrew and Polish words and eventually gave rise to Yiddish.[236]

Gavri'el ben Yehoshu'a Schossburg, the seventeenth-century Hebrew chronicler, described the situation of Jews in early Poland as "a delight to all the lands of the Exile for its Torah, honor and greatness."[237] For centuries, a special legislation "bestowed on Jews a privilege granted to neither burghers nor peasants. That privilege was nobility, granted to Jews who converted to Christianity."[238] Although few Jews took advantage of the law, a conversion of 500 Jews in 1751 was particularly meaningful as it sparked a debate about the "Polonization" of the Polish Jews, and the "Judaization" of Polish Catholics. Adam Mickiewicz was against such a Polonization, regarding "Jews in Polish lands as a priceless value that must never be surrendered."[239] By the end of the seventeenth century, Poland had the highest Jewish population in all of Europe. Until World War II,

> the majority of Jews in the world could trace their ancestry to this region. Jews in Poland enjoyed extensive autonomy and collective economic prosperity, while developing sophisticated institutions of communal governance. [...] Later generations have often regarded the precedents set by Polish Jewry in such areas as communal autonomy, education, halakhah, and Jewish self-definition as classic models.[240]

Currently, it is estimated that as many as "80% of Jews across the world can trace their roots back to Poland."[241]

During the period of struggles for Polish independence, following the partitions of 1772, 1773 and 1775, "there was a need to gain the support for the national cause of the numerically significant Jewish minority. That is why every manifestation of Polish patriotism by that minority was registered and highlighted. One relevant example is Norwid's splendid poem 'Żydowie polscy' [Polish Jews], devoted to Jewish participation in the demonstrations preceding the Uprising of 1983."[242] The Jewish fighter Berek Joselewicz, who fought in the Kosciuszko Uprising and died in an 1809 battle, and Rabbi Dov Berush Meisels of Warsaw, who participated in the Polish rebellions of 1830–31 and 1863, "took on iconic status as symbols both of Jewish sacrifice for Poland and Polish–Jewish amity."[243] Until World War I, Poland continued to be a prime Jewish destination. Following the Russian pogroms of 1905, there was a wave of migration of Russian Jews to Poland's Galicia, the Southern part of Poland under Austro-Hungarian occupation, the least oppressed and most politically independent of all three partitioned parts of Poland.[244] Famously, in *Fiddler on the Roof*, Chava and Fyedka escape Ukraine, with its Tzarist pogroms, and go to Cracow, the unofficial capital and cultural center of Galicia, which was seen at that time as a Jewish safe haven, with its Jewish neighborhood, Kazimierz, often referred to as the Galician Jerusalem.

There is a reason why for centuries Jews flocked to Poland in search of a peaceful life. Perhaps because of Poland's history of oppression under the Russian, Prussian and Austro-Hungarian occupation during centuries of partition, or Polish diasporic experience, Polish aristocracy developed an honor code of ethnic and religious tolerance, and a sense of acceptance towards their Jewish compatriots. Based on historical accounts, it appears that Gentiles and Jews lived in peace in a syncretic Polish culture. A 1885 newspaper, for example, describes an intermission during the performance of a Jewish play, attended by both Jews and Gentiles, as "a mixture of voices, languages, social classes, manners, moods; a veritable Tower of Babel of people linked only by hope of relaxation, freedom and entertainment."[245] Among other things, the persecution of Jews in Russia contributed to the blending of Polish and Jewish cultures, in theatre in particular. In 1883, the Tzarist government banned theatrical performances in Yiddish. As a result, many Yiddish plays with Jewish themes were translated into Polish and performed by both Polish and Polish-Jewish actors for both Gentile and Jewish audiences.[246]

Poland's legacy of partitions created unique conditions in different parts of the country. The Tsarist government incited Polish–Jewish antagonism; thus, the Russian-occupied area saw some violent incidents. The Austro-Hungarian government, on the other hand, preferred to incite Polish–Ukrainian conflicts, which accounted for the relatively peaceful coexistence of Jews and Poles in southern Poland, the so-called Galicia.[247] During that time, in southern Poland, any antipathy to Jews was connected in general to the fear of modernity and progress, with country Jews – associated with the idyllic Poland of the feudal past and rustic folklore – being the "good ones," and the city Jews – associated with industrial progress and speculation – being the "bad ones."[248] This theme of country versus city emerges in plays of the era, performed for both Jewish and Gentile audiences.[249] However, during the wave of migration of Russian Jews into Galicia, the first roots of conflict began to sprout, particularly among the uneducated lower classes of Polish peasants and middle-class gentry, who, for the first time, began to see the foreign Russian Jews as competitors for scarce resources. In Galicia, the Russian Jews were often seen simply as Russians, widely disliked in Poland due to the centuries of partitions.[250]

Before World War I, Jews in Poland "represented a tremendous force."[251] At the beginning of the twentieth century, 37 percent of Warsaw's 500,000 inhabitants were Jewish. Following the war, after Poland gained independence in 1918, one-third of the entire Polish population was Jewish: "According to the 1921 Statistical Yearbook some 750,000 Jews used Polish as their native tongue."[252] In addition to Polish Jews, the Polish Republic at that time had large populations of Belarusians, Lithuanians and Ukrainians, many of them also Jewish. Altogether, 37 percent of the population consisted of minorities, which made the Polish state "inherently unstable" *vis-à-vis* its European neighbors.[253] The push for a unified national identity led to increasingly anti-Semitic rhetoric; regardless, the Jews were the only politically active minority in Poland at that time.[254] Roza Pomerantz-Meltzer, for example, was the first woman elected to the Sejm, the lower house of the parliament, in 1919, as a member of a Zionist party.[255] Many Jews also occupied the highest echelons of Polish social, economic and intellectual life, which led to the conflation of anti-intellectual and anti-Semitic sentiments in a populist surge of newly emerged nationalism. Sandauer writes:

> Jewish Poles were an extremely varied group encompassing converts, those with a dual sense of belonging, and lastly those who spoke Polish but felt themselves to be Jews. [...] At the same time the important role of Jews in the general culture kept on growing. [...] Since these people created a considerable part of Polish culture, one could not oppose them without opposing this very culture. Hence the coalescence of antisemitism and anti-intellectualism and the rise of plebeian racism.[256]

The result was increasing resentment towards Jews, though, as Sandauer points out, it was rarely backed by action. Jan Błoński even expresses surprise that, despite the heated rhetoric, "words were not followed by deeds."[257] Kantor himself reminisced that in his hometown, Wielopole, Polish and Jewish communities "lived in an agreeable symbiosis," each cultivating its own holidays and traditions.[258] In his article "Hebrew-Yiddish-Polish: A Trilingual Jewish Culture," Chone Shmeruk (1989) also suggests that the various strata of Polish–Jewish culture lived in relative harmony, with different social and cultural identities cultivating their own sense of belonging. Shmeruk writes:

> In addition to the traditional religious culture that was still predominant in Poland between the two world wars, three modern post-Enlightenment cultural systems existed among Polish Jewry. They were generally distinguished by linguistic and ideological characteristics. The cultural systems in the Jewish languages – Hebrew and Yiddish – were usually identified with defined Jewish nationalist ideologies. Hebrew culture relied on Zionist ideology, whereas modern Yiddish secular culture was built primarily by Bundists and their adherents, and to a lesser extent by Zionist socialists, Folkists, and those Jewish communists who did not advocate the assimilation of Jews.[259]

Parallel to these two cultural systems, there also existed a Polish cultural system in which the "striving for Jewish self-preservation [was] less apparent."[260] Shmeruk distinguishes between "the thin stratum of Polish intelligentsia of Jewish descent, including renowned Polish writers, who were totally assimilated into Polish culture and identified themselves as Poles – even despite certain sporadic expressions of Jewish self-identification to which they were pushed by hostile forces over which they had no control"[261] and those Jews "whose exclusive or partial cultural language was Polish [but who were either] Zionist in ideology or nonaffiliated and politically apathetic [and who] certainly never denied their Jewish identity."[262] Schmeruk argues that Poland had a complex multilayered culture. He writes:

> The true and great power of this culture lay not in isolation of these linguistic areas but in their interaction, an interaction that included the traditional religious cultural system as well. The full picture of the culture of Polish Jews can only be perceived by approaching it as a polysystem in which the power of its components comes from the force of their mutual, dynamic interaction, and not in their isolation.[263]

The multiculturalism of Polish society and blending of three discernable linguistic and cultural traditions set Poland apart from other European countries. Compared with the anti-Semitic violence that at that time was sweeping France, Germany and Russia, the situation of Polish Jews appeared not as volatile. Błoński suggests that it was, ironically, Polish Catholicism that both fueled the violent rhetoric and, in the end, kept people from committing acts of violence.

Right before World War II, in 1939, 3.3 million Jews lived in Poland. This population constituted 40 percent of all European Jewry at that time. "In 1942, there were four Jews for every eight Poles in Warsaw."[264] Half of the European Jews who died in the Holocaust were of Polish origin. Just as many non-Jewish Poles, nearly 3 million, also died in concentration camps and uprisings. The Nazis built concentration camps on Polish soil precisely because it was efficient – it saved on transportation costs since most European Jews were concentrated in Poland. With such numbers and the strong connection between Polish and Jewish cultures in Poland prior to the war, it was impossible for the Polish and Jewish communities not to develop deep personal bonds. Writing in 1966, Lichten notes that

> Contrary to some opinions, there was a fairly strong sense of community solidarity in the early days of the occupation. As time wore on, it slowly evaporated, with considerable assistance from Nazi propaganda. And as fear of the death penalty for aiding fellow citizen drove the separating wedge deeper, it became easier – far easier – for the latent inhumanity which exists in all men to emerge in some. [...] Such was the climate of Poland's occupation: the collapse of the communitarian sense, a *désengagement* between ghetto-dwellers and those outside the city. Like poisoned air, this atmosphere made its own somber contribution to the Armageddon which was unrolling in Poland and elsewhere. Against this background, the individual and group actions of fraternity toward the Jew stand in even stronger relief. A number of

influences contributed to the climate of alienation. The first of these was the plans, policies, and attitudes of the Germans toward the whole of the Polish population. It is a well-known and ironic fact that the Nazis themselves left massive documentation dealing with the future of the Polish Nation – slated as the next mass victim after the Jews. [...] Particularly important are the regulations pertaining to penalties for any form of assistance extended to a Jew.[265]

During the early days of the Nazi occupation, Jews and Gentiles felt solidarity against the common enemy. Poland was the only Nazi-occupied country in which helping Jews was punishable by death, and many Poles risked their lives to save their Polish-Jewish friends and neighbors. Many others were killed while trying to save them. As Błoński notes: "There is a place in Israel commemorating people who saved Jews during the war. Thirty percent of the names on that list are Polish names."[266] We will never know how many of those who tried perished. As records also indicate, "there were persons notorious for their anti-Semitic feelings and activities before the war who, in view of the tragedy of the Jews, became their committed friends and supporters."[267] There was an official underground Polish organization, Żegota, the Council to Aid the Jews, which had branches in Warsaw, Cracow and Lwow, that organized forged documents, mainly identity cards and birth certificates, and placed Jewish children in Gentile families, or hid them in monasteries and orphanages. Żegota kept communication with Ghetto dwellers by smuggling food and newspapers printed by the Polish Home Army in Polish, Yiddish and Hebrew.[268] During the Ghetto Uprising, Żegota helped to deliver weapons and to sneak people in and out of the Ghetto. During the most desperate fighting of the uprising, the white and red Polish flag fluttered alongside the white and blue of the Jewish standard.

One of the most heroic and tragic examples of Polish resistance fighters was Witold Pilecki, the founder of the Secret Polish Army (Tajna Armia Polska) and a member of the Polish Resistance Home Army (the AK). The AK had about half a million members, and it took orders from the Polish government in exile, stationed in London during World War II. In 1940, Pilecki volunteered for Auschwitz as part of a secret resistance operation to gather intelligence and help prisoner morale. He was supplied with false documents and deliberately got himself caught in the street roundup. While in Auschwitz, Pilecki organized the resistance movement, and prepared the first ever intelligence report on the camp. The report was delivered to the Western Allies, which until then thought that Auschwitz was either an internment or a labor camp. In 1943, Pilecki escaped from Auschwitz to participate in the Warsaw Uprising. After the war, he returned to communist Poland from exile, and began collecting evidence of Soviet atrocities and persecution of Poles. The Soviets considered the Polish Home Army an arm of the USA and Great Britain. When the communists took control of Poland, the members of the AK were labeled traitors (fascist/capitalist/imperialist sympathizers). Many of them ended up in Stalinist prisons, tortured and killed. In 1948, Pilecki, like many other members of the AK, was accused of working for the "foreign imperialists," and was executed by Stalin's secret police.[269] Until 1989, information about Pilecki's heroic life and tragic death was strictly censored by the communist government (as was any other information on the sacrifices of the Polish Home Army fighters, including the facts of the Warsaw Uprising), and only a handful of people in Poland and abroad knew of his life. Pilecki was one of only a few men to volunteer for Auschwitz, and his heroic attitude exemplifies the aristocratic ethos of self-sacrifice and moral responsibility that drove many Polish underground fighters. He was one of many Polish Don Quixotes. Sadly, the communist government erased their lives and sacrifices from Polish history, and it erased their role in helping their Jewish compatriots. Michael Schudrich, the Chief Rabbi of Poland, said Pilecki was "an example of inexplicable goodness at a time of inexplicable evil. There is ever-growing awareness of Poles helping Jews in the Holocaust, and how they paid with their lives, like Pilecki. We must honor these examples and follow them today in the parts of the world where there are horrors again."[270] Pilecki's tragic death, at the hands of the Stalinists – after so many sacrifices and years of serving the Polish and Jewish cause – illustrates the circumstances of Poles under the Nazis and under the postwar Stalinist government. To represent men like Pilecki, who were silenced and whose memory was erased by the Stalinist government, as "raging anti-Semites" in American pop culture is a great injustice.[271] In 2012, Aquila Polonica published Pilecki's 1945 report about his two and a half year undercover mission as a prisoner at Auschwitz. Titled *The Auschwitz Volunteer: Beyond Bravery*, the report was translated by Jarek Garlinski, and was published in English for the first time.

Despite many heroic acts, some Poles did choose to settle private scores and get rid of their Jewish neighbors. As Lichten notes: "The immediate postwar years saw the appearance of hundreds of personal testimonies to both human cruelty and human decency."[272] Ringelblum "recounts cases of ruthless denunciation of Jews but he likewise describes many moving gestures of sympathy and decency. He tells of seeing Gentiles accompany Jews to the ghetto with flowers, and embrace their friends before leaving them at the gate, to the astonishment of the watchful German gendarmes."[273] Ringelblum writes: "The most beautiful novel may be written in the future about the courage of Poles, about the noblest idealists, who were not frightened by the threats of the enemy which rained down on them from the red posters."[274] The stories and statistics of that era reflect a gamut of human behaviors, from heroic to horrific:[275] "'How do we proceed, then?' – Lichten asks – 'Do we take a huge balance sheet, marking down acts of decency on one side and acts of evil or indifference on the other? If so, might not individual deeds of bravery in face of certain death carry greater merit than the negative weight of inaction of betrayal through terror?'"[276] What makes each story particularly painful and layered is the deep and long history of Polish–Jewish relations: each incident, each choice, was personal, yet each had implications on both the individual and the national scale.

More than 90 percent of Polish Jews were murdered by the Nazis. Most of Poland's 300,000 Holocaust survivors left the country for the USA or Israel immediately after the war. Before the war, the Polish and Jewish cultures were tightly interwoven, with language, customs, cuisines, art, and literature intertwining in a hybrid Polish–Jewish national identity. After the war, the ethnic makeup of Poland changed drastically, and with it, the Polish national identity. Jewish homes were empty, Jewish friends and family members were gone, synagogues were destroyed, *shtetls* burned. At the same time, the communist regime completely rejected the ethos of acceptance that had drawn so many Jews to Poland before World War II. Members of the Polish intelligentsia and nobility who might have stood against it had largely perished during the war in concentrations camps, at Katyń,[277] and in the Warsaw Uprising. With no mitigating force to counteract the communist government's program of Jewish scapegoating, the 1960s – and the year 1968 in particular – marked a period of infamy in the history of Jewish–Polish relations. In the beginning of 1968, 40,000 Jews still lived in Poland; by the end of that year only 5,000 remained.[278] The combination of anti-Semitic propaganda and purges created an atmosphere in which the subject of Auschwitz as foremost a Jewish-Polish experience was taboo. It's not that the discourse was completely absent from the public debate; on the contrary, it was very much present, but it was framed by a particular political slant that minimized the Jewish aspect of the history, and never seriously addressing the role that anti-Semitic Poles played in the Holocaust. As Lichten noticed writing in 1966: the "reluctance to analyze the recent past does exist, and, not surprisingly, only a very few works bearing directly on the subject of our investigation have been published."[279] What was published was often distorted for political purposes; for example, Emmanuel Ringelblum's *Notes from the Warsaw Ghetto* "differ[s] significantly in the Yiddish, Polish, and English editions," most likely due to political considerations.[280] On the one hand, it might have been a simple case of delayed mourning – some time had to pass before some issues could be addressed head-on. On the other hand, the silence around the subject was motivated by the communist regime's own objectives. The result was a gaping hole in Polish national consciousness, a sense of irrevocable cultural loss that one could neither acknowledge nor discuss. The subject of the Holocaust as a primarily Jewish experience was expunged from the national discourse, as was the entire prewar Jewish culture that used to be an integral part of Poland and Polish national identity.

The country never came to terms with the Holocaust nor with the fact that Poland was its epicenter.[281] Following Czesław Miłosz, in 1987 Jan Błoński called on Polish literature to do the necessary soul-searching and to tackle the stigma of the Holocaust that had "stained" Polish soil.[282] Błoński writes:

> On more than one occasion Czesław Miłosz has spoken in a perplexing way of the duty of Polish poetry to purge the burden of guilt from our native soil, which is - in his words - "defiled, blood-stained, desecrated." [...] What Milosz means here is neither the blood of his compatriots nor that of the Germans. He clearly means Jewish blood, the genocide which – although not perpetrated by the Polish nation – took place on Polish soil and which has stained that soil for all time. That collective memory which finds its purest voice in poetry and literature cannot forget this bloody and hideous stigma. It cannot behave as if it never happened.[283]

Błoński's essay, written almost two decades after the events of 1968, touched a nerve, unraveling the years of silence around the Holocaust.[284] In 1968, however, the anti-Semitism; the grief and shame; the destruction of the intelligentsia; and the strictures of totalitarian rule – with its Cold War dynamic contingent on Middle East politics – converged to create conditions in which genuine discourse on a catastrophic national event was impossible. There was no mourning, no redemption, no reconciliation. As many scholars noted: "With the Holocaust, nearly the entire Jewish population was erased from Poland, and with it a large portion of their common history."[285] A third of the Polish nation – nearly all of its Jewish population – had disappeared, and Poles couldn't discuss it directly.

The silence around Jewish issues, in fact, extended to all areas of life, including theatre scholarship. Conducting research on Yiddish plays in nineteenth-century Poland, Michael C. Steinlauf notes that the Polish theatre scholar Witold Filler, "in a manner typical of most Polish scholars under communism, does not directly address the Jewish content of these plays, but rather only hints at it, or rather, winks at it. This is symptomatic. There are great silences about these issues [in Poland]."[286] Jewish culture has always been an integral part of Polish culture, and the silence that surrounded the Jewish history and Jewish aspect of the Holocaust during the years of communist rule, culminating with the 1968 events, had a significant impact on Polish culture, including Polish theatre. Like scholars, theatre artists were forced to hint and wink at the issues.

Created under the postwar circumstances, in which Poland was trying to come to terms not only with what had happened during the Holocaust but also what was happening at the moment (rampant anti-Semitic government rhetoric as well as mass deportations of Polish Jews to Israel), both Grotowski's *Akropolis* (developed between 1962 and 1967 – right before the 1968 deportations) and Kantor's *Dead Class* (created in 1975 – only a few years after) engage the issue of the Holocaust in a way that addresses the Polish past and present; they respond to history, while both speaking and not speaking of the taboo subject. As Grzegorz Niziołek puts it:

> *Akropolis* is not just a representation of a concentration camp; it also clearly articulates the subject of the Jewish Holocaust. The subject of the Holocaust appears in both Kantor's *Dead Class* and his earlier works. It's difficult to interpret *Akropolis* and *Dead Class*; it's difficult to understand what they're really about, and what "happens" in their enactment. The disruptive representational strategy of these works is foremost connected to the issue of the Holocaust, and to the taboo with which the Holocaust is associated in our national consciousness. In both cases, the viewer is placed in an unfamiliar situation and forced to confront something located "beyond the pleasure principle." The moment of shock, of emotional and cognitive disturbance, that these spectacles trigger is extremely important; they're vital. […] The idea of Grotowski's "poor theatre" was formed as he worked on *Akropolis*; Kantor's concept of the Theatre of Death was developed while he worked on *Dead Class*. The revolutionary, far-fetched ideas developed from the ground up in these works radically transformed Polish postwar theatre and are impossible to understand without facing the issue of the Holocaust. It cannot be a coincidence.[287]

Niziołek points out that the formal inventions of both directors, Grotowski's theory of Poor Theatre and Kantor's Theatre of Death, were responses to the trauma of the Holocaust. Following Adorno's claim that "unresolved antagonisms of reality" find their expression in artworks as "immanent problems of form,"[288] Martin Harries suggests that there is a tension, an "antagonism" – two contradictory impulses that come into play in a post-traumatic historical retrospection: the impulse to look and the impulse not to look. Form in art is a function of that tension. Harries writes, "If serious historical retrospection – the contemplation of the Holocaust – forces the spectator into a kind of self-destruction, is the choice to make the turn toward this historical retrospection not itself a form of masochism? The imperative to remember collides with the angels' warning: do not look back."[289] In *Akropolis* and *Dead Class*, the two contradictory impulses come into play in the respective creation and reception of each work. Grotowski's and Kantor's formal experiments with actors, props and *mise-en-scènes* grew out of a long "sedimentation of history," but also out of the tensions of a particular historical moment. Likewise, their critical receptions were driven by contradictory impulses. Polish contemporary reviews of the two spectacles avoided the subject of the Holocaust altogether, focusing instead on aesthetic, visual or theoretical aspects. Many critics skirted the issue of the Holocaust, veiling it in acceptable language. This avoidance of direct address can be blamed on the censorship that controlled much of the public debate; but perhaps it was also prompted by a certain resistance on the part of the audience, "resistance which prevented the viewers from deciphering or even seeing the clues."[290] This same resistance – the fear of seeing that plagued Polish critical reception – also pervaded the foreign response to both productions. *Dead Class*, for example, was customarily referred to as a satire on "traditional educational conditioning,"[291] or as "a satire on the educational process,"[292] with the trauma reduced to "the haunting effects of childhood upon adult life."[293] The rare audience that seemed to read the missing cues of Kantor's masterpiece was the Jewish audience. Krzysztof Miklaszewski recalls that when *Dead Class* was shown in Israel in December 1985, "audiences were left weeping."[294]

If Polish scholars were constrained by a political system that governed most of the discourse, as well as by a post-traumatic delay, American theatre scholars were simply not interested in the topic. They chose to completely decontextualize both *Akropolis* and *Dead Class*, avoiding any assessment that could be politically controversial in the Cold War climate. The critical trend away from "the literature of theater," which has historically been the source of Polish political discourse, and towards "gestures and non-verbal communication" also neutered any political impact that either of these works could potentially have had – in Poland and abroad.[295] Both *Akropolis* and *Dead Class* are deeply political (despite the claims that their authors made against such interpretations) and, as "export products" to beyond the Iron Curtain, they were also secret messages in a bottle, "written" in a coded language, to be decoded by those outside of the Soviet prison. Yet, to this day, they remain undecoded.

Following the fall of communism in 1989, Polish–Jewish relations underwent significant reevaluation. First, new research by American and Polish scholars, such as Jan T. Gross, Barbara Engelking and Jan Grabowski, brought to light incidents of pogroms of Jewish survivors who returned to their hometowns and villages during the immediate postwar period. Particularly unnerving was Jan T. Gross's book *Neighbors: The Destruction* of the Jewish Community in Jedwabne, Poland (2001), and *Fear: Anti-Semitism in Poland after Auschwitz; An Essay in Historical Interpretation* (2006). Gross's research finally – after more than 40 years of silence – opened a debate, and led to soul-searching in Polish society.[296] The results were an increasing interest in the Jewish roots of Polish culture, and attempts to straighten out the record – to strengthen Polish–Jewish relations, and most of all, to reclaim whatever was left of the 800 years of Jewish history in Poland.[297] Poles began discussing and openly acknowledging the anti-Semitism that swept Poland before World War II as well as the postwar pogroms,[298] clarifying the actual historical facts as well as emphasizing the heroism of Poles who risked their lives during the Nazi occupation to save their Jewish compatriots.[299] Simultaneously, for the first time, Poles also began to question the representation of Poles in American pop culture and media. One of the issues, for example, involved the representation of the death camps in the international media. For years, the international press habitually referred to the death camps as "Polish concentration camps." This geographic designation created misleading impressions as to who were responsible for building and running the camps, thus shifting the blame for the Holocaust from German Nazis to Poles. Despite the efforts of the Polish government, the American and German media, including *Der Spiegel* and the *New York Times*, and in 2012, even President Obama (in a White House ceremony celebrating Jan Karski) continued to refer to the camps as "Polish."[300] The effort to clarify the historical facts, to acknowledge both the heroism and the ignominy, has strengthened the ties between Poland and Israel by emphasizing the common suffering endured by both Poles and Jews at the hands of the Nazis.[301] (Before World War II, 1.3 million people lived in Warsaw. In 1945, following the Warsaw and Ghetto Uprisings, only about 1,000 survived among its ruins.) Acknowledgment of the common tragedy as well as the depth and breadth of Jewish roots in Poland before World War II also led to the rediscovery and renewed celebration of Jewish-Polish heritage. Jewish music and theatre festivals are now organized in major Polish cities, and synagogues and neighborhoods are being rebuilt and restored. In Warsaw, a new Jewish museum is to be built with the goal of reviving "the spirit of what was once Europe's largest Jewish community" – as the *Guardian* reported – "the multi-million-pound museum will be on the site of the notorious wartime Warsaw ghetto and will be next to the ghetto memorial. […] The plans are part of a widespread and ongoing effort since the fall of communism to revive Poland's past as a rich site of Jewish culture, which has seen the reemergence of Jewish theatres, restaurants and bookshops, as well as a renewed enthusiasm for Yiddish."[302] The goal of the museum is to remind the world of the rich history of the Jews in Poland, to show how deeply the two cultures were connected and to present Poland as "more than just the world's largest Jewish graveyard."[303]

In 2009 the *New York Times* called the post-1989 shift in Polish–Jewish relations "the greatest ethical transformation of any country in Europe."[304] Many scholars and commentators have interpreted the recent Jewish Renaissance in Poland as a form of post-traumatic acting-out. Finally, after the years of forced silence, Polish society is able to speak about and embrace its Jewish roots, and come to terms with its own history. As Lehner notes: "Many Poles find in Jewishness an activist project, a way to bear witness to unspoken losses, a possibility for a better future."[305] A second wave of Polish-Jewish writers, such as Henryk Grynberg, Antoni Marianowicz, Michał Głowiński and Arnold Mostowicz, have begun for the first time to write about their own wartime experiences. For these writers, "writing about wartime survival as Jews became part of a delayed process of integrating these experiences into their often fractured identities."[306] The political and cultural shift in the Polish–Jewish debate led to a reexamination of Polish history, as well as a reexamination of the Polish literary canon, including Romantic national literature. The form of what could be called "reading against the Jewish grain" allowed the rediscovery of Polish literature, while making visible what had been previously ignored: Jewish mythology and symbolism; the blending of Christian and Kabbalah rituals; the many references and allusions to Yiddish culture and language; and the intermingling of Polish and Jewish life that for many centuries was taken for granted. The new readings and rereadings have also opened a dialogue in the field of Polish studies abroad. This includes the theory and history of Polish theatre, with particular emphasis on the works of Grotowski and Kantor. For the first time, their theatrical works can be viewed as traumatic products of a particular historical moment in Polish–Jewish relations. For the first time, they are being decoded.

Theatre and Theory

Since 1989, there has been a significant shift in the field of Slavic studies, from the purely historiographic research favored for many years, to critical theory, including a broader, interdisciplinary view of Central and Eastern European history, now being reexamined through the prism of trauma studies and postcolonial theory, with particular emphasis on the cultural hybridity of Polish national identity.[307] The shift, which began in historical research, has affected the field of literary studies as well.[308] As Halina Filipowicz notes,

> Profound disciplinary change has occurred in the field of literary studies (including one of its subfields, Slavic studies) in [the USA,] and has forced us to redefine and adjust the tools of our inquiry. What has changed in the last decades is, for example, the breadth and intensity of an interest in the internationalization of literary studies. It is not merely that the language of literary studies has changed – as documented by the popularity of such terms as "border crossing," "cross-cultural," "diaspora," "hybridity," "imagined communities," and "nomadism" – but also that many of its procedures have been or are being adjusted. One of the consequences of this seismic shift is the realization that all national traditions are plural rather than singular, that they are heterogeneous, even polyvocal, and hence to understand them requires the use of methods from across a wide range of fields.[309]

This shift in Slavic studies has led to a much deeper, more complex, and subtle understanding of Polish–Jewish history and relations.[310] As more archival documents are unveiled, we learn more and more about how these relationships are influenced by the Stalinist[311] and Nazi regimes; how they are influenced by centuries of partitions, World War II and, finally, Cold War Middle East politics. Between 1772 and 1989,

Poland was an independent nation for exactly 21 years (from 1918 to 1939); as Polish–Jewish relationships evolved throughout the centuries, they developed under partitions and eventually in the shadow of two of Europe's most murderous totalitarian powers – Russia and Germany. As Edward Lucas points out, Polish–Russian relations, for example, are marked by such a long history that pathological trauma is inevitable. Lucas writes:

> From the partitions of Poland in the late 18th century to the crushing of the 1863 uprising against Tsarist autocracy, to the Red Army's march on the infant Second Republic (foiled by the Miracle of the Vistula in 1920), to the Molotov–Ribbentrop Pact of 1939 which divided Poland between the Nazi and Soviet empires, to the Katyń massacre in 1940 and the Soviet-backed imposition of martial law in 1981 – the list is so long and so tragic that pathological historical trauma seems the normal and inevitable response.[312]

The most common and effective strategy of a totalitarian regime is to inflame the internal ethnic tensions, scapegoating groups against each other in an attempt to draw attention from the regime's own agenda. As Fatouros famously wrote on account of Sartre's essay on colonialism: "The colonial system is led by its own internal necessity to corrupt and demoralize the colonized, to impoverish them, to destroy their social structures and disrupt their social relationships."[313] Although the postcolonial approach to Poland's complex history does not answer all of the questions, it provides a multilayered and nuanced understanding of the historical circumstances that have surrounded centuries of Polish–Jewish relations. To quote a recent essay: "As the demons of Absolutism, Nationalism, Fascism and Communism raged in Europe, Poland was particularly stricken. Jews and Poles were pitted against each other, causing great suffering. This history has left us today with a set of unresolved problems, but for the first time, these issues can be addressed in a democratic, liberal context."[314] For theatre scholars, the changes in Polish–Jewish relations and the postcolonial approach to Polish studies allows us to see Grotowski and Kantor's work not only for what it says but also, to quote Gayatri Spivak again, for what it "cannot say" – or, rather, for what it couldn't say. We can analyze what's there, visible, but also what's not there, what's missing, unspoken, and invisible. We can try to find meaning in its "negative ontology."[315]

Trauma (from the Greek for "wound") is defined as a violent rupture in the social and psychological order that fundamentally alters an individual's concept of the self and the world. The origins of contemporary trauma studies date back to 1980, when post-traumatic stress disorder (PTSD) "was first included in the diagnostic canon of the medical and psychiatric professions."[316] Within the field of trauma studies, experts – including psychologists, psychiatrists, and those who specialize in contemporary critical theory – disagree about the precise definition of PTSD; however,

> most descriptions generally agree that there is a response, sometimes delayed, to an overwhelming event or events, which takes the form of repeated, intrusive hallucinations, dreams, thoughts or behaviors stemming from the event, along with

numbing that may have begun during or after the experience, and possibly also increased arousal from (and avoidance of) stimuli recalling the event.[317]

The response to trauma is often delayed and fragmented.[318] Roberta Culbertson adds that "Most disturbingly, bits of memory, flashing like clipped pieces of film held to the light, appear unbidden and in surprising ways, as if possessed of a life independent of will or consciousness."[319] When one becomes either numbed to or entrapped by one's traumatic memories, a way out of the closed circuit of one's psyche is to be able to tell one's story: "a therapeutic process – a process of constructing a narrative, of reconstructing a history and essentially, of re-externalizing the event – has to be set in motion."[320] But the movement from silence to words is difficult because, as Cathy Caruth argues, "To cure oneself – whether by drugs or the telling of one's story or both – seems to many survivors to imply the giving-up of an important reality, or the dilution of a special truth into the reassuring terms of therapy."[321]

Caruth calls PTSD a pathological symptom: not a symptom of the unconscious, but "a symptom of history." She writes, "The traumatized, we might say, carry an impossible history within them, or they become themselves the symptom of a history that they cannot entirely possess."[322] Bernhard Giesen argues that "a collective trauma transcends the contingent relationships between individual persons and forges them into a collective identity."[323] Arthur Neal suggests that national traumas have been created by "individual and collective reactions to a volcano-like event that shook the foundations of the social world."[324] In defining national or cultural trauma, Jeffrey Alexander suggests that "Even when the nature of the pain has been crystallized and the identity of the victim established, there remains the highly significant question of the relation of the victim to the wider audience."[325] The relationship between the victims and the audience, particularly an audience that has been implicated in the victim's traumatic history, is always already marked by a now-shared collective memory and post-memory. The shared historical memory that has been forged between the two groups "leaves indelible marks upon their group consciousness, marking their memories forever and changing their future identity in fundamental and irrevocable ways."[326] Or, as Martin Harries puts it: "Can an artwork transmit trauma? [...] The problem of the transmission of trauma from person to person, and from generation to generation, is one of the most contested points surrounding trauma, and this controversy is germane."[327]

Trauma studies are a relatively new trend in critical studies; however, the vocabulary has been used intuitively for quite some time. In the case of *Akropolis* and *Dead Class*, a few critics noted the odd, psychologically complex quality of these productions. Writing about *Akropolis*, the American critic John Simon, for example, commented that "Politically, it is the image of a people brutalized successively by Catholicism, Nazism and Communism incessantly and hideously licking their wounds."[328] Writing about *Dead Class*, the Polish critic Anna Boska noted that "*Dead Class* resembles a spiritualist séance, bringing back ghosts. In fact, it is bringing up the dead world of the past, which only appears dead. It is still alive in our subconsciousness. We carry it within us; it comes back to haunt us."[329] For Jan Skotnicki, *Dead Class* brings back all the memories of war that he cannot escape: "It's a gallery of incredible faces, as if cut out from the old fashioned daguerreotype… No, it's a veil of our memory…our dreams, and our nightmares, memories stubbornly coming back with more force, with the passage of time…"³³⁰ Józef Szczawiński, as if trying to shake his own ghosts, asked with regard to *Dead Class* whether it is possible to live in memory: "Can you enter the river twice in the same place?"³³¹ Szydłowski too asked a similar question: "This show refers to other wars that plagued humanity. Should we remember them now?"³³² Eugenio Barba made a similar and very personal observation about Grotowski's group, suggesting that it could never escape the irrevocable loss of World War II:

> "Mourning" is the term I associate with Grotowski's actors. I recall my mother who lost her husband at the age of thirty-three. She could laugh, enjoy herself, talk or flirt with other men. But in the darkest corner of her heart lurked the awareness of an irreplaceable loss or of an irrevocable liberation, the memory of being struck by lightning and surviving while the house in which you grew up is reduced to ashes.³³³

Akropolis and *Dead Class* each struggle with the issue of representation, giving voice to feelings and emotions that Poles were forced to suppress. Within the political context in which they were created, these spectacles are also perhaps the purest theatrical expressions of PTSD, addressing the unspeakable subject of the Polish–Jewish experience in a veiled, nondirect way.

The evolution of trauma studies, and the changes in Slavic studies that encompassed the renewed interest in Jewish roots of Polish literature and culture, as well as the postcolonial approach to Eastern European history, all allow us to reevaluate *Akropolis* and *Dead Class* in a new, previously undiscernable context that also enriches the fields of theatre and performance studies. Both *Akropolis* and *Dead Class* have become catalysts for the collective experience, ways to process the trauma of the Holocaust and to attempt to come to terms with the fact that it was perpetrated on Polish soil. Both were also created in political circumstances that forbade open and free expression, short-circuiting the natural process of mourning and healing. Grotowski and Kantor developed aesthetically drastically different works, each of which nonetheless seeks to respond to the trauma of the Holocaust. This correspondence has had broad consequences not only for our understanding of their work, but also for our understanding of the ways that translating trauma through the prism of performance can significantly alter and deflect the meaning and reception of theatrical works outside and within their cultural and historical context. Or, as Hans-Thies Lehmann puts it in *Postdramatic Theatre*: "The postdramatic theatre of a Tadeusz Kantor with its mysterious, animistically animated objects and apparatus, [his] historical ghosts and apparitions […] exists in this tradition of theatrical appearances of 'fate' and ghosts, who, as Monique Borie has shown, are crucial for understanding the most recent theatre."³³⁴ Kantor's and Grotowski's formal innovations have altered our sense of both what theatre means and how we are to approach drama within – and outside of – its context. Niziołek notes that "Trauma always resurfaces at the wrong time. There is never a good time for it because it always ruins something, brings destruction in our reality."³³⁵ Entering into a dialogue with the Polish Romantics in the context of the Holocaust, *Akropolis* and *Dead Class* ruptured the structure of Polish literary and dramatic tradition, marking Polish memory forever, and changing the theatre world "in fundamental and irrevocable ways."[336]

What follows are two sections, one on *Akropolis* and one on *Dead Class*. Each section provides background information on the many literary and dramatic works that both Grotowski and Kantor reference. Both show how each director adapted the Polish literary tradition to suit his own aesthetic goals, and how his aesthetics evolved *vis-à-vis* the historical circumstances in which he was forced to create. The analysis of Grotowski's *Akropolis* focuses on the ways that Wyspianski's drama and Borowski's writing style allowed Grotowski to develop his own understanding of the audience–actor relationship, as well as his own acting methodology. The analysis of *Dead Class* focuses on a myriad of Polish theatrical and literary works, including those of Mickiewicz, Ansky, Schulz, Gombrowicz and Witkacy, that influenced Kantor's understanding of the actor–object relationship as well as his concept of the bio-object. Each section also compares and contrasts the Polish and American receptions of each work, analyzing the complex political, historical and cultural aspects that influence a particular interpretation of the director's style. What I hope to show is – to bring up Adorno again – how form in art becomes a function of history, or, perhaps, how history becomes a function of form.

Part I

OUR AUSCHWITZ: GROTOWSKI'S *AKROPOLIS*

Chapter 1
JERZY GROTOWSKI: A VERY SHORT INTRODUCTION

Born in 1933, Jerzy Grotowski graduated with a degree in acting from the State School of Theatre in Cracow. He went on to pursue directing at the Lunacharsky Institute of Theatre Arts (GITIS) in Moscow, where he studied the acting and directing techniques of Stanislavsky, Vakhtangov, Meyerhold, and Tairov. After returning to Poland, Grotowski began working as a teaching assistant at the Theatre School in Cracow. He continued to study directing, and the year 1957 marked his directing debut with a production of Eugene Ionesco's *The Chairs*. In 1958, Grotowski directed a workshop production of Prosper Mérimée's *The Devil Made a Woman*, and a production of *A Jinxed Family* by Jerzy Kszysztoń, a troubled and relatively unknown Polish playwright. Conceptualizing this early production, Grotowski not only changed the title to the *Gods of Rain*, but weaved in a number of other poetic and film texts, including lines from Polish poets and Shakespeare's *Hamlet*, as well as texts from contemporaneous media, such as newspaper articles.[1] During those early theatrical experiments, Grotowski was interested in developing a unique directorial relationship to the script. An interview conducted on account of the opening of the *Gods of Rain* is one of the first records of Grotowski's emerging views on directing: "As far as the director's relationship to the dramatic text goes," Grotowski says, "I believe the text should only serve as a theme for the director, on the basis on which he should construct a brand new work of art, *his* spectacle."[2] In the program notes to the production, Grotowski wrote: "To choose a play doesn't necessarily mean that one needs to agree with its author."[3] The production was a breakthrough for Grotowski, insofar as he began to strongly believe that text should not bind a director. While in 1959 he wrote that "Theatre begins with a vision, one person's individual truth, the playwright's subjective vision,"[4] in his subsequent productions he slowly replaced the vision of the playwright with the vision of the director. Grotowski eventually came to believe that the traditional dramatic text should be the last and least considered element of a theatrical production, which needs its own language – its own autonomous text. Following this path, all of his productions were free adaptations and were appropriately labeled with the phrase "according to," beginning with the 1959 production of *Uncle Vanya According to Anton Chekhov* at the Old Theatre in Cracow.

At that time in the USA, Grotowski's loose treatment of text was considered revolutionary. It was, in fact, one of the main reasons why the New York theatre boheme embraced Grotowski's theatrical formula, considering it a beacon of progress in the battle between dated affectation – with the "literature of theater" – and the postmodern emphasis on "gesture and 'nonverbal communication'" as the primary mode of theatrical exchange.[5] In Poland, however, Grotowski's strategy was quite common and, for number of reasons, it evoked varied critical responses. In 1962, in a review written on the occasion of the opening of *Kordian*, an anonymous critic praised the "linguistic and physical showmanship" of Grotowski's group, noting that "We can see here really hard work with the language, beautifully recited verses with phenomenal memorization, but still…there is something off."[6] (At that time, Grotowski began using text only for its melodic quality, disregarding the meanings of the words and sentences – text was nothing more than raw material for the training of the actor's vocal apparatus.) Following Grotowski's successes abroad, in 1967, Roger Planchon, a well-respected French theatre director, accused Grotowski of not being able to discern the specificity of dramatic language:

> Grotowski's reputation rests on his one statement that text belongs to literature, not to theatre. We could, however, flip that argument. Grotowski argues that the essence of theatrical work lies outside of text. It's true that everything that has been written can be considered literature: Mallarmé's poem, a silly marketing slogan, a newspaper article and an essay on Plato. We could, therefore, argue with Grotowski that he doesn't see the specific nature of a dramatic text. Since Sophocles, the playwrights have attempted to find a language that differs from that of poetry and epic (and from dance and pantomime). In other words, dramatic language/text always was, and continues to be, different from "literature."[7]

Many Polish critics and theatre artists echoed Planchon's sentiments. In 1969, Adam Hanuszkiewicz, director of the National Theatre of Poland, for example, wryly noted that "Grotowski's attitude to the dramatic text is basically like a Mime's approach to the scenario of the story. For the Mime-actor of the Commedia dell'arte, centuries before Grotowski, the text had the value of a scenario."[8] Like Planchon, Hanuszkiewicz was not impressed by Grotowski's method of free adaptation, considering it a dilettante's approach.

Hanuszkiewicz's dismissive gesture was partially prompted by the fact that the strategy of free adaptation wasn't particularly innovative in Poland at that time. In fact, to varying degrees, it was a very conventional way to direct. The majority of Polish national dramas written in the nineteenth and the early twentieth centuries were written without any intention of ever being staged – because the government would not allow them to be staged. Most were political in nature, and there was simply no possibility that any theatre in partitioned Poland would be permitted to produce them, whether under Prussian, Russian, or even the most lenient of the three, Austro-Hungarian, censorship. Tymon Terlecki suggests that Romantic drama was "intimately linked with the theater of its era. These works were not *Buchdrama* or *Lesedrama*. They became such, in time, out of a spirit of contradiction and opposition, out of necessity, out of desperation that they would never be produced on stage."[9] Jan Kłossowicz confirms that, due to necessity, Romantic drama "came into being entirely outside the theatre and reached the theatre stage only in the 20th century."[10] Daniel Gerould rightly notices that the unique situation of Polish Romantic drama evolved from its peculiar political situation; all three, Mickiewicz, Słowacki, and Krasiński, wrote their plays in exile, never expecting them to be performed. They wrote plays "for a theatre that existed only in the imagination of its authors and designed to transcend the bounds of reality and the prosaic stage that imitated it."[11]

Often these dramas more closely resemble poetry than dramatic works (for that reason they are sometimes refered to as "dramatic poems"). Thus, irrespective of political issues, there are also practical considerations; the Wagnerian grandeur and syncretic structure of the Polish Romantic dramas make them challenging for the stage. Mickiewicz himself wrote that "We should not expect to see a Slavic drama realized on the stage in the near future, for no theatre would suffice to present [it]."[12] Since these plays were not staged in their time, no one really knows the true staging intentions of their authors.[13] As a result, following the regaining of independence in 1918, the interwar Polish directors who attempted to stage any of the canonical works from the Romantic period didn't feel the need to stay true to the text. To quote Jan Kott: "It was very characteristic of the theatre in the interwar period to use the text of even the great classics merely as raw material."[14] Thus, as Kathleen Cioffi points out, due to the historical circumstances, the Polish tradition of free adaptation evolved "into a more avant-garde form than [was] typically seen in Anglophone theatre."[15] Simultaneously, there was an increasing emphasis on the role of "the director as *auteur* of a theatrical production." The interwar Polish theatre artists believed that "the director/theatre artists should have absolute control of their productions extended to the text itself, and therefore they often wrote their own adaptations both of prose and even of plays that had already been written."[16] Such an approach, which became known as free-directing, was especially promoted by Leon Schiller, a Polish theatre and film director, theoretician and critic, founder of the directing department at the National Theatre Arts Institute, and the artistic director of Warsaw's Great Theatre.[17] Himself influenced by Gordon Craig, Schiller is often considered the father of modern Polish theatre, and his approach to directing has influenced future generations immensely. As Kathleen Cioffi notes:

> Schiller represents the main Polish link between the Great Reformers from the prewar period to the postwar tendency to adapt. He had personally known Gordon Craig, had worked with Craig on his journal, *The Mask*, and had organized an exhibition of Craig's stage designs in Warsaw. In fact, he wholeheartedly adopted Craig's notion of the director as "theatre artist" who is the "author" of the theatrical production rather than the mere interpreter of the playwright's work. As Korcelli mentions, Schiller was especially fond of adapting others' texts for the stage.[18]

Describing the training of young directors advocated by Schiller, Kazimierz Braum points out that the student director was trained "to control all the elements of the performance, to be the sole and unique 'author of the production' who creates all aspects of the piece. This control began with the text, he or she had to learn how to make adaptations, directorial versions of the classics, cuts, etc."[19] In the 1920s and 1930s, Schiller himself directed a number of grand, visionary and often cubist productions in the style of Eisenstein and Reinhardt. Schiller's training, combined with the tradition of free adaptation, permeated Polish theatre, establishing the standard way of approaching the dramatic text. As Konstanty Puzyna notes: "After World War II, and especially after 1955, the Schillerian tradition – at least as a model – became compelling even in provincial theatres."[20]

Following World War II, under the Soviet regime, the great Romantic dramas were, again, considered a political liability due to their strong liberatory themes. Under the circumstances, the role of the director was then not just to make theatrical sense of what were essentially untheatrical texts, but also to say things between the lines that were censored in public discourse. Raymond Temkine poignantly describes the situation:

> [T]he plays performed most often [in today's Poland] are those of the great Romantics of the nineteenth century, Mickiewicz, Slowacki, the poets of emigration, who came to Paris to escape the Tsarist oppression. Written rather freely and without the slightest consideration for theatrical conventions, these playlets, today, have turned into remarkable dramatic vehicles, capable of seducing both directors as well as the most outspoken members of the avant-garde.[21]

It is only natural that, during communism, the tradition initiated by Schiller combined with the need to navigate one's way through the minefield of strict political censorship only further strengthened the position of director. In fact, the position of director became much stronger than that of playwright. "Our directors have killed our playwrights," one dramaturg noted many years later.[22]

Due to the historical circumstances, the necessary *laissez-faire* approach to theatrical texts has been quintessential to Polish directors for many years, and Grotowski's voice, though loudest of them all, wasn't all that revolutionary in the context of the entire Polish theatre scene of his era. On the contrary, his experiments very much conformed to the prevailing theatrical conventions. From the American perspective, however, Grotowski's approach appeared innovative and revelatory. Dominated by realist, kitchen-sink dramas, American theatre of the postwar period lacked a strong avant-garde tradition, so anything that moved beyond the traditional, realist convention of verisimilitude to the dramatic text appeared to be a theatrical breakthrough. Ironically, in Poland today, many young artists consider Grotowski's approach to the text to be too conservative. For example, Igor Krentz, a member of the performative group Azzoro, made this telling, offhand remark in 2009: "Grotowski treated text as a point of departure. That's very different from the performative arts that don't use literature at all."[23]

Regardless of how innovative Grotowski was, or was not, in his treatment of the texts he chose to use, his directorial palette – though international in scope – was strongly rooted in the Polish national canon, and tightly bound by its native historical, social and political context. In 1959, Grotowski wrote: "I consider those who claim that we should embrace foreign texts because Polish drama is poor and inadequate to be nothing more than demagogues."[24] Although later on he ventured outside of the

Polish canon, rendering the works of, among others, Cocteau, Calderón, and Kalidasa, the foundation of Grotowski's oeuvre rests firmly on the Polish dramatic tradition. It is a fact that is hard to escape, but which has been customarily ignored by American avant-garde circles, which readily dismiss the rich textual and contextual framework of Grotowski's direction. As Temkine puts it, "Jerzy Grotowski is Polish and strongly rooted to his origins. So are those who surround him. The tendency to forget that causes misunderstandings."[25] By 1972, when Temkine's book was published in English, the American reception of Grotowski had already generated layers of misreadings around his work.

In 1959, Grotowski moved to Opole to become the artistic director of the Thirteen Row Theatre. At the same time, Ludwik Flaszen assumed the title of literary director. The Thirteen Row Theatre had been founded a year earlier, in 1958, by Stanisław Łopuszanski and Eugeniusz Ławski. Both men came from the Jan Kochanowski Theatre, at that time Opole's one and only state owned and operated theatre. The leadership transition from Ławski to Grotowski was difficult, with Ławski's proponents resisting the theatre's new management and artistic direction. The small provincial city of Opole was hardly an artistic mecca in 1959; Grotowski's reasons for moving there were a source of both speculation and ridicule. One of Grotowski's earliest critics, Jan Paweł Gawlik, wrote sarcastically of one of Grotowski's early productions:

> Grotowski's method is a method of blackmail with "hipness," supported by loud and overwhelming self-promotion. [...] If Grotowski were to only try his experiments in a private theatrical space, without his annoying self-promotion and advertising, the risks would be minimal; it would be his private artistic risk. But since he promotes himself as the official artistic director of the "professional experimental theatre" in Opole, a city that is both culturally important and neglected – it ceases to be a private matter.[26]

Considering Opole's provincial status, and the awkward transition of leadership at the Thirteen Row Theatre, Grotowski must have anticipated some local hostility towards his avant-garde theatrical experiments. Why then, did he choose to leave Cracow and go to Opole? At that time Cracow was the cultural and theatrical epicenter of Poland. Grotowski leaving the vibrant and sophisticated city for the less attractive Opole could have derived from a number of aspirations, from his desire to escape Cracow's competitive atmosphere, to his long-term plans for greater artistic freedom and control. What is perhaps most striking about Grotowski's decision to pull up stakes in Cracow, however, is that it came precisely at a moment of great opportunity in Polish cultural life. 1959 marked the culmination of a decade's worth of historic political change in the Eastern Bloc. In 1953, Stalin died and Khrushchev came to power as the new head of the Soviet Union. In 1956, under pressure from the emerging new guard, Khrushchev denounced Stalinist atrocities, ushering in a new era of Soviet history. Although Krushchev's indictment of Stalinist regime was delivered behind closed doors to a circle of Party insiders, he never intended his gesture to remain secret. Thanks to the CIA, his speech was quickly disseminated, convincing the West that there was genuine change afoot in Soviet Union. Although the changes were not as profound as expected, the implications of Khrushchev's move resonated throughout the Eastern Bloc, initiating a new era of greater artistic and political freedom. In Poland, the period starting in 1956 is often referred to as The Thaw, or Polish October. The former members of the Polish underground partisan army, the Armia Krajowa (AK, the Home Army), were finally released from prisons. During World War II, they served under the Polish government in exile in London; and during the Stalinist regime they had been imprisoned by the Soviets as the agents of "foreign governments." Simultaneously, the Communist Party, under the rule of Władysław Gomułka, loosened its grip on the country's political and cultural life. Though censorship remained ubiquitous, the sense of fear and terror that permeated Poland during Stalin's reign gave way to a more hopeful vision of the future. In drama, film and literature, the former obligatory style of socialist realism gave way to unfettered abstract experimentations, which were finally officially allowed. Playwrights such as Sławomir Mrożek and Tadeusz Różewicz, inspired by the absurdist experiments of Beckett and Ionesco – as well by those of Polish absurdists Stanisław Witkacy and Witold Gombrowicz, whose pre–World War II works were suppressed by the Stalinist regime and only now were beginning to be rediscovered – began creating an absurdist language that tackled both transnational existential themes and, specifically, Polish political and cultural issues. This was also the time of the rebirth of Polish cinema, a moment in which Andrzej Wajda, Roman Polanski and Andrzej Munk began their film careers, spearheading a distinctly Polish filmmaking style, the so-called Polish School (1956–1962).[27] The artists were hungry for new forms of expression.[28] So why, at this particularly rich moment in Polish cultural life, did Grotowski choose to leave Cracow, with its vibrant artistic milieu and open-minded audiences, for small, provincial Opole, where there was no audience for his work and where he was actually met by open hostility?[29] According to Flaszen, both he and Grotowski sought a secluded spot in which to concentrate. Lacking other evidence, we must take Flaszen at his word.[30] The move, however, indicates Grotowski's tendency to distance himself – for whatever reasons – from the Polish theatre circles of his time. Unlike Kantor, who stayed and worked in Cracow his entire life, drawing inspiration from the city, Grotowski was never attached to a place, moving easily from one city to the next, from one country to the next. This lack of a fixed geographic locale placed Grotowski always on the fence, on the border between his native context and the universal audience to which he strove to appeal.

Grotowski's time spent in Opole, however, was productive. In 1959, he mounted an adaptation of Jean Cocteau's *Orpheus*. A year later, he free-directed three productions: George Byron's *Cain*, Vladimir Mayakovski's *Mystery Buffo*, and Kalidasa's *Shakuntala*. Stagings of the "theatrical montages,"[31] *Tourists* and *Clay Pigeons*, as well the Polish national Romantic drama, Adam Mickiewicz's *Forefathers' Eve*, followed in 1961. In 1962, Grotowski directed another Romantic national drama, Juliusz Słowacki's *Kordian*. Both plays, *Forefathers' Eve* and *Kordian*, are considered canonical in the Polish national repertoire, and frequently prove pivotal to directors' artistic and intellectual development; it was customary that every director at some point in his or her career tackle at least one of them. The year 1962 also saw the first variant of Grotowski's

Akropolis, According to Stanisław Wyspiański, followed by *The Tragic Fate of Doctor Faust, According to Christopher Marlowe* (1963), and *A Study of Hamlet*, based on Shakespeare's play and Wyspiański's essay of the same title (1964).

While in Opole, Grotowski also began working on a new acting method and, in 1965, in an issue of *Odra*, he published the article "Towards a Poor Theatre." The concept of "the poor theatre" itself came from a review by Józef Maria Święcicki, published in *Tygodnik Powszechy*. Interestingly, the review was not at all about theatre. In fact, Święcicki was a conservative Catholic who wrote about "poor" and "rich" methods in church homiletic practices. Święcicki was inspired by minimalist philosophy and initiated the development of new minimalist homiletics. In his review of sermons by Władysław Mirski, a Catholic priest, Święcicki praises Mirski's sermons for their concision and lucidity, writing admiringly: "The author [Mirski] rejects baroque rhetorics, aiming for the simplest, most direct and honest expression, accomplished with the poorest possible means. [Mirski's] style is characterized by short sentences which arrange themselves organically with rhythmic cohesion; it's a style completely opposite to pathos and phraseology."[32] In one interview, Flaszen reminisces that Grotowski's company used Święcicki's terms during rehearsals: "We talked about 'poor' and 'rich' methods in the technical and aesthetic sense."[33] Eventually, those terms were simplified. *Teatr ubogi* (poor theatre) came to mean a theatre of poor means, as opposed to a rich theatre with elaborate costumes and sets. The word "poor" denoted material poverty. It meant focusing on an actor as the principal and most direct means of expression. Jan Kott ironically (or as some have suggested, cynically) notes that "The renunciation of material goods, given conditions in Poland, was probably the easiest decision. A far more difficult one was the renunciation of the theatre of politics."[34] It was a time of persistent shortages. Everything, including theatres, in Poland at that time was "poor."[35] Regardless of whether it was inspired solely by Święcicki, or helped by the economic circumstances, Grotowski's minimalism came to form the theoretical core of his aesthetics.

In 1968, "Towards a Poor Theatre" was translated into English. That same year, the publishing house Odin Thearets Forlag released the article as a book in Denmark, soon followed by a publication in the USA by Simon and Schuster, with a preface by Peter Brook. Brook was not shy in praising Grotowski, proclaiming that "no-one since Stanislavski [...] has investigated the nature of acting, its phenomenon, its meaning, the nature and science of its mental-physical-emotional processes as deeply and completely as Grotowski."[36] At that time, Brook was one of the most highly regarded theatre directors in the world; his preface naturally accorded with Grotowski's immediate legitimacy in the international theatre circles. Echoing Brook's accolades, the USA's reception of *Towards a Poor Theatre* was nothing short of a second coming. In 1970, Richard Gilman wrote in the *New York Times* that "*Towards a Poor Theatre* is a book of unequaled significance not only for the theater but for something a great deal more central: the state of our thinking about the nature of esthetic creation and about the place of imagination in an increasingly utilitarian world."[37] In the years that followed, *Towards a Poor Theatre* was reprinted in dozens of countries. However, ironically, despite its international renown, the book wasn't published in Poland until 2007, when the

Grotowski Institute, under the leadership of Grzegorz Ziółkowski and Jarosław Fret, finally released its first Polish edition. The Polish edition includes Brook's introduction, articles by Eugenio Barba and Denis Bablet, and Richard Schechner's interviews with Grotowski. The reason why it took so long for *Towards a Poor Theatre* to be published in Poland was Grotowski's own reluctance to grant the copyrights to the book, but who, when, and if anyone at all in Poland was actually trying to obtain them remains unclear.[38]

In 1965, Grotowski and his ensemble moved to Wrocław, a large metropolitan city, which would become their home for the next decade. The group was offered a prominent, centrally located space at the city center on the market square. According to the Laboratory Theatre's records, "a special governmental commission in Warsaw decided that Opole was not the proper setting for Grotowski's theatre. […] By 1965, when the move was made, the group's artistic accomplishments and growing international reputation could hardly be ignored."[39] Working in Wrocław proved fruitful for Grotowski; while there, he mounted what are now considered his three most mature productions: Juliusz Słowacki's *The Constant Prince*; *Apocalypsis cum Figuris*, based on the Bible, Fyodor Dostoyevsky, T. S. Eliot, and Simone Weil; and Stanisław Wyspiański's *Akropolis*. In fact, besides his book *Towards Poor Theatre*, these three productions provided the basis for Grotowski's international fame.

Chapter 2

NATIVE SON: GROTOWSKI IN POLAND

By 1969, Grotowski "[enjoyed] a god-like status among the experimental troupes of the West."[40] Following his 1968 Edinburgh success, where he was referred to as "the Edinburgh Festival's biggest theatrical catch,"[41] his position in Western European and American avant-garde circles was well-established. Even before arriving on American soil, Grotowski's troupe was "preceded by its reputation for being one of the most important experimental companies in the world,"[42] and "perhaps the most celebrated acting troupe in the world."[43] Grotowski was called "an unquestioned genius of modern dramatic innovation"[44] "one of the greatest artists in the theatre that has ever lived"[45] and "the third great original theater mind of the century [after Stanislavsky and Artaud]."[46] Writing for the *New York Times*, Clive Barnes rhetorically asked and answered: "Is Grotowski one of the great theatrical innovators of our time? Yes."[47] The accolades, some sincere, some ridiculously pretentious, seemed to come from every direction, prompting Ronald Bryden to sardonically note, "Grotowski: such is the theatre's newest name of God. He is the magis' mage, guru of the gurus: the ultimate to which Living Theatre, Peter Brook and the *Tulane Drama Review* bow down."[48]

However, while Grotowski was acclaimed abroad, particularly in America, his position in Poland was ambiguous to say the least. Both Polish theatre professionals and audiences treated him with suspicion, mostly ignoring his work and his group. Jan Kłossowicz, a well-regarded Polish theatre scholar, notes that

> [I]n 1969, when Grotowski was making a triumphant tour in the western hemisphere, the "Bread and Puppet" company aroused tremendous interest and gained high appraisal of important theatre critics in Poland. In the course of a couple of months, more was written in Poland about this company than once about Grotowski in a couple of years.[49]

In a similar tone, in 1970, at the peak of the American Grotowski craze, Jan Kott reports unenthusiastically:

> I saw Grotowski's Laboratory Theatre for the first time about seven or eight years ago in Opole, a small town in Silesia. The audience was restricted to twenty-five, but that evening only four or perhaps five guests from Warsaw and two young girls from the local school came to the performance of *Akropolis*. I saw Grotowski's theatre for the second time three years later. He had already moved to Breslau [Wrocław], where he was given space in the old town hall […] At Grotowski's theatre the audience was again

restricted to thirty or forty, but at that performance of *The Constant Prince* there were no more than a dozen or so. Grotowski already at that time had his enthusiasts and his enemies, but the number in both camps could be counted on the fingers of both hands. During all those years Grotowski's theatre did not enter into Poland's theatrical life; it did not attract even the young. It was in Poland, but really did not exist in Poland.[50]

The controversy surrounding Grotowski in Poland remained unaddressed for a long time. For example, reviewing Temkine's book, the Polish critic Witold Filler notes that Temkine "avoids any mention of the controversy that surrounds Grotowski's work in Poland. But it is here, at the heart of this controversy, where Grotowski's theatre explodes for us Poles, with an intensity surprising for us."[51] Baffled by Grotowski's popularity abroad, Filler continues: "It is the third book now written in Europe on Grotowski, none of which are written by Polish authors. [...] Abroad, Grotowski is being called the most important and prolific theatre artist of our time. And us? What do *we* think about all that?"[52] Indeed, reading the rare native responses to Grotowski's international success, one quickly notices a sense of puzzlement among the Polish critics. Writing for the official party newspaper, Wisz, for example, cleverly reframes Grotowski's success abroad as a success of the socialist system: "[Socialism] creates a social structure that supports the discovery and development of world-class talents, even if we ourselves don't always understand them. The fact that our political system discovers, produces, nurtures and promotes them testifies to its success."[53] Since there seemed to be no logical explanation for the discrepancy between the Polish and foreign receptions of Grotowski's work, Grotowski's international success was tactfully ignored by the Polish press through most of the 1960s. Although the Grotowski Institute's archives are full of press releases – dutifully drafted by Flaszen, Barba, and Grotowski himself – heralding the Laboratory Theatre's European and American successes, rarely did the releases reach a readership broader than the Ministry of Culture, which paid for the group's international travels.

In the late 1960s, Grotowski's name began to appear more often in the Polish press. The Polish theatre community, however, remained largely indifferent towards him. In a 1965 issue of the *Times*, an anonymous British critic wrote hopefully:

> At last, Jerzy Grotowski's talents as a director and trainer of actors are getting to be appreciated at home in Poland. For a long time Poland seemed far behind the rest of the world in its interest in this theatrical revolutionary who turns traditional plays inside out and teaches actors to make use of Yoga and thereby to project an intensity rare on any stage. [...] In Poland itself, Mr. Grotowski is beginning to seem less like the leader of an isolated heretical cult. It is now possible to find Polish theatre people who will speak favorably of him or will at least temper their criticism.[54]

The assessment, however hopeful and optimistic, was overstated and premature. At that time, both the Polish theatre community and the audiences were genuinely uninterested in Grotowski, his theatre, or his methodology. In fact, Polish theatre professionals mistrusted anyone from the West who came to Poland to learn about

Grotowski's methods, and were not in the least shy about expressing their feelings on the subject. Hovhannes I. Pilikian, one of a few Westerners who visited Poland in 1969 in search of Grotowski's roots, poignantly described his reaction to what he perceived to be an almost ostentatious contempt towards Grotowski from his Polish peers: "It was [...] something of a shock to discover that in his own country Grotowski is 'put in his place' by those who know him and that there is no ambiguity in their attitude."[55] Pilikian's discovery of Grotowski's hapless position in Poland was shocking because it completely diverged from the image of a theatrical guru that Grotowski created and cultivated abroad.

Little has changed since 1969 with respect to Grotowski's reputation in Poland, although contempt has given way to polite indifference. In 1999, following Grotowski's death, *Dialog*, one of Poland's leading literary and art journals, asked Krzysztof Jędrysek, then Dean of Acting at the famed State School of Theatre in Cracow, to comment on Grotowski's passing. Although Jędrysek tried to be diplomatic, his ponderous comment reflected the current reality: "For many people, the name Grotowski doesn't even ring a bell."[56] Ten years later, in 2009 – a year marking the 10th anniversary of Grotowski's death, the 50th year since Flaszen and Grotowski assumed leadership of The Thirteen Row Theatre in Opole, and the 25th anniversary of the Laboratory Theatre's dissolution[57] – the Grotowski Institute, in collaboration with UNESCO, announced 2009 as the Year of Grotowski. Conferences, symposiums, workshops, and screenings of Grotowski's televised theatre pieces and documentaries were scheduled around the world from New York to Tokyo. Finally, even in Poland, the celebrations were hard to ignore, and events, conferences and screenings were scheduled across the Polish cultural, theatrical and academic landscapes. Trying to explain and come to terms with Grotowski's near complete absence from Polish theatrical discourse, *Didaskalia*, Poland's leading theatre journal, devoted its June 2009 special issue to the subject. In one article, Beata Guczalska, for example, shared a poignant anecdote about four international student directors who had recently visited Poland to study directing at the State School of Theatre in Cracow. They had come to Cracow from Yugoslavia, Columbia and Israel, having learned Polish with the sole purpose of studying the famed Grotowski method at its source. As they soon discovered, nobody at Cracow's prestigious theatre school was teaching the Grotowski method. Moreover, scarcely anyone knew, or was even remotely interested in, what this method might entail.[58] Guczalska suggests that the anecdote illustrates the unspoken "pact of silence" around Grotowski's figure and methodology that persisted for many years in Polish theatre circles. Although this "silence" was breached, briefly, during the Year of Grotowski, the awareness of his art remains the province of a specialized few. In 2009, Joanna Wichowska, a contemporary theatre critic, melancholically noted that "Nobody here [in Poland] misses [Grotowski], and what's left of him is the legend of a guru, surrounded by a group of actors-devotees who have been completely dependent on him."[59] For its part, *Didaskalia* sheepishly concluded that, to this day, the Polish theatre community continues to widely believe that the "proper place for Grotowski is at the universities and university presses, not theatres and theatre schools."[60] Unlike in the West, in Poland Grotowski's acting method continues to be viewed as a mere object of academic study, and not at all as an applicable tool for the practical training of actors or directors.

Both Grotowski's supporters and detractors have, in their own ways, contributed to the long-standing Polish silence about Grotowski's work. His collaborators have been protective, to the point of secrecy, of his legacy. Their defensiveness comes from the desire to evade critics, who would not mince their words if given the chance. While nearly worshiped abroad, in Poland Grotowski was customarily called a "con man," a "sect leader," and a "manipulator."[61] The Laboratory Theatre was often described as a cult that attracted only those with weak psyches and unstable families: a substitute for one's unfulfilled childhood longings and neuroses.[62] Gustaw Holoubek, one of Poland's most prominent theatre and film actors, called Grotowski and his actors "artistic impotents, emotional cripples without talent and with sick and limited psyches, who look at art as compensation for their emotional shortcomings. They sell their own emotions, which are most likely twisted and pathological, in an act of 'disgusting exhibitionism,' 'an invitation to voyeurism.'"[63] Unfortunately, Holoubek's assessment captured the sentiments that many had expressed. Some of Grotowski's collaborators and peers who did speak of him publicly were no less forgiving. Ewa Lubowiecka, for example, one of Grotowski's former actresses, called him a "charlatan and manipulator."[64] Lubowiecka recalls in vivid details and without sympathy:

> Grotowski gave us shoes that didn't fit, so our feet would hurt. [...] He spurred us against each other because he knew he could manipulate us. He treated us like objects. [...] In *Akropolis*, he dressed us in potato sacks. I had a hole in the sack that revealed my breasts. It was humiliating and incomprehensible.[65]

Many Polish critics accused Grotowski of fostering a pathological dynamic within his group. Krystian Lupa openly called him "a suspect intellectual, always looking to advance his own interests." He was also, in Lupa's eyes, a "false prophet."[66] (The statement was a sarcastic allusion to Martin Buber's short essay "False Prophets," which Grotowski considered one of his primary inspirational sources.[67]) Grotowski was often accused of treating his actors inhumanely. There was a feeling that something creepy was happening within his troupe. As Guczalska observes:

> There was something wrong with him, his actors were overexploited and died prematurely. Grotowski crossed some borders that weren't supposed to be crossed. [...] Professional actors always treated him with distrust, convinced that – thanks to his charisma and cruelty – he coerced his actors to sacrifice their lives for him.[68]

There are dozens of complaint letters, preserved in various archives, that reveal the horrible working conditions at the Laboratory Theatre: a 135 square-foot dressing room, stuffed with costumes and props, shared by eight actors, a wardrobe person, and two electricians, without showers or hot water.[69] Grotowski seemed to have ignored his actors' complaints, which prompted many of them to leave the Laboratory Theatre. The recent recollections of Grotowski's collaborators, Maciej Prus, Waldermar Krygiera,

Urszula Bielska and Ewa Lubowiecka, provide a complex picture of the company's inner workings. What attracted Western theatre artists – and the Western press – to Grotowski was a perception of the group's powerfully collaborative spirit; neither the letters of troupe members written during the 1960s nor the recent recollections, however, reveal much of the *esprit de corps* so widely celebrated in the West.

For a long time, Grotowski had very few supporters in Poland. Among them were Irena and Tadeusz Byrski, two former members of Osterwa's Reduta company; the director Konrad Swinarski, known in the West for the world premiere production of *Marat/Sade* in East Berlin; and Tadeusz Łomnicki, one of Poland's leading actors. Their voices, however, were exceptions to the overwhelming animosity of the majority of both Polish theatre artists and the Polish public. Although eventually Grotowski's support among Polish artists widened (and included Halina Gall, Wladysław Broniewski, and Jacek Woszczerowicz), to this day, despite his international reputation, Grotowski and his work are approached with mistrust and distance.[70]

Chapter 3
GROTOWSKI: THE POLISH CONTEXT

In 1969, in his review of Grotowski's production, Irving Wardle quotes Polish critic Boleslaw Taborski as saying that "Grotowski's company was little prized in its own country until it won its reputation abroad, that is: from spectators who knew not a word of Polish and were dependent for understanding on non-Polish speaking converts like Raymonde Temkine and Grotowski's own statements of intention in *Towards A Poor Theatre*."[71] Contrary to what Wardle suggests, however, Grotowski's fame abroad was never the basis for his purported recognition in Poland. On the contrary, the fact that Grotowski became a guru to America's flower-power generation actually contributed to marginalization of his work and his methods in Polish theatrical circles. This contradiction may seem bizarre at first, but praise for an Eastern European artist in the West, with a corresponding loss of prestige in his native country, was not unique to Grotowski. Czesław Miłosz, the Polish poet and writer who served as cultural attaché of the communist People's Republic of Poland in Paris right after World War II, and who defected and received political asylum in France, is another example of how success in the West often diminished the status of the Eastern European artist in his homeland. In 1960, Miłosz emigrated to the USA, and shortly thereafter became an American citizen. After Miłosz's defection, he was branded a traitor and his books banned by the communist government. In 1980, at the height of heated political protests in Poland, and when the Solidarity movement was just beginning to gain momentum, Miłosz won the Nobel Prize in literature. In fact, many Poles heard about him for the first time on the day that the prize was announced. Although Poles generally embraced Miłosz's Nobel, they were not quite convinced that he had won it on merit. On the contrary, many interpreted it as a political nod to the Polish Solidarity dissidents – a welcome gesture, but one suggesting the prize was not awarded on the basis of Miłosz's literary talents alone. The Polish response to Miłosz's Nobel Prize was additionally understandable insofar as Miłosz, who never actually lived under the communist regime, was seen by Western academics as an expert on Polish life under communism. This paradox was viewed as yet another example of the fashionable, but hollow, tokenization of an intellectual from behind the Iron Curtain. Miłosz's *Captive Mind*, a study of the behavior of intellectuals under the totalitarian regime and a masterwork in its own right, was perceived in Poland as a signature book that built Miłosz's political, rather than literary, identity. Moreover, the Polish public, as well as members of Polish literary circles, saw the works of many other writers – among them the poet Zbigniew Herbert, poet-playwright Tadeusz Różewicz, experimental poet Miron Białoszewski, and poet Wisława Szymborska (who won her own Nobel in 1996), to name a few – as far superior to Miłosz's. These artists stayed in their home country, for better or worse. This decision contributed to their lack of visibility in the West but enhanced their reputations and credibility at home. Staying in the country meant learning to write between the lines, or often writing "into the desk drawer,"[72] an effort both hopeless and heroic.[73] While Miłosz enjoyed his life in Berkeley, Herbert and Różewicz consciously sentenced themselves to oblivion, food shortages, censorship and political instability.

For a long time, many Poles felt that the West, particularly American intellectual and creative elites, developed a tendency to fetishize artists whose works had been banned or censored by their own governments. Depending on the unfolding events in Eastern Europe, they would become favorite *causes célèbres* for the bored New York artistic socialites, who often held highly idealized, misinformed and foolish views of Eastern European socialism.[74] One interesting example is Eugenio Barba's honest description of his encounter with Polish socialism *vis-à-vis* his idealized, leftist vision:

> In this society which defined itself as socialist, my left-wing ideas collided with endless examples of injustice, abuse of power, bureaucracy, indifference and cynicism. My ingenuousness vanished, and in its place I felt acquiescence and apathy creeping in. I was confused. All my theories, both political and theatrical, dissolved. [...] I had come to Poland because I believed that "communism restored its fertility to the human race." But, as I saw it, socialism was an obscure caricature, often even a nightmare.[75]

Does an idealized political view skew the formation of cultural tastes amongst foreign audiences? Many Poles thought so. Although many prominent Polish artists like Roman Polanski, Krzysztof Kieślowski and Andrzej Wajda, to name a few, succeeded abroad and continue to be revered in Poland – in fact, their Polish fame is often boosted by their international success – those who were initially not highly regarded in Poland, but who did succeed abroad, especially in the USA, were perceived as doing so by humoring and manipulating the utopian political impulses of the American left, rather than on the merits of their own work. While this opinion was prominent among Poles, it was also a message emanating from communist propaganda, which makes the task of differentiating between genuine and manipulated sentiment *vis-à-vis* the American art scene a difficult one. Many Poles see Miłosz as having been made something of a poster boy for the liberal Western cultural establishment – which to this day, even despite his now-iconic status, continues to fuel some measure of Polish ambivalence about his literary virtues.

Polish theatre circles were similarly suspicious of Grotowski's international success. Critics questioned the degree to which his success was based on artistic merit rather than his usefulness as a position statement for the politically-engaged, New York avant-garde, a fad that would pass with the first winds of political change. Adam Hanuszkiewicz, director of the National Theatre of Poland, bluntly sums up the prevailing sentiment, questioning the Western motives for embracing Grotowski:

> Anything exotic always fetches good prices on the Western market! Grotowski is a "child" of Stanislavsky, and his theatrical father-figure creates all the problems for

him. I despise mystification. Grotowski's theatre lacks a truthfulness of purpose and is typified by a confusion of intentions. It is a hybrid, a deformed birth of naturalism and expressionism. He starts with physiological naturalism and ends up in his own cul-de-sac of stylization and formalism. It is too real to be art, and yet it is too contrived to be real or spontaneous in the manner Grotowski intends us to believe it is. I respect immensely the Living Theatre. Its members are not hypocritical. They come and touch you in the audience. I would not mind if they spat at me, and hit me as a member of the audience they would like to activate. In Grotowski's Theatre on the other hand, to profess utmost naturalism or realism with all its sexuality, and tend to audience-involvement, and then at the same time ignore that there even is any audience, *not involve* them, or even attempt to do so, to respect them as others, it is sheer hypocrisy; it defeats its original purpose and is a new guise for the old Fourth Wall business. Grotowski's is a theatre of peepholes… The audience is put in a position of Peeping-Toms. To witness therefore, the reactions of disgust on the part of the audience is a more rewarding theatrical experience than the actual performance. […] To defy respect-worthy critics is all very exotic-esoteric for you in the West, but it will soon wear out though. Inevitably it happens to all art that lacks truth! To philosophize on laboratorial improvisation and then spend weeks discussing whether the forefinger or the middle finger must come forward in a certain pose the actor strikes, is cheating one's own principles, and is a betrayal of one's audience.

I have personally two arguments against Grotowski's type of theatrical expression. Firstly, theatre, by definition, by its very nature and essence is a live, collective art and must make sense to the masses, from the child to the professor. Good theatre cannot be limited to an audience of initiates, familiar to the secret rites of their society. Secondly, if Grotowski were serious in his commitment to discover in the theatre an equivalent to religion in an atheistic society, then he would not limit his audience to a select few. The concept of the Chosen is basically an expression of a negative, fascistic attitude. Religion shares the same essence with Theatre, it is meant for the masses, the child and the professor must be able to pray together in the same church. The utmost Grotowski may hope to evolve would be a Cult, a mystery-cult of a Secret Society, which is never a Religion.[76]

As Hanuszkiewicz cannot see any redeeming qualities in Grotowski's work, he concludes that explanation for its popularity in the West is the West's own appetite for exotic cultural treats. Although Hanuszkiewicz's statement may seem reductive and dismissing, to fully understand its implications we need to understand the psycho-political framework of Polish postwar culture.

One of the primary reasons for Grotowski's poor standing in the Polish theatre scene had to do with what appeared to be his exceptional political status. In their 1986 article, Jerzy Tymicki and Andrzej Niezgoda captured the complexity of Polish sentiments towards Grotowski during the early days of his international career:

In those days, Grotowski was in a very special position. He was both conservative and radical, compliant and blasphemous. He was backed by the authorities, having been a member of the Party for years (as were his actors). Critics praised him as an innovator. Groups of youths regarded him as a guru. At the same time, he was never accepted by the larger Polish public because he rejected traditional national and religious values and beliefs. Grotowski's deconstructions of Polish classics (Mickiewicz's *Forefathers' Eve* and *Kordian*, Słowacki's *The Constant Prince*, and Wyspianski's *Akropolis*) were regarded as offenses against national treasures. *Apocalypsis cum Figuris*, with its scene of fucking the sacred bread, caused people to cry, "blasphemy." Abroad, Grotowski's reputation was much stronger. In Poland he was accused of manipulating his actors and spectators. Indeed, people said, Grotowski appeals only to the youth because they are easier to manipulate. When in the mid-1970s Grotowski announced his "exit from the theatre," many felt relief. He ceased to be a challenge and a provocation.[77]

As Tymicki and Niezgoda suggest, there was something uneasy about Grotowski's relationship with the communist regime. Under the Soviet regime, it was literally impossible for the average Pole to obtain a passport, yet Grotowski visited Russia, China and India. Such travels were unfathomable for anyone who was not somewhat connected to the Communist Party; Polish citizens were simply not allowed to travel beyond Polish borders. Only those who somehow collaborated with the Communist Party were permitted to travel. As Barba recalls, a passport was "a document that nobody possessed in a socialist country. [...] Poland was a prison, where you could neither have a passport nor travel abroad as could citizens in capitalist Europe. The secret police were omnipresent and the friendliness of a girl could conceal the interest of an informer."[78] In 1956, Grotowski traveled extensively abroad, even writing an article on his travels, titled "Between Iran and China." These early travels alone put Grotowski in a politically questionable position. Eugenio Barba recalls his conversation with Grotowski, about Grotowski's meeting with the Russian theatre director Yiru Zavadsky, "the grandson of a Polish aristocrat who had been deported to Siberia during the Warsaw insurrection of 1863. [His] productions were in the worst socialist-realistic style and had won him innumerable honours."[79] While hosting in his apartment in Moscow, Zavadsky showed Grotowski his passport, bragging, "I can go to Capri or to London tomorrow if I want to see a show in the West End." Then Zavadsky led Grotowski "to the window and pointed out two large ZIM limousines parked in the courtyard, each with its own chauffeur inside. 'The Soviet people put them at my disposal day and night. I have lived through dreadful times and they have broken me. Remember Jerzy, *nie warto*, it is not worth it. This is the harvest of compromise.'"[80] According to Barba, Grotowski talked about "this moment as of a turning point in his life. [...] Zavadsky had been his great master."[81] One can't help wondering why...

When reading Grotowski's newspaper articles from that period of the late 1950s to the early 1960s – and knowing the historical currents that governed Poland's political life at that time – one is struck by a certain blatant opportunism glaring from Grotowski's writings. In 1955, at the height of socialist realism, Grotowski openly denounced artists who choose to engage in any kind of private, and therefore unchecked, art making. He wrote: "We often hear of a peculiar double life among artists. They create one kind of art for the critics and the official exhibits, and another kind of art for themselves, their friends and their families. This is the art in which they reveal their true selves."[82] In denouncing such double lives, Grotowski called for everyone to embrace socialist realism: "We ask for an atmosphere in which we could openly speak the same way that we speak in private. [...] The common goal: Socialist Realism. The strategy: honesty, bravery of expression and artistic exploration."[83] The language that Grotowski used in this article echoes the clichéd language used by the Communist Party in its propaganda materials. In another article from 1955, Grotowski literally used the same vocabulary that had become a signature party line: "We, the young would like to dedicate ourselves to a theatre that evokes revolutionary passion, love, class brotherhood, cult of heroism, and hate towards capitalist oppression."[84] In 1956, at the height of the October Thaw, Grotowski again opportunistically followed the trend – this time, however, denouncing Stalin and socialist realism. In the October issue of *Dziennik Polski*, he writes: "From the mid-1930s, that is, from the era of the cult of Social Realism, Stalin has drastically limited the creative freedom of Soviet artists."[85] By then, socialist realism was no longer "one common goal" and Grotowski modified his position to fit the current political winds. In 1957, however, the wave of temporary freedoms was again slowly receding, and Grotowski again renewed the call for socialism, repeating the propaganda slogans of the Communist Party in a communist youth journal: "We are obliged to fight against those who want a return of capitalism, who want the land to be returned to the landowners, who want the factories to be returned to their owners. We need to fight against those who want the return of dictatorship over the proletariat."[86] Reading Grotowski's writing from this period, one finds it difficult not to at least suspect Grotowski of collaboration with the regime. As the times changed, the tone and message of his articles always paralleled the official party line. In his book, *Grotowski: Przewodnik* [Grotowski: A Handbook], Dariusz Kosiński writes about a 1997 meeting with young students, during which they accused Grotowski of having an "unclean" political record, on account of running an official theatre in what was a totalitarian country. Defending himself, Grotowski reportedly responded: "We could do nothing and lose our only chance or try to do as much as we could under the circumstances."[87] Kosiński wonders if the compromises were always necessary, and about the extent to which Grotowski availed himself of politically expedient solutions.[88] Whatever the answer, Grotowski's ambivalent political sympathies put him in the communist camp, which made him suspect amongst Polish artistic circles, which generally opposed the regime. As could be expected, anyone suspected of collaborating with the Party was automatically suspected of being an informer, and, needless to say, informers were unwelcome in artistic circles – their presence inhibited private conversations, and, more importantly, could be dangerous. Of course, there remain many unanswered questions swirling around the communist past: who collaborated with whom and for what reasons? Who now wants to know, and why? Was it at all possible to be even slightly successful without appearing as if one collaborates with the regime? What did that collaboration entail, and how far did it go? How are we to judge it from the current political perspective?

Another reason why Polish theatre circles shunned Grotowski is rooted in both the historical strategies for coping with totalitarian oppression, and the ways in which such political strategies influenced Polish acting. Both Nazis and Communists took themselves extremely seriously. As Wittgenstein rightly noted in 1948, there was no humor in Nazi

Germany: "Humor is not a mood but a way of looking at the world [*Weltanschauung*]. So if it is correct to say that humor was stamped out in Nazi Germany, that does not mean that people were not in good spirits, or anything of that sort, but something much deeper and more important."[89] Communists offered a similar vision of the world, a world in which they were unable to laugh at themselves because the very existence of the totalitarian regime they perpetuated was threatened by laughter; it was a world without irony. In his 1984 book *Carnival!* Umberto Eco suggests that: "The most repressive dictatorships have always censured parodies and satires but not clowneries; [that's] why humor is suspect but circus is innocent."[90] Since dictatorial power is grounded in fear, and fear is disarmed by laughter, dictators fear irony, or as Peter Sloterdijk puts it: "An essential aspect of power is that it only likes to laugh at its own jokes."[91] Neither communism nor fascism was able to withstand irony because, like any totalitarian system, they were unable to withstand self-criticism.[92] Thus, as a coping mechanism under the years of totalitarian oppression, Poles developed a proverbial form of resistance: an intellectual distance from the oppressive ideology. Peter Sloterdijk calls it kynicism, "a rejection of the official culture by means of irony and sarcasm."[93] It was a peculiar form of "pissing against the idealist wind" of the ardent party *apparatchiks*.[94] As Sloterdijk puts it:

> Cheekiness has, in principle, two positions, namely, above and below, hegemonic power and oppositional power. [...] The kynic, as dialectical materialist, has to challenge the public sphere because it is the only space in which the overcoming of idealist arrogance can be meaningfully demonstrated.[95]

In Poland, years of partitions, followed by Nazi and then Soviet occupation, created a society that couldn't approach existential questions other than through sardonic self-debasement. For decades, the language of kynical dialectic permeated every aspect of Polish culture, from music to literature, from high- to lowbrow – including Polish theatre.[96] Kynicism established lines of communication between the theatres and their audiences; actors, directors and playwrights learned to speak between the lines, using metaphors, symbols, or sometimes just a wink, to communicate their anti-establishment sentiments to their audiences. As a result, people went to the theatre to see the wink, the smile, small gestures that told them they were not alone in their contempt for, and struggle against, the regime. It was genuinely political theatre because there was genuine political oppression.[97]

The kynical strategy affected the training and development of Polish actors, who were naturally inclined to engage in subtle, ironic exchanges, rather than exaggerated theatrical passions. Konrad Swinarski perfectly described this phenomenon when, in 1967, he defended the exuberant emotionality of Grotowski's acting style against the ironic tendencies of generic Polish acting:

> One thing that is both a good and bad aspect of Polish acting is that the Polish actor is a born comedian, but a comedian who only knows how to make jokes. He will make fun of everything, even of himself, because he believes that everything is relative and thus deserving to be mocked. Most of our actors cannot play a great passion simply

because they have never known it, or they weren't taught how to do it. In Grotowski's theatre, the actors can play great passions – and I don't care whether it happens on the borderline of hysteria, or as a form of theatrical expression.[98]

For Swinarski, the tragic nihilism of Polish postwar culture infected Polish actors, who were no longer able to commit to any steady worldview, and thus no longer able to either feel or play emotions.[99] They were able, however, to make clever jokes about the system. The tradition of Polish acting is founded on Stanislavsky's methodology, but in the form that he developed later in life; the role is supposed to be a "product of mind, not of heart," as Holoubek put it.[100] Theatre is a place of artifice that should attempt to recreate the world of ideas; it is a place of subtle and refined intellectual engagement, not a place to search for unbridled passions and emotions. Creating a role requires total concentration, not hysterics.[101] The political framework of Polish culture contributed significantly to such an understanding of what was and wasn't acting, with kynicism as the major contributing factor.

Grotowski's theatre trended towards a completely different direction; it took itself, its projects and its guru extremely seriously. As Hanuszkiewicz comments: "A theatre where one cannot laugh is inhuman to say the least. Grotowski's is a theatre of no-laughter, (he has literally banished laughter from his theatre), no sense of humour, no irony."[102] Trained as an audience to laugh at the world, themselves, life, death and oppression, Poles were not used to the full pathos, piety and exuberant emotionalism that Grotowski's theatre offered. Grotowski's approach to theatre went against the Polish actor's training, as well as the cultural strategy of kynical resistance. Many years later, Grotowski reportedly defended his approach, arguing that his theatre was, in fact, apolitical in order to be political. He also suggested that his complicated relationship with the communist regime and Polish culture was multilayered and ironic.[103]

The last, but no less important, reason why Grotowski was not accepted in Poland has to do with the general character of his theatre, which challenged perceptions concerning the role theatre played within Polish culture. The Laboratory Theatre was founded in 1959, six years after Stalin's death. It was a period of political thaw, but it did not change the basic fabric of Polish society. Influenced by years of partitions, World War II, the Holocaust, and the Stalinist purges, Poles considered life to be fundamentally and fatalistically tragic, but felt that one's own existential tragedy in the face of the overwhelmingly brutal forces of history was not something one should dwell on with hopes of finding salvation, especially not in theatre. If Poles felt pain, it was "a pain with a smile and a shrug."[104] What Grotowski proposed, however, was something completely opposite: acting as "a creative process of self-search."[105] Grotowski based his training on Osterwa's prewar dictum that the role of the "actor was not so much to *play* a role as to *be*, to *live* on stage."[106] Quoting Grotowski: "We want to work through our own impulses and instincts, through our own inner beings and through our own individual responses."[107] Or, as Peter Brook put it, for Grotowski "the theatre [was] a vehicle, a means for self-study, self-exploration; a possibility of salvation."[108] Grotowski's company, Brook wrote, "ha[d] a sacred aim."[109] Such an approach was contradictory to the very core of Polish identity. It's not to say that kind of pathos and piety – a soul searching without cynicism – has been absent from Polish society.

On the contrary, it has always been part of the everyday experience; however, the kind of piety and pathos that Grotowski proposed has been solely reserved for the religious sphere. In contemporary Poland, "where 'holiness' both commonly and officially belongs entirely to the institution of the Catholic Church, there is a constant need for reiterating the term's meaning [...] When speaking of 'sacral theatre,' we remain removed from both confession and theology."[110] In the context of the historically strong Catholic framework, Grotowski's "sacred aim" appeared not only blasphemous, but nearly pathological.[111] For Poles, theatre was not meant to be a place of salvation; that's what church was for.[112] Theatre was a place to think, not to pray. Looking for salvation in dogmatic theatre projects was not just profane, it was also considered intellectually immature, naïve, narcissistic, and altogether too self-indulgent to be considered a legitimate response to the tragic fatalism of single human existence or communal political fate. It was also too self-important, and therefore, ironically, it rang false. To quote Hanuszkiewicz again: "[Grotowski's theatre] is too real to be art, and yet it is too contrived to be real."[113]

Through years of Nazi, then Communist, regimes that were rooted in self-importance, Poles grew suspicious of those who took themselves too seriously; Grotowski's lack of distance from himself and his work for a long time evoked both professional and personal disdain.[114] In Jan Kott's 1980 essay titled "The End of the Impossible Theatre," for example, he passionately accuses Grotowski of leading the Western theatre onto a self-destructive path of pseudo-religious, cultish revelations.[115] The same year, Lech Raczak published an article in *Dialog* titled "Para-ra-ra," that was a virtual attack on Grotowski's paratheatre. Raczak's article was particularly painful for Grotowski because Raczak was himself a leader of the newly emerging political counterculture. As Leszek Kolankiewicz summarizes it, Raczak described Grotowski's theatre as "unfinished," "poor in intellectual engagement," and "a bunch of aimless physical exercises having nothing to do with intellectual activity."[116] He accused Grotowski of promising his followers an egalitarian engagement with their feelings while in fact he merely turned them into a mindless herd of sheep: "It seems that the route from the mothership to *Daily News* [*Daily News* was a propaganda piece on Polish TV, rightly despised by the Polish public] is quite simple. [...] Time has scorned the prophets: their choice has shown itself to be illusory; their escape from civilization came to halt in the blind alley of the industrial wasteland."[117]

Krystian Lupa was openly annoyed by what he called Grotowski's "holy seriousness." Lupa went even further, confessing that he was personally "repelled by that solemn anointment with which they tried to feed me, the viewer, their work, the supposed 'spiritual nourishment' wrapped in some kind of Eucharistic pretense. [I am suspicious] of anyone whose arguments are addressed only to the 'true believers.'"[118] Lupa's comments articulate a prevailing sentiment towards Grotowski that continues to dominate the Polish theatre community.[119]

Because it ran against the grain of the Polish cultural framework on multiple levels, Grotowski's acting methodology was generally not considered useful for professional training. Citing Hanuszkiewicz again, Grotowski's approach was considered

> naïve, childish, inconsistent, amateurish! His actors may be good yoga performers, but not even mimes – let alone good actors. They are professionally very bad, useless!

Except for Grotowski, nobody can work with them. They are limited and single-track minded. Surely, a professional actor must be capable of working with different directors. But not those of Grotowski's Theatre.[120]

Andrzej Seweryn, one of only a few Polish actors invited to perform at the Comedie Française, put it succinctly: "I am confident that Grotowski has no influence on Polish theatre. Whatsoever! I speak about professional theatre. I am not saying it as a reproach because how was this influence supposed to manifest itself? That suddenly everyone would start rolling on the floor?"[121]

As a nation only recently recovering from the trauma of the war, Poles didn't go to the theatre to see pain or passion; no theatrical experiments could match the real pain caused by the experience of the war, the Holocaust, and the Stalinist regime. It was, however, only natural that Grotowski's "creative process of self-search" found fertile ground in New York's avant-garde circles, which could afford the luxury of such self-search. Poles had neither the time nor the energy for "self-study" and "self-exploration"; they were happy to have escaped Hitler and Stalin, and were trying merely to survive and not get shot or arrested by the SB (Security Bureau).[122] As Jan Kott puts it: "Grotowski was welcomed by [the New York] theatres as a great guru. He taught violent means. In fact, the language of social and sexual revolution, Marx and Freud, Lenin and Artaud, became intermixed. [...] The theatres of the New Left felt that revolution could enter the mind only through the skin."[123] For obvious reasons, a combination of Marx and Lenin was not an ideological mix that Polish youth found appealing. It was, however, a perfect fit for the do-your-own-thing-find-yourself counterculture of 1960s New York. Kott continues:

> Sit-in, teach-in, love-in – these are forms of instant liberation, Utopias acted out, and thus theatre. The Woodstock Festival was a real *Paradise Now*. It was also an *Apocalypsis cum figures*, but the figures were different. One can accept one of the apocalypses or reject both, but one cannot accept both of them at the same time.[124]

Grotowski's self-centered acting methodology seemed an ideal vehicle for young Americans looking to escape the nine-to-five routine while searching for exotic thrills and the meaning of life, and trying to fill the existential void left by their affluent, suburban adolescence. They rejected the institutionalized religion of their parents, replacing it with what Ross Wetzsteon calls the "chic spirituality" of communes and performance groups.[125] Compared to "spiritual" trips to India, and to LSD, Grotowski offered a more sheltered, but equally exotic and enigmatic, adventure on the journey towards self-discovery. Ironically, he himself was quite aware of his status as *fad-du-jour*; he played up his inscrutable Eastern European mystique, and openly spoke about it a number of times.

What attracted American theatre artists to Grotowski was what most Poles found repellent: the quasi-religious, cult-like structure of his group.[126] For Andre Gregory, for example, meeting Grotowski was a moment of personal epiphany. In a 1975 interview, he said: "My life has changed because I saw Grotowski's art. I am not just talking about my theatre, that it changed. I saw Grotowski's theatre and something inside me opened up. I made a certain discovery about myself; and that is why I needed Grotowski's theatre. I needed it not as a theatre professional, but as a human being."[127] Like many others enraptured by the redemptive vocabulary of Grotowski's theatre, Richard Schechner too reverently wrote in 1969 that "Grotowski speaks of his theater in religious terms, of 'novitiates' and 'disciples.'"[128] In an essay, "Exoduction," published in *Grotowski Sourcebook*, Schechner goes as far as to suggest that Grotowski's theatre replaces the holy place. Schechner wrote that "In Grotowski's terms, this search for the Shekhinah is his 'Theatre of Sources,' his 'Objective Drama,' his 'Art as Vehicle.'"[129] Many years later, in 2008, Schechner verified his assessment, writing: "I realize that Grotowski did not intend to found a religion. But undeniably, his utterances are suffused with religious imagery and allusions. Those devoted to his work behave as if Grotowski's inner work has the quality of a sacred."[130] Following Grotowski's death, Allen Kuharski poignantly summed up Grotowski's cult-like appeal for the American avant-garde:

> The appeal [of Grotowski's work] was irresistible: a marriage of ethics and virtuosity that promised to renew and redeem the frivolous and increasingly irrelevant institution of the theater. [Grotowski's] work seemed to imply that such a sanctified yet secular art theatre could assume a role of ethical leadership and renewal in a society at large, and that the authority of church and state might even pale in comparison. Though Grotowski was scrupulously modest in his statements on these scores, his language implies a kind of theatrical messianism [...] A very seductive idea to theater people in any context [...] A seduction to which I must admit, like so many others, I succumbed from afar.[131]

As Kuharski admits, Grotowski's "theatrical messianism" was seductive, but also ethically questionable. Like Kuharski, many others succumbed to it without questioning it. Richard Gilman's reverent review from 1970 captures the strange, cult-like mysticism described by Kuharski. According to Gilman, theatre – thanks to Grotowski – "has felt itself in the presence of something very like a redemption."[132] As opposed to life, which "in the present is inauthentic," Gilman writes, Grotowski's theatre offers something "pure" and "true." In Grotowski's theatre, Gilman continues, "[a]lmost every movement and sound is what can only be described as 'pure,' without precedent and predictability, yet wholly inevitable, accurate, created, true."[133] Gilman's reverence is exactly the attitude that evoked consternation among Polish theatre practitioners in regards to Grotowski.[134] Many of them felt uneasy about the strange cultish atmosphere that surrounded the Laboratory Theatre.

Although rooted in Polish Romantic drama, Grotowski's religious language of messianism and redemption also resembles the cult of personality that dominated the totalitarian aesthetic.[135] Martin Harries writes that the trend to recapture the notion of the sacred in postwar theatre was a way to reclaim from the state what the state took from theatre through grand spectacles of totalitarian power: "Theatre artists were at once threatened and flattered by massive state ceremonies that also aspired to a grasp on the sacred. [...] Theatre artists saw the state seizing a theatrical power, and longed for an efficacy to equal that of the state."[136] Michał Masłowski suggests that the religious aspect of Grotowski's work was a response not so much to the political circumstances in Poland as to the more general crisis of faith that followed World War II. Masłowski argues that following Auschwitz, Catholicism – or more generally, Christian values – was exhausted and no longer answering the basic existential questions.[137] Thus, theatre became a substitute environment in which one could renew the search for answers. In Polish Romantic drama, the redemptive and messianic themes are closely connected to the Judeo-Christian tradition that pervaded the contemporaneous Polish exilic discourse; however, in postwar Poland, the relationship between politics, theatre and religion is much more complicated. If, for Romantic poets, theatre served as a unifying force that blurred the boundaries between the sacred and secular worlds in a political call for mass revolt against the oppressors (particularly in Adam Mickiewicz's *Forefathers' Eve* and in Juliusz Słowacki's *Kordian*), in Grotowski's theatre, the insertion of the sacred into a secular context seems to lack political purpose. As Konstanty Puzyna puts it: "With full awareness, [Grotowski] pushed aside the political aspects of Romanticism, as well as its historical interest and close poetic observation of contemporary reality. He sought in it instead myth and ritual, that which is timeless and unchanging. One may well judge that he completely academicized these dramas."[138] Without political motivation, Grotowski appears to blaspheme for blasphemy's sake, which, from the Polish point of view, is pointlessly "irresponsible eccentricity, exhibitionism, excess, and mumbling."[139] Grotowski's theatre promised redemption, but it was never clear from what. There was a particular circular – perhaps even tautological – framework in Grotowski's soteriological combination of theatre and religion that made many Poles uncomfortable.

Such are the many reasons behind Grotowski's lukewarm reception in Poland. But what mechanisms structured the epistemology of Grotowski's theatre in America? And how did the meaning of who and what was Grotowski develop outside of the context that formed him? How did such knowledge – literal, temporal and historical – develop? How was meaning around Grotowski and his work created?

Chapter 4

GROTOWSKI, THE MESSIAH: COMING TO AMERICA

In 1962, Eugene Barba, who was a student at Warsaw's Państwowa Wyższa Szkoła Teatralna (PWST, the National School of Theatre), came to Opole as part of his internship. Eventually, he became one of Grotowski's closest collaborators and his most ardent foreign supporter. Shortly after meeting Barba, Grotowski participated in the Eighth World's Youth Festival in Helsinki, where he also met Raymonde Temkine. She visited Opole in 1963, watched a special performance of *Akropolis*, and was greatly impressed by Grotowski's theatre. Those two contacts augmented international perspectives of Grotowski, but to reach wider audiences, Grotowski needed a concrete theatrical piece that would appeal to international tastes. As Dariusz Kosiński notes:

> Grotowski was becoming more ambitious and certain of his artistic direction. What he needed was a model spectacle which would showcase both his theory and methodology, but which would also be international in its character. The adaptation of Wyspiański's *Akropolis* became such a spectacle. If we assume that Grotowski consciously constructed a spectacle to show the full range of his theatre's possibilities, then we can also assume that he chose the play as well as its setting because they naturally interest both Polish and international audiences.[140]

As a showcase spectacle for a broader international audience, *Akropolis* fulfilled its function, but in Poland, initial reviews were mixed, to say the least. Puzyna notes that the production "provoked extremely tempestuous discussions."[141] One critic, Aunt Agnieszka, passionately argued that the "normal theatre goer is not interested in horror in theatre. He is overwhelmed, demobilized and weakened by such shows. [...] If we could put all of the tyrants of history together and show them *Akropolis* as part of their punishment, that would be all right. But us? What for?"[142] She sarcastically called the show "an adventure of a construction company," noting that "One man was sitting there with tears in his eyes, looking at the set. Apparently, as I learned later, he was remodeling his bathroom and he couldn't find the much-needed pipes anywhere in the stores. The actors promised to give him the coveted pipes from the set once the show was over."[143] Although Aunt Agnieszka's review wasn't particularly sophisticated, it did capture the general sentiment of Grotowski's Polish audiences.

Abroad, however, the situation was different. From 1962 to 1967, the Laboratory Theatre traveled with *Akropolis* throughout Europe, including Holland, France, Belgium and Italy. The show drew predominantly positive reviews; *Het Parool* called it "brilliant," while *Vaterland* wrote: "The symbolism of the spectacle leaves the viewer with a long-lasting impression. The tension grows systematically thanks to the skills of the actors, who show remarkable control over their bodies, which they use as tools for emotions."[144] In Brussels, *Akropolis* was shown only four times, but *Het Lasstse Nieuws* was very much impressed, and *Het Volk* compared it to Dante and Hieronymus Bosch.[145] *La Libre Belgique* proclaimed the Laboratory Theatre "the most famous acting troupe in the world."[146] In Paris, the group received mostly positive reviews, with Bertrand Poirot-Delpech of *Le Monde* writing, "…beyond hysterical glances, the slobbering and the shuddering of the muscles, is expressed the most spiritual resistance to order and violence."[147] Among all the positive reviews, there were also a handful who couldn't decide what to think. C. van Hoboken of the *Amsterdam* newspaper, for example, asked philosophically, "Is Jerzy Grotowsky a genie or a charlatan?"[148] In many European reviews from that time, the word "experiment" reappears, suggesting that many reviewers considered the show to be a work in progress. In 1969, Grotowski again took his troupe abroad, travelling to Great Britain, Mexico, and France. The group gave eight performances of *Akropolis* at Edinburgh, thirty in Paris, and eighteen in Aix-en-Provence, cementing the role of *Akropolis* as the group's signature show.[149] In France, particularly, Temkine noticed "admiration was expressed by the very ones who were not always in agreement on the principles."[150]

In late 1968, Grotowski and his Laboratory Theatre were planning their first visit to the USA. The trip, however, was cancelled following the revocation of American visas for the group. The revocation was a response of the American government to the Soviet invasion of Czechoslovakia, which quashed the ongoing student protests. Because Poland's army, under the leadership of the meek and Soviet-friendly Gomułka, joined the Soviet invasion, the US government considered Poland to be an aggressor nation as well. Inadvertently, Grotowski's group was swept up in the overall boycott of the Eastern Bloc. The refusal of visas was met with protest in New York by 62 leading theatre figures, including Albee, Miller, Hellman, and Robbins, who wrote an open letter protesting the revocation of visas.[151] The letter, published in the *New York Times*, proclaimed that "the performances of [the Laboratory Theatre] could be most important to the future development of the American theater."[152] Shortly after, the signatories formed the National Committee to Welcome the Polish Laboratory Theatre. Co-chaired by Ellen Stewart and Ninon Tallon Karlweis, the committee soon grew to over 100 members, and included the cream of the crop of New York's cultural elites. Like many before him, Grotowski became a new favorite *cause célèbre*, a fresh symbol of the struggle against the repressive policies of the US government.

Despite the protests, however, Grotowski's troupe was not permitted entry into the USA, and the group went to London instead. Under the patronage of the Ford Foundation, Lewis Freedman – the producer of the Public Broadcast Laboratory – decided to record Grotowski's production, believing wholeheartedly "that the loss [would] damage American knowledge of international theater."[153] As a result, in 1968, from 27 October to 2 November, *Akropolis* was filmed by James MacTaggart, a leading producer and director in his era, in Twickenham studios near London. As the legend goes, Grotowski never again agreed to the filming of any of his shows.

(Years later, he did permit Italian television to record *Apocalypsis cum figures*, but never gave permission to release it. In 1989, he also allowed the Workcenter's performance to be recorded.)[154] Grotowski believed "that theatre is an independent art, and there is no need to use other technologies. Poor theatre should use its own resources, that is, actors and space; the relationship between the actors and the audience is the most important."[155] The use of the camera disrupts and denatures it. This time, however, Grotowski gave permission to MacTaggart to film *Akropolis*. Forestalling potential criticism of this decision, Grotowski spoke at length about the reasons behind it and the process:

> We decided that *Akropolis* was almost impossible to present on television. The others were quite impossible. *Akropolis*, like our other productions, is organized in a certain area of space. It's not broken up into the stages and the auditorium. It's an osmosis of a place where there's action, and a place where there's the spectator. The action happens in the middle of the spectators, around them. Each spectator makes a selection of what he will watch. [For television] we decided that we would do a reportage on our production of Akropolis. In the short time available to us for taping the television production here in London, we decided to observe both actors and spectators from outside, with the camera serving as observer. The man who's the spectator in the audience brings the man who is at home into the theater. It's now a production for a spectator who's never seen one of our productions before, or how it works. *We've* had to make the choice of what to look at in place of the one the spectator would make in the theater. It would be dishonest to pretend the production was ever originally designed for television. It's not elegantly done. It's as though we had grabbed something quickly as it passed by.[156]

Reportedly, Grotowski discussed the production with MacTaggart at great length, but when the actual taping took place, for the first two days he is said to have just watched, rather like an author: "I could suffer like the authors of the plays we do, though of course, they're dead! Suffer in silence. On the third day, as it were, I rose again and left the tomb, suggesting things for the details we were still recording."[157]

Following the renewed appeal to American immigration authorities, Grotowski was finally given a one-week entry visa to the USA and permitted to travel to New York to help edit the film.[158] The film was in Polish and without subtitles, but with a lengthy, half-hour introduction by Peter Brook that aimed to contextualize and explain Grotowski's piece. Finally, after months of speculation and anticipation, spurred by the positive reviews from Europe and the publication of *Towards Poor Theatre*, the American public was able to see the famed Laboratory Theatre. *Akropolis* aired in the USA on WNET (National Educational Television) the evening of Sunday, 12 January 1969, immediately sparking vigorous critical debate, and cementing Grotowski's iconic status among American theatre critics, scholars, and practitioners.[159] Initial critical reviews of the film, however, were mixed and tended towards discussion of differences between the recorded and live versions. Mark Shivaslondon, for example, began his editorial about the film by asking, "how on earth any of Grotowski's productions could be transferred to television."¹⁶⁰ Leo Mishkin of the *Morning Telegraph* found the entire experience emotionally overwhelming:

> *Akropolis* turned out to be highly stylized, strange and eerie work that pretty well bore out Mr. Brook's words. It was the director's aim, according to the notes I have at hand, to present a sort of Apocalyptic vision of the history of mankind through a set of figures building a crematorium at, of all places, Auschwitz. […] the total effect is of such size and stature as to leave you open-mouthed with astonishment. We have already had, on and off-Broadway, the Theatre of the Absurd, the Theatre of Cruelty, and more lately, the Theatre of Involvement. The Polish Laboratory Theatre apparently has now struck out in an entirely new direction, possibly to be eventually termed the Theatre of Mankind's Guilt and Conscience.¹⁶¹

Jack Gould of the *New York Times* acknowledged that the TV recording

> had to cope with such successive matters as explaining Mr. Grotowski's methodology, overcoming the difficulty of the play's being done in the Polish language, and televising on the small screen a work clearly designed for staging in the round. […] The TV version may have been unfair to the Polish director's intent. The receiver itself represented an intrusive proscenium arch, and preoccupation with irrelevant close-ups tended to erase the totality of mood of the unorthodox staging. The succession of brief snippets defeated a sense of enveloping rhythm of the inmates remembering their past and reincarnating their Greek and Hebraic ancestors."¹⁶²

After having seen the live theatre performance in 1970, Stanley Kauffmann wrote that

> The difference between the theater performance of *Acropolis* and the PBL film was the difference between an event and the report of an event […]. The event was so utterly theatrical that the film was utterly irrelevant. To sit *amidst* those Polish actors at *Acropolis*, almost to smell them, to see them setting down the wheelbarrow an inch from my foot and find myself not flinching because I had confidence in them, knowledge that they knew I was there, were doing it all for me and at the same time that they didn't care whether I was there or not… […] It was not merely the patent fact of their and my physical presence, it was a sense of not being acted *on* but of collaboration.¹⁶³

Months later, when Grotowski's group finally performed live in New York, Ross Wetzsteon of the *Village Voice* preferred the TV version to the live show, writing: "[T]he play seemed more moving when it appeared on television last winter, for in the theatre, the action has a kind of dimly lit and cluttered diffuseness overcome by the in-drawing nature of the TV image, by the use of close-ups in particular."¹⁶⁴

The *New York Times* reviewer, John Simon, however, wasn't as forgiving as others, criticizing both the production and the TV version, and calling the first "a Keystone Komedy with a dash of bitterness," and the second, "the reduction of a reduction."¹⁶⁵ In his second review of the live performance, Simon was even more derisive: "It is a sad comment on our age that Grotowski should have become the most revered and sedulously emulated figure in world theatre."[166] Simon continued mercilessly:

> Esthetically, it looks like a cross between recreation period in an idiot school and an aboriginal blood rite in the rain forests of the Amazon. Morally, it is a combination of sadomasochistic agonizing with mythopoeic self-aggrandizement. This self-styled Theatre of the Poor is, in fact, just poor theatre. [...] In all these productions there is so much carefully rehearsed movement, falling somewhere between second-rate modern dance and calisthenics gone berserk.[167]

In a rebuke to Simon's review of the filmed version, William Kinsolving, also of the *New York Times*, accused Simon of not just misunderstanding the production, but of even failing to "cover up the fact that he did not understand what Grotowski was about."[168] *Akropolis* – Kinsolving writes – "is a vitally important development in theatre, and seeing Grotowski's work put the Living Theatre and Schechner in perspective and in the shade."[169] Responding to Simon's main complaint that the characters were homogenous and indistinguishable, lacking individuality and expressiveness, Kinsolving argues that their apparent homogeneity is a deliberate artistic decision, intended to evoke broader and more complex abstract concepts:

> Simon should remember that the careful line drawings of character in our realistic/naturalistic theater, no matter how beautiful or exquisite, are limitations. When one is dealing with whole concepts, ideas, beliefs, one can portray them in the theater with a device larger than the realistic. Concepts cannot be confined in careful line drawings. Grotowski uses symbols for these concepts which, it is to be hoped, cause the audience to create the limitless in their minds. He purposefully seems to take away the individuality of a specific actress, not to reduce her, but to enable her to expand, to represent all women, all men, every concept, idea, belief, that might come up in the play.[170]

Kinsolving's review implied that dismissing Grotowski's work is a sure sign of bigotry and a lack of sophistication, thus dismissing Simon as something of a provincial simpleton. The exchange between Simon and Kinsolving, however, set up an interesting dilemma: which of the two critics, and for what reason, could rightfully claim a monopoly on understanding a work that, literally, neither of them understood?

Kinsolving's review was an implicit challenge to the members of the New York avant-garde to embrace Grotowski based on the visual, while ignoring the textual and contextual aspects of his work. The challenge was promptly picked up by a number of theatre artists, including Andre Gregory, Joseph Chaikin and Richard Schechner.[171] For Chaikin, "Grotowski was one of the people who went the furthest in their experiments. In that sense, he influenced all of those who work in theatre, and all of those who go to theatre."[172] Chaikin, however, was against "mimicking Grotowski's work," concluding that those who try to follow him "spend five, six years doing something that's basically only an empty noise."[173] With Schechner, the case was different for number of reasons.

It has been suggested that "Schechner's whole sudden rise to prominence as a theater director [has been] tied with the beginning awareness of [Grotowski's] work."[174] Schechner's "expertise" on Grotowski was initially developed from the collaboration between Grotowski and *The Drama Review* (*TDR*), which published three of Barba's articles on Grotowski, even before the Laboratory Theatre arrived in the United States. The articles were sent to Schechner by Barba, and their publication didn't require any particular research on, or knowledge of, either Poland or Grotowski. *TDR* made an error, attributing one of Barba's articles to Grotowski himself.[175] Ironically, that 1964 article, "Dr. Faustus in Poland" was published in a special issue on Marlowe. Based on these three articles by Barba, Flaszen's description of *Akropolis*, Grotowski's essay "Towards a Poor Theatre," and Henry Popkin's article on Polish Theatre,[176] Schechner became an expert on Polish theatre.[177] Most importantly, however, the evolution of Schechner's Grotowskian expertise appears to be a foundational turning point in the development of methodology and critical practice in the field of performance studies. Inserting himself in the critical debate between Simon and Kinsolving about Grotowski, Schechner proclaimed the supremacy of "gesture and nonverbal communication" over the "literature of theatre," formulating for the first time the premise of performance studies as an artistic and critical method. In 1969, in an article he wrote for the *New York Times*, Schechner reframed the Simon–Kinsolving debate around Grotowski's work by arguing that

> The war has organized itself around two pivotal battles. One pits language – the "literature of theater" – against gesture and "nonverbal communication." The other argues the benefits of a participating versus a watching audience. […] Those who most effectively practice traditional theater are not very articulate. Thus we have the spectacle of articulate advocates of nonverbal communication ranged against inarticulate defenders of the literary faith; and practitioners against critics who – for what might seem to be obvious reasons – feel compelled to say that finally words are what matters in theater.[178]

Framing the debate in such simplistic boundaries, Schechner dismissed the "literature of theatre" and with it any contextual and historical considerations, thus establishing the critical trope that was to dominate performance and theatre scholarship for the next four decades. Posing the problem as conflict between those who cling to old notions of literary text and those who are brave enough to venture into the realm of their "self-exploration" based on "gestures and non-verbal communication" – between those who get it and those who don't – Schechner defined a mode of critical thought that took pride – like Tyszka's New York University (NYU) student – in not knowing. According to Schechner, knowing the text means not knowing the production. Likewise, being ignorant of the text is a key to understanding the essential core of the production. Schechner presented himself as particularly versed in Grotowski's work, having had special access to one of his workshops: "I was a member of one such seminar in which I learned (by doing) some of the basic Grotowski exercises and disciplines."[179] Thus, the argument successfully inverted epistemological practice: not knowing Polish, and being unfamiliar with the Polish literary and cultural context that formed Grotowski's work, meant somehow knowing the *true* – universal – Grotowski. This intimate, universal knowledge of Grotowski required absolute ignorance of the historical and cultural framework of his work.

To further solidify his point, Schechner drew what he considered an obvious equivalence between his work and that of Grotowski: "There is a strong, identifiable relationship between Grotowski's *Dr. Faustus, Akropolis, The Constant Prince* [...] and the Performance Group's *Dionysus in 69*," adding that "All attempt new spatial uses of the theater, new audience-performer relationships, new outlooks on what the theatrical function is."[180] For Schechner, such a quasi-religious structure offered an opportunity for a movement:

> A movement not generated by playwrights and protected by critics; but one sponsored by directors and performers. A movement not yet sealed in books but revealed in many productions and bringing together in a new synthesis such diverse influences as yoga and the Kathakali of southern India, the visionary outcries of Antonin Artaud, the rituals of many nonliterate peoples, the passion for systemization of Stanislavski, and the peculiar anxieties of today's Western world.[181]

The movement was to draw on many exotic sources under the broad term of "performativity," but none of the sources were to be studied in depth, since intuitive "loving descriptions" of one's own subjective perceptions were sufficient epistemological practice. The movement became the discipline known as performance studies.

In the book *Theatre as a Vehicle* (2001), Leszek Kolankiewicz analyzes some of Schechner's writings on Grotowski, particularly his essay "Exoduction," which ends Schechner's 1997 *Grotowski Sourcebook*. Parsing the essay, Leszek Kolankiewicz ironically notes that some of Schechner's divagations on the ethics and politics in Grotowski's work, for example, would be clearer were Schechner "to know the meaning of Polish word 'walenrodyzm,' and if he were to know the relationship between Polish culture, history and literature."[182] *Walenrodyzm* derives from Adam Mickiewicz's Romantic, narrative dramatic poem, *Konrad Wallenrod*. The title character sacrifices his life and his honor in defense of his country; he realizes that there is no other way to conquer the ruthless enemy but through betrayal. He suffers because sacrificing his moral code is more heartbreaking than sacrificing his life; his infamy will outlast him. This motive appears and reappears in Polish drama, resurfacing in Wyspiański and Grotowski as well. Kolankiewicz suggests that Schechner has no knowledge of Polish Romanticism – which fundamentally shaped Grotowski's work and sensibility – and adds that "Schechner looks at Grotowski's work from the American perspective," without understanding the long literary tradition, based on generations of political and cultural discourse that formed twentieth-century Polish theatre.[183] Citing an anecdote about another director, Kolankiewicz jokingly suggests that Schechner "doesn't even understand the word 'understand.'"[184] Ironically, as if responding to Kolankiewicz's jab, Schechner wrote in 2008: "This real Grotowski is not available. Strangely, and I can't wholly explain what I mean."[185]

Not knowing the "real" Grotowski, however, didn't stop Schechner and others from trying to imitate Grotowski's style. These attempts were based on the assumption that if one were to replicate the formal aspects of Grotowski's theatre, one could achieve the same level of insight. For Grotowski's imitators, it would have been sacrilegious to suggest that form in Grotowski's theatre is an extension of a cultural and historical framework that cannot be replicated. In 1991, Jan Kott sums up his sentiment towards Grotowski's imitators: "The spectacles of those who mimic Grotowski, especially those in America, remind me of Italian restaurants in which you can follow the preparation of your dish. But in this restaurant, that is all you're getting: your plates remain empty until the very end."[186] Schechner's directorial attempt, *Dionysus in 69*, wasn't deemed successful.[187] Robert Brustein wryly notes that

> This very loose adaptation of *The Bacchae* uses less than one-third of Euripides' text, and fills the rest of its three-hour length with improvised interpolations concerning the players' opinions on politics, sex, their own neuroses and their director Richard Schechner [...] its only function is as a springboard for calisthenics, puberty rites, group therapy and a prolonged orgy.[188]

The apparent sloppiness of Schechner's attempt to incorporate Grotowski's ideas was widely noted. Elenor Lester writes:

> The strange acting techniques in *Dionysus* also follow Grotowski's ideas that the actor should shift between his real self and his role and that he should change roles and styles rapidly during the performance. However, it is inevitable that the intense, highly-disciplined Grotowski theatre of ultimate confrontation should undergo dilution in the hands of a group of American kids whose basic philosophic stance is the holiness of Do Your Own Thing.[189]

Grotowski's aesthetics were an extension of sedimented historical tensions. They grew organically from a particular historical moment, which could not be artificially transplanted and replicated. As Clurman points out: "And that is why most productions done à la Grotowski must be largely fraudulent. His theatre has its roots in a specific native experience. It is organic, with a lived tradition which was shattered and defamed by unimaginable inequity and boundless shame."[190] It is not surprising that productions such as *Dionysus in 69* made Grotowski very skeptical of American imitators of his ideas. As Robert Brustein recalls:

> Grotowski seems very eager to dissociate himself from what he calls the "illegitimate children I refuse to recognize." [...] In a recent interview in *Le Monde*, Grotowski complains about the impostors who claim to have mastered his technique after completing a few exercises, and then show off the process to the public instead of completing their training – all in the name of "self-expression." "The word 'non-conformism' is bandied about," he says, "and yet there's complete conformity in the sense that every professional milieu has its five or six pet slogans (i.e. personality,

freedom of the individual, sexual revolution, new society, etc.)… instead of getting things done…we create group hysteria and try to show that that is 'alive' and 'spontaneous.' There can be no confession without control; confession implies clarity, lucidity, and structure. Plasma and change are a confession of dilettantism."[191]

In 1970, a symposium was held at NYU, at which Grotowski set out to clear up "misconceptions in the United States about the Grotowski method." During the event, Grotowski "categorically disowned his imitators, disengaged himself from critics who interpreted his work narrowly, discredited some of his own work, disenchanted those who followed him blindly, defined his purpose and studiously declined deification."[192] Grotowski's skeptical attitude towards his American followers was no secret. He often discussed the cultural schism between his experiences and those of his American followers, fully aware that like all other exotic attractions, he too was a temporary fad of American theatre elites:

> Grotowski warns against slavish imitation. His method – a trial and error process – cannot be successful without one's own independent research. And those who use his name without understanding his intent are bound to fail, he feels. He is particularly unimpressed by "American infantilism" – actors searching for new gurus each decade to solve their artistic and personal problems. "Americans never develop a technique of their own to its ultimate end," he said. "One year it's Zen, another yoga, then Grotowski, and then, who knows?"[193]

Chapter 5

THE MAKING OF AN AURA

In his famous 1935 essay "The Work of Art in the Age of Mechanical Reproduction," Walter Benjamin defines the concept of what he calls an "aura of the work of art" as "that which withers in the age of mechanical reproduction."[194] Mechanical reproduction strips the work of art of its aura because it "substitutes a plurality of copies for a unique existence."[195] The aura, Benjamin argues, is inevitably connected to the ritualistic, religious aspect of the work of art:

> Originally the contextual integration of art in tradition found its expression in the cult. We know that the earliest art works originated in the service of a ritual – first the magical, then the religious kind. It is significant that the existence of the work of art with reference to its aura is never entirely separated from its ritual function. In other words, the unique value of the "authentic" work of art has its basis in ritual, the location of its original use value.[196]

Benjamin separates film from theatre, arguing that the theatrical event preserves the aura, while the cinematic one destroys it. Film is easily available and reproducible, while the theatrical experience, by necessity, is singular and of limited availability. Benjamin writes:

> The aura which, on the stage, emanates from Macbeth, cannot be separated for the spectators from that of the actor. However, the singularity of the shot in the studio is that the camera is substituted for the public. Consequently, the aura that envelops the actor vanishes, and with it the aura of the figure he portrays.[197]

That which is not easily viewed and obtained becomes veiled in mystique, and shrouded in myth. But if replicability and availability destroy an aura, the conscious restriction of access to an object should enhance it. An aura, built on gossip, desire, snobbism, fashion and envy, adds value and creates the meaning of an object. If theatre – by its very nature – preserves the aura of a live and therefore ephemeral performance, restricting access to a theatrical event only adds to its mystique, making it even more meaningful and important. Thus, we can argue following Benjamin's argument that restricted access boosts the theatrical work's aura.

When in 1969 Grotowski's troupe eventually came to the USA on the invitation of the Brooklyn Academy of Music, Ninon Tallon Karlweiss and the American

Committee for the Laboratory Theatre, *Variety* reported in the fall of 1969 that "The Brooklyn Academy of Music [...] has imported the culturally fashionable Polish Laboratory Theatre for a six-week engagement at stiff prices before small audiences."[198] Apparently, everyone expected the performances to take place in Brooklyn, but Grotowski found the performance space unsuitable and "so there started a frantic search for a church, vacant, adaptable and amenable for Grotowski's purposes."[199] Reportedly, when Grotowski found out that "he could not remove the pews from the Brooklyn church, a search for another, more flexible church was undertaken. Six churches were examined before the Washington Square church was found."[200] The Washington Square church couldn't host very many people, and that was precisely the point. Robert Findlay noted that Grotowski's prominence "rest[ed] on a relatively small number of productions seen by relatively few people."[201] As a custom, Grotowski's group performed for audiences of no more than 40 to 100.[202] Only 100 people at a time could watch *Akropolis*. In fact, according to Stuart W. Little's report, in the USA "about ninety persons watched each performance of *The Constant Prince*, between 100 and 120 saw *Acropolis*, and about forty saw *Apocalypse*."[203] The tickets for the opening night of *Akropolis* reportedly sold for $100,[204] and for $200 on the black market.[205] Adjusted for inflation, that's about $590, and $1,180, respectively. (At that time, an average salary in Poland was about $25–30 per month.) As Simon recalled, "Many people were unaware of the change of location; moreover, the starting time was announced one way on the ticket [...] and another way in the *Times*."[206] Because of the change of venue, the house was reportedly oversold by 30 percent, which resulted in near-riots. This is how Leonard Lyons described the ensuing mayhem of that opening night: "There are no reserved seats for Jerzy Grotowski's Polish Laboratory Theatre. The customers rush to find places on the long benches at the side of the balcony. A few days ago there was a riot because too many big-seated people were jammed in."[207] Richard Coe of the *Washington Post* ironically noted that "Only the opening night list of *Coco* – with the allure of the names of Katharine Hepburn and Chanel – [was] as hard to crash"[208] Tickets for *Akropolis* were so hard to find that Eric Bentley, in an open letter to Grotowski published in the *New York Times*, pleadingly – if sarcastically – complained:

> You have been a traumatic experience for New York and while this might do New York a lot of good, it would certainly seem that our city had a lot to put up with. Have you any idea how many people have suffered rebuff, if not insult, in their attempts to see the Polish Laboratory Theater? I seem to have spent most of October and November visiting the wounded. Their cries still ring in my ears. Church doors have not suffered such blows since Martin Luther drove great nails into them – rumor has it that Theodore Mann, for one, went on pounding on yours all through the night and never did get in – though he had tickets.[209]

Grotowski's limited-audience approach met with diverse opinions. Richard Coa praised the strategy, writing that "Grotowski is quite right to limit his audience to 100.

One doubts that such tensions could be imposed, expressed and communicated to a larger group."[210] In a similar tone, Margaret Croyden, apparently one of the lucky few permitted to enter the church, wrote:

> Grotowski insists the audience be part of this "psychic struggle," and he deliberately limits their number to 100, so that the viewers can sit close enough "to smell the actor's sweat." But rather than being "assaulted" verbally or physically, as was the viewer at the Living Theater, the spectator is a "persona" in the play by virtue of his proximity to the action. [...] The audience in *Acropolis*, grouped around the stage and almost impinging upon the action, are the living ones watching the dead re-enact their agony.[211]

Similarly enthralled, James Roose-Evans wrote that:

> Grotowski is concerned with the spectator who has genuine spiritual needs and who really wishes, through the confrontation with the performance, to analyze himself. The very physical proximity of the actors and audience is intended to assist the collective self-analysis to take place. Does this imply a theatre for an élite? The answer is a positive, yes.[212]

However, not everyone appreciated Grotowski's strategy. Particularly unforgiving was again John Simon, who wrote dryly in response to Roose-Evans: "People who come to the theatre specifically to be psychoanalyzed are not an elite, but a plurality of neurotics and psychotics in need of help, help that they can get much better elsewhere."[213] And in his *New York Theatre* review, Simon went even further, admitting:

> What I find most repellent about the Grotowski operation is the sacerdotal mystique surrounding it. Audiences are admitted in absurdly small numbers, a few at a time, after unconscionable waiting periods outside the doors. They are seated as uncomfortably as anchorites at penance, squeezed together, and hectored by ushers all the way. [When you leave, you are handed] a kind of icon, woodcut emblematic of the play, along with a lengthy statement from the Master explaining with hierophantic modesty and in absurd detail how these productions are group efforts in the truest sense. Sold also are expensive, mystagogic and totally unreadable books in which the Master set forth his teachings. And the program notes, by Grotowski and his literary advisor, Flaszen, consist of the most portentous lucubrations this side of scientology.[214]

The tone of Simon's annoyance with Grotowski's "sacerdotal mystique" paralleled the Polish sentiments. Likewise, Stuart Little sarcastically noted that "[t]he total audience for the whole engagement would scarcely have filled the Majestic Theater for the two performances on a matinee day of *Fiddler on the Roof*."[215] Describing the hysteria that surrounded the ticketing and admission to Grotowski's shows, Clive Barnes cited an anecdote, according to which Harvey Lichtenstein, director of the Brooklyn Academy and a man who invited Grotowski to the USA, was unable to see the performance: "Harvey Lichtenstein [...] naturally felt that he and his hard-pressed press cohort, together with a couple of people who had actually paid for their tickets, might unobtrusively stand at the back. The feeling was misplaced. They were thrown out."[216] "The hoopla surrounding Grotowski,"[217] as Barnes put it, was grander than what even the most theatrical divas were used to: Grotowski "certainly carries eccentricity to unusual lengths."[218] Grotowski himself famously wrote that he is "not concerned with just any audience, but a special one" that undergoes a "creative process of self-search."[219] Apparently, in New York in 1969, that "special audience" consisted of anyone strong enough to push their way through the crowds.

Regardless of his motive, in artificially limiting access to his performance, Grotowski did accomplish one major objective; he turned himself into a luxury good of the New York theatre boheme, in the same way that Hermès bags or Playboy bunnies were made into luxury goods.[220] Limiting the number of spectators also meant that the audience predominantly consisted of inner circles of theatrical connoisseurs. As Martin Gottfried put it: "For serious theatre people as well as professional avant-gardists, the most talked-about and influential stage person in all the Western world is Jerzy Grotowski, director of the Polish Laboratory Theatre, even though, in a real sense, his American reputation is the work of theatre elitists and fashionmongers."[221] It almost seems as if Grotowski managed to replicate in New York a scene characteristic of Poland at that time: persistent shortages of everything led to long lines in front of stores customarily provoking mayhem among the weary *kolejkowicze* (persons who stand in line for a long time, sometimes doing so professionally for someone else). The shortages and the long lines naturally made goods, whatever they were, veiled in the missing aura. It was perhaps this mechanism of privileged access that Grotowski so well orchestrated in New York, as well as the combination of coincidences and political climate that allowed him, against all odds, to assume the reins of American avant-garde theatre for the next four decades.

Chapter 6

ON NOT KNOWING POLISH

Robert Findlay notes that "Grotowski has been hailed by many of his contemporaries as the most significant twentieth-century theatrical figure since Stanislavsky."[222] Specifically, Findley points out *Akropolis*, "as a true ensemble work, […] set the style and tone for much of the avant-garde experimentation of the late 1960s and early 1970s, both in Europe and in North America."[223] Martin Gottfried adds that "*Acropolis* is an extraordinary kind of theatre utterly unlike anything that came before it."[224] Likewise, in his 1968 Paris review of the performance, Thomas Quinn Curtiss writes: "This *Akropolis* of Mr. Grotowski is an imposing achievement of the modern stage, a work that will have a wide and beneficial influence."[225] Considering the accolades that both the play and the director received throughout the years, how is it possible that *Akropolis*, a work of unquestionable international impact, escaped any serious dramaturgical inquiry in the countries that embraced it and gave it its reputation? The esteem in which Grotowski was held by American scholars and theatre practitioners – despite the fact that, as Findlay points out, "his performances have been in Polish, a minor European language spoken and understood outside Poland by almost no one except émigrés"[226] – raises pressing questions about how the meaning and context of theatrical works are formed and transformed cross-culturally. How do critics and theatre scholars tackle their lack of language or cultural context when assessing the value and impact of international theatre pieces? What is the value of a work of theatre outside its cultural, historical, and social context, and how should or shouldn't that value be assessed? How are theatrical tastes produced and propagated?

Regardless of the buzz that surrounded *Akropolis*, most of the interest was focused on the acting and the *mise-en-scène*. The fact that the show is based on an obscure Polish modernist drama evoked little critical comment. Although the film's voiceover translated some lines of the play, the dialogue was not the main focus of the commentary about the film or the criticism about the play that followed the film's release. In fact, in his introduction to the film, Lewis Freedman honestly warned:

> The language is Polish, the actors are members of the Polish Laboratory Theatre, and the play is written by Stanisław Wyspiański at the turn of the century. Good Evening, I'm Lewis Freedman and actually, I don't speak Polish. And it's possible that some of you don't either. We are presenting the play tonight entirely in Polish because we believe that it's a fascinating and moving experience in the theatre.[227]

Gould recognized that "the language problem was a handicap and made the production seem further remote and detached."[228] But most reviewers confidently disregarded language altogether, suggesting that not knowing Polish was not a noteworthy obstacle to their understanding the show. Martin Gottfried boldly wrote: "This is easy enough to follow and an understanding of Polish is unnecessary especially since, as has become clear, Grotowski has no interest in language anyway. Even in Polish, the words are purposely garbled and rechanneled into incantation, ritualized expression, repetition and finally word-destruction."[229] With similar confidence, Clive Barnes also assured his readers "that even Polish speakers can understand nothing that is being said until the play's conclusion."[230] In another review, Barnes did admit that "without any knowledge of Polish [he] couldn't identify [which] myths specifically [the play refers to]."[231] However, he then quickly dismissed any notion that knowledge of Polish was an issue, adding, "I am far from certain whether a knowledge of Polish would offer any more enlightenment – I have a suspicion that many of the guttural and sonorous sounds and songs that the actors offer are gibberish."[232] Many critics followed the same route, dismissing the language and, with it, the historical and cultural context of the show. Irving Wardle, for example, noted that "the company makes an impact that bypasses language."[233] Harold Clurman wrote that "the lines [of Grotowski's adaptation] spoken at incredible speed are not dialogue; they are tortured exclamations projected in the direction of another being, but with no shape or personal address. It has been said that a knowledge of Polish does not make the lines readily intelligible."[234] Likewise, Stefan Brecht voiced the opinion that "some Poles have alleged they did not understand more than a word of two."[235] Edith Oliver asserted that "Even if we had not earlier read some of what they are saying, our lack of Polish wouldn't matter a bit, […] Their posture and their voices on that darkened stage tell us everything we need to know."[236] Moving towards the nonverbal communication of gestures, postures and *mise-en-scène*, most American critics shrewdly sidestepped discussing text, language or cultural context altogether. Replacing such discussions with dehistoricized, decontextualized "ethnography of performance," they argued that one does not need to understand the language in order to understand the production; the production itself, not its context, offers us "everything we need to know."

But this was *not* the opinion of Polish critics. Polish critic Witold Filler framed the sentiment succinctly, writing "it is impossible to understand Grotowski without knowing anything about Mickiewicz and Wyspiański, without ever entering into Borowski's dark world."[237] Everyone who knows Mickiewicz, Wyspiański and Borowski must agree with Filler; without its historical, cultural and literary context, Grotowski's *Akropolis* is merely an empty shell of what it is meant to be. The only Polish critic who shared the American critics' viewpoint that language was not important was Bohdan Drozdowski, who wrote:

> Of course, nobody at the Edinburgh Festival understood Polish, nor did they read Flaszen's program notes, but everyone submitted to the mysticism of the actors: their grimaces, gestures and body movements. Watching *Akropolis* in Edinburgh – one of a few who actually understood the text – I came to the sacrilegious conclusion that Grotowski's actors could be reciting anything else, newspaper articles or a phone book for example, in place of Wyspiański's text and the effect would be the same.[238]

However, even Drozdowski quickly acknowledged that "without knowing the language, you could not philosophically understand the essence of the spectacle."[239] Knowing Polish *does* make the lines intelligible, and the dialogue is *not* all gibberish. On the contrary, as Drozdowski points out, the essence of the spectacle comes through the text. Wolfe Kauffman of the *Herald Tribune*, as one of a very few foreign critics who do speak Polish, was clear that his own understanding of Polish very much affected his interpretation of the show:

> It was, said Jean-Louis Barrault, managing director of the Théâtre des Nations, "a vital and terrifying theatrical experience." He might be right. He had the advantage of not understanding Polish. Unfortunately, I do [...] maybe it would have worked easier (with this audience) if it were not a play I knew or a language I recognized. It is a sort of mass yoga or hypnosis that is attempted here. And I think it works with most of the audience, or did on the opening night. [...] Yes, it works. As theatrical experiment. But not at all, not for a minute, as theatre.[240]

For Kauffman, knowing the language provided additional layers of understanding that made him question the objective of the entire performance. Indeed, the literary framework of *Akropolis* is rich in meaning and steeped in a complex historical and dramatic context. Unfortunately, in lieu of dramaturgical understanding, most American theatre scholars preferred to argue that not knowing is what actually creates knowledge.

Very few critics besides Kauffman actually acknowledged the language barrier. Irving Wardle was one of them, cautioning scholars and audiences about too formal an approach, which could limit interpretative tropes. Not knowing Polish, Wardle wrote, creates a "perception of [*Akropolis*] affected by reputation and ignorance of the language. There is a temptation to see what you have been told to see."[241] What the critics, theatre scholars and practitioners saw were choreographed movements and chantings, all of the audio-visual Eastern European mystique that – to a large degree because of the incomprehension of language – evoked a complex but not complete emotional response. In a way, the misapprehension was the source of the enigma that provoked emotive reception. Harry Harris wrote that "Despite the language barrier, the performance, played at barely arms' length from a solemn audience, had great emotional impact."[242] Grotowski's two other productions shown in New York in 1969 were often described in a similar vein. Ronald Bryden, for example, succinctly captured the problem: "Without understanding a word, distanced from the performance by seating which forces you to peer down into an enclosure like a bull ring or operating theatre, you're held shaken and exhausted by a torrent of fantastically controlled movement, sound and emotion."[243] Sandra Schmidt of the *Los Angeles Times* stressed the Laboratory Theatre's formalism, which generates its emotionality:

> Without words – the play is in Polish – the thing I find most extraordinary about Grotowski's group is their force. The entire play is presented at a constant level of very high intensity. [...] Actors, in striking themselves or other actors, do not pull their punches, yet the punches seem strong expressions rather than out-of-control

explosions of violence. It is force rigidly contained, and therefore amplified, within a specific form.[244]

Allan Lewis shared a similar experience of being enraptured by the audio-visual effects: "I did not understand a word of the staccato rhythmic percussion Polish, but it did not matter very much. I sat spellbound for one hour deeply involved, thrilled by a revolutionary theatrical revelation."[245] Likewise, writing about *Apocalypsis*, Henry Hewes too stressed the theatricality and intensity of the performance: "*Apocalypsis* delivered as it is in Polish moves us not by its story, which we cannot really follow, but by the intensity and theatricality of its performance."[246] Decontextualized and dehistoricized, Grotowski's work becomes a found object in the "systemic play of difference" within the foreign field of semiotic and cultural markers. It fascinates because it is unknown, but the fascination itself negates the will to knowledge. As Martin Harries pointed out, to know means to lose both the magic and the innocence of formal spectatorship. For twentieth-century post-Auschwitz art, it also means that one is forced "to contemplate her own destruction, [...] to think about mass death" in categories that go against the pleasure principle.[247]

A very few foreign critics even acknowledge the Polish roots of *Akropolis*, or admit that in lacking a knowledge of its text and context, one lacks a fundamental understanding of the work itself.[248] Robert Findley was the rare reviewer who noted that, without understanding the text, one misses all of the subtleties of the production:

> [A]s in most theatrical performances, the more intricate and subtle nuances have depended as well upon essentially literary elements: namely, the dramatic form of the performance, the words spoken by the actors, and perhaps most importantly, some awareness by the audience of the original text from which the performance has evolved.[249]

Similarly, Frank Marcus wrote that "The roots of Grotowski's art are deeply embedded in the tragic history of Poland. There are characteristic traces of the Gothic, of the grotesque, of cruelty, even of a romantic, aristocratic disdain, but above all, of Catholicism."[250] Joseph Papp openly suggested that formal aspects of *Akropolis* were tied to its cultural circumstances:

> I was absolutely overwhelmed by the *Acropolis*. It is a fantastic piece of work, both in its content and in its technique. I recognized that it was not simply one production but that it came out of years and years of work. As for us, we have to find ways of expressing our particular ideas. It was no accident that this work came out of Poland.[251]

Michael Kustow also wrote: "I argue that this play is a peculiarly Polish classic, steeped in romanticism, and marked by extreme idealism which Polish writers poured into their work because of their impotence to change the condition of Poland, which was for so long the plaything of Prussia, Russia, or Austria."[252] However, he added, "I speak no Polish, so I cannot tell you exactly how the text had been cut or transposed."[253]

Chapter 7

"IN POLAND: THAT IS TO SAY, NOWHERE"

If Wyspiański's *Akropolis* is an attempt to capture, condense and understand the Polish psyche at the end of the nineteenth century, Grotowski's *Akropolis* is an attempt to capture, condense and understand the new twentieth-century Polish consciousness, one forever framed by the smoke from the Auschwitz ovens. The fact that Grotowski chose *Akropolis* as his framework for a performance piece that seeks to respond to the trauma of the Holocaust is not accidental. Grotowski enters into a dialogue with Wyspiański, but to gain an understanding of what this dialogue entails, we must first understand the historical context surrounding the publication and production history of Wyspiański's drama. At the turn of the twentieth century, around the time Jarry wrote *Ubu*, Poland – in tune with its bleak European image – was swept by Romantic dreams of national greatness characterized by a combination of ironic self-awareness and fatalistic determination. As Margaret Croyden sums it up: "Periodically invaded, partitioned, dismembered, oppressed, and brutalized, and itself guilty of oppression and backwardness, Poland has embodied the modern tragedy in a world dominated by great powers. It has also come to symbolize heroic resistance to those powers, resistance depicted through the years by its great writers, poets and composers, and in our time by its film and theater directors as well."[254] Writing *Akropolis*, Wyspiański followed the tradition of engaging in political dialogue about Poland's liberatory project. The play was written in 1904 (eight years after Jarry wrote *Ubu*), at a moment when the underground currents of liberation ran in all directions, from martyrological fantasies of grandiose national uprising, filled with pathos and glory, to passive and pragmatic assessments of Europe's current political and military situation, to cynical (or kynical) attempts at irony and sarcasm as a way to survive and withstand the cultural and political repression imposed by the partitioners.

At that time, Wyspiański – born in 1869 and educated within the Philosophy Department of Jagiellonian University and at the School of Fine Arts in Cracow – was already renowned as both a painter and a playwright. Wyspiański's paintings and writings attempted to combine the Romantic style of Polish national painters with that of French impressionism. From 1890 to 1895, Wyspiański travelled extensively, visiting Italy, Switzerland and France. In France he studied at the private atelier Académie Calarossi. While traveling, Wyspiański became an avid theatregoer and saw some of the greatest productions of Shakespearean and Ancient dramas of that time. Greatly impressed by the expressive potential of theatre, Wyspiański began to write, and by 1904, he had completed all of his greatest plays: *Warszawianka* [*Varsovian Anthem*]

(1898); *Protesilas i Leodamia* [*Protesilas and Laodamia*] (1899); *Meleager* [*Meleager*] (1899); *Klątwa* [*The Curse*] (1899); *Legion* [*Legion*] (1900); *Wesele* [*The Wedding*] (1901); *Wyzwolenie* [*Liberation*] (1903); and *Noc listopadowa* [*November Night*] (1904). All of the plays combine Polish national themes with ancient and classical elements and modernist forms. Each was instantly performed or printed, asserting Wyspiański's status as Poland's foremost playwright and thinker. *Akropolis* was, in fact, Wyspiański's last great drama, followed by the lesser-known *Skałka* [A Small Rock] (1907); *Powrót Odysa* [*Return of Odysseus*] (1907); and *Zygmunt August* [Zygmunt August] (1907, unfinished). Among all of Wyspiański's dramas, *The Wedding*, *Liberation* and *Akropolis* are considered his masterworks. Among those three, it can be argued that *Akropolis* is the most complex, multilayered and polyvocal.

Akropolis appeared in Cracow bookstores five weeks after Wyspiański finished writing it, on Good Friday in 1904. The date of release was a symbolic choice that drew on the long-established parallel between Poland's dreams of national emancipation and Christ's resurrection (in line with the national liberatory theology that had haunted Poland since the late 1800s). In anticipation of the publication, the press speculated about which theatre would stage it. After publication, some sources even provided updates on the progress of the first upcoming production. According to Leon Schiller, each time a Wyspiański play was published, the event was anticipated with the same enthusiasm that is typical of theatre openings, and the gossip surrounding the publication ran wild. The play became the main topic of discussion in Cracow's artistic circles.[255] Reviews, though, were mixed, characterized by sentiments that ranged from outrage, to misunderstanding, to reverence. The responses are best summarized by Witold Noskowski, who many years later wrote in his review of the 1932 production of the play in Poznań, "The question of what *Akropolis* means is not as important as what *Akropolis* is. To answer this question though, you need to use your imagination and empathy, not your reason."[256] From the start, *Akropolis* was a cultural enigma, one that even Poles had to absorb on a subconscious, subnational level. The play was Wyspiański's third and final installment in a series that includes *Wesele* [*The Wedding*] (1901) and *Wyzwolenie* [*Liberation*] (1903). Tadeusz Sina called the trilogy a Polish *Divine Comedy* in which *The Wedding* represents Hell, *Liberation* Purgatory, and *Akropolis* Heaven.[257] Władysław Prokesch, in a 1904 review, proclaimed that "[following] *The Wedding*, and *Liberation*, which express the contours of Wyspiański's artistic thought, in *Akropolis*, his historio-sophy finally crystallizes."[258] And Antoni Mazanowski noted that, although the obvious connections between the three dramas are elusive, there are some clear similarities: "The ending appears to connect all three, *Akropolis*, *Liberation* and *The Wedding*. *The Wedding* announces that the plot will move to Wawel, and both *Liberation* and *Akropolis* do take place at Wawel. Also, in both, the character of Apollo has a similar function: he's a symbol of a song of resurrection."[259] All three dramas, Mazanowski noted, belong to the genre of so-called "symbolist poetry."[260] Wyspiański expected the play to be staged before it was published,[261] and it was scheduled to be staged right away at the Słowacki Theatre in Cracow,[262] but after a series of misunderstandings and bitter exchanges of letters with its then artistic director, Józef Kotarbiński, about its stage value,[263] Wyspiański severed all connections with Słowacki, and for the next year and a half – that is, not until Solski took over – none of Wyspiański's plays were staged there.[264] Kotarbiński's tastes were rather traditional, tending towards the Shakespearean structure and psychological realism that dominated European stages of the late nineteenth century. He considered *Akropolis* a visual work inappropriate for staging.[265]

Akropolis was partly inspired by actual events. After years of failed Polish attempts to regain control of Wawel Cathedral, in 1905 the Austro-Hungarian government at least ceded it to the Polish council of Galicia (a partially self-governed Polish state that remained under Austro-Hungarian control). Austrian troops, however, did not completely leave the Wawel hill until 1918. After years of exploitation, the cathedral needed significant renovation, and as early as 1888, the first renovation committee met to arrange the fundraising. Wyspiański, collaborating with a well-known Polish architect, Władysław Ekielski (1855–1927), designed a series of sketches for extensive restoration that included a set of opulent, Tiffany-style stained-glass windows. Faced with a choice between Wyspiański's grand visions and the conservative approach of Sławomir Odrzywolski, another Polish designer, the castle administrators eventually chose Odrzywolski's designs. Wyspiański's sketches were never realized, although they were eventually published posthumously in 1908,[266] to the great chagrin and regret of everyone involved.[267] Describing the projects, Franciszek Pułaski wrote that "the magnificent designs are freeing to your imagination"; they are "mystical," with a touch of modernism.[268]

When the renovation of Wawel Cathedral began in 1895, the workers uncovered Gothic and Baroque frescoes concealed beneath layers of paint in one of the crypts. A few years later, Wyspiański received official permission to view the frescoes. The experience affected him greatly. The figures, which had been painted centuries before, seemed to Wyspiański to come to life. He wrote:

> On both sides of the room, large figures of angels, both female and male, strong, burly men with unconventional but expressive faces. They have "character," beautiful youths. They hold in their hands various instruments for torture – everyone has a different tool.[269]

The main theme of *Akropolis*, of historical figures in a tapestry coming to life, is inspired by Wyspiański's symbolic interpretation of his encounter with the freshly uncovered frescos. Analyzing this aspect of *Akropolis*, Wojciech Bałus notes that the idea of resurrecting statues is not new in European literature; an example is the statue of the Commander that comes to life in almost all of the versions of Don Juan.[270] But by setting the play in Wawel, yet renaming it *Akropolis*, Wyspiański follows the modernist tradition of figurative replacement. As with Joyce's Ulysses, whether the hero is called Hector or Achilles is not as important as the fact that he is an archetype. Similarly, *Akropolis* is a figurative replacement for Wawel and vice versa; both are conduits for history, memory and identity – *Akropolis* for Europe, and Wawel for Poland.[271]

Wyspiański, however, wasn't the first to make this analogy. There were a number of nineteenth-century Polish writers and philosophers, among them Józef Kremer and Leon Zienkowicz, who had compared the political and national role of the Greek Akropolis to the Polish Wawel, so the analogy was known in educated circles.[272]

Chapter 8
AKROPOLIS/NECROPOLIS

Historically, Wawel was the royal castle when Cracow was the Polish capital, but even after the capital was moved to Warsaw, Wawel remained a major royal residence. More importantly, Polish monarchs were buried in its crypts. In Polish culture, Wawel is considered a seed of national self-definition, the place where history mixes with artifacts and nostalgia for past greatness. In 1845, Józef Mączyński called it a "national bible."[273] Kazimierz Kosiński called it a "holy place":

> Wawel is a Polish sacred hill [...] The emotions one experiences while there are religious in nature. It is here where religious and patriotic feelings blend together, paralleling the track of Polish literature since the 16th century [...] There is an overwhelming sense of death permeating the Cathedral. Entering it, we feel like pilgrims; going up the hill, we get tired and, once we get there, we feel relieved. Right away, we're struck by the view of St. Stanisław's coffin. To visit the royal graves, we have to go downstairs into the basement. It is here that we also encounter the graves of the great Polish Romantic poets. Once we're out, the shining sun conflicts with our mood. But then, we're directed to see the newly renovated part of the castle, and here, we experience brand new feelings of revival. It is here that Wawel becomes a symbol of national resurrection. Leaving the castle, one no longer enters the basement, but goes out on the other side with the view of the Vistula river.[274]

Wawel's position as the seed of Polish nationality hasn't changed. Even today, the Wawel website touts it as "a place where one can best understand Poland and Poles."[275]

During the partition of Poland, the castle was often referred to as a Polish necropolis – a cemetery where Polish history and the Polish sense of national selfhood lay buried in its cathedral under piles of dust and time. Wyspiański aptly called it "the cemetery of the tribes" – a phrase that became one of the refrains of Grotowski's production. Kosiński aptly points out that

> Wyspiański struck an emotional connection with Wawel in his childhood. He knew that the place had deep irrational value in the national subconscious, as a place of recollections, where one could undergo almost mystical transformation, a grand epiphany revealing the essence of life that wins over death by its pure will to resurrection.[276]

Wyspiański designed his ill-fated and never-realized stained-glass window for Wawel to channel "the visions of decomposing bodies deposited in the cathedral, forcing the viewer to rethink the role of the national necropolis for Polish society, its function as a source of identity, vitality and hope for the future."[277] The renovation of Wawel, with the discovery of the hidden frescoes, became a ghostly event, or so it seemed to Wyspiański, who wrote his *Studium o Hamlecie* [A Study of Hamlet] with Wawel in mind. Hamlet's uneasy relationship with the ghost of his father closely parallels Wyspiański's own emotions when confronted with the ghosts of Polish history that suddenly emerge from the frescoes. A number of Polish critics have suggested that Wawel is the actual hero of *Akropolis*, and that its works of art play the roles of actors.[278] Because of its place in Polish history, Wawel has always had a nearly sacred status; it is a place where religious and national trajectories intertwine in the literal "body politics" of the buried royals. In locating his drama in the castle's cathedral, Wyspiański, whether consciously or unconsciously, blurs the line between art and the sacred. The play becomes a form of *mysterium tremendum*, a ritual performed by and for the few initiates who understand the weight of history and its sacred dimension. Jan Błoński points out that the entire Polish Romantic tradition, starting with Adam Mickiewicz (1798–1855) and Juliusz Słowacki (1809–1849), and proceeding through Zygmunt Krasiński (1812–1859) and Wyspiański (1869–1907), is framed by the religious context in which drama is seen as a ritualistic celebration uniting its participants within the sacred aura of illusions and conventions.[279] The reasons for such development of Polish drama are many, including deep-rooted religious, messianic and Romantic traditions. The primary function of Romantic dramas was symbolic: to unite the conquered nation under the common goal of national liberation. As Daniel Gerould put it, "Although seemingly alone and defeated, the heroes of these romantic dramas embody a supra-personal ideal and identify themselves with the entire nation, for which they become willing martyrs."[280] The readers are asked to join in the common martyrology, to sacrifice themselves on the altar of national greatness. Since the call for action asks for nothing less than death, it has a transcendent, sacred dimension. Like his predecessors, Wyspiański follows the same Romantic tradition, and it is this sacred, ritualistic aspect of his drama that eventually captures Grotowski's imagination.

Chapter 9

THE VISION AND THE SYMBOL

Tymon Terlecki writes that *Akropolis* is, "perhaps, the strangest and most baffling of Wyspiański's dramatic works."[281] At the crossroads between the Romantic and avant-garde traditions, in many ways Wyspiański was ahead of his time, anticipating the twentieth century's crisis of representation. Łempicka notes that *Akropolis* is a literary hybrid both structurally and thematically: part drama, part opera and part poem, with themes that stretch across cultures and epochs. It was partially this conglomeration of themes, motives, and genres that prompted Solski to reject the idea of staging it.[282] A few literary critics of the time agreed with Solski, suggesting that the play is proof of Wyspiański's weakening mental condition, of the "disintegration of the great talent's creative elements," claiming that "such chaos and disorder was never before seen in poetry." Critics contended that the play reflects Wyspiański's "sick imagination," that "the entire first act is an aberration," and that the play "is maddening and sick."[283] More generous, Antoni Mazanowski stressed the stylistic inconsistency of the playwriting:

> Each act of *Akropolis* could stand on its own. Like tapestries and sculptures which ended up in the cathedral accidentally and can be moved somewhere else without losing their meaning, so the acts of *Akropolis* share the same arbitrariness. They are not connected either by their common time and place, common theme, or common feeling.[284]

"In *Akropolis*, there is not an ounce of reality; everything is a vision and a symbol,"[285] Mazanowski continued reproachfully, but he eventually acknowledged that "[i]t is a beautifully written work."[286] The play breaks with prevalent, late nineteenth-century realist conventions while drawing on newly emerging avant-garde trends. Elżbieta Kalemba-Kasprzak pointed out that "Wyspiański questions in his drama the rule of '*repraesentatio*' that dominated the nineteenth-century theatrical space [...] His reality is multi-perspective, multi-dimensional, and symbolic."[287] In 1904, Jan Stena's review of the play contained similar observations:

> For me, *Akropolis* does not have a plot; I don't understand why these particular images are assembled here together in this particular order [...] But, it is the style that is important – the soul of the poet [...] Whoever is mystified by life's enigmas won't be able to pass by this work in indifference. Whoever wants to listen to the soul of the poet will find him here more accessible, more familiar than in his other more mature works.[288]

Responding to all the criticism, in 1932 Karol Homolacs, a Polish painter, wrote a passionate editorial reminding the critics that Wyspiański was foremost a painter, and then a poet: "Wyspiański […] begins writing his dramatic work by drawing the sketch of a scene on a piece of paper."[289] But, in 1969, contradicting Homolacs, Wojciech Natanson commented: "It is often said that Wyspiański was a great poet, but a bad writer."[290]

Indeed, critics' ambivalence towards *Akropolis* stems from the fact that the play borders the threshold of two trajectories: lingering nineteenth-century Romantic tradition steeped in nationalistic and revolutionary longings, and European modernist tradition framed by post-national avant-garde aesthetics. Konstanty Puzyna considered Wyspiański a Romantic, though Puzyna also noted that Wyspiański's fascination with modernist designs, especially those influenced by Gordon Craig's ideas, places him on the border between Romanticism and Modernism.[291] Terlecki suggested that *Akropolis* "is governed by the laws or the logic of dream, not the laws or the logic of waking life. […] we are dreaming a dream in the form of a drama."[292] The objects that come to live belong to the liminal space between the waking and oneiric states. For that very reason, Terlecki argued, "*Akropolis* presents itself as an anticipation of surrealist poetics."[293] Nina Taylor classified it as a symbolist drama in the "Maeterlinckian vein of mood and metaphysical suggestion."[294] Drawing on Mickiewicz's call for grand, dramatic works that unite all of the arts into one monumental stage production, Wyspiański's work brings together a number of art forms into one autonomous vision. Wyspiański was fascinated by Wagner's concept of *Gesamtkunstwerk*, particularly his inclination towards ancient stories, themes and characters. Wyspiański advanced Wagner's ideas by becoming the harbinger of the Great Theatrical Reform, particularly of the theories of Edward Gordon Craid and his concept of an autonomous "art of theatre."[295] Gordon Craig himself repeatedly acknowledged Wyspiański as the front runner of the movement and even devoted an issue of his journal, *Mask*, to Wyspiański following the poet's death in 1907. Wyspiański's *Akropolis* is an autonomous work of art, functioning according to its own internal logic of a dream. It exists in an alternative universe that parallels the world only on the symbolic and metaphorical level. It operates completely independently from the historical moment, while simultaneously condensing multiple epochs and geographic locations into one psycho-visual landscape.[296]

At the time of its publication in 1904, *Akropolis*, full of symbols, allegories, and modern conventions, was considered "the most fantastical"[297] of all Wyspiański's dramas. But it was also a nationalist drama in the same sense that *Wesele* and *Wyzwolenie* were considered nationalist dramas.[298] Kazimierz Kosiński suggests that, following the 1863 January uprising against the Russians, which ended in an overwhelming Polish defeat and brought on further persecutions from the partitioners, the Poles' outlook grew increasingly gloomy. Collaboration with the partitioners became more predominant, and hopes for resurrection slowly faded, giving way to passivity and acceptance of the status quo, and thus reawaking the urgency in some quarters to revive the national passion for independence.[299] Drawing on the liberatory Romantic tradition established by Mickiewicz and

Słowacki, Wyspiański saw the role of playwright-poet as that of both clairvoyant and leader, and that of the conscience of the nation. In this sense, *Akropolis* "is both a religious and a political statement to a then nonexistent Polish nation."[300] Indeed, in writing *Akropolis*, Wyspiański attempted to capture Poland's ambivalence towards its history, its present and its future, and sought to recreate the ephemeral effect, the sense of loss and hope that Wawel embodied. Wawel was the place where the death struggle over the Polish national soul was going to happen.[301] But first and foremost, the play was an attempt to represent through allegories and metaphors a sense of Polish national consciousness, with all of its conscious and subconscious elements, both sacred and profane.

The play consists of four acts, which at first glance appear to have nothing to do with each other. They take place in four different places around Wawel: "In what has been likened to the four mansions of a Chichester mystery play, the four separate frames in which four separate actions take place, this setting provides the only unity."[302] Act 1 takes place in the national corpus of the cathedral; it focuses on national themes and draws on Zygmunt Krasiński's 1840 play *Trzy Myśli Henryka Ligenzy* [Three Thoughts of Henryk Ligenza]. The four stone angels from the tomb of St. Stanisław Szczepanowski (the medieval patron saint of Poland) come to life, and they carry his coffin, beckoning other figures to rise up. In addition to the angels, Wyspiański resurrects the Lady figure and the Cupid figure from the monument to Andrzej Ankwicz, a Roman Catholic archbishop of Prague (1833–1838) who was born and ordained in Cracow; the Lady figure from the memorial to Stanisław Skotnicki (1894–1939), the general of the émigré brigade in Switzerland; and the Cleo figure from the memorial to Roman Sołtyk (1790–1843), the Polish general of Napoleon's Russian campaign. The tone of act 1 is dark and ominous. It opens with a prologue that narrates what has just happened: "They have left and are leaving,/ they left the heavy cloud of smoke circling above the church/ […] They have left,/ and smoke and darkness grows heavier."[303] The angels grow weary under the heavy weight of the coffin, asking God if he hears their pleadings: "Does He hear us talking,/ or does he only hear our wailing?" – to which the second Angel replies:

> Can you smell it? – the incense smoke
> weaves the fog
> like a spider web – ?
> Ah, the candles! I thought they would smoke out the flame.
> I was burning in this fiery halo
> weak under the weight of the coffin
> my eyes blinded by the light.[304]

The death and love themes intertwine, in a melancholic *danse macabre* of love, loss and desire. As Nina Taylor notes, "The latent eroticism and theatricality of Baroque aesthetics take flesh, and the sacred love of paschal worship turns swiftly to profane love as figures from other sepulchral monuments wake up, and give vent to their erotic urges in scenes of mutual seduction."[305] The love theme quickly gives way to the sense of desperate sadness and muted mourning which overwhelms the play. The Angels struggle to hold back the tears for something, or someone, they have lost:

ANGEL:	Don't cry and don't curse.
MAIDEN:	Don't cry? Don't complain?
ANGEL:	Don't wail – don't weep.
MAIDEN:	Don't remember – nothing?[306]

The hopeless melancholy of the first act, with its somber and dark undertones, the images of Angels suffering under the weight of the coffin, the smoke rising above the church, and those who unjustly perished and who must be mourned in silence, all quickly bring to mind Auschwitz. The sensory imagery is strikingly similar, and the association is inevitable for a modern reader (as it was for Grotowski); though of course, it is not inscribed in Wyspiański.

Wyspiański drew on other scenes from the tapestry for the themes of the play's remaining three acts. Act 2 focuses on the Greek story of Hector and Andromache, and act 3 on the Hebrew story of Jacob and Esau. Act 4 revolves around David, the king of Israel, who in this version becomes a Polish prophet. In *Akropolis*, Greco-Roman mythology intertwines with Judeo-Catholic sacrum, all of which intermingle with references to Polish national literature and military culture. As Kalemba-Kasprzak notes, "The integration of Wawel with *Akropolis*, Troy, Mount Sinai, and Jerusalem allows one to define European tradition as a space of common mythical identity."[307] In 1927, in response to its first full production, at the Słowacki Theatre in 1926, an anonymous critic confidently wrote: "It is not difficult to see in this oratory mysterium of Easter revival, the ideas of polygenesis, the Helleno-Nietzschean idea of eternal recurrence, Hectorian sacrifice and biblical references to Christ whose benevolence unites all of the quarreling nations."[308] The rediscovered Baroque and Gothic frescoes and the Greek mythological figures of royal ghosts come to life to tell their dramas and become allegorical representations of Polish national tragedy as framed within the larger European context. Terlecki argues that "*Acropolis* is a drama of civilization, of culture in an inner sense. It embraces the widest prospects of the cultural entity which in the course of time has been called European, Western Mediterranean, Atlantic, Judeo-Greco-Latin-Christian."[309] As Terlecki rightly notes, "there is not a single real, living person in the play."[310] It operates entirely on the level of symbols, myths and metaphors. Or, as Nina Taylor observes, *Akropolis* "provides a condensed evocation of consecutive cultures and centuries, and a portrayal of the metaphysics underlying the Greek, Judaic and Christian heritage, in which works of art are considered as the main residue of civilization, and cultural layers are superimposed and fused into the entity which we call Western culture."[311] It is important to note that, architecturally, Wawel is a syncretic building, which architecturally combines Romanesque, Gothic, Renaissance, Baroque and Neoclassical elements.[312] Likewise, bringing them all together, *Akropolis* attempts to condense the essence of Western culture and identity as framed by the tragic struggle between conflicting values and paradigms. It is this aspect of Wyspiański's *Akropolis* that Flaszen had in mind when he argued that, in

Grotowski's adaptation, "the century-old values of European culture are put to a severe test."[313]

Drawing on Krasiński's plays *Three Thoughts*, as well as on Homer's *Iliad*, and Jewish *Tanakh* (the Hebrew Bible), Wyspiański attempted to recover and restructure the historical moment of his era. Like Krasiński, Poland's renowned Romantic poet, Wyspiański merges together in his *Akropolis* the location, the cathedral, the time, the night, and the idea of angels coming to life. The Trojan myth from Homer's *Iliad* is about the "conscious acceptance of one's death, apathy, and the fatality of faith. The biblical Hebrew story of Jacob is all about action, dynamism, struggle with one's destiny."[314] The dichotomy between apathy and action, fatality and self-determination, reflects a particular Polish schizophrenia. Thus, along with the dreams of greatness and images of resurrection, *Akropolis* also contains resigned undertones:

> The dead won't rise.
> Their bodies will turn to ashes
> Full of the ashes is this crypt
> Today, the dust that is left
> Does not have the strength
> To rise and to be.
> We're only immortal
> In spirit – .[315]

The fatalism of the first act of *Akropolis* is a theme that Wyspiański, like many Poles, had been pondering for almost a decade. In 1896, he began work on illustrations for a new publication of *The Iliad*. That same year, he visited Paris, where he saw an adaptation of Sophocles' *Oedipus Rex*, another thematic source for *Akropolis*. He also read Aeschylus' dramas around this time.[316] The Greek heroes, living and dying on the gods' playgrounds, became models for the Polish sense of national fatalism, framed by centuries of oppression and uprisings, and forever etched in the national memory. Juliusz Kleiner (1938) defined fatalism as the "tragedy of the dual nature of one's acts."[317] It is the Oedipal tragedy of a man whose motives, actions and outcomes misfire terribly, confirming rather than averting his fate. In 1907 in his study *Life and Death in the Works of Wyspiański*, Stanisław Brzozowski wrote that "Wyspiański once more relives the historical legacy of Poland to prove that one cannot live on memory alone. Memories do not exist. But Wyspiański doesn't know the world of the living. He simply defends himself from the madness of memory."[318] In this context, Wawel, at once a cemetery and a repository of Poland's national legacy, becomes fatalistically entangled in the myths of national martyrology and revival. One of the most prominent images of the first act is an eagle, Poland's national coat of arms, in the half-opened coffin. There are many interpretations of this image; everyone agrees that an eagle represents the partitioned Poland, but there are disagreements about whether the half-opened coffin suggests that the eagle should not be awakened as it is too early for the uprising, or whether it implies that it will never be the right time.

Akropolis is set in the castle during the Night of the Resurrection, a holiday just before Easter that, according to folk legend, is a night of miracles. The setting also alludes to Christ's resurrection. (In Polish, Easter – *Wielkanoc* – literally means "the Great Night.") The exact time is from midnight to four o'clock in the morning, the liminal hours. Bałus argues that "the religious liminality, the condition between sacred and profane, can never be sustained for too long. There will always be 'something' separate created in the space/time of 'in-between.' Between the cemetery and the village, there is a wall. This is the place to bury suicides. Two fields are always separated by the balk. This is the place where the ghosts appear." (In Polish, the word for "balk," *miedza*, comes from the word *między*, which literally means "in between.")[319] The in-betweenness of time is important in *Akropolis* because it denotes the "something" that is created in the space between the sacred and the profane, and that parallels what is created between the West and the East. This is the space of Polish national identity: a space in constant geo-psychological struggle with itself and its surroundings. The play is a meeting place between the living and the dead, who resurrect themselves in order to brandish their sacrifice and pass judgment on the living. It is a confrontation between history, the present and the vision of the future, which depend on the dialogue between the living and the dead.

Acts 2 and 3 take place outside of Wawel, on the steps to the cathedral. Before the restoration of Wawel, the tapestries depicting the mythical figures that Wyspiański brings to life had hung inside the cathedral. Although when he was writing the play the tapestries were no longer in place and he instead used the illustrations of Ignacy Polkowski, Wyspiański considered the tapestries an integral element of the cathedral. The mythical setting of act 2 also changes; the Vistula River, which passes through Cracow, changes into the ancient Scamander River, which passes near ancient Troy. Drawing on *The Iliad*, Wyspiański retells the Greek story of Priam, Hector, Paris and Helena. To allow Paris and Helena their happiness, Hector follows his fate and goes to war, knowing well that he will die. He believes he will return in spirit, wrapped in everlasting glory. In the meantime, Paris and Helena romance each other, unaware of their tragic destiny. Wyspiański's Priam, the King of Troy, and father of both Hector and Paris, in vain chastises Paris: "Do you know that your folly means our unhappiness?" To which Paris replies: "And isn't it your virtue/ that we can be as foolish as we want to/ under the majesty of your will/ and your strength?" [320] The exchange is a bitter allusion to Poland's political situation; Poles who accept the protectorate of their occupants are foolish, Wyspiański seems to suggest. The act ends with a battle between Hector and Ajax. Standing ominously among the scavenging ravens, Cassandra tries to calm Andromache, Hector's desperate wife, who wanders aimlessly through the battlefield, sensing the looming tragedy.

This act is structured around the opposition between Hector and Paris, and between Hector and Apollo. Tymon Terlecki points out that Paris and Hector represent "two opposite tensions in culture. The one embodied by Hector is exaltingly altruistic, self-denying and sacrificial, and can be called the heroic ideal. It is opposed to the attitude of Paris – egotistical and given to pleasure and joy of life."[321] Wyspiański's Hector is more aware of the inevitability of his death than he is in *The Iliad*. In this sense, Hector symbolizes the Polish soldier who is aware of the futility of his fight and the inevitability of his death, yet is unable to resist the battle because he is driven by the heroic myth of immortal glory. Paris symbolizes those Poles who prefer to focus on their private lives rather than devote themselves to the national struggle. In 1905, Antoni Mazowski noted the parallels between Troy and Poland: "Everything is in the scene: knightly honor, idyllic love, youthful love, marital love, love that's changed into friendship over one's lifespan. It looks like it's all taken from heroic Troy, but in fact, it all breathes of a small pastoral, like the ones woven in our own old hamlets. Really, it's a true image of Polish Troy."[322] Thus, the pairings of Hector and Paris, and Hector and Apollo represent the immediate problems of the Polish national struggle. According to Władysław Zawistowski, the conflict between Hector and Achilles is not a drama of either a colonized or colonizing nation: "It is a two-faceted analysis of freedom; it is a process of becoming aware of what is not freedom, but free life, not the problem of freedom, but the problem of normal, everyday free life."[323] The play ponders a deeply paradoxical sense of Polish identity; Poles send their children to wars (Wyspiański seems to say) with all the patriotic pathos and fanfare that such endeavor entails, yet they are fully conscious of the inevitable failure. They believe (and yet they do not believe) in the greatness and nobility of personal sacrifice on the altar of national and international struggles. They are resigned to absurdity just as they are resigned to pathos, balancing perpetually on the border between them; they are at once Europe's greatest Romantics and its greatest cynics. Tymon Terlecki notes that "At the basis of *Acropolis* and its cultural philosophy lies the fundamental opposition of life and death, the taste for living and the fascination with the poetry of graves."[324] Wyspiański is philosophical about the trope of Polish martyrology; on the one hand, he sees the necessity of the struggle and sacrifice, but on the other, he remains ambivalent about their costs and results. There is a fatalistic tone to *Akropolis* that juxtaposes private life with national obligation. Kalemba-Kasprzak notes that "Love and death in this act are defined not only in existential terms, but also in ethical: as necessity (fate) and honor (recognition)."[325] Likewise, Tadeusz Sinko argues that Wyspiański's Greece is different from the "sensual and beautiful poetic marble of French or Italian neoclassicism; it is a mysteriously gloomy, passionate and archaically colorful place. It is Greece looked at through the pessimistic lens of Nietzschean philosophy."[326] Drawing strongly on the themes of Ancient Greece, Wyspiański is able to develop a mythic framework that illuminates the political situation in partitioned Poland. This stylistic gesture is very much in tune with Wagnerian aesthetics, but it also anticipates Brecht's epic theatre.

As much as it draws on Greek mythology, *Akropolis* is also steeped in biblical references. Kretz-Mirski (1910) points out that, of the twenty-five scenes in *Akropolis*, only two are wholly original.[327] Some are taken directly from the Hebrew Bible, and some retell the biblical story with changes. In 1926, J. Mirski made a table that compares and contrasts scenes from *Akropolis* with those from the Book of Genesis (see Appendix).[328]

Act 3 of *Akropolis* also takes place on the stairs of the cathedral, and focuses on the Hebrew story of Jacob and Esau. Wyspiański's version of this tale opens as the two brothers prepare to go hunting – Esau sent by the father and Jacob by the mother.

Since Esau is the firstborn, he is the one Isaac wants to bless. The Abrahamic blessing that Isaac intends to give would ensure that Esau's descendants be the chosen people. However, Esau, aware that God pronounced that Abraham's descendants would be enslaved for 400 years before they would be allowed to return to their homeland, sells his birthright for a bowl of lentil soup. He is eventually outwitted by Jacob, who receives Isaac's blessing and thus becomes the one whose descendants are forever blessed. Wyspiański portrays Esau as the victim, who passively accepts his fate, and Jacob as the one who (albeit reluctantly) betrays him. Although he is ordered to do so by his mother Rebecca, Jacob feels guilty and doubts whether a blessing received by deceit is legitimate. Tymon Terlecki argues that "The conquering dynamic and the persevering passive hero do not contradict but complement one another. They represent two equally important levers to human existence, to progress and to the development of civilization."[329] Maria Stobrecka suggests that Wyspiański's Esau represents Poles who both mistrust their legacy and feel robbed of it.[330] A similarly symbolic role is Laban, who tricks Jacob into marrying his older daughter Leah instead of the promised Rachel, violating the social norms of primogeniture, and thus uprooting all of the Children of Israel. Laban is fully aware that, in going against Jacob, he goes against himself, against the very essence of his being. Regardless, he chooses to accept and follow through on his fate.[331] Wyspiański further describes Jacob's travel to Haran and his struggle with the angel, who blesses him and his descendants but also confirms that his descendants will suffer centuries of struggles. When asked, "Who are you?," the angel replies: "Necessity." After twenty years of pilgrimage, Jacob eventually returns to Esau's home and Esau forgives him. Esau is portrayed as "noble, knightly and magnanimous."[332] Józef Rachwał writes, "Life, for Wyspiański, is eternally ambivalent, and thus, an eternal struggle in which man never comes out as the winner […] For this reason, the temporal triumph is itself tragic because it contains the element of inevitable defeat."[333] In this sense, like Hector, Jacob and Esau are both tragic characters. Each is fully aware of the fundamental absurdity of his predicament; one is betrayed, the other is forced to betray.

Act 4 takes place on the ground level of the cathedral. The characters are the sculptures of King David and Christ-Salvatore, a Catholic saint known for healing the sick. King David's sculpture comes to life carrying a harp, which suggests that he represents Wyspiański the poet himself. The Vistula River, depicted as Troy's Scamander River in act 1, now becomes the Jordan River. The final act alludes to Mickiewicz's messianic idea of Poland as the "Christ of the nations": suffering for others but eventually destined for glorious resurrection. The half-opened coffin indeed cracks open and an eagle from the first act flies away. Christ-Salvatore resurrects and stands above the poet, who descends to Earth, into a human domain.

Wojciech Bałus notes that there are two ways of reading Christian sacred architecture. The Byzantine churches are constructed in a way that places Christ on the highest point of the church's cupola, an arrangement that symbolizes neoplatonic hierarchy, both ontological and axiological; everything comes from and focuses on God. The movement of mosaics and the interior architecture of the church thus follow from top to bottom. In Western churches, the structure is focused on man, who looks up in his search and yearns for God. The movement of the interior design is thus from the bottom up. In *Akropolis*, Wyspiański reads the design of the cathedral as Western; the movement is from the poet up to Christ-Salvatore.[334] This shows that Wyspiański identified more with Western than with Eastern ontotheology. Bałus also notes that this figure of Christ-Salvatore is referred to as Apollo, who "represents Polish Resurrection."[335] The conflation of the figures suggests once again the ethnic and cultural hybridity of Polish identity.

In the final scene, Wawel collapses and St. Stanisław's coffin is destroyed, accompanied by thunder and fire. Eventually Apollo arrives, riding in a golden chariot pulled by four white stallions. He sings a paean to the resurrected Christ and concludes the play with a mournful statement: "The trumpets sound like cannons/ like in the olden days;/ as if Poland has been resurrected/ [...] / And the song can be heard over the nation and the land/ over the bleeding land of the Polish Akropolis."[336] Simultaneously, new light rises over the ruins. Fusing the iconography of Apollo with Christ into "one symbolic entity," Wyspiański once again reiterates the Greco-Christian unity of Polish tradition.[337] Tymon Terlecki suggests that the grandiose musical finale has "a Wagnerian, Berliozian immensity" and that the scene itself "has the grandeur of both a catastrophe and of apotheosis."[338] The double meaning of the finale has many implications. Józef Rachwał suggests that the coffin, and by extension Wawel, represents the past that suffocates the living spirit of the nation: "Escaping from under its spell and its weight would allow the nation to live in the moment and look forward to the future."[339] *Akropolis* also illustrates the prevailing conflict between Romantics and Classicists in Polish literature and culture at the turn of the twentieth century, one calling for action, the other for pragmatism.

Chapter 10

"THIS DRAMA AS DRAMA CANNOT BE STAGED"

Because of its scope, multilayered setting and constant balancing between pathos and irony, *Akropolis* is difficult to stage. Some Polish directors and critics regard it as poetry rather than drama. Starting in 1904, Władysław Prokesch unequivocally proclaimed *Akropolis* to be "unsuitable on stage, despite the fact that Wyspiański included sheets of music composed by Bolesław Raczyński."[340] Elżbieta Morawiec, writing about the 1978 production directed by Krystyna Skuszanka, stated that "In the history of Polish theatre, this production remains yet another attempt to resurrect a play that in this form cannot be resurrected."[341] Jerzy Bober suggested that the play does not have a "dramatic form."[342] Maciej Szybist concurred: "This drama as drama cannot be staged."[343] As Marta Fik noted, "One false step, and instead of originality and genuine pathos, you get falsity and pretension."[344] Krzysztof Pleśniarowicz pointed out that Wyspiański's play presents two challenges. One is the issue of stylistic consistency, as the play comprises four one-act plays of different structures and styles. The second is the fact that it is virtually impossible to stage the final scene, with its dual challenge of Apollo-Salvatore entering the stage riding a chariot drawn by horses and the castle getting destroyed.[345] Thus, the play has been generally avoided by Polish theatres. Parts of the play were sung by the choir at the Teatr Miejski in Lwów on 28 September 1904, and Leonard Bończa staged the first and fourth acts on 1 December 1916 in Cracow's Słowacki Theatre, under the artistic direction of Adam Grzymała-Siedlecki. Bończa's production was prepared in an attempt to commemorate both Wyspiański's death and the anniversary of the November uprising against the Russians in 1830, which ended in Poland's defeat. Zygmunt Wierciak designed the scenery and Zbigniew and Andrzej Proszanek designed the costumes.[346] This production evoked mixed reactions, with Teofil Trzciński writing one of the most laudatory reviews: "Someday, in the years to come, when all other Wyspiański dramas will perhaps be seen as mere historical footnotes, *Akropolis* will be viewed as a timeless, eternal work, the Festspiel of Polish theatre."[347]

Some, however, questioned the wisdom of staging only two acts while completely cutting act 3. The theatre justified its choice, explaining that it wanted to focus on the motif of resurrection rather than the usual martyrological theme. The approaching end of World War I brought hopes of Polish independence (indeed, 1916 is called the "year of Polish hopes"), and with it a feeling of relief from 200 years of struggle. That optimistic atmosphere clearly influenced Bończa's interpretation of *Akropolis*. Fittingly, Teofil Trzciński called the play "a moment of respite for the Polish conscience."[348]

Akropolis was staged in its entirety for the first time 22 years after its publication, following a conflict between the Słowacki Theatre (under the artistic direction of Zygmnunt Nowakowski) and the National Theatre in Warsaw regarding who should premiere the play, a dispute the Słowacki Theatre won. The play opened on 29 November 1926, and featured Józef Sosnowski as both director and actor, with a set design by Bolesław Kudewicz. Although the play eventually attracted great acclaim among both critics and audiences, Leon Schiller did not like it. He wrote, "*Akropolis* got stuffed in the box of Cracow's scene among decorations copied verbatim from Wawel architecture, a choice that turned the play into some kind of postcard from Cracow, unnecessarily allegorical."[349] In this production, the final scene showed the cathedral falling apart into the darkness as the back wall rose, revealing Apollo-Salvatore riding a chariot driven by four white stallions. This version too provoked mixed reactions, with some critics praising "the cinematic effects" while others considered them inappropriate for the "national mysterium."[350] The last production staged before World War II was the 1932 version directed by Teofil Trzciński that opened on 26 November at the Teatr Polski in Poznań. The set was designed by Zygmunt Szpingier, who based his design on Wyspiański's drawings and Wyczółkowski's graphics. Schiller liked this production, declaring: "Teofil Tczciński, in Poznań, was able to mount – against difficult odds – a memorable, incredibly clear and successful production."[351] As in previous productions, the final scene had liberatory underpinnings, with a golden Wawel emerging in the background.[352] Both Iwo Gall and Leon Schiller later attempted to stage the play, and sketches of their designs are preserved in Polish archives, but the concepts were never realized.[353] After the war *Akropolis* was staged by Kazimierz Dejmek in 1959 without great success. In 1966, Mieczysław Kotlarczyk directed a production at Teatr Rapsodyczny in Cracow.[354] According to Osiński, Dejmek chose to interpret Hector as a symbol of "Polish madness" and the entire play as a condemnation of Polish Romanticism.[355] Both Dejmek and Kotlarczyk chose to interpret *Akropolis* foremost as a national drama. In February 1978, Krystyna Skuszanka directed yet another version of *Akropolis* at the Słowacki Teatr in Cracow, with the set designed by Ewa Tęcza and the music by Adam Walaciński. The reviews were lukewarm. Jerzy Bober asked: "Does *Akropolis*, this unsettled drama-poem, have any chance for a coherent staging? In my opinion, it does not."[356] *Akropolis* wasn't staged in Warsaw, the Polish capital, until 2001, under the direction of Ryszard Peryt.

The relative lack of interest in staging *Akropolis* runs counter to the near obsession with Wyspiański's other dramas (such as *The Wedding* and *Liberation*), which have been in the repertoire of almost every Polish theatre since they were written. Knowing the convoluted production history and the controversies surrounding various attempts at staging, one can't help but credit Grotowski for taking up the challenging project. Grotowski was the first one to bring *Akropolis* back to the Polish stage in the second half of the twentieth century.[357] The unofficial world premiere of Grotowski's version of *Akropolis* is marked as either October 9 or 10, 1962 (depending on the source), and the official premiere as October 20, 1962. At that time, the line between rehearsal and public performance was somewhat blurry; Grotowski would often rehearse a piece with an invited audience or show a piece to the public, then withdraw it to rework it some more. This was the case with his production of *Akropolis*, which was shown at various stages of its development beginning in early 1962.[358] According to Józef Kelera, there are five versions ("variants") of the production, each considered by Grotowski's group to be a separate work with its own opening.[359] Osiński lists them as October 10, 1962, Opole (variant I); 1962, Opole (variant II); 1964, Opole (variant III); 1965, Wrocław (variant IV); and 1967, Wrocław (variant V).[360] The cast included Zygmunt Molik as Jacob, the harpist and the leader of the dying tribe; Rena Mirecka as Rebecca and Cassandra; Antoni Jaholkowski as Isaac; Zbigniew Cynkutis and Mieczysław Janowski as Angel and Paris, respectively; and Ryszard Cieślak as Esau. The set and props were designed by Józef Szajna. Each of the five variants presented a slightly different version of the show.[361]

Chapter 11

TWO NATIONAL SACRUMS

Akropolis was relatively better received in Poland than Grotowski's other productions. However, it generated as much discussion and controversy as his other shows.[362] At a symposium to commemorate Wyspiański's 100th birthday in 1969, organized by Jagiellonian University, there was a lone suggestion that Grotowski's staging of *Akropolis* was the most successful production of any of Wyspiański's dramas.[363] However, most critics voiced their discomfort at the production. In his program notes for the production, Flaszen (1962) points out that Grotowski did not add any new lines to the play but merely stripped it to the bare bones of its poetics.[364] Grotowski did make a drastic change in its staging, however, moving the play from Wawel Cathedral to an Auschwitz crematorium. Summarizing the Polish response to this transposition, Konstantyn Puzyna writes: "Like Schiller, Grotowski connects romantic tradition with the twentieth-century avant-garde. This connection was so shocking at that time that it was not easily accepted or understood. […] Grotowski's attempt to profane the two 'national sacrums seemed particularly sacrilegious.'"[365] In response to Puzyna, Tadeusz Kudliński firmly questions the alternatives:

> Grotowski attempts a brave, and sometimes impossible struggle with Romantic poetry and attitude, an attempt at re-evaluation of our deeply rooted mystical and heroic myths. This attempt often evokes offense. But let's ask ourselves what's better? To leave this repertoire in the museum, stage it conventionally as part of one's honorary national pastime? Or use all of our passion to challenge it to see what's left of our Romantic traditions?[366]

Grotowski used the strategy of "ironic inversion." As Findlay puts it, "Whereas Wyspiański's original is an optimistic affirmation of the centuries-old traditions of Western culture and civilization, Grotowski deliberately submit[s] these values to the tests of mockery and blasphemy. Wyspiański's values thus [become] ironically inverted."[367] Or as Margaret Croyden puts it, based on Flaszen's essay: "[Grotowski's] intent is to test the old masterpieces against modern sensibilities. This is done by the 'dialectic of apotheosis and derision' – the actors play multiple roles and there is a montage of scenes juxtaposing classical ideals with grotesque mockery or self-parody."[368] Flaszen argues that, thanks to such a strategy, "the profaned values are revived, renewed, on a higher, more sublime level through the shock [of these juxtapositions]. The destitution of the human condition, culminating in excess, allows the viewers to reach *catharsis* in its almost archaic form."[369] However, Grotowski's irony is very different from that utilized by other Polish directors of that time. Grotowski replaces one sacred with another; the religious mysticism of Judeo-Christian sacred, which forms the basis of Wyspiański's mythological framework, is replaced with religious-like secular mysticism of a group ritual formally structured – with chants, movements and trance-like episodes – in order to replicate what it disowned. As Michał Masłowski puts it, it turns into a "secular mass without God."[370] Or as Agnieszka Wojtowicz notes, Grotowski attempts to "cure a romantic attitude with romantic attitude," replacing one sacred with another, thus never escaping the tropes he wants to challenge. Simultaneously, there is no clear, established framework for redemption: from what and towards what? As Mateusz Lipko notes, despite using Christian terminology, Grotowski's concept of salvation is not grounded in any coherent system. The actors are asked for self-sacrifice, but since there is no God in Grotowski's liturgy, there is no one to sacrifice oneself to nor anyone from whom to receive redemption.[371] Because of its tautological structure, Grotowski's commentary is never self-referential and *Akropolis* never engages with itself. It never acknowledges its own implication in the process of making and remaking the sacred. There is no kynicism in Grotowski's approach; ironic inversion reaches its limits at the shores of the self that remain intact.

Grotowski's main goal, however, is not to merely reenact or represent the condition of the concentration camp, but to somehow embody it in a ritualistic fashion. In this sense, instead of just acting their parts, actors transform the audience into witnesses. In an interview, Grotowski argues that the theatrical space means "everything: Wawel Cathedral, concentration camp, entire world and cosmos."[372] Waldemar Krygier's image for the poster for the 1962 performance was stylized like a Greek pantheon. It was an allusion to the original script and its own modernist transpositions. The text itself is used very loosely, a single sentence from Wyspiański here and there, barely recognizable except to those familiar with the original script. Such sparse interpretation prompted Konstantyn Puzyna to write, "Dialogue is no longer subjected to the literary structure of the drama. It becomes a matter of game, play […] The actors are no longer subjugated to the text; the text is subjugated to the actors."[373] In his review, Jan Paweł Gawlik, a Polish theatre critic, calls the show "radical" precisely because it uses the text as one of its elements rather than as an anchor.[374] Another Polish reviewer openly warns: "Some will be inspired and some will be offended by 'the parody of Wyspiański.'"[375] With such limited connection to Wyspiański, why set *Akropolis* in Auschwitz? If Auschwitz, why *Akropolis*? If *Akropolis*, why Auschwitz?

In an interview, Grotowski said, "The Royal Palace is not a sanctuary any more; it is not what it was for Wyspiański in the 19th century: the cemetery of our civilization. That's why Wyspiański called the Royal Palace the *Akropolis*: it was Europe's ruined past."[376] He continued: "We asked ourselves a painful and paradoxical question. What is the cemetery of our civilization? Perhaps a battleground from the war. One day I knew without a doubt it was Auschwitz."[377] To quote Mark Fortier, "The simple belief in eternal life or the progress of civilization is replaced by an interwining of life and dead: the acropolis, the height of western civilization, is equally the necropolis, the death camp, the cemetery of civilization."[378] At that time, many Europeans asked themselves the same question. German society seemed to be the epitome of the European culture. As Jean Améry puts it:

> No doubt: whatever abominations we may have experienced, they still do not offset the fact that between 1933 and 1945 those things of which I speak in my writings took place among the German people, a people of high intelligence, industrial capacity, and unequaled cultural wealth – among the people of "Poets and Thinkers." For me this is a fact that until this day remains unclarified and, despite all the diligent historical, psychological, sociological, and political studies that have appeared and will yet appear, at bottom probably cannot be clarified.[379]

Capturing the same sentiment, Grotowski's objectives were complex, focusing on Wyspiański's text only insofar as it serves to explore the modern world, epitomized, Grotowski believed, by the concentration camp. Grotowski explained this in an interview years later:

> I reworked [*Akropolis*] to analyze not only the great myths of the past but the biblical and historical traditions as well. It dramatized the past from the point of view of heroic values. Since World War II we have noticed that the great lofty ideas of Western civilization remain abstract. We mouth heroic values, but real life proves to be different. We must confront the great values of the past and ask some questions. Do these values remain abstract, or do they really exist for us? To discover the answer we must look at the most bitter and ultimate trial: Auschwitz. Auschwitz is the darkest reality of our contemporary history. Auschwitz is the trial of humankind. What has been our goal in this play? To put two opposite views on the stage, to create brutal confrontation in order to see if these past dreams are concrete and strong, or only abstractions. In other words, we wanted to confront our ancestral experiences in a situation where all values were destroyed, and that is why we chose Auschwitz. What was the reaction to this play? The audience watches the confrontation; they observe the dreams of the prisoners, and the dreams of the great people of our past. Past dreams appear annihilated by the reality of Auschwitz. But in another sense, the dreams survive because they give weight and depth to the prisoners, for they feel themselves part of the collective past. Man in that situation is being tested, pitted against past ideals. Does he survive the test? The audience will decide.[380]

Raymonde Temkine succinctly summarizes Grotowski's point: "The question is put this way: what will make us germinate in our soil, what is nourishment from which we can live, we for whom there is no more God?"[381] Correspondingly, writing about one of the earliest versions of Grotowski's *Akropolis* in 1963, Jerzy Panasewicz, another Polish critic, poignantly ponders the connection between Wyspiański and Auschwitz: "I can't say if, by looking at *Akropolis* through the prism of the concentration camp, Grotowski tells us something new about Wyspiański's play. On the contrary, it might be more appropriate to say that he tells us something new about the concentration camp."[382] Indeed, Grotowski was as much, if not more, interested in exploring the issues around the Holocaust as he was interested in Wyspiański's text. In fact, he was exploring the topic of German–Polish–Jewish relations long before he decided to stage *Akropolis*. The play, in a way, became a vehicle for continuing earlier experiments.

Before he became focused on *Akropolis*, Grotowski devised short shows based on the speeches of Hitler, Himmler and Goering, which explored the German–Polish–Jewish relations. The actress Ewa Lubowiecka, dressed in a black minidress, recited the texts with scenes from Auschwitz running in the background. The company toured those shows along the Polish western border. The audience, mostly of German origins, clapped and cheered to Hitler's speeches about Poles who, as slaves, needed to be conquered. Once the audience members understood the real – ironic – sub-context of the speeches and the intentions of the actors, they began throwing tomatoes onto the stage.[383] In many ways, *Akropolis* thus became a culmination and extension of Grotowski's earlier work on the problem of Holocaust.

While working on the next version of *Akropolis*, in 1964, Grotowski also adapted Wyspiański's *Studium o Hamlecie* [A Study of Hamlet], which Wyspiański wrote around the same time he wrote *Akropolis* (*Studium* was published in 1905, a year after *Akropolis*). Both of Wyspiański's plays share many similar themes, including an encounter with ghosts, an exploration of national and European identity, and a quest for Polish self-definition within the larger politico-cultural context. Both plays were written with Wawel – and, as a result, with Wyspiański's viewing of the newly discovered frescos – in mind.[384] In his adaptation of *Studium*, Grotowski continued the same theme of Polish–Jewish relations which he pondered in *Akropolis;* however, this time the emphasis was placed on the persecutions of Jews under the Communist regime. As Zygmunt Molik recalls, in *Studium*, "Hamlet was a Jew, and the courtiers were the government police and secret bureau."[385] As Agnieszka Wojtowicz notes, in light of the intense anti-Semitic rhetoric that came from the communist regime, Grotowski's adaptation was "politically impossible to defend from the censors."[386]

Chapter 12

"HOLLOW SNEERING LAUGHTER": MOURNING THE COLUMBUSES

Although they admired Grotowski's formal theatrical strategies, foreign scholars and critics remained unaware of the relationship between Grotowski and Borowski. In Poland, however, it was common knowledge that both the form and content of Grotowski's *Akropolis* were inspired by Borowski's writing and the style of his prose. In fact, many have suggested that in his theatrical strategy, Grotowski replicated Borowski's writing style. As Osiński points out, that relationship was completely overlooked, however, in European and American circles.[387] Tadeusz Borowski (1922–1951) was a Polish writer, poet and essayist who survived Auschwitz, wrote a highly acclaimed series of concentration camp stories (published in the USA under the title *This Way for the Gas, Ladies and Gentlemen*), and committed suicide in 1951 by inhaling gas from an oven. Borowski's 1942 volume of poetry has an "apocalyptic and catastrophist tone [that] stands out against the poetry of his generation, which was shot through with a grand romantic urge to fight."[388] The poster for *Akropolis* quotes an epitaph from a poem by Borowski. The poem cited by Grotowski goes like this:

> *Nad nami – noc. Goreją gwiazdy,*
> *dławiący, trupi nieba fiolet.*
> *Zostanie po nas złom żelazny*
> *i głuchy, drwiący śmiech pokoleń.*
> Above us – night. Smoldering stars,
> stifling, putrid purple of the sky.
> We'll leave behind us iron scraps
> and hollow sneering laughter [of those – generations – who'll come after us].[389]

In Poland, the last two lines of Borowski's poem are considered a kind of sacred motto of the so-called Columbus 20 generation, the generation born in the 1920s. The term comes from Roman Bratny's novel *Kolumbowie. Rocznik 20* [Columbuses: Generation 1920s], which was published in 1957.[390] The novel chronicles the stories of young intelligentsia partisan fighters, spanning the years 1942–1948. They were in their late teens and early twenties when the war broke out. They fought in the underground resistance army (AK, Armia Krajowa [The Home Army]) during the Warsaw uprising; they studied at the secret universities; and they died in concentration camps and Nazi prisons. They were the lost generation – those who died, and those who survived but never truly recovered from the horrors of the war. Bratny called them the Generation of Columbuses because, as he said, they were the ones who discovered Poland, meaning that when faced with the very real prospect of their nation being obliterated, they put aside their private lives, dreams and desires to defend it.[391] Borowski was considered one of the Columbuses, and his poem acknowledges the tragic truth of this generation: the fundamental, cosmic inconsequentiality of their sacrifice. It also asks, implicitly and bitterly, for remembrance. This remembrance was intrinsic to the postwar nation-building of communist Poland, but, because it was wrapped in the newly installed communist regime, it inevitably became a part of Soviet propaganda. The new establishment equated fascism with capitalism, and emphasized the Soviet victory over both. Communist leaders cultivated wartime memories for their own purposes: the dead were to serve as a constant reminder of the military deliverance and the military might of the Soviet Union.[392] Thus, the everyday life of Poles revolved around national holidays commemorating the people, the battles, the victories and the defeats of the war.

The war existed in Poland's national consciousness on two levels: the personal and the political. Personal mourning progressed along its natural course through works of literature, poetry and film. But this mourning never had a chance to work itself out fully because it was perpetually reinforced and redefined by the artifice of the official, politically sanctioned mourning, framed and imposed by the governmental structures that regulated all the media, celebrations, school ceremonies and numerous other secular rituals of remembrance, most of which seemed to never end. Eric Santner argues that, since Germans were the perpetrators, they were not allowed to officially mourn their own dead and thus experienced a process of failed mourning: a form of self-denial.[393] If Germans as the perpetrators were not allowed to openly mourn their dead, Poles in a way were doomed not just to mourn theirs forever, but to live with them in the constant, frozen presence of Soviet propaganda. The national post-traumatic stress disorder was ingrained in the very fabric of the political regime, and became an essential part of the postwar Polish psyche.

Historically speaking, unlike the Columbuses, Grotowski's generation, those born during or just before the war, did not remember the war from an adult perspective; Grotowski was born in 1933 and thus six years old when the war started, and 12 when it ended. But Grotowski and his peers were the children of the Columbus 20 generation and lived in the same psychic reality their parents had. It is no accident that Grotowski chose Borowski's poem for his poster. It is also no accident that he chose to set Wyspiański's play in Auschwitz. Since World War II, Auschwitz has been a part of the Polish self-definition, the knowledge of it ingrained in the national consciousness and passed on as part of the nation's epistemology. Ewa Lubowiecka, one of Grotowski's actresses, recalls a childhood experience of visiting Auschwitz:

> When I was a little girl, my mom took me to Auschwitz. My shoes got stuck in the mud with protruding white human bones. In the barracks, thousands of shoes, hair, some made into braids, children's buggies, purses, glasses, suitcases. Incredible numbers. This memory became vivid in *Akropolis*: we repeated: shoes, shoes or hair, hair, hair.[394]

Lubowiecka's experience was typical for Polish children of her generation, and her memories of Auschwitz were shared across the spectrum of Polish society. Grotowski captured this feeling in one of his interviews: "I didn't do Wyspiański's *Akropolis*, I met it. I didn't illustrate Auschwitz from the outside; it's the thing in me which is something I didn't know directly, but indirectly I knew."[395] He added:

> We eliminate those parts of the text which have no importance for us, those parts with which we can neither agree nor disagree. Within the montage one finds words that function vis-à-vis our own experience. The result is that we cannot say whether it is Wyspiański's *Akropolis*. Yes, it is. But at the same time it is our *Akropolis*.[396]

Clurman noted that "*Akropolis* takes place on the threshold of mass extinction."[397] Raymonde Temkine summarized her interpretation in one sentence: "*Akropolis* is the story of the extermination of all people after an outbreak of barbarism pulverizes them."[398] In his 1963 review, Bogdan Bąk wrote that the play might as well have been titled *Akropolis from the Epoch of the Ovens*.[399] And, writing on the occasion of Grotowski's death in 1999, Holger Teschke referenced both the Katyń massacre of Polish officers by the Soviets and Auschwitz in his description of *Akropolis*: "Grotowski's *Akropolis* was constructed within the socialist camp, whose enclosures included the forest of Katyń. […] It lives in the darkness of Cracow's cathedral, where the shadows of Veit Stoss's figures sleepwalk in the night; it reaches up toward the dark clouds of Auschwitz, toward the smoke rising in spirals."[400] None of the foreign critics, however, delved into the details as to the literal meaning of Grotowski's images they so praised.

The original program for Grotowski's production also included a few fragments from Borowski's *At Our Auschwitz* (the title is hard to translate into English in a way that would preserve Borowski's bitter nonchalance; in French, it would be "Chez-Nous Auschwitz," suggesting a restaurant, a family retreat or a summer camp). The passages inserted in the program go as follows:

1) We work beneath the earth and above it, under a roof and in the rain, with the spade, the pickaxe and the crowbar. We carry huge sacks of cement, lay bricks, put down rails, spread gravel, trample the earth… We are laying the foundation for some new, monstrous civilization. Only now do I realize what price was paid for building the ancient civilizations. […] If the Germans win the war, what will the world know about us? They will erect huge buildings, highways, factories, soaring monuments. Our hands will be placed under every brick, and our backs will carry the steel rails and the slabs of concrete. They will kill off our families, our sick, our aged. They will murder our children. And we shall be forgotten, drowned out by the voices of the poets, the jurists, the philosophers, the priests. They will produce their own beauty, virtue, and truth. They will produce religion.[401]
2) One day I was goalkeeper. […] Between two throw-ins in a soccer game, right behind my back, three thousand people had been put to death.[402]
3) Not long ago, the labour Kommandos used to march in formation when returning to camp. The band played and the passing columns kept step with its beat. One day the DAW Kommando and many of the others – some ten thousand men – were ordered to stop and stood waiting at the gate. At that moment several trucks full of

naked women rolled in from the FKL. The women stretched out their arms and pleaded:

> "Save us! We are going to the gas chambers! Save us!"
> And they rode slowly past us – the ten thousand silent men – and then disappeared from sight. Not one of us made a move, not one of us liftend a hand.[403]

4) But this is how it is done: first just one ordinary barn, brightly whitewashed – and here they proceed to asphyxiate people. Later, four large buildings, accommodating twenty thousand at a time without any trouble. No hocus-pocus, no poison, no hypnosis. Only several men directing traffic to keep operations running smoothly, and the thousands flow along like water from an open tap. All this happens just beyond the anemic trees of the dusty little wood. Ordinary trucks bring people, return, then, bring some more. No hocus-pocus, no poison, no hypnosis.[404]

Borowski's passages fittingly grounded the conceptual framework of Grotowski's production.[405] The set of *Akropolis* was bare, stripped to its essentials: pipes, bags of cement, wooden planks, a wheelbarrow. Designed by Józef Szajna, himself an Auschwitz survivor, the set was an attempt to reflect the bareness of the camp. As Grotowski reminisced:

> These scenic elements – pipes, shoes, wheelbarrows, costumes – were very intentionally found. It's no accident that [Szajna] picked these elements. He has always been called abstract. The scenic elements of *Akropolis* were not abstract, but neither were they realistic. These elements were concrete objects, things from bad dreams, but all completely "untheatrical." Szajna found these objects in flea markets and junk shops.[406]

Szajna's contribution to *Akropolis* has been widely acknowledged, and in Poland he is credited as the show's co-author, although with time many have diminished his role. In fact, he collaborated with Grotowski on the text as well as the set. Szajna came to the theatre from painting. Before joining Grotowski, he was already established as a successful artist and set designer. For his art, Szajna drew inspiration from his own experiences as an Auschwitz prisoner. Born in 1922, he was sent there as a boy. After a failed attempt at escape, he was sentenced to death and was miraculously saved from the group of prisoners being led to their execution. *Akropolis* is Szajna's best-known spectacle, but it was followed by the critically acclaimed *Replica* (in its four versions) and an adaptation of Tadeusz Hołuj's *Puste pole* [Empty Field].[407] Both shows attempt to illustrate the experience of Auschwitz by using metaphors, symbols and visual parables. In *Empty Field*, produced in 1965, the prisoners, dressed in the characteristic striped uniform, run onto the stage accompanied by the ominous clicking of wheelbarrows. In *Replica*, often called *Requiem*, a pile of trash – rags, shoes, pipes and pieces of mannequins – covered with dirt greets the entering audience. After a pause, an outstretched hand reaches out from beneath the pile, greedily grabbing a piece of dry bread. Soon enough, the dead resurrect; horribly massacred bodies emerge slowly from the pile of trash, indistinguishable from the surrounding objects.[408] Likewise, in *Akropolis*, Szajna wanted to portray "a day from the life of a man who became a number." As he said, "I filled the space with piles, wheelbarrows and old tubs, because the prisoners were ordered to build a grave-crematorium for themselves. Their costumes consisted of old burned-out potato sacks, with wounds and bodies carried like clothes. The low-set berets emphasized their faces – musselmen's masks – and wooden shoes clunked with the movement of millions of legs in the process of camp misterium."[409] Many critics, including Gurawski, suggested that Szajna lacked a fundamental understanding of the theatrical space, as he used similar props (prisoners' garb, clogs, wheelbarrows, pipes) in *Empty Field*.[410] Szajna, in his defense, cited his camp experiences as fundamental to his theatrical choices: "Our production – with its Akropolis-Oświęcim association as a symbol of modernity, [...] found its inspiration in my personal experiences as the prisoner in Auschwitz-Birkenau, which were essential for us."[411] Szajna brought to *Akropolis* his experiences but also his own aesthetic. The fact that he was an Auschwitz survivor searching for a means to process and express his experience adds to our understanding of the show as foremost a post-traumatic work meant to retell the experience. Other members of Grotowski's creative team shared similar experiences. Ludwik Flaszen, for example, spent the war with his family in an internment camp in Uzbekhistan, due to their partially Jewish heritage, and Zbigniew Cynkutis' father was among those killed during the Katyń Massacre.

Like the cast's personal experiences, Szajna's experience in Auschwitz influenced his approach to set design while he worked with Grotowki on *Akropolis*. Raymonde Temkine notes that during the performance of *Akropolis* the set transforms into a symbolic wall, trapping the audience members in the space of the camp:

> The room is hung with ropes set in the shape of a spider web which the spectators hardly notice when they enter the room. But, at the end of the production, the pipes nailed to the ground are hung on the ropes, enclosing them in a metallic trap. Thus, the spectators, too, are caught in the concentration-camp universe.[412]

In his review of the show, Gawlik compares the staging to a scene from one of the paintings of Jerzy Adam Brandhuber (1897–1981), an Auschwitz survivor and one of the founding members of the Auschwitz museum site, whose series of paintings *Forgotten Earth* depict scenes from daily camp life.[413] French reviewer Emile Copermann, in his review of Grotowski's Paris premiere, compares the staging to Bosch's *Hell*.[414] Other reviewers compare it to Marc Chagall.[415] Raymonde Temkine marvels at the affinities "between Grotowski and certain painters – Caravaggio, Rembrandt, and Ribera."[416] Responding to those painterly comparisons, Clurman argues that they are incorrect, as Grotowski's minimalist aesthetics lack the opulence of the painters to whom he has been compared. Clurman writes: "The names of Breughel, Bosch, Grunewald are frequently invoked for purposes of comparison; but that is misleading, for there is sumptuousness in those artists. Grotowski's stage, architecture, costuming are bare. Everything has been stripped to the bone."[417] The struggle of both critics and scholars with the contextualization of Grotowski's piece derives from their strategy of focusing on *mise-en-scène*, trying to interpret the play through the prism of known visual markers. Lacking the specificity of the cultural framework, critics and scholars turn to "sharp and loving descriptions" as a way to draw the familiar parallels and thus make meaning out of the dense, multilayered theatrical text. Margaret Croyden, for example, was but one of the few American critics whose "sharp and loving descriptions" make the problem of decontextualized reading apparent:

> To see the Laboratory Theater is to be transplanted into a black, brooding world of classical myth and contemporary degradation, depicted in an atmosphere of horror, executed with the delicacy of a poet. [...] Against the eerie screeching of a violin and the dead silence of the audience, the inmates work in unison – hammering, lifting, and hanging their pipes and chimney stoves on vertical wires – building their Acropolis turned crematorium. Intermittently they re-enact ancient myths with the stylized precision of acrobats or mimes. Dressed in torn, worn-out sacks, heavy, oversized brown wooden clogs, and colorless skull caps that negate their sex, the prisoners move with exquisite control, their arms and legs dangling with the grace of a mobile sculpture. Their faces (untouched by make-up) are gray death masks: eyes turned inward, smiles frozen, foreheads ossified – creatures from another land, tortured wrecks, brutalized automatons. They speak, chant, whisper, and intone, creating an unrelenting rise and fall of sounds quite unlike anything usually heard in Western theater.[418]

"Sharp and loving," Croyden's description lacks specifics. She reads the show in the broader context of universal horror that she knows from TV and books.

Yet Grotowski's *Akropolis* has no plot resembling an episode of TV or short story; there is only action that parallels Borowski's description: the prisoners working in the camp, carrying pipes, planks and bags of cement. Grotowski describes the action of the play:

> The prisoners worked all the time. They took metal pipes that were piled in the center of the room and built something. At the start, the room was empty except for the pile of pipes and the spectators were disseminated through all the space. By the end of the production the entire room was filled by the metal [...] We organized it all into the rhythm of work in the extermination camp, with certain breaks in the rhythm where the characters refer themselves to the traditions of their youth, the dreams of their people.[419]

Within this camp structure, Wyspiański's *Akropolis* enters the production in a metatheatrical fashion as a play within the play. Grotowski did not stage Wyspiański's *Akropolis* within Wyspiański's story; he staged it within Borowski's. The story provides the primary setting of the production.[420] "The actors did not play prisoners, they played what they were doing – people plunged into absurd, detailed routine."[421] To amuse themselves, to pass the time, and to take their minds off their work, the prisoners in *Akropolis* "reenact scenes from the Old Testament and Homer" during breaks in their labor. The religious aspect of the enacted texts also appears in Borowski book, which wryly describes everyday camp life: "Directly beneath me, in the bottom bunk, lies a rabbi. He has covered his head with a piece of rag torn off a blanket and reads from a Hebrew prayer book (there is no shortage of this type of literature at the camp), wailing loudly, monotonously."[422] As Borowski notes, the religious wailing was a background noise in camp's daily life, while piles of prayer books of all religions and in all sort of languages needed to be processed daily. One can imagine a single page or two carried away by the wind towards the working prisoners.[423]

This framework of the production parallels very closely the actual conditions of the camp. As Bruno Bettelheim notes in his autobiographical essay about his time at Dachau and Buchenwald, he and the other prisoners were often forced to perform nonsensical tasks,

> such as carrying heavy rocks from one place to another, and after a while back to the place where they had picked them up. [...] They resented such nonsensical work. [...] They felt debased when forced to perform "childish" and stupid labor, and preferred even harder work when it produced something that might be considered useful.[424]

Elsewhere, Bettelheim writes:

> Every prisoner was confronted with the problem of how to endure performing stupid tasks for from 12 to 18 hours. One relief was to talk, when the guards did not prevent it. During the hours of early morning and late evening twilight the guards could not see whether the prisoners talked. That provided them with at least two hours a day for conversation while at work.[425]

In his review of *Akropolis*, Polish theatre critic Jerzy Panasewicz emphasizes that Grotowski didn't mean to immediately shock the audience, but rather to build the tension through the gradual awareness of the details, gestures, poses and sounds. They emerge piecemeal as if from a fog, revealing the gruesome atmosphere of the place. Panasewicz writes:

> Grotowski doesn't want to shock or surprise. On the contrary, it seems as if he wants to lull the viewer, calm him, let him feel the magic of theatre, let him forget that he is in a theatre. So, the first scenes are played slowly, lazily, as if on the sly. The room slowly fills with construction, the atmosphere grows heavier. The movements become sharper, swifter, the voices grow deeper and more complex, the contrasts are more and more brutal and assaulting.[426]

It is the boredom, the slowness, the "banality" of life at Auschwitz, as Hannah Arendt puts it, that horrifies. Against the background of a routine day, filled with back-breaking, mentally exhausting labor, the prisoners escape into a fantasy world combining myths and religiosity. Kalemba-Kasprzak poignantly notes that "this ambivalent play-acting of grandiose mythic scenes brings both hope and despair."[427] Lisa Wolford emphasizes that the actors are "performing archetypes of Western cultural mythology," but the choice of archetypes is not accidental; they are the characters from Wyspiański's drama.[428] Flaszen notes that "The ancient myths and motivations are played by the fragments of humanity on the fringes of experience to which we have been driven by our twentieth century."[429] Wyspiański's text enters Borowski's structure as if on the sly: the fragments of *Akropolis* are performed by the prisoners to kill time and boredom, and, perhaps, to cling to some external world in which myth and the sacred still matter.

However, the double layering of the texts, Borowski's and Wyspiański's, is skewed, and "the framework for identification with the mythical heroes is suspect, or even impossible. Jacob kills Laban while arguing over Rachel, who can be replaced by either a pipe or a man, while Jacob's fight with the Angel remains unresolved."[430] The myths and rituals of Wyspiański's text are replicated with a strange combination of both reverence and contempt, seriousness and disregard. Grotowski explains that in the scene of marriage between Rachel and Jacob, woman can be replaced by a pipe because in this world, it makes no difference; nothing really matters nor has any meaning: "The biblical characters who come to life in Wyspianski's original, [...] have been replaced by the lifeless fetish objects of the concentration camps: Christ is a headless rag doll; Rachel is a stove pipe; the hair of the dead is a strip of gauze or plastic – signifiers radically alienated from what they represent."[431] In one interview, Grotowski describes the role of the objects:

> A prisoner takes a piece of pipe, there is nothing else, and he begins to look for a woman. He touches the pipe as if it were a woman. To the other prisoners it becomes a reality and some of them answer, with proper text, as if the pipe were a woman. For the first prisoner it is the pipe that has answered. The marriage procession is that of tragic farce.[432]

The skewed layering of the play's structure and the pairing of the two texts are not accidental. Bettelheim recalls that "the prisoners [were forced] to hit one another, and to defile what the guards considered the prisoners' most cherished values. For instance, the prisoners were forced to curse their God, to accuse themselves of vile actions, accuse their wives of adultery and of prostitution."[433] They were to be broken, both physically and psychologically. It wasn't enough to kill them. The Nazis wanted to destroy their humanity, any sense of their human dignity; there was to be no meaning in their lives and death. They were to die not even like animals, whose death is inscribed in the cycle of nature's destruction. No, the Nazis' victims were to die like worms, crushed pointlessly under the shoe of a psychopathic child. Borowski's stories capture both the absurdity and banality of evil; but what Grotowski calls a "tragic farce," for Borowski was something else, a "tragic cynicism," a deep, profound awareness of one's implication in the unbearable. If farce implies distancing from the evil, with some degree of autonomy, cynicism suggests complete integration, dissolution of the self into a world with no values. In postwar Poland, many Auschwitz survivors were writing wartime memoirs, but it was Borowski's story that Grotowski chose as a framework for Wyspiański's drama. To understand his choice and its cultural and stylistic implications, one needs to know more about life in Auschwitz, and about Borowski and his writing.

Chapter 13

AGAINST HEROICS

Borowski is often considered one of the most tragic figures in Poland's Columbus 20 generation. In Miłosz's book-length essay *The Captive Mind*, Borowski is presented as one of the "captive" types.[434] Borowski is Beta, the unhappy lover who survives Auschwitz and becomes zealously entangled in the Soviet regime, believing wholeheartedly that it is the only way to protect humanity from fascism. Disappointed and disillusioned, realizing he has become a part of the regime he sought to fight, Beta takes his own life. Like Beta, Borowski survived Auschwitz and eventually reunited with his fiancée Maria, who survived the women's camp. During their stay at Auschwitz, Maria was seriously ill and Borowski repeatedly risked his own life to smuggle medicine, food, and his letters to her. After the war, Borowski stayed at various prisoner camps, searching for Maria. He eventually found her in a Swedish hospital and they both returned to Poland. This was the time when Soviets began using the fear of fascism as their primary propaganda tactic, and Borowski, like many intellectuals who survived the war, came to sympathize with the Soviet regime.[435] His former colleagues instantly accused him of betrayal and, once his stories were published, of distorting the reality of camp life and writing "amoral" prose.[436]

Borowski wrote about Auschwitz with nonchalant distance. There is none of Elie Wiesel's moral outrage or Primo Levi's philosophical outrage in his writing.[437] Raymonde Temkine describes Borowski's work as "one of the most gripping novels that an escapee from the fields of death ever consecrated to the hell in which he lived and because of which Borowski finally died, committing suicide some years after his liberation."[438] Borowski describes daily life in Auschwitz in a casual, deadpan tone, embedding himself completely in its reality: there are no heroes here. The line between victim and perpetrator blurs, and survival means acceptance and normalization of horror. No one is without guilt, and Borowski implicates himself as much as anyone else. Andrzej Wirth, in the *Polish Review* (1967), notes that "In the Auschwitz cycle the narrators […][are] […] victim[s] collaborating in crime. Within the system of extermination he [finds] a comparatively comfortable position of a mediator between victims and their tormentors and plays this role with relish."[439] After his stories were published, many readers confused Borowski the man with his literary alter-ego, and accused him of perpetrating the acts his alter-ego commits. Actual witness accounts contradict Borowski's story.[440] He was reportedly one of the rare few who retained their human impulses, regularly helping his fellow inmates. For example, Borowski gave up his job as an Auschwitz orderly, a privileged position in the camp's hierarchy. Although the post offered a greater chance of survival, Borowski felt obliged to "share the common lot of the other prisoners."[441] Eventually, the lack of heroics in Borowski's writing ran counter to both communist propaganda and the long-standing national mythology, as Wirth writes: "Borowski's conscious anti-heroism displayed in his attitude to the occupation and the concentration camps represents a ruthless revision of the romantic sentimental myth then prevalent in Polish literature."[442] Thus, Borowski became the subject of criticism from both camps: the regime and the opposition. Both communists and Catholics accused him of nihilism, decadence, "cynicism, moral indifference and uncontrollable 'moral insanity.'"[443] For Borowski, though, sheer survival was enough to implicate the survivors, and he challenged them to tell the truth:

> The first duty of Auschwitzers is to make clear just what a camp is [...] But let them not forget that the reader will unfailingly ask: But how did it happen that you survived? [...] Tell, then, how you bought places in the hospital, easy posts, how you shoved the 'Mussulmans' [prisoners who had lost the will to live] into the oven, how you bought women, men, what you did in the barracks, unloading the transport s[...] tell about the daily life of the camp [...] But write that you, you were the ones who did this. That a portion of the sad fame of Auschwitz belongs to you as well.[444]

Through his Auschwitz experience, Borowski came to believe that the human being is a fundamentally cruel and merciless creature, capable, with a slight shift in circumstances, of the most appalling acts,[445] and his writing, with its normalization of camp ethics, makes this realization intolerably pervasive: "One is shocked into an awareness of the unnaturalness of mass extermination because it is presented as natural."[446] The result is the "alienation effect [...] brought about by the description of unimaginable crimes as if they were something almost natural, [something normal and ordinary]."[447]

Borowski writes about Auschwitz as though he were writing about summer camp, with a chilling distance. Irving Howe, in the *New Republic*, summarizes Borowski's style: "Borowski writes in a cold, harsh, even coarse style, heavy with flaunted cynicism, and offering no reliefs of the heroic."[448] One is astounded by "his absolute refusal to strike any note of redemptive nobility."[449] Jan Kott adds, "The most terrifying thing in Borowski's stories is the icy detachment of the author."[450] Wirth points out that Borowski's "tone is one of apparent cynicism, moral indifference and uncontrollable 'moral insanity.'"[451] Bogdan Wojdowski calls it "tragic cynicism."[452] But stylistically Borowski's writing is not just a skillful use of dark humor. There is some Swiftian irony in its self-incrimination, but the style is also fully steeped in the tradition of the Polish grotesque, following the likes of Witold Gombrowicz and Bruno Schulz. It has a particularly Polish *je ne sais quoi* detachment in the face of utter despair and the overwhelming, brutal force of history. Borowski's hero is not faced with any moral choice simply because, to quote Wirth again, he is "*deprived of all choice*. He finds himself in a situation without a choice because every choice is base. The tragedy lies not in the necessity of choosing but in the impossibility of making a choice."[453] For Borowski's heroes, every choice is laughable.

In *Akropolis*, Grotowski transposes Borowski's writing style into theatrical language. In his interview with Margaret Croyden, Grotowski said about Auschwitz:

> It is true that in the extermination camps many who survived found solidarity. For many, this produced a sense of absolution and nobility. But if we really want to confront the Auschwitz experience, we must confront its darkest aspects: the mechanics of the camp. For instance, the air itself was limited for one. To live meant to breathe the air that another one lacked. If we want the truth, we must show Auschwitz as a giant mechanism with all its cruelty. The mechanics of the camp were arranged for a specific goal and they worked. We cannot avoid this reality. It is a choice we made: the mechanism of Auschwitz in confrontation with past values.[454]

Like Borowski, Grotowski frames the violence in the cool detachment of the mundane, the absurd and the poetic. But in theatrical space, the detachment is threefold: it is the detachment of the spectators from the actors, of the actors from their roles as prisoners, and of the prisoners from the mythical roles they reenact. Grotowski plays with three planes: the reality of spectators, the reality of the concentration camps, and the reality of Wyspiański's drama, which the prisoners reenact. There is also a fourth layer: Wyspiański's own skepticism about the national ideals of Polish martyrology, a kind of *ad absurdum*, double remove that is both ironic and quixotic in light of Auschwitz. Thus, Grotowski's *Akropolis* is not just metatheatrical; the structure of the performance is that of a Russian *matryoshka* doll – a play within the play within the play within the play – that nonetheless leaves the actors on the outside, beyond any of the structural frames, in a reality untouched by text, context, or historical memory. The distancing is accomplished by the textual framing, the setting of the audience, the acting and the structure of the play.

Chapter 14
REPRESENTING THE UNREPRESENTABLE

In "Essay on Cultural Criticism and Society" (1949), Theodore Adorno puts forth a dramatic thesis: "to write a poem after Auschwitz is barbaric."[455] Adorno's statement implies that the experience of Auschwitz altered our relationship to language. In a way, Adorno argues, the Holocaust leaves us speechless. Following Adorno, artists, writers, poets, painters and filmmakers, as well as literary critics, have struggled with the issue of representation: how, if at all, should the Holocaust be represented? What does representing it mean if every representation is connected to the European project of Enlightenment, the very idea of humanism, its failure and aftermath? Among other things, the Holocaust reduced death from a unique experience that defines our humanity to mass production. Jean Améry, for example, argues that Auschwitz altered the European aesthetic of death and dying. After the Holocaust, death could no longer be seen through the prism of art:

> The first result was always the total collapse of the *esthetic* view of death. What I am saying is familiar. The intellectual, and especially the intellectual of German education and culture, bears this esthetic view of death within him. It was his legacy from the distant past, at the very latest from the time of German romanticism. It can be more or less characterized by the names Novalis, Schopenhauer, Wagner, and Thomas Mann. For death in its literary, philosophic, or musical form there was no place in Auschwitz. No bridge led from death in Auschwitz to *Death in Venice*. Every poetic evocation of death became intolerable, whether it was Hesse's *Dear Brother Death* or that of Rilke, who sang: "Oh Lord, give each his own death." The esthetic view of death had revealed itself to the intellectual as part of an esthetic mode of life; where the latter had been all but forgotten, the former was nothing but an elegant trifle.[456]

How to aestheticize Auschwitz, and to what ends? A significant number of scholars and writers agree with Adorno and "view the Holocaust as virtually unrepresentable in language."[457] Some, such as Claude Lanzmann, suggest that trying to represent, or even to understand, the Shoah is in itself an act of "obscenity." The Shoah is beyond human understanding: "There is an absolute obscenity in the very project of understanding," Lanzmann famously claimed.[458] Others, such as Michael Bernstein, wonder whether anything "about human nature or values can be learned from a situation in extremis except the virtual tautology that extreme pressure brings out extreme and extremely diverse behavior."[459] Bernstein argues that,

> because so much of our culture is still strongly bound to the belief that the truth lies in the extreme moments which "ordinary bourgeois life" covers over and that it is only at the (appropriately named) "cutting edge" of the unthinkable that the most valuable insights remain hidden, it has become possible, by a truly grotesque inversion, to interpret the ruthlessness of the Shoah as offering the most authentic – because most horrendous – image of the underlying reality of our world.[460]

Thus, in representing the Holocaust, Bernstein implies, one runs into the risk of sensationalizing it without revealing anything profound about the human condition.

When faced with the decision of how to commemorate Auschwitz, a committee formed by former prisoners, under the leadership of Tadeusz Wąsowicz, decided to simply leave the site as it was – as no artistic representation, no work of art, seemed adequate, seemed able to capture the horror of the place.[461] When Grotowski chose Borowski's stories to frame his interpretation of *Akropolis*, he was faced with the same problem of representing the Holocaust, which dominated postwar literary discourse. But in this respect, theatre is even more problematic than film or literature: how does one represent "a reality that is too strong to be expressed theatrically?"[462] It is no accident that Polish postwar theatre generally avoided the topic and that, with the exception of the 1949 drama *Germans* (a collection of moral vignettes by Leon Kruczkowski about "ordinary" Germans and their mindless, self-interested collaboration with the Nazi regime) and Szajna's 1965 adaptation of *Empty Field*, there were no major plays that dealt directly with either the war or the Holocaust. When in 1962 Grotowski tackled the subject of Auschwitz, he knew the challenges that such a project entailed, but he also knew one thing for sure: he wanted "no realistic illusions."[463] The representation had to be nondirect because, as he pointed out, "We cannot play prisoners, we cannot create such images in the theatre. Any documentary film is stronger. We looked for something else. What is Auschwitz? Is it something we could play today? Auschwitz is a world which functions inside us. In the performance the SS men were not visible, only prisoners."[464] In many ways, Grotowski's solution was simple; he used the same strategy that Borowski used in literature.

> Grotowski submitted the facts of Auschwitz itself to the tests of mockery and blasphemy. His prisoners of the death camp were pitiful yet somehow beyond pity; they were simply there – an objective fact for the audience to ponder. They were hardly the noble victims our culture has raised nearly to a level of sainthood. Rather, they were human beings simply confronted with the ultimate in inhumanity. Like the unsentimentalized characters in the death-camp stories of Tadeusz Borowski, Grotowski's actors presented figures submitted to "the din of an extreme world" [...] who had cracked and become living dead.[465]

In the introduction to MacTaggart's recording of the play, Peter Brook argues that Grotowski was able to actually capture the spirit of the concentration camp:

> The horror that is at root of the very notion of [a] concentration camp actually emerged. *Akropolis* has something of the dangerous nature of a Black Mass. [...] In a Black Mass [...] there comes a point when all the showy and theatrical things, people dressed up in bizarre ways, becomes unimportant, and what actually happens is that a certain quality of pure evil actually manifests itself. [...] In *Akropolis*, by the same sincerity and mastery of deep rhythmic elements, the pulse of life in a concentration camp actually came out in the open, and I had a feeling of something truly nasty, truly repellent, and one that stops speech.
>
> At certain moments in *Akropolis*, because a nameless horror was not described, was not referred to, was not brought into our imagination as something that once happened in a place called Auschwitz, it actually was brought into being there. [...] One takes the greatest nightmare, the incomprehensible nightmare of our times, which is the concentration camp, and one is tempted to think that the greatest reality that you can find about [a] concentration camp is its own reality. In other words, a documentary approach: what can go beyond the statistics, the books that tell us the facts about the concentration camp? [...] Trying to be more artistic would have been cheap. You can't do more than that. [...] Grotowski, through *Akropolis*, proves that there is an exception that defies this rule. He has made an imaginative work of art, which at first sight has the trappings of art. [You can say:] this is art theatre, it takes place with a lot of actors doing stylized semi-balletic movements, chanting in ritualistic ways and one could say, this is turning the naked reality of a concentration camp into something inferior, an attempt of an artist to make a beautiful work of art. [But] gradually, as one enters into [Grotowski's] intentions, and into what is achieved by his actors, one sees that this is not what happens. What [the actors] are doing is making the spirit of that concentration camp live again for a moment, so in a sense, their work is more realistic, because even the statistics refer to the past, the man describing in the courtroom what happened refers to the past. Grotowski does something that no film can do. (The film also refers to the past.) He actually makes the sense of concentration camp for a moment reappear, and it is there. And you can taste it, sense it, touch it and feel it, and you can't say that doesn't exist anymore in this world, that has nothing to do with the mankind, that it is a terrible Hitlerian dream, something we mustn't forget because it happened then. There it is again. A group of men makes it come back, and it that sense, it is like a Black Mass.[466]

As mentioned earlier, when Grotowski's troupe eventually came to the USA, the director chose to perform *Akropolis* at the Washington Square Methodist Church. In the opening paragraph of his *New York Times* review, Clive Barnes wrote about the effect that such a setting evoked: "It is a room, except it isn't a room, it's a church. And inside the room, which is the concentration camp Auschwitz, are prisoners. And inside the church are spectators. The spectators are mixed up with the prisoners, so that the actors and the audience are in a constant position of emotional confrontation."[467] The choice of a church as a staging venue captured the multilayered subtleties of Grotowski's adaptation. However, Grotowski never intended to represent the concentration camp literally. On the contrary, as Flaszen puts it in his notes: "The spectacle was supposed to be a poetic paraphrase of the concentration camp. Literalness and metaphor intertwine like in a dream world."[468] Literal representation was impossible formally, conceptually and ethically.

Chapter 15

TRIP TO THE MUSEUM

During the first twenty years following World War II, in Poland, Auschwitz was a site of political and ideological manipulations, where numerous political interests intertwined, structuring and restructuring its meaning. In the early years, Auschwitz served as a symbol of national struggle, but also as a tool of Cold War propaganda, a site of antifascist/anticapitalist manifestations. It is here, for example, that the Polish government staged a demonstration against the Korean War to denounce the "imperialistic" policies of the USA. And in the 1950s, at one of the exhibits, pictures of Auschwitz prisoners were placed alongside photos of New York's homeless and caricatures of American soldiers.[469] In 1955, following Stalin's death, nationalist sentiments resurfaced: a new exhibit was opened that again stressed the national, rather than the ethnic, identities of the Auschwitz victims.[470] As a result of all the political propaganda, in the early 1960s Auschwitz became a principal destination of school groups and workplace trips, visited more often than Wawel.[471] In homage to Borowski, in 1959 Tadeusz Różewicz even wrote a short story, "Trip to the Museum" [Wycieczka do muzeum], attempting to capture the sheer horror and superficiality of those trips.[472] Using Borowski's deadpan tone, Różewicz coolly describes the stream of tourists wandering the Auschwitz site. In search of excitement, carelessly quoting sentimental clichés and propaganda slogans, they eagerly ask where they can see "the hair." The trip to the museum doesn't teach anything despite the best efforts of the guide, who weaves in "the specifics: numbers, kilograms of clothing, women's hair, thousands of shaving brushes, combs and bowls, and millions of burned bodies, with moral and philosophical aphorisms, quotations from school books, etc."[473]

As for Polish literature and cinema during this period, such media was almost solely devoted to the experience of the war, particularly the Holocaust, but often the stories were co-opted by the communist regime for its own purposes.[474] The image of the Auschwitz prisoner as a heroic fighter was actively created and promoted in the Polish media as an emblem of Polish patriotism. Many artists, whether through conviction or lack of other options, bought into that story. Marta Wróbel suggests that it wasn't so much the Soviet propaganda, but the fact that the enormity of Nazi crimes weighed heavily on Central Europe's consciousness, generating a group impulse against the overwhelming nihilism and loss of faith in fallen European civilization and in human beings in general. As a result, for example, Polish cinema of the 1940s was "sentimental, melodramatic and full of lofty national emotions."[475] Wanda Jakubowska, director of the film *Ostatni etap* [*The Last Stage*], considered by many to be one of the very first films about Auschwitz, said that she "consciously avoided showing the stages of the final degradation of men to avoid steering the movie into the realm of the macabre, thus instigating unhealthy emotions in the audience. [She preferred to focus] on the heroic rather than suffering element."[476] Jakubowska's film ends with one of the main heroines, Marta Weiss, who is about to be hanged, spurring on her fellow inmates to keep fighting back. "The Red Army is coming soon!" Marta screams, slashing her own wrists, as Soviets airplanes fly over the camp, wreaking havoc among the German guards. Jakubowka's film was treated as a national treasure by the Communist media, winning multiple awards at Polish and Eastern Bloc film festivals. Many survivors found the movie cathartic; however, many others criticized the film for presenting too clean, too polished an image of Auschwitz life: "Why didn't Jakubowska show the daily struggles over crumbs of bread? Over one spoon of soup? Why didn't she show the massive transport of the 'human mass' that needed to be processed?"[477] Outside the official media, the general perception was that "at the end of the movie, the main emotion felt by the viewer was supposed that of overwhelming gratitude to the Red Army for liberating the camp."[478] It is said that Stalin himself approved the screenplay, which reportedly brought tears to his eyes. Jakubowska herself recalls that "in one of the scenes, the Russian prisoners pray to Stalin to save them. There was truth to it, as indeed some of them viewed Stalin as their savior."[479] Wojciech Roszewski suggests that the skewed sentimental image of Auschwitz presented by Jakubowska wasn't a result of artistic or ethical miscalculation, but rather an expression of against-all-odds faith in the humanistic order of the world.[480] Regardless of the reasons, the tendency to focus on the heroic struggle rather than the suffering and degradation of the victims dominated the Polish politics and culture of the postwar era.[481] The story was slightly different with the 1948 film *Ulica graniczna* [*Border Street*] directed by Aleksander Ford. The movie tells the story of the relationships, choices and fates of a group of children and their families, Jewish and Polish, living on the Border Street. Ford's movie does not have a happy ending, as Ford wanted "the viewer who watches it to realize that the issue of fascism and racial oppression is not over."[482] Grzegorz Niziołek recalls how the censorship commission, which was to permit the film for release, had trouble with the realistic portrayal of the Holocaust, arguing that society as a whole was not ready to accept it.[483] Despite winning the 1948 Grand Prix at the Venice Film Festival, the film didn't premiere in Poland until 1949.

Unlike any other art produced in Poland at that time, however, Borowski's writing hit with an uncanny, brutal force, perhaps because rather than trying to make a point, he simply presents reality as it was, with all of its horrifying details. Jean Améry, himself an Auschwitz survivor, wrote eloquently about the horrifying isolation of an intellectual in Auschwitz:

> In Auschwitz, however, the intellectual person was isolated, thrown back entirely upon himself. Thus the problem of the confrontation of intellect and horror appeared in a more radical form and, if the expression is permitted here, in a purer form. In Auschwitz the intellect was nothing more than itself and there was no chance to apply it to a social structure, no matter how insufficient, no matter how concealed it may have been. Thus the intellectual was alone with his intellect, which was nothing other

than pure content of consciousness, and there was no social reality that could support and confirm it.[484]

Reason and moral judgment simply failed when confronted with Auschwitz's reality. To try to create a social reality that could support intellectual or ethical engagement within the reality of the camp was, for Borowski, impossible. His stories simply are, with all their twisted logic, without any external, supporting ethical structures; they are untouched by moral interpretations, testifying to the barbarism of the human race by the sheer power of their horrifying presence. For Borowski, there is no outside. To quote Michael Bernard:

> Borowski's stories – seem […] almost to remind us that the self-enclosed world of the concentration camp, with what passes for logic, cannot be circumscribed by logic at all, and that there is something outside of our capacity to describe that world, that universe, which also limits our ability to reason those things that we would otherwise believe or hope to be so.[485]

Like Lanzmann, Borowski too seems to believe that Auschwitz is beyond our comprehension. To make that which one considers beyond human reason seem natural and reasonable must have been excruciatingly painful. In many ways, Borowski's suicide, by inhaling the gas from his own oven four days after the birth of his only daughter, seems almost inevitable; unlike other survivors, who often found relief in "a process of constructing a narrative, of reconstructing a history and essentially, of re-externalizing the event,"[486] Borowski never found such comfort. He refused to compromise, even, or perhaps foremost, with himself. As Wojdowski puts it, in inscribing himself as the antihero of his stories, "Borowski was an author who had the courage to kill himself during his own lifetime."[487] Borowski's attitude, Wojdowski writes, was a form of "intellectual heroism" that perhaps "only one writer in a century is capable of."[488]

Chapter 16

BEARING THE UNBEARABLE

One of Borowski's most dramatic gestures was to break the prevailing taboo against representing the figure of the *Muselmann*, or Muslim, which stood in complete opposition to the figure of the heroic fighter persistently promoted by the Polish government.[489] "Muselmann" was an Auschwitz term for a prisoner who, in total exhaustion and despair, withdraws into himself, losing the will to survive. As Wolfgang Sofsky puts it, "The *Muselmänner* are persons destroyed, devastated, shattered wrecks strung between life and death."[490] Jean Améry writes a similar definition in his memoir: "The so-called Mussulman, as the camp language termed the prisoner who was giving up and was given up by his comrades, no longer had room in his consciousness for the contrasts good or bad, noble or base, intellectual or unintellectual. He was a staggering corpse, a bundle of physical functions in its last convulsions."[491] Aldo Capri also recalls in vivid details:

> I remember that while we were going down the stairs leading to the baths, they had us accompanied by a group of *Musselmänner*, as we later called them – mummy-men, the living dead. They made them go down the stairs with us only to show them to us, as if to say, "you'll become like them."[492]

As Agamben points out, the origins of the word *Muselmann* are unclear; however, it was a specific jargon term used in Auschwitz. In Majdanek, "the living dead were termed 'donkeys'; in Dachau they were 'cretins,' in Stutthof 'cripples,' in Mathausen 'swimmers,' in Neuengamme 'camels,' in Buchenwald 'tired sheikhs,' and in the women's camp known as Ravensbrück, Muselweiber (female Muslims) or 'trinkets.'"[493] The *Muselmänner* spent their time crouching on the ground, shivering. "Seeing them afar, one had the impression of seeing Arabs praying. This image was the origin of the term used at Auschwitz for people dying of malnutrition: Muslims."[494] The word *Muselmann* also referred to Islam in the spiritual sense:

> It is the meaning that lies at the origin of the legends concerning Islam's supposed fatalism, legends which are found in European culture starting with the Middle Ages. [...] But while the Muslim's resignation consists in the conviction that the will of Allah is at work every moment and in even the smallest events, the Musselmann of Auschwitz is defined by a loss of all will and consciousness.[495]

Kogon called them "men of unconditional fatalism."[496]

There were two stages of severe malnutrition that *Muselmänner* underwent. Ryn and Kłodzinski point out that the first stage was characterized by "weight loss, muscular asthenia, and progressive energy loss in movement." The second stage began

> when the starving individual lost a third of his normal weight. If he continued losing weight, his facial expression also changed. His gaze became cloudy and his face took on an indifferent, mechanical, sad expression. His eyes became covered by a kind of layer and seemed deeply set in his face. His skin took on a pale gray color, becoming thin and hard like paper. [...] In this phase, they became indifferent to everything happening around them. They exclude themselves from all relations to their environment. If they could still move around, they did so in slow motion, without bending their knees. They shivered since their body temperature fell below 98.7 degrees.[497]

Finally,

> In a final stage of emaciation, their skeletons were enveloped by flaccid, parchment-like sheaths of skin, edema had formed on their feet and thighs, their posterior muscles had collapsed. Their skulls seemed elongated; their noses dripped constantly, mucus running down their chins. Their eyeballs had sunk deep into their sockets; their gaze was glazed. Their limbs moved slowly, hesitantly, almost mechanically. They exuded a penetrating, acrid odor; sweat, urine, liquid feces trickled down their legs. The rags that covered their freezing frames were full of lice; their skin was covered with scabies. Most suffered from diarrhea. They ate anything they could lay their hands on – moldy bread, cheese wriggling with worms, raw bits of turnip, garbage fished from the bins.[498]

Along with the physiological changes, the *Muselmänner* underwent psychological changes as well. A number of scholars and researchers suggest that their mental condition deteriorated to the point of autism. They lost their will to live and became pure bodies:

> Their psychological and mental condition has been interpreted as a loss of the will to live, an enigmatic apathy and surrender to fate. Psychopathology talks about "affective anesthesia," an "annihilation," a radical destruction of the meaning of life. [...] The mental and psychological changes to which the Muselmann was subject were closely linked with physical emaciation and the destruction of social relations. Immiseration implies a simultaneous destruction of the social sphere, the *vita activa* and *vita mentalis*.[499]

In the end, "they were no longer the masters of their own bodies. The soma collapsed into its component parts. The unity of bodily existence was dissolved."[500] In his 1943 essay "Individual and Mass Behavior in Extreme Situations," Bruno Bettelheim chronicles his one-year stay at the two biggest concentration camps for political prisoners, Dachau and Buchenwald. One of the goals of the camp was to "break the prisoners as individuals and to change them into docile masses from which no individual or group act of resistance could arise."⁵⁰¹ The camp rules and structure aimed to change the prisoners' personalities to the point where they became objects useful for the Nazi state. The result was a form of detachment and rejection of reality that evolved as a defense mechanism. "The prisoners lived, like children, only in the immediate present; they lost the feeling for the sequence of time, they became unable to plan for the future or to give up immediate pleasure satisfactions to gain greater ones in the near future."⁵⁰² Eventually, "A feeling of utter indifference swept the prisoners. They did not care whether the guards shot them; they were indifferent to acts of torture committed by the guards. The guards had no longer any authority, the spell of fear and death was broken."⁵⁰³ In the end, they became like autistic children, completely detached from reality and enclosed in their own world. "What was external reality for the prisoner is for the autistic child his inner reality. Each ends up, though for different reasons, with a parallel experience of the world."⁵⁰⁴ Giorgio Agamben writes about the process:

> Just as autistic children totally ignored reality in order to retreat into an imaginary world, so the prisoners who became *Muselmänner* substituted delirious fantasies for the relations of causality to which they no longer paid any attention. In the semi-crossed-eyed gaze, hesitant walk, and stubborn repetitiveness and silences of Joey, Marcie, Laurie, and the other children of the school, Bettelheim sought a possible solution to the enigma that the Muselmann had confronted him with in Dachau. Nevertheless, for Bettelheim, the concept of "extreme situation" continued to imply a moral and political connotation; for him, the *Muselmann* could never be reduced to a clinical category. Because what was at stake in the extreme situation was "to remain alive and unchanged as a person" (Bettelheim 1960: 158), the *Muselmann* in some sense marked the moving threshold in which man passed into non-man and in which clinical diagnosis passed into anthropological analysis.⁵⁰⁵

The Muselmann existed outside of understanding, outside of ethics, and outside of definitions: "At times a medical figure or an ethical category, at times a political limit or an anthropological concept, the *Muselman* is an indefinite being in whom not only humanity and non-humanity, but also vegetative existence and relation, physiology and ethics, medicine and politics, and life and death continuously pass though each other."⁵⁰⁶ Agamben adds: "The *Muselman* is a limit figure of a special kind, in which not only categories such as dignity and respect but even the very idea of an ethical limit lose their meaning."⁵⁰⁷ *Muselmänner* were generally ignored by the other prisoners, as they testified to some horrible limits on survival:

> To survive as a man not as a walking corpse, as a debased and degraded but still human being, one had first and foremost to remain informed and aware of what made up one's personal point of no return, the point beyond which one would never, under any circumstances, give in to the oppressors, even if it meant risking and losing one's life. It meant being aware that if one survived at the price of overarching this point

one would be holding on to a life that had lost all meaning. It would mean surviving – not with a lowered self-respect, but without any.⁵⁰⁸

Muselmänner often invited abuse, as "[t]heir lethargy was frequently mistaken for laziness, or a form of passive resistance against the orders of the supervisors and prisoner functionaries. [...] Their apathy was provocative; it stirred the rage of their tormentors."⁵⁰⁹ The prisoners avoided them so as not to be reminded of what they themselves might become: "The prisoners wrote them off – in order not to have to write themselves off. To watch the *Muselmann* die was to preview one's own dying, a dying that was more frightening than death."⁵¹⁰ As Agamben put it: "The sight of *Muselmänner* is an absolutely new phenomenon, unbearable to human eyes."⁵¹¹ Or as Wolfgang Wolf framed it: "Like the pile of corpses, the *Muselmänner* document the total triumph of power over the human being."⁵¹²

In writing about the *Muselmänner* openly, Borowski crossed a line in Polish literature that wasn't supposed to be crossed. In 1961, a year before the premiere of *Akropolis*, a Polish medical journal finally published the first-ever account of the Auschwitz experience on the human body and mind. The journal issue, devoted solely to the figure of the *Muselmann*, broke the taboo around the issue.⁵¹³ The same year, Bogdan Wojdowski published an article on Borowski, calling him the one true and honest chronicler of his times, and suggesting that it is with Borowski's text that real analysis of Auschwitz should begin.⁵¹⁴ In fact, Wojdowski begins the article by stating definitively that contemporary literature starts with Borowski's poem "Pieśń," the very poem quoted by Grotowski on the poster for *Akropolis*.⁵¹⁵ Grzegorz Niziołek notes that both of these events had enormous effect on the public debate around Auschwitz, and both of them took place a year before Grotowski began rehearsing *Akropolis*.⁵¹⁶ In 1970, Antoni Kępiński published yet another milestone article titled "KZ-Syndrome," which summarizes his ten years of research on Auschwitz survivors and the figure of the *Muselmann*.⁵¹⁷ In his article, Kępiński makes a number of points that shed light on the long-term psychological consequences of surviving Auschwitz. First, Kępiński notes that survivors tend not to form deep, intimate bonds with anyone other than other survivors. They move through life as if wearing a mask, always detached from people and events around them: "In normal contacts with people, they prefer superficial relationships, hiding behind the mask of social conventions, unable and afraid to get close to anyone."⁵¹⁸ Having seen what the human being is capable of when the veneer of civilization is removed, they don't trust or engage with anyone who hasn't shared their experiences. The only time they come alive is when they talk about the camp:

> They come alive. Their eyes begin to sparkle as if they suddenly became younger, turned back to the times of the concentration camp. Everything becomes alive and fresh again in their memories. They can't escape the magic circle of the camp life. In this world, there are things horrible, things beyond human understanding, but there are also beautiful things, the lowest and highest of human nature: nobility and dignity alongside ruthlessness and horror. They got to know the human being from all sides and perhaps, because of that, they constantly wonder who he is.⁵¹⁹

All of the survivors, though they may suffer a myriad of different ailments, share one characteristic: they all seem to exist in a different world. The detachment, the otherness of the survivors, Kępiński suggests, comes from very particular aspects of their experience:

> First, camp provided an unbearable range of emotions: one was as much shocked by the brutality as by the unconditional kindness. Second, one underwent an extreme experience of one's psycho-physical oneness. In everyday life, a normal person can distinguish between his *psyche* and his *soma*. In the camp life, however, such differentiation became impossible. In that sense, the experience of the camp can be compared to that which psychoanalysis diagnoses as a regression to childhood when the body is the site of one's whole psychological life. The final result is descent towards autism as an attempt to establish one focal point that would mobilize one's survival instinct, permitting one to negate all mechanisms of the external reality.[520]

To a smaller or larger degree, all prisoners underwent a similar form of what Kępiński calls "camp autism." In fact, it was a necessary "adaptation" to camp life; one simply couldn't survive without it. The prisoner, Kępiński suggests, withdrew into himself and became autistic in order to survive; it was the only way he could protect his psyche: by eliminating its connection to the outside world and becoming solely body. The most extreme case of camp autism was the *Muselmann*, whose condition reached a state of "woodening," a complete internal indifference. Kępiński's article was the first significant medical assessment of the camp life, and of the psychological reality of a *Muselmann*. The article was widely read and discussed. Niziołek suggests that, besides Borowski's writings, the 1961 issue of *Przegląd Lekarski* and Kępiński's 1970 article were primary influences on Grotowski's *Akropolis*. In fact, Niziołek argues, we can effectively ask "whether Grotowski used the extreme and shocking historical situation to explore and demonstrate the validity of his methods, or *vice versa*, the extreme experience became, in fact, a basis for his anthropology."[521] There are ethical and formal issues at stake in the Niziołek question. To put it differently, in Adorno's terms, is form a function of history in *Akropolis*, or is history a function of form?

Akropolis is the exploration of the elements of the historical, psychosomatic reality of Auschwitz's Muselmann, as described by the medical studies of that time: the autistic condition experienced by the Muselmann; the psychological detachment felt by the survivors; and finally, their "coming to life" to tell their stories, much like Wyspiański's mythical figures. In many of his writings and interviews, Grotowski stresses the actor's need to search for authentic emotions: "We wish to confront our art without costly devices or commercial accoutrements. We want to work through our own impulses and instincts, through our own inner beings and through our own individual responses."[522] Part of that search is what Grotowski calls "an absolute act," the moment in which the actor becomes one with himself; his body and psyche function on the same level, thus there is no distance between psyche and soma, thought and action. In a sense, the actor's body, like the Auschwitz prisoner's, becomes the site of his whole psychic life: psyche collapsed into soma while the actor becomes one with himself. The goal of Grotowski's acting training was thus "to eliminate from the creative process the resistances and obstacles caused by one's own organism, both physical and psychic (the two forming a whole)."[523] Or, as Jennifer Levy puts it, "the absolute act" is "the crux of an actor's art through which one reveals oneself completely to another (the spectator) in a self-reflexive act that does not distinguish between character and self."[524] Eugenio Barba calls it "a non-duality in which the object does not differ from the subject. [...] This is the Perfect Wisdom, the enlightenment that can be attained through *via negativa*, denying worldly categories and phenomena to the point of denying the self and, by so doing, reaching the Void."[525] In a number of ways, in the moment of the "absolute act," the actor approaches, or rather mimics, the autistic condition of the Auschwitz *Muselmann*. Grotowski himself defines the concept of "absolute act" in his 1969 article "Theatre Versus Ritual," in which he writes that during the absolute act, the distance between thought and feeling, body and soul, collapses. This is, Grotowski writes, what happens in the final scene of *Akropolis*:

> The absolute act happens in the final scene of *Akropolis*, when the prisoners all go to the crematorium. When the absolute act takes place, then the actor, the human being, moves beyond the temporal to which we all are confined in our everyday life. The distinction between thought and feeling, body and soul, consciousness and subconsciousness, seeing and impulse, sex and reason disappears. The actor who accomplishes this becomes whole with himself. [...] He is no longer acting.[526]

However, modeling the acting process on the condition of the *Muselmänner* raises a number of ethical and theoretical questions. In reviewing the show, a number of critics touched upon some of the issues, offended by what they perceived to be an "acting exercise" serving as representation of the horrors of Auschwitz. In an open letter to Grotowski published in the *New York Times*, Eric Bentley, for example, accuses Grotowski of reducing the experience of the Holocaust to an abstract theatrical exercise: "Your version of Auschwitz in Acropolis is over-esthetic and therefore distressingly abstract. [...] In New York, thousands of whose families lost relatives in the extermination camps, you show us an Auschwitz that is of technical interest to theater students!"[527] Likewise, John Simon found the entire viewing experience "repulsive." Simon writes:

> A little reflection will show that all this, apart from its obvious ugliness, is nonsense. For if the prisoners were enacting visions that are supposed to fill them with hope and a sense of the transcendent, they would not portray them as ghastly travesties. If, on the other hand, the prisoners are jeering at their cultural and spiritual heritage, their actions become a grim charade so nihilistic that no one would bother enacting it in the shadow of death. Grotowski has confused – inadvertently or deliberately – the horrible experiences of prisoners with their hopeful fantasies; the result is not harrowing enough to convey the death-camp experience, and sheds no new light on it; even less is it able to express the persistence of human dignity and imagination, for which task it lacks poetry. [...] For me, *Akropolis* produced only one effect – of studied repulsiveness, which made the incineration of these creatures come none too soon.[528]

For Simon, Grotowski's production not only failed to communicate the experience of Auschwitz in a tangible or convincing way, but presented the camp experience in a way that made one morally queasy. Neither Bentley nor Simon, however, understood the connection between Grotowski's representation and the studies on the condition of the *Muselmänner* that pervaded Polish discourse at the time. Thus, neither one of them fully understood where their emotions came from or what is at stake in the questions they've asked. Likewise, no theatre or performance studies scholar has pursued this line of research.

To use Adorno's framework again, in Grotowski's work, the "unresolved antagonisms of reality" find their expression in the "immanent problems of form."[529] Grotowski's formal experiments with the historical psychosomatic reality of the *Muselmänner* grew not only out of the "sedimentation of history," but also out of tensions of a particular historical moment: the taboo placed on the representation of the *Muselmänner*; the post-traumatic tension within the Polish discourse at the time between contradictory political, historical and psychological impulses; and, finally, Grotowski's troupe's own experiences with camp reality (particularly Szajna's Auschwitz experience and Flaszen's internment camp experience). Grotowski was exploring the *Muselmann*'s autistic-like condition – which many Polish researchers analyzed at that time – as a way to conceptualize the acting processes, but the ethical question as to whether such treatment delimits the *Muselmänner* as a transhistorical and anthropological category remains open. In presenting a vision of history that acts as both a rupture from, and repetition of, the past, did Grotowski inadvertently void the history of its spatio-temporal location, its singularity, and, by proxy, did he deprive the very victims of their singularity? Was such a gesture an appropriate artistic means to represent man, who – in Szajna's words – "became a number"? And most importantly, was such a gesture of replicating the history revelatory, cathartic or morally objectionable? How are we to see the relationship between spectators, actors and the real victims? Who is a witness and who is a proxy witness; whose authority of experience are we to trust, and to what end?[530] If, as Adorno reminds us, form is a function of history, does it inadvertently mean that history becomes a function of form and, if so, are art's moral issues inescapable?

In addition to ethical issues, there are also formal questions involved in Grotowski's experiment. In defining his concept of "bare" life, Agamben notes that *Muselmänner* could not communicate their own internal experiences; or, to put it differently, they failed to communicate their own lives – their own self-awareness of their own existence – in way that could be read and understood by others. They remained completely enclosed in their own autistic-like reality. Modeling his acting process on the *Muselmänner*'s conditional collapse of distance between psyche and soma, did Grotowski also have to confront their failure to communicate their internal experience? Was that why he was eventually led to abandon theatrical practice in favor of paratheatrical activities in which the spectators – and therefore any need for external communication – are completely superfluous? Is there a correlation between the condition of the *Muselmann* as expressed in *Akropolis* and Grotowski's later decision to move away from theatre as fundamentally a "mediated" practice? Or, in other words, did he eventually hit the proverbial conceptual/theoretical/formal wall?

Chapter 17

THE LIVING AND THE DEAD

The ethical and formal relationships between survivors and those who had not undergone such experiences became the basis for the "detailed investigations of the actor-audience relationship."[531] Grotowski wrote that, in *Akropolis*, he consciously (and counterintuitively) mixed the actors with the spectators. As Walter Kerr put it: "He has put the audience and the actors together in an extraordinarily close relationship without insisting upon that false intimacy, that overbearing directness of contact, that marks and mars the work, say, of the Living Theatre."[532] The goal was for the spectators to remain distant, like witnesses, but also to immerse them in the theatrical reality. In an interview, Grotowski said: "In *Akropolis* the audience represents the living watching the 'dead' inmates in the nightmare dreams. Ultimately the audience must give its own answer. Will mankind retrieve its past dreams? Can it survive the greatest brutality of the century? Is there hope?"[533] Or as Flaszen put it:

> The action takes place in the entire space, among the viewers. But this time, they are not invited to participate. On the contrary, there is a total lack of contact between the actors and the viewers. They exist in two different, impenetrable worlds: those who are inducted into the final experience and those who aren't, who understand only everyday life – the dead and the living. Physical closeness only enhances psychological distance: the viewers, placed face to face, are ignored. The dead appear in dreams of the living, strange and incomprehensible. And, as in a nightmare, they surround us from all sides.[534]

Although actors and spectators intermingled, they were separated by a cognitive distance, and functioned as though inhabiting two separate worlds: the world of the living and the world of the dead.[535] Flaszen added that the viewers and actors live in

> two separate and mutually impenetrable worlds: those who have been initiated into ultimate experiences, and the outsiders who know only everyday life; the dead and the living. The physical closeness on this occasion is congenial to that strangeness: the audience, though facing the actors, are not seen by them. The dead appearing in the dreams of the living seem odd and incomprehensible. As if in a nightmare, they surround those living on all sides.[536]

Grotowski added: "Emotive osmosis is impossible – and to create the distance between the two worlds, two realities, two different human reactions, you need intermingling."[537]

The spectators

> were treated as people of another world, either as ghosts which only got in the way or as air. The actors spoke through them. The personal situation of the spectators was totally different from that of the characters. The spectators functioned both as spectators and within the context of the play. They are in the middle and at the same time they are totally irrelevant, incomprehensible to the actors – as the living cannot understand the dead.[538]

Robert Findlay described the phenomenon in greater detail:

> Perhaps it was most distressingly confrontational to an audience member that the actors' eyes looked dead. The performers looked through audience members as if the latter were glass windows. Thus, despite the intimate proximity of performers and spectators, Grotowski's actors constructed a clearly impenetrable psychological barrier between themselves and those witnessing their activities. The performers were, indeed, figures of another world, another time – they were the dead performing for the living and thus creating for the spectators an atmosphere of nightmare.[539]

In *Akropolis*, actors looked through spectators as if they were transparent. As Jennifer Kumiega noted: "There was in *Akropolis* no attempt to make direct or elicit response from the audience. There were deliberately created effects of rejection and alienation, the psychological imposition of the initiated upon the uninitiated."[540] Kumiega added: "This psychological barrier was an effective way of preventing conventional catharsis."[541] This detachment, however, was not meant to translate into a lack of emotion. On the contrary, it was a detachment intended to create emotion. Based on writings from the Thirteen Row Theatre workshops, Osiński wrote: "Grotowski simultaneously 'directs' two groups – actors and viewers, that is, he treats them as one community, integrated in theatrical time-space. […]1 The action takes place in the entire space – the 'scene-auditorium' on the border between those two groups: actors and viewers. It is here that the theatrical experience happens."[542] Although Grotowski never aimed for the cathartic experience in the Aristotelian sense of the word, he was aiming to achieve some kind of emotional reaction in the psychological empty space between the actors and the viewers. Raymonde Temkine offered one of the most chilling and poignant descriptions of that mechanism:

> The spectator would be relieved if a real contact could be established, a communion through pity; but he is rather horrified at these victims who become executioners – one need only refer again to Borowski's work to know what was necessary for survival in the camps – and who repulse or frighten more than they evoke pity. They escape, they repulse. They sneer at love; they break family ties; they ask Cassandra about the future. They turn to the Wailing Wall to get out of it. Because the spectators are the living, they find themselves rejected by the dying, who know more than they do about life and feel strongly their absolutely uncommunicable experience. So what good is it

to try to be something other than a nightmare? They take refuge in the superiority of the initiated. They cross through you and you do not exist.[543]

There are opposing views as to how successful Grotowski was in achieving his goal. Edith Oliver of the *New Yorker* was very much bothered by the lack of conventional catharsis:

> The production is an engrossing technical display, and you've never seen anything like it. And yet…Is it possible to see a play about Auschwitz without being moved? It now is possible. "The image of mankind projected on the background of the monstrous and perverted civilization of the extermination camp is meant to set in motion the poetic process of pity and horror." It does not. Fascination, yes, and a tension that responds to the almost incredible tension of the actors, and admiration for some of the most effective and powerful scenes. […] But catharsis, no.[544]

Ross Wetzsteon, on the other hand, was taken by the emotional distance and the emotions it created:

> Most striking in its stage presentation, however, was the fact that, unlike most avant-garde troupes which carry the action into the audience, the performers seemed to insist not on "breaking down the barrier between performance and audience," but on maintaining an inalienable distance. This distance-in-closeness, reminiscent of D. H. Lawrence's insistence that a membrane remain between two beings even in the most intimate relationships, exemplified the complicity-yet-alienation theme of the Auschwitz plot far more effectively than the grim audience-participation set and those agonized writhings in our laps.[545]

In a 1958 interview, Grotowski said that he was interested in the form of medieval European morality plays, which employ a kind of psychic dialogue between the audience and the performers.[546] In *Towards a Poor Theatre*, he explains how the sense of the sacred that emerges from that dialogue can be cathartic:

> The theatre, when it was still part of religion, was already theatre: it liberated the spiritual energy of the congregation or tribe by incorporating myth and profaning or rather transcending it. The spectator thus had a renewed awareness of his personal truth in the truth of the myth, and through fright and a sense of the sacred he came to catharsis.[547]

However, Grotowski's idea of the sacred didn't necessarily read in the way he intended it. Martin Gottfried, for example, wasn't convinced: "Despite some extensive rationalization on the part of Jerzy Grotowski and his literary advisors at the Theatre, *Acropolis* is a presentation of cruelty and horror without any ascension into mysterious spiritual sanctity. It is a vision of western civilization as a culture of agony, degradation and death."[548]

The actors in *Akropolis* are like ghosts who move "as in a nightmare, in which the dead haunt the living, surround them from all directions."[549] Their faces are like masks, frozen grimaces of indifference, created through the use of facial muscles only: "Each actor kept a particular facial expression, a defensive tick, without make-up. It was personal for each, but as a group it was agonizing – the image of humanity destroyed."[550] Walter Kerr noticed that in Grotowski's poor theatre, "The actor's function [...] has been entirely altered. He has ceased being an instrument and has become an object. [...] He is his own man now, and alone. He is alone with his own body, his own capacity for making sounds, his own personal stripped-down truth."[551] Even as early as 1965, Grotowski wrote extensively about this process:

> The actor provokes by provoking himself; removing the mask of everydayness, and through excess, profanation and sacrilege, attempts to approach some truth about himself. The viewer then experiences something similar. When the actor no longer demonstrates his body for the highest bidder, but frees it from any external pressures and barriers from spiritual experience, when he burns his body, makes it cease to exist, he no longer sells his body, but gives it away in sacrifice, in a redemptive gesture, approaching something sacred, holy. [...] The body should cease to exist.[552]

Thomas Richards wrote,

> The facial masks in Akropolis were not frozen, constructed for some formal reason, but rather directly linked to the inner logic of the persons in their specific circumstances. The basis [...] was the situation of Jews in Auschwitz, and particularly those who were kept alive in the camp before being exterminated. [...] [I]n extreme oppression there comes an inner way of speaking, a repeated formula [...] Each actor discovered his facial mask by repeating a specific inner formula and allowing it to sculpture his face, almost giving the wrinkles. [This is] what Stanislavski called the inner monologue.[553]

Leaving actors without makeup and specific costumes, which would have helped define their characters, Grotowski was after a very specific effect. He asked himself: "[How can we] find a human expression that remains cool, distant? We took some elements from classic pantomime, but we changed it [...] We wanted to create a struggle between structure and impulse."[554] Actors' faces were to remain frozen throughout the entire show, like the faces of *Muselmänner*.[555] Their faces were "like images of misery and acceptance, their voices [...] dehumanized, their entire manner represent[ing] humanity in such a condition of degradation that the humanity itself [...] flicker[s] like a guttering candle."[556] The actors appeared like empty shells, wreckages of their former selves, completely enclosed in their own world, indifferent to the external reality: they were like autistic children, untouched by the effect they evoked.[557] Edith Oliver was very much bothered by this effect: "I want to see masks become faces," she wrote.[558]

Thomas Quinn Curtiss vividly described the unbearable atmosphere of the performance: "One suspects that one has been locked up with a pack of dangerous lunatics as – uncomfortably near – these grotesques rush about."[559] Likewise, Flaszen wrote: "There is no hero, no character set apart from the others by his own individuality. There is only the community which is the image of the whole species in an extreme situation."[560] By bringing his actors to the brink of human awareness, Grotowski wanted to challenge the spectator to reveal something about him/herself, in the same way that the earlier morality plays challenged their spectators: "A spectator willing to be shocked into casting off the mask of life, a spectator ready to accept the attack, the *transgression* of common norms and representations, and who – thus denuded, thus disarmed, and moved by a sincerity bordering on the excessive – consents to contemplate his own personality."[561]

Chapter 18

JACOB'S BURDEN

Grotowski was very much influenced by Hasidic philosophy. He admittedly read Martin Buber's *I and Thou*, and *Gog and Magog*, and was greatly impressed by Buber's philosophy of history and religion. Buber, an Austrian-Jewish philosopher who believed in the Hasidic principle of the unification of religious practices with everyday life, was fluent in Polish, and his writings were quite popular in postwar Poland. As Karen Underhill pointed out,

> Buber's early lectures on Judaism and his and his wife Paula Buber's retellings in German of Hasidic tales appealed particularly to those who had moved away from traditional religious practice, had been educated in German, Polish, or Czech, and had joined, or hoped to join, a cosmopolitan, secular European culture as citizens of their respective countries. Estranged from their ethnic and religious traditions, and often no longer speaking a Jewish language, whether Hebrew or even Yiddish, many in this generation developed a more or less-articulated longing for a revived relationship with Jewish tradition. […] He was able to appropriate the image of the Jew as Oriental, to make it a sign of how Jews had in themselves and in their tradition a source of deep spirituality that modern European intellectuals and artists were now seeking. […] Buber describes a particular type of individual (variously described as the Oriental, the Jew, the mystic) who is open and susceptible to the perception of that authenticity and wholeness."[562]

Grotowski was particularly interested in the relationship between Hasidic and Polish messianism. He believed that Poland was a cradle of Hasidic thought, and that Hasidic philosophy influenced Mickiewicz's Romantic messianism.[563] In the same way that Wyspiański considered Poland to be rooted in the traditions of both Old and New Testaments, Grotowski saw a deep bond between Polish and Jewish cultures. Grotowski's insistent emphasis on the Jewish aspect of *Akropolis*, however, ran counter to political propaganda that constructed the image of Auschwitz as foremost a place of national Polish and universal human suffering. As Grzegorz Niziołek pointed out, Auschwitz was used by the Polish Communist Party to solidify a sense of national unity by reflecting the unprecedented national sacrifice. The proclamation of 2 July 1947 establishing the Auschwitz Museum, for example, stated that the museum's role is to "commemorate the suffering of the Polish Nation and other Nations."[564] The Jewish side of the story was woven into the general narrative about the camp. Ewa Lubowiecka, who participated in rehearsals for the first version of *Akropolis*, described the atmosphere of that period:

> Today we think differently about Auschwitz, but back then, the concentration camp was a symbol of Polish martyrology. Nobody talked about Jews. It was obvious that they also died there, but nobody knew that Auschwitz was built specifically to exterminate the Jewish people. But even back then, Grotowski already thought that this shouldn't be a secret.[565]

In many ways, by drawing attention to Jewish mythology and Jewish martyrology, Grotowski very consciously broke with the government-established national narrative.

The Jewish motive that Grotowski took from Wyspiański is particularly important. In fact, Grotowski changed the order of the second and third acts so that, in his version of *Akropolis*, Jacob's story becomes a leading narrative. The switching of the two acts has a double meaning: Jacob, the biblical patriarch who receives the blessing for himself and his people, becomes the Greek Priam lamenting the destruction of his people; he becomes the leader of the dying tribe. Jacob's mother, Rebecca, becomes the Greek Cassandra, daughter of Priam. In Greek mythology, Cassandra is given the gift of prophecy from Apollo, but because she doesn't return his passion, he curses her so that no one takes her prophecies seriously. Cassandra's knowledge and powerlessness symbolize humanity's existential tragedy, and her madness "evokes the same awe, horror and pity as do schizophrenics."[566] In *Akropolis*, Rebecca/Cassandra was played by Irena Mirecka, and in the final 1967 version of the spectacle, her figure, alongside that of Jacob/Priam, eventually came to dominate the story. Jacob was played by Zygmunt Molik, who opened the play with violin music. The image of the prisoner-musician is emblematic: an orchestra of Jewish musicians was customarily ordered to play joyous songs to accompany prisoners' marches to the gas chambers. Jacob's song, *Tango Milonga*, was an international hit before the war; it was written by two Polish-Jewish musicians, Jerzy Petersburg and Andrzej Własta. The song was often played during the selection process at Auschwitz, and eventually it came to represent a symptom of the "hate of music" that Pascal Quignard describes in his philosophical essay *La haine de la musique* (1997).[567]

Following Borowski, Grotowski also used the Jewish aspect to broach a very difficult subject: the participation of Jews in the extermination of other Jews. The heroic, fighter image of the Auschwitz prisoner that dominated Polish politics and culture in the postwar era demanded that the prisoners were always represented as a unified force against the Nazi oppressor. There was a kind of taboo around stories of collaboration between prisoners and Nazis, especially those involving Auschwitz prisoners, and in particular the *Sonderkommando*, a special unit of Jewish prisoners that assisted in the killing process. The *Sonderkommando* supervised the selection process and the gassing of the prisoners; they segregated the possessions of those killed, pulled their gold teeth and burned their bodies in the ovens. The units were also responsible for covering up the Nazis' crimes. Often, they witnessed and participated in the deaths of their loved ones. The *Sonderkommando* lived separately from other prisoners; they were allowed to take food they found in the belongings of the dead and they were often healthier and better fed than others. As witnesses to the killing machine, members of the *Sonderkommando* were perfectly aware that they would also eventually be killed; nevertheless, they agreed to their fate in hopes of a miraculous survival.[568]

Writing about *Sonderkommando* and their tragedy in his short stories, Borowski broke yet another taboo. Andrzej Wirth points out that the classical concept of tragedy, with the hero of superior moral standing succumbing to larger forces, fails when faced with the enormity and anonymity of the Holocaust. Focusing on the ambiguity between the criminal and the victim in his stories, Wirth argues Borowski creates a shattering condemnation of the Nazi system in which human beings lose any sense of their singularity, becoming a formless mass of flesh that needs to be processed and disposed of: "The de-individualization of the hero [leads to] a *de-individualization of the situation.*"[569] There is no emotional, intellectual or any other kind of relationship between the murderer and the victim. Wirth writes:

> Ultimately, murder is committed by machines: and it is led up to by countless limited decisions taken by countless people as if in the void, without any emotional or even intellectual link with the objects of crime. [...] The victims are inhuman, nondescript and either they do not represent any values or they represent negative ones like fear, degradation and willingness to collaborate with the tormentor.[570]

Following in Borowski's footsteps, Grotowski used the same artistic strategy of alienation and "de-individualization." Appropriately, Clurman's observations of *Akropolis* nearly parallel Wirth's critical take on Borowski's stories. Clurman poignantly notes:

> In *Akropolis*, the executioners and their victims become nearly identical: they are kin. [...] The prisoners themselves have been reduced to savage blasphemy. They are no longer individuals but the debris of humanity. If pity and terror are evoked in the spectator, if his moral sensibility is affected, it is through a kind of impersonal revulsion, from which he recovers as if from an anxiety dream he remembers as something intolerably spectral. One cannot normally sustain or assimilate such experience.[571]

In a similar tone, Ludwik Flaszen eloquently writes :

> Trapped at its roots, this image of the human race gives rise to horror and pity. The tragi-comedy of rotten values has been substituted for the luminous apotheosis which concluded the philosophic-historic drama of the old poet. The director has shown that suffering is both horrible and ugly. Humanity has been reduced to elemental animal reflexes. In a maudlin intimacy, murderer and victim appear as twins.
>
> All the luminous points are deliberately snuffed out in the stage presentation. The ultimate vision of hope is squashed with blasphemous irony. The play as it is presented can be interpreted as a call to the ethical memory of the spectator, to his moral unconscious. What would become of him if he were submitted to the supreme test? Would he turn into an empty human shell? Would he become the victim of those collective myths created for mutual consolation?[572]

Irving Wardle notes that "Grotowski's method is to expose classical myth to the test of modern experience and what he does here is to remove the action to a death camp and ask how far the classical idea of human dignity can withstand our latest insight into human degradation."[573] Grotowski's *Akropolis* asks spectators not just to remember the dead but also to question their own humanity, as Robert Findlay points out: "The audience members inevitably were trapped in a merciless self-confrontational questioning: under similar circumstances, what would I do? What would happen to all my polite, civilized values? Would I too crack? What would become of me?"[574] In his *New York Times* review, Clive Barnes puts it more explicitly: "Grotowski's purpose in *Akropolis* is to challenge the audience to see itself in the context of Auschwitz. To accept some iota, a scintilla of that horror, to be involved in that web of human choices and squalid heroism."[575] In such circumstances, Kalemba-Kasprzak notes, "The Aristotelian concept of catharsis escapes aesthetic categories and begins to carry psycho-social functions. Grotowski's vision of the *Akropolis*-necropolis is as much of an image of the twentieth century as it is a process of descending into the dark and unspoken realms of our subconscious."[576] And, finally, Peter Brook specifically addresses audience experience: "The experience is there to be taken or not by the people who come. The experience is for the receiver, if he wishes […] You *do not* have to participate, you *do not* have to take what is there, but few people who get there can resist."[577] Like Borowski, Grotowski challenges the spectators to tell the truth, foremost about themselves, and, like Borowski, he questions the line between victim and perpetrator. As he frames it:

> We did not show victims but the rules of the game: in order not to be a victim one must accept that the other is sacrificed. At that moment we touched something essential in the structure of the extermination camps. For example, the scene between Jacob and Angel: Prisoner "Jacob," kneeling, carries the wheelbarrow on his back and in it is the prisoner "Angel." The Angel must lie there, but Jacob will die if he does not rid himself of his burden. During the fight Jacob says the words with very beautiful, elevated melody – all of the stereotypes of the meeting between Jacob and Angel.[578]

Flaszen describes this scene in more detail:

> The struggle between Jacob and the Angel is a fight between two prisoners: one is kneeling and supports on his back a wheelbarrow in which the other lies, head down and dropping backward. The kneeling Jacob tries to shake off his burden, the Angel, who bangs his own head on the floor. In his turn the Angel tries to crush Jacob by hitting his head with his feet. But his feet hit, instead, the edge of the wheelbarrow. And Jacob struggles with all his might to control his burden. The protagonists cannot escape from each other. Each is nailed to his tool; their torture is more intense because they cannot give vent to their mounting anger. The famous scene from the Old Testament is interpreted as that of two victims torturing each other under the pressure of necessity, the anonymous power mentioned in their argument.[579]

The poetic aspect of this scene clashes with the reality of the camp; to survive, Jacob participates in the extermination of an Angel, whose body becomes a limp object to be gotten rid of.⁵⁸⁰ In another scene, Jacob kills Laban by stepping on his throat. Robert Findley describes the scene:

> Jacob comes to his uncle Laban (Cynkutis), and there is a death struggle over Laban's daughter Rachel, symbolized by the piece of plastic wrapping which earlier symbolized the hair of the corpses. The struggle is a tug of war between two prisoners over a seemingly near worthless object. Eventually the prisoner playing Jacob overcomes, pressing his foot to the throat of the prisoner playing Laban, whose eyes suddenly go dead.⁵⁸¹

The scene is short and brutal. Flaszen points out that Jacob's "relationship to Laban is not governed by patriarchal law but by the absolute demands of the right to survive."⁵⁸² Similarly, the scene between Isaac and Esau is not about the filial violence of brother against brother, but about the necessity of violence: "Esau tips the wheelbarrow so that Isaac's body rolls out into the bathtub. Esau says: 'Jacob, Jacob. I will kill Jacob my brother.'"⁵⁸³ Margaret Croyden notes that "Not only Auschwitz but the whole world appears to be a concentration camp. People kill each other swiftly and smoothly."⁵⁸⁴

Grotowski models both Jacob and Esau on Abramek, a Jewish *Sonderkommado* from one of Borowski's stories. Abramek is a Polish diminutive of the name Abraham. In the Hebrew Bible, "Abraham is imagined as the vehicle for revealing God's splendor to the world. [...] Although the Bible begins with Creation, the narrative of Western cultural origins begins with Abraham."⁵⁸⁵ In Jewish eschatology, it is through Abraham that the divine enters human society, and it is with him that God makes the covenant. Abraham is the first patriarch in the social sense as well. The story of his willingness to sacrifice Isaac, his son, as proof of his faith is the first narrative to connect death with the language of the sacred in a larger, socio-political context; it creates the fraternity of faith that demands and gives death as the price of belonging. In a way, Abraham's story provides a framework for the Western, Judeo-Christian understanding of the sacred. In Borowski's story, however, Abramek is an antithesis of the biblical Abraham. For Borowski, there are two kinds of Auschwitz prisoners, the *Muselmann* and the *lagered*. Abramek is a man *lagered*, a symbol of the complete dehumanization of the human psyche; he is a prisoner who cynically accepts and adjusts to camp life. He remains indifferent to everything that happens to him: ovens, orchestra, hangings, gas chambers. He learns the rules of survival and accepts them as given, skillfully navigating the reversed moral code of Auschwitz reality. In a deadpan voice, Borowski narrates his conversation with Abramek, who tells him about a new method of burning children's corpses. To amuse himself and make the job easier, Abramek treats the corpses like toys:

> "So, you're still alive, Abbie? And what's new with you?"
>   "Not much. Just gassed up a Czech transport."
>   "That I know. I mean personally?"

"Personally? What sort of 'personally' is there for me? The oven, the barracks, back to the oven… Have I got anybody around here? Well, if you really want to know what 'personally' – we've figured out a new way to burn people. Want to hear about it?"

I indicated polite interest.

"Well then, you take four little kids with plenty of hair on their heads, then stick the heads together and light the hair. The rest burns by itself and in no time at all the whole business is *gemacht*."[586]

"Congratulations." I said drily and with very little enthusiasm.

He burst out laughing and with a strange expression looked right into my eyes.

"Listen, doctor, here in Auschwitz we must entertain ourselves in every way we can. Otherwise, who could stand it?"[587]

In *Akropolis*, Abramek reemerges, as Grotowski includes this fragment of Borowski's story in the program notes. Complicating the issue of the victims' participation in the Holocaust, Grotowski, like Borowski, creates a world of inverted values, in which there are no moral lines to be drawn because everyone is implicated in one way or another in the mass murder. On a larger scale, *Akropolis* thus implicates the humanity (and the Polish nation) as a whole: everyone has the potential to become *lagered*.

Chapter 19

THE FINAL DESCENT

Thematically and structurally, Grotowski's theatrical vision of European civilization negates Wyspiański's: resurrection is replaced by voluntary descent into the underworld. In the final scene, the prisoners follow the headless ragdoll into the crematorium which they have just built, shutting the covers behind them. As they disappear into the hole, they sing a triumphant song. Are they oblivious? Ironic? Defying? Grotowski describes the scene as an inversion of Wyspiański's ending, a form of cruel variation on the Easter procession:

> At the end of Wyspiański's play, the Savior arrives. But in Auschwitz the savior never came for those who were killed. […] The final procession was the march to the crematorium. The prisoners took a corpse and they began to sing: "Here is our Savior." All the processions disappear into the hole during the song of triumph.[588]

Kalemba-Kasprzak notes that there is an element of "religious fervor" in the prisoners' procession, as "One by one, they disappear into the trunk that now is their coffin. Once the last prisoner is gone and the cover is shut, the voice coming from inside recites two lines from Wyspiański's text: 'they're gone – and smoke circles linger above.'"[589] The scene attempts to represent metaphorically one very specific aspect of Auschwitz life. Customarily, Germans would employ a number of strategies to prevent the creation of martyrs, whose elevated status could inspire and unite the prisoners. Bettelheim describes one such strategy:

> If a prisoner tried to protect a group, he might have been killed by a guard, but if his action came to the knowledge of the camp administration then the whole group was always more severely punished than it would have been in the first place. In this way the group came to resent the actions of its protector because it suffered under them. The protector was thus prevented from becoming a leader, or a martyr, around whom group resistance might have been formed.[590]

In *Akropolis*, the beatification process is mocked to reflect the reality of the camp. Thus, the savior, the redeemer who could inspire or lead, is nothing more than "a headless, raggedy doll rag."[591] He is denied humanity, as there is no difference between human body and trash; both are treated the same. The purpose of the camp was not just to eliminate millions of people, but to create the moral conditions that would justify that purpose. The victims had to be deprived of any sacral, any human, dimension; they had to agree to acknowledge their own status as objects. Flaszen writes that in the final scene of *Akropolis*,

> [t]he procession evokes the religious crowds of the Middle Ages, the flagellants, the haunting beggars. Theirs is the ecstasy of a religious dance. Intermittently, the procession stops and the crowd is quiet. Suddenly the silence is shattered by the devout litanies of the Singer, and the crowd answers. In a supreme ecstasy, the procession reaches the end of its peregrination. The Singer lets out a pious yell, opens a hole in the box, and crawls into it dragging after him the corpse of the Savior. The inmates follow him one by one, singing fanatically. They seem to throw themselves out of the world. When the last of the condemned men has disappeared, the lid of the box slams shut. The silence is very sudden; then after a while a calm, matter-of-fact voice is heard. It says simply, "They are gone, and the smoke rises in spirals." The joyful delirium has found its fulfillment in the crematorium. The end.[592]

In a similar tone, Jerzy Gurawski adds: "The finale had a shocking effect as the actors disappeared into a big trunk, in which they stacked themselves up according to a pre-designed plan."[593] In one of the first reviews of the show from 1963, the critic Jerzy Panasewicz notes that "The final scene, when the crowd disappears into the crematory oven, is dramatic in its final moments of silence."[594] Not everyone, however, was taken by those final moments. One Polish reviewer sarcastically commented: "The actors disappeared into a box, and we were told to leave quickly because they wouldn't come out while we're around, and they might suffocate. I would suggest that the next time, they drill some holes in the box. Better to be safe than sorry."[595] (Anticipating criticism of her criticism, however, the reviewer also rightfully points out that "Just because the subject matter is sacred, doesn't mean that the form cannot be criticized.")[596]

Robert Findlay points out that, at the end, "the audience typically does not applaud; it simply leaves the theatre."[597] Peter Brook suggests that the lack of applause can be explained by the fact that the performance appears to leave most people shell-shocked: "most people go away silent because they have seen something with their own eyes that they would rather, much rather, have heard about, and not have seen."[598] Jack Gould adds: "conventional applause at the play's end was basically a cop out. A witness does not cheer his own conclusions or discoveries."[599] Or as Robert Findlay puts it:

> One does not applaud a ritual, because one would be applauding oneself as a participant. Nor would it have been appropriate at the end to applaud the seven performers obviously cramped together under the black box in the central area. One is awed by their integrity as performers, but simply leaves without ceremony in order to facilitate their quick exit.[600]

Osiński points out that the structure of Wyspiański's *Akropolis* "is ascending, framed by and culminating in the myth of resurrection. Grotowski's version of *Akropolis*, however, is descending, framed by the myths of death and sacrifice. Such an approach makes explicit the tragi-grotesque character of Grotowski's work, and allows one to define the entire theatrical reality in the context of the absurd, suffering and irony."[601] Osiński notes that Grotowski's use of juxtaposition – resurrection versus mass graves, cathedral versus crematory ovens – is a technique known since the Middle Ages, the so-called *coincidentia oppositorum*, the aim of which is to create a larger, overarching synthesis.[602] "We looked for ways to express a tragic situation in an unsentimental way," Grotowski writes.[603] This unsentimental – some would say cruel – strategy was taken directly from Borowski.

Chapter 20

TEXTUAL TRANSPOSITIONS

Grotowski's relationship to the dramatic text is complicated; although he disregards the playwright's intentions, he also considers the text a framework of already-established, cultural signposts on which the director is to build his own version of the show. In *Towards a Poor Theatre*, Grotowski elaborates on his relationship to the classic text:

> The strength of great works really consists in their catalytic effect: they open doors for us, set in motion the machinery of our self-awareness. My encounter with the text resembles my encounter with the actor and his with me. For both producer and actor, the author's text is a sort of scalpel enabling us to open ourselves, to transcend ourselves, to find what is hidden within us and to make the act of encountering the others. […] In the theatre, if you like, the text has the same function as the myth had for the poet of ancient times.[604]

Ludwik Flaszen points out that "Grotowski took Wyspiański's drama and fashioned a montage, with fragments, scenes, and with the concentration camp. So, there was a script of sorts, although this script made no sense as a drama, because the whole structure was destroyed in it."[605] Thus, the outline of Wyspiański's drama serves as a departure point for skewed transpositions of themes, symbols and metaphors. Robert Findlay describes in detail one such transposition:

> In the original, for example, two angels bring to life the statue of a woman, telling her that she is alive and should be happy. In Grotowski's treatment, the same dialogue functioned for a cruel scene in which two prisoners, seemingly functioning as guards, mercilessly interrogated a third, pushing the prisoner back and forth between them. At other moments, the use of a single word or phrase from the original served as the central image for an entire scene. In Wyspiański's text, another angel brings to life a female statue and alludes to his own silvery braided hair ("to włosy mi brzęczą srebrzystych splotów zwojem"), and this image for Grotowski became a brief scene in which two prisoners of the death camp were seen sorting the hair of the corpses.[606]

In another essay, Flaszen notes that "the balance of the text has been somewhat altered by the deliberately obsessive repetition of certain phrases such as 'our *Akropolis*' or 'the cemetery of the tribes.' This liberty is justified because these phrases are the motifs around which the play revolves."[607] But in addition to those selective phrases from *Akropolis*, Grotowski also uses an excerpt from a letter about *Akropolis* that Wyspiański wrote to Adam Chmiel: "Reading the scenes from *Akropolis*, I am pleased with them, and I feel like each scene has behind it the lightness of the air."[608] And he uses one sentence from Zenon Parvi's 1904 review of the play: "This drama, the fantastic and symbolic dimension of which is unprecedented, reflects an image of evolving humanity, its fighting and its shepherding aspects, that nonetheless remains dominated by the power of the song."[609] In a Brechtian maneuver, the two fragments are spoken in the prologue of the production by the harp player, framing the text of *Akropolis* in its metatheatrical context.

The symbolic transposition of *Akropolis* to Auschwitz brings structural and stylistic parallels. Kalemba-Kasprzak astutely notes:

> It seems that the two authorial visions – Wyspiański and Grotowski – could not be farther apart in their conceptual and stylistic framing, but it does not mean that they are not connected. Although their structural relationship is complex, and it does not have anything to do with the traditionally understood notion of "interpretation," nonetheless, the connection is there, not only in terms of construct, but also audience reception. Both versions show "the drama of civilization," both attempt to create a global vision of European culture, both epitomize the theatrical accomplishments of their epochs. Wyspiański's play is a synthesis of the nineteenth century, opening up well-established theatrical conventions. Grotowski's production communicates – on different levels – the crisis of the twentieth century, while announcing the inevitable crisis of representation that is to dominate all future theatrical endeavors.[610]

By reframing Wyspiański's work in the context of the Holocaust, Grotowski turns it into a prism that can capture, translate and respond to a particular historical moment. The success of subsequent attempts to do so can be debated, but the fact remains that by moving Wyspiański's play from its hermetic nationalistic context into Auschwitz, an internationally recognized symbol of the twentieth century, Grotowski not only deconstructs the "unrepresentable" but also draws attention to the roles that context and form can and should play in a theatrical production. Writing in a review of the Paris production, Thomas Quinn Curtiss notes: "What Mr. Grotowski has done is not to stage the written play, but to dramatize the spirit that lies at its heart. By transferring the incidents of the script to an alien background he exposes them for fresh interpretation."[611] By offering a vision of Auschwitz that tackles some of its most sensitive taboos, Grotowski's *Akropolis* channels the historical tensions into a formal structure that simultaneously remains in a dialogue with both past and present. Wyspiański's drama serves as a symbol of the past: the dead monuments of Wyspiański's *Akropolis* once again are revived to testify and to witness.

Chapter 21
AKROPOLIS AFTER GROTOWSKI

Since Grotowski's death, there have been a number of attempts in Poland to stage *Akropolis*, either Wyspiański's or Grotowski's version. In April 2001 *Akropolis* was revived at Teatr Narodowy under the direction of Ryszard Peryt (set design by Ewa Starowieyska), who is better known as an opera director than a theatre director. Peryt's production was not successful.[612] It stressed the national and religious character of the play while adding one more character from another Wyspiański play, *Wyzwolenie* [*Liberation*]. Konrad, a hapless, Polish Romantic hero who turns into Hector, Jacob and King David, contains in himself all of the major characters, thus unifying the plot structure of the play. Wyspiański took Konrad originally from Mickiewicz's *Forefathers' Eve*, a Polish Romantic drama with undertones of the Hamletian dilemma of action versus inaction. Roman Pawłowski, writing in *Gazeta Wyborcza*, mocked Peryt's choice as an unfortunate attempt to reframe the national liberatory theology in a new European context ("Poland, the Christ of the nations, becomes Poland the Europe of the nations"), thus replicating the closed-minded pathos of the national–religious eschatology – something that, Pawłowski notes, both Wyspiański and Grotowski luckily escaped.[613] "The difference between Wyspiański's work and Peryt's," Pawłowski wrote, "is like the difference between the Bible and its radio talk-show interpretation."[614] He added:

> Peryt does not look for contradictions in Wyspiański's work; he is not interested in the dialectic of apotheosis and mockery on which Grotowski [built] his spectacle. The drama which was an attempt to sum up the European civilization in one tradition of antiquity, Judaism and Christianity, in Peryt's version becomes reduced to Polish Catholicism, a mistaken belief that all highest European values come from Poles.[615]

What you get is a theatre of the pseudo-absurd: "Peryt's spectacle claims that Troy was defended by Poles, only Homer forgot to mention it in his *Iliad*. Our man was also in the Bible; he even gave rise to one of Israel's tribes. One thing I don't understand, though, is why our hero, in the third act, like the biblical Jacob has two wives. And how does bigamy relate to proper Catholicism?"[616] Mockingly, Pawłowski added: "If Wyspiański's *Akropolis* was an attempt to bring Polish culture out of its restricted locality into the broader paradigm of European civilization, Peryt's version brings it back to its restricted national roots."[617]

In 2004, in the USA, the Wooster Group mounted a show, *The Poor Theatre: a series of simulacra*, meant as a tribute and a postmodern reenactment of Freedman's film of Grotowski's *Akropolis*. The performance consisted of members of the Wooster Group reenacting the movements of Grotowski's actors, as captured by Freedman's film, which ran in the background. *The Poor Theatre* premiered in Warsaw to mixed reviews. Some regarded it as a "faded copy," and others as a "new look at Grotowski."[618] Schechner called it an "enactment of absence," writing: "*Poor Theatre* is all about death – death of artists in and close to the Performance Group and Wooster Group [...] and the death of the avant-garde itself."[619] *Poor Theatre* makes no allusion to Holocaust, a decision which Joanna Wichowska called a "respect for trauma, which the Wooster Group cannot claim to understand."[620] Joanna Targoń noted that the Wooster Group's enactment is meant to be a parody, a form of letting go of one's past, no matter how sacred. Targón writes that, in *The Poor Theatre*, "the morbid piety and pathetic seriousness of Grotowski's disciples becomes an object of mockery, a mockery which is foremost aimed at the Wooster Group members themselves."[621]

In 2009, another adaptation of *Akropolis* was mounted in the Wrocławski Teatr Współczesny [Modern Theatre] under the direction of the Greek director Michael Marmarinos. Titled *Akropolis. Reconstrukcja* [*Akropolis Reconstruction*], the show opened on 11 December. The music was composed by Piotr Dziukeb, the set designed by Dominika Skaza, and the choreography arranged by Leszek Bzdyl. The show's aim was to combine Wyspiański's text with Grotowski's version of *Akropolis*. Marmarinos once again asked a question about the Polish Akropolis: what, and where, is it now? The interesting fact, however, is that he doesn't speak Polish; thus, his interpretation of Poland, and hence the Polish Akropolis, was that of an outsider. Marmarinos was attracted to the play because of his fascination with the "Polish soul," as he called it, the cultural and contextual complexity of Polish national identity:

> The structure of the Polish soul speaks to me. I like your way of dramatizing everything. And I like the fact that it is often a source of your problems. I like that, because it gives you a depth, an understanding of the essence of things. It also pushes you towards a very specific sense of humor, which is also very interesting. You can also see all of the contradictory forces that were at play in making the Polish soul so complex. I refer here to both the historical context and your geographic location between the two mythical powers – Russia and Germany.[622]

The press release described the spectacle as a

> unique experiment, attempting to erect a theatrical museum of our common historical memory. A museum for the twenty-first century, in which the spectator is provoked by all means available, to make a judgment as to what he sees and why he sees it in the order in which he sees it. The Greek director and Polish actors, like a group of tourists, invite their audience on a journey in search of the Polish Akropolis. This uncommon visit to the Akropolis focuses on linguistic signs but also on colors, shapes and sounds. Wyspiański's texts (from 1904) and Grotowski's spectacle (from 1962) function as tour guides. How does their experience relate to ours? We have to find out. The spectacle is not only an attempt to reconstruct "the highest place in the city-state" (such is the etymological meaning of the word "akropolis"), but foremost an attempt to define it

once again. It is an attempt to figure out what mechanisms rule our national memory and to reconstruct our national identity – group and individual diagnosis at the end of the year 2009.[623]

The first act is a staging of Wyspiański's first act: the monuments come to life. In the second act, the actors replay Grotowski's spectacle based on archival slides, projected in the background. The actors literally replicate the movements of Grotowski's actors and the fiddler plays the same song as in Grotowski's version. Marmarinos moves the second act of Wyspiański's text to the end, thus also replicating Grotowski's structure.[624] Marmarinos, however, adds additional text, his own humorous anecdotes, and other elements.[625] He said about the production: "We approach what they [Grotowski's actors] have done as a historical accomplishment. We take a certain form; let's say, we take a picture, which captures a certain moment in time, and try to return to the source of its origins to discover something deeper."[626] The production's motif was water; the set contained a pool of water, and the show opened with actors coming out of the pool. The pool was "a symbol of all cultural contexts, in which a person is submerged his whole life. The program notes also contained a short blurb: "The body of a man with the weight of 70 kg has about 45 liters of water. If he were to lose 1.5 liters a day, he would die in six days." Thus, Marmarinos seems to suggest that a man without cultural baggage, like a man without water, is doomed to disappear.[627]

The project received mixed reviews. Krzysztof Kucharski called it a "group creation reminiscent of hippie communes."[628] Kucharski also asked a rhetorical question about the contemporary relevance of such explorations: "Does anyone ever wonder about which place in Poland is the most important for him/her?"[629] Reflecting popular perception of Wyspiański's dramas as being passé, Leszek Pułka humorously noted: "My son said that if he ever wanted to punish his children, he would have them watch Wyspiański's *The Wedding*." Pułka then asked, "Is the return to *Akropolis* a return to something we haven't been missing at all?"[630] Critics were also ambivalent about the spectacle's relationship to Grotowski's production. Wojciech Sitarz flatly stated that "At the present moment, it is impossible to stage *Akropolis* and not to have it compared with Grotowski's production, which is widely acknowledged as groundbreaking."[631] Sitarz continued: "It is difficult to say who is more important for Marmarinos, Grotowski or Wyspiański. But it is not important to make this decision. Marmarinos clearly showed us that you can't treat our cultural heritage in a vacuum, because it forms us, even if we don't realize it."[632] Joanna Targoń sadly concluded that Marmarinos' spectacle is "like a spiritualistic seance that fails from the get-go because it assumes that bringing up the very ghosts it's trying to bring up is an impossible endeavor."[633] Marmarinos himself said: "I ask myself one question – what is *Akropolis* for Poles today? I think there is only one answer – *Akropolis* is Grotowski. Just like Acropolis is an important place for European history, Grotowski's *Akropolis* is an important point for the history of European Theatre."[634] Joanna Derkaczew liked the connection to Grotowski: "The spectacle is an attempt to bring fresh new perspective to Grotowski's work. If this is the strategy for modern artists tackling his legacy, there is a chance that Grotowski will cease being a museum piece with a 'don't touch' sign."[635] On the other hand, Katarzyna

Kamińska wrote that "The reconstruction never happens. The dialogue with Grotowski is unclear. Marmarinos makes a number of references to Grotowski's production, but the references do not comment on or bring anything new to Laboratory's version of *Akropolis*."[636]

Wyspiański's *Akropolis* has always been notoriously difficult to stage. By all accounts, the most recent attempts have failed to some degree to capture Wyspiański's monumental, syncretic vision. What is, however, interesting in all these attempts is that they engage not just Wyspiański's text, but also Grotowski's. In a way, following Grotowski's production of *Akropolis*, it became impossible to stage Wyspiański's version without at least acknowledging Grotowski's. Translated through the trauma of Auschwitz, Wyspiański's text as a cultural object has been deflected by Grotowski's performance. Interpretation of Wyspiański's *Akropolis* can no longer exist independent of Grotowski's interpretation; its meaning has been permanently altered.

Figure 1. *Akropolis*, 1963, dir. Jerzy Grotowski, set design by Józef Szajna – The prisoners building the crematorium. Courtesy of The Grotowski Institute.

Figure 2. Auschwitz crematorium. 2010. Photo by Bill Huston. Courtesy of the photo author.

Figure 3. *Akropolis*, 1963, dir. Jerzy Grotowski, set design by Józef Szajna – The prisoners building the crematorium. Courtesy of The Grotowski Institute.

Figure 4. Auschwitz crematorium. 2010. Photo by Bill Huston. Courtesy of the photo author.

Figure 5. *Akropolis*, 1963, dir. Jerzy Grotowski, set design by Józef Szajna – The prisoners building the crematorium. Courtesy of The Grotowski Institute.

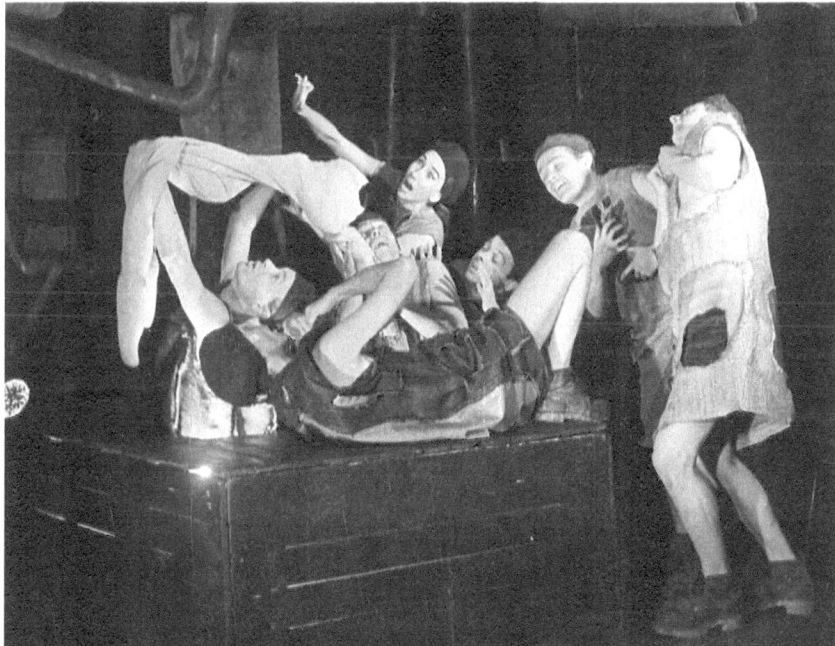

Figure 6. *Akropolis*, 1963, dir. Jerzy Grotowski, set design by Józef Szajna – The prisoners building the crematorium. Courtesy of The Grotowski Institute.

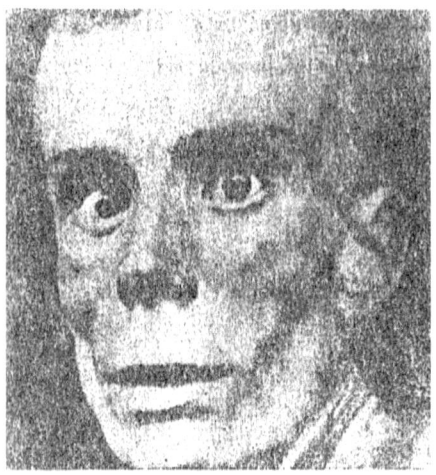

Figure 7. Characteristic dead face of the *Muselmann*, with expressive, shiny eyes. Photo reprinted from André Leroy and Maximilian Attila, *Le deportation* (Paris: Le Patriote Résistant, 1968), inside cover. Author of the photograph unknown.

Figure 8. Actors' masks for *Akropolis*, 1963. *Akropolis*, dir. Jerzy Grotowski, set design by Józef Szajna. Courtesy of The Grotowski Institute.

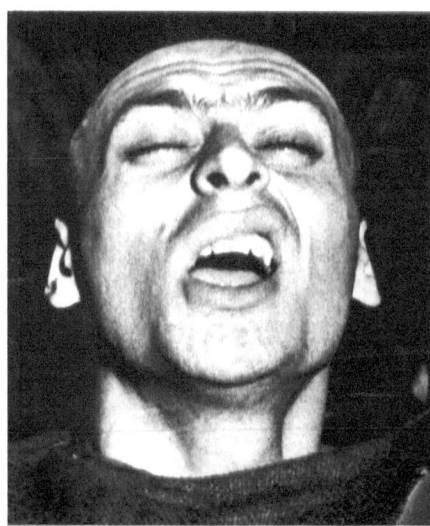

Figure 9. Actors' masks for *Akropolis*, 1963. *Akropolis*, dir. Jerzy Grotowski, set design by Józef Szajna. Courtesy of The Grotowski Institute.

Figure 10. *Akropolis*, 1963, dir. Jerzy Grotowski, set design by Józef Szajna. PBL Episode 207: Polish Lab Theater (1969). Courtesy of WNET.

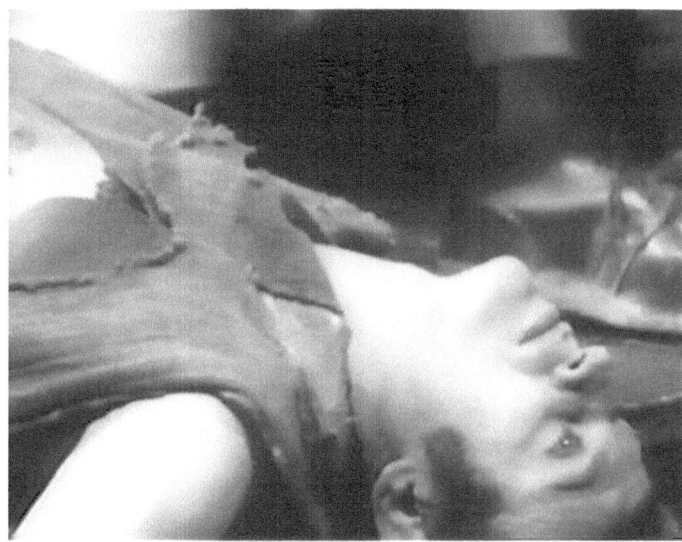

Figure 11. *Akropolis*, 1963, dir. Jerzy Grotowski, set design by Józef Szajna. PBL Episode 207: Polish Lab Theater (1969). Courtesy of WNET.

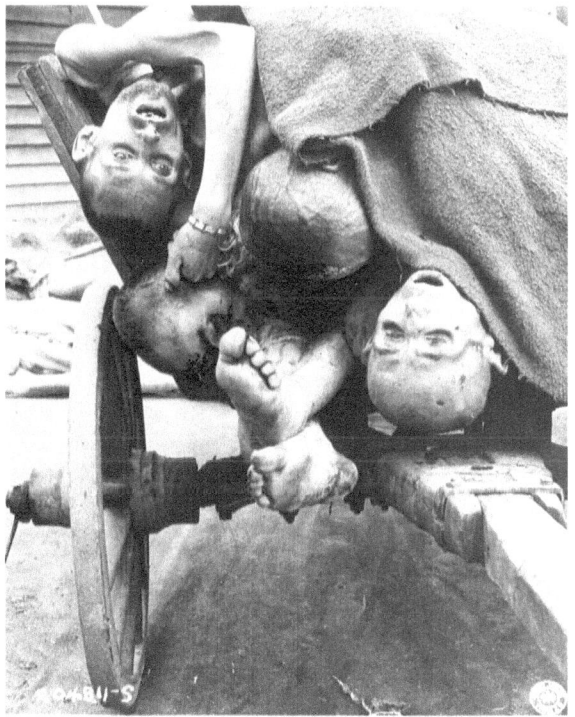

Figure 12. A cart laden with the bodies of prisoners. Saturday, 5 May 1945–Saturday, 12 May 1945. Gusen, [Upper Austria] Austria. Photo by Sam Gilbert. National Archives and Records Administration, College Park Time/Life Syndication United States Holocaust Memorial Museum. Courtesy of Bud Tullin, Harold Royall and Stephen Adalman.

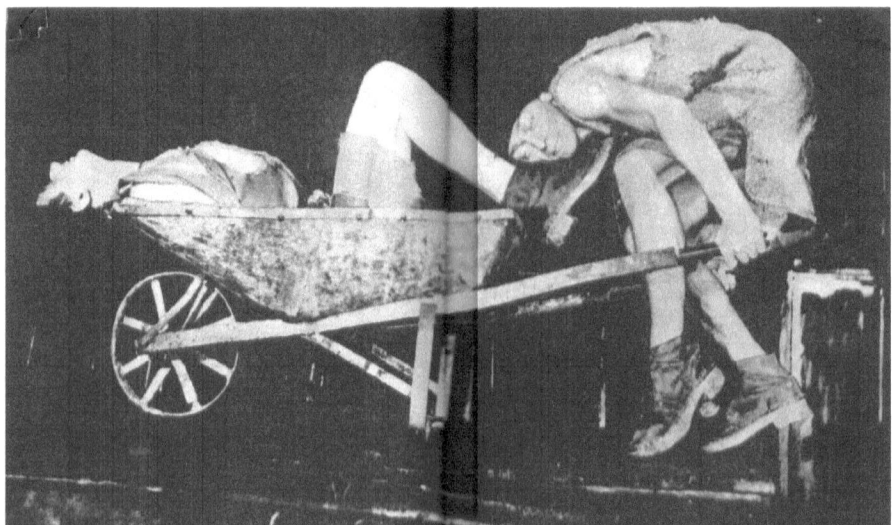

Figure 13. Corpses are piled on a cart in the Gusen concentration camp. Saturday, 5 May 1945–Thursday, 10 May 1945. Gusen, [Upper Austria] Austria. United States Holocaust Memorial Museum. Courtesy of Eugene S. Cohen.

Figure 14. *Akropolis*, 1963, dir. Jerzy Grotowski, set design by Józef Szajna. PBL Episode 207: Polish Lab Theater (1969). Courtesy of WNET.

Figure 15. Corpses at Mauthausen concentration camp. Liberation scene at Mauthausen. 1945. Mauthausen, [Upper Austria] Austria. Photo by Donald Dean. Courtesy of Center for Holocaust and Genocide Studies, University of Minnesota.

Figure 16. *I Shall Never Return*, 1988, dir. Tadeusz Kantor. Photo by Tommaso Lepera. Courtesy of the photo author.

Figure 17. View of a cart laden with the bodies of prisoners who perished in the Gusen concentration camp. Saturday, 5 May 1945–Saturday, 12 May 1945. Gusen, [Upper Austria] Austria. United States Holocaust Memorial Museum. Courtesy of Benjamin Ferencz.

Figure 18. Corpses at Auschwitz concentration camp. Courtesy of the Holocaust Research Project. <www.holocaustresearchproject.org>

Figure 19. Survivors and piles of corpses in the Gusen concentration camp. Saturday, 5 May 1945–Saturday, 10 May 1945. Gusen, [Upper Austria] Austria. United States Holocaust Memorial Museum. Courtesy of Benjamin Ferencz.

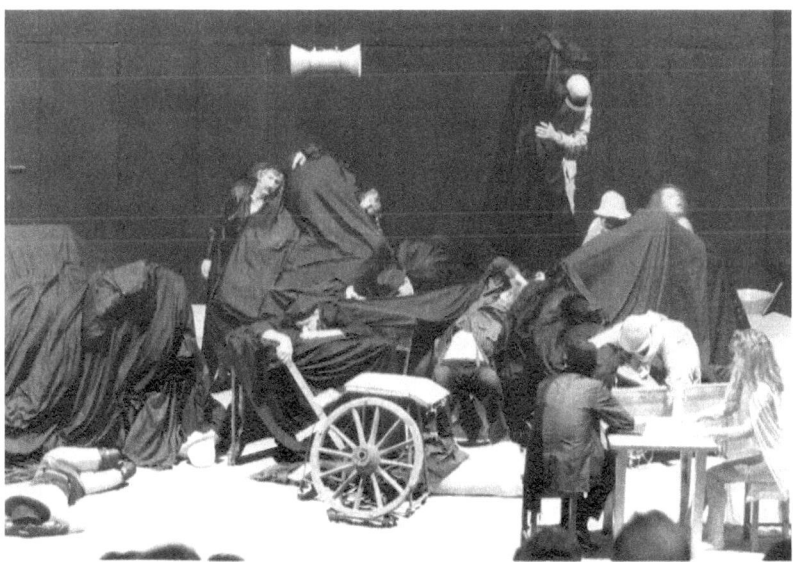

Figure 20. *I Shall Never Return*, 1988, dir. Tadeusz Kantor. Photo by Tommaso Lepera. Courtesy of the photo author.

Figure 21. *Let the Artists Die*, 1984, dir. Tadeusz Kantor – Final Emballage. The Last Work of Master Veit Stoss: Barricade. Photo by Witold Górka. Courtesy of Dorota Krakowska and Cricoteka.

Figure 22. Auschwitz, pile of suitcases left by the victims. Courtesy of Auschwitz-Birkenau Museum.

Figure 23. Emballage, 1961, drawing by Tadeusz Kantor. Courtesy of Dorota Krakowska and Cricoteka, Centre for the Documentation of the Art of Tadeusz Kantor.

Figure 24. Auschwitz, pile of suitcases left by the victims. Courtesy of Auschwitz-Birkenau Museum.

Figure 25. Jew Wanderer [Hajduk i Żyd]. Drawing from Kazimierz Władysław Wójcicki and Wincenty Smokowski, *Obrazy Starodawne* [Pictures from Olden Days] (Warsaw: G. Sennewald, 1843), 108.

Figure 26. Tadeusz Kantor's Artist Wanderer. Photo by Konrad Pollesch. Courtesy of the photo author.

Figure 27. *Kurka wodna* (*The Water Hen*; 1967). Photo by Jacek Stoklosa. Courtesy of the photo author.

Figure 28. *Kurka wodna* (*The Water Hen*; 1967). Photo by Jacek Stoklosa. Courtesy of the photo author.

Figure 29. Costume design for *Kurka wodna* (*The Water Hen*; 1967), dir. Tadeusz Kantor. Courtesy of Dorota Krakowska, and Cricoteka, Centre for the Documentation of the Art of Tadeusz Kantor.

Figure 30. Prisoners arriving at Auschwitz concentration camp. Courtesy of Auschwitz-Birkenau Museum.

Figure 31. Prisoners arriving at Auschwitz concentration camp. Courtesy of Auschwitz-Birkenau Museum.

Figure 32. Prisoners arriving at Auschwitz concentration camp. Courtesy of Auschwitz-Birkenau Museum.

Figure 33. Prisoners arriving at Auschwitz concentration camp. Courtesy of Auschwitz-Birkenau Museum.

Figure 34. Costume for Absent Old Man. *Dead Class*, 1975. Photo by Piotr Oleś. Courtesy of the photo author.

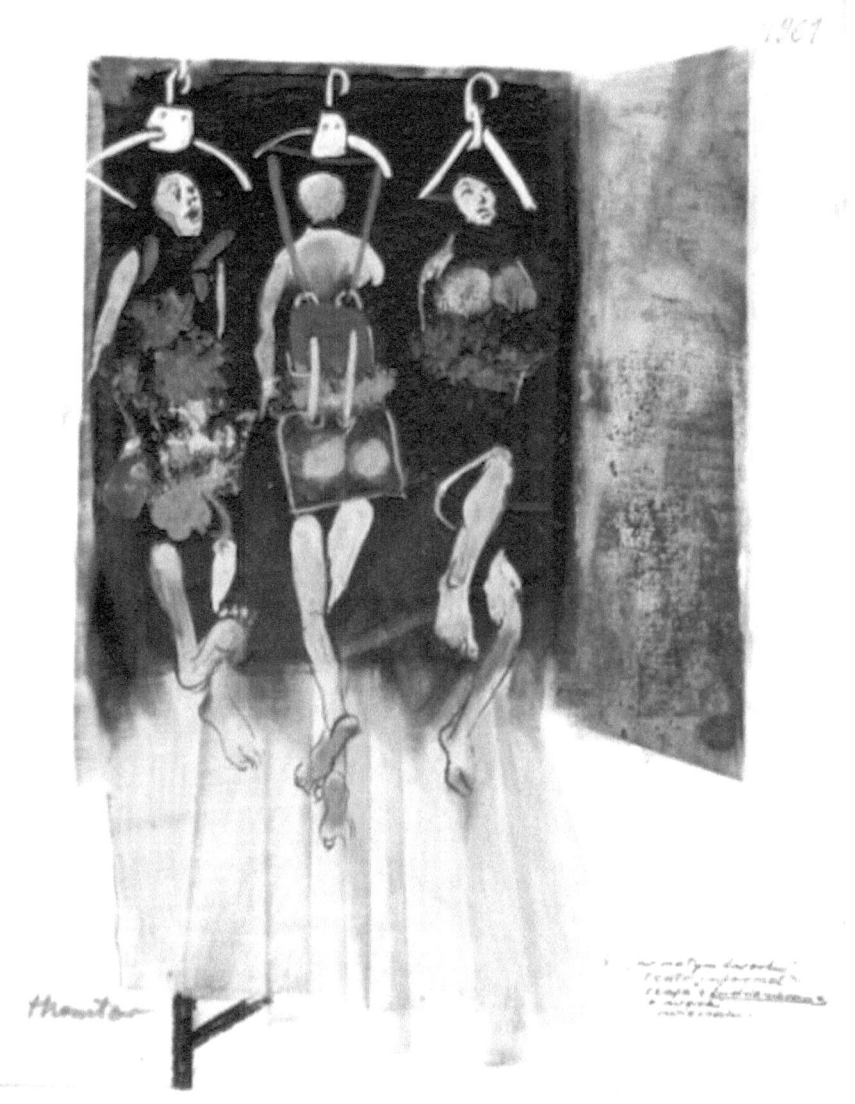

Figure 35. Design drawing for *The Country House*, 1961, dir. Tadeusz Kantor. Closet. People as Coats on the Hangers. Courtesy of Dorota Krakowska and Cricoteka, Centre for the Documentation of the Art of Tadeusz Kantor.

Figure 36. *Dainty Shapes and Hairy Apes*, 1973, dir. Tadeusz Kantor. Coatroom. Exhibit "Tadeusz Kantor od *Małego dworku* do *Umarłej klasy*" [Tadeusz Kantor: From *The Country House* to *Dead Class*], 2010. Photo by W. Rogowicz. Courtesy of the National Museum in Wrocław.

Figure 37. *Dainty Shapes and Hairy Apes*, 1973, dir. Tadeusz Kantor. Sketch. Coatroom and 40 Mendelbaums. Courtesy of Dorota Krakowska, and Cricoteka, Centre for the Documentation of the Art of Tadeusz Kantor.

Figure 38. Bruno Schulz, "The Old Age Pensioner [Self-Portrait] and the Boys." Dated before 1937. By permission of Marek Podstolski. Courtesy of the Museum of Literature, Warsaw.

Figure 39. Bruno Schulz, "The Old Age Pensioner [Self-Portrait] and the Boys on the Bench." Dated before 1937. By permission of Marek Podstolski. Courtesy of the Museum of Literature, Warsaw.

Figure 40. Bruno Schulz, "Chassids by the Well, waiting for Messiah," 1934. By permission of Marek Podstolski. Courtesy of the Museum of Literature, Warsaw.

Figure 41. *Dead Class*, 1975, dir. Tadeusz Kantor. Photo by Andrzej Lojko. Courtesy of the photo author.

Figure 42. *Dead Class*, 1975, dir. Tadeusz Kantor. Wax Figures of Children, 1989. Photo by Janusz Podlecki. Courtesy of the photo author.

Figure 43. *Dead Class*, 1975. Exhibit "Tadeusz Kantor od *Małego dworku* do *Umarłej klasy*" [Tadeusz Kantor: From *The Country House* to *Dead Class*], 2010. Photo by W. Rogowicz. Courtesy of the National Museum in Wrocław.

Figure 44. *Dead Class*, 1975. Exhibit. Ośrodek Propagandy Sztuki in Park im. H. Sienkiewicz, Łódź, Festiwalu Dialogu Czterech Kultur, 2008. Photo by Grzegorz Michałowicz. Courtesy of Polska Agencja Prasowa (PAP).

Figure 45. Senator Alben W. Barkley of Kentucky, a member of a congressional committee investigating Nazi atrocities, views the evidence firsthand at Buchenwald concentration camp. Weimar, Germany, 24 April 1945. Department of Defense. Department of the Army. Fort Leavenworth, Kansas. 18 September 1947. (Online version available through Archival Research Catalog (NAIL Control Number: NRE-338-FTL(EF)-3134(2)) at <http://arcweb.archives.gov/>. Accessed 1 August 2011.)

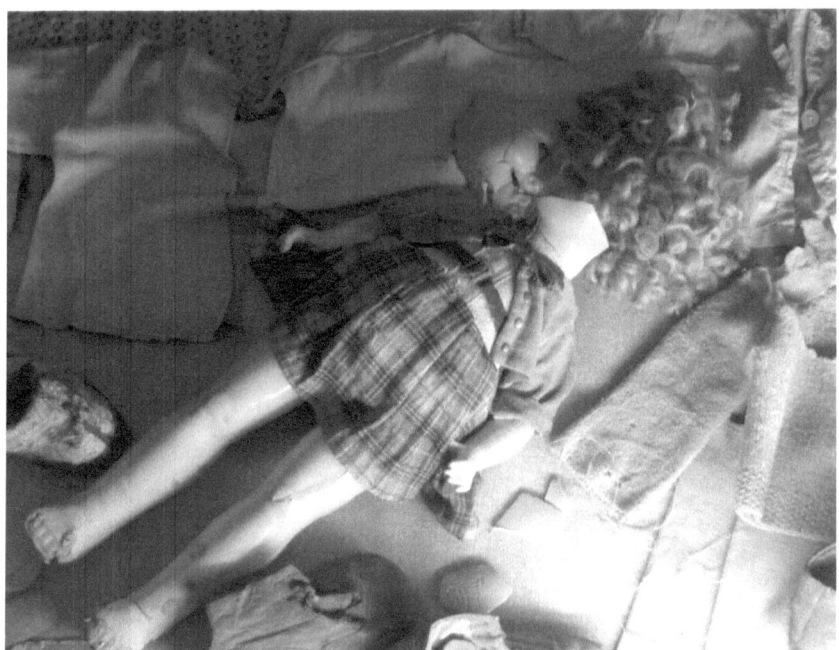

Figure 46. Objects left by the victims who died in the gas chambers. Auschwitz Museum exhibit. Photo by Bill Huston. Courtesy of the photo author.

Figure 47. Objects left by the victims who died in the gas chambers. Auschwitz Museum exhibit. Photo by Bill Huston. Courtesy of the photo author.

Figure 48. *The Dybbuk*, 1922, dir. Yevgeny Vaktangov, Moscow. The Beggars' Dance at Leah's Wedding. In the middle, as the Bride: Shoshana Avivit, who preceded Hanna Rovina in the part. Reprinted with permission of IDCPA, Tel-Aviv University and Habima Theatre.

Figure 49. *Wielopole, Wielopole*, 1980, dir. Tadeusz Kantor. Photo by Andrzej Lojko. Courtesy of the photo author.

Part II

OUR MEMORY: KANTOR'S *DEAD CLASS*

Chapter 22

TADEUSZ KANTOR: A VERY SHORT INTRODUCTION

Born in 1915 in Wielopole Skrzyńskie, a small Polish-Jewish town in Southern Poland, Tadeusz Kantor grew up in a world dominated by both Christian and Jewish mysticism. Today, in the house where Kantor was born, there is a small museum, with souvenirs from his childhood and props and drawings from his spectacles. During his childhood, every aspect of daily village existence, from birth to death, had religious ramifications that were imminently embedded within the entire sociocultural context of each congregation. The two worlds, Kantor remembers, "lived in an agreeable symbiosis," each cultivating its own traditions.[1] The synagogue and the church stood on opposite sides of the city; Jewish and Christian ceremonies were performed parallel to each other. Ruled by the cycles of their religious rituals, each community was oriented more towards sacred than earthly values. As Kantor reminisces, "beyond its everyday life, the little town was turned towards eternity."[2] The coexistence and intermingling of the two cultures, and the spiritually charged atmosphere of timelessness and mysticism they evoked, were resurrected time after time in all of Kantor's spectacles. The town – constructed like a theatrical space in which the predictable intertwined with the accidental, the grotesque with the profound, the sacred with the profane – became the framework for the juxtapositions Kantor investigated over years of theatrical experiments. Built around the everlasting oppositions between life and death, form and matter, illusion and reality, consciousness and object, Kantor's "religious dramas" attempt to simultaneously reconcile these poles and show the impossibility of doing so. Like a parallel universe belonging to neither fiction nor reality – a universe of neither form nor matter, in which characters are neither dead nor alive, neither people nor objects – Kantor's theatre forces the viewer to rethink the meaning of basic concepts.

Although spending his childhood in the enigmatic Wielopole significantly shaped his artistic vision, Kantor's theatrical vocation actually began in Cracow. While attending the Cracow Academy of Fine Arts, Kantor mounted his first production, a marionette version of Maeterlinck's *Death of Tintagiles*. His first truly avant-garde theatrical event, however, took place in 1942 during the German occupation of Poland, when he staged Wyspiański's *The Return of Odysseus* at the Cracow Underground Independent Theatre. Hans-Thies Lehman points out that, in the production, "Kantor placed the figure of the returning Odysseus at the centre of his work: a figure symbolically returning from the realm of the dead, who, as Kantor says, 'established a *precedent* and a *prototype* for all the later characters of [his] theatre.'"[3] In this staging, Kantor made his first attempt at blurring the border between fiction and reality. Staging the play in a real house ruined by bombs, Kantor relocated the audience from the fictional Ithaca it expected into the reality they wanted to escape. As Daniel Gerould puts it, *The Return of Odysseus*, "Wyspiański's dark and sinister drama[,] is interpreted as the contemporary story of a soldier-homecomer back from the war."[4] Describing the opening scene, Kantor himself writes in his production notebook:

> Wearing a muddy uniform and a helmet, Odysseus passes through the audience; very long triumphant sounds of a parade march are heard; Odysseus sits heavily on a gun-barrel, hunched over, forming a shapeless mass; it is unclear what he is…[Finally,] an actor who plays the Shepherd begins talking to Odysseus [in order to move him off the stage]. Suddenly, the spectators notice Odysseus' violent gesture and see a club hitting the Shepherd's head…[5]

As the Shepherd falls down dead, Odysseus begins his first line: "I am Odysseus, returning from Ithaca…"[6] Years later, Kantor reminisces about the production:

> Odysseus was not a Homeric hero but a figure from our day-to-day life. He was a German general in a faded overcoat coming back from his war, returning to a destroyed room on Grabowska Street in Krakow. The room itself was art. It was the first environmental art. The audience was inside a work of art; surrounded by debris, different objects such as a broken wheel, decayed wooden boards, a stolen loudspeaker which was used to broadcast Homeric odes, etc.[7]

Setting the play within the reality of the German occupation had a terrorizing effect as the audience slowly realized that the rugged soldier was actually an actor. As a real soldier, he was so much a part of the surrounding reality that his psychological and physical condition became a function of reality and hence made him invisible. Yet, as an actor playing a soldier, he belonged to fiction, and hence his condition remained foreign. It was in the moment that reality became fiction, and vice versa, that his tragedy was discovered, and the play gained the power to shock and transform. "It was then," Krzysztof Pleśniarowicz writes, "during wartime, that the 29-year-old Kantor discovered the basic idea of his theater: the principle of the impossibility of representation; the impossibility of placing a pre-existing drama, plot and character in reality."[8] In his notebook from 1944 Kantor writes: "Odysseus must return for real. It would be hypocritical to try to create the fake illusion of Ithaca."[9] The shock of discovering that the soldier was an actor completely altered the viewers' relationship with the character. Spectators no longer saw an actor playing the soldier – they saw a real soldier. As Kantor put it: "*The Return of Odysseus* established a precedent and a prototype for all the latter characters of my theater. There were many of them. The whole procession that came out of many productions and dramas – from the Realm of Fiction – were all 'dead'; all were returning to the world of the living, into our world, into the present."[10]

During the performance of *The Return of Odysseus*, Kantor placed a sign on the entrance door to the theatre saying: "You cannot enter the theater with impunity."[11]

This statement – which was literally true since, at that time, the Germans persecuted anyone involved in any sort of cultural activity – after the war became a metaphor for the emotional impact that Kantor's plays were meant to have on his audience. The viewers, Kantor claimed, enter the theatre with the conviction of their own untouchability; they "[treat] theatrical work as a spectacle, which can be viewed without moral consequences."[12] Belonging to the sphere of illusion, theatrical space projects a sense of security; beyond the limits of the stage, the viewer remains protected from fictional tragedy. For Kantor, however, the goal of theatre is "to bring the theatrical production to a point of tension at which only one step separates drama from life, the actor from the spectator."[13] In other words, Kantor wanted to create conditions that would destroy the viewer's superficial sense of security by making theatre a place of authentic emotions. *The Return of Odysseus* raised a number of questions that eventually became essential for Kantor's future experiments with space, text, actors and objects.

Tracing the history of Kantor's theatre is not easy. He is known to have meticulously constructed a narrative of his work by changing the chronology of events. Jacek Stokłosa, the graphic designer and photographer for Cricot 2, recalls philosophically:

> Kantor followed the rule "the ends justify the means." He had to follow this rule to get anything done in the Poland of that time; sometimes, though, his actions were just ridiculous. He would date his drawing – made in sharpie – as 1945! They didn't have sharpies back then! He would write the manifestos to his plays after they premiered and backdate them. He would take photographs I took for him and mark and date them in some strange order that only he understood. But I remembered exactly when I took them. For that reason, I think, scholars who study Kantor have a hard nut to crack. Maybe trying to verify all his dates is not a worthwhile endeavor; maybe it's just best to leave things in the order he left them in…[14]

Indeed, prior to the 1975 premiere of *Dead Class*, Kantor's archives are a maze. We can only speculate as to which experiment influenced which spectacle, or which spectacle influenced which theory.

After World War II, Kantor largely focused on painting and stage design, mainly for the Stary Teatr im. Heleny Modrzejewskiej [Helena Modrzejewska Old Theatre] in Cracow. In 1947, he traveled to Paris, where he encountered contemporary avant-garde paintings. At that time, Polish art was beginning to be dominated by socialist realism, and any nonrepresentational art was considered dissident. Kantor's instant fascination with abstraction was spurred mainly by his rebellious streak and his rascally contempt for authority. Unfortunately, with the communist regime's increased pressure on artists, Kantor abandoned painting for nearly eight years. In 1955, on the verge of the October Thaw, Kantor decided to exhibit all his postwar paintings, but he no longer considered himself just a painter. That same year, 1955, he founded Cricot 2 and became a theatre director.

Over the next forty years, Cricot 2 was Kantor's life's work and the source of his greatest masterpieces. The name Cricot 2, an anagram of the Polish words meaning "it's a circus," references the interwar, avant-garde theatre named Cricot, where Witkacy's plays were performed (hence the "2" in Cricot 2). It also alludes to the informal, circus-like character of Kantor's theatre.[15] Influenced by expressionism, Kantor perceived theatre as a process in which the final product remains unknown and comes forth through the development of the artist's emotions and ideas. Through its experiments with actors, objects and space, Cricot 2 underwent a progressive transformation, from the Autonomous Theatre (1956) through the Informel Theatre (1960–62), the Zero Theatre (1962–1964), the Happening Theatre (1967), the Impossible Theatre (1971–72), and, the final period, the Theatre of Death (1975–1990). Each stage in the development of Cricot 2 was announced in a manifesto written by Kantor in order to crystallize his newly evolved idea.

For its first 20 years, Cricot 2 would "play with Witkacy" – that is, it would loosely adapt Witkiewicz's plays, transforming them into happenings and what Kantor called *cricotages*. Kantor was fascinated by Witkacy, and he adapted nearly all of Witkacy's plays: *Mątwa* [*The Cuttlefish*] (1956), *W małym dworku* [*Country House*] (1961), *Wariat i zakonnica* [*Madman and the Nun*] (1963), *Kurka wodna* [*The Water Hen*] (1967), *Nadobnisie i Koczkodany* [*Dainty Shapes and Hairy Apes*] (1973). In subsequent productions, Kantor moved further and further from Witkacy's texts towards abstract representations of Witkacy's theoretical concepts. Święcicki points out that "During Kantor's period of 'playing with Witkacy,' the action taking place onstage couldn't be just an illustration of the text. What's more, there could be no relationship whatsoever between the fiction of the drama and staged action."[16] Following the avant-garde tradition of the Great Reform Kantor, like Grotowski, considered theatre an autonomous work of art, with text serving mainly as one of its components, not a stencil on which to build theatrical reality. As Kantor once put it: "The theatre is not a place for the reproduction of literature. The theatre is an autonomous art."[17] Witkiewicz's texts, because of their absurd and fantastic structure, provide the kind of raw material that Kantor was seeking. In 1978 the American critic Charles Edelman, fascinated by Kantor's theatre, poignantly described Kantor's relationship with Witkiewicz:

> Kantor has been one of the leading figures of the Polish avant-garde since 1965, and is unusual in that he has only six productions to his credit since then. With the exception of one work, they have all been either productions of Witkiewicz's plays, or based on his notes and theories. Cricot 2 is formed anew for each production, which is rehearsed exhaustively, toured, and then abandoned, never to be revived. Kantor is unique in his dedication to exploring Witkiewicz's world of nonsense and madmen, and then bringing it to life as a momentary but unforgettable vision of chaos.[18]

Daniel Gerould points out that, by embracing Witkiewicz's theatre of the absurd, Kantor made as much an aesthetic gesture as a political one, rebelling against the prevailing trend of socialist realism. Cricot 2's first adaptation of Witkiewicz's *The Cuttlefish*, "a play about art and totalitarianism, [was] the first post-war performance of any of Witkacy's work, until then banned from the stage, and an important step in liberating the Polish theatre from the constraints of Stalinism."[19] In this production Kantor also introduced many ideas that would later become his signature style, among them the "silent movie" sequences. He also began to experiment with the notion of chance and unpredictability, staging situations in which actors and viewers had to respond spontaneously. Put in a cage, tied up or left alone, the actors were provoked to create their own stage directions. Asked to interact with machines they did not know how to operate, they were cut off from any external points of reference and had to devise their own chain of events, conditions and situations that often countered the text or even completely deviated from it.[20] Kantor called this period of theatrical activity the Informel Theatre. These activities marked the beginning of serious theatrical experiments that eventually grew into full-fledged masterpieces of the Theatre of Death.

The next step, however, was the Zero Theatre. Seeking real experiences, Kantor placed actors in situations in which they would not only act spontaneously but also experience genuine feelings. Reducing their movements to an absolute minimum, the Zero Theatre transferred the action towards the actors' emotions. In 1961, in a production of Witkiewicz's play *Country House*, Kantor "hung" a group of actors on clothes hangers and stuffed them into a closet. As Agata Miklaszewska describes the scene: "Humiliated and helpless in the face of the piles of rags and bulging bags surrounding them on all sides, the actors themselves became more and more similar to torpid objects – unnecessary, worn out, stored pointlessly in a rickety wardrobe."[21]

In the 1963 production of *Madman and the Nun*, Kantor went even further, reducing the action to an absolute minimum, but also reducing the role of the dramatic text. To quote Daniel Gerould: "CRICOT 2 presents Witkacy's *Madman and the Nun* as Theatre Zero, in which there is radical destruction of the dramatic text and the stage creates its own reality. The play itself is not performed, but the text is quoted, commented upon, and repeated."[22] Following the Polish directing tradition, like Grotowski, Kantor was interested in text only insofar as it provided raw material for theatrical fiction.

Daniel Gerould rightly notes that "As a stage designer and as a pioneer in the development of Happenings, Kantor has exerted a profound influence on the new generation of theatre artists in Poland."[23] In 1965, Kantor mounted Poland's first-ever happenings – *Cricotage* and *Linia Podziału* [*The Dividing Line*]. Two years later, he staged the famous *List* [*The Letter*] and *Panoramiczny happening morski* [*Panoramic Sea Happening*]. In *The Letter*, two postmen carry an enormous letter across the city. In *Panoramic Sea Happening*, Kantor, the maestro, "conducts" the ocean waves, with beachgoers behind him watching the "symphony." Starting in 1957 with the Informel Theatre, Kantor also organized a series of happenings called emballages, during which "living human insides" are packaged, single or together, in rolls of paper or other materials.[24] Kantor writes about the concept:

> The space of the stage was filled out with an immense black sack. All the actors and a few supernumeraries were inside it. Only their heads and hands were visible through the narrow openings in the sack. The heads would come closer and then move apart. The heads moved and "lived" independently of the actors – they were autonomous… All the conflicts taking place inside would be transmitted through and intensified by subtle movements and different tensions in the external surface of that emballage.[25]

The point of an emballage was to transform a human body in a way that caused it to lose all of its natural abilities. Constrained, the body has to discover new ways of functioning. In dis-emballages, on the contrary, Kantor "undressed" his subjects, searching for deeper knowledge of their psyches via the hidden crannies of their pockets. Kantor saw clothing, like emballage, as another form of wrapping. Covering the human body, it covers the deepest human mysteries. "I am interested in clothing," – Kantor writes – "Especially from underneath. When you unstitch lining. Which is a sort of bottom. Closer to the body. You uncover successive layers of clothing like layers of skin."[26] The dis-emballages, like the *Anatomy Lesson Based on Rembrandt*, for example, during which Kantor dissects the clothes of his actors, became a way to uncover "the true uncontaminated side of individuality."[27] In his script for the happening, Kantor notes: "Just make the first step/ take the courage to separate something,/ and you discover suddenly the new inner world."[28] The purpose of both the emballages and dis-emballages was to analyze the relationship between man – a living being – and his physical, objective reality, which was represented by the package he was wrapped in, be it paper or clothing.

In 1972, Kantor staged another play by Witkacy, *Nadobnisie i koczkodany* [*Dainty Shapes and Hairy Apes*], which incorporated a number of elements from the happenings. In *Dainty Shapes and Hairy Apes*, Kantor traps his audience in a nightmarish coatroom in which viewers are brutally stripped of their coats. Part of the audience, "The 40 Mandelbaums," are selected and given Jewish *tallits* (shawls) and beards. The Mendelbaums are closed in a separate room that looks like a large shower. As Daniel Gerould describes it: "Actors and objects are fused […] The 40 Mandelbaums, who are found in Witkacy's text, are costumed as Hasidic Jews with beards, black hats, and gowns, and are played by members of the audience, coached by the head Mandelbaum (a Cricot actor). Voices for the Mandelbaums heard over a loudspeaker are based on the cries of Jews approaching the gas chambers."[29] Grzegorz Niziołek points out that, in *Dainty Shapes and Hairy Apes*, "Kantor brings us into the very center of the death machine."[30] Ironically, not one Polish reviewer mentioned the meaning of those scenes. It might have been a political issue, since censorship would most likely remove any Holocaust references. But, as Niziołek points out, it was also as if the audience and reviewers were unable to consciously decipher the play's clues. Stunned by the sheer impact of the production, they were unable to discern its direct visual references, and could only absorb them subconsciously. As Niziołek puts it: "Kantor wanted to make a literal reading of those associations difficult. He purposely created a work which would allude to the Holocaust and resonate on a subconscious level."[31] Arthur Sandauer was the only Polish critic to even mention the Holocaust, but even he couldn't do it directly, writing only that the image of man in this spectacle is horrifying and that the experience of viewing it is cruel.[32] Eventually, the coatroom from *Dainty Shapes and Hairy Ages* became a springboard for Kantor's *Dead Class*. Kantor spoke about that transition:

> When in 1972 we began working on *Dainty Shapes and Hairy Apes*, it was supposed to be called *The Grammar Lesson, or The 40 Mandelbaums*. We made school benches, but it

didn't work, so we moved everything to the coatroom. Now, I return to the benches again. [...] Emptiness leads to death. In this spectacle, *Dead Class*, death becomes art. This reality that I am building here – it is a return to school, the benches with people touched by death, some of them already gone...[33]

In Happening Theatre, Kantor also introduced the idea of a Journey, creating "the Eternal Wanderers," an array of figures carrying "parcels, bags, suitcases, rucksacks." In 1963, Kantor wrote about the idea:

I met a clochard who, according to the motto of his clan, *omnia mea mecum porto*, was a monstrous camel; he was wearing many coats, blankets, sheets, hats, a mass of bags of all kinds, large and small, bulged, hanging on ropes and bands... He propped himself with a small old ladder. Isolated from the outer world by an enormously thick layer, consolidated inside, he was an integral whole.[34]

Zuzanna Jastrzębska describes Kantor's traveler: "A man with baggage carries with him his history, his destiny, his hopes. The journey is a constant state of waiting. Waiting for the train, which didn't come, waiting for his dreams to come true."[35] Kantor's traveler is modeled on the iconic image of the Jew Wanderer, an image deeply embedded in the Polish psyche since the Poles' own diaspora of the Romantic era. The Eternal Wanderers carry all they own with them: they are forever homeless, seeking a lost arcadia. The image of people driven from their homes, forced to carry their possessions with them, evokes memories of Jews transported to concentration camps. On account of *The Water Hen* production, Kantor wrote: "In my theatre, *The Water Hen*, there was a troupe of wanderers with exaggerated attributes of travel – in their tiresome, hallucinatory 'march' they became a living message of that idea: of the concept of adventure, the unknown and surprising, the flow of time, extermination [...]."[36] During World War II, the image of the displaced wander, carrying with him his entire life, was part of everyday reality; the Auschwitz archives have preserved thousands of photos of prisoners being loaded and unloaded from the trains, bending under the heavy weight of their bags and suitcases, which were stuffed with essentials but also with family souvenirs and treasures. Customarily, the Germans instructed Jews destined for camps to bring their valuables with them. The Jews were gassed when they arrived at the camps; their things were sorted, catalogued and shipped to Germany, to be distributed among Germans.

Separated from the reality of life and enclosed within his own world, Kantor's clochard eventually became the model for the bio-object, a theatrical form in which an actor is connected with an object. Eventually, Kantor utilized this form to assemble his famous "Human Nature Preserve," a gallery of bio-objects: actors and objects connected in strange, lugubrious symbiosis. Figures such as the Man With a Suitcase, the Man With a Sack and Its Unknown Contents, the Woman Drowned in a Bathtub, the Man With His Door, the Helpless Man with a Table, reappeared time after time in subsequent productions, becoming the essential elements of Kantor's theatre, evolving to signify questions of life and death, reality and illusion. During these early experiments, prior to *Dead Class*, Kantor's theatre probed the relationship between form and history. In fact, in Kantor's theatre, to bring up Adorno's thesis, the form was always a function of history. The concept of the bio-object was developed as a metaphorical representation of a man displaced, sentenced to eternal homelessness, modeled on a centuries-old image, and reinforced by recent history. During the period of Zero Theatre, actors stuffed into tight closet spaces represented prisoners on their way to Auschwitz, stuffed like cattle into the windowless boxcars. Kantor devised various torture and death machines that recall the torture machines used by Nazi doctors in concentration camps for "experiments" on human subjects. In *Madman and the Nun*, the Annihilation Machine traps the actors and makes their escape impossible. In *The Water Hen*, the Torture Machine elongates the body of a mannequin to a grotesque size. In a 1973 adaptation of Witkiewicz's *Dainty Shapes and Hairy Apes*, a huge rat trap machine installed on a hospital trolley is designed to snap at any moment, breaking the transported patient's neck. A full-size human skeleton, attached to the gurney where the IV usually is, watches over the grisly procedure. Is he the Angel of Death, Doctor Mengele? Kantor's various torture machines and elaborate stage props resemble those found in Auschwitz that were famously used for both medical and aesthetic purposes. Detaching these signposts from their Auschwitz context, Kantor gives them new aesthetic meanings, yet – perhaps on some subconscious level – they remain familiar to his audiences, both simultaneously recognizable and unrecognizable, visible and invisible. Buried perhaps by the post-traumatic history into the furthest recesses of memory, they still somehow remain oddly familiar, oddly recognizable. Although no Polish critic ever mentioned Auschwitz when responding to Kantor's *Dead Class*, not one of them ever claimed that his images, tableaux or formal gestures were too difficult, too abstract, too incomprehensible or too artificial to understand. They understood – so it seems – without knowing or understanding what it was that they understood.

Chapter 23

DEAD CLASS: THE MAKING OF THE LEGEND

The premiere of *Dead Class* inaugurated the period of the Theatre of Death. Kantor was no longer experimenting as he had before. *Dead Class* was his first fully grown, fully mature work, standing on its own, testifying to Kantor's fully developed, individual aesthetic as a director and an artist. *Dead Class* was followed by four major plays, which all belong to Kantor's Theatre of Death: *Wielopole, Wielopole* (1980), *Let the Artists Die* (1984), *I Shall Never Return* (1988), and *Today Is My Birthday* (1991). The less well-known cricotages, *Where Are the Snows of Yesterday* (1982) and *Machine of Love and Death* (1987), also belong to this period, but are generally not considered fully developed productions.

Rehearsals for *Dead Class* began, according to various accounts, in December 1974 or January 1975.[37] Fragments of the spectacle were first performed on 11 September 1975, for the 140 participants of the XI Congress of the International Association of Art Critics (AICA).[38] Its official premiere, however, took place on 15 November 1975, at the Krzysztofory Gallery in Cracow.[39] Located underground in a Gothic basement off Cracow's Main Market Square, the Krzysztofory Gallery had a somber, tomblike atmosphere ideally suited to Kantor's play. The cast of the first version of the play included Maria Stangret-Kantor as the Woman with a Mechanical Cradle, Zofia Kalińska as the Somnambulist Prostitute, Andrzej Wełmiński as the Man with the Bicycle, Maria Górecka as the Woman Behind the Window, Bogdan Grzybowicz as the Stranger, Mira Rychlicka as the Man in the Toilet, Zbigniew Bednarczyk as the Old Man Exhibitionist, Roman Siwulak as the Old Man Pederast, Wojciech Łodyński as a Regular Old Man, Lika Krasicka as the Absent Old Man from the First Bench, Jan Książek as an Absent Old Man from the Last Bench, Zbigniew Gostomski as the Man Passing Obituaries, and Kazimierz Mikulski as the Beadle in Past Perfect. Later on, the Beadle would be played by Krzysztof Miklaszewski. For years, Stanisław Rychlicki played the Cleaning Lady, though in 1989, in Paris, Leszek Stangret had to fill the role.[40] This first version of the play featured both Kantor's amateur actors and professional actors from the Cracow Bagatela Theatre. Eventually, Kantor assembled an unusual group of people: professional actors, amateur actors, artists, painters, one authentic countess, two world-class diamond polishers and one locksmith. Once in a while a foreigner would leave his or her life and family behind to join Kantor's circus.[41]

According to Andrzej Wełmiński, the first version of *Dead Class* "was more offensive, less comical, very dramatic, and stronger, deeper than the next version" of the play.[42] It was this first version that was recorded by Andrzej Wajda and his Zespół X in 1976. At that time, Wajda was filming *Man of Marble* in Cracow, and so one evening he went over to the Krzysztofory Gallery to see *Dead Class*. Many years later he recalled: "It was fantastic, such a small, corner theatre. The actors act as if for themselves, allowing us in merely to watch. The second time I came in, Kantor was surprised that one director wanted to see another director's show. I told him I wanted to film *Dead Class*. It took us three days to film it – that was the length of our break from filming *Man of Marble*."[43] Barbara Kazimierczyk noted that "*Dead Class* fascinated Wajda to the point that he wanted, as he said, to see it from the inside out. He wanted to know how it developed, how it reached its climax. Wajda spoke openly about how difficult it was to capture the ephemeral atmosphere of Kantor's spectacle. He said: 'I thought that even if I couldn't capture the whole spectacle on film, I might at least be able to show Kantor at work within it.'"[44] In 1977, *Dialog*, one of Poland's leading journals, conducted a discussion on Kantor. Participants included Konstanty Puzyna, Andrzej Wajda and Tadeusz Różewicz. During the discussion, Wajda vividly described the challenge of filming *Dead Class*: "Kantor waits for his audience. He stands and waits, 'Here I am, I am ready, and here are my actors. We are waiting. Please, come in, sit down.' To replicate it with the camera is difficult. I only show two shots: Kantor and the audience. It could mean something or it could mean nothing."[45] Kazimierczyk noted that Wajda's main challenge was to remain on the margins of the artistic process:

> Wajda knew from the beginning that his film wouldn't replicate the show exactly. The camera only records the result, not the process. [...] Wajda's film, as if standing at a crossroads, reveals production artifices to film viewers that would not be apparent to an audience viewing the play in a theatrical setting. [...] During the promenade scene – when the old people all go outside for the springtime walk – we are reminded of the surrealistic sequences from Buñuel's *Le Chien Andalou* or *Discreet Charm of Bourgeoisie*. We regret that Wajda didn't do his own separate film version of *Dead Class*, and that he remained at the level of an archivist. Why did Wajda, as an artist, suddenly grow so humble?[46]

Echoing this sentiment, Zuzanna Jastrzębska argued that the differences between Kantor's theatrical production of *Dead Class* and Wajda's film version are insurmountable, and that it would have been more interesting if Wajda had done his own version of *Dead Class*, rather than trying to record Kantor's:

> [Wajda's version] is a work of art in its own right, different from Kantor's, and might be considered confrontational even by those who saw the theatrical production of *Dead Class*. Kantor believes that the camera revealed too many of the spectacle's secrets. In the movie, everything looks literal; there are no illusions. In theatre, illusion is fundamental. It has to be, so that the viewer can weave in his own visions and memories, reconstruct his own history.[47]

The legend goes that, while they were filming in Kazimierz – a former Jewish quarter of Cracow, the prewar "Slavic Jerusalem"[48] – Kantor asked for a pile of trash to be placed on the set. Apparently, that morning he'd seen a passing truck carrying a load of beige cardboard that seemed perfect for that purpose. Wajda spent the day searching for the truck and eventually tracked it down. Then, when Kantor saw the desired pile of cardboard, he asked to have it hosed with water, but after the pile was hosed down, he decided that it needed to be burned first because the water hadn't softened the edges of the cardboard sufficiently. So, Wajda ordered someone to bring gasoline and burn the cardboard.[49] Watching Wajda's film, one easily notices the pieces of cardboard debris flying around the Woman with a Mechanical Cradle. She rocks back and forth in a tragic stupor to the rhythm of the two wooden balls thudding inside the otherwise empty cradle, vacantly singing Kaddish to her nonexistent child, small and desolate on the street of the postapocalyptic landscape of Cracow's Kazimierz. Many years later, Kantor disowned Wajda's film version precisely because of this scene. In fact, Miklaszewski notes that "Kantor totally rejected Andrzej Wajda's decision, in his film version of *Dead Class* (1979), to move three of the play's scenes into the Jewish–Cracow landscape. Whenever he could, Kantor would criticize Wajda's film."[50] For Kantor, Wajda's vision was too literal, too palpable, too representational.[51] Kantor was never interested in representation. Instead he chose to reflect, as Frank Rich put it, "the agony and hardware of official humiliation," to represent the effects of "torture and mass murder without attempting to simulate unspeakable crimes that defy representation on stage."[52] Perhaps Kantor was right – the scene, in all its cinematic brilliance, testifies more to Wajda's than to Kantor's aesthetic – although its tragic, forsaken despair does capture the broken, ravaged spirit of their generation. Despite Kantor's protests, however, Wajda's recording of *Dead Class* was shown on Polish television a number of times, becoming a recognizable staple of his work and, ironically, turning him into a household name.

After a string of performances in Cracow, in 1976 *Dead Class* went on a six-week *tourneé* of England, Wales and Scotland, where it won a number of awards at the Edinburgh Festival. Upon the troupe's 1977 return to Poland, Kantor fired the Bagatela Theatre actors. The reported reason was Kantor's growing need for flexibility in the face of an increasingly intense schedule of international travel. Despite the scepticism of naysayers, Kantor managed to mount a second version of the play. The second version lacked some characters from the first version, including The Regular Old Man, and the Stranger. It also lacked the grammar-lesson scene. But Kantor added a number of new characters: the Twins, the World War I Soldier, and the Girl.[53] This second version, recorded by Denis Bablet (CNRS, Le Centre national de la recherche scientifique), was distributed worldwide, helping to fuel Kantor's international success.[54] However, neither Wajda's nor Bablet's version is considered a complete recording of the show. There are two other, also incomplete, recordings of *Dead Class* available at Cricoteka. In December 2005, to celebrate the 13th anniversary of the show's premiere, Polish television showed a film montaged from all four recordings. To this day, many Polish critics lament the lack of one complete recording of the show.[55]

Chapter 24

DEAD CLASS IN POLAND

Dead Class was received in Poland as a symbolic closing of contemporary art's neo-avant-garde era.[56] Many critics wondered at its subtle density of meanings, pointing out the self-contained nature of Kantor's work. Roman Szydłowski wrote: "There [was] not one empty space in this spectacle."[57] In a similar tone, in his essay "Signs and Significations in the Theatre of Tadeusz Kantor," Olgierd Jędrzejczyk argued that every visual and aural element of Kantor's spectacle was embedded with a multiplicity of signs, each one as important as all the others:

> Even the most vulgar gestures seem like an innocent child's play, in this pageant of our fears about our future, about passing the exam of life. In Kantor's theatre, every sign signifies, every gesture has meaning, every flicker of light is important. If you were to take away even one idea, there would be nothing left: everything is perfectly integrated. That is why Kantor and his troupe pay special attention to every, even the most minuscule, detail, even in the midst of what appears to be chaos. That's how they created a show that's like a poem in which great passions compete with lugubrious observations about the world.[58]

Many critics noted that assigning all of the spectacle's elements – actors, props, music, set, text – equal footing creates a natural tension between them, with each element struggling to assert its dominance, or at least to reclaim a traditional sequence of meaning. Magdalena Hniedziewicz pointed out that "The tension is built anew each time. It is created not by artificial tricks, but by the structure of the work itself."[59] Krzysztof Pleśniarowicz explained that phenomenon in a review aptly titled "The Symbolism of *Dead Class*," writing:

> The symbolic rule of equivalencies in *Dead Class* creates tension between universal meanings and universal values. This goal is accomplished by the degradation of traditional aesthetic conventions: unraveling the fascinating and revolting ambiguity of the actor's condition, depriving an actor of his dignity, equating him with an object, a representative of "Reality of the Lowest Rank," […] "reality degraded."[60]

Kantor's concept of the "Reality of the Lowest Rank" was borrowed from Bruno Schulz, but it also echoes the Nazi philosophy that equates a human being with an object, treating human bodies as a raw mass that is to be either disposed of or processed into useful objects (soap, mattresses, paper weights, lamp shades, etc.).

In Poland, *Dead Class* received unanimously glowing reviews. In 1976, at the Wrocław Theatre Festival, *Dead Class* was called "a hit, a true work of art, unlike all other attempts at mechanical 'artisanship.'"[61] In fact, the spectacle was not part of the juried festival, but an independent production. The jury, however, was so taken by the performance that they decided to break the rules and award it a special jury prize.[62] The jury praised *Dead Class* as a one-of-a-kind work that captures the twentieth century's spirit and aesthetic. Many critics stressed the impact that the spectacle had on its audiences. Henryk Bieniewicz summarizes that sentiment:

> Kantor's *Dead Class* needs to be placed in a completely different category. Its extraordinary acting, visual and sound effects all resonate with aesthetic, philosophical, and emotional implications. It's an exceptional spectacle, both cruel and profoundly humanistic, enamoring with the breath of the author's invention and deeply touching. No one can remain indifferent – and I think that no one was left indifferent – after seeing it.[63]

In a similar tone, Marta Fik notes the impact of *Dead Class*, writing: "*Dead Class* is Kantor's most interesting work yet, and one of the most interesting theatrical events of recent times [...] *Dead Class* remains in one's memory; in fact, you may never forget some of its images."[64] Likewise, Puzyna melancholically points out that "There is something in *Dead Class* that you remember it even months after seeing it."[65] Tadeusz Różewicz called *Dead Class* "one of a kind," adding: "For me as a man – not a playwright or author, but as a human being – the most precious surprise was joy and wonder."[66] Andrzej Wajda bluntly stated that "As a spectacle, [*Dead Class*] is integral."[67] He added, "It's the most moving spectacle I have ever seen in Polish theatre."[68] Wajda also pointed out that *Dead Class* received unanimous acclaim: "Everyone agrees that *Dead Class* is a brilliant work of art. This spectacle does not have any enemies. I have yet to meet anyone untouched by it, who would say either that it's not a brilliant work of art, Kantor's best work, or something that goes beyond what we are accustomed to seeing in the theatre."[69] Konstanty Puzyna, too, wondered: "What strange enthusiasms we've bestowed – and continue to bestow – on *Dead Class*. We're always disagreeing and arguing with each other, different in our tastes and likes – and then, suddenly, we're in unanimous agreement about this spectacle. Full national – and even international – accord."[70] In fact, in Poland, even those who previously dismissed Kantor's forays into avant-garde art couldn't hide their admiration for *Dead Class*. Maciej Szybist and Józef Kelera, who admitted they didn't like or follow Kantor's art, were so taken by *Dead Class* that, upon seeing it, Kelera tried to immediately shame the city of Cracow into filming Kantor's work,[71] and Szybist enthusiastically wrote: "Kantor accomplished something unbelievable: He managed to say something about our world in the language of the avant-garde art."[72]

The Polish reception of *Dead Class* stands in stark contrast to that accorded Grotowski's *Akropolis*. In fact, many Polish critics reviewing *Dead Class* often described it in terms of what it was not, while simultaneously making subtle jabs at the "other" self-proclaimed theatrical avant-garde. Although very much in disagreement in terms of their interpretations of Kantor's strategies *vis-à-vis* his audience, both Jan Kłossowicz and Wiesław Borowski, for example, agreed about what Kantor is not; he is not Grotowski. Their analysis has a strong, though implicit, criticism of Grotowski's aesthetics. While praising *Dead Class*, Kłossowicz sarcastically writes:

> [*Dead Class*] is formulated on a simple, old-fashioned formula of a relationship between the author and his viewer. There are none of the hip new tricks of the "open" theatre, none of its group work, improvisation or audience participation. The viewers sit in a normal position, on the chairs, and the actors act on a free space in front of them, creating what is called a scene. [...] In this composition, nothing is said directly. The viewer is not asked to do anything, nor is he bored by personal stories or attacked by the clichés of "feelings," "nudity," "copulation," or "agitation."[73]

In a similar vein, though offering quite a different version of Kantor's relationship to his audience, Wiesław Borowski explains that

> [Kantor] comes in contact with the void, not with his audience. He creates a genuine sense of that void, without relying on tricks like contemplation or meditation, all favorites of the pseudo-avant-garde groups that – with grim literalness – move programmatically, and irreversibly, away from the theatre.[74]

In many ways, Kantor is embraced by Poles because he fits the Polish sociocultural framework; unlike Grotowski, Kantor is not perceived as someone incapable of ironic self-reflection. It was as if there was, suddenly, an avant-garde that doesn't embarrass with overt emotional exhibitionism, that speaks about Poland's tragic history with both humility and dignity, but also with a touch of self-irony. Andrzej Górny, for example, praised Kantor's "distance from himself." In *Dead Class*, Górny writes, Kantor suggests that "the artist should not rebel, but be humble and mocking, distanced from himself as a creative being."[75] Unlike Grotowski, who treated himself and his work with "holy pomposity," Kantor offers a profoundly disturbing vision of the world while at the same time trying to capture, against all odds and better judgement, a sense of ironic self-detachment. In 2009, Krystian Lupa, who always speaks of Kantor with reverence, explained that difference between Kantor and Grotowski, in not-so-subtle terms:

> [Unlike Grotowski's work], I absorbed Tadeusz Kantor's spectacle with fascination. He wasn't pretending to offer me something, like some kind of angel of wisdom. On the contrary, he came to theatre with all of his ebullient energy, revealing all of his human smallness. He had no deep strategy to con me, the viewer, to sell me his goods, his art, as something better than what it was in reality.[76]

Chapter 25

THE POLISH HISTORY LESSON

There are many reasons Poles were enraptured by *Dead Class*: Kantor captured the trauma of the national history in a way that was profound but indirect, tragic but dignified, sorrowful but also fatalistically ironic. Jan Kłossowicz poignantly claimed: "I don't know who today could write a play with equal emotional impact, a play as rich in meaning and as immersed in its own cultural tradition."[77] And in 1986, eleven years after the premiere of *Dead Class*, Jerzy Tymicki wrote that Kantor's "*The Dead Class* (1975) and *Wielopole, Wielopole* (1980) were wise, deep, spectacular and expressive performances – perfect alloys of traditional and modern art, theatre and happenings, the culture of the exterminated Polish Jews, and national archetypes."[78] Indeed, *Dead Class* alludes to Polish history via a multilayered theatrical structure, embedded within the broader literary and artistic canon. First, it refers to the early twentieth century, right before World War I, which many consider something of a magical period in Polish history. During the last few years leading up to World War I, Poles were quietly and with trepidation anticipating the eventual victory; they were both hopeful and resigned. Hopeful because the approaching conflict offered the possibility of independence, and resigned because, judging by the past failed attempts, the war could also mean yet another pointless bloodbath. The writers of that period permitted themselves to use the national struggle solely as a background for a personal *Bildungsroman*, very much in the style of those written by other European modernist authors. In that sense, *Dead Class* can be read as a form of metaphorical, postmortem *Bildungstheater* for that generation.

Recalling the experience that inspired *Dead Class*, Kantor vividly described the memory of an encounter with an old, abandoned classroom from that era:

> It was 1971 or 72. In a small village. Like a hamlet. One street. Small, poor, squat huts. And an even poorer school. It was summer, vacation time. The school was empty and abandoned. It had only one classroom. You could peek into it through two small, dusty windows that were placed low, right above the road. It seemed as if the school had sunk below street level. I glued my face to the glass. I was a small boy again, sitting in a small, poor class, in a bench marked by pocket knives, browsing with my ink-stained fingers the pages of my first book. The wooden floor was pale from constant washing. It was perfect for the bare feet of country boys. Whitewashed walls, with paint peeling on the bottom, and a black cross on the wall. Today, I know that there by the window something important happened to me. I made a certain discovery. Somehow, very clearly, I came to feel the EXISTENCE OF MEMORY.[79]

Dead Class fills that old classroom with the "debris of dusty school books" and ghastly old men and women, wearing macabre, pale blue makeup and school uniforms.[80] Some of them carry objects, something from their childhoods – a bicycle, a cradle, a window – and all of them carry wax, child-size mannequins symbolizing the lost alter egos of their childhoods. There is the Somnambulist Prostitute, the Woman with a Mechanical Cradle, the Woman Behind the Window, the Old Man with a Bicycle, the Old Man from the Lavatory, the Old Man Pederast, the Paralytics and the Repeat-A-Year Hourglass Bearer. The Beadle from the Good Old Days and "Charlady-Death keep up their good work as the spiritual guardians of these 'eternal pupils.'"[81] The pupils are ghosts, memories of what they could have been. *Dead Class* recalls their childhood, but primarily refers to their tragic adolescence – the Holocaust and World War II, during which most of them perished. This is the second historical layer of the production; the ghosts now return to their childhood classroom, looking back on their lives, their beginnings and ends each marked by these two historical benchmarks. Roman Szydłowski, one of Kantor's childhood friends, poignantly comments on *Dead Class*'s relationship to World War II:

> For me, *Dead Class* was homage to the victims of war and fascism. When I first saw it, I couldn't shake the impression that *Dead Class* is the gymnasium that both of us, Kantor and myself, attended. Those were our friends who died during World War II, who return now to our classroom, carrying with them their tragic lives. Watching it today, I also see it through the prism of modern times. Kantor's Theatre of Death is also a warning against the apocalypse of war. It's no longer just a look back; it's also a vision of the theatre of death that we would face in our future.[82]

Wacław Janicki, one of Kantor's Twins, expresses a similar sentiment: "*Dead Class* does not have a dramatic structure; it is a record of a personal, existential experience."[83] Elżbieta Morawiec calls the show an "Apocalypse According to Kantor."[84] And Maciej Szybist writes that "this spectacle is a confession: personal, dramatic and lyrical."[85] Combining the two historical periods, World War I and World War II, onto a photographic memory plate,[86] Kantor creates a spatial moment that traps his generation in one post-traumatic gesture; walking in circles, the pupils cannot escape their lives and deaths: they cannot undo what has happened. They can only repeat, compulsively and tragically, the movements and gestures of their childhood lessons, as if hoping that, if they do so, they will get one more chance, one more shot at life.

Chapter 26
DEAD CLASS ABROAD

In his review of *Dead Class*, Bogdan Gieraczyński confidently wrote that "*Dead Class* is the most important and original Polish spectacle of the last decade. It is also one of the most famous, one which I believe will have a long and illustrious life abroad."[87] Shortly after its Polish premiere, *Dead Class* toured Holland, West Germany, France, Iran, Yugoslavia, Belgium, Italy, Australia, Venezuela, the USA, Switzerland and Mexico. It played in London, Paris, Amsterdam, Nancy, Belgrade, Milan, Syndey, Barcelona, Graz, Lyon, Lille, Stuttgart, Majorca, Caracas and New York City. In June, 1981, six years after its premiere, *Dead Class* was reported as having been performed 550 times worldwide.[88] Altogether, in the 17 years of its travels, the spectacle played over 2000 times all over the world.

In the first week of the Edinburgh Festival, *Dead Class* won the *Scotsman* award for originality and high artistic value. Reviews were unanimously positive: "The visual impact of the performance is tremendous. [...] it is quite simply agonizing. [...] simply astounding"[89] – wrote *Fringe*'s Brian Barron. Gordon Parson of the *Morning Star* called the show "Outstanding."[90] An anonymous account of Cricot 2's visit to Edinburgh reveals the level of anticipation surrounding Kantor's show:

> [The] enthusiasm of some informal Scottish cultural circles resulted in special care offered to the actors who were provided, for instance, with extremely attractive though distanced (over 30 kms from Edinburgh) lodgings in an old Scottish manor house of Mrs. Matilda O'Brien at Peebles. [The i]nitiative, devotion and personal commitment of Richard Demarco, owner of the art gallery and David Gothard, a young stage director, helped enormously to build an excellent atmosphere around the Polish troupe. The Edinburgh premiere was honoured by the presence of the Polish Ambassador to Great Britain, Mr. Artur Starewicz.[91]

The anticipation around *Dead Class* was palpable, and the show made a great impact on its audiences. Richard Calvoressi of Studio International poignantly summed up the influence of *Dead Class* on Edinburgh audiences:

> Quite the most remarkable event in the Festival was the visit of Tadeusz Kantor's Cricot 2 Theatre from Poland. [...] A grubby, claustrophobic little corner was found and *The Dead Class* held Edinburgh audiences spellbound for a fortnight, paving the way for Cricot's London visit and the exhibition of Kantor's work at the Whitechapel.[92]

Following its performance at the Edinburgh Festival, Cricot 2 went to Cardiff, Wales, where *Dead Class* was shown in "the excellent[ly] equipped, though small, auditorium of the Sherman Theatre, an experimental university stage. The two scheduled appearances immediately hit the headlines in local newspapers," spreading the group's fame.[93] The *Glasgow Herald* critic wrote, fascinated: "Whatever this is, it's excellent. […] It is intensely interesting: it can't be labeled, but it lives in the mind as a strong and cohesive statement largely because of the perfect and convinced manner of its performance."[94] Following the accolades, BBC 2 did a show about *Dead Class*, which it broadcast twice.

As a result of all the reviews coming from Edinburgh and Wales, Cricot 2 was invited to London, where it "was awaited with great impatience, revealed not only in the festival gossip and newspaper announcements but, what is equally important, by a TV broadcast of the fragments of the play, transmitted twice on BBC 2."[95] All the anticipation resulted in sold-out shows. There were even rumors circulating in London crediting *Dead Class* with saving the Riverside Studios from near-bankrupcy.[96] The anonymous report described the performance:

> The London opening [of *Dead Class*] was attended by "everybody": critics, artists, and other celebrities of the city's cultural circles, the Polish Ambassador and the Mayor of Hammersmith. All tickets were booked long in advance and despite two additional nights (there were nine performances altogether) many had to leave the box-offices empty handed.[97]

On the day of the London premiere, "there was a notice in the foyer saying that, at Kantor's request, no one would be allowed into the theatre until he gave permission. Finally, 15 minutes after the scheduled opening, everyone was allowed in. The wait was worth it."[98] In London, as in Edinburgh, critics unanimously hailed the show as a "masterpiece."[99] Ann McFerran of *Time Out* called it "a furious show of fantastic shapes and bizarre connotations consisting of a stunning sequence of dream-like images evoking a forgotten era."[100] Michael Billington, of the *Guardian*, wrote: "Kantor here provides us with one of the greatest images of modern drama: a dust-laden, disintegrating classroom filled with ancient pupils living out old memories and obsessions."[101] John Barber, of the *Daily Telegraph*, voted *Dead Class* Best New Play. Frank Marcus, of the *Sunday Telegraph*, gave Kantor the title of Best Director. And John Elsom, of *Listener*, voted it best production in the design category. *Dead Class* was unquestionably perceived as representing the best of Polish theatre: "[The] Edinburgh and London centers of international critical opinion were not only struck by the direct emotional and visual experience provided by the 'Cricot-2' production and the 'Emballages,' but maybe also by the radical artistic ideas born of Polish tradition but new to the English soil."[102] In France, responses were similar. *Politique Hebdomadaire* called it a "truly terrifying show."[103] Hubert Gignaux considered *Dead Class* the most significant event of the Nancy festival,[104] and Raymonde Temkine joined the chorus, calling it a "masterpiece."[105]

Although Kantor's artworks were first shown in New York in 1958, it took another 20 years for his theatre to reach American shores. *Dead Class* had its New York premiere in 1979 at La MaMa Theatre. Almost 40 years later, Ellen Stewart, La MaMa's founder and artistic director, reportedly recalled the initial missteps around the reception of the show:

> The first performance of *Dead Class* in 1979 brought in maybe 20 people. I actually stood out on the street, trying to bring some people in, because I was embarrassed that New York didn't recognize this masterpiece. Then, *The New York Times* ran Eder's review, which called it "a satire on educational process." When *The Times* realized who Kantor was, they threw Eder out. The next review was intelligent and enthusiastic – and I had a full house from then on.[106]

It is quite possible that, many years after the event, Stewart embellished the story a bit for dramatic effect. First, Eder's review, though puzzling, is not negative. In fact, he writes that, after the show, "We are left with an impression that is at once troubling, vivid and obscure."[107] Second and most importantly, according to accounts printed at the time, following the buzz from Edinburgh and London, *Dead Class* was a must-see event of the New York theatre season. The show was attended, as Tish Dace humorously noticed in her own review, "by nine-tenths of the city's important experimental directors, playwrights, performers and producers. […] If some disaster, natural or man-made, had sent those spectators to their just or unjust rewards, the Off-Broadway theatre would have required many years to recover."[108] The conflicting accounts of the performance perfectly capture New York's ambivalent attitude towards Kantor's work. Although without exception all subsequent reviews were laudatory, expressing a mixture of fascination, horror and bewilderment, Kantor himself never inspired the kind of cultlike devotion and mimickry among the American theatre scholars and practitioners that Grotowski did.

Though most critics were unable to figure out exactly what they saw, they were unanimously taken by *Dead Class*'s breathtaking beauty. Marilyn Stasio (1979) called it "the most electrifying piece of avant-garde theatre to strike in a long time. […] Most beautiful and most horrifying… […] As a political metaphor, *The Dead Class* is devastating. As an existentialist view of the living, it is deeply unsettling. As theatre, it is dynamite."[109] Merle Ginsberg (1979) of *Villager* unambiguously declared: "*The Dead Class* is such a monumental and serious work that it is almost ridiculous to call it the most important theatrical event in New York at the present moment – it simply cannot be compared to anything."[110] Ginsberg reiterated. "*The Dead Class* is magical, dark and as exciting as it is brooding – a lesson in life."[111] *Dead Class* won the 1979 OBIE award and, according to Pleśniarowicz's records, *Newsweek* called it the greatest theatrical piece in the world.[112] *Dead Class* visited New York twice, and was performed on each occasion at La MaMa. Its second staging, in 1991, came after Kantor's death.

Chapter 27

ON NOT KNOWING POLISH, AGAIN

Dead Class was not just Kantor's breakthrough, but unequivocally one of the most transformative theatrical events of the late 1970s, one of only a few theatrical pieces that captured the spirit of the century. Peter Brook famously said: "*Dead Class* was a great shock for me. This play contains the suffering of all of Europe. I think that theatre is nothing more than an attempt to condense everything in existence. *Dead Class* was just that: the experience of humanity condensed in one image."[113] Writing about *Wielopole, Wielopole* three years after the New York premiere of *Dead Class*, Margaret Croyden summarizes Kantor's impact on the international theatre scene:

> [Kantor's] work is popular; he has played in almost every capital of the world, winning more than 15 international prizes and awards, and enjoying a splendid reputation. [...] Those who see it experience something very special, painful perhaps, or astonishing, but an artistic phenomenon which cannot easily be dismissed or forgotten.[114]

Despite the impact of *Dead Class* on the contemporary avant-garde (from Richard Foreman to Robert Wilson to Krystian Lupa), there's a surprising lack of in-depth scholarship about this work. The universal Kantor appealed to twentieth-century universal tastes and anxieties, but the Polish Kantor, like one of his vagabond artists, carried with him the entire baggage of national trauma and psychosis, the "hollow and sneering" laughter of his generation's ghosts. This Polish Kantor was too difficult to translate, too opaque to understand and too dense to attract foreign attention. As was the case with Grotowski's *Akropolis*, with *Dead Class* foreign critics and scholars slipped easily into a comfortable, superficial reception of Kantor's work. They bypassed any attempt at deeper comprehension, and resigned themselves to mere descriptions of what they saw. Many Western critics justified their lack of contextual understanding by asserting that such information was a distraction that obscured these works' broader messages.

    Critical responses to the role of language and history in Kantor's *Dead Class* can be grouped into the same categories as Grotowski's *Akropolis*. The first category of critics asserted that language doesn't mean anything, or that the work itself requires no critical – and thus no linguistic – engagement. French critics in this category include Michael Boue from *L'Humanité Dimanche*, who raved that "this unparalleled piece completely escapes from the clutches of criticism."[115] Matilde La Bardonnie suggested in *Le Monde* that "Neither the visual aspects of the production nor the gripping music require any sort of interpretation."[116] Henri Chapier in *Le Quotidien de Paris* called the performance "wordless."[117] In Edinburgh, an anonymous critic argued that language is being used as "pure sound": "They do use words, in Polish naturally, but they give the impression of being used as pure sound, rather as paint might be, to express mood rather than meaning."[118] Rosalind Carne echoed a nearly identical sentiment: "Even a non-Polish speaker can sense that language is used primarily as sound; the choral chanting of the lessons becomes a ritual cry."[119] Another critic tried to assure his audience, writing that

> The fact that he uses a Polish text does not obscure his success, particularly in the opening moments when the audience is confronted with a group of doll-like creatures, old, dusty and grim, squeezed on school benches. One by one they shuffle from the room to return to the swelling sound of a waltz encumbered by actual manikins of children, of themselves as children, which cling round their necks or are dragged along at their sides.[120]

Likewise, Julie Elwall assured her audience that not knowing Polish would not detract from their enjoyment of the play: "While all the dialogue is in Polish, this does not detract from the soaring intensity of the action."[121] Even Martin Esslin, always a careful critic, couldn't resist dismissing the role of language: "There is music here and mime and speech in Polish – but it is not at all vital for the audience to understand the words spoken, their sound values, which Kantor treats as objects, are strong enough without a knowledge of their dictionary meanings."[122] Reynolds, on BBC's "Critics' Forum," argued that "They use language which of course one doesn't understand, Polish, but which has a kind of meaning and very often I've talked to Poles about them, very often you don't need to understand what's being said, a lot of it is almost like a chorus in a Greek play."[123] In London, Christopher Hudson, of the *Standard*, also asserted that since one cannot explain it, *Dead Class* needs no explanation. Hudson wrote:

> It breaks all the rules of theatre but manages to be supremely theatrical. There is no ordered sequence of events: no proper communication between the characters. What jabberings of speech it has are in Polish and German. But the scene it set for us, of dead men and women trying pitifully to recapture some spark of humanity by re-enacting the behaviour of their childhood, is powerful enough to need no explanation.[124]

Reactions in the USA weren't too different. Eileen Fisher made a similarly dismissive comment in her 1979 review:

> The dialogue of *Dead Class* is mostly in Polish with bits of French, Yiddish, Hebrew, and one English sentence ("The war has begun") thrown in. But verbal comprehension matters little here. Apprehension suffices because the dialogue does not seek to inform but rather to evoke. What is more, there is no traditional plot, no character in the usual sense, no linear narrative.[125]

How, without "verbal comprehension," could she have known if there was or wasn't a linear narrative? Glenn Loney evokes a similarly dismissive sentiment, arguing that the text can be ignored because "much of the action is pantomime, pantomime which is quite specific in its detail."[126] Harold Clurman followed suit, confidently asserting, "Simultaneous translation of the spoken text would not be of much help to comprehension; nor would be a scenario of the action. The *Dead Class* consists mostly of macabre movement; the players are puppet-like characters – and people-like puppets."[127] How did Clurman conclude that "simultaneous translation of the spoken text would not be of much help to comprehension"?[128] Other anonymous critics echoed that judgment, arguing, "You don't have to understand Polish, European politics of the beginning of this century, or even life itself to be overwhelmed by such a theatrical coup de theatre, simply a receptive human being. *The Dead Class* is not for applauding, but for receiving."[129, 130]

The second group of critics responding to *Dead Class* argued that, even if its words mean something, it doesn't matter what they mean because actual, symbolic or metaphorical meanings of specific words and phrases are irrelevant to the play's overall symbolic or metaphorical meaning. Tish Dace, for example, suggested that Polish-speaking and non-Polish-speaking audiences would experience no difference in their responses to the play:

> Kantor asks any audience to react instinctively, so when we respond without benefit of verbal cues – we are not, I gather, at a markedly greater disadvantage than a Polish audience would be. The costumes and make-up, the often bizarre pantomime, sounds effects, and music, the vocal effects and the objects – both stage props and hand props – communicate, if not often a discursively paraphrasable incident or situation, at least a macabre mood, a distorted image, a visual or auditory impression.[131]

Dace went even further, suggesting that watching *Dead Class* could actually induce an understanding of Polish in audience members, claiming the play is so "Artaudian in its presence of repetitive non-verbal modes that it is almost accessible to an audience unfamiliar with Polish."[132] Likewise, Eileen Blumenthal wrote that "not understanding Polish isn't a crippling handicap for spectators. The play's impact is largely visual and musical, and much of the verbal material either obviously is gibberish or contains recognizable keys ('Sarajevo,' 'Cleopatra,' 'Aleph,' 'Beth')."[133] Merle Ginsberg went a step further, arguing that the language barrier actually enhances *real* understanding of the piece:

> I cannot report on what the play, if it is such a thing, is about, if it is about anything. *The Dead Class* is in Polish, and even the book sold on its contents does not make any attempt to translate it verbatim. The language barrier, however, is not a barrier to a real understanding of the piece, and in fact, enhances its music-like quality, and places it further out into the realm of the unknown, where Kantor wants it to be.[134]

The third group of critics bashfully admitted that – as Marilyn Stasio (1979) of the *New York Post* put it – "a rudimentary acquaintance with Polish would […] help."[135]

Richard Eder, in his *New York Times* review, pointed out that "The mood varies continually from torpor to shouting hysteria; the shouting is done in untranslated Polish, which leaves us at something of a disadvantage."[136] In Great Britain, two *Guardian* critics, Nicholas de Jongh and Cordelia Oliver, raised the possibility that *Dead Class* might have a linguistic dimension. Oliver cautiously noted that "knowledge of the original would no doubt sharpen one's appreciation by adding yet another layer of meaning."[137] Venting his frustration, the flabbergasted de Jongh wrote: "Obviously much is missed, since we have no means of understanding the Polish that the characters speak, and after ninety minutes the effects [begin] to induce a sort of bewildered torpor, but the extended stage pictures root in the mind."[138] Self-conscious about not knowing the language, Brian Barron of *Festival Times* jokingly interpreted some of the action onstage as a response to the audience's ignorance: "At one point the splendid 'absent old man from the first bench,' who otherwise says and does nothing, comes forward and addresses the audience. But we don't undertand (how can we? It is in Polish, isn't it?) and he dismisses us with a derisory gesture that is perfectly clear."[139]

Finally, the last group of critics were unable to even decide what to think about the role of language in the play, let alone the meaning of the play itself. They often sought recourse in Kantor's program notes, with some finding them helpful, others finding them as obscure as the play itself. John Tatzer wrote, "The Polish text is dense and impenetrable: the message, even with Kantor's wordy programme notes, obscure and ambiguous."[140] Likewise, Richard Eder found the program notes incomprehensible, writing sarcastically: "As the lengthy program notes, translated with perfect incomprehensibility from the Polish, tell us: 'It would be unjustified bibliophilic pedantry to attempt to find those missing fragments necessary for a complete "knowledge" of the subject of the plot of this play.'"[141] Rosalind Carne, on the other hand, found the program notes superfluous: "A programme note explains the episodes and a wealth of bookstall literature outlines the genesis of this Theatre Of Death, but most spectators will find ample food for contemplation without any written assistance."[142] A frustrated Mel Gussow, of the *New York Times*, pointed out that the program notes were not perfectly aligned with the performance:

> A guide in the program offers a step-by-step map of the journey, but there are ellipses and divergences. For one thing, though camels are indicated in the outline, they never appear in performance. One signpost admits that "important events are lost within the dream in progress." Surprises await, even in scenes that are repeated. The effect is hypnotic as we watch the disturbing stage pictures – a mountain of battered books as refuse, the washing of corpses, a mass grave of doll-like children.[143]

Charles Edelman found the program notes helpful, though his interpretation of *Dead Class* as a "nightmare of death within the ordinary rituals of life" is a significant misunderstanding of the production:

> Performed in Polish, with the aid of some excellent program notes describing the action, the play is a horrific but often hilarious nightmare of death within the ordinary

rituals of life, acted out by characters dressed all in black on a Spartan black set, accompanied by a rather schmaltzy rendition of Viennese waltzes.[144]

Edelman further suggested that the program notes are the only way to access *Dead Class*:

> Perhaps the only way to give an idea of the action is to draw upon the program notes: OLD MAN IN A W.C./ WOMAN IN A WINDOW/ FALLING ASLEEP/ HISTORICAL HALLUCINATIONS/ SOLDIER FROM THE FIRST WORLD WAR/ PHONETIC BLOTS/ BELL BREAK. These feverish images, performed by a remarkably skilled and disciplined company, last for about ninety minutes without interruption. Then the play ends suddenly, as "all repeat their arrested gestures, which they will never finish, imprisoned by them forever."[145]

Perhaps the most straightforward linguistic assessment of *Dead Class* was provided by Michael Billington in *Arts Guardian*, who commented cryptically on the metatheatrical relationship between Kantor's pupils and foreign critics:

> Only a Pole could grasp all the play's historical and political references. But what comes clearly across is Kantor's ability to marry image and sound (birth is represented by a terrifying leg-widening mechanical contraption and the amplified sound of metallic balls rolling round a wooden box) and his ability to anchor his impression of human life in the concrete and particular. Like Beckett, he reminds us "We are born astride a grave;" but the image you carry away is of rotting books, Dickensian desks and of aged, ashen-faced pupils locked into a persona they did not ask for and cannot understand.[146]

These reviews that dismissed the linguistic aspect of *Dead Class* contributed to a persistent, general misunderstanding of Kantor's work. These reviews condoned and established the cultural paradigm for foreigners, such that omitting the significance of language became an empirical, unquestioned reality, instead of a flawed interpretation. A note in the *Chambers Biographical Dictionary* (2007) is just one of many examples of that outcome. *The Chambers* reductively describes *Dead Class* as "a largely silent piece with actors portraying corpses in a school classroom," with no mention of the historical or cultural framework of the production.[147]

Chapter 28

THE VISUAL AND THE PUERILE

Two of the strategies that foreign critics used to grapple with *Dead Class* deserve special attention. One was to rely on the work's visual aspects as a primary access point (the "what you see is what you get" approach). The second was to reductively interpret *Dead Class* as – to quote Anne Barry – "a satire on the educational process."[148] If the first strategy attempted to frame *Dead Class* in the broader European canon of art, the second one completely missed the point, failing to see the deeper historical roots of Kantor's masterpiece. Evoking a number of dramatic comparisons, Harold Clurman attempted to locate *Dead Class* somewhere along the spectrum of theatrical landscape based on its *mise-en-scène*:

> It is reminiscent of German expressionist drama, without expressionism's literary emphasis. The fascination of the *Dead Class* is largely visual (its director, Kantor, was first a painter), and it succeeds by the mordancy of its physical metaphors: its weird suggestiveness and, above all, by the mastery of its performances.[149]

This *mise-en-scène* approach, however, seemed an inadequate framework for understanding Kantor's works, as another critic noted:

> Mr. Kantor's work is anti-theatre. He is attempting to create a new kind of drama, a form that has the abstract qualities of music or sculpture as well as something of the unnerving aspects of a happening. I'm not sure I want him to succeed, valuing theater for just those qualities of humanism that he would banish. But *The Dead Class* is undeniably fascinating as well as disquieting.[150]

Michael Billington pointed out that what makes Kantor's work a masterpiece is that it straddles the borders of theatre and visual art:

> The greatness, I think, lies partly in the universality of its image: we all sat in class and all carry through life the emotional luggage of childhood. [...] But the greatness also comes from the feverish animation of Kantor's production, which he literally conducts from on stage, and from its visual humour, the camera shutter that unfolds like an elephant's tusk, the charwoman who sweeps up a monstrous pile of books and then deliberates where to insert one tiny scrap of paper, the man who constantly pulls a piece of string through his head. Kantor, a former painter, vibrantly bridges the gap between the graphic and the dramatic arts; and if *The Dead Class* is not a masterpiece, then the word has no meaning.[151]

Following Billington's lead, many critics – as they had with *Akropolis* – found it more constructive to compare *Dead Class* to various paintings than to other plays. Mel Gussow noted that watching Kantor conduct his actors felt "almost as if [one] were looking at *Guernica* while Picasso was painting it."[152] Paul Overy of the *Times* compared *Dead Class* to "a series of animated tableaux from Bosch."[153] Hubert Gignoux compared it to Munch.[154] Merle Ginsberg also noted that *Dead Class* was like "Edvard Munch on stage."[155] Richard Eder compared the show to Grosz's painting.[156] Martin Esslin compared it to drawings by Toulouse-Lautrec[157]; and Marilyn Stasio compared it to Cranach and Bosch.[158] Frank Marcus of the *Sunday Telegraph* noticed a resemblance to Chagall.[159] Michael Billington described *Dead Class* as "Will Hay cross-fertilized with Magritte."[160]

In his book on Kantor, Noel Witts wrote that "one of the reasons why Kantor's productions were able to speak to so many audiences that did not understand Polish was because the visual clarity of the works conveyed much of their essential meanings."[161] Witt's assessment, to a large degree, stemmed from initial responses to Kantor's work, which minimized the historical, linguistic and cultural aspects of *Dead Class* while elevating its visual elements. It is true that the visual impact of *Dead Class* might have been sufficient enough to draw an international audience, but Witts' assessment – that most of Kantor's essential meanings are conveyed only through visuals – is reductive.

Missing the many metaphorical and symbolic levels of *Dead Class*, a number of critics offered a literal and rather myopic interpretation of Kantor's production, as a satire on "traditional educational conditioning."[162] To be fair, some of the very first translations of the play's title emphasized the school motif: *Umarła klasa* was originally translated as *The Dead School-Form*.[163] It is difficult to pinpoint which came first, the reviews or the translation. The comments of John Barber in the *Daily Telegraph*, who voted *Dead Class* the Best New Play of 1976, are among the most trivial: "Kantor invokes a traumatic experience that has damaged us all: school. He reminds us that it was in the classroom that we suffered our first indignities, first bled inwardly under the bullying of our fellows and the incomprehension of our masters."[164] For Kantor's generation, calling a prewar childhood a traumatic experience – *vis-à-vis* the experience of World War II and the Holocaust – is absurd. Oblivious to history, Barber pressed on with his pseudo-Freudian analysis, explaining further that he "chose *The Dead Class* because it imposes a powerful and probably unforgettable image to convey a central and universal experience never before explored so painfully: the haunting effects of childhood upon adult life."[165] William Harris, in *Soho Weekly News*, offered equally perfunctory insights, suggesting that the essence of the suffering expressed in *Dead Class* is part of the "human condition" and lies in the "disciplining and humiliation" experienced in childhood. Harris wrote: "In *The Dead Class* Kantor has found a uniquely universal metaphor – the classroom with its austere regimented desks – to convey his satire of the human condition. The disciplining and humiliation we all experience at one time."[166] But Barber and Harris weren't the only ones to reduce the entire historic and existential baggage of *Dead Class* to a comic strip on the pains of growing up. An anonymous reviewer in the *West London Observer* wrote, "Tadeusz Kantor's *The Dead Class* is a comic and horrific picture of 'the best days of your life.'"[167] He continued, asserting that "Comic touches include a charwoman sweeping up a pile of books then wondering where to put a scrap of paper and a man pulling a piece of string through his head. The full horror comes through – even though the text is in Polish. If you have sat through school classes you should sit through this."[168] Another anonymous critic called *Dead Class* "A satirical comedy on education using a lifesize mannequin and actors."[169] For these two critics, the horror references the traumatic experience of school, not of war or the Holocaust. Gordon Parson, from *Morning Star*, wrote: "Kantor, the director, conducts his living puppets though a series of grotesque, farcical and bitter games, reflecting on the blindness to human needs of traditional educational conditioning."[170] And Jasia Reichardt of *Architectural Design* saw the play's intensity as a way to illuminate a childlike sensibility. She confidently wrote: "Everything happens in childhood with an intensity which is rarely matched in later years, and so these people in their dotage go through grammar lesson[s], birth, crucifixion, they go for walks, discover sex, and the classroom char, Death, is seen at the end as a prostitute."[171]

However, the most misinformed reviews were those that saw *Dead Class* as a Marxist critique of class struggle and capitalist institutions. This naïve interpretation of *Dead Class* as Marxist critique fails to grasp the fact that Kantor worked under and against an oppressive communist regime he opposed. Apparently blind to that fact, Gordon Parson wrote: "Surprisingly missed by critics was the area of reference to the death of a social class – the bourgeoisie. These senile children learn nothing as frenetically they repeat their actions to the swelling and dying chords of a romantic waltz."[172] Eileen Blumenthal added: "The piece mourns both the decline of a society and the victims of its ossification."[173] She then broadened the reference to include all institutions: "Entering, the audience finds a dozen gray-faced characters seated on small, old-fashioned classroom benches, fidgeting, staring. Dressed in black, of ambiguous sex and age (though mostly oldish), these people could be the peon-clients of any institution – a welfare agency, prison, school."[174] Kantor indeed refers to childhood, but not in the literal sense as many critics interpreted it. In *Dead Class*, childhood functions – as it does in Witkacy, Schulz and Gombrowicz – as a metaphor for death. The first stage of life becomes a mirror image of the last one: life and death, childhood and old age, are the bookends of human life. For Kantor they don't exist separately and cannot be analyzed in their own solipsistic categories. For his particular generation, they also serve as two bookends of the twentieth century's bloodiest highlights, with World War I and World War II marking their childhoods and their deaths.

Chapter 29

THE NATIONAL AND THE TRANSNATIONAL

Dead Class was successfully performed all over the world. In each new city, as Klaudiusz Święcicki put it, "Every viewer came to the spectacle with his or her own cultural system of significations. Hence the many interpretations of this work."[175] Since neither language nor historical context was available to international audiences, foreign critics used other strategies to structure their responses to Kantor's elusive masterpiece. Reading those initial reviews is important because they provide a framework for the process of making meaning, the entire epistemological enterprise that eventually came to surround Kantor's work. The foreign critical response to Kantor's work reflects the innate difficulty of finding a critical framework to address its meaning. Critics' inability to grasp its geographic, historical, artistic or aesthetic meanings underscores the difficulty with which works like *Dead Class* are classified, taught and shown. Many foreign critics argued that Kantor's work is intrinsically transnational, even though it clearly bears the marks of its Polish origins. As early as 1977, Raymonde Temkine wrote of *Dead Class* that although "the performance has a trans-national meaning, one can feel an exceptionally strong sense of Polishness running through it."[176] Jean-Pierre Leonardini suggested: "To argue that *The Dead Class* is performed in an exclusively Polish cultural context is misguided."[177] Nella Bielski saw it in the context of European postmodernism.[178] In 1976, Mitchell, trying to both tie Kantor to the Theatre of the Absurd, and to defend his universal appeal, compared him to Beckett (and even to Jim Dine, an American pop artist with neo-Dadaists impulses):

> We are talking about him very much in Polish terms so far, surely he's very much an international artist, the happenings things, the whole idea of man as a voyager on a bicycle reminds one inevitably of Samuel Beckett and the use of objects in pictures, like these umbrellas which are everything which we haven't mentioned. It reminds one of Jim Dine and the American school. He doesn't seem to me to be at all a parochial artist.[179]

Mitchell's disconnected associations reveal his struggle with the critical conceptualization of *Dead Class* outside its Polish context.

Some critics considered the Polish "esoterism" of Kantor's work to be a selling point: "*Dead Class*, done with that supercharged force which the best Polish theatre has, horrifies and intrigues and amuses."[180] Others, however, like Cordelia Oliver of the *Guardian*, didn't consider Kantor's Polishness a good thing. She wrote, rather cryptically: "It has to be emphasised that Kantor's Cricot Theatre from Poland is no esoteric, elitist group relentlessly peeling away the layers of onion till only emptiness remains."[181] Others, writing in a similar tone, assured audiences that *Dead Class* is not an incomprehensible Polish musing. Eileen Blumenthal of the *Village Voice* wrote: "Despite *Dead Class*'s very Polish background and framework, though, it speaks directly to an audience only casually familiar with those roots."[182]

Another group of critics considered what they viewed as Kantor's specifically national vision to be an apt metaphor for the broader human experience of the violent twentieth century. Rosalind Carne from the *Financial Times* wrote: "Polish history has lent a biting edge to that nation's theatre, and this extraordinary work by Tadeusz Kantor speaks loudly, if not always clearly, about humankind on the brink."[183] Marina Vaizey, during a BBC discussion about Kantor's work, suggested that it is in fact the very Polishness, born of Poland's tragic history, that provides Kantor's work with its transnational character:

> I think it's an intensely Polish show which I find very interesting because Poland [...] is one of the most oppressed European countries there's ever been. [...] Poland is a country which seems to me to be about survival. [...] I think Kantor has done something which Western European artists would find much more difficult to do. He has made an art which is basically and unashamedly about the human condition.[184]

Frank Rich also considers Polish history a metaphor for twentieth-century European history, as reflected in Poland's postmodern art forms: "As Mr. Kantor is a witness to the Poland shredded by two world wars and countless repressions and dislocations, so is he a child of a fractious age in art."[185]

For many critics, a culturally specific Polish experience is at the heart of Kantor's work. Reynolds pointed out that

> There is an agony of expression which you don't find in the work of a lot of western European artists; particularly in the works of playwrights like, say, Vaclav Havel, you find this intense agony, the memory of the pain and the suffering of the war expressed [...] much more deeply.[186]

Interestingly, Yosunari Takahashi, a Japanese critic, was the only one who considered the play more a commentary on World War I than on World War II, a kind of homage to times long past. He wrote that

> one cannot unambiguously assert that the anger and bitterness of a nation which has repeatedly found itself the prey of a barbaric imperial thirst for conquest is unequivocally woven into the performance. Nevertheless, two scenes provide evidence of this fact. The first is when the character rising from the dead sings the Austrian national anthem with such hatred; the second is where the old folk exit, to dance a waltz out of pure cussedness, containing all the prewar symbolism of la belle époque. In these scenes it is difficult not to see and to hear the voice of stifled anger and bitterness bursting in a great cry from the soul of the nation.[187]

Harold Clurman reached even further, suggesting that the production reflecting both the centuries of Polish partition and Romantic tradition, is invariably connected to Poland's liberatory national longings:

> This background points in part to the special nature of *Dead Class*, first produced in 1975. Its mood, one of pained, even hysterical, romanticism, is characteristic of Polish drama in general since 1900. Polish history is tragic – for hundreds of years the country has been the victim of oppression, and its rebellions have constantly been crushed by alien forces. There is nearly always a political vein in Polish plays. "In Poland," Kott writes, "even a striptease may have ideological overtones."[188]

Some critics suggested that the play had a contemporary political meaning simply because "[I]t's impossible to do anything in Poland without it having a political meaning."[189] Marina Vaizey argued that contemporary Polish theatre, in Brechtian fashion, uses historical dramas as a way to veil current political problems: "I think that's absolutely true and this [Brechtian strategy] is absolutely true of the arts in Poland at the moment. I mean they will perform nineteenth-century plays which are about Polish nationalism because they won't perform 1976 plays which are about Polish nationalism."[190]

Since the nineteenth century, Polish national dramas have been infused with political meaning, and Poles remain viscerally responsive to performances of the great national Romantic dramas despite the fact that they are over a century old. For example, a 1967 production of Adam Mickiewicz's *Forefathers' Eve*, which deals with the eighteenth-century Russian partition of Poland, provoked street demonstrations. Kantor's theatre, however, was never openly political in the way that Western critics consider political theatre to be. Kantor said a number of times that art and politics should not mix: "Art must not be mixed up with politics. It's always bad for art when it tries to make a political point – look at Russian Socialist Realism."[191] Kantor never publicly acknowledged any political subtext in his work.[192] Some foreign critics didn't understand how it was possible for *Dead Class*, which, "goodness knows, doesn't embody Socialist Realism," to be made in Poland under the Soviet regime. "[W]hy, on a strictly esthetic level, does the Polish government countenance and even fund what in other central European countries – witness Squat in Hungary – would be branded counter-revolutionary?" Tish Dace asked.[193] Kantor's work existed in Poland, in the form in which it existed, because it used the abstract language of avant-garde art to speak about something that Poles couldn't, or weren't able to, openly address: the Holocaust. Kantor's work fulfilled a psychological need that could neither be openly expressed nor acknowledged. Although he himself never spoke of politics, *Dead Class* is political in the way that the best works of art are political: it doesn't try to advance any point. It merely wonders at man's entanglement with political forces that most often devour him.

Only one foreign critic referenced the Holocaust directly as the core of the show. Frank Rich, bewildered at the range of Kantorian vocabulary, asked honestly: "In his subconscious, the conventional memories of a village childhood – early intimations of God, sex and death – intermingle with the specters of a Holocaust history. How does one put a canvas of that size and idiosyncratic tilt on stage?"[194, 195]

Chapter 30

WITKIEWICZ'S TUMOR

Dead Class is a web of references to Polish culture and literature, as well as to the Bible, the Old Testament and Greek and Roman mythology. These references form the basis of a rich tapestry of wordplay that's lost without an understanding of Polish. As Marek Jodłowski puts it: "*Dead Class* is a poem, made of predominantly extralingual components, but then again, so is poetry, whether phonic or visual, always extralingual."[196] Each word evokes a multitude of meanings, symbolic and literal, and layers of historical and literary significations. Nevertheless, while few audience members outside Poland understand the play's language, it is perhaps the lack of understanding that gives *Dead Class* an aura of enigma, exoticism and international magic. Brian D. Barron describes the process: "When we are all silent, [the actors] slowly animate into Polish words and gestures that are strangely gripping."[197] If one does not understand the words, they become whatever one wants them to be; the enigma fascinated audiences and fueled their imaginations.

The images Kantor used to create *Dead Class* reflect the so-called Polish School of Grotesque.[198] Eileen Blumenthal, alone among American critics, rightly noted that "Kantor's vision of the death of culture is very close to themes in Grotowski's work, although his sensibility is linked to a more general tradition of Polish surrealist writing, including the works of Bruno Schulz, Witkiewicz and Gombrowicz."[199] Kantor called *Dead Class* "a dramatic séance."[200] He frequently explained the idea: "Why séance? The idea came from Artur Sandauer. Because it is not a play but a spiritualist séance to which *Tumor Brainiowicz*, Witkacy, Schulz and the actors of Cricot 2 are all invited."[201] Katarzyna Fazan noted that Kantor's allusions to Gombrowicz, Witkacy and Schulz are easily recognizable, but they function in *Dead Class* as new art objects.[202] *Dead Class* functions on many levels – visual, metaphorical and symbolic. The Polish literary tradition is only one component, but understanding how it works and what it means changes one's perception of the work completely. Textually, *Dead Class* rests on Witkacy's play *Tumor Brainowicz* (1920). Visually and conceptually, however, it draws on a number of Polish dramatic and literary works: Witold Gombrowicz's cult novel *Ferdydurke* (1938); Bruno Schulz's *Street of Crocodiles* (1934, particularly "The Treatise on Tailor's Dummies") and *Sanatorium Under the Sign of The Hourglass* (1937, particularly the story "The Old Age Pensioner"); S. Ansky's Yiddish play, *Dybbuk or Between Two Worlds* (1920); and Adam Mickiewicz's romantic drama, *Forefathers' Eve* (1823). Zygmunt Greń argues that *Dead Class* cannot be seen merely in the context of the works it references, but needs to be seen in the context of Polish culture and history:

> To talk about *Dead Class* with some sense, one has to talk about it within the broad context of Polish culture. Its literary inspirations, Schulz and Witkiewicz, should be secondary considerations. Their presence in Kantor's work could be accidental or personal. *Dead Class* doesn't stage their texts and I caution against including *Dead Class* under their names in their encyclopedic entries. In fact, *Dead Class* eludes clarification. It can be understood only in broader cultural categories.[203]

Though Greń is right, and neither Witkacy, Schulz nor Gombrowicz should be viewed in a merely literary context, looking at Kantor's *Dead Class* through the prism of their works helps shed light on the multilayered, semiotic landscape of Kantor's séance. Their works capture the spirit of their times as well as the complexity of Poland's cultural response to its political position. Their writings, with their existential anxieties, dark, swaggerly humor, poetry and goof, reflect the Polish post–World War I sensibility: a combination of hope and despair, deep humanism and profound fatalism, childish naiveté and brutal cynicism. To understand how Kantor fits into this hermitic world, one needs to get in on the Polish joke he shares with Witkacy, Shulz and Gombrowicz.

Often credited with being the first absurdist playwright, Stanisław Ignacy Witkiewicz, pseudonym Witkacy (1885–1939), was the son of Stanisław Witkiewicz, the painter and art critic. Witkacy was a dramatist, poet, novelist, painter, photographer, art theorist and philosopher. He spent his childhood in Zakopane, where he was homeschooled and allowed to engage in any creative or intellectual activity he wished. He was widely known as a child prodigy, writing his first play, *Cockroaches*, at the age of eight, and beginning to paint as a teenager. From 1904–5, he studied at the Academy of Fine Arts in Cracow, but he gave that up to travel, visiting Italy, Germany and France. In 1914, he joined Bronisław Malinowski, a famous Polish traveler and ethnographer, on his trip to Australia and Polynesia. Witkiewicz returned at the outbreak of World War I to enlist in the Russian Army. Although he did so to fight the Germans, his father was crushed by the decision and never forgave him for it. After the war, in 1924, Witkacy started a commercial portrait firm, which swiftly made him famous in Polish art circles, although he himself considered the entire enterprise a joke.[204] Witkacy quickly outgrew his father, becoming one of Poland's most influential twentieth-century avant-garde artists. Witkacy's theoretical works on art include *New Forms in Painting and Misconceptions Around Them* (1919), *Theory of Pure Form* (1921–32), and two volumes of theoretical writings on painting and theatre published as *Notes on Aesthetics* (1922) and *Theatre* (1923). He also authored 38 plays, written mainly from 1918–25. They include *Pragmatists* (1921), *The Water Hen* (1922), *Country House* (1923), *Madman and the Nun* (1924), *Jan Karol Maciej Hellcat* (1925), *The New Deliverance* (1925), *Tropical Madness* (1926), *Metaphysics of a Two-Headed Calf* (1928) and *The Cuttlefish* (1933). His most famous play, *The Shoemakers*, written between 1931 and 1934, was not staged until 1957.[205] His two most famous novels, *Farewell to Autumn* (1927) and *Insatiability* (1930), are considered masterpieces of Polish modernist literature. Witkacy committed suicide in 1939 upon learning that the Soviet Army had entered Poland. He was buried somewhere in a forest in what is now Ukraine. In 1985, his body was ceremoniously and with great fanfare returned to Poland, and buried in a cemetery in Zakopane. However, even after death, Witkacy played yet another joke. The public soon learned that the body brought from Ukraine was not Witkacy's but that of a young girl.

Although today Witkacy is widely credited with being a precursor of the Theatre of the Absurd, his work was not recognized in Poland or internationally until years after his death. Not until the 1960s were his plays and theoretical writings, particularly his *Theory of the Pure Form*, finally translated, influencing many absurdist playwrights and directors. Witkacy was considered *persona non grata* by Poland's communist regime, which, having expunged the 1939 Soviet invasion from its version of history, officially disregarded Witkacy's protest/suicide and, for that matter, Witkacy himself. The fact that his paintings and writings oppose the formerly prevailing trend of socialist realism was another pretext for banning Witkacy from public discourse. For many years, even mentioning his name was considered a subversive political gesture. Thus Poland was slow to recognize Witkacy – in good part because of his outcast status under the communist regime – which kept him from receiving the international acclaim he deserved.

Witkacy was also not well understood or appreciated during his lifetime. As Olga Kiebuzinska notices, following 1918 – the year Poland finally regained its statehood – an explosion of "nationalistic fervor, chauvinism, and competing ideologies" dominated public discourse: "Since Witkacy's novels and plays, and indeed even his very persona, were considered to be too decadent for the fostering of the national literature, his work was often ignored or castigated by the press."[206] Yet despite his marginal position, or perhaps because of it, Witkacy managed to create an impressive body of work that escapes any contemporary category, foreshadowing the postmodern turn in postwar drama and literature. According to the Polish critic Jan Kott, author of the influential *Shakespeare, Our Contemporary*,

> Between the wars, Witkacy was the most eminent writer in Poland and one of the most interesting in Europe. But he was also – and this may be more astonishing – one of the most original precursors of the intellectual and artistic climate of the 1960s. [...] Witkacy, who came too early, seemed to his contemporaries to be a man who came too late. [He was] one of the most universal European minds.[207]

Witkacy's plays, Kott argues, are symbolic images of "the agony and decay of the first years of the century." Politically, they toy with the idea of "the end of civilization fatally threatened by the egalitarian revolution coming from the East and by Western consumerism and mechanization."[208] There is, in Witkacy's life and work, a strong correlation between artistic and political impulses: his works reflect foremost a prewar anxiety of decadence and looming apocalypse. As Jan Błoński puts it:

> It is easiest to understand Witkiewicz as a social prophet and forecaster of the decline of civilization. [...] Like so many others, he announced the end of art, the destruction of individuality, the decline of sensitivity to the metaphysical, though his

argumentation was highly original. He believed that these virtues would be defeated by the increasing democratization of life, which would generate a society of robots who would be completely content but also perfectly dull.[209]

Structurally, Witkacy's theories of theatre are often compared to those of Artaud and Tzara. Like Artaud, Witkacy proposed the theatrical dissolution of standard epistemological codes into grotesque violence, and absurd and nonsensical macabre. Like Tzara, he glorified controlled chaos and serendipity as a foremost strategy for creating new, disquieting meanings. As Boy-Żeleński puts it: "The unreality of Witkiewicz's theatre mitigates the effects of its brutality, which in any other 'normal theatre' would be evoked by a mere one-tenth of what Witkiewicz proposes."[210] Witkacy, Kott writes, "continues the destruction of naturalistic theater exactly from the point where Strindberg stopped."[211] In Witkacy's theatre, Kott continues, "the congruity of the nineteenth-century dramatic structures was torn apart as abruptly as the coherence of nineteenth-century social and political systems."[212] The postmodern worlds of Witkiewicz's plays function according to their own fantastic rules. Jan Błoński calls them caricatures of Shakespearean tragedies and comedies.[213] They're full of characters that resemble robots, dummies or near-corpses. They come from all walks of life, and are often "disguised in fantastic or historical costumes, scattered around the world, from the great metropolis to Malayan jungle, with sophisticated names, titles and nicknames."[214] Like Ionesco's heroes in *The Bald Soprano*, they recite their lines like automatons, detached from themselves and each other. In Witkiewicz's theatre, the line between living and dead is blurred; "corpses get up and continue conversations, and suicides, jumping out of windows, come back through the front door."[215] Like Kantor's figures, many of Witkacy's heroes are "located on the vague borderline between life and death. They resemble either the corpses of 'caballi' or the corpses of 'zombies.'"[216] However, they are not supernatural beings in the traditional sense, but are more like battery-operated, grotesque toys. Witkacy completely breaks with "the centuries-old convention of portraying the return of the dead in European theatre."[217] There is nothing strange or bizarre in Witkacy's returns of the dead: they're visible to all, and their resurrections are natural and commonplace occurrences. Kott suggests that Witkacy's approach was revolutionary because it combined Western and Eastern ideas of distanciation well before Brecht did so. Kott writes: "The theater in which the dead are puppets, and in which the dead get up and walk […] originated in the fascination with the Oriental theater."[218]

For Witkacy, representation is always more symbolic than literal. His characters are symptoms of their times. As Ewa Szkudlarek points out, in Witkacy's world, "All that is physical is marked with illness, decay and death. No wonder a human being takes the shape of a dummy."[219] In all of that, however, Witkacy never veers into aesthetic pomposity or political self-righteousness. An element of swagger, if sometimes also of a bittersweet sneer, permeates the pages of his writings. Boy-Żeleński argues that Witkiewicz is one of those artists who looks at art not for artistic emotions, but for answers to his most basic existential questions: "He is in a constant state of metaphysical questioning"; and his work is characterized by "derisive grimace and autoirony."[220] Witkiewicz's dramas, Boy-Żeleński argues, shouldn't be discussed in aesthetic terms, because they are merely records of dreams, "a record of an incredible nightmare of life, occasionally turning into a spasmodic laughter of either derision or despair, which then quickly dissolves away into astonishment and profundity."[221] Or, as Kott puts it: "Witkiewicz's theatre is sometimes bitter, but always scoffing."[222]

Like his plays, Witkacy's theory of pure form was neither accepted nor understood during his lifetime. According to Witkacy's theory of pure form, dramatic language is separate from anything else: the play has to function according to its own internal logic, not according to the logic of the natural world:

> The point is to be able to deform life as one wishes, according to one's imagination, to create a world guided not by psychology or someone's ideas about the irrefutable "facts of life" but by the logic of its own internal, purely theatrical construct. […] Coming out of the theatre, a person should feel as if he's waking from a strange dream in which even the most mundane things had a bizarre charm.[223]

Anticipating Theatre of the Absurd works by Beckett and Ionesco, Witkacy's dramas function in their own solipsistic space; any "action" is always futile and circular. Boy-Żeleński writes that Witkacy's theatre is "like a 'brothel' in which his skewed philosophical theories and his paintings meet."[224] According to Andrzej Wirth, Witkacy's style can also be compared with that of Gertrude Stein, mainly because of their similar dismissal of psychology and their sharp focus on language and image.[225]

After World War II, the first short critical essay about Witkacy, authored by Alina Grabowska, appeared in 1957, in *Dialog*.[226] As Grabowska recalls, she had to avoid connecting Witkacy's suicide to the Soviet invasion, writing instead that the Soviet army had entered Latvia (though, as she points out, everyone knew what she meant).[227] The first postwar production of a Witkacy play was Kantor's 1956 adaptation of *Mątwa* [*The Cuttlefish*]. In choosing Witkacy, Kantor "ostentatiously reverted to the tradition of the much-maligned avant-garde" that the Communist government wished to suppress.[228] Following Kantor's production in the late 1950s, the Polish avant-garde theatre began slowly – if furtively – discovering Witkacy. However, as Janusz Degler pointed out in 1985, "the rehabilitation of [avant-garde] tradition after 1956 did not mean that resistance to Witkacy disappeared. He was still performed rarely, with great caution and distrust."[229] In fact, the first edition of Witkacy's collected plays wasn't released until 1962, 33 years after his death. In the few years following the publication of his plays – between 1964 and 1969 – there were 42 premieres of Witkacy's work. A decade later, from 1980–81 (the period of martial law and the Solidarity movement), Witkacy was the third most widely performed playwright in Poland (behind Fredro and Mrożek).[230] In 1986, Jacek Sieradzki gloomily suggested that the only way to stage Witkacy's plays is as shallow comedies, since treating Witkacy's catastrophic vision of the world seriously contradicts both Marxism (which assumes a dialectical progress of history) and Polish Catholicism (which asserts the supremacy of transcendental values over the material ones).[231]

In a critical preface to *Tumor Brainowicz*, Witkacy writes: "Deformation for deformation's sake, nonsense for nonsense's sake, unjustified in purely formal categories, is something that deserves utter condemnation."²³² *Tumor* was Witkacy's first staged play, and it was supposed to be a test of his *Theory of Pure Form* and its applicability to real theatre. It opened on 3 June 1921 at the Słowacki Theatre. To stage the play, the director, Teofil Trzciński, had to persuade censors – who considered its incomprehensibility potentially subversive – as well as the general public – who were skeptical of Witkacy's flamboyant writing style – of *Tumor*'s legitimacy and worth. When finally the show was green-lighted, it didn't go as smoothly as Witkacy had hoped. The actors refused to perform *Tumor Brainowicz* because they considered the play too absurd. Trzciński had to assure everyone that the play would be staged solely as an experimental piece for an invitation-only audience of friends and theatre connoisseurs. The incident established a pattern. Most of Witkiewicz's dramas provoked similar controversies, with actors refusing to act in his plays or audiences boycotting them. Following the performance, Witkacy conceded that the actors acted "wonderfully"; he was "thrilled" – he wrote – regardless of the fact that some of them might consider his compliments unwelcome.²³³ Interestingly, Witkacy didn't attend any rehearsals (how does that compare with today's process of "play development"?) and saw the play, like everyone else, on the day of its opening. Trzciński directed the play in a naturalist style, believing that "Witkacy's world is sufficiently grotesque and bizarre [such that] there's no need to embellish it with a flamboyant *mise-en-scène*. Its heroes have so much 'fantastic psychology' that it would be superfluous to emphasize it with non-traditional acting tricks."²³⁴

The play was performed in its entirety twice, eventually closing to critical "outrage and disgust."²³⁵ Most critics agreed that the play, like Witkacy's theories, was full of nonsense. Their "unfriendly or even hostile attitude, vilifying and ridiculing and accusing Witkacy of propagating nonsense and pure piffle," was directed not so much at Witkacy or his play, but at the entire contemporary avant-garde movement he represented.²³⁶ Emil Haecker subtly suggested that Witkacy had lost his mind, sarcastically noting that "any poor newspaper boy, if paid well enough, would have produced – with the same director and the same advertising – comparable results."²³⁷ Szyjkowski asserted that Witkacy's play "look[ed] like a lunatic's hallucinations in the last stage of paralysis," and that obviously Witkacy "confuses theatre – an art based on words – with painting and music. He shows Picasso's calf on the stage and asks it to talk, which is a sin against nature."²³⁸ Szyjkowski accused Witkacy of "rejecting all realism, all normatives, all associations, […] all subjects, all sense and feelings."²³⁹ Wilhelm Fallek began his review proclaiming that "*Tumor Brainowicz* is written in a language that's understood only by those with a sixth sense. Those with five senses can never understand it." Witkiewicz, Fallek continues, "turns logic on its head and throws out all traces of psychological truth. None of *Tumor*'s characters has a logical personality. […] [The play] is a slap in the face to all traditional dramatic formulas […] and each scene looks like it was a mere caprice." Fallek also notes that Witkacy's characters "love and hate in the same minute; they are both comic and tragic at the same time."²⁴⁰ Skoczylas complained that "all the actors could be easily replaced by the marionettes. By accepting their parts, the actors must have a priori agreed to give up all of their individuality."²⁴¹

Some reviewers, however, were not critical, and perceived the play as having its own logic, in the same way naturalist plays do.[242] Boy-Żeleński called *Tumor* a "grotesque dream fantasy on a mathematical theme."[243] He concluded that Witkiewicz's theatre would not be a beacon of modern theatre, but would find a place somewhere on theatre's respectable margins. *Tumor*, he wrote, is "arch-intellectual, suffering with too many mental shortcuts."[244] On the opposite end of the spectrum was Anatol Stern, a self-proclaimed futurist, who accused Witkacy of not being radical enough and of clinging to old notions of order – of not being able to liberate himself from the constraints of form and, more precisely, of creating "nonsense for nonsense's sake." Stern wrote:

> Witkacy's struggle against pure nonsense, nonsense for nonsense's sake, is a struggle of tragism against humor. Pure nonsense is nothing but an inner sense of humor; it is a denial of any higher order, any metaphysical form and content. […] Witkacy's German tragism, which pushes him to struggle against unfounded nonsense, prevents him from understanding his own *Theory of Pure Form*. He cannot understand that one can and should strip things of their metaphysical values, deny their 'in-itself' existence. That is, he cannot heroically accept the world and human beings as they are: acknowledging both their intrinsic value and the subjective malleability of that value. The moment of acceptance is the moment at which tragism flips into humor, where tragism loses its grounding and is thrown into the outer sphere.[245]

Stern classified Witkacy as a German expressionist, accusing his play of being structurally too logical to be truly avant-garde. Stern wrote that *Tumor Brainowicz*, "from the beginning to the end, is one of the most normal, most appropriate plays in the world. […] No wonder it was acted in naturalist fashion."[246] According to Stern, Witkacy used a method of free association, thus, every seemingly illogical phrase or sequence can be unlocked with its proper key: "This drama has everything, except one thing, one treasure – the will to embrace the illogical, that beautiful, ephemeral point at the end of modern art."[247] For Stern, Witkacy's writing is not avant-garde enough.

Following the reviews, Witkacy wrote a number of rebuttals, inciting heated theoretical debate among Polish theatre artists and critics. He proclaimed forcefully: "I am happy!! The experiment was successful: Pure Form works on stage."[248] Then, he proceeded to respond to critics individually, implying in less than subtle language that they were either lazy or unintelligent; he called one of them a skunk and another an ignoramus. But he was also aware of his hopeless position: "My situation is fatal: for futurists, there is too much sense in my plays; for naturalists, too little."[249] As a result of all the rebuttals, Witkacy earned the nickname "nonsense's apologist." He was perceived as "torn on the cross between theory and practice," unable to reconcile his two contradictory impulses.[250]

Tumor Brainowicz had a very short performance history. Warsaw's Teatr Mały planned a second production in 1926, but it was cancelled when actors once again refused to perform it and went on strike after the first read-through. There are drawings of the unrealized set, designed by Feliks Krassowski. The first fully realized production of *Tumor*

Brainowicz finally took place in 1974 in Olsztyn, at the Teatr im. Stefana Jaracza. Directed by Wanda Laskowska, with set design by Zofia Pietrusińska and music by Andrzej Zarycki, the production attracted little notice, though it did arouse the interest of the theatrical inner circle. On 25 February 1985, to celebrate the 100th anniversary of Witkacy's birthday, a documentary on his life and work ran on Polish television. Titled *Witkacy's Tumor*, it was directed by Grzegorz Dubowski and starred Janusz Zakrzewski as Witkacy, Jerzy Binczycki as Tumor, and Anna Seniuk as his wife. The movie wove together documentary footage and performances from Witkacy's plays. In 1998, the Jan Kochanowski Theatre in Opole staged another full version of *Tumor Brainowicz*, directed by Jan Nowara, with choreography by Iwona Olszowka, set by Marek Mikulski, and music by Tomasz Bajewski. Two years later, in 2000, the same production was shown at the Wojciech Bogusławski Theatre in Kalisz. Reviewing the play, Krzysztof Piech wrote:

> A burly, boorish, genius mathematician; his demonic wife; a fallen aristocrat (with a rabbit-like ability to breed); and a stunning, sensual and inaccessible step-daughter. A revolutionary mathematical discovery, and bureaucrats stopping at nothing to prevent its dissemination. Degenerate European civilization and the exotic – as in an opium-eater's dream – island of Timor. [...] It's a brilliant visual show right down to its last detail.[251]

In 2002, *Tumor* had its Warsaw premiere, with a production at the Theatre Academy, directed by Jarosław Gajewski with set design by Agata Ochman. The New York premiere of *Tumor Brainowicz* (not counting Kantor's *Dead Class* version), was in 2003, at La MaMa Experimental Theatre Club (La MaMa ETC). It was performed by the Theatre of a Two-Headed Calf (named after Witkacy's play, *Metaphysics of a Two-Headed Calf*) under the direction of Brooke O'Harra.

Witkacy's heroes are often mathematical or metaphysical geniuses, Titans tortured by their "insatiable" urge to create. As Jan Kott puts it: "The Titan endures all the pain of limitation of individual existence; he is burnt out by his permanent urge to perform; he finds no outlet for the energy exploding within him; he cannot sleep, foam bubbles from his mouth."[252] Eventually, Titans turn into dictators:

> [B]ored with themselves and the automatic world, Titans become the most cruel dictators simply to fill time with action. They carry on gigantic financial operations of found subversive organizations to rule the world through terror. They murder, rape, and torture without scruple solely in order to experience a metaphysical shock.[253]

Like Witkacy's other Titans, Tumor is a long-haired mathematical genius, tortured by both an unquenched need to create and his insatiable intellectual and sexual appetites. He proclaims: "I feel so insatiable that my brain turns into mush [...] Now, I will finally overcome this dull democracy. I will be a cruel and formidable ruler, and then I will establish a complete socialism. Let those sheep suffocate in their own shit."[254] But, unlike other Titans, Tumor cannot become a dictator, though he does try – and fails – to rule the secluded and exotic island of Timor. Confronted with the dignified pride of the island's natives, Tumor's sense of European identity crumbles. Unlike native kings and princes, Tumor himself is of very humble birth, the son of a quick-witted peasant. He suffers horribly, knowing that while he aspires to the life of an aristocrat, he's really just a simple hillbilly. Tumor has many children, so many in fact that he cannot identify all of them. His new wife, Rozhulantyna [The Unhinged], impatiently awaits her brand new son, Izydor Brainowicz. She's "a terribly desirable woman" who fantasizes about living on a deserted island where, like a rabbit, she could endlessly procreate with a genius. Rozhulantyna is of noble birth; she married Tumor for his raw, plebeian "animalism." With long monologues, grotesque scenes of the macabre, and unnatural reactions, *Tumor* represents "the theater of the absurd with a vengeance."[255] Like *Ubu Roi*, Tumor is a commentary on rising dictatorships, and the inconsequential position of an individual, whose dreams and passions are laughable in the face of overwhelming historical forces. According to Witkacy, the human being, with his grandiose self-image, might as well be a mumbling child or the village idiot. Indeed, acts one and two take place in a nursery where "adults play absentmindedly with toys strewn on the floor."[256] The play's criticism of postcolonial powers questions the validity of European imperial ambitions. As Daniel Gerould puts it: "The contrast between East and West, colored and white, savage and civilized, as developed by Joseph Conrad [another Polish writer, and author of *Heart of Darkness*], becomes fundamental to Witkacy's worldview. [In *Tumor Brainowicz*] half-naked, smelling of raw meat, and fearfully superstitious, the savages are nobler than the conquering Europeans, who lack absolute values."[257] But Witkacy's subtle jabs are never one-sided or supercilious. On the contrary, he mocks the self-righteous fetishization of the "noble savage," as much as he does the trappings of postcolonial power and ideology.

How did Kantor use Witkiewicz's text, and to what degree does the answer matter? Olgierd Jędrzejczyk writes:

> Witkacy is believed to have said that he dreamt of someone staging his plays in a realistic fashion, with realistic sets and costumes, with traditional acting methods. [...] Something like that, Kantor couldn't do. That is why his stage shows a total integration of acting, visual and musical elements, with clear focus on surrealist effects.[258]

It is difficult to believe that Witkacy was serious when he shared this "dream" about the realistic production of his plays. If he was, it had to be in hopes that such productions would serve to enhance the surrealistic nature of his texts. Kantor's version of *Tumor* is peculiar in the sense that it is both a Witkacy text and a fully autonomous Kantor play. For many years now, Polish critics have been puzzled as to how to describe the critical and creative relationship between Kantor and Witkacy. Ryszard Smożewski puts it most succinctly: "Kantor and Witkacy have been in love for a long time now, but what we have here is a form of literary necrophilia, so we don't know how Witkacy would take Kantor's courtship."[259] Cricot 2, the name of Kantor's theatre, was taken directly from the interwar avant-garde theatre Cricot, where Witkacy's plays were performed.[260] Witkacy's texts have been used in most of Kantor's productions, starting in 1956 with *Mątwa* [*The Cuttlefish*], so the fact that he chose another Witkacy text for *Dead Class* wasn't in itself surprising. The question is what *Dead Class* owes and doesn't owe to Witkacy.

Wojciech Owczarski argues that "*Dead Class*, even though it references *Tumor Brainiowicz*, doesn't owe Witkacy anything."[261] Jan Kłossowicz suggests that "*Dead Class* has lots of citations from *Tumor*, but it doesn't have anything in common with Witkiewicz. [...] It quotes from *Tumor*, but the point is that the characters 'take up some roles,' but no play is being performed."[262] Klaudiusz Święcicki, on the other hand, claims that "*Tumor Brainiowicz* is the constructive axis of [Kantor's] drama."[263] According to Wiesław Borowski, Kantor believed it would be almost impossible to stage any of Witkacy's plays literally: "outside the literary imagination, Witkiewicz's complicated dramas must turn into shallow and silly farces."[264] Finally, Barbara Kazimierczyk rightly observes, "It is worthwhile to note that though the show itself is saturated with the climate of Schulz's prose, it actually uses direct citations not from Schulz but from Witkiewicz's *Tumor Brainiowicz*."[265] Why not simply use Schulz's text, Kazimierczyk wonders?

Kantor himself was coy about *Dead Class*'s relationship to all three: Witkacy, Schulz and Gombrowicz. Early on, he admitted that Witkacy's text plays a significant role (although not as significant as Schulz and Gombrowicz) in *Dead Class*. In an interview given right before the opening of *Dead Class*, he is quoted as saying:

> In *Dead Class*, there is my artistic reality plus traditional literary connections, that is, Witkiewicz, Schulz, and Gombrowicz. Witkiewicz's text provides my theatrical framework, but Schulz's work is closer to me (more so than Gombrowicz's) because of its atmosphere.[266]

In another 1975 interview, Kantor stressed that "*Tumor Brainiowicz* scarcely exists in my production. Now you see it, now you don't: it is not my intention that my production should be a production of Witkacy's play."[267] Years later, he completely denied associations with any writer: "Why I don't stage the plays of various authors? Because I think it is not the truth, that is, not my truth."[268] In 1977, Kantor disowned Witkacy completely, denying any connection to *Tumor Brainiowicz*:

> Attention: It would be the unreasonable pedantry of a bibliophile to try to figure out all the missing fragments for a "full" knowledge of the play. It would be the surest way to destroy the utmost important sphere of FEELING! That is why it is *not* advisable to read or even to know Witkiewicz's play *Tumor Brainiowicz*. This text only serves us to accomplish the above-mentioned objectives.[269]

The objective of *Dead Class* is to perform *Tumor*'s text as if on the sly: "The actors are to behave 'like animals in a zoo' – they take care of their own business, watching those who watch them. They are watched or rather viewed by the audience."[270] The text is an add-on to the primary reality of the classroom. Like Wyspiański's *Akropolis* performed within Grotowski's version of Auschwitz, Witkiewicz's *Tumor Brainiowicz* is performed within Kantor's world of *Dead Class*. As Kantor puts it:

> The actors of *Dead Class* subscribe loyally to the rules of theatrical ritual, taking up some kinds of roles, in some kind of play, here and there. Yet, they don't seem

to ascribe much importance to what they're doing, performing as if automatically, from habit, as if almost ostentatiously rejecting their roles, repeating someone else's sentences and gestures, abandoning them easily and without scruples. Those parts- as if badly memorized - constantly fall apart, creating gaping holes in the structure of the play. All we have left is our intuition and feelings.[271]

The acting is based on the appearance of acting, on "careless makeshift recitations, cheap half-felt attempts, fragments of sentences here and there, fading movements, unclear intentions, mystifications, as if they [are] really acting some play, or trying to."[272] Konstanty Puzyna even wonders whether perhaps there was a class during Kantor's school years that had staged a play that stayed in Kantor's memory in bits and pieces.[273]

Dead Class consists of "readymades": found men, found objects and found language, with Witkacy's text serving as one more *objet trouvé* that constitutes the characters' fragmented identities. In the program notes to *Dead Class*, Kantor writes:

> As if stuck and patched together from various bits and pieces left over from childhood, from the fortunes experienced in their past lives... From their dreams and passions, they keep disintegrating and transforming themselves in this theatrical movement and element, relentlessly making their way towards their final form, which cools off quickly and irrevocably, and which is to contain their whole happiness and their whole pain, THE WHOLE MEMORY OF THE DEAD CLASS.[274]

Kantor's actors pick up the fragments of Witkiewicz's text at what appear to be random moments. The Woman Behind the Window speaks Rozhulantyna's lines, inviting the children for a spring walk; her voice slowly transforms, and the invitation becomes abuse. The spring walk becomes a torture. In another scene, the Woman with a Mechanical Cradle ecstatically proclaims her desire to be in endless labor giving birth to a multitude of geniuses. Two men with fake wooden penises mimic the postcolonial, sexual anxieties that Witkacy mocks in *Tumor*.

One of the most profound connections to Witkacy, however, happens not so much on the level of text, but on the level of metaphor. *Dead Class* features both dummy children and characters oscillating permanently between the worlds of the living and the dead – very much like Witkacy's characters. Kantor borrows from Witkacy the existential metaphor of childhood as a reminder of death: childhood and old age, birth and death, are the parentheses, the bookends of human existence. The prologue to *Brainiowicz* provides a stunning image that is the crux of the entire play:

> Żywych jaszczurów napiętnowane mordy
> Gęgają w rudą przestrzeń bezimiennej planety.
> Pokarbowane w mękę nadisteń,
> Poząbkowane w niemowlęce *fałdki*,
> *Pofałdowane* w starcze uzębienia.

Unfortunately, Daniel Gerould's translation of *Tumor* fails to capture the point of this passage:

> Living salamanders' branded mugs
> Cackle in the nameless planet's red expanse.
> Serrated in the torment of surexistence,
> Denticulated into baby *puckers*,
> *Enfolded* into old senile dentures.[275]

Gerould successfully translates the wordplay on denticulated/dentures, but he misses the point of *pofałdowane/fałdki*. In Polish, the noun *fałdka* (singular of *fałdki*) can mean both "a ruffle on a baby's dress" and "a facial wrinkle." The adjective *pofałdowane* – a derivative of *fałdka* – can, not surprisingly, mean "ruffled," or "puckered," but, more importantly, it can also mean "wrinkled" (as in "facial wrinkle"). In this sense, the word pair *pofałdowane/fałdki*, functions as a pair of bookends, linguistically and symbolically breaching the mental and existential space between the two poles of human life: birth and death, from a baby's puckers to an old man's wrinkles and dentures. Gerould's translation, "puckered/enfolded," fails to capture that essential, existential meaning in Witkiewicz's wordplay. But the wordplay unifying birth and death at the heart of Witkiewicz's play becomes the conceptual core of Kantor's *Dead Class*. To quote Barbara Kazimierczyk, *Dead Class* "is a *mysterium tremendum* of human existence, stretched between its two poles: childhood and death. It is a poetically condensed struggle with the spectra of annihilation and oblivion, a struggle with oblivion that man, a mortal being, constantly faces."[276] Or as Marek Jodłowski puts it, "The women wear long black dresses; the men wear black coffin suits. And when – at first slowly, shyly, and then zealously – they raise their hands, fingers, the coffin suits begin to resemble school uniforms (the identification of birth and death?)"[277] The bookend structure is important because it parallels the trauma of two wars, with Witkacy's own life, and suicide on the eve of the second war, echoing the historical narrative.

Besides providing textual and metaphorical subtext to *Dead Class*, Witkacy, particularly his theory of pure form, greatly influenced Kantor's understanding of theatre and theatrical space. Describing Kantor's aesthetic style in *Postdramatic Theatre*, Hans-Thies Lehman poignantly argues that Kantor's work is thoughtfully postmodern, as it is dismantling traditional dramatic formulas. Lehman writes, "There is a search here for a 'state of non-acting' and non-continuous plot structure, but instead repeatedly expressionistically condensed scenes, combined with a quasi-ritualistic form of conjuring up the past: 'This process means dismembering logical plot structures, building up scenes, not by textual reference, but by reference to associations triggered by them.'"[278] Lehman, however, locates Kantor's highly sophisticated aesthetic language in a broader postdramatic category, forgetting about Witkacy's theory of pure form and its influence on Kantor's theatre. Marek Jodłowski, on the other hand, explains the connection, suggesting that Witkacy's theory of pure form, in fact, brings forth all other literary layers of *Dead Class*:

> Kantor calls Schulz and Witkiewicz "participants in his séance." This is not only because some scenes were derived from *Tumor Brainowicz* (The Old Man in the Toilet becomes Tumor, and the Woman with a Mechanical Cradle, his wife, Rozhulantyna, etc.); and not only because there are echoes of Schulz short stories like "The Retired," "Mister," or "Treatise on Mannequins." What most significantly characterizes Kantor's debt to Schulz and Witkiewicz is the way he manages to evoke the density of Schulz's prose, and the way in which his thought mirrors the categories of Witkacy's *Theory of Pure Form*.[279]

Following Witkacy's premise of a theatrical work's coherence within its own system of signification, Kantor famously said *"Dead Class* is a closed work. It works alternately by provoking fascination and repulsion. It could even evoke the feeling of shame in a viewer who realizes that he is permitted to become a voyeur peeking into final matters."[280] Or, as Anna Hoffman puts it: "*Dead Class* has no beginning and no end in the traditional sense."[281] The play's structure is like an Escher dragon, eating its own tail, or a Mobius strip that defies spatial logic. Its circular structure resists gratuitous critical engagement. According to Witkiewicz's *Theory of Pure Form*, language in theatre affects the viewer on many levels by its sound-rhythm, meaning and imagery. Thus, sound is as important as visual images. Following Witkacy's footsteps, "Kantor had his sound engineer take care of the musical effects, which were most effective, and often evoked Polish fantasies of prewar extravagance. *Valse Française*, also known as *Walczyk Babuni* (Grandma's Waltz), was a constant feature in family song books."[282] The music was intended to capture the prewar atmosphere of cafés and salons. Composed by Adam Karasiński in 1907, "the diabolic Waltz Français brings to mind characters from Witkacy and Gombrowicz, conjuring Cracow's coffee houses and the mad avant-garde that filled them."[283] The music, the images, the cavalier approach to Witkacy's text, and the entire structure of *Dead Class* are all meant to capture the forgotten worlds of both Cracow's avant-garde and small, Polish-Jewish *shtetls*. Frank Marcus of the *Sunday Telegraph* is one of the few foreign critics who points out the dense mixture of images and music aimed to evoke a particular time and place within the structural context, reminiscent of the Theatre of the Absurd:

> The action is grotesque, macabre, and farcical, reflecting the Gothic splendour of [Kantor's] hometown, Cracow, its sense of tragic destiny coupled with an awareness of its absurdity. Witkiewicz, the poet and artist whose ideas inspired Kantor, had affinities with Artaud and anticipated the Absurdist movement. I shall long remember these mature, black-hatted pupils, recalling in their attitudes the etching of Chagall, tripping with their marionettes to the strains of romantic waltz.[284]

In *Dead Class* the motif of old, small-town Galicia intertwines with fragments of Witkacy's *Tumor Brainiowicz*, capturing the anxious, early twentieth-century culture.[285] To quote Krzysztof Miklaszewski: "I have never seen any other play that capture[s] so deeply all the anxieties of modern civilization, as expressed by the author of *Tumor Brainiowicz*."[286] In that sense, *Dead Class* is as much a "history lesson" as it is a theatre work.[287] It recalls times gone that return to the subconscious in dreams and nightmares, mixing longing, horror, pain and laughter.[288] How, then, does Witkacy fit into Kantor's "history lesson"? He provides both structure and texture to *Dead Class*: its absurd but internally coherent postdramatic overtext; its multilayered visual, auditory and textural subtext.

Chapter 31

AN AGE OF GENIUS: BRUNO SCHULZ AND THE RETURN TO CHILDHOOD

Kantor's second literary inspiration was Bruno Schulz, a Polish-Jewish writer of the interwar period, widely regarded as one of the most imaginative writers of his generation. His collection of short stories, *Cinnamon Shops* (published in English as *The Street of Crocodiles*), was first published in 1934 in Warsaw. A second collection, titled *Sanatorium Under the Sign of the Hourglass*, was published three years later, and included a series of illustrations that Schulz created especially for the book. A third collection, *The Messiah*, was lost during World War II. A collection of Schulz's personal letters, titled *Book of Letters*, has only recently been published. Born in 1892 in Drohobycz, a small, predominantly Jewish town located near Lvov, Schulz spent most of his life in his hometown, rarely leaving. He considered Drohobycz a microcosm of the modern world, a place where small and grand passions play out against the canvas of drudgery-filled, day-to-day existence. He drew his inspiration from the town's daily rhythms, proving himself to be an accurate observer of its life and inhabitants. During World War II, Schulz's visual talents earned him protection from a Gestapo officer, Felix Landau, who was stationed in Drohobych and who admired Schulz's drawings. Schulz was eventually shot by another Gestapo officer as payback for Schulz's protector shooting the officer's own "personal Jew," a dentist. The bitter irony of Schulz's own death has never been lost; in fact, it has become a part of his legend, always present in the consciousness of those who come to admire his writing. Indeed, Schulz's writing has been recognized worldwide by the likes of Bohumil Hrabal, Danilo Kis and John Updike. His life is the subject of Cynthia Ozick's novel *The Messiah of Stockholm*. To commemorate the 100th anniversary of his life, and the 15th anniversary of his death, UNESCO designated 1992 the Year of Bruno Schulz.

The main protagonist of Schulz's short stories is young Józef (the author's alter ego), and Jacob, his father (modeled on Schulz's own father). The father is a demiurge, a demigod, who has control over the material world and the ability to make things out of nothing. Yet, he is also a slave to his passions and relinquishes his creative powers, unable to resist the spell of young women. Narrated from the child's point of view, Schulz's stories follow the form of *Künstlerroman*, a subgenre of the *Bildungsroman*: a coming-of-age novel that specifically maps the growth of an artist from childhood to creative maturity. An acute observer, Józef surveys people, objects, places and his overall surroundings, all of which provide inspiration for his artistic growth. Although Schulz never moved away from Drohobycz, his two short story collections are widely recognized as masterpieces of surrealist writing. They're packed with rich descriptions, eccentric characters, multilayered figurative language and surprising metaphors, neologisms and regionalisms.

How does Kantor's *Dead Class* capture or relate to Schulz's rich, dense prose?[289] Like Witkacy and Kantor, Schulz was also a visual artist. Using a rare printing technique called *cliché-verre*, Schulz produced a series of sketches of daily scenes of his native Drohobycz, some of them illustrations for his short stories. Schulz's visual imagination is apparent in his writing, which is characterized more by rich imagery and vivid descriptions than by dialogue or action. For that reason alone, Miklaszewski suggests, Schulz's prose is difficult to adapt to the stage. Dialogue and action are the typical domains of theatre, more accessible than image and description. Therefore, Miklaszewski argues, "Every attempt to adapt Schulz's stories must end in failure."[290] Bronisław Mamoń agrees, concluding that "Schulz's prose, when stuffed into a dialogue, immediately becomes dead, falling apart into cheap, impressionistic images."[291] Commenting on Wojciech J. Has' film adaptation of Schulz's *Sanatorium Under the Sign of the Hourglass*,[292] Puzyna notes that "The Jewish aspect was very well developed in terms of costumes, sets, language. You could feel the presence of the consultants, advisors, etc. But you could no longer feel Schulz."[293] Responses to Has' film version vary: some critics declared "Schulz's death at the hands of Has," while others acknowledged that, because the structure of Schulz's novels is virtually impossible to represent, Has deserves credit for at least trying.[294]

However, despite their nearly unanimous conviction on the untheatrical nature of Schulz's prose, critics also unanimously agree that Kantor's interpretation of Schulz's work is an exception to the rule. Writing about *Dead Class*, Krzysztof Miklaszewski admits that he "could never imagine that anyone could capture the sensual metaphors of Bruno Schulz" in the way that Kantor does.[295] Many critics shared Miklaszewski's sense of wonder, fascinated by the uncanny way that *Dead Class* evokes the atmosphere of Schulz's mysterious world of the long-gone Polish *shtetl*. Artur Sandauer writes that, in *Dead Class*, "traces of Witkacy disappear [...] and Schulz resonates more clearly."[296] Puzyna argues that Schulz "dredges from Kantor's unconscious the elements that Witkacy could not."[297] Unlike Has' film, Kantor's *Dead Class*, Puzyna suggests, "captures the atmosphere, the climate of those days, ideally."[298] Nina Király explains that Kantor succeeded because "In drama, ritual is a primary resource from which theatrical myth is constructed. Kantor uses Schulz's texts in the same way, by constructing a mental reality, in which – as in a dream – the difference between reality and illusion dissolves."[299] Schulz's short stories and drawings provide a blueprint for the rich imagery of Kantor's *Dead Class*. Like Schulz, Kantor operates with mental shortcuts, visual imagery, and rich, nightmarish dreamscapes. As in Schulz, in *Dead Class*, Kantor's objects are deprived of their utilitarian function: a chair is not for sitting; a cradle is also a coffin; at every turn of the bicycle wheel, a wax corpse of a child pops up; a window is detached from the wall. Objects live their own lives, function in their own time-space.[300]

Understanding the literary context of Kantor's ideas provides a much more profound understanding of the visual signposts that construct the play's most evocative landscapes. Kantor not only shares with Schulz a dreamy sense of a pre-1914 village life, he actually borrows from Schulz, as Puzyna notes, a number of specific elements:

> Mannequins, a Cheder, a small-town Galicia gymnasium, archaic, warped characters in black costumes, perverse erotic allusions, double entendres, the entire sphere of psychoanalytical and psycho-social insinuations, allusions and secret relations, […] old, dusty books, necrologs, a shameful sense of something forbidden happening there in the corner, a forgotten pile of junk coming back to life, emanating its own existence only to be thrust back into eternity. Almost all of Schulz is there, in *Dead Class*, everything, except one sentence literally quoted from Schulz's text.[301]

Two motifs that frequently reappear in Schulz's work, both his drawings and writings, particularly fascinated Kantor. One of them is an image of an old man returning to a classroom, a final trip down memory lane before he faces eternity. This image is taken directly from Schulz's short story "The Old Age Pensioner." The second motif is the recurring image of an adult carrying a child, a smaller version of himself, in his arms, trying to come to terms with his life by reexamining his childhood. These two images, essential for Schulz's creative imagination, invest Kantor's *Dead Class* with a complex web of meanings and associations that encompass broader existential themes as well as a specifically Polish aesthetic.

In "The Old Age Pensioner" (sometimes translated as "The Retired"), a short story from *Sanatorium Under the Sign of the Hourglass*, Schulz wanted to portray, as he wrote to his friend, Romana Halpern, "the human fear of loneliness, of the barren land of an unnecessary and marginal life."[302] In the story, an old, decrepit man, Simon, is harassed by a crowd of young boys: "Sometimes they [the boys] venture up to my bench in their lunatic chases, throwing over their shoulders some obscure abuse at me. Their faces seem to come off their hinges in the violent grimaces that they make at me. Like a pack of busy monkeys, in a self-parody of clowning, this bunch of children runs past me, gesticulating with a hellish noise."[303] Trying to win them over, the elderly Simon adopts some of their behaviors: he makes silly faces, improper gestures and hellish noises. Enjoying the childish pranks and games, and longing for some human contact, he decides to go back to school, and politely asks the headmaster not to be "treated differently in any way, [than the other boys], even with regard to corporal punishment." Led by the headmaster, old Simon enters the classroom, "looking around the mobile, awkwardly grimacing faces, the same situation [as] fifty years before." Eventually, he is accepted by the boys and becomes one of them, "engrossed in a thousand affairs, intrigues, and interests." He "[becomes] a complete child."[304] However, the "blissful period of childhood solidarity with the other boys"[305] is suddenly interrupted when, one day, Simon gets picked up by a gust of wind and is "carried higher and higher into the unexplored yellow space."[306] His disappearance is barely noticed and elicits only a sly, bitter smile and a cool, matter-of-fact statement from the schoolmaster: "We must cross his name off the register."[307]

Schulz ascribed a different literary form to each stage of life: "Monologue and lyricism belong to youth. Dialogue and the novel belong to adulthood, and theatre is a domain of old age. [...] That is the main reason why Schulz propagate[d] the idea of 'a return to childhood.' For Schulz, a return to childhood [did]n't mean a return to immaturity. On the contrary, it mean[t] reaching maturity through different, more effective means."[308] Schulz considered childhood an "'age of genius,' a time when no barrier existed between an inner psyche and the outer world, between dreams and reality, between desire and fulfilment, between the intellectual and the sensual – the time of the origins of poetry."[309] For Schulz, childhood is a mythic age during which one is completely submerged in the world. To quote Jerzy Ficowski, "As a whole, Schulz's stories are really reconstructions of a mythic 'book of childhood,' and he terms its symbolic prototypes the Book of the Authentic."[310] For Schulz, "There is no return to childhood 'in general,' however; Schulz returns to his own particular childhood and it is there that he finds the elements of his poetic constructs. His own childhood supplied what he termed the 'iron capital' of his imagination and his 'archetypes.'"[311] In a 1936 letter to one of his friends, Andrzej Pleśniewicz, Bruno Schulz wrote:

> What you say about our artificially prolonged childhood – about immaturity – bewilders me somewhat. Rather, it seems to me that this kind of art, the kind which is so dear to my heart, is precisely a regression, a return to childhood. Were it possible to turn back development, achieve a second childhood by some circuitous road, once again have its fullness and immensity – that would be the incarnation of an "age of genius," "messianic times" which are promised and pledged to us by all mythologies. My ideal goal is to "mature" into childhood. This would really be a true maturity.[312]

One of the recurring images in Schulz's writing is that of a child carried in his father's arms. It was an image archetypical of Schulz's creative memory, and he described it a number of times in different contexts. One of his most evocative descriptions appears in a letter to Witkacy:

> I don't know why some images from our childhood stay with us. They are like threads in a web of meanings that crystallize around us while we try to make sense of the world. One such image has always been for me that of a child carried by his father in his father's arms through the night, conversing with the darkness around them. The father enfolds the child tightly in his arms, protecting him from the element that speaks and speaks, but for the child, these arms are diaphanous. The night penetrates them, and between the father's calming whispers, the child hears the constant, pervasive moaning of the darkness. Tortured and overcome with fatalism, the child responds to them with tragic readiness, fully submerged in elements from which there is no escape. These early images delineate for artists the boundaries of their art.[313]

This image haunts Schulz's writing; he often described it as a fundamental image, which eventually established a framework for his artistic sensibility. As he put it: "These early images mark out for artists the boundaries of their creative powers. [...] they do not discover anything new after that, they only learn how to understand better and better the secret entrusted to them at the outset."[314] The same image of a father and child appears in another short story, titled "Spring":

> A man walks under the starry grist spilling out of the mills of night; he walks hugging a child in the folds of his cloak; constantly on his way in his continual wandering though the endless spaces of night. The distant worlds come quite close, frighteningly bright, they send violent signals through eternity in mute, unutterable statements – while he walks on and on and soothes the little girl endlessly, monotonously, and without hope, helpless against the whispers and sweet seductions of the night, against the one word formed on the lips of silence, when no one is listening to it…[315]

Schulz's poetic fascination with childhood reflects a longstanding tradition. Krzysztof Miklaszewski notes that the *fin-de-siècle* fascination with childhood originates in Romanticism:

> The fascination with childhood – like with the motif of a doll or marionette – comes from Romanticism. The child became then, according to Christian principles, a symbol of innocence and purity. As a being closer to nature, the child acts on impulse; it reads the world more directly. […] Eventually, the world as seen through children's eyes becomes even more important. […] Sad melancholic children are portrayed as possessed by grown-up passions; they play and replay the dramas of love and jealousy, hate and death.[316]

The early twentieth century, partially under the influence of Freud's psychoanalytical interpretation of childhood as a source of self-knowledge, was a period of renewed interest in child psychology, especially with regard to the differences between adults' and children's points of view. For example, in their 1918 book *The Psychology of Childhood*, Naomi Norsworthy and Mary Theodora Whitley wrote: "The difference between adults and children in imagination may be discussed under three heads: differences in kind of images, differences in vividness of images, and differences in number of images. […] Children visualize more. It is probable that in childhood the proportion of visual images is greater than at any other time."[317] Many European writers of the late nineteenth and early twentieth centuries, from Proust to Joyce, looked to childhood for the key to self-knowledge. The newly independent Poland of the interwar period focused its hopes and attention on a fresh generation of children; a passionate pedagogical discussion took place in schools and in public discourse. One pedagogical trend, the so-called New School, rejected traditional education and focused on developing a separate language that would adequately describe and discern the specificity and uniqueness of child psychology and experience.[318] All these efforts resulted in a renewed interest in childhood as a source of knowledge and creativity, inspiring a number of autobiographical *Bildungsroman* and *Künstlerroman*. In autobiographical *Bildungsroman* and *Künstlerroman*, the author often juxtaposes childhood experience *vis-à-vis* the modern world, in order to comment on contemporary values. In a sense, the return to childhood becomes a way to reject present reality.

For Schulz, becoming aware of one's existence allows one to "return to childhood, that is, to mature and consequently develop an attitude towards the world that enables engagement with the world through authentic values."[319] In this sense, Schulz's poetic vision of childhood channels the general anxiety of the interwar period. Schulz viewed childhood as a lost arcadia, a moment when one is unaware of the true dangers facing one's world and imaginary monsters have superhuman powers. Because children are sheltered from the outside world of artificial wants and desires (*vis-à-vis* the child's authentic emotions), childhood is also an infinitively tragic moment of oblivion, destroyed in a minute by the crushing realities of the world and human existence. Childhood is thus for Schulz a time suspended in an existential vacuum, and his writings are permeated with ominous visions of death and misery, intertwined with grotesque attempts to embed meaning into an otherwise meaningless human existence. Combining the idea of childhood with that of old age – a kind of existential montage that forces us "to see the adult in a disturbing and true light [...] not as an acclamation of experiences, but as a child who is just a lot closer to death"[320], Kantor was influenced predominantly by Schulz's philosophical ideas about childhood.

Schulz's idea of the return to childhood forms the basis of Kantor's *Dead Class*. The play opens with An Absent Old Man – the "MAIN IDEA," as Kantor called him – slowly taking his place on the school bench. As with Schulz's Old Age Pensioner, Kantor's Absent Old Man returns to the classroom to remember – if only briefly – the atmosphere of his childhood. He remains still for a moment, staring vacantly into the eternity before him. As Wiesław Borowski notes: "The stillness of the first scene both fascinates and repulses."[321] Eventually, the Absent Old Man leaves, or rather is led away by another man. They quickly return but, no longer alone, they're accompanied by a group of adult pupils, dressed like them, in black garb and long, black dresses. Each pupil carries a mannequin of a child in his or her arms. If the child lives in a world dominated by imagination, adulthood is a world of rational and pragmatic thinking. To quote Święcicki, "According to Kantor, the child mannequins embody the memory of childhood, abandoned and forgotten by the pragmatism of life."[322] Or, as Kantor puts it:

> The Absent Old Man – I call him THE MAIN IDEA. The basis for the entire spectacle. In one happy moment, I came up with the idea of connecting the actors, old men who return to their classroom to remember their childhoods, with the figures of wax children, dressed in school uniforms. To connect literally and forever…these are rather children's corpses… The old people carry them like their own childhoods… dead children fall down, held by the last thread, some are dragged as if they are a burden, a "ball and chain," as if they crawled onto those who, aging, killed their childhoods with their socially sanctioned adulthoods…[323]

Or, as Daniel Gerould comments on that most famous Kantorian image:

> In *Dead Class* the pupils are senile old people at the edge of the grave, sent back to school bearing with them little dummy-children, who are the dreams lost in the pragmatic

process of living and growing up. They endlessly repeat the same suspended gestures, which they will never finish, because they are forever imprisoned within them.[324]

The old people, wearing bluish-white makeup, look like "cadavers, ghosts, or mannequins. Wearing mostly black and dusty clothing against two black backdrops, these actors have a pale green, deathly pallor. Most are gray-haired and old. Some men play old women, while some women play men. Appearing particularly treacherous, though, is one 'live' man in a black velvet suit."[325] They sit still, staring vacantly at the audience "with the glazed knowledge of a nightmarish world. Suddenly, with a thunderous music, the 'dummies' arise, and under the quizzical eye of their mentor Kantor, enact their ritualized education. The figures erupt in the space, one with a bicycle attached to his leg, another with a window pressed anxiously to her face, a third yields a bare breast. Marching and whispering, they arise and subside rhythmically, anarchically enacting their ferocious rituals of birth and death."[326] The pupils parade to the sounds of a waltz, moving rhythmically in a somnambulist stupor. Carrying the child mannequins, they form Kantor's famous bio-objects: theatrical forms that combine a living actor and an object. Clinging to the actors, the wax figures of children constrain them twofold: physically (as baggage the actors cannot get rid of) and metaphorically (as symbols of their dead childhoods). Urszula Rzewiczok vividly describes the images:

> In *Dead Class*, actors are the alter-egos of the dead. They are made up as old people, carrying the backpacks and the effigies of themselves from their childhoods. They parade around their benches in a helpless march, freezing once in a while like in a photograph. They speak in fragments, which include words in Latin and Hebrew, quotes from the Bible, mythology and history, and school rhymes. Once in a while, the sound of Waltz François blasts from the speakers. The pulsating rhythm of their attempts breaks and disintegrates into apparent chaos. Tadeusz Kantor, present all the time on the stage, conducts his actors with impatient gestures. The layering of words, meanings, and symbols is very dense.[327]

The wax children look like bizarre growths, parasitizing the bodies of the old men and women, who cannot or are unable to shake them off. Kantor's succinct description captures the image's essence: "Some of [the wax figures] are swaying inertly, clinging with a desperate movement, hanging, trailing, as if they were the remorse of conscience, curling up at the actor's feet, as if creeping over these metamorphosed specimens...human creatures unashamedly exhibiting the secrets of their past...with the EXCRESCENCE of their own CHILDHOOD..."[328] In his interview with Michal Kobialka, Kantor elaborates on the ideas behind his own fascination with childhood:

KOBIALKA: This notion of journey, this quest for intimate and distant memories, seems to me to be closely connected with the concept of a child's perspective on life as discussed by Evgeni Zamyatin in his "On Literature, Revolution, and Entropy." He wrote that "children are after all the boldest philosophers;

KANTOR: they come into life naked, not covered by one single small leaf of dogma or creed. That is why their questions are always so ridiculously naive and so frighteningly complicated."[329] This journey is the journey of a man who, like a child, poses questions which sound banal to us who are dominated by the system but are at the same time frighteningly complicated.

KANTOR: What you have just mentioned was shown in The *Dead Class*. Each of those old men murdered the memory of his childhood. They are cantankerous. Each of them carries a wax figure of a child whom they killed. What was a true spirit in a child becomes a stilted and false convention. That image was also a leading force of Those Serious Men, which was exhibited at the Pompidou Centre in Paris. Those serious men – ministers, directors – are caught performing childish activities; they pick their noses, undress and dress up, ride on bicycles, etc. In The *Dead Class*, there was a special mechanism with a plastic finger to pick one's nose. A child not only has a vivid imagination but also true responses. Maybe if all politicians had something of the child in them we would live in peace.[330]

Like Schulz's Old Age Pensioner, the pupils revert to infantile pranks, which seem both immature and a matter of life and death. To quote Daniel C. Gerould, "Reversion to the infantile, the childish pranks and degraded experiences of the schooldays, seems immature from the adult point of view, but is in fact the original matter of life."[331] The pupils reveal their dark sides with something resembling the perverse pleasures of an exhibitionist: "The images overlap. Black clad and dusty with matching faces, the middle-aged-to-elderly relive childhood in school, seminal in more senses than one – excretory, sexual, emotional, lonely, ambitious, resigned, mediocrity and nothingness."[332] The Somnambulist Prostitute randomly exposes her left breast, or the Man with the Bicycle takes off his pants in a gesture of childish anger. They perform this one gesture *ad infinitum*, as if under a magic spell, trapped and unable to escape their childhood habits. Kantor takes the concept of Brecht's *gestus* to the extreme, exaggerating or perhaps even satirizing it:

> Occassionally the class acts in unison, reciting a lesson or staging a funeral, but mostly they revert in isolation to the obsessive habits of their schooldays: wheeling a bicycle, sitting on the lavatory, grimacing through a windowpane, exhibiting themselves shamelessly since even shame is behind them now. This zombie zoo, with their wrinkled faces and gaping mouths, is made extraordinarily poignant by the silent participation of the dummy children, at one moment discarded like firewood on the ground, at another sitting helplessly at the desk as if their presence could redeem the lives that were to be debauched by war and corruption.[333]

In addition to a wax figure of him- or herself, each pupil also carries objects from childhood, symbolizing its humiliations and "incidents, passed over in embarrassed silence," shameful and pitiful aspects of each character.[334] Functioning as signs, the objects become more powerful than the characters themselves. Like all of Kantor's bio-objects, the characters have no names other than those given to them by the objects they are carrying. Hence, the characters of *Dead Class* are An Old Man in the Lavatory, An Old Man with a Bicycle, A Woman Behind the Window, A Street- and Sleep-Walker, and the Woman with a Mechanical Cradle. The anonymity forced on the pupils by the objects is terrifying, as it denies them not just their own personalities, but their very lives. In the realm of fiction, they come to "define [the] character and the whole past of the actor."[335] The strange attachment of the pupils to their objects brings them constant humiliation. Crying over her cradle, the Woman with a Mechanical Cradle is spit on and cursed by the whole class, who take advantage of this moment of vulnerability. Humiliated, she is placed on the Family Machine, an object with "two wings, provided with footholds, [which moves] to the movements of human legs."[336] Her legs are pulled apart by two pupils, and everyone laughs at her with a sickening, degenerate cackle. Treated as an object, she metamorphoses into an empty copy of herself, a half-insane creature screaming out loud lines from Witkiewicz's *Tumor* about the infinite pleasures of childbirth and her insatiable desire to be permanently in labor. Strapped to the machine, she becomes a new form, inanimate and alien to herself. To retrieve her identity, she must transcend her role as well as her body. Her individuality "has to permeate and revive this new organism."[337] Although she eventually leaves the machine and comes back to her bench as though nothing has happened, her torture starts a cyclical process of humiliation and recovery. Every couple of minutes one of the pupils breaks down in a spasm of "agonizing excess reaching the stage of cruelty, feverish raving, dying," and, after being humiliated by the class, he comes back to his bench as though the incident never happened.[338] Her condition, genuine and tragic, transmits itself to the audience. As Kantor puts it: "The emotions [of the spectators] appear first of all as a consequence of this sudden metamorphosis. The scene of cruelty ceases to be a spectacle. It deepens."[339]

As with Schulz, childhood for Kantor has multiple meanings: "the parade of the dead children is more than a symbol, more than a striking pattern, it is quite simply agonizing."[340] It is agonizing to watch because Kantor's show captures Schulz's subtly ominous vision, with its broad and lugubrious framework for understanding things to come. As Zuzanna Jastrzębska puts it: "Tadeusz Kantor brought into *Dead Class* the poetry, philosophy, and artistic vision of Bruno Schulz. There was, in Schulz's drawings and writings, foreboding of the horrifying crimes of fascism, all the sufferings that beleaguered humanity during World War II."[341] Or, as Rolando Perez poignantly frames it: "Throughout Schulz's work one is confronted with a certain quiet anxiety about the fate of material existence either because of the limit of Spirit as it resides in matter or because, looming in the not too distant future, are (human) forces operating without our knowledge that threaten to bring life to an end."[342] For those born in the 1920s, childhood was an ephemeral moment of escape from the horrors to come. For those born later, childhood was a nightmare that many did not survive. Yet, despite the ominous tone that Kantor takes from Schulz, in *Dead Class* there is also a kind of tragic, quiet and dignified resignation to life, against all odds. As Richard Calvoressi puts it, *Dead Class* "is a terrifying 20th century Dance of Death, full of violent gesture, distortion and noise, but there is an irrepressible life in the antics of these mannequin-like creatures, however weighed down and imprisoned they seem by their childhood selves."[343]

Chapter 32

CONVERSING WITH GOMBROWICZ: THE DEAD, THE FUNNY, THE SACRED AND THE PROFANE

If Witkacy provides the structural and textural framework of *Dead Class*, and Schulz gives it its philosophical and existential framework, then it is Gombrowicz who provides the play's subtly ironic and iconoclastic undertone. In *Dead Class*, Kantor, as he himself explains it, reads Schulz through Gombrowicz, paying homage to Gombrowicz's cult novel, *Ferdydurke*.[344] In his review of Kantor's show, Jan Bończa-Szabłowski points out that, besides Schulz, "The child-mannequins carried by the old people remind us of Gombrowicz's thesis about an eternal childhood lasting into old age, but also of the vision of the world as a classroom. The place where we still have some delusional hope that we will learn something, find some definitive meaning to our actions, feelings and dreams."[345]

Born in 1904, Gombrowicz studied law in Warsaw while simultaneously pursuing his literary ambitions. His first volume of short stories was published in 1933, and his first comedy, *Iwona, Princess of Burgundy*, was published two years later. In 1939, Gombrowicz traveled to Argentina for two weeks, but war broke out, and he ended up staying in Argentina for over 20 years, working at a bank to support himself. For a long time, Gombrowicz was considered a dissident writer by the Polish postwar communist government, and he published his work through *Kultura*, a magazine for Polish intellectual émigrés in Paris. In 1950 Gombrowicz published his novel *Trans-Atlantic*. It was followed by another novel, *Pornography*, in 1960, and by *Cosmos* in 1965. Following their unexpected and overwhelming success, Gombrowicz's works were once again banned in Poland. It would be many years before his books were again published in his homeland.

In 1967, Gombrowicz was awarded the International Literary Prize. He died two years later of heart failure.[346] Since his death, Gombrowicz has become one of Poland's most revered writers, celebrated worldwide for his innovative writing style, which combines sardonic black humor with subtle, offhand profundity. His novels are seen as precursors to the surrealist experiments of the 1950s and 1960s. His theatrical plays also make him a precursor of the Theatre of the Absurd, though Gombrowicz flatly denied this on many occasions: "my theatre is not an 'absurd' theatre and I am basically against the obsessions of the absurd and the tone of present day literature," he said in his last interview.[347]

Published to critical acclaim in 1937, *Ferdydurke* became the standard-bearer of Polish avant-garde writing of the prewar era. Its publication immediately inspired passionate commentaries and arguments. In a 1938 review of the book, Jan Lorentowicz wrote that *Ferdydurke* "simply bursts with talent."[348] The only problems that Lorentowicz saw with the novel was its "lack of good taste" and its going too far in terms of its implicitly sexual undertones.[349] J. W. Skiwski wrote that *Ferdydurke* appeared to him as "deeply unsympathetic."[350] Bruno Schulz called *Ferdydurke* "genius," proclaiming in his review that everyone must read it.[351] Alfred Łaszowski called it "auto-satire."[352] And Gustaw Herling-Grudziński declared his "cool admiration" for the novel.[353] As the book drew accolades from literary circles, so it attracted sharp critiques from the radical right and left, which condemned its individualistic vision of the world, refusal to take political positions, and blunt, unabashed mockery of all ideological viewpoints. Natalia Wiśniewska even went so far as to accuse Gombrowicz (and Schulz by extension) of supporting fascism, writing that: "They [Gombrowicz and Schulz] will raise their right hands and march 'nach Osten,'[354] worshipping their über-man, made in the image of the mannequin."[355] Stanisław Baczyński wrote that "both Schulz and Gombrowicz are suspended in a vacuum, lacking any real foundation on which the experiences of their books can be framed."[356] He accused *Ferdydurke* of "deforming reality," which can lead to "uncontrolled buffoonery." And, in a way, Baczyński had a point.

The events in the novel are preceded by a warning that it's half-dream and half-fantasy, blurring the reader's sense of what constitutes reality. *Ferdydurke*'s title is nonsensical, and the book "is meant as a parody and is an anti-novel at best."[357] The tone of the novel is always half-serious, with flowery idioms and idiotisms elevated to the level of seriousness that flips to nonsense, with poetic metaphors and neologisms that unravel even the most rigid, pompous discourse. As Rochelle H. Ross puts it: "Gombrowicz deals in a similar manner with every convention, and he does so in his original use of language, in the exaggerated humor, and in the mock-serious tone bordering on the ridiculous."[358]

Ferdydurke also mocked the literary canon of the 1920s. Built around the liberatory and martyrological motifs of the Romantic tradition, nineteenth-century Polish literature became a dominant source of post–World War I Polish identity, which dictated the trends of postwar literature. One of these trends was a rapidly emerging nationalism that quickly turned to xenophobia, constructing an image of Poland as a country squeezed between two totalitarian powers. It was this image that *Ferdydurke* attacked.[359] Yet, for all its clowning, *Ferdydurke* is also strangely ominous. In the foreword to its Spanish edition, Gombrowicz reminds readers that the book was published a year before the start of World War II, and that "one should keep this in mind when desiring to enter and understand its climate."[360]

In the novel, 30-year-old Joey (Józio), who is unable to grow up and "be something definite," is suddenly thrown back into the classroom and reduced to the mindless repetition of worn-out patriotic clichés.[361] Not being able to face "maturity" and all that it entails, particularly the lack of vagueness, Joey gets "pupa-fied" – reduced to a child: "My idiotic, infantile pupa had paralyzed me, taking away all my ability to resist."[362] In Polish, *pupa* means "bum" or "booty" and is an expression that mothers often use in conversations with their children. In *Ferdydurke*, *pupa* also means something else: it has a symbolic meaning that designates something big, a powerful, omnipotent and omnipresent force that is able to constrain one's spirit. Pupa also means "the fat pink bottom of the good bourgeois baby which [a grown] man becomes in *Ferdydurke* under the pressure of social idealism."[363] Going back to the classroom, Joey undergoes a quick process of "maturification," "for there is nothing that the Mature hate more, there is nothing that disgusts them more, than immaturity."[364] Yet, here, maturity and immaturity are reversed, and the idiotic literature lessons with the robotic Prof. Pimko turn into nonsense and grotesque. Under the circumstances, Joey tries to resist, "unafraid to say anything that comes to his mind, unaware of his own exaggerations, believing wholeheartedly in his own brilliance, digressing from joke to joke that often turns to ridicule."[365] Another method of escape from pupa-fication is to make a horrible *gemba* (or, *gęba*) (trans. "face; grimace"). In fact, the boys stage elaborate gemba duels, in which the loser is the one who is unable to take the look of the opponent's warped gemba. As a result of schooling and all the boyish games and pranks aimed to combat it, Joey slides further and further into immaturity, unable to resist the lightness of thought that it offers. As Robert Boyers notices, in *Ferdydurke*, the educational system "specializes not merely in the education of youngsters, but in the reduction of adults into children…"[366]

Jelenski argues that the Poles' enthusiastic postwar reception of *Ferdydurke* was partially due to the fact that they "recognized in *Ferdydurke* the image of their own situation in the face of that monstrous Sunday School which Stalinism was imposing on them."[367] After the war, *Ferdydurke*'s brazen dismissal of school authority and glorification of individualism was naturally seen as subversive. This of course turned the novel into a forbidden fruit. Łukasz Garbal cites Marek Hłasko, who recalls borrowing the novel for an hour from a friend, with a watch as collateral. As Łukasz Garbal points out, in the 1960s, *Ferdydurke* was part of the political discourse; Gombrowicz's vocabulary (especially the words *pupa* and *gemba*) entered vernacular language, particularly in reference to oppressive political structures.[368] But there was something more to it. For postwar Poles, *Ferdydurke* accidently, if ideally, captured the essence of the beaten swagger of the Polish spirit, the "hopeless hope" and pain, "but a pain with a smile and a shrug."[369]

Ferdydurke is a paean to freedom of thought, while simultaneously mocking the seriousness and pathos of national sacred values. Here's a typical exchange Joey has with the literature professor Pimko:

> [Pimko] took his spectacles off his nose, wiped them with his handkerchief, and placed them back on his nose, the nose that had now become indomitable. It was a truly nasal nose, trite and inane, consisting of two parallel, finite tubes. And he said:
> "What do you mean, a spirit?"
> "My spirit!" I exclaimed. He then asked:
> "You mean the spirit of your home, your country?"
> "No, not of my country, my own spirit!"
> "Your own?" he asked amiably, "we're talking about your spirit then? But are we at least familiar with the spirit of King Ladislas?"
> What, King Ladislas? I felt like a train suddenly shunted to the siding of King Ladislas. Stopped in my tracks, my mouth open, I realized that I was not familiar with the spirit of King Ladislas.

"And are we familiar with the spirit of the times? How about the spirit of Hellenic civilization? And the Gallic, and the spirit of moderation and good taste? And the spirit of the sixteenth-century bucolic writer, known only to myself, who was the first to use the word 'umbilicus'? And the spirit of language? Should one say 'use' or 'utilize'?"[370]

In another iconic scene, Miętus (Minty), one of Joey's friends, is asked to be enraptured by a great poet. Since he cannot make himself enraptured by the poet, he is told by Professor Bladaczka (Paleone) that "Great poetry being great and being poetry, cannot help but enrapture us." Near convulsions, Miętus replies desperately, "But I don't understand, how I can be enraptured when I am not enraptured!" Miętus' sentence entered the Polish vernacular permanently, denoting the absurd difference between the obligatory need "to be enraptured" by something that doesn't enrapture, and the reality of one's true feelings. Although originally the sentence referenced the national pathos of Romantic poetry, following World War II it became a cryptic code sentence referencing the communist system. Russell Brown offers poignant analysis of this scene:

> Unlike Schulz, Gombrowicz concentrates on negative aspects of school life; the teaching is mechanical and uninspired, and the boys are forced to admire a certain poet simply because he is considered great and ultimately because the teacher's job depends on the boys' uncritical acceptance of the standards of taste and the values of the system.[371]

Ferdydurke mocks everything that Poles found holy, including the cult and glorification of the dead, with everything – all the baggage of "cultural values," national history, and memory – that such veneration entails. In this context, maturity then means agreeing to participate in the national pathos, while immaturity means the irreverent mockery of that pathos. In fact, Prof. Pimko exemplifies the absurdity of this idea of 'maturity' stretched to its logical limits:

> The memory of the dead, said Pimko, "is the ark of the covenant between the new times and the old, just like the songs of the people (Mickiewicz). We live the life of the dead (A. Comte). Your aunt is dead, and this is a good reason, even a compelling reason, to extol her contribution to cultural thought. The deceased had her faults (he enumerated them), but she also had her good points (he enumerated them) which benefited everyone, all in all not a bad book, that is, I meant to say "C" plus – well then, to make a long story short, the deceased was a positive force, my overall assessment of her is rather favorable, which I consider it my pleasurable duty to tell you, since I, Pimko, stand guard of the cultural values your aunt undoubtedly still personifies, especially since she's dead.[372]

Ferdydurke is full of dark humor, but its mockery of the dead is effective only because of the profound reverence that Polish culture pays to its dead. Gombrowicz never crosses into the realm of sacrilege or profanity. He mocks the dead relatives, historical and literary figures and the national pathos that they stand for, as if they were living; they are, in many ways, part of the dialogue.

Ferdydurke is a book of serious ridicule. It ponders absurdity with a philosopher's profundity, perpetually oscillating between a joke and a scream. Yet, as Miłosz notices, Gombrowicz's dark humor has a "triumphant and joyous" tone.[373] Kantor captures that sense, revealing to us both the profundity and the absurdity of our existence. As Marian Sienkiewicz puts it: "Kantor recalls all of the password-signs, flawlessly capturing Gombrowicz's sardonic tone. He's also doing it with a sharp wit, revealing just how easy it is to recall our school past with a few words."[374] As a performance "Conversing with Gombrowicz," to quote Kantor, *Dead Class* engages *Ferdydurke* on multiple levels: "The Old Men are eternal boys who, when put on classroom benches, begin to act like children. It was enough to merely change their circumstances, just slightly, for the bubble of convention to burst."[375] Or, as Kantor puts it, "The Old Men 'slide' into being boys. This metamorphosis is rather shameful. This 'sliding' – they do it as if it were the last (forbidden) sexual pleasure. They 'slide' into boys, 'sucking up' to the boys."[376] Here, one of them drops his pants in a gesture of childhood defiance, revealing his pupa for all to see; there, others engage in gemba duels, making horrible and funny faces at each other, trying to scare each other and perhaps threaten death.

The interwar Polish educational canon focused on two things: re-establishing a sense of common national identity, which was lost during the years of partition, and defining Poland's position *vis-à-vis* its European legacy. Hence, on the one hand, a high school education stressed the history and glory of the Polish army, with a particular focus on the cult of Józef Piłsudski, who was a provisional leader of the newly reinstated Polish state during the years 1918–22, and who led a successful war against the Bolsheviks, thanks to which Poland was able to sustain its eastern borders. On the other hand, an interwar Polish education also stressed the study of Greek and Latin, and of ancient history and mythology. Thus, in Kantor's *Dead Class*, Judeo-Christian motifs, Cheder, the Hebrew alphabet, and so forth intertwine with Greek and Roman mythology. Solomon is mentioned along with Cleopatra and Prometheus. Kantor's Old Men and Women randomly exclaim names from Greek mythology and Roman history, the two paramount subjects of a pre–World War I Polish education. Dislodged from their context, dredged up from the long-forgotten corners of memory, and shouted out at random, these bits and pieces of the European literary canon symbolize the fragmentation and dissociation of European identity at the turn of the century. These literary bedrocks of European culture – which embody "the spirit of Hellenic civilization" – no longer signify the power of history, or the cultural heritage that guards centuries of European domination. Decontextualized, stripped of dignity, they become "small and defenseless," ridiculously discarded in the despised domain of mundane childhood Sunday-school lessons. *Dead Class* "lessons," such as "Solomon" and "Prometheus," expose the vulnerability of the ancient mythological and biblical heritage, the ambivalence of its staying power, and the fundamentally meaningless role that the proud "spirit of Hellenic civilization" has played in controlling or halting the fascist impulse that swept through Europe.[377] Pathos mixes with grotesque, equating low and high European culture. Like *Ferdydurke*, *Dead Class* mocks national sacrums and, like *Ferdydurke*, it questions both Polish and European legacies.

Inspired by Gombrowicz, *Dead Class* engages the dead with the same nonchalant attitude, a mixture of complete and utter reverence, and swaggering, offhand familiarity. This approach to death is deeply rooted in Polish literature; it appears and reappears in the works of Witkacy, Schulz, Gombrowicz and many others. In his book on Polish black humor, Tomasz Bocheński notes that "Death is egalitarian, dying is not. [...] Laughing at death is a privilege not granted to everyone. [...] Black humor thrives among monads, loners who laugh at their own and others' helplessness in final situations."[378] (Perhaps this is why Polish culture is rooted in black humor.) Kantor talks about death "without relying on macabre or symbolism. He avoids any kind of religious vision of 'resurrection' or any mysticism of 'eternal Tao.' Instead, he focuses on the external – cultural, social and biological symptoms of death: rituals, commentaries, monuments, cabinets of wax figures. [...] Thus, death is a cultural event, and not just an existential one."[379] In *Dead Class*, Death is represented by an Old Charwoman, dressed in black, who is both starkly severe and ridiculous. Many have compared Kantor's mixture of dark humor and existentialist themes to Beckett, but as Brian Barron points out, "Kantor is not Beckett. His symbolism is straightforward and always self-deflating, thus the black, black charwoman has a comic solo scene with the director, and her triumph as an Allegory-of-Death is marked by the unnatural swelling of her bosom and backside. And the jokes are all on us: they are enjoying themselves, they are actors, we are 'the others.'"[380] Kantor's fascination with, and nonchalance towards, death is deeply rooted in Polish culture; it's an attitude that some find too complex, even pathological. As Glenn Loney puts it:

> Whence comes this fascination with death? Is this by any chance from the same gangrened artery, connected to the same poisoned heart that gave us the cold ironies of Polanski's *Dance of the Vampires* or the tempestuous theatricality of Grotowski's *Poor Theatre*? For someone struggling to distance themselves from such tormenting thoughts, the obsessive vision of Kantor's *The Dead Class* might look like just one more contribution to the genre of the "Polish joke." But this really is not the case. What we are talking about is the very serious business of death.[381]

If *Dead Class* is Kantor's Polish joke, it is both tragically serious and hysterically funny.

Chapter 33

PANIRONY: "A PAIN WITH A SMILE AND A SHRUG"

Dead Class successfully combines horror and humor, pathos and the grotesque. Its moments of horror are reinforced by humor; moments of pathos are reinforced by the grotesque. Without an understanding of the context and meaning of what the actors say, the humor is lost, and the delicate line between pathos and grotesque turns into sentimentality.[382] Writing about Witkiewicz's humor, for example, Artur Sandauer asks: "What is Witkacy's humor about? What does it make fun of? After all, all laughter is laughter at something. To answer this question: Witkacy's humor, foremost, makes fun of realism. [...] The second object of Witkacy's parody is the Young Polishness, which he knows well enough as he himself is its product. Finally, Witkacy's third victim, besides naturalism and Young Polishness, is himself."[383] The Young Polishness (*młodopolszczyzna*) that Sandauer mentions refers to a turn of the century literary movement in Polish literature that "attempted to revive the religious faith of a bygone age, treating the rites of Catholicism as a source of creative inspiration."[384] For the poets of "Young Poland," "even the messianistic pathos of the great Romantic predecessors became an aesthetic impulse."[385] Due to its pathos and "stylistic extravaganza," the Young Polishness acquired a pejorative connotation, inviting the scorn and disdain of the emerging avant-garde, with Witkacy and Gombrowicz leading the way. It also embodied the nationalistic, xenophobic impulse that became essential for the interwar period of nation-building, but that also had portentous undertones. The satirical, self-mocking trend in Polish literature derided ardent prewar nationalist Catholicism, among other things.[386] After World War II it gave impetus to the subversively cynical attitudes of Polish society *vis-à-vis* the communist regime. As for today, in making fun of the Young Polishness, Witkacy's and Gombrowicz's "writings, although now so much part of the canon in Poland that they are studied in high school, continue to provoke by poking fun at such Polish sacred cows as Catholicism and Romanticism."[387] Grotowski, with his ambition of a holy theatre, rejected this cynicism. In fact, as Cioffi points out, any attempt at staging *Ferdydurke* would have been incompatible with Grotowski's methodology: "*Ferdydurke* [...] rejects Grotowski's aspirations to holiness for his theatre – it is defiantly irreverent."[388] *Ferdydurke*'s tone, however, lends itself effortlessly to Kantor's style.

Kantorian and Grotowskian mockeries of national sacrums have different origins and premises, yet that is not to say that Kantor was disinterested in the national pathos. In 1932, while studying at the Tarnów Gymnasium, he "designed and constructed sets for the Third Act of Wyspiański's *Wyzwolenie* (Liberation) and the Fourth Act of

Wyspiański's *Akropolis* as produced by the gymnasium amateur players in Sokol Hall."[389] Kantor spoke admiringly about Wyspiański's *Akropolis* on a number of occasions: "this maniacal and genius poet-decadent used a weird, for his times, method: he placed antique mythology in the old walls of Cracow's castles, and, responding to his call, the crowds of Greek heroes marched from Hades to the Polish Akropolis, the royal Necropolis."[390] Kantor eventually seemed to outgrow Wyspiański, and once stated tersely: "Wyspiański's Necropolis is simple: Necrophilia – as seen, of course, through the eyes of a Great Artist."[391] Unlike Grotowski's adaptation of *Akropolis*, however, *Dead Class* makes no attempt at grand syntheses of sacred proportions; on the contrary, it is "a frightening and disturbing mixture of comedy and horror."[392] Like *Ferdydurke*, Kantor's work is defiant of not just nationalistic pathos, but of any totalitarian structure that constrains and threatens the life and freedom of the individual. Humor, or its absence, delineates the oppressor's reach. To quote William Harris: "Kantor can't abide much European experimentation because of its lack of humor. 'To be without humor is to be without intelligence.' [For Kantor] [t]he Russians are humorless and therefore dangerous.'"[393]

Tomasz Bocheński points out that, in Schulz's work – as in Witkacy's and Gombrowicz's – "laughter behind the curtains of life fulfills the function of *catharsis*, emphasizing the pathos (tragedy) of our existence, and allowing us to see ourselves as small marionettes (mannequins)."[394] Schulz called this amusing theatre of existence a "panirony": a realization of the inconsequentiality of one's being. Mixing humor with pathos, panirony sneers at death and tragedy; it's a form of rebellion and a survival strategy. In a 1934 letter to Witkacy, Bruno Schulz discussed his own prose: "My inventiveness, my form or my writer's 'grimace' leans, just like yours, towards aberration, persiflage, buffoonery, and self-irony."[395] Or, as Dorota Głowacka puts it: "Schulz's text, saturated with language almost to the point of spilling into nonsense, is obsessed with the images of excess, overgrowth and proliferation."[396] Bogusław Gryszkiewicz frames Schulz's black humor in the context of modernist literature, particularly the gallows laughter of various avant-gardist groups whose work focuses on war and destruction. Modris Eksteins notes that, following World War I, humor became bitter and black.[397] Black humor was a "cult signature of the world isolated from conventional norms."[398] It allowed one to control an unbearable reality by trivializing it, while simultaneously building bonds between the oppressed. Gryszkiewicz points out that Schulz's humor is the humor of a world "after apocalypse [in which] there is nothing sacred, no bonds, laws or dogmas [...] in which everything is allowed and everything can be expected."[399] Gryszkiewicz argues that Schulz's humor is that of an ironist, or, to quote Adorno, in Schulz's writing "There is laughter because there is nothing to laugh at."[400]

Gryszkiewicz frames Schulz's writing in the tradition of Eastern European Jewish humor, which evolved as a survival strategy. Ofra Nevo describes the development of Jewish humor:

> What is identified in world-wide professional literature as Jewish humor refers to the humor that originated in 19th-century Eastern Europe. There, Jews lived under harsh conditions, confronted with real danger to their lives. Jews were intimately familiar

with feelings of hopelessness and the necessity to be passive when confronted with overwhelming forces and hostile people. For centuries, Jews have lived as unwelcome aliens in foreign lands. With no country of their own, they spread all over the world, at best tolerated, and usually persecuted or driven out. They learned to carry on in these oppressed, painful conditions through dedication to their religious beliefs, scholarship, culture and communal life. They clung to the belief that they were the chosen people, and this helped them feel superior despite being treated as inferiors. Best of all, they learned the usefulness and joy of humor, which enhanced their self-esteem and helped them cope with their intolerable predicament.[401]

Despite the despair that drives the Eastern European tradition of Jewish humor, there is an element of hope and a "zest for living." As Elliot Orling points out,

Humor is transcendent when it reflects the unwillingness of the individual to surrender to the impossible conditions of existence and attempts to achieve a measure of liberation from the social, political, economic, and even cosmic forces that remain beyond one's control. Jewish humor is thus conceptualized as transcending the conditions of despair and consequently is distinctive in its reflection of an unperturbable [sic] optimism and zest for living.[402]

Bruno Schulz's humor comes from this tradition. Grounded in Schulz's work, Kantor follows in his footsteps. In *Dead Class*, "we find both bitterness and humor as inseparably bound together as in real life."[403] To quote Oliver Cordelia: "[W]hat Kantor offers is all humanity in microcosm – the comedy and the tragedy, the passion, the petty and the piercing anxiety."[404] Or, as Jerzy Jarzębski puts it: "The essence of *Dead Class* rests on its ability to balance between metaphysics and a spoof. It is a bit like a dance of death, like a mysterium tremendum in which horror and grotesque go hand in hand. Perhaps only Kantor could combine them so effectively."[405] In Kantor's words, *Dead Class* is a chain reaction of "death – shame – circus – dry-rotted wood – sex – glitz – kitsch – humiliation – putrefaction – pathos – absolute…"[406]

It could be effectively argued that Kantor's humor also has its roots in Purim, the carnivalesque Jewish holiday celebrating the story of the *Megile* (the Book of Esther), which narrates the miraculous saving of the Jews of Persia. According to the story, during the fifth century BCE, Haman, the prime minister of King Ahasuerus' regime in Persia, intended to kill all the Jews in the kingdom. However, Mordecai, a Jewish sage, and Esther, his young and beautiful niece, devised a plot to stop him. Using her charms and her intelligence, Esther won over the king's heart and, as Queen, persuaded him to spare the Jews. Finding out about the plot, the king hanged Haman on the same gallows on which Mordecai was to be hanged. Purim is celebrated each year in the Hebrew month of Adar (February/March), and it includes a variety of performances; "masquerade, pranks, intoxication and general licentiousness pervade the holiday and contribute to the inversion of the social order that is its hallmark."[407] Having been performed by Jewish communities across Poland from the sixteenth century onwards, Purim "commemorates Haman's plan to annihilate the Jews, and their miraculous rescue. [... It] has remained an occasion for collective catharsis over a people's deliverance from its enemies; [...] a saturnalian and carnivalesque [...] mimesis of vengeance against evil."[408] Purim is at once a carnivalesque celebration and a symbolic victory over the oppressor. The performers are amateurs; dressed in homemade costumes, they move from home to home, disguised beyond recognition. Historically, Purim players (*Purimshpilers*), usually poor *yeshiva* students (students of Talmud), would write and rehearse the Purim play (*Purim Shpiel*) themselves and perform them going from home to home. The performances – based on the text of *Megile* – would draw in entire families which often gathered in living rooms to enjoy the show. At the end of the performance, the actors would ask for coins and sweet treats as a payment for their effort.

The cross-dressing, drunken-like abandon and amateurish quality of Kantor's actors, who pick up and drop the text in a carnivalesque fashion, captures the spirit of Purim. Growing up in multicultural Wielopole, Kantor most likely saw the Purim plays performed a number of times. In *Dead Class*, the celebration of Purim blends with the Mourner's Kaddish in a melancholic and profound mixture of sadness, despair and grotesque. Purim spiels are no longer celebrated across Poland, and perhaps Kantor's attempt to capture the spirit of these celebrations is both an homage to a world gone and a tragically ironic commentary on the *Megile* story itself; following the Holocaust, the story of Haman's failed plot to annihilate all the Jews of Persia, and the Jewish rescue, can never again be retold with the same joyful, carnivalesque abandon.

In his book *Postdramatic Theatre*, Hans-Ties Lehman, citing Monique Borie, eloquently describes the role of post-traumatic yet life-affirming humor in Kantor's work, vis-à-vis other influential twentieth-century avant-gardists:

> [Kantor's] theatre is marked by past terror and, at the same time, by the ghostly return. It is a theatre whose theme, as Monique Borie says, is the remains, a theatre *after* the catastrophe (like Beckett's and Heiner Müller's texts); it comes from death and stages "a landscape beyond death" (Müller). In this it differs from drama, which does not show death as proceeding, as the basis of experience, but instead depicts life moving towards it. Death in Kantor's work is not dramatically staged but ceremonially repeated. Hence, it also lacks the dramatized question about death as a moment in which the decision about the meaning of a life occurs [...]. Rather, every ceremony is actually a ceremony of the dead; it consists in the tragicomical annihilation of meaning and the showing of this annihilation – a showing which as such somehow reverses the annihilation. Thus, when the figure who obviously represents death in *Wielopole, Wielopole* or *The Dead Class* is dusting the old books, "humiliating" and destroying them, the scene also communicates a paradoxical zest for life in its comic drive.[409]

This theatrical game of "playing with the void," as Kantor calls it, takes place on multiple levels, with innocuous humor turning into horror, and vice versa. Evoking the nightmare world of the Holocaust, the first layer is that of classroom horror, a mixture of childish pranks that border on – and eventually turn into – cruelty. To quote Krzysztof Miklaszewski:

> *Dead Class* (1975) became a gold mine of childish humor. Parodies of school lessons, excavated from the senile memories of old people; caricatures of their teachers, and their methods, tricks and mockeries; bullying for no apparent reason – all of that creates the atmosphere of childish humor. And when you add to it the comedy of adolescent eroticism and the first discoveries of the opposite sex; if you add the catalog of quite unpedagogical punishments; if you add meanness, sucking up and denouncements, merciless domination and cruelty towards the weakest; that is, if you add up all the ways "to improve one's student status," the condensation of all that evokes both laughter and horror.[410]

Anna Hoffman's 1976 review of *Dead Class* adds that "Kantor's entire spectacle is grounded in grotesque and farce. Spectators burst out laughing: funny gestures and faces, funny repetitions of nonexisting words, a funny old man, frozen with his little bicycle, funny young men with attached 'deux fois grandeur naturelle' penises, funny names of the dead, like Józef Wgrzdągiel."[411] Michael Billington of the *Guardian* is one of very few foreign critics to recognize Kantor's combination of pathos and the grotesque:

> [W]hat makes Kantor's theatre remarkable is its combination of what Brook would call the rough and holy. There is much vaudeville humour in the rapacious female pupil edging up to the nervous male, the man who pulls a piece of string through his head, the camera shutter that extends like a concertina, the face-pulling, snook-cocking attitude to authority. Yet there is something gravely mysterious about the way the class rises and falls to the swelling sound of an ubiquitous 1930s café waltz as if in memory of past pleasure; and something funny and chilling in the way class's spring outing starts at a merry, shining faced trot and is gradually reduced to a laborious trudge through quicksand.[412]

The humor of *Dead Class* is not gratuitous. It is meant to heighten horror by diminishing the audience's defense mechanisms. Humor turns and heightens the moments of cruelty. (In that, Kantor very much follows the Shakespearean formula; discovering King Duncan's dead body is so much more horrifying because it happens right after the antics of the drunken porter.) In *Dead Class*, the meaning of what appear to be innocent childhood pranks quickly turns into something else; laughter morphs into uncomfortable giggles; pranks turn into tortures. For example, following her humiliating ordeal on the Family Machine, the Woman with a Mechanical Cradle crouches on the floor. She is spat at and bullied. Finally,

> Death – the Cleaning Lady – brings in the MECHANICAL CRADLE, which looks more like a small coffin. The cradle rocks two wooden balls back and forth inside it, mercilessly thudding inside the empty cradle. It's the Cleaning Lady's cruel prank… birth and death – two complementing systems.[413]

Death places the cradle in front of the Woman. She slowly begins swaying back and forth in a tragic stupor to the ruthless rhythm of the two thudding balls. She vacantly sings a lullaby to her nonexistent child, and tenderly caresses the dirty bundle of rags in her arms. Abandoned and desolate, "spat on and trash thrown on her, she begins singing a lullaby that sounds more like a despairing scream."[414] The lullaby soon reveals itself as the Kaddish, the Jewish prayer of mourning for the dead. What started as a satire on schoolyard bullying becomes a profound metaphor of inconsolable loss and mourning.

The humiliation and objectification of the Woman with a Mechanical Cradle also bring to mind familiar scenes from life at Auschwitz. The cruelty of laughing boys is reminiscent the cruelty of SS men, who found joy in the gratuitous suffering and death of others. They too were once children. In another scene, the Old Man pulls down his pants, revealing his "pupa" to everyone. In the context of the schoolyard banter, the gesture appears funny, but it "is not a joke. It is a recollection of a memory – the SS-men, guards, policemen waiting in front of the houses," looking for Jews whom they would identify by circumcision.[415] Oscilating between pathos and grotesque, the scene also alludes to Gombrowicz's *Ferdydurke*. In another scene, the Old People begin to mock each other, pointing fingers and incanting "finger, finger." Suddenly, as if in a trance, they start rocking back and forth, holding their heads between their hands in a gesture of despair; the incantation turns into wailing. In another scene, one of the twins playfully replaces the other on the bench; they repeat the skit, and it suddenly turns ominous. They replace each other as if on the death machine's assembly line; they cease to be unique human beings, and become objects processed by the death machine. Mel Gussow describes the mechanism of the routine:

> As one of the twins is forcibly evicted from his desk – the actor moving as limply as a ragdoll – his deadpan doppelganger pops up in his place. That sequence is repeated as in a silent movie comedy. At other times, as the actors march in a grand parade to the tune of plangent music, the play becomes a Polish variation on a Fellini film.[416]

The grotesque representation of the Nazi death factory turns into a madman's dreams. The hyperreality of the Holocaust operates in a language that only those in the know understand. The play is filled with subtle Holocaust allusions that are veiled and easily missed by those removed from their cultural context: the deathlike appearance of the Old Men and Women; the gratuitous, casual violence; the pile of children's corpses and burned books; the necrologs; the names of the dead called out loud; the somnambulist march to the backstage's dark gaping hole, into which actors disappear as if into a death chamber.

Leszek Kolankiewicz poignantly argues that the source of Kantor's humor is a form of magical thinking. *Apotrópaios* means "the one that exorcises the evil." Kantor wards off the "waiting lady of death" with humor. Kolankiewicz compares Kantor to Molière, whose wit sharpened on his deathbed. Playing the Imaginary Invalid, "Molière believed that by pretending that his sickness was the invention of a hypochondriac's mind, he would – through the magic of theatre – be able to keep at bay his very real illness and approaching death."[417] Kantor's humor, like Molière's, reaches into the humor of *commedia dell'arte*. "Happy Death, like all that is joyful in the world, is best expressed by the grotesque. In the grotesque, death is a comic character from the carnival, like on Halloween. Kantor's personifications of death are always grotesque. In *Dead Class*, Death the Cleaning Lady is an old hag in a rascally skewed hat, dressed in drag, whose black dress clings to her muscular body."[418] She has strong, manly legs, which are bent; she tries to walk in ridiculous, wooden female shoes. She wears vulgar makeup and carries a broom that can at any moment become a sickle. At the end of the play she turns into a common street whore.

Dead Class is full of symbols and references that form a diaphanous web of significations, holding the play in the iron grip of historical memory. Emilia Zimnica-Kuziola writes:

> [Kantor's] spectacles were shown all over the world, and often compared to musical works (based on their repeating, composition-like themes, such as war, the extermination of European Jewry, totalitarianism, [and] death). His theatre was full of dissonances, with metaphysical and grotesque elements. The tragic and comic elements, reality and illusion, literal and symbolic meanings, intertwined. Kantor wanted to provoke strong emotions – tears, laughter and fear, but also to provoke an intellectual engagement with the symbols inscribed in his work.[419]

The smooth transition from the innocence of the grotesque to the symbolic sphere of the Holocaust heightens the sense of horror. The juxtapositions create a nightmarish, nauseating moment of clarity. *Dead Class* is "full of dark humor because it is usually the kind of humor one uses in the moments of danger and fear."[420] Such humor leads to a grotesque that straddles laughter and tragedy, joke and pathos. It's a madman's laughter – hysterical, helpless laughter in the face of absurdity of the world, death and survival, the overwhelming brute force from which there is no respite. The English critic John Elsom points out that "There is a vein of savage comedy in mid-European drama which we can find in Wedekind, Brecht, Toller and others which we have never managed to realize in this country. It may be lucky that we cannot do so, for we may not have suffered those experiences […] Kantor shows us, with a shudder, what we are missing."[421] In a 1976 BBC Critics' Forum on *Dead Class*, Marina Vaizey called Kantor's laughter "the laughter on the gallows,"[422] and Barker called it "bitter gaiety."[423] Mitchell, however, argued that because of the subject matter, there can be no real humor in *Dead Class*:

> When Marina Vaizey talked about it being about the human condition it seems to me that it's really about the experience, the 20th century experience of dehumanization, the lowest object he says is the paper bag which is the equivalent to the human skin and that man is a kind of junk and…or has been turned into that, he's been de-natured and that's why I found it not very humorous, I mean it may have occasional jokes in it but it seems to me a fundamentally extremely despairing view of the world.[424]

The dramatic differences in the perceptions of *Dead Class* have been constant during its long run. Katarzyna Boruń-Jagodzińska observes that "*Dead Class* is a phenomenon so removed from categorization, that even with a full house, and undeniable success, you could observe completely opposite responses to the play (while at certain moments some laughed, others sat there with horrified expressions on their faces)."[425] Writing for the *Financial Times*, B. A. Young also suggests that some of the humor is lost because of the language barrier: "Much of what goes on is very funny, and much of it would doubtless be funny if one knew more Polish. It is also subtly disturbing."[426] Because most of the play's funny moments take place on the level of gesture, the humor and grotesque are much easier read without knowing the language than the horror, which is veiled beneath layers of symbol and allusion. These qualities nevertheless coexist, making it impossible to characterize the play as either funny or horrifying. It is in fact both; Kantor's laughter may at any minute become Munch's mute scream.

Barker, of the BBC Critics' Forum, notes that in *Dead Class*, "there is a joke there, there is a Polish joke."[427]

Chapter 34

RAISING THE DEAD

Although *Dead Class* makes no direct reference to Auschwitz, it relives the anguish of the Holocaust, which returns as flashes and bits of haunting memory: "Kantor negates both physical presence and the present, concluding that only thought and memory are important."[428] Thus, the references to the Holocaust are hidden behind the script and the visual landscape; they are and are not there, both visible and invisible. Memory is important because after a traumatic event, one lives only in memory, dwelling in the moment of trauma, reliving it over and over again. That is why the circular structure of *Dead Class* is important: the pupils parade round and round, always returning to the same point in time and space; they become lively and excited in one moment, only to dissolve in desperate cries in the next. There is a horrifying compulsion in those gestures. Repeated continuously, they become absurd and devoid of meaning. The characters seem to be stuck, unable to move on, to go forward, as if they are stuck in the moment of trauma and lost in it forever. Tish Dace vividly describes the experience: "The identity of the characters and the significance of their activities seems far less important than the compulsions; and the nightmare quality of their experiences – together with an occasional garish bit of humor – infects our psyches so forcibly that Kantor's precise intentions don't much matter."[429] Although Kantor occasionally allows characters to rebel and free themselves from their baggage, they are unable to free themselves from the objects' hegemony. As Miklaszewski describes Death the Cleaning Lady:

> [The Charlady] represents the Putzfrau – the type of person who cleans school buildings – and she is weighed down with all the tools of her trade: brooms and brushes big and little, shovels and buckets. In particular, she has a huge brush that takes the place of a scythe. A completely expressionless face; movements which are set, precise, mechanical, and repeated hundreds of times.[430]

The repetitions, patterns, rhythms and mechanical evocations of routines create a comic atmosphere, functioning like *commedia dell'arte* lazzi; they can, however, become horrifying at any moment. All of the characters are "branded with the 'arrested gesture' which traps each of the characters, and which will never reach completion."[431] As many psychiatrists have noted, the repetition compulsion is a symptom of post-traumatic stress syndrome. Bessel A. van der Kolk, for example, points out that "Unbidden memories of the trauma may return as physical sensations, horrific images or nightmares, behavioral reenactments, or a combination of these. […] [I]ndividuals become fixated on the trauma [...] 'as if their personality development has stopped at a certain point and cannot expand anymore by the addition or assimilation of new elements.'"[432] Freud writes that traumatized individuals "repeat the repressed material as a contemporary experience instead of [...] *recollecting* it as something belonging to the past."[433] They are trapped in the traumatic moment, unable to escape it, repeating it again and again, hoping for a different outcome. In *Dead Class*, compulsive repetitions have a horrifying quality, as characters seem to unable to snap out of their mechanized destinies. Richard Eder notices that the rhythms and repetitions also create a strange sense of beauty: "This sounds hermetic and pretentious. What we see is certainly hermetic; frequently repetitious and without means of access into its purpose or pattern. But it is not pretentious; there are power and beauty in its images and sharpness and highly controlled artistry in their execution."[434] Glenn Loney points out that there is something sickly in these repetitions, which void everything of meaning, reducing the actors to mechanized puppets:

> Of course it's no novelty now to see someone drop his pants; to see a woman bare her breasts; to see a man pathetically exposed and humiliated. But somehow with Kantor's troupe, the effects were rather different. The aim was not to shock a stuffy, middle-class audience, or to titillate the young swingers among the spectators. How could nudity be exciting when it reveals only corpse-like flesh? And the compulsive, even mechanical repetition of the exposure of the breast makes its own comment on lust and desire, stunned, killed by endless, meaningless, joyless encounters.[435]

Cathy Caruth calls PTSD "a symptom of history." She writes, "The traumatized, we might say, carry an impossible history within them, or they become themselves the symptom of a history that they cannot entirely possess."[436] In *Dead Class*, old people carry the corpses of themselves as children, unable to get rid of them or assimilate them into their current condition. In a world defined by trauma, Hartman suggests, "mediation through speech has become impossible."[437] The Absent Old Man from the First Bench epitomizes that phenomenon: he sits on the bench, silent and still as if "frozen with grief."[438] Words fail him because his suffering is beyond language. Eileen Fisher notes that

> [*Dead Class*] operates in many dimensions. The dead past historically refers to the extinction and disappearance of nearly all Polish Jews and the death of millions of soldiers since 1914. Moreover, the ghostly return of the dead past upon the backs of the dead present suggests a now dying civilization which is being killed by both history and the deadly present. On a theatrical and metaphorical level, the parade signifies a dance of death. This image resonates long enough for the audience to experience the virtual essence of death – on stage and within themselves.[439]

A number of reviewers implicitly read *Dead Class*'s return of the dead as a poetic manifestation of post-traumatic stress syndrome. To quote Faulkner, "The past is never dead. It's not even past."[440] Roman Szydłowski writes that *Dead Class* is a "meditation on man and his fate, everything that's pathetic and tragic that happened to him in our century, and everything else that will happen to him."[441] Anna Boska writes that "*Dead Class* resembles a spiritualist séance, bringing back ghosts. In fact, it is resurrecting the dead world of the past, which only appears dead. It is still alive in our subconsciousness. We carry it within us; it comes back to haunt us."[442] Jan Skotnicki somewhat hopelessly acknowledges that, for him, *Dead Class* brings back all the memories of war that he cannot escape: "It's a gallery of incredible faces, as if cut out from an old-fashioned daguerreotype… No, it's a veil of our memory…our dreams, and our nightmares, memories stubbornly coming back with more force, with the passage of time…"[443] These descriptions summarize an almost clinical definition of post-traumatic stress disorder. Likewise, Tish Dace directly references trauma in her review:

> What transfixes the spectators in *The Dead Class* is a spectacle in which the men and women ranging from their 30s to their late 50s relive childhood and adolescent emotions and situations. Kantor's written material stresses death and the dead, and the setting – 1914 or so – with the ashen makeup and the moldering schoolbooks, suggest a group of cadavers reliving brief ordeals of their youth. Repetitive sections bear out this surmise by creating a sense of obsessive dwelling on isolated moments of trauma.[444]

One of the dominating motifs in *Dead Class*, besides the return to childhood, is that of raising the dead; the Old Men and Women of *Dead Class* are like the living dead, ghosts returning to "their childhood schoolroom where they pose as for a post-mortem reunion photograph."[445] Jan Kott calls Kantor a great Charon, "who takes the dead to the other side of the Styx river, but who can also bring them back."[446] Kantor's living dead, however, are very different from those that traditionally haunt Western drama. Jan Kott points out that, in Western theatre, the dead who return to the world of the living are always outsiders:

> There is a long theatrical history behind characters who, after their death, come back on stage in order to haunt living people to give them moral lessons. The dead come back on stage both in Shakespeare and in other Elizabethan theater, both in Romantic and in modern drama. The dead come back either as ghosts or as hallucinations. The ghost is a metaphysical statue; the hallucination is a psychological situation. But both imply, in the properly theatrical sense, that the ghost or hallucination can be seen only by some of the characters on the stage, that it behaves in a different way from the "living" characters, it speaks differently, it moves differently, it often wears the costume of a ghost, and if it does not have a costume, then it must have some special traits or marks.[447]

Yet in Kantor's *Dead Class*, the dead retain their liminal space. Likewise, Artur Sandauer points out that, in Schulz's short story about the Pensioner, Schulz "insinuates that the condition of an Old Age Pensioner is ambivalent. We can't convincingly answer who he really is: an old pensioner or an apparition, a phantom or a 'traveler from the other side.' Kantor retains this ambivalence, only giving us many variants on Schulz's old Pensioner."[448] Like Schulz's Pensioner, Kantor's Old Men and Women are not of the other world. They are very much part of reality; they live and dwell in memory. They exist on the border between the living and the dead, belonging and not belonging to either world.

The liminal quality of Kantor's *Dead Class*, which takes place in between the world of the living and the world of the dead, is influenced by Schulz on many levels. In Schulz's title story, *Sanatorium Under the Sign of the Hourglass*, Joseph goes to the underworld to visit his deceased father. To get there, he takes a train. As Russell Brown reminds us, the motif of the descent into the underworld is "one of the great archetypes of world literature [...] from the Greek Orpheus and Odysseus and the Babylonian *Gilgamesh*[,] to Dante's *Divine Comedy* and Goethe's *Faustus*, to many modern examples."[449] Shalom Lindenbaum points out that, unlike other mythical tales of returning to the underworld, Schulz's story is subjective; we don't know whether his father has really died, whether he's sick and dying, or whether the whole incident is a dream or a metaphor.[450] Joseph crosses a footbridge that separates the world of the living and the world of the dead. In Schulz, the world of the dead looks like a sanatorium, very much like any other in the world of the living (Schulz was inspired in this image by Thomas Mann's *Magic Mountain*). Joseph is told that everyone is asleep: "Here everybody is asleep all the time [...] Besides, it is never night here."[451] Near the sanatorium is a town similar to the one Joseph left behind. When he finally sees his father, he realizes his father is as sick as he was at home; he is dying for a second time, despite already being in the afterlife. Schulz's story conforms to the archetypal motif: "the death of one father today is like the deaths of fathers and other loved ones in the past and in epic records in that the living want to visit them, to regain the intimacy and security interrupted by death."[452] Since the world of the dead is like the world of the living, the line between the living and the dead blurs: just as Joseph goes into the underworld, the dead can return at any time to the world of the living.

Chapter 35

DEAD CLASS AS KADDISH…

Jan Kott once called *Dead Class* a form of Kaddish, the Jewish mourner's prayer. Jewish law requires that the Kaddish be recited by selected mourners for the first 11 months after the death of a loved one, and then on each anniversary of the death. The Kaddish is a mourning prayer recited in Aramaic that praises the greatness of God, asking him for peace for all. It never refers directly to that which it is about: death. In Hebrew and other Semitic languages, the name of God is written without vowels, as it was strictly forbidden to pronounce it. In mystical theology, the supreme experience of being, that is, the perfect name of God, is the experience of meaning of the *gramma* itself, "word that is written but not read" (*Quere wela³ ketib*).[453] As Agamben explains it, "as the unnamable name of God, the *gramma* is the final and negative dimension of meaning, no longer an experience of language but language itself, that is, its taking place in the removal of voice."[454] According to Derrida, the sign stands in for the thing it signifies; by being there, the sign signifies the absence of the thing it designates. The sign thus is a pure negativity. It establishes its meaning on the basis of difference from other signs, other negativities. Thus, language is a play of negatives that negate themselves in relation to themselves, and which negate the very things they signify. As Derrida puts it:

> The sign is usually said to be put in the place of the thing itself, the present thing, "thing" here standing equally for meaning or referent. The sign represents the present in its absence. It takes the place of the present. When we cannot grasp or show the thing, state the present, the being-present, when the present cannot be presented, we signify, we go through the detour of the sign. We take or give signs. We signal. The sign, in this sense, is deferred presence.[455]

The sign signals being, which simultaneously is and is not: being. Like the Kaddish, and Jewish mysticism, *Dead Class* is veiled behind a screen of signs and symbols.

Holocaust allusions in *Dead Class* function on the level of ritual, myth and metaphor. Raising the dead, *Dead Class* is a memory plate drawing on Jewish, Christian and pagan traditions to relive and retell the story of a world that's vanished forever:

> Kantor's theatrical séances reflect the irredeemable loss of a quintessential Polish childhood in a multicultural society where Jewish rabbis and Catholic priests dance together a nostalgic tango in *The Dead Class*. At the same time, his séances reflect the wound of post–World War II Poland – the almost total disappearance of its Jewish

population, as well as the destruction of the Polish intelligentsia by the Nazi and the Communist regime that invaded Poland from both borders.[456]

Krzysztof Miklaszewski writes that "*Dead Class* is the most Jewish of all Polish returns to childhood. [...] *Dead Class* is a memory lesson about a world that no longer exists. It is a snapshot of a Jewish world within Poland that no longer exists."[457] Kantor's own background is somewhat ambiguous. His close friends, like Krzysztof Miklaszewski, speak openly of Kantor's Polish-Jewish origins. Others never mention it. Kantor himself was guarded when speaking about his Jewish background. Because of the Polish communist government's anti-Semitic propaganda and the 1968 expulsions, it was often necessary to hide one's Jewish roots. Kantor would repeatedly brush the question aside, framing it in a larger context: "I think there are some Jewish roots in my family, but it's not important to me. What is important is the fact that Jewish culture is incredibly important for Polish culture."[458] The first time he spoke of his Jewish father openly was in a foreign interview in 1982: "My mother was Catholic. Pure. My father was Jewish, and he converted to Catholicism. But he got lost in the First War."[459] The 2008 exhibit at the Jewish Museum in New York titled "Theatres of Memory: Art and Holocaust" noted that Kantor himself preferred to keep his origins vague, while always stressing Jewish aspects of Polish culture at large:

> Kantor kept his Jewish roots purposefully ambiguous. Yet his work from the very beginning was founded on remembrance of the "Jewish, amputated part of Polish culture." For an artist who grew up between the omnipresent Catholic Church and the Jewish cemetery of his hometown, the cross and the ghost-like figure of the body of a young boy serve as universal symbols for death, martyrdom, and loss.[460]

Kantor himself said many times that, in his hometown of Wielopole, the two communities lived in harmony, each focused on its own cycle of rituals and celebrations. Kantor's uncle was a priest who lived with his family; he would often engage the local rabbi in long philosophical discussions. Kantor would also play with the rabbi's son, and together they would visit both church and synagogue to observe the local ceremonies.[461] Kantor would evoke this memory – priest and rabbi, Catholic and Jewish rituals performed alongside each other – time and time again in his Theatre of Death. In fact, the intertwining of Jewish and Catholic motifs, the transcendental and mystic atmosphere of otherworldly engagement, is the foundation of *Dead Class*. Elżbieta Morawiec once wrote that "Tadeusz Kantor was like a Jew – the Eternal Wanderer who travelled the world, all over Europe, well acquainted with the most fashionable trends, only to return, in the end, to his provincial Wielopole, somewhere on the edge of a lost civilization, to his lost childhood, between church and synagogue."[462]

Krzysztof Pleśniarowicz points out that "the Jewish motif of the *Dead Class* is not stable. It appears and disappears like an echo, like the 'historical apparitions' of World War I [...] Jewish motifs dominate moments of consternation, when the motifs are consolidated (statements from the Old Testament, wailing from the 'Cheder, Hebrew alphabet, Yiddish lullaby')."[463] In *Dead Class*, Jewish motifs appear and disappear like ghosts. They float through the play, occasionally and briefly directing attention to Jewish suffering. Eileen Blumenthal points out that "Images suggesting Polish Jewry, shtetl life, and the holocaust intensify the play's sting and sense of mourning. Pupils study the Hebrew alphabet; a woman sings an old Yiddish lullaby to an empty, mechanical cradle, the children are piled on a mass grave-pyre of old, worn books."[464] In veiling Jewish themes, Kantor follows an early twentieth-century literary tradition that evolved as a response to rising anti-Semitism on the one hand and, on the other, secular Jews' desire to remain part of the broader European discourse while preserving their Jewish heritage. Karen Underhill notes that many secular Jewish writers and philosophers from the interwar period – including Walter Benjamin, Gershom Scholem, Franz Kafka, Martin Buber and Franz Rosenzweig – make no reference to their Jewish origins in their work. Underhill also argues that Bruno Schulz belongs to this group:

> Schulz and his work can fruitfully be placed within a constellation of assimilated Jewish intellectuals of his generation, whose work reveals an attempt to incorporate Jewish philosophical and mystical heritage into modern, often secular systems of thought [...]. [They] have incorporated into their language and imagery, elements of Jewish mystical and messianic philosophy – including attitudes towards language drawn from kabbalah, certain elements drawn from Hasidic philosophy, and the Hasidic storytelling tradition [...] and in particular Eastern European Hasidic tradition.[465]

Underhill notes that, in Schulz's writing, Jewish motifs are woven into the text, hidden in the poetic language of metaphor and symbol. His work reflects a tension between the desire to reclaim and embrace Jewish heritage and an impulse to disengage from it. It's a source of renewal – and a doomed culture. A dark, ominous tone intertwines with lyrical musings on the enigmatic, fragile world of the Jewish *shtetl*. As Underhill writes:

> The ways that Jewish elements appear in Schulz's text – often coded in allusive or allegorical references that also become some of his most powerful, many layered metaphors – reveal a simultaneous rejection and embracing of Jewish sources. [...] On the one hand, Schulz pushes Jewishness to the margins and proclaims it dead, banishing direct discussion of it from the body of the text. On the other hand, his entire oeuvre works to enshrine precisely marginality, and the Underworld – the land of the dead. Thus, in Schulz's work we confront both the subtle identification of Jewishness with death, marginality and misshapenness, and the constant recuperation of that which is marginal – of the scrapheap or the shards – and of that which is dead, abandoned, or decayed.[466]

In 1975, right before the opening of *Dead Class*, Kantor admitted that "Our generation was raised in the shadow of Schulz. Many of us forgot about it. It wasn't until the 1960s when we began to rediscover Schulz's prose. But at that time we were discovering it only in relation to our own artistic pursuits. Schulz's work didn't become clear to us until the 1970s. His concept of 'Degraded Reality' – 'Reality of the Lowest

Rank' – eventually became fundamental to my own work."[467] Schulz's heroes exist as if "on the outside," in a "degraded reality of the lowest rank." Writing about Schulz's sense of foreboding about the Shoah, Rolando Perez points out that "Time and again, Schulz refers to 'those people,' who remain unnamed as a people with a distant past, having a history all their own. Their homes are old and in them reside all the elements of a tradition, a way of life that is on the verge of disappearing."[468] Kantor's concept of "Degraded Reality" or "Reality of the Lowest Rank" – the reality of discarded, forgotten objects which nonetheless emanate their own quiet beauty – was borrowed from Schulz. The idea became essential for Kantor's work and for his concept of *teatr biedny* – poor theatre. Kantor fills his classroom with poor, discarded, found objects, and poor, discarded men. Degraded, forgotten and eventually annihilated, the Jewish-Polish world of Kantor's childhood becomes, as in Schulz, the world of the living dead.

If in Schulz's writing there is a sense of doom, a premonition of looming apocalypse, then in Kantor's world there is postapocalypse. As Zygmunt Greń notes:

> There are emotions in Kantor's work. Each movement, each gesture, is logical and [...] painful. In *Dead Class*, Kantor shows us the tragic history of the Jewish people, history that took place on Polish soil during World War II. [...] The child mannequins thrown onto the pyre symbolize the extermination of the nation. The iron ball rhythmically rocks in the mechanical cradle instead of a crying child. Precisely, scene by scene, Kantor measures out the judgment of their fate and history. He doesn't illustrate it, but conjures it with signs, symbols, bringing back into memory those who can remember or who can imagine.[469]

Like the Kaddish, which never directly references that which it is about, death, Kantor's *Dead Class* never directly references that which it is about, the Holocaust – yet the sense of mourning for a world vanished, forever, pervades Kantor's performance with images reconstructed from memory.

Chapter 36

DEAD CLASS AS *DYBBUK*, OR THE ABSENCE

One of *Dead Class*'s main Jewish influences is *Dybbuk or Between Two Worlds*, a play by Szymon Ansky about a restless soul unable to find her way to God. *Dybbuk* was first staged in Moscow by the Jewish Habima Theatre, directed by Evgeny Vakhtangov, in 1922. Vakhtangov and his touring company brought the play to Cracow's Theatre Bagatela in May 1926, and returned for subsequent productions in Cracow in April 1930 and April 1938.[470] It is unclear when Kantor saw the play, but its main theme, of a ghost entering the body of another, affected him greatly, and its influence is clearly visible in *Dead Class*. The title *Dybbuk* comes from *dibuk meruach raa*, which literally translates as "possessed by a bad spirit." In Jewish folklore, the term *dybbuk* refers to a dead person's soul. In Jewish mysticism, the soul is always on borrowed time during life; in death, it is returned to its rightful owner, God. Ansky's *Dybbuk* is a love story with mystical overtones; the father marries off his daughter, Lea, to a man other than her beloved Chanan. Heartbroken, Chanan commits a mortal sin by pronouncing the unpronounceable name of God and dies. Because he has sinned, his soul cannot find peace, and Lea invites it to her wedding. Chanan's soul enters her body, and she breaks off her engagement to the other man. Through Kaballah, the father soon realizes that Chanan is the son of a deceased friend; the father and this friend had agreed that their children would one day marry. Thus, fate brings the two lovers together, even if it's in the afterlife.

Dybbuk takes place in the liminal space between life and death; the dead are always present, their souls moving among the living, making demands, entering and exiting the living's bodies, and influencing the living's lives. In Kaballah, the word *gilgul* means a form of reincarnation, the transmission of souls: at the moment of death, the soul leaves one's body and enters another. But untimely death leaves a soul with unfinished business. It is suspended in limbo: it is neither holy enough to go to heaven nor debased enough to enter an animal or a stone. But it is also not so innocent as to pass into another body. Thus, possessing someone, attaching itself to someone and purifying itself, is its only chance.[471] The idea of eternal wandering, of souls unable to find peace, of the dead always suspended and always present among the living, greatly influenced Kantor's aesthetics. He returned to the notion of staging *Dybbuk* time and time again, though he never produced it. In *Dead Class*, however, the *gilgul* motif reappears. The Old People exist on the border between the living and the dead. For Kantor, the dead are "honored and rejected/irrevocably different and infinitely strange, and again: somehow deprived of all significance, to be left out of account, without the smallest hope of taking some place in the full relationships of our life which is accessible, familiar and comprehensible to us only but meaningless to them."⁴⁷² As living corpses, they straddle life and death; they arouse both fear and anxiety because, belonging to neither world, they are bound by neither world's laws.

In the context of *Dybbuk*, *Dead Class* could also be read as a mystical meditation on the Holocaust: what happened to all the souls whose earthly lives were cut short? Do they live among us, entering and exiting our bodies at will, demanding justice, closure, remembrance? In his article "The Unburied Ones," Zygmunt Greń poignantly describes *Dead Class* as "*Antigone* revisited." Greń writes: "Kantor's gesture is a magnificent homage, full of pathos, a grand mass for the souls of those whose bodies were left unburied as ordered by the custom. The Polish artist evokes the memory of the Holocaust and its victims, raising a monument to them in the spiritual realm of their nation's culture."⁴⁷³ Another critic called *Dead Class* "Dada in Auschwitz."⁴⁷⁴ But Kantor is not so much concerned with representing Auschwitz as he is with exploring the human condition before and after Auschwitz. Instead of literal representation, Kantor aims at capturing absence, the overwhelming feeling of irrevocable loss. *Dead Class* is meant to evoke what Dominick LaCapra suggests happens "when loss is converted into absence": never-ending, unquenchable mourning. As LaCapra writes, "One faces the impasse of endless melancholy, impossible mourning, and interminable aporia in which any process or working through the past and its historical losses is foreclosed or prematurely aborted."⁴⁷⁵ *Dead Class* captures the experience of infinite, uncontainable loss and, most importantly, captures not so much the presence as the absence – the horrifying absence – of millions who vanished. As Zygmunt Greń puts it:

> To say that Kantor joined the group of authors who record their wartime memories would not be enough. He decided to take upon himself responsibility for his characters. He personally brought them back to life, and sentenced them to an inhuman death. Serious, or with a slight, barely visible smirk, with his large, black scarf wrapped around his neck like a funeral sash, it is Kantor all by himself who does this. Nothing else – its grotesque or lyricism, humor or bitterness or sentimental memories – could carry this spectacle's baggage, explain its mystery, or provoke the shock we experience when faced with *Dead Class*.⁴⁷⁶

In his travel journal, Krzysztof Miklaszewski writes that, when *Dead Class* was shown in Israel in December 1985, "audiences were left weeping."⁴⁷⁷ Kantor summarizes that response: "Because the Jewish nation suffered…suffered…suffered. Human suffering is a way to understand art. People who have never suffered, they don't bother. No. They consume."⁴⁷⁸ Klaudiusz Święcicki adds that "Closed in a mythical Arcadia, the fate of the students in *Dead Class* becomes for viewers a peculiar experience of *pathei mathos* ('through suffering comes knowledge')."⁴⁷⁹ Ansky's *Dybbuk* provides another layer of meaning to *Dead Class*, alluding to the Holocaust by evoking the absence it created. Through the mystical and literary framework of *Dybbuk*, Kantor creates an elaborate ritual that captures the effects and aftereffects of trauma. *Dead Class* rereads Ansky's play via the lens of the Shoah, embedding the text with new meaning.

Chapter 37

THE DEAD AND THE MARIONETTES

In *Dead Class*, Kantor is interested in representing absence, and he does so by two aesthetic means: one, he places his actors on an equal footing with objects, thus creating his bio-objects, combinations of actor and object; and two, he models his actors on marionettes. *Dead Class*, however, wasn't the first work in which he explored these concepts. Kantor used mannequins in *The Water Hen* (1976) and *The Shoemakers* (1970). In his staging of Słowacki's *Balladyna*, Kantor had mannequins as doubles of the real actors.

In modeling his actors on marionettes, Kantor was partially influenced by the theories of Heinrich von Kleist and Edward Gordon Craig. In a pivotal essay written in 1810, "About the Marionette Theater," Kleist introduces the idea of the intrinsic supremacy of the puppet over the human actor. On an ontological scale, Kleist locates man somewhere between God, the supreme being, and the marionette, the absence of being, both of which represent similar degrees of perfection as complete opposites of each other. The marionette's lack of consciousness and the centralization of all of its movements from one point of gravity make it an absolute and finished form, one for which nothing can be improved. Because all the puppet's movements are controlled from one point, it can be fully coordinated, creating the sort of ultimate, divine grace attainable only by that other perfection, God.[480] For Kleist, marionettes "are members of only one world, responding 'naturally' and 'gracefully' to divine guidance. This is underscored by their apparent weightlessness. They hardly touch the floor; they are not bound to the earth, for they are drawn up from above. They represent a state of grace, a 'paradise lost' to man, whose conscious and willful or 'free' self-assertions make him 'self-conscious.'"[481]

Following Kleist's premise, Gordon Craig, in his 1908 essay "The Actor and the Über-Marionette," formulates a theory according to which the limitations of an actor's body make it an insufficient vehicle for precisely expressing a director's idea. The human body, Gordon Craig claims, is subject to internal and external laws, which prevent it from carrying an artistic message.[482] According to Gordon Craig, because of the "'accidental' influence of man's unpredictable emotional behavior, human inconsistency [is] the 'enemy of design, and hence of art.'"[483] Gordon Craig sees the human body, which is enslaved by subjective emotions, as useless material for the theatre.[484] In order to attain the desired perfection, the actor "must go" and be replaced by what Gordon Craig calls the "über-marionette." Arguing for the superior precision of the über-marionette over a living being, Gordon Craig, like Kleist, ascribes to it the same enigmatic and godlike beauty. Because of its mysticism, the über-marionette embodies a superior model of being, one that "will not compete with life – rather will it go beyond it. Its ideal will be not of flesh and blood but rather the body in trance – it will aim to clothe itself with a death-like beauty while exhaling a living spirit."[485] The exaggerated morbidity of the puppet does not negate life, but, on the contrary, Gordon Craig claims, glorifies it. Through its artificiality, the marionette reaches beyond the essence of life, becoming its improved version, "the last echo of some noble and beautiful art of past civilization."[486] Gordon Craig was fascinated by death, believing that theatre should come "from that mysterious, joyous, and superbly complete life which is called Death."[487] As the marionette embodies death, Gordon Craig calls for "the return of the image – the über-marionette to the Theatre; and when he [the über-marionette] comes again and is but seen, he will be loved so well that once more it will be possible for people to return to the ancient joy in ceremonies – once more will Creation be celebrated – homage rendered to existence – and divine and happy intercession made to Death."[488]

However, while Kleist and Gordon Craig were inspirational, *Dead Class* is foremost influenced by Schulz's story "A Treatise on Mannequins." In "A Treatise on Mannequins," Schulz muses on the strange, hidden lives of tailor's dummies, as he writes: "We wish to create man a second time, in the shape and semblance of a tailor's dummy."[489] Dummies are not objects, Schulz writes, because "There is no dead matter, […] lifelessness is only a disguise behind which hide unknown forms of life."[490] The dummies live some horrifying secret life that's trapped within them:

> Figures in a wax museum, even fair-ground parodies of dummies, must not be treated lightly. Matter never makes jokes: it is always full of the tragically serious. Who dares to think that you can play with matter, that you can shape it for a joke, that the joke will not be built in, will not eat into it like fate, like destiny? Can you imagine the pain, the dull imprisoned suffering, hewn into the matter of that dummy which does not know why it must be what it is, why is must remain forcibly imposed on a helpless block, and ruling it like its own, tyrannical, despotic soul? […] Have you heard at night the terrible howling of these wax figures, shut in their fair-booths; the pitiful chorus of those forms of wood or porcelain, banging their fists against the walls of the prisons?[491]

For Schulz, however, the most important thing is the equivalency of human body and object. As Wiesław Borowski points out: "The resemblance of the human body to the material thing – Schulz said – 'the essence of materiality devoid of any traces of psyche,' leads inevitably to the creation of the mannequin."[492] And Tomasz Bocheński notes:

> Schulz treats the wax figures as metaphors for beings which froze in one final form. That is why there is a semblance between wax figures and people who stopped changing, who froze in one expression, one grimace. It's that semblance which makes it difficult to distinguish between the living and the dead. The living can become embalmed alive. This embalming, lack of change, "statism" – those are signs of death – or madness.[493]

Schulz was fascinated with the idea of the human body devoid of its human quality, objectified and used for its material properties: "Ancient, mythical tribes used to embalm their dead. The walls of their houses were filled with bodies and heads immured in them: a father would stand in a corner of the drawing room – stuffed, the tanned skin of a deceased wife would serve as a mat under the table."[494] Schulz's fascination with the body-as-object had an ominous echo to it, as if Shulz foresaw the complete degradation of the human being. In his essay on Schulz's Holocaust vision, Rolando Perez writes:

> Firstly, the Nazis' total and absolute depersonalization of the Jews in the camps: turning the bodies of human beings into material objects of use, e.g. ashtrays. One cannot help but recall the horror of seeing on film thousand of bodies bulldozed into ditches – human bodies that, in the docility of their lifelessness, resemble tailor shop manikins. Secondly, and perhaps more in line with what Schulz had in mind, are the objects of clothing worn by the victims of the camps: the combs, the striped uniforms, the wallets with the family photographs in them, those mementos which make up so much of our lives, and yes, especially the shoes, the thousands of shoes of victims as they are on display at the Holocaust Museum in Washington, D.C. It is impossible to look at these objects and not feel their spirit.[495]

As Bozena Shallcross notes, "the physical remains of human victims – their jewelry, shoes, clothes, and even their hair – have become the Holocaust's dominant metonymy. […] Anyone who contemplates the material legacy of Auschwitz-Birkenau is struck first of all by both its shabby everydayness and the simple utility of the objects on display – a utility determined by the demands of survival."[496] Deported prisoners believed they were being displaced, and they were encouraged by the Nazis to bring with them all of their most valuable belongings. Upon arrival to Auschwitz, the victims were robbed of everything they carried; their belongings were sorted and send to the Third Reich, with most valuables hidden across Hitler's Europe. Shallcross argues that "the Holocaust, with its agenda of human extermination, promoted a fetishization of objects; the acts of looting, amassing, and sorting gave uprecedented centrality to the fragmented material object-world."[497] In retrospect, Schulz's approach to the human body was prescient, as was his concept of the Reality of the Lowest Rank – the reality of objects and people abandoned.

Schulz's fascination with mannequins and objects, and the Reality of the Lowest Rank, which emanates its own hidden life, became primary sources for Kantor's aesthetics. All of Kantor's objects have metaphorical meanings, and all of the meanings are connected to the trauma of the Holocaust: the piles of abandoned books symbolize the Jewish books of prayer, which were a constant presence at Auschwitz; the pile of children's corpses recalls the dead whose bodies were burned in the Auschwitz ovens; the abandoned objects dropped on the floor testify, like mute witnesses, to the horrifying absence of their former owners. Influenced by Schulz, Kantor was interested in mannequins and objects insofar as they represent negativity, which is to say absence. In his essay "Sketch of the Modern Erotic," Różewicz writes, "the most expressive description of bread is a description of hunger [...] the absence of the body is a description of love."⁴⁹⁸ Like Schulz, Kantor thought that life could be expressed through "the absence of life, through an appeal to DEATH, through APPEARANCES, through EMPTINESS and the lack of a MESSAGE."⁴⁹⁹ For Kantor, unlike Gordon Craig and Kleist, the marionette has to become a "model for the living ACTOR."⁵⁰⁰ As Kantor notes in his "Manifesto of the Theatre of Death": "The Mannequin in my theater must become a MODEL through which passes a strong sense of DEATH and the conditions of the DEAD [...] The mannequin in my theatre is designed to serve as a model through which the powerful sensation of death, and the lot of the dead, may be experienced."⁵⁰¹ And elsewhere: "Among the elements of the spectacle, the mannequin has a place between object and actor – it is an object, yet it looks like an actor, and, in the mind of a viewer, it brings a completely different association than some thing or machine."⁵⁰² Devoid of essence, the marionette epitomizes the body as a condition of nonbeing. Made in the image of man, it negates existence while also suggesting it. As Neal Ascherson puts it, Kantor's actors "convey to an audience the sense of simultaneous likeness and terrible difference which they would experience on looking at a corpse."⁵⁰³ In *Dead Class*, actors become dead like mannequins, and mannequins become like actors; the distinction between living being and inanimate object is erased. Irving Wardle notes that the equivalence of actors and mannequins plays a major role in creating *Dead Class*'s nightmarish quality. Wardle writes, "the passage of time is set vibrating like a violin string; and nothing contributes more to this than the affinity Kantor establishes between the dolls and the live actors. They meet, it seems, at an equal point of accomplishment."⁵⁰⁴ Richard Cork similarly marvels at the perfect illusion: "The spectators are never quite sure at any given point whether they are looking at real actors or inanimate dummies; the performance begins with a motionless congregation of effigies, and Kantor refuses to distinguish with total clarity between humans and mannequins throughout his 'play.'"⁵⁰⁵ Likewise, Marina Vaizey also notes, "you often can't tell the mannequins from the real actors until somebody moves and the mannequins very cleverly move…"⁵⁰⁶

For Kantor, the model for an actor should be the marionette, a form which is both dead and alive. Straddling life and death, the marionette simultaneously negates and asserts life. Becoming semi-puppets, the actors in Kantor's Theatre of Death multiply the meanings of their presence; they illustrate both the condition of death through the apparent absence of life (like a marionette), and the condition of life through their apparent presence (as human beings). Hovering ambiguously between life and death, they become alternately either the body devoid of essence, or the essence separated from the body. The identity of the actors is simultaneously destroyed and brought forward through this destruction. As Lehman notes: "In a kind of exchange with the living bodies and together with the object, they change the stage into a landscape of death, in which there is a fluid transition between the human beings (often acting like puppets) and the dead puppets (appearing as if animated by children)."⁵⁰⁷ The actor is simultaneously a marionette – the body – and, as Schreyer puts it, "the bearer of the marionette" – the soul. He is the object and the subject, the body devoid of essence, and the soul trying to assert its being.

Mel Gussow quotes Jan Kott, who movingly writes about Kantor's "games with the void":

> In his analysis of the performance art of Tadeusz Kantor, Jan Kott speaks of his Polish countryman as a creator of "a theater of essence." With Kantor, he explains, "essence is the aftermath… as final as the Last Judgment." It is "a trace, like the still undissolved imprint of a crustacean on stone." Kantor's archeological imprint is transmitted through images, many of them, as Kott says, expressing the director's horror and fascination with "the still life of the dead." Kantor transports us to a world in which the dead play restless roles.[508]

Eileen Fisher of *Theatre Journal* also poignantly notes that, during the performance, one can actually feel the physical presence of death onstage:

> In a highly significant sense, the dead past – in the form of children's corpses – returns to complement the dead present who compose the dead class. Now, the live actors who "play dead," dead insofar as they too performed as corpses until Kantor as medium invoked them to life in the séance's opening segment, carry and incarnate the "real dead." This haunting image transcends generic barriers – linguistic, historical, ideological, theatrical, and temporal. […] On a theatrical and metaphorical level, the parade signifies a dance of death. This image resonates long enough for the audience to experience the virtual essence of death – on stage and within themselves. One wishes the awesome dance of death would stop because of one's instinctive fear of the actual existence of death, but Kantor prolongs this segment from the sidelines. His waving hands and piercing looks push the company and the spectators to living apprehensions of death's essential, not existential, reality. Never before have I witnessed death as a stage property. Kantor concretely dramatizes various conjugations of dying: past, present, and past perfect.[509]

Chapter 38

MEN AND OBJECTS

Adapting Duchamp's concept of the "readymade" object, Kantor invents the idea of "readymade" man: an actor as is. As he said in one of his *New York Times* interviews: "For example, there's a creature I call 'The Found Character,' precisely like Marcel Duchamp's 'objets trouvés.' In folklore a 'found' object is believed to possess links with the world of the dead; it is purposeless, gratuitous, a pure work of art."[510] Tish Dace notes that "Kantor achieves an additional grotesque quality, a non-living creepiness. Kantor's fascination with found objects instead of stage props – he uses two wooden balls in place of a baby doll in the mechanical cradle, for instance – further detaches us from the action."[511] Although Kantor often referenced Duchamp in his international interviews, Kantor's most prominent influence was Schulz's Reality of the Lowest Rank. Like Schulz, Kantor was interested in the lowest objects, abandoned and forgotten pieces of human existence; he saw the human being as a mere replica of this overlooked detritus. Like Shulz, Kantor was also interested in objects *vis-à-vis* their relationship to human beings. As Richard Calvoressi puts it in his review of the Edinburgh performance of *Dead Class*:

> The performance space is blocked with junk: heaps of dusty books, old newspapers, weird Tinguely-like machines, a fire-iron, a wooden school lavatory, a row of scratched benches. But these are not props in the normal sense; Kantor believes that they are simply there, on an equal footing with the actors. And there is a sense in which the objects in *The Dead Class* are actors, obstacles which threaten to take on a life of their own and dominate the human action. Kantor cultivates what he calls the "poor objects," a real thing taken from life. [...] The association and memories, the fragments of past life which rise to the surface from all this detritus, made *The Dead Class* an unforgettable experience and Kantor's visit the most exciting thing that has happened to the visual arts at the Edinburgh Festival for a long time.[512]

Finally, after many years of experiment, Kantor created what he called "BIO-OBJECTS," theatrical forms brought into existence by joining the living actor with inanimate objects, such as a chair, a bicycle, a mannequin or an additional pair of legs. Forcing an actor into a symbiotic relationship with the object, Kantor consciously placed him in a situation which demanded that the actor reinvent the role assigned him. Although Kantor first used the term bio-object in his essay "The Theater Place," written in Italy in 1980, the idea was first introduced in the 1950s with the production of Witkiewicz's *The Cuttlefish*. Kantor noted that "BIO-OBJECTS were not props which the actors used. They were not 'decorations' in which you 'act.' They made indivisible wholes with the actors. They exuded their own autonomous 'lives,' not related to the FICTION (content) of the play."[513] The bio-object became a fundamental device with which Kantor could destroy and create illusion. With an object attached to his body, the actor is trapped between the role he's hired to perform – that of his character – and the one he performs unwillingly, that of himself struggling with the rigidity of the form infringing on him. "The objects grown into their bodies [make] it impossible for the actors to create a coherent image of a character."[514] In their struggle for identity, the object and the actor interact with each other by interchangeably imposing themselves on each other. The physical presence of an object locates the actor on the border between illusion and reality. In both reality and fiction, his subjective existence is obliterated by the object; in both reality and fiction, his movements must at least partially adjust to the object. Describing one of his bio-objects, the Man with Two Bicycle Wheels Grown into His Legs, Kantor writes:

> [he] is completely separated from
> reality of a different kind
> and is enclosed in an inhuman,
> but at least for him natural,
> feeling for speed
> and motion
> that can be realized with the help of his legs,
> with the consciousness of vehicle.[515]

The actor, both as himself and as the character he portrays, must redefine himself in the new physical situation. Mutating the actor's body, the wheels transform his sense of reality and of himself both on- and offstage. As Michal Kobialka notes:

> [The actors'] bodies could be treated as an intricate field of interplay between two parallel systems, that is, the illusion of being another character and the actor's own Self. Because illusion "was merely a reflection,/ just like a moonlight,/ a dead surface," actors in this system needed to eliminate dependence on the arrangement that existed outside them and to gain autonomy by exposing only themselves, rather themselves than their characters.[516]

The struggle to retrieve his identity, to recreate himself anew, belongs to a world that is not subservient to any laws, to neither those of fiction nor those of reality. Since the actor cannot completely control the object, and the object cannot control the actor, interaction between them is intrinsically based on chance. Consequently, the motions of the bio-object are always authentic and generated on the spot, escaping both life and theatre. "Through the 'life' of those BIO-OBJECTS, FICTION (the content of the play) '[shines] through,' in an endless process of losing itself and coming back," writes Kantor.[517]

The function of bio-objects is to initiate these primal tensions. As forms placed on the border between object and subject, they also exist on the border between fiction and reality, life and death. The intrinsic antagonism between actor and object alternately enhances and eliminates the differences between the juxtaposed notions. "This contradiction between death and life correspond[s] to the opposition between fiction and reality."[518] Each pair of contradictions becomes a means to construct and deconstruct the viewer's sense of the world and of oneself. "Our goal," writes Kantor, "is conditions so organized and formed that the audience loses its stiffness, its position of being prepared in advance for more or less indifferent observation of what is happening on stage [...] the on-stage reality should shock the viewers more or less on the level of their everyday life."[519] Setting up a world of fundamental oppositions, which parallels the spectator's notion of the world and within which he secures the spectator, Kantor then proceeds to destroy these familiar frames by creating a world in which none of the oppositions are relevant. In this sense, Kantor's theatre could be compared to certain structuralist premises. To make the world comprehensible, man constructs it around binary oppositions. Exposing this mechanism allows him to step outside of himself, yet it leaves him in an existential vacuum, in a world devoid of a subjective experience that can no longer be imagined within the onto-linguistic context. Kantor's maneuver eliminates the subject in order to reconstruct it. For Kantor, the subject is essential, but it can only be comprehended after a complete "descent into body." In such a world, viewers are "intentionally deprived of 'the right to distance, to a feeling of superiority and an opportunity to pass judgment' and other privileges granted to them in 'normal theater.'"[520] In the relationship between actor and spectator, "the actor is forced to reveal to the viewer his ridiculousness, his poverty, sacrificing even his dignity. He must stand before the audience powerless and without any protective or false covers."[521] The moment in which an actor – a "human shell, exhibitionist, con artist" – chooses to "make public what used to be most hidden," he gains the power to shake the audience's sense of reality.[522] His exhibition is an ultimate act of rebellion and arrogance against the omnipotent rules of self-protection. As Aldona Skiba-Lickel explains, Kantor's actor crosses the border of shame, yet, as she notices, "it is in the crossing of the border that the taste of mystery becomes detectable."[523]

The bio-object's intrinsic qualities permitted it to create conditions in which actors must exist on equal terms with objects. As early as 1944, Kantor, discussing objects used in *The Return of Odysseus*, wrote: "[the object] WAS,/ [it] EXISTED/ on equal footing with the actor./ [The object] WAS THE ACTOR!" He later observed how, in a performance exploiting the bio-object, "The actors became its live parts, its organs. They were, one could say, genetically joined to it [...] They tried] to adjust to it physically, 'relate' to it, 'find measure,' get in touch with it..."[524] Although on the physical level object and actor were equated, the bio-object altered not just the actor's physical state, but his mental state as well. The physical struggle between actor and object to control the other's movements parallels the psychological struggle to control one's own identity. Belonging to intrinsically opposite categories, both actor and object impose their essence on the bio-object. As Krzysztof Pleśniarewicz notices, "In specific situations it was sometimes the 'object' side that dominated and sometimes the 'human.'"[525] Though an object restricts an actor's movements, occasionally the actor liberates himself from the object's domination and confers upon it the elasticity of his own body. The split repeats itself, and the bio-object becomes either a living organism or a soulless wreck. "Kantor created a quasi-functional principle of the theatrical game dominated at one point by the subjective and by the objective – an illustration of the eternal conflict between matter and mind, a rivalry of two alien, independent forces," Pleśniarewicz writes. He asserts that, in Kantor's performances, "The rivalry between objectivization and the recovery of subjectivity also destroyed all connections between actor and […] character as 'written' in the dramatic text[,] on which the performance was based."[526] The actor struggles with the object as both the character he is performing and as himself; on- or offstage, physical interaction between actor and object remains subject to the same laws. Kantor's bio-objects transform an actor into a hollow copy of himself, a semi-automaton, a marionette, a form that is able to project more emotion than an actor pretending to be someone else. Controlling the actor's movements, the bio-object extends its control over the actor's emotions.[527] The intrinsic antagonism between man and space creates a milieu in which the actor cannot escape the objectivization forced upon him by the stage's spatial design. The only way to retrieve man's subjectivity is for him to merge with surrounding objects, and "to use [his] body as [a means] of visually exploring the abstract laws of the theater [space]."[528] "Characters, objects, become a function of space and its transformation."[529] As Pleśniarewicz notes:

> This space and the laws that governed it leveled the dramatic text with the theatre, the actor with the object, the living with the dead, and made possible the creation of the BIO-OBJECT – the connection and disconnection of actors and objects into completely new participants in the game, created and destroyed over and over […].[530]

In *Dead Class*, the classroom forces adults to act like children. They become total objects through their adaptation to a space that objectifies them. "In the photographs of dead memory the pupils melt into the homogenous mechanism of the class," writes Pleśniarowicz. "The uniformity of their black 'funeral' costumes and the deadly pallor of their faces dominates (Kantor called this 'a clear case of a bio-object,' since 'the benches and the pupils make up one organism')."[531] Seated on benches, they reenact the movements encoded in their minds in a manner appropriate to the setting. They seem to be conditioned to raise their hands and to attempt to give answers even though nobody asks them any questions. It is an impulse incited by the situation in which they have been placed, the classroom of their childhood. Each one of them makes some effort to remember the scenes they used to be a part of, yet, since years have passed, all they can recall are "bits and pieces left over from childhood, from the unfortunate experiences in their past lives (not always repeatable), from their dreams and passions."[532] In the general confusion of meaning, some characters assume the role of teachers, punishing those who appear least competent. Finally, the actors play not just the role of students, but the role of children as well. They start making faces and mock each other. Their progressive infantilization turns them into semi-automatons, puppets emptied of their subjective essence. Carrying the mannequin children, the old people "are turning into BIO-OBJECTS, they began to live through the emanation of their own death."⁵³³ The audience cannot relate to the actors playing these childish roles as much as those playing the dead, yet the audience cannot experience the same blatant fascination that they reserve for the real dead. Bio-objects as "forms empty of subjectivity"⁵³⁴ epitomize life and death, living organisms and inanimate matter, in the struggle for space and identity.

Estranged from their theatrical roles, the actors in *Dead Class* foreshadow the split between body and soul. "They act as if automatically, out of habit; we have even the impression that they ostentatiously refuse to own up to these roles, as if they were only repeating somebody else's sentences and actions, tossing them off with facility and without scruples; these roles break down every now and then as if badly learnt."⁵³⁵ Pretending to pretend to be someone else, rather than pretending to be someone else, Kantor's actors play themselves playing someone else. Alienated from their roles, they remain objectified and somewhat exposed: "The very condition of BEING ESTRANGED, which places them on a par with the condition of an OBJECT, removes biological, organic and, and naturalistic [expressions of] life."⁵³⁶ Hans-Ties Lehman explains the antinaturalistic mechanism behind Kantor's objects:

> The vulnerable human players become part of the whole structure of the stage, the damaged objects being their companions. This is also an effect enabled by the postdramatic gesture. For even when it is shown with a Naturalistic intention – where the milieu appears in its authority over people – the theatrical "environment" in dramatic theatre functions in principle merely as a frame and background to the *human* drama and the human figure. In Kantor's theatre, however, the human actors appear under the spell of objects. The hierarchy vital for drama vanishes, a hierarchy in which everything (and every *thing*) revolves around human action, the things being mere props. We can speak of a distinct thematic of the object, which further de-dramatizes the elements of action if they still exist. Things in Kantor's lyrical-ceremonial theatre appear as reminiscent of the epic spirit of memory and its preference for things.⁵³⁷

In *Dead Class*, objects are not chosen at random merely to agitate the actor's mental states through their presence. In the realm of fiction (the content of the play), they come to "define character and the whole past of the actor."⁵³⁸ Describing one of the pupils, Kantor writes, "An Old Man With Bicycle will not be parted from it, a piteous and battered toy from his childhood… he constantly goes for nocturnal trips on it, only the place has curiously shrunk to the classroom, around the benches…"⁵³⁹

> His BIKE is standing next to the desk, ready for
> Nighttime escapades. A body of a boy
> in a school uniform spread on it like a cross is his
> dead childhood. The bike carries it along
> in its futile wanderings.⁵⁴⁰

For an Old Man with a Bicycle, the Woman Behind the Window, a Street- and Sleep-Walker, the Woman with a Mechanical Cradle, the object attached to the actor is real;

the actor knows that the audience, whether it knows his stage name or not, defines him by the object he carries with him. He no longer plays the Man with a Bicycle – he is one. If only for the length of the performance, the object gives the actor a new identity; he ceases to be himself – that is, an actor performing his role – and becomes a generic Man with a Bicycle, his character.

In *Dead Class*, the characters are engaged in a perpetual struggle between two states. The objects attached to them not only force their identities upon the actors, but also "sentence [them] to the repetitive fulfilling of their peculiar destinies: the Woman with a Mechanical Cradle must take part in rituals defined by death and futile childbirth; the Old Man in the Toilet continually returns to the 'shameful place' assigned to him; the Old Man with a Bicycle keeps pushing the weird vehicle…"[541] Reduced by their objects to semi-automatons repeating movements in numb oblivion, they lack essence. As Krzysztof Miklaszewski notes:

> Just as one of the old men raises his finger, rousing himself to answer a question, another takes advantage of the opportunity to thrust his hand out, groaning to show how badly his bladder aches. And that is how it begins, with an air of schoolboy rivalry, this "pantomime of erect fingers." Each one's irresistible urge to score a victory over his classmates leads to a gradual retreat from the benches, and finally to the withdrawal of the entire class. In this succession of movements, the spectator is able to make the startling observation that among the dozen or so participants, there are a couple of people who are paralyzed and dependent on friends to move about; their existence is restricted to the mechanical repetition of actions which are "predetermined" for them by their environment.[542]

Kantor's approach was partially influenced by Meyerhold's experiments with biomechanics. According to Meyerhold, an actor that relies solely on emotions, as Stanislavsky's methodology dictates, becomes paralyzed and unable to control his or her voice or body. Only by discovering the body's proper kinetics can an actor create a role anew, in a way that truly involves the audience. According to Meyerhold, "all psychological states are determined by specific physiological processes. By correctly resolving the nature of his [or her] state physically, the actor reaches the point where he [or she] experiences the excitation which communicates itself to the spectator."[543] Although Kantor did not apply the rules of biomechanics directly, the interaction between actor/bio-object and spectator is partially based on Meyerhold's principles. Limiting the actor's array of gestures, the object forces the actor's body to follow the rhythm of its movements which, unnatural as they are for the actor, automatically metamorphose him or her into an inert, rigid creature. The mechanization of the actor's movements creates a situation in which, struggling to retrieve his or her subjectivity and conquer the morbidity projected on the body by the object, the actor experiences genuine feelings of constraint and violation, which transmit themselves to the audience. Objectified on each level of his or her being, as actor, as self, and as the character, the actor cannot protect him- or herself from the total annihilation of the self other than by exhibiting this self to the public. As Daniel C. Gerould puts it:

> All psychological and biological processes are reified, through the use of machines that are infantilely primitive and without any practical utility, such as the Family Machine, which makes the victim's legs keep opening and closing. Death the Sweeper, the ultimate confrontation with the great Void, brings on the Mechanical Cradle, which looks like a small coffin.[544]

In his 1988 essay "To Save From Oblivion," Kantor asserts this principal premise of his theatre. The contemporary world, with its "mass movements, mass ideologies, mass wars, mass crimes," deprives the individual being of all significance. The "Small, Poor, Defenceless, but magnificent history of individual human life" disappears under the burden of "collective life," "the consumerism of the world." The role of the artist is to "save from oblivion 'the individual life' of a human being." "It is only in this 'individual human life,'" Kantor writes, "that TRUTH, DIVINITY and GRANDEUR are preserved. They should be saved from oblivion, saved from all the 'powers' of the world, despite the awareness of impending failure."[545] Theatre is a means of saving from oblivion one's individual self by exposing it on stage and glorifying it as a work of art. In one of his essays, Kantor writes:

> A human being, who is amazingly fragile and delicate,
> who is unable to deal with his own Self,
> H I D E S in himself certain things,
> which I will call "sacred."
> A human being does not want to R E V E A L,
> at any price,
> that which is hidden
> because the act of revealing will always signify
> R E D U C T I O N and
> W E A K E N I N G.
> A human being wants to conceal
> all that contains the essence of life.[546]

Chapter 39

DEAD CLASS AS *FOREFATHERS' EVE*

Finally, Kantor's most eminent literary inspiration was Adam Mickiewicz's Romantic, four-part drama-poem, *Dziady* [*Forefathers' Eve*]. Written while Mickiewicz was in exile, *Forefathers' Eve* consists of four parts, each distinct in form. They can be, and customarily were, performed separately. In 1832, in a letter to his colleague Joachim Lelewel, Mickiewicz wrote: "I place great hopes in our nation and in a course of events unforeseen by any diplomacy. […] I would think only that our aspirations should be given a religious and moral character, distinct from the financial liberalism of the French and firmly grounded in Catholicism."[547] For the next 200 years, Mickiewicz's martyrological, liberatory vision of a Poland as expressed and solidified in *Forefathers' Eve* came to dominate Polish literature and art. It also became a primary source of Polish self-definition and nationalistic identity. Written in 1820–21, Part II, the so-called Vilnius–Kaunas part, focuses on folklore, particularly a Christianized version of a pagan ritual concerning the raising of the dead. The ludic ritual is viewed as a source of creativity and a manifestation of the early Romantic ontological and ethical attitude towards the mystical and supernatural. Part IV, written in 1821–2, is a spiritual, Romantic love story. It tells the tale of the unfortunate and exalted lover Gustav, who commits suicide upon seeing his beloved marry someone richer than he. Gustav returns from the dead to recount his story, lamenting his love and the suffering it brought him. Part III, written in 1832, is based on Mickiewicz's own life and his political activities under the Tsarist regime. Connecting politico-historical, mystical, messianic and martyrological themes, this part is considered a masterpiece of Polish Romantic drama. Its main hero, Konrad, rebels against God, blaming Him for all the evil, and asks Him to cease His omnipotence and let others recreate the world. Finally, Part I, chronologically the last one to be written, consists of loose scenes describing various cemetery rituals and choric sequences. This part was never finished.

Forefathers' Eve has had a tumultuous production history, mainly due to its strong political and liberatory themes. The drama-poem was not written with hopes of ever being staged under the regime of partitions. The Tsarist Government Commission for Internal and Religious Affairs banned Part III immediately after its publication in 1833; "The Petersburg Committee of Foreign Censorship confirmed the ban, defining the work as 'an outpouring of poisonous bile against the Russian government and imperial family.' Rewards were offered for handing in copies and fines imposed for possession, although the arbitrariness of Tsarist justice allowed for sentences of 25 years military service for individuals caught with the work."[548] As a result of the censorship, there were many official and unofficial performances, of student and underground productions, with different parts produced here and there. In fact, different sources provide different dates for what was the first official full staging of *Forefathers' Eve*. Part IV, titled *Gustaw*, was performed by Seweryn Malinowski in 1835, and in 1848, excerpts from Part III under the title *Senator Nowossiltzoff czyli Śledztwo zbrodni stanu na Litwie* [Senator Nowossiltzff, or an Investigation of a Coup d'état in Lithuania] were performed. Part II, accompanied by the music of Stanisław Moniuszko, was produced under the title *Phantoms* in 1865.[549] Some critics cite Wyspiański's 1901 version as the official premiere, since it "utilized all the parts and tailored them into a single show."[550] Wyspiański, however, cut 46 percent of the text, so other critics don't consider it a "full staging." A full staging, however, as Kazimierz Braun points out, would take nine hours.[551] The second significant staging of the drama took place at the Polish Theatre in Vilnius in 1921, when Poland had regained its independence. A number of other productions followed, one in 1932, at the Teatr Miejski in Lvov, and another in 1934 at Warsaw's Teatr Polski. Following World War II and the Soviet occupation of Poland, *Forefathers' Eve* once again became a politically volatile work, as the parallels between the Tsarist and Communist regimes were hard to miss, and the strong anti-Russian slant was read as an anti-Soviet metaphor.[552] Although *Forefathers' Eve* was obligatory reading in Polish high schools, the government-controlled educational system differentiated between anti-Tsarist and anti-Russian sentiments while promoting the Polish–Soviet relationship. Regardless of pro-Soviet propaganda, the Polish public saw *Forefathers' Eve* as a subversive work, and it was often staged as such. Kazimierz Braun provides a short summary of the play's performance history:

> The first production of the play after 1945 was mounted by Szyfman at the Teatr Polski in Warsaw in 1955, directed by Aleksander Bardini. Its impact contributed significantly to "October 1956" [the 'October Thaw' following Stalin's death in 1953] in the Polish theatre. The next production was not permitted until 1961, but fourteen different stagings of the play followed between 1961 and 1967; from 1973 to 1980 it was staged seven more times. All in all between 1960 and 1980 there were twenty-two productions of *The Forefathers' Eve*. Additionally, fragments of the work served as elements of various montages and scenarios.[553]

The play's most explosive production took place in 1967, at the National Theatre in Warsaw, under the direction of Kazimierz Dejmek. Although the play was scheduled to tour the Soviet Union, the Polish government decided to close it down after only a few performances, because audiences wildly cheered its anti-Russian passages. Braun suggests that some of the cheers were started by provocateurs planted in the audience by a dissident faction of the Communist Party, as a ploy in party infighting; they were joined by students as the government began to lose control of the situation.[554] Eventually, "[t]he closure of the play on 30 January 1968, officially due to the illness of its central actor, Gustaw Holoubek, resulted in a march by students of Warsaw University, protesting against what was widely seen as Soviet interference."[555] Further suppression of the intelligentsia and Polish Jewry prompted many to emigrate. Gomułka, then the first secretary, called *Forefathers' Eve* "a knife in the back." *Forefathers' Eve* was banned for five years.⁵⁵⁶ Since then, *Forefathers' Eve* has become a thermometer for "the political temperature in Polish society as a whole."⁵⁵⁷ "I read *Dziady* fifteen times, and I have to admit with horror, that this work is a curse," confesses Jan Nowicki, one of Poland's most revered actors. "The fact that we have *Dziady* and we revel in it is a symptom of our national illness. I always thought what a healthy nation the English are with their Shakespeare, or the French with their Molière."⁵⁵⁸

In his book on Gogol, Stephen Moeller-Sally points out that the literary celebrations can "mediate persons into the collective abstraction of national identity."⁵⁵⁹ That is what happened to Mickiewicz. The redemptive ideas in *Forefathers' Eve*, Part III – particularly the notion of Poland as "the Christ of nations," sacrificing its independence for Europe's redemption and the regeneration of European civilization (and humanity in general) – became the core of Polish liberatory theology and the source of a renewed Polish nationalism. Although recent scholarship on Mickiewicz disputes the Christian interpretation of *Forefathers' Eve* (Halina Filipowicz, for example, argues that Mickiewicz is not the author of the famous phrase "Poland, the Christ of nations," but that the phrase was coined by an anonymous writer in 1840 to describe the prevailing idea in Mickiewicz's whole body of work⁵⁶⁰), this exegesis has dominated the Polish sense of selfhood for centuries, invariably bound up with dreams of Polish independence and resurrection. Filipowicz poignantly argues that Mickiewicz

> was (and still is) construed as the national patriarch, as the patron saint of Polish cultural legitimacy, even superiority, indeed of Poland itself. Since the vicissitudes of modern history rendered the geographic and political concept of Poland elusive or fragile, Mickiewicz's life and art have been claimed as a kind of homeland. Mickiewicz troped as Poland is a figure of monumental consistency that stands guard over the illusion of Polish culture as an essentially monolithic one.⁵⁶¹

This interpretation of Mickiewicz's work and celebrity dominated both the Polish literary and educational canons. Before World War I, Mickiewicz's body of work served as a phantom stand-in for the lost homeland. During the interwar period of Polish independence, it fueled the nation-building process, prescribing Catholicism and nationalism as the new nation's two main forces. After World War II, the view of Mickiewicz as an essentially Polish signifier served both the Communist regime's attempt to uphold the illusion of Polish culture as homogeneous (thus effectively erasing the nation's diverse cultural and ethnic roots), and, for the opposition, as a tool of strategic essentialism aimed at strengthening the sense of national identity *vis-à-vis* the Soviets.

Parallel to the Catholic interpretation of *Forefathers' Eve*, another interpretation emerged, which stressed the Hasidic influences in Mickiewicz's work. In 1982, Artur Sandauer argued that Mickiewicz in fact called for a renewal of Christianity through its re-Judaization, a return to its Judaic roots. Mickiewicz believed, Sandauer writes, that Christianity had become corrupted and needed to return to its origins.⁵⁶² As Sandauer also points out, "It took a great many years to decode Mickiewicz's admission that his mother was Jewish. This message is encoded in a stanza of Dziady that mentions a 'foreign mother and her son Adam,' identified by the letters D and M which in Hebrew add up to 44."[563] Following Sandauer's work, a number of Polish and American scholars began to read *Forefathers' Eve* in a way similar to how Wyspiański's *Akropolis* is read: as an agglomeration of Judeo-Christian mythology, Hasidic mysticism and pagan rituals, a testimony to Poland's multiethnic heritage. For example, in her 1990 book, Jadwiga Maurer provides a compelling and in-depth analysis of Mickiewicz's connection to the world of Polish Jewry, including the symbolic and religious dimension of Kaballah.[564] The most recent international scholarship on Mickiewicz follows the same trajectory. In his 2001 essay "Konrad and Jacob: A Hypothetical Kabbalistic Subtext in Adam Mickiewicz's *The Forefathers' Eve*, Part III," Stuart Goldberg brings up this once-neglected view of Mickiewicz's work, pointing out the similarities between Konrad and Jacob, and citing numerous references to Kaballah found in Mickiewicz's writings.[565]

In 1932, Kantor traveled to Lvov to see Leon Schiller's staging of Mickiewicz's *Dziady*. The set was designed by Andrzej Pronaszko. The production made a great impression on the young Kantor.[566] As he puts it:

> I spend a lot of time thinking about *Dziady*. In 1937, I even designed its staging. I was aware that Zaduszki (Dziady) is understood by the whole world. [...] It is well known that in the 1860s, Lautréamont (who died in 1870), who was a protoplast of modern surrealism, wrote that he would not have been able to write his profane poetry if he hadn't read Mickiewicz's *The Great Improvisation*. For Lautréamont, Mickiewicz was a great blasphemer in relationship to God and in relationship to all established and sanctioned social, religious and national values. I consider Romanticism to be avant-garde, one of the greatest ones, greater than Surrealism or Dadaism. When Romanticism appeared, it destroyed the entire surface of hitherto prevailing culture, and Mickiewicz was one of those who contributed to that, with his *Dziady*. But, whereas *Hernani* was quickly staged, *Dziady* became known – and much, much later – only to Polish audiences. It never reached international audiences. And here is also the fault of our interpretation. Our art is interpreted by historians, critics, theatre directors, directors and other writers, and *Dziady* was interpreted in purely national terms. Nobody – in my opinion – interpreted *Dziady* as a great work of the great European avant-garde. Unfortunately, it is our fault that Mickiewicz stands at the very end of that line, and that *Hernani* – which is in fact very boring – became a revolutionary and emblematic Romantic drama, and *Dziady* did not. It is not Mickiewicz's fault, it is our own. It is the fault of Polish modernity, which poured our national sauce all over him, and still sees him in such a narrow framework. I think it is the same thing with Wyspiański. Wyspiański was used as a flagpole for the national struggle, and it was forgotten that he was one of the greatest representatives of the turn-of-the-century avant-garde, symbolism and secession.[567]

Helen Fagin poignantly explains that "the only difference perhaps between Mickiewicz of Poland and Byron of England or Schiller of Germany is that the Polish poet's national situation and circumstances demanded his total commitment and his dedication to the problems of his country, whereas the European romantics were free to address themselves in their works primarily to the world of the individual and his place in the society."[568] Kantor saw *Forefathers' Eve* in the context of European literature, unjustly neglected and limited by a too-narrow nationalistic (and Catholic) interpretation.

Kantor was fascinated by *Forefathers' Eve*. Like Grotowski, Kantor's interpretation of Mickiewicz's *Forefathers' Eve* offered a polyvocal view of the Polish bard's work as invariably rooted in long-standing Hasidic, and even pagan, traditions. In *Dead Class*, Kantor weaves in the pagan ritual of the raising of the dead described in *Forefathers' Eve*, Part II. Writing about Dziady, the ceremony of bringing up the dead, in his short introduction to *Forefathers' Eve*, Mickiewicz explains:

> *Dziady* is a ritual, a ceremony performed by villagers in Latvia, Prussia and Kurlandia, to commemorate "dziady" – dead people. The ceremony has its origins in paganism, and it used to be called a Goat Ceremony, led by Kozlarz [Piper], Huslaw, Guslarz, priest and the poet. In modern times, as enlightened priests and landowners wanted to get rid of any rituals they considered based in superstition and profanity, the poor took it underground, performing it secretly at roadside altars and in empty, old houses near cemeteries. They brought food and drink, and called on the dead.[569]

In *Forefathers' Eve*, Part II, the first ghost is the soul of a child, Angel, who can't get into heaven because during his lifetime he never experienced "the bitterness of life." He refuses food and drink and asks for "two grains of bitterness" because "he who hasn't experienced the bitterness of life will never find the sweetness of heaven."[570] The second ghost is The Damned, who suffers horrible tortures because his soul cannot leave his body. He would rather go to hell than further suffer such painful uncertainty. During his lifetime, The Damned was an evil man, and he received no mercy from the ritual's participants because "He, who was never human, can never be saved by the humans."[571] The third ghost is the spirit of a 19-year-old virgin girl who refused to get married and therefore died without experiencing the joys and sorrows of love. Now, she longs for the touch of a young man, because "he who has never walked on earth will not find his way to heaven."[572]

In the Polish language, *dziady* has a double meaning. In modern Polish, *dziady* refers to old, poor or homeless people. The idiom "*Zejść na dziady*" [go in the way of dziady] means to deplete, to become impoverished, whether financially, morally or intellectually. In Kantor's *Dead Class*, the twin meanings of *dziady* play out as the old people are both ghosts who return from the dead, and depleted, destroyed copies of what they used to be. Leszek Kolankiewicz wrote at length about the connection between *Dziady* and Kantor's *Dead Class*:

> Kantor's theatre is comparable to *Dziady*, Part II, which focuses on the ritual of raising the ghosts of the dead. In this sense, Kantor is like Guślarz, who has the power to speak to the dead. To answer Zbigniew Majcharowski's question about whether the form of *Dead Class* is closest to that of Mickiewicz's *Dziady*, we can say yes. Kantor's séance should be called the Twentieth-Century Dziady, as it reaches back into the

archaic modes of pre-Poland: the obligation of the living to the poor, lost souls of the departed, which have to be fed and kept warm. Kantor's vision speaks to modern viewers because its cryptoreligious effectiveness does not demand a confessional attitude as its precondition.[573]

Artur Sandauer compares *Dead Class* to a spiritual séance, suggesting that Kantor's very definition of theatre is formulated on Mickiewicz's poems. *Dead Class* and *Wielopole, Wielopole*, Sandauer writes, "are séances calling on the spirits of the dead. Kantor believes that theatre, in its fundamental sense, is *The Forefathers' Eve*."[574] Klaudiusz Święcicki draws religious connections between *Forefathers' Eve* and Kantor's *Dead Class* in the context of the Catholic Mass:

> The religious references in *Dead Class* go beyond ritual into Christian liturgy. The scenes of "Too Long Forefathers' Eve" and "Ceremonial Funeral" make reference in their structure to the *uniwersa fraternisa* of an old Christian Mass. In pre-Gregorian liturgy, after the ceremonial deposition of gifts, there was a long litany of names. The called names were of the dead and the living. Mixing the living with the dead was supposed to emphasize the unity of the Church. In Kantor's spectacle, old people reading large, black obituaries emphasize their connection to the departed. *Dead Class* becomes a community of memory for the artist, actor and viewer.[575]

Although Kantor's *Dead Class* neither quotes nor directly references *Forefathers' Eve*, it captures the spirit of Mickiewicz's poem in a way that creates its own independent frame of signification. In his review of the 1996 production of *Forefathers' Eve*, directed by Jerzy Grzegorzecki at the Stary Teatr in Cracow, Wojciech Szulczynski notes that "the spirit of *The Dead Class*, Kantor's legendary production, which by dint of sheer force introduced to experimental theatre around the world the problem of the decline, collapse, and death of modernist culture," hovered over the production.[576] So, it now seems impossible to stage *Forefathers' Eve* without acknowledging Kantor's veiled interpretation of Mickiewicz's poem.

Kantor's *Dead Class* draws on many sources of Polish literature and drama to paint a multilayered, post-traumatic landscape without a single literal allusion. The show is a meditation on the Holocaust, on absence and on history, which can swallow us at any moment in its merciless grip. Kantor's characters are living dead, coming back to demand justice, to reminisce on their lost lives and lost childhoods, asking for one more chance. Historical and critical analyses of Grotowski's *Akropolis* and Kantor's *Dead Class* allow us to examine the ways that both directors represent Auschwitz. Such analysis can offer a new critical understanding of the ways that translating trauma through the prism of performance can alter and deflect the meaning and reception of theatrical works, outside and within their cultural and historical contexts.

Chapter 40

DEAD CLASS: THE AFTERLIFE

Following Kantor's death in 1990, *Dead Class* was performed by his actors in Poland and abroad for a short while. The same year, the play was again staged in New York, but without Kantor's presence, it lost some of its magic. As Mel Gussow poignantly notes:

> Kantor's early opus, *The Dead Class*, returned this week to La MaMa to reintroduce theatergoers to the work of this icon of experimentalist drama. The director died in December and his company, Cricot 2, is carrying on his work. In the company's previous visits to the United States, all of them at La MaMa, Kantor was himself integral to the performance. A brooding totemic figure, he appeared onstage with his actors, serving as conductor, stagehand and silent watchman. His presence added an immeasurable dimension to the theatrical experience.[577]

The play was last performed in 1992, by Cricot 2 in Prague and Bremen. It was then that they decided to dissolve the troupe. Some eventually regrouped into an ensemble called Former Cricot-2 Actors. Others considered such an idea sacrilege.

In 2001 Krzysztof Miklaszewski directed *Scenes from Dead Class*, performed by the graduates of the Academy of Theatrical Practices, which was founded by the Gardzienice Theatre. Kantor would have rolled over in his grave – the Gardzienice Theatre is rooted in Grotowski's tradition (the company founder, Włodzimierz Staniewski, collaborated with Grotowski for years, until in 1977 he founded his own company). However, the director, Miklaszewski, was an actor at Cricot 2 for 17 years, and is the current artistic director of Warsaw Theatre Rampa. For *Scenes*, Miklaszewski used his own notes from the time he played the role of the Beadle, as well as Kantor's partitura (the "script" of the performance written post-performance) of *Dead Class*. The show premiered on 24 October at the Lublin Theatre Festival, to much anticipation and controversy. It received mixed reviews. Roman Pawłowski didn't know how to respond, writing:

> Miklaszewski's show, however, is not a copy of Kantor's spectacle, but a reduction. Miklaszewski voided *Dead Class* of its most important two elements: the past and death. There are no Schulz-like mannequins sitting in the school benches next to the living pupils, there is no Old Man, no necrologs, no old newspapers from 1914, no scene of washing the dead corpse. There is, however, the strength and joy of life, which radiates from Miklaszewski's show.[578]

According to Miklaszewski, *Dead Class* has to be retold through the eyes of a new generation:

> The return to the past in the case of these young people means something completely different. Today's generation has completely different memories. Even for me, some subjects that Kantor recalled in his shows – World War I for example – were alien. For them, not only World War II but even the Solidarity movement are alien. That is why I cleansed *Dead Class* of its death motif. Otherwise, it would be hypocrisy to try to capture that spirit with these students.[579]

Roman Pawłowski further notes that it would be impossible to stage *Dead Class* today, with all of its existential, cultural and political baggage:

> Miklaszewski does not imitate *Dead Class*, but rather enters into a conversation with Kantor's work. He says that today, black-and-white Kantor, submerged in the past, is impossible for most viewers to digest. In his show, Kantor's role as conductor is taken up by a young punk with a black leather jacket and purple mohawk. In the final scene, he leads the pupils off the stage only to return a minute later, screaming to heavy metal music a manifesto of a generation with past and without a future: "I am bad, I am dirty." In order to stage Kantor's show today, Miklaszewka had to remove from it what was essential: its existential experience of death. What was left from *Dead Class* was class – a satire on school. Raising hands, which in Kantor's show was a macabre image of struggle over life and death, in Miklaszewski's show became just raising hands. Theatre of Death without death, becomes, in a way, dead.[580]

Ironically, without its existential, cultural and political baggage, *Dead Class* becomes what it has always been to foreign critics: "a satire on the educational process."
  Wacław Janicki, one of Kantor's famous Twins, completely disagreed with Miklaszewski, arguing that *Dead Class* is Kantor's personal, individual confession, which cannot be repeated: "*Dead Class* does not have a dramatic structure, it is the record of a personal, existential experience, which was for Kantor a theatrical séance. It was successful not only because it was artistically successful, but because Kantor was present during the entire show."[581] Janicki was very much opposed to meddling with Kantor's legacy in any way: "I wonder to what degree staging *Dead Class* is a courageous gesture, and to what degree it is abusing Kantor's legacy. An artist can raise the bar as high as he wants to, but I don't see anything in Miklaszewski's previous experience to justify such a move."[582] Włodzimierz Staniewski, on the other hand, notes that, thanks to Miklaszewski, one can see "how Kantor organized everything."[583] Miklaszewski himself acknowledges the controversy: "The title is both modest and arrogant. Maybe too risky. Maybe. But twenty-eight years ago, I risked even more, crossing the threshold of Krzysztofory Gallery."[584] Krzysztof Pleśniarewicz, a longtime Cricoteka director, suggests that one shouldn't consider Kantor's theatre untouchable: "Kantor himself built his artistic position on playing with other authors – particularly,

Witkacy. I would love to see a theatre that would similarly play with Kantor, without replicating or mimicking his work."[585]

Following Kantor's death, versions of his shows were mounted in a number of countries. However, Miklaszewski's attempt to revive *Dead Class* was the first of its kind in Poland.[586] The French theatre scholar Georges Banu claims that there's a trend in late twentieth-century art which he calls "*le kantorisme*." "Oftentimes, Kantor's experiences are taken literally: I have heard of one American professor who showed students videos of *Dead Class* and instructed them to mimic the actors."[587] In 2005, on the occasion of the play's 13th anniversary, a montage version of *Dead Class* was shown on Polish TV, accompanied by press coverage, private screenings and lectures. At that time, Jacek Cieślak poignantly asked what *Dead Class* could possibly mean for contemporary young people. "Although they grew up in computerized classes, writing and reading literature on the internet, the sequence with old, moldy books has to make a great impression on them. Maybe they will think that every class, even the younger one, will have to die one day."[588]

Since Kantor's death, his actors have performed the same ritual every year. "Every December 8th, on the anniversary of Kantor's death, right by Cricoteka, on Kanonicza Street, thirteen live monuments take their places. Two Chasids with the Desk of Last Resort and the Eternal Wanderer, bent beneath the weight of his baggage, take their place for 15 minutes to the sounds of Jewish music."[589]

POSTSCRIPT

Just because we are postscript, it doesn't mean that the script is not there. On the contrary, to paraphrase Derrida, there is nothing but the script.

I have decided to call Kantor and Grotowski's theatre post-traumatic rather than postdramatic, recognizing that these two concepts, one derived from psychology and the other from theatre theory, are fundamentally connected. In her introduction to Hans-Ties Lehman's milestone book on *Postdramatic Theatre*, the translator, Karen Jürs-Munby, explains that the 'post' in 'postdramatic' is to be understood

> as a rupture and a beyond that continue to entertain relationships with drama and are in many ways an analysis and 'anamnesis' of drama. To call theatre 'postdramatic' involves subjecting the traditional relationship of theatre to drama to deconstruction and takes account of the numerous ways in which this relationship has been refigured in contemporary practices since the 1970s.[1]

As Jürs-Munby notes, 'postdramatic' denotes a rupture between drama and theatre *vis-à-vis* their symbiotic past. Likewise, trauma is defined as a violent rupture in the social and psychological order that fundamentally alters an individual's concept of the self and the world. Trauma denotes a rupture between the individual and the world: just as postdrama is no longer bound to theatre ("there can be theatre without drama"), the traumatized individual is no longer bound to the world that betrayed him. What is the rupture that made the postwar theatre postdramatic? Can we argue that it was the trauma of the war that made the drama postdramatic in the first place? Which came first? Jürs-Munby explains further that "The experiences of World War II, the Holocaust and Hiroshima […] have fundamentally shaken the belief in this historical model, which explains why postwar practitioners such as Samuel Beckett, Tadeusz Kantor and Heiner Müller eschew the dramatic form in the wake of these events."[2] In other words, Jürs-Munby suggests that the historical traumas of World War II led to the social, political and cultural rupture within the hitherto prevailing grand paradigms – which, in turn, led to the postdramatic moment.

Lehman himself notes that "Postdramatic theatre is also theatre in an age of omitted images of conflict."[3] Likewise, to be in a post-traumatic condition means to not be able to verbalize, or sometimes even to properly recall, the traumatic event – to replace it with bits and flashes of memory, with metaphors and surrogate symbols. Postdramatic, post-traumatic theatre circles around trauma, often veiling it in the visual and metaphorical language that is post-and-beyond the word. Perhaps theatre had to detach itself from drama and become postdramatic because the language of drama was no longer sufficient to express the inexpressible. Although Lehman devotes an entire chapter to Kantor, considering his work to be quintessentially postdramatic, he barely mentions Grotowski, including him in the litany of other postwar practitioners who could potentially be classified as postdramatic. Is Grotowski postdramatic in the same way that Kantor is? Yes and no. Grotowski still believes in words; Kantor does not. If we follow Lehman's recommendation and think deconstructively, we must recall Derrida's thesis that the word signifies the death of the very thing it designates, "death of the pure idiom reserved for the unique."[4] To give name to a unique thing is to eliminate the difference, the absolute, that marks it as unique, and to "inscribe it within a difference [of the language...], to suspend the vocative absolute."[5] The deconstructive relationship between drama and theatre is inscribed in the post-traumatic inability to give name to the thing, in an ironic resistance to the suspension of the vocative absolute, a resistance to the pronouncement of the unpronounceable, to the erasure of the self in the postheterotelic difference of history.

APPENDIX

Table 1. Chronology of Events

1973 – Americans leave Vietnam.	**1979** – *Dead Class* premieres in New York at La MaMa.	
1969 – Woodstock festival.	**1975** – *Dead Class* premieres in Cracow.	
1968 – Martin Luther King is assassinated.	**1969** – *Akropolis* premieres in New York.	**1968** – Expulsion of the remaining Jews from Poland. Following the expulsions, only 5,000 Jews remain in Poland.
	1968 – *Akropolis* is filmed in London.	
1967 – Six-Day War in the Middle East. The United States allies with Israel while the Soviet Union sides with the Arab Nations.	**1962–1967** – *Akropolis*, in variants I–V, is shown in Poland.	
1965 – Bombing of North Vietnam begins. Americans begin protesting the war.	**1965** – Founding of Grotowski's Laboratory Theatre in Wrocław.	
1963 – President John F. Kennedy is assassinated.	**1959** – Grotowski moves to Opole to become the artistic director of the Thirteen Row Theatre.	

APPENDIX

		1956 – Polish October Thaw.
		1955 – Founding of Kantor's Cricot 2 Theatre.
1950–1953 – The Korean War.	1953 – Stalin dies.	
1948 – The State of Israel is proclaimed.		
	1947, 14 June – The Auschwitz site becomes a museum.	
	1946–1948 – Borowski publishes his Auschwitz stories.	
1946 – Churchill delivers the "Iron Curtain" speech. Cold War begins.		
		1945–1947 – Most of Poland's 300,000 Jewish Holocaust survivors leave the country immediately after the war.
		1945–1953 – Socialist realism is a predominant art form approved in Poland and the Eastern Bloc.
1945 – The US drops two atomic bombs on Japanese cities; World War II ends.	1945, 4–11 February – Yalta Conference between the "Big Three," Churchill, Roosevelt and Stalin. Poland becomes a Soviet satellite.	
	1944 – The Warsaw Uprising.	
	1943 – The Warsaw Ghetto uprising.	
1941 – The US enters World War II.		
		1939–1945 – Over 6 million Poles perish in WWII, approximately twenty percent of Poland's prewar population, including 3 million Polish Jews.
	1939 – World War II begins.	1939 – 3.3 million Jews live in Poland, constituting forty percent of all European Jewry at that time and more than one-third of the Polish population.

(*Continued*)

Table 1. Continued

1938 – Gombrowicz's *Ferdydurke* published in Warsaw.	
1937 – Schulz's *Sanatorium Under the Sign of The Hourglass* is published.	
1934 – Schulz's *Street of Crocodiles* is published.	
1933 – Jerzy Grotowski is born in Rzeszów.	
1926 – Ansky's *Dybbuk* is shown in Cracow (the show returns in 1930 and 1938).	
1921 – Witkacy's *Tumor Brainiowicz* is written, premieres in Cracow.	
1915 – Tadeusz Kantor is born in Wielopole.	**1918**, 11 November – Poland regains independence
	1914–1918 – World War I
1904 – Wyspiański's *Akropolis* is published in Cracow.	
1820–1932 – Mickiewicz's *Forefathers' Eve* is written.	**1772, 1793, 1795** – The three partitions of Poland. Poland loses its independence and becomes partitioned between the Russian, Prussian and Austro-Hungarian empires.

Table 2. Comparison between Wyspiański's *Akropolis* and *Genesis*

Akropolis, Act II			Genesis			
Scene	1		Exac.	Chapter	XXVI	verses	1–4
"	2		"	"	"	"	6–13
"	3		Orig.				
"	4		"				
"	5		Der.	Chapter	XXVII	verses	14–17
"	6		Sign.	"	"	"	18–19
"	7		"	"	"	"	32–41
"	8		Exac.	"	"	"	42–46
"	9		"	"	XXVIII	"	1–4
"	10	(Jacob's dream)	Sign	"	"	"	11–22
"		(Jacob and shepherds)	"	"	"	"	2–10
"	11		"	"	"	"	11
"	12		"	"	"	"	13–15, 12–19
"		(Wedding pantomime)	"	"	"	"	20–23
"	13		Orig.	"	"	"	25
"	14		Exac.	"	"	"	25–27
"	15		Sign. & Chan.	"	"	"	28–35
"			"	"	XXX	"	1–24
"	16		Exac.	"	"	"	25–34
"	17		"	"	XXXI	"	5–7, 9, 11–15

(*Continued*)

Table 2. Continued

Akropolis, Act II			Genesis	
"	(Pantomime)	"	"	17–21
18		"	"	22, 23–25
20		"	"	26–32
21		"	XXXII	4
22		Sign.	"	7–8
23		Exac.	"	9–12
24		"	"	13–20
25		Chan.	"	24–32
25	(Reconciliation)	Sign.	XXXIII	5–16
		Orig.		

Exac. — Parallels exactly or with small changes
Sign. — Parallels with significant changes
Chan. — Scene completely changed
Orig. — Original
Der. — Derived

Table 3. Comparison between Grotowski and Kantor

KANTOR	GROTOWSKI
1. Aesthetics inspired by Gordon Craig, Kleist, Meyerhold, constructivism and Dada.	1. Aesthetics inspired primarily by Stanislavski.
2. *Dead Class* influenced by the "Polish School of Grotesque": Stanisław Witkiewicz, Witold Gombrowicz and Bruno Schulz (also by Yiddish playwright S. Anky and Adam Mickiewicz)	2. *Acropolis* influenced by Polish national literature: Stanisław Wyspiański and Polish Romantics (also Tadeusz Borowski)
3. *Teatr Biedny* – Poor Theatre – an ontological concept, referring to a psychological condition vis-à-vis history. All the elements of the spectacle have the same value: actors, objects, set, text, audience – they all are equal. Theatre without psychology. Theatre of amateurs.	3. *Teatr Ubogi* – Poor Theatre – a material concept, referring to staging technique: theatre with no objects, no props, no costumes, no sets, with only the naked body of an actor. Emphasis on the actor. Actors undergo physical training and psychological-spiritual training. "We consider the personal and scenic technique of the actor as the core of theater art."
4. Time is trapped in one post-traumatic gesture: repetition-compulsion.	4. Time is continual, narrative, linear.
5. Theatrical event should be distanced from the audience: actors are like the dead, "irrevocably different and infinitely strange."	5. Theatrical event should replicate religious, ritual experience. Theatre with "a sacred aim." The actors and spectators interact in the same way that participants in a religious ritual interact.
6. Emphasis on the emotions of the audience. The lack of emotions in the actor. Actor as a mannequin, semi-puppet. Actor on equal footing with the mannequin. Actor as half-dead. The Theatre of Death: "a game with void."	6. Emphasis on the authentic emotions of the actor. Theatre as psychotherapy: acting with the ideal partner. The audience is secondary: theatre without the audience: "We don't strive to be avant-garde, we confront our own experience."
7. Purpose of rehearsals is to bring the actor closest to the condition of the object. Emphasis on tableaux: "There is never action, only photographic plates."	7. Purpose of rehearsals is to bring to actor to the most emotionally charged state, to the breaking point, the source.
8. The body of an actor connected to the object becomes a bio-object. The audience responds to the objectification of the actor.	8. The body of the actor is a vehicle of his emotions. Actor undergoes "trance." The audience responds to the emotions of the actor: "full identification of the viewers with the actors."
9. Attempts to make body more physically present: body as a physical entity – matter.	9. Attempts to diminish the distance between impulse and reaction: the body disappears, the actor becomes "whole" during "an absolute act."
10. Believes it is impossible to represent the past and its heroes. Stages the inability to resurrect drama, plot, characters and regions of memory.	10. Believes it is possible to reveal the inner, archetypal self of the actor at the moment of the performance.
11. Believes in the multiplicity of the Self.	11. Believes in the Universal Self.

NOTES

Foreword

1 Romana Konieczna, "Przed premierą 'Pechowców.' Rozmowa z reżyserem" [Before the Opening of the "Jinxed": Conversation with the Director], *Trybuna Opolska* 265 (1958): 4.
2 Seth Baumrin, "Ketmanship in Opole: Jerzy Grotowski and the Price of Artistic Freedom," *TDR: The Drama Review* 53, no. 4 (Winter 2009): 49–77. Baumrin borrowed the term "Ketman" from Czesław Miłosz, who borrowed it from Arthur Gobineau's book *Religions and Philosophies of Central Asia*. Travelling through Asia, Gobineau noticed the Persian practice of hiding one's true feelings and opinions behind a mask of false identity. See footnote 73 in Part 1 for a more detailed explanation.
3 Konstantyn Puzyna, *Półmrok* [Twilight] (Warsaw: Wydawnictwo PAN 1982), 135.
4 Andrzej Żurowski, "Pulling Faces at the Audience: The Lonely Theatre of Tadeusz Kantor," *New Theatre Quarterly* 1 (1985): 367.
5 Kathleen Cioffi, "ZAR and Other Microcultures of 'Grotland,'" *Slavic and East European Performance* 28, no. 2 (2008): 20–29.
6 Richard Schechner, *The Grotowski Sourcebook*, ed. Richard Schechner and Lisa Wolford (London: Routledge 1997), xxv.
7 Blanka Zizka, "Arriving in Warsaw – Part One," Wilma Theater website (blog), 28 July 2011, <https://wilmatheater.org/blog/arriving-warsaw-part-one> (accessed 30 April 2012).
8 "Tadeusz Kantor: Twenty Years Later," ed. Natalia Zarzecka and Michal Kobialka, special issue of *Polish Theatre Perspectives* 1, no. 2, forthcoming.
9 David Bordwell, *Making Meaning: Inference and Rhetoric in the Interpretation of Cinema* (Cambridge, MA: Harvard University Press 1996) 274.
10 Kantor, quoted in Miklaszewski, *Tadeusz Kantor: Między śmietnikiem a wiecznością* [Tadeusz Kantor: Between Garbage and Eternity] (Warsaw: Państwowy Instytut Wydawniczy 2007), 32.

Introduction

1 Theodor W. Adorno, "Trying to Understand *Endgame*," in *Notes to Literature: Volume 1*, ed. Rolf Tiedemann, trans. Shierry Weber Nicholson (New York: Columbia University 1958), 242.
2 By "drama," Adorno means not only a dramatic text but also a theatrical performance.
3 I thank Elinor Fuchs for bringing this review to my attention.
4 Gita Honegger, "Lost in Translation, or 'Rather than bury Zadek, I come to praise him!'" *Theater* 40, no. 3 (2010): 116–27, at 119.
5 Günther Rühle, quoted in Honegger, "Lost in Translation," 127.
6 Michel Foucault, *Language, Counter-Memory, Practice* (Ithaca, NY: Cornell University Press 1980), 138.
7 I thank my colleague Lawrence Switzky for bringing this essay to my attention.
8 Virginia Woolf and Andrew McNeillie, "On Not Knowing Greek," in *The Common Reader* (San Diego: Harcourt Brace Jovanovich 1984), 23, 29, 36–7.
9 "What differs? Who differs? What is difference?" – Derrida asks (Jacques Derrida, "Difference," in *Margins of Philosophy*, trans. Alan Bass (Chicago: University of Chicago Press 1985), 15).

10 Ibid., 11.
11 Theodor Adorno, *Aesthetic Theory*, trans. Robert Hullot-Kentor (Minneapolis: University of Minnesota Press 1998), 35.
12 Bordwell, *Making Meaning*, 264.
13 Susan Sontag, *Against Interpretation, and Other Essays* (New York: Picador 1966), 7.
14 Ibid., 9.
15 Ibid., 12.
16 Ibid., 14.
17 Bordwell, *Making Meaning*, 264.
18 Ibid., 267.
19 Ibid., 265.
20 Ibid., 274.
21 Ibid., 269.
22 Ibid., 273.
23 Richard Schechner, "Want to Watch? Or Act?" *New York Times*, 12 January 1969, D1.
24 As Aristotle privileges dramatic text over spectacle, Western critical tradition privileges drama over performance. The shift away from the "literature of theatre" began with the early twentieth-century avant-garde, and accelerated in the 1960s with the development of performance art. It was followed by the conceptualization of the field of performance studies, which was no longer at all "interested in drama as such" (W. B. Worthen, "Disciplines of the Text/Sites of Performance," *TDR: The Drama Review* 39, no. 1 (1995): 13–28, at 26).
25 As Halina Filipowicz notes, although "[the] move away from the traditional understanding of theatre as a servant of drama has escaped the hegemony of the text on page, [by] merely reversing the terms of the binary [...] inversion remains within its limiting framework" (Halina Filipowicz, "Performing Bodies, Performing Mickiewicz: Drama as Problem in Performance Studies," *Slavic and East European Journal* 43, no. 1 (Spring 1999): 1–18, at 4).
26 Adorno, "Trying to Understand *Endgame*," 262.
27 Silence in theatre is as important as words, precisely because it stands in their place. To quote Heiner Müller: "[T]he basic thing in theatre is silence. Theatre can work without words, but it can not work without silence" (Arthur Holmberg, "A Conversation with Robert Wilson and Heiner Müller," *Modern Drama* 31 (1988): 453–8).
28 Patrice Pavis, *Languages of the Stage: Essays in the Semiology of Theatre* (New York: Methuen 1982), 1.
29 Ibid.
30 Adorno, "Trying to Understand *Endgame*," 242.
31 Honegger, "Lost in Translation," 116.
32 Shannon Jackson, *Professing Performance: Theatre in the Academy from Philology to Performativity* (New York: Cambridge University Press 2004), 6. In her review of Jackson's book, Heidi Bean poignantly notes that the word "performance" itself opened up a debate that necessarily led to interdisciplinary sloppiness:

> The generic literary subdiscipline of drama has only recently yielded its place to the more charged, interdisciplinary, and ambiguous term "performance." This shift opens the way for a wider methodological scope and troubles the taxonomies that once dominated literature and theater departments. Indeed, as any performance scholar knows all too well, the concept of performance has become a very large and shaky common ground for a variety of disciplines and practices, including music, art history, anthropology, philosophy, literature, and, of course, theater. (Heidi R. Bean, "'Professing Performance: Theatre in the Academy from Philology to Performativity' (review)," *Cultural Critique* 71 (Winter 2009): 151–4, at 151)

33 As a result of such questionable epistemology, the most celebrated American "experts" on Kantor and Grotowski are unable to say as much as "hello" in Polish, while teaching – at the country's top universities – courses on Kantor and Grotowski. Such a situation would be unacceptable in any other area of critical studies. It's difficult to imagine a French department with a Proust expert not speaking French, or a Russian department with an expert on Chekhov not speaking any Russian. Yet, in the field of performance studies, this is an acceptable practice. While students and theatre critics can't possibly be expected to learn the language of every show or play they review, read, or study, scholars should speak the language of their research.
34 Richard Schechner and Victor Turner, *Between Theatre and Anthropology* (Philadelphia, PA: University of Pennsylvania Press 1985), 252.
35 Performance studies reportage analysis "gives a blow-by-blow description of the performance, examines how it affects us [...] and how the waves of meaning are generated through the multiplicity and simultaneity of signs." The problem is, however, as Patrice Pavis notes, that in reader-response analysis, "our Western cultural habits" and "our ethno- or Euro-centrist gaze determines and often mortgages our perceptions" (Patrice Pavis and Christine Shantz, *Dictionary of the Theatre: Terms, Concepts, and Analysis* (Toronto: University of Toronto Press 1999), 254–60).
36 In his 1997 essay on the state of current theatre research, Patrice Pavis suggests that by shifting away from "literature" in the 1970s, theatre needed to establish itself as independent of literature; however, Pavis argues, the focus on dramatic text is making a comeback as text is being recognized once again as an important element of theatre's semiotic field. Pavis writes:

> Theatre semiology established itself as the dominant academic discourse of the seventies because theatre (since Artaud) felt the need to be treated as a discipline in and for itself, as an autonomous language and not as a branch of literature. Its principal concern has thus been to start with the stage, with the large moments or stage units, and to examine the text as it is enunciated on stage. As a result, the semiology of the text was neglected or even disqualified, the text and the stage were radically separated as were dramaturgical analysis and "theatrical language." But now the dramatic text is making a marked comeback: theatre is no longer simply considered as a performance space, but once again, albeit in a different way, as textual practice. (Patrice Pavis, "The State of Current Theatre Research," *Applied Semiotics / Sémiotique appliqué* 1, no. 3 (1997): 203–30, at 208)

37 Zbigiew Osiński, "Grotowski and the Reduta Tradition," in *Grotowski's Empty Room*, ed. Paul Allain (London: Seagull Books 2010), 31.
38 Wojciech Szulczynski, "Review: 'Forefathers' Eve: Twelve Improvisations,'" in "Eastern European Transitions," special issue, *Theatre Journal* 18, no. 4 (December 1996): 499–503, at 499.
39 Jerzy Tymicki and Andrzej Niezgoda, "New Dignity: The Polish Theatre 1970–1985," *TDR: The Drama Review* 30, no. 3 (Autumn 1986): 13–46, at 22.
40 Szulczynski, "Review: 'Forefathers' Eve: Twelve Improvisations,'" 499.
41 Halina Filipowicz, "Demythologizing Polish Theatre," *TDR: The Drama Review* 39, no. 1 (Spring 1995): 122–9, at 125.
42 The original title of both Wyspiański's and Grotowski's works is *Akropolis*. In the English-language literature and press, both versions, *Akropolis* and *Acropolis*, are used interchangeably. Whenever possible, I use the original title, *Akropolis*.
43 The original English-language posters and program notes list the title as *Dead Class*. The English-language reviews from the 1970s and 1980s use both *Dead Class* and *The Dead Class*. Michal Kobialka uses *The Dead Class*. Whenever possible, I follow the original posters and use

Dead Class since I believe that's how Kantor himself wanted it. Without the article, the title is more ambivalent, less assertive – poorer.
44 Irving Wardle, "Haunted Visions of Museum of Memory," *Times*, 18 November 1982, 8.
45 Jackson, *Professing Performance*, 6.
46 Robert Findlay, "Grotowski's 'Akropolis': A Retrospective," *Modern Drama* 27, no. 1 (March 1984): 2.
47 Ludwik Flaszen, "Wyspianski's *Akropolis*," in *The Grotowski Sourcebook*, ed. Richard Schechner and Lisa Wolford (New York: Routledge 1997), 64–72. Originally published as Ludwik Flaszen, "A Theatre of Magic and Sacrilege," *TDR: The Drama Review* 9, no. 3 (1965): 64.
48 Jane Turner, *Eugenio Barba* (London and New York: Routledge 2005), 4.
49 Findlay, "Grotowski's 'Akropolis': A Retrospective," 8.
50 Daniel Gerould, "Jerzy Grotowski's Theatrical and Paratheatrical Activities as Cosmic Drama: Roots and Continuities in the Polish Romantic Tradition," *World Literature Today* 54 (1980): 381–3.
51 Mark Fortier, *Theory/Theatre: An Introduction* (London: Routledge 1997), 77.
52 James Slowiak and Jairo Cuesta, *Jerzy Grotowski* (London: Routledge 2007).
53 Milly S. Barranger, *Theatre: Ways of Seeing* (Florence, KY: Wadsworth Publishing 2005), 62–3.
54 Jennifer Kumiega, *The Theatre of Grotowski* (London: Methuen 1985), 60.
55 The collections were published under the titles *Le Monde de Pierre* and *L'Adieu à Maria*. *Farewell to Maria* was published in Poland in 1947, and *The World Made of Stone* was published in 1948. In America, *Farewell to Maria* was published in 1976 under the title *This Way for the Gas, Ladies and Gentlemen*. The collection was supplemented by a few stories from *The World Made of Stone* and from another collection, *Byliśmy w Oświęcimiu* (1946) [*We Were in Auschwitz*]. The title, *This Way for the Gas, Ladies and Gentlemen* [*Proszę państwa do gazu*], was taken from one of the stories included in *We Were in Auschwitz*.
56 Neal Ascherson, "The Artist as Traitor," *The Scotsman*, 28 August 1976. Cricoteka Archives: CRC III/000184.
57 Tadeusz Kantor, quoted in "Kantor profeta dell'avanguardia," interview with Enrico Piergiacomi, *Sipario* 383 (1978): 18–22 (quoted in Krzysztof Pleśniarowicz's lecture "Kantor–Grotowski: między maglem a wiecznością" [Kantor–Grotowski: Between the Calender and Eternity] given at the conference "Grotowski: samotność teatru. Dokumenty, konteksty, interpretacje" [Grotowski: Loneliness of the Theatre. Documents, Contexts, Interpretations], Cracow, 25–27 March 2009. Reprinted in Krzysztof Pleśniarowicz, "Kantor–Grotowski: między maglem a wiecznością" [Kantor–Grotowski: Between the Calender and Eternity], *PERFORMER* 2 (2011), <http://www.grotowski.net/performer/performer-2/kantor-grotowski-miedzy-maglem-wiecznoscia#footnote3_w8f1j6n> (accessed 15 February 2012)).
58 William Harris, "Tadeusz Kantor: Exploring the Dead Theater," *Soho Weekly News*, 22 February 1979, 27.
59 Quoted in Zbigniew Osiński, *Jerzy Grotowski: Źródła, inspiracje, konteksty* [Jerzy Grotowski: Origins, Inspirations, Contexts] (Gdańsk: Słowo/Obraz Terytoria 1998), 332.
60 Despite those efforts, however, there remains much suspicion among the most ardent supporters and scholars of both directors.
61 See <http://www.grotowski.net/en/performer>.
62 Ellen Stewart, quoted in Zbigniew Basara, "Kantor wrócił do Nowego Jorku" [Kantor Returned to New York], *Gazeta Wyborcza* 265 (13 November 2008): 21.
63 Konstanty Puzyna, "My, Umarli" [We, the Dead Ones], in *Półmrok, Felietony teatralne i szkice* (Warsaw: Państwowy Instytut Wydawniczy 1982), 102–14, at 102.
64 Tish Dace, "The Class of the Living Death," *Soho Weekly News*, 15 February 1979. Cricoteka Archives: CRC III/000487.

65 Krzysztof Jędrysek, quoted in Beata Guczalska, "Polskie środowisko teatralne wobec Grotowskiego" [Polish Theatre Community's Relationship towards Grotowski], *Didaskalia, Gazeta Teatralna*, June 2009, 21 [Originally published in *Dialog* 6 (1999): 135].
66 Wisz, "Grotowski i inni" [Grotowski and Others], *Trybuna Robotnicza* 51 (1–2 March 1969). Grotowski Institute Archives.
67 Robert L. King, *The Ethos of Drama: Rhetorical Theory and Dramatic Worth* (Washington, DC: Catholic University of America Press 2010), 1.
68 Paul de Man (1973) writes an account of Derrida's famous philosophical/grammatological question:

> Jacques Derrida – who asks the question "What is the difference" – and we cannot even tell from his grammar whether he "really" wants to know "what" difference is or is just telling us that we shouldn't even try to find out. Confronted with the question of the difference between grammar and rhetoric, grammar allows us to ask the question, but the sentence by means of which we ask it may deny the very possibility of asking. (Paul de Man, "Semiology and Rhetoric," *Diacritics* 3, no. 3 (Fall 1973): 29)

69 Holger Teschke, "Jerzy Grotowski, 1933–1999," *Theater* 29, no. 2 (1999): 4–15, at 6.
70 Peter Brook, *Empty Space* (Austin, TX: Touchstone 1995), 59.
71 Ibid.
72 Joanna Targoń, "Don Kichot w okularach dla krótkowidzów" [Don Quixote in Glasses for the Nearsighted], *Gazeta Wyborcza* 67 (20 March 2009): 10.
73 Tamara Karren, "'*Umarła Klasa*' Kantora" [Kantor's *Dead Class*], *Tydzień Polski*, 9 October 1976, 7.
74 Tadeusz Kantor, "Teatr Śmierci (manifest)" [The Theatre of Death (manifesto)] (Warszawa Biblioteka Galerii Foksal 1975). First published in English in *Canadian Theatre Review* 16 (Fall 1977), translated by Voy T. and Margaret Stelmaszyński. Reprinted in Tadeusz Kantor, *A Journey Through Other Spaces: Essays and Manifestos, 1944–1990*, ed. Michal Kobialka (Berkeley: University of California Press 1993) 106.
75 Quoted in Krzysztof Miklaszewski, *Encounters with Tadeusz Kantor*, trans. George M. Hyde (New York: Routledge 2001), 36.
76 Harris, "Tadeusz Kantor: Exploring the Dead Theater," 27.
77 Tadeusz Kantor, *A Journey Through Other Spaces: Essays and Manifestos, 1944–1990*, ed. Michal Kobialka (Berkeley: University of California Press 1993), 275.
78 Ibid., 481.
79 Bogdan Gieraczyński, "Na przykład 'Cricot 2'" [For Example Cricot 2], *Tygodnik Demokratyczny* 38 (18 September 1976): 16.
80 Glenn Loney, "Kantor and the *Dead Class*," *Other Stages*, 8 February 1979, 11.
81 Kathleen Cioffi, "Review of *Ferdydurke*," *Theatre Journal* 54, no. 2 (May 2001): 301–3, at 303.
82 Ibid., 301.
83 This is also how they saw themselves: Grotowski always considered himself an "heir of the Polish Romantics, [...while Kantor] viewed himself as the one true avant gardist" (Zbigniew Osiński, "Tadeusz Kantor i Jerzy Grotowski Wobec Romantyzmu" [Tadeusz Kantor and Jerzy Grotowski versus Polish Romanticism], in Dariusz Kosiński, *Tradycja romantyczna w teatrze polskim* [Romantic Tradition in Polish Theatre] (Cracow: Towarzystwo Naukowe Societas Vistulana 2007), 157–8).
84 Adam Hanuszkiewicz, quoted in Hovhannes I. Pilikian, "Grotowski: Seen from Poland," *Drama: The Quarterly Theatre Review* 95 (Winter 1969): 63.
85 Paul Overy, "Surrealism without Surfeit," *Times*, 31 August 1976. Cricoteka Archives: CRC III/000189.
86 Jan Kott, quoted in Leszek Kolankiewicz, *Wielki mały wóz. Teatr jako wehikuł* [The Big Small Dipper: Theatre as a Vehicle] (Gdańsk: Słowo/Obraz Terytoria 2001), 260.

87 Jerzy Jarzębski, "'Umarła klasa' po 30 latach" ['Dead Class' after 30 Years], *Gazeta Wyborcza*, 15 November 2005, 2.
88 Konstanty Puzyna, "Grotowski i dramat romantyczny" [Grotowski and Romantic Drama], in *Półmrok, Felietony teatralne i szkice* (Warsaw: Państwowy Instytut Wydawniczy 1982), 132–40, at 133. For an alternative view, see also Małgorzata Dziewulska, "Ogniokrad" [Fire Stealer], *Teatr* 47, no. 3 (1992): 12–21.
89 Andrzej Walicki, *Philosophy and Romantic Nationalism: The Case of Poland* (Oxford: Clarendon Press 1982), 240–41.
90 Jan Kott, "Czemu mam tańczyc w tym tragicznym chórze..." [Why Should I Dance in That Tragic Chorus], in Jan Kott, *Kamienny Potok. Eseje* (London: Aneks 1986), 109–10. Translation mine. This essay was reprinted in English as Jan Kott, "Why Should I Take Part in the Sacred Dance?" trans. Edward J. Czerwinski, *TDR: A Journal of Performance Studies* 14, no. 2 (T46) (Winter 1970): 199–203.
91 Ibid., 114.
92 Bruno Schulz, "Wędrówki sceptyka" [Skeptic's Travels], *Tygodnik Ilustrowany* 6 (9 February 1936): 112.
93 Kantor, quoted in Osiński, "Tadeusz Kantor i Jerzy Grotowski Wobec Romantyzmu" [Tadeusz Kantor and Jerzy Grotowski versus Polish Romanticism], 161.
94 Konstanty Puzyna, "Polska tradycja i dramat współczesny" [Polish Tradition and Modern Drama], in *Półmrok, Felietony teatralne i szkice* (Warsaw: Państwowy Instytut Wydawniczy 1982), 97–101, at 100.
95 Interestingly, Zbigniew Osiński, a longtime admirer and the leading Polish scholar of Grotowski's work, argues the exact opposite, suggesting that Grotowski's theatre offers hope and redemption, while in Kantor's theatre, "there is no place for hope or salvation." For Kantor, "man dies like a rat," alone, "in the face of loneliness and death" (Osiński, "Tadeusz Kantor i Jerzy Grotowski Wobec Romantyzmu" [Tadeusz Kantor and Jerzy Grotowski versus Polish Romanticism], 164).
96 Tomasz Bocheński, *Czarny humor w twórczości Witkacego, Gombrowicza, Schulza – Lata trzydzieste* [Black Humor in the Works of Witkacy, Gombrowicz, Schulz – 1930s] (Cracow: Towarzystwo Autorów i Wydawców Prac Naukowych UNIVERSITAS 2005), 8.
97 Ibid.
98 Ibid., 7.
99 Milan Kundera, *Encounter* (New York: HarperCollins 2010), 119.
100 Tamara Trojanowska, "Many Happy Returns: Janusz Glowacki and His Exilic Experience," in *Living in Translation: Polish Writers in America*, ed. Halina Stephan (New York: Radopi 2003), 270.
101 Milan Kundera, *Vanek Plays* (Vancouver: University of British Columbia Press 1987).
102 As Agnieszka Wójtowicz ironically notes, thanks in no small part to their precarious historical circumstances, Poles have developed an "ability to take things seriously, while at the same time ridiculing them" (Agnieszka Wójtowicz, "Próba leczenia postawy romantycznej za pomocą postawy romantycznej (Grotowski i narodowe myty)" [An Attempt to Cure Romantic Attitude with Romantic Attitude (Grotowski and the National Myths)], in Kosiński, *Tradycja romantyczna w teatrze polskim* [Romantic Tradition in Polish Theatre], 187).
103 Osiński, "Tadeusz Kantor i Jerzy Grotowski Wobec Romantyzmu" [Tadeusz Kantor and Jerzy Grotowski versus Polish Romanticism], 162.
104 Konstanty Puzyna, "Grotowski i dramat romantyczny" [Grotowski and Romantic Drama], in *Półmrok, Felietony teatralne i szkice* (Warsaw: Państwowy Instytut Wydawniczy 1982), 132–40, at 138. Translation mine. Puzyna's text was reprinted in English in 1988 as "Grotowski and Polish Romantic Drama," trans. Jacob Conrad, *Theatre Three* 4 (Spring): 44–50.
105 Claire Fanger, Richard Kieckhefer, and Nicholas Watson, *Conjuring Spirits: Texts and Traditions of Medieval Ritual Magic* (University Park, PA: Penn State University Press 1994), 261.

106 David S. Ariel, *Kabbalah: The Mystic Quest in Judaism* (Lanham, MD: Rowman & Littlefield Publishers 2005), 147. In Kabbalah, in addition to demons, dybbuks and golems who restlessly wander the earth atoning for their past sins, liminal time when the soul is caught between the earth and another world is called *shivah*, a seven-day mourning period during which the soul of the dead "travels back and forth between the grave and his earthly residence and participates as mourner over his own body" ("Selection from the Writings of Rabbi Yehudah HeChassid: Life after Dead," in *Kabbalah: Selections From Classic Kabbalistic Works from Raziel Hamalach*, by Avraham Yaakov Finklel (Jerusalem: Targum Press 2003), 129).
107 Mickiewicz, quoted in Filipowicz, "Performing Bodies, Performing Mickiewicz," 15.
108 Michał Masłowski, "Od obrzędu żałobnego do świeckiej mszy" [From Funeral Rite to Secular Mass], *PERFORMER* 1 (2009), <http://www.grotowski.net/performer/performer-1/od-obrzedu-zalobnego-do-swieckiej-mszy> (accessed 10 August 2011).
109 Ludwik Flaszen, quoted in Masłowski, "Od obrzędu żałobnego do świeckiej mszy" [From Funeral Rite to Secular Mass].
110 Jerzy Grotowski, quoted in Dariusz Kosiński, *Grotowski: Przewodnik* [Grotowski: A Handbook] (Wrocław: Instytut Im. Jerzego Grotowskiego 2009), 144.
111 Kantor, quoted in Krzysztof Pleśniarowicz, *Teatr nie-ludzkiej formy* [The Theatre of the Un-Human Form] (Cracow: Jagiellonian University 1994), 25.
112 Leszek Kolankiewicz, *Dziady. Teatr święta zmarłych* [Dziady: Theatre of the Forefathers' Eve] (Gdańsk: Słowo/Obraz Terytoria 1999), 407.
113 Zbigniew Osiński, "Tadeusz Kantor i Jerzy Grotowski Wobec Romantyzmu," [Tadeusz Kantor and Jerzy Grotowski versus Polish Romanticism], 180–81. Likewise, Mickiewicz himself believed "in the basic unity of all the mythological systems" (Wiktor Weintraub, *Literature as Prophecy: Scholarship and Martinist Poetics in Mickiewicz's Parisian Lectures* (The Hague: Mouton & Co. Publishers 1956), 70).
114 Quoted in Helen N. Fagin, "Adam Mickiewicz: Poland's National Romantic Poet," *South Atlantic Bulletin* 42, no. 4 (November 1977): 103–13, at 103.
115 Ibid.
116 Kundera, *Encounter*, 85.
117 Halina Filipowicz, "Mickiewicz: 'East' and 'West,'" *Slavic and East European Journal* 45, no. 4 (Winter 2001): 605–731, at 606.
118 Benedict Anderson, *Imagined Communities: Reflections on the Origin and Spread of Nationalism* (London: Verso 1983).
119 Jerzy Ziomek, "Epoki i formacje w dziejach literatury polskiej" [Époques and Formations in the History of Polish Literature], *Pamiętnik literacki* 77, no. 4 (1986): 23–54, at 23.
120 Milan Kundera, "The Tragedy of Central Europe," *New York Review of Books* 31, no. 7 (26 April 1984): 33–8, at 33 (originally published as "Un Occident kidnappé ou la tragédie de l'Europe centrale," *Le Débat* 27 (November 1983): 3–22).
121 Kundera notes that after World War II, "the border between the two Europes shifted several hundred kilometers to the west, and several nations that had always considered themselves to be Western, woke up to discover that they were now in the East [...] The part of Europe situated geographically in the center [found itself] culturally in the West and politically in the East" (Kundera, "The Tragedy of Central Europe," 33).
122 Roger Cohen, "The Glory of Poland," *New York Times*, 13 April 2010, <http://www.nytimes.com/2010/04/13/opinion/13iht-edcohen.html?_r=1&emc=eta1> (accessed 10 August 2011).
123 It is ironic that Karl Marx himself called for the Polish borders to be restored to their pre-partition lines.
124 Quoted in Oscar Halecki, "Poland's Place in Europe 966–1966," in *Studies in Polish Civilization*, ed. Damian Wandycz (New York: Institute on East Central Europe, Columbia University and The Polish Institute of Arts & Sciences in America 1966), 16.

125 Neal Ascherson, *The Struggles for Poland* (New York: Random House 1988), 4.
126 Norman Davis, *God's Playground: History of Poland* (New York: Columbia University Press 2005).
127 Pedro Calderon de la Barca, *Life is a Dream* (Middlesex: Echo Library 2007).
128 Alfred Jarry, *Ubu Roi*, ed. Drew Silver (Mineola: Dover Editions 2003), vi.
129 Christine Olga Kiebuzinska, *Intertextual Loops in Modern Drama* (Madison, NJ: Fairleigh Dickinson University Press; London: Associated University Presses 2001), 48.
130 Harold B. Segel, *Polish Romantic Drama: Three Plays in English Translation* (Ithaca, NY: Cornell University Press 1977), 9.
131 Daniel Gerould and L. Ploszewski, "Introduction, From Adam Mickiewicz's 'Lectures on Slavic Literature' Given at the Collège de France," *TDR: The Drama Review* 30, no. 3 (Autumn 1986): 91–7, at 91–2.
132 Filipowicz, "Performing Bodies, Performing Mickiewicz," 4.
133 Ibid.
134 Harold Segel, *Polish Romantic Drama: Three Plays in English Translation* (Ithaca, NY: Cornell University Press 1977).
135 Ibid., 10.
136 Harold Segel, *Polish Romantic Drama: Three Plays in English Translation* (Amsterdam: Harwood Academic Publishers 1997).
137 Miroslawa Modrzewska, Catherine O'Neil, Peter Cochran and Bill Johnston, *Poland's Angry Romantic: Two Poems and a Play by Juliusz Slowacki* (Cambridge: Cambridge Scholars Publishing 2009).
138 Manfred Kridl, Józef Wittlin and Władysław Malinowski. *The Democratic Heritage of Poland* (London: G. Allen & Unwin 1944).
139 Manfred Kridl, *An Anthology of Polish Literature* (New York: Columbia University Press 1957).
140 Manfred Kridl, *A Survey of Polish Literature and Culture* (New York: Columbia University Press 1967).
141 Czesław Miłosz, *The History of Polish Literature* (New York: Macmillan 1969).
142 Tymon Terlecki, *Stanisław Wyspiański* (Boston: Twayne 1983).
143 Roman Koropeckyj, *Adam Mickiewicz: The Life of a Romantic* (Ithaca, NY: Cornell University Press 2008).
144 Kazimierz Braun, *A History of Polish Theater, 1939–1989: Spheres of Captivity and Freedom* (Westport, CT: Greenwood 1996).
145 There is also Wiktor Weintraub's thin and poorly written 1956 *Literature as Prophecy: Scholarship and Martinist Poetics in Mickiewicz's Parisian Lectures*, which, as the title indicates, provides a brief overview of Mickiewicz's lectures (Wiktor Weintraub, *Literature as Prophecy: Scholarship and Martinist Poetics in Mickiewicz's Parisian Lectures* (The Hague: Mouton & Co. Publishers, 1956).
146 Daniel Charles Gerould, *Theatre, Theory, Theatre: The Major Critical Texts from Aristotle and Zeami to Soyinka and Havel* (New York: Applause Theatre & Cinema 2000).
147 William B. Worthen, ed. *The Wadsworth Anthology of Drama* (Boston, MA: Thomson/Wadsworth 2004).
148 Michael L. Greenwald, Roger Schultz and Roberto Darío Pomo. *The Longman Anthology of Drama and Theater: A Global Perspective* (New York: Longman 2001).
149 Bernard Frank Dukore, *Dramatic Theory and Criticism: Greeks to Grotowski* (New York: Holt, Rinehart and Winston 1974).
150 Oscar Brockett, *History of the Theatre*. 10th ed. (Boston: Pearson 2008).
151 Sharon Boak, "The Reflection of the Napoleonic Legend in Adam Mickiewicz's *Pan Tadeusz*," *Slovo* 20, no. 2 (Autumn 2008): 107–18, at 118.
152 Segel, *Polish Romantic Drama*, 31.
153 Ibid.

154 Abraham G. Duker, "Some Cabbalistic and Frankist Elements in Adam Mickiewicz's 'Dziady,'" in *Studies in Polish Civilization*, ed. Damian Wandycz (New York: Institute on East Central Europe, Columbia University and The Polish Institute of Arts & Sciences in America 1966), 213–35, at 213.
155 Ibid.
156 Ibid.
157 Duker, "Some Cabbalistic and Frankist Elements in Adam Mickiewicz's 'Dziady,'" 227.
158 Ibid., 223.
159 Only recently did Polish and American scholars begin again to look at Mickiewicz's work through the prism of Hasidic tradition. The earliest treatment of Mickiewicz's drama in the context of Kabbalah appears in Duker, "Some Cabbalist and Frankist Elements in Adam Mickiewicz's 'Dziady.'" Duker's essay, however, written in 1966 at the height of anti-Semitic propaganda, went without a ripple in Poland. More recent essays include Jadwiga Mauer's poignant analysis of the strategies used by canonical Polish scholarship to avoid discussing Jewish aspects of Mickiewicz's work (*"Z matki obcej": Szkice o powiązaniach Mickiewicza ze światem Żydów* ["Of Foreign Mother": Essays about Mickiewicz's Connections with the Jewish World] (London: Polska Fundacja Kulturalna 1990)); and Stuart Goldberg, "Konrad and Jacob: A Hypothetical Kabbalistic Subtext in Adam Mickiewicz's *Forefathers' Eve*, Part III," *Slavic and East European Journal* 45, no. 4 (Winter 2001): 695–715.
160 Krzysztof Pleśniarowicz, *Teatr Śmierci Tadeusza Kantora* [Tadeusz Kantor's Theatre of Death] (Chotomow: VERBA 1990), 107–52.
161 Daniel Gerould, *Theatre/Theory/Theatre: The Major Critical Texts from Aristotle and Zeami to Soyinka and Havel* (New York: Applause Books 2003), 30.
162 Walicki, *Philosophy and Romantic Nationalism*, 304. Emphasis mine.
163 Adam Mickiewicz, "Slavic Drama," in Gerould, *Theatre/Theory/Theatre: The Major Critical Texts from Aristotle and Zeami to Soyinka and Havel*, 330–31.
164 Ibid., 330.
165 Segel, *Polish Romantic Drama*, 43.
166 Dariusz Kosiński, *Teatra Polskie: historie* [History of Polish Theatre] (Warsaw: Wydawnictwo Naukowe PWN, Instytut Teatralny 2010), 118.
167 Ibid., 124.
168 Tymon Terlecki, "A Critical Appraisal of Mickiewicz's Lecture About Theatre," in *Studies in Polish Civilization*, ed. Damian Wandycz (New York: Institute on East Central Europe, Columbia University and The Polish Institute of Arts & Sciences in America 1966), 278.
169 Wyspiański's ideas about scenography greatly influenced Gordon Craig, and following his death, in 1909, Gordon Craig's journal *The Mask* published a long essay on Wyspiański.
170 Nina Taylor, "Stanisław Wyspiański and Symbolist Drama: The Work of Art as '*dramatis persona*,'" *Slavonic and East European Review* 66, no. 2 (April 1988): 198–209, at 199.
171 Ibid., 60.
172 Małgorzata Dziewulska, *Artyści i pielgrzymi* [Artists and Pilgrims] (Wrocław: Wydawnictwo Dolnośląskie 1995), 140; Kolankiewicz, *Dziady. Teatr święta zmarłych* [Forefathers' Eve: Theatre of the All Soul's Day]; Dariusz Kosiński, *Polski teatr przemiany* [Polish Theatre of Transformation] (Wrocław: Instytut im. Jerzego Grotowskiego 2007).
173 Jerzy Grotowski, "'Dziady' jako model teatru nowoczesnego. Rozmowa z dyrektorem Teatru 13 Rzędów w Opolu Jerzym Grotowskim, rozmiawiał Jerzy Falkowski" ['Forefathers' Eve' as a Model for Modern Theatre: A Conversation with Jerzy Grotowski, Jerzy Falkowski], *Współczesność* 21, no. 101 (1–15 November 1961): 8; Jerzy Grotowski, "Teatr a rytuał" [Theatre Versus Ritual], *Dialog* 8 (1969); Jerzy Grotowski, "O praktykowaniu romantyzm" [Practicing Romanticism], *Dialog* 25, no. 3 (1986): 91–2; Tadeusz Kantor, *O powinnościach artysty, rozmowa z Tadeuszem Kantorem, Krzysztof Miklaszewski* [About the Responsibilities of an Artist, Conversation with Tadeusz Kantor, Krzysztof Miklaszewski] (Cracow: TVP, 1985).

174 Tadeusz Kantor, quoted in Osiński, "Tadeusz Kantor i Jerzy Grotowski Wobec Romantyzmu" [Tadeusz Kantor and Jerzy Grotowski versus Polish Romanticism], 164.
175 Katarzyna Fazan, *Projekt intymnego teatru śmierci: Wyspiański, Leśmian, Kantor* [The Project of the Intimate Theatre of Death: Wyspiański, Leśmian, Kantor] (Cracow: Wydawnictwo Uniwersytetu Jagielonskiego 2009), 276.
176 Osiński, "Tadeusz Kantor i Jerzy Grotowski Wobec Romantyzmu" [Tadeusz Kantor and Jerzy Grotowski versus Polish Romanticism], 165.
177 Kathleen Cioffi, *Alternative Theatre in Poland 1954–1989* (London and New York: Routledge 1996), 86.
178 Zbigniew Osiński, *Teatr Dionizosa. Romantyzm w polskim teatrze współczesnym* [Dionysian Theatre: Romanticism in Polish Contemporary Theatre] (Cracow: Wydawnictwo Literackie 1972), 183.
179 Harold Clurman, "Jerzy Grotowski," in *The Grotowski Sourcebook*, ed. Richard Schechner and Lisa Wolford (New York: Routledge 1997), 161–3, at 161. Originally published in 1974 as a chapter titled "Jerzy Grotowski" in Harold Clurman, *The Divine Pastime* (New York: Macmillan 1974), 221–6.
180 Kosiński, *Polski teatr przemiany* [Polish Theatre of Transformation], 426–7.
181 Leszek Kolankiewicz, *Na drodze do kultury czynnej: O działalności instytutu Grotowskiego Teatr Laboratorium w latach 1970–1977* [On the Way to the Active Culture: About Grotowski's Laboratory Theatre 1970–1977] (Wrocław: Instytut Aktora 1978), 11.
182 Walicki, *Philosophy and Romantic Nationalism*, 241.
183 Wójtowicz, "Próba leczenia postawy romantycznej za pomocą postawy romantycznej (Grotowski i narodowe mity)" [An Attempt to Cure Romantic Attitude with Romantic Attitude (Grotowski and the National Myths)], 187.
184 Osiński, *Teatr Dionizosa. Romantyzm w polskim teatrze wpółczesnym* [Dionysian Theatre: Romanticism in Polish Contemporary Theatre], 193.
185 Peter Brook, introduction to *Akropolis*, stage dir. Jerzy Grotowski, film dir. James MacTaggart, prod. Lewis Freedman (New York: Arthur Cantor Films 1968).
186 Osiński, *Teatr Dionizosa*, 200.
187 Ahuva Belkin, "Ritual Space as Theatrical Space in Jewish Folk Theatre," in *Jewish Theatre: A Global View*, ed. Edna Nahshon (Lieden; Boston: Brill 2009), 15.
188 Jan Klossowicz, "Grotowski in Poland," *Le Théâtre en Pologne / Theatre in Poland* 5 (1971 [special issue devoted to Jerzy Grotowski]): 3–10, at 3.
189 Juliusz Tyszka, *Widowiska Nowojorskie* [New York Spectacles] (Wydawnictwo ARS NOVA: Poznań 1994), 201.
190 Ibid.
191 Ibid.
192 Ibid., 202.
193 Ibid.
194 Gayatri Chakravorty Spivak, "Can the Subaltern Speak?" in *The Post-Colonial Studies Reader*, ed. Bill Ashcroft, Gareth Griffiths, and Helen Tiffin (London: Routledge 1995), 28. Reprinted from Gayatri Chakravorty Spivak, *A Critique of Postcolonial Reason: Toward a History of the Vanishing Present* (Cambridge, MA: Harvard University Press 1999).
195 Kantor, quoted in Krzysztof Miklaszewski, *Tadeusz Kantor: Między śmietnikiem a wiecznością* [Tadeusz Kantor: Between Garbage and Eternity] (Warsaw: Państwowy Instytut Wydawniczy 2007), 32.
196 Kantor was fully aware of the paradox he was faced with: the need to be and not to be both a national and international figure. He said:

> Wyspiański is also impossible to understand. *Wyzwolenie* (*Liberation*) can't be understood by any foreigner. And it's not a question of snobbism. Art needs to be international, especially theatre. THEATRE NEEDS TO BE UNIVERSAL TO BE NATIONAL.

Take *Wielopole*, for example. After its opening, they wrote that I am the most [...] national of all Poles, although this spectacle was compared to *Amacord*. It could be the same with Mickiewicz. (32)

One detects a note of bitterness in Kantor's assessment at what he perceives to be an unjustified neglect of Polish drama on European and world stages. He largely blames Polish directors who, enclosing their work in the hermetic tradition of Polish literature and culture, failed to communicate the transnational merit of Polish drama. Kantor raised eyebrows in Poland's theatre community with his frequent complaints that plays like *Dziady* [*Forefathers' Eve*] and *Wesele* [*The Wedding*] were staged so that "no-one outside Poland could understand them." He insists: "I believe you could show it [...] universally. Without changing anything because you can't change it, but also without solely focusing on all the traditional, national themes" (Kantor, quoted in Pleśniarewicz Krzysztof, *Teatr nie-ludzkiej formy* [The Theatre of the Un-Human Form] (Cracow: Jagiellonian University, 1994), 11). Did Kantor himself succeed? Irving Wardle noted that *Dead Class* "acknowledges a heavy debt to Gombrowicz and Witkiewicz. Kantor, however, is one of the few artists who have succeeded in making this hermetic [Polish] tradition partly available to cultural outsiders" ("Haunted Visions of Museum of Memory," *Times*, 18 November 1982, 8). Likewise, Polish scholar Krzysztof Pleśniarewicz made a similar observation, arguing that "Tadeusz Kantor managed in a unique way to resolve the dilemma of the Polishness and the universality of his art" (*The Dead Memory Machine: Tadeusz Kantor's "Theatre of Death,"* 56).

197 Ibid.
198 Spivak, *A Critique of Postcolonial Reason*, 307.
199 Grotowski, quoted in Raymonde Temkine, *Grotowski*, translated from the French by Alex Szogyi (New York: Avon Books 1972), 29.
200 Temkine, *Grotowski*, 29.
201 Findlay, "Grotowski's 'Akropolis': A Retrospective," 12. See also Tyszka, *Widowiska Nowojorskie* [New York Spectacles], 202.
202 For more on the topic, see Joseph Warren Beach, *The Concept of Nature in Nineteenth-Century English Poetry* (New York: Macmillan 1936) or Myra Reynolds, *The Treatment of Nature in English Poetry between Pope and Wadsworth* (New York: Gordian Press 1909). I extend my thanks to my colleague Larry Switzky for familiarizing me with this poetic trope.
203 Tyszka, *Widowiska Nowojorskie* [New York Spectacles], 202.
204 Clive Barnes, "Jerzy Grotowski's 'Acropolis': 1904 Drama Is Adapted for Polish Group," *New York Times*, 5 November 1969, 40.
205 Martin Gottfried, "Acropolis," *Women's Wear Daily*, 5 November 1969, 63.
206 A. W., "A Painting Comes Alive," *Glasgow Herald*, 23 August 1976, 5.
207 Blaise Pascal, *Pensées*, trans. W. T. Trotter (Oxford: Benediction Classics 2011), 162.
208 Thornton Wilder, *The Ides of March* (New York: Harper & Bros 1948).
209 *Idy marcowe* [*Ides of March*] dir. Jerzy Gruza (Warsaw: Teatr Polski Telewizji 1962).
210 *Marcowe migdały* [The Almonds of March] dir. Radosław Piwowarski (1989).
211 In 1939, Hitler and Stalin divided Poland and attacked it from both ends. During the 1945 Yalta conference, Joseph Stalin, Winston Churchill, and Franklin D. Roosevelt divided Europe between different spheres of influence, leaving Poland under Soviet control.
212 Adorno, *Aesthetic Theory*, 3.
213 Ibid., 6.
214 Ibid., 17.
215 Martin Harries, *Forgetting Lot's Wife: On Destructive Spectatorship* (New York: Fordham University Press 2007), 9.
216 Likewise, drawing on Adorno's and Hannah Arendt's theories on the relationship between modernity and the Holocaust, the Polish-Jewish philosopher and sociologist Zygmunt Bauman argues in his books *Modernity and Ambivalence* (Ithaca, NY: Cornell University Press

1991), and *Modernity and the Holocaust* (Ithaca, NY: Cornell University Press 1989) that the Holocaust was an extension of the Enlightenment idea of progress. Jews, as the ultimate "strangers" *par excellence* – the society's *indécidables* – who refused to be categorized into the modern social categories, were eliminated because they stood in the way of social progress.

217 Margaret Croyden, "Images that Recall the Polish Past," *New York Times*, 9 May 1982, D4.
218 Osiński, "Tadeusz Kantor i Jerzy Grotowski Wobec Romantyzmu" [Tadeusz Kantor and Jerzy Grotowski versus Polish Romanticism], 164.
219 Quoted in Peter Novick, *The Holocaust in American Life* (New York: Houghton Mifflin 1999).
220 Eugenio Barba, *Land of Ashes and Diamonds: My Apprenticeship in Poland* (Aberystwyth, UK: Black Mountain Press 1999), 10.
221 Jonathan Huener, *Auschwitz, Poland and the Politics of Commemoration, 1945–1979* (Athens: Ohio University Press 2003), xiv.
222 Michael Steinlauf, "Poland and the Memory of the Holocaust," address at the Sholom Aleichem Club in October, 1998 < http://www.csjo.org/resources/essays/poland-and-the-memory-of-the-holocaust/> (accessed 20 December 2011).
223 Joseph L. Lichten, "Some Aspects of Polish–Jewish Relations during the Nazi Occupation," in *Studies in Polish Civilization*, ed. Damian Wandycz (New York: Institute on East Central Europe, Columbia University and The Polish Institute of Arts & Sciences in America 1966), 154–75, at 162.
224 Mark Kramer, "Memo from Warsaw: 'Origins' of the RRC," *Novosti* 16, no. 1 (Fall 2010): 7.
225 Allen Kuharski, "Jerzy Grotowski: Ascetic and Smuggler," *Theater* 29, no. 2 (1999): 10–15, at 11.
226 Ibid.
227 Tyszka, *Widowiska Nowojorskie* [New York Spectacles], 202.
228 The peasants are surprised that such a cultivated man doesn't know what everyone knows. But his ignorance also confirms their conviction that Westerners do not care about anything, surely not about them. Westerners are not interested in the fate of such a small country as Poland, and hence do not know its history very well. Such a view of the West is based on the events of the German invasion of 1939, the Yalta conference, and the Nazi and Soviet occupations.
229 Following Lanzmann's film, the first March of the Living took place in 1988, starting the Holocaust tourism industry, a rite of passage for many Jewish youths and a tradition which, ironically, hasn't initially contributed to the bettering of Polish–Jewish relations:

> In the early years of the March, participants were banned from contact with Poles regardless of religion, and Poles had no opportunity to participate in the March. Today, the March continues to relax their restrictions on who may participate; still, there is lingering resentment amongst some Poles over their treatment by March organizers (Taube, 2006). Konstanty Gebert [...] points to language once used as part of the regular literature for the March, which preempted participants' personal reactions to the trip by telling them that they would feel "hate" for the Poles they encountered. Thus, Jewish travelers were essentially expected to experience emotions that were not necessarily productive, positive, or even authentically their own. Gebert's criticism of the March, however, also extends to the ways in which Poles react to Jewish visitors. Not only do many regard the March and similar trips as an intrusion into their towns and locales, but they often come to resent what they perceive to be wealthy, comfortable individuals marching through their relatively impoverished towns. The result is that the Jewish visitors often leave with an unnecessarily skewed image of Poles, while Poles similarly develop negative and resentful images of Jews. (Kamil Kolata, Barbara Pieta and Ira Stup, "Never Again? Contemporary Anti-Semitism and Representations of Jews in Modern Poland," *Humanity in*

Action, 2009, <http://www.humanityinaction.org/knowledgebase/63-never-again-contemporary-anti-semitism-and-representations-of-jews-in-modern-poland> (accessed 14 November 2011))

Coming to Poland in the early 1980s from the rich West, Lanzmann was most likely perceived in the same way by the Polish peasants he interviewed. At that time, Poland was reeling from one of the biggest challenges in its postwar history: the 1981–83 martial law, with its government curfews, searches, arrests, travel restrictions, general poverty, and persistent food shortages. Dealing with serious everyday issues, the peasants most likely considered it a kind of luxury to spend time dwelling on the past. For them, the war has left a residue that was never really completely eradicated, intimately woven into their everyday life under the communist regime.

230 Quoted in Lichten, "Some Aspects of Polish–Jewish Relations," 159.
231 The American representation of Poles in a negative light might have something to do with a certain avoidance and denial of America's own attitudes towards Jewish refugees before and during the war. It might be a kind of displaced guilt, or perhaps a simple lack of historical knowledge amongst those of the general population, many college students and even academics. Before and during World War II, time after time, German Jews were refused the status of refugees. In fact, at the 1938 conference of the League of Nations, "none of the thirty-two countries represented at the conference was ready to accept a substantial number of the wandering Jews" (Lichten, "Some Aspects of Polish–Jewish Relations," 162). In 1943, when many of the Jews had already perished, the same conference brought the same results. Tellingly, when in 1940 Americans were asked to accept British dog refugees, "the appeal produced what the editors called 'a most gratifying response.' Several thousand Americans wrote back, saying that they were ready to provide a haven for a refugee dog [...] No one thought of anything similar for the Jews" (Gideon Hausner, *Justice in Jerusalem* (New York: Herzl Press 1978), 231). As Leonard Dinnerstein observed, "FDR's tenure in the White House coincided with the worst period of anti-Semitism in the history of this country" (Leonard Dinnerstein, *Antisemitism in America* (New York; London: Oxford University Press 1995), 102). Since Roosevelt was very attuned to the public mood, he modulated his immigration policies to fit national sentiments. Perhaps the most telling was the USA's decision not to save 20,000 German-Jewish children (the famous Wagner–Rogers Bill of 1939), while Great Britain accepted 9,000 of them. Following the failure of the bill, the decision rested with FDR, who ultimately refused to sign it through the Executive order. Another famous story is that of the *MS St. Louis*, which in May 1939 carried on board 937 Jewish refugees from Nazi Germany. They were refused entry into the USA, and the ship was forced to return to Europe. These events are not part of the mainstream American narrative about World War II, and they do not appear in popular Hollywood movies. At the time of the war, America was not under anyone's occupation, and Americans didn't risk death by hosting Jews. Thus, the representation of Poles in American pop culture is problematic on many levels, though we can only speculate why.
232 Michael Kimmelman, "Poland Searches Its Own Soul," *New York Times*, 8 April 2009, <http://www.nytimes.com/2009/04/09/movies/09abro.html?_r=2> (accessed 21 March 2011).
233 Gene A. Plunka, *Holocaust Drama: The Theatre of Atrocity* (Cambridge: Cambridge University Press 2009), 19.
234 Susan A. Glenn and Naomi B. Sokoloff, eds, *Boundaries of Jewish Identity* (Seattle: University of Washington Press 2010).
235 Kamil Kolata, Barbara Pieta and Ira Stup, "Never Again? Contemporary Anti-Semitism and Representations of Jews in Modern Poland," *Humanity in Action*, 2009, <http://www.humanityinaction.org/knowledgebase/63-never-again-contemporary-anti-semitism-and-representations-of-jews-in-modern-poland> (accessed 14 November 2011).

236 Artur Sandauer, *On the Situation of the Polish Writer of Jewish Descent in the Twentieth Century* (Jerusalem: The Hebrew University Magnes Press 2005), 16.
237 Moshe Rosman, "Poland: Poland before 1795," in *YIVO Encyclopedia of Jews in Eastern Europe*, 14 March 2011, quoting *Petaḥteshuvah*, 1651 4a. <http://www.yivoencyclopedia.org/article.aspx/Poland/Poland_before_1795> (accessed 14 March 2011).
238 Sandauer, *On the Situation of the Polish Writer of Jewish Descent*, 16.
239 Ibid., 17.
240 Rosman, "Poland: Poland before 1795."
241 Kate Connolly, "Museum to Mark Jewish Life in Poland: Director Says Million-Pound Site in Warsaw Will Show Poland Is 'More than Just the World's Largest Jewish Graveyard,'" *Guardian* (London), 18 July 2002, 16.
242 Sandauer, *On the Situation of the Polish Writer of Jewish Descent*, 19.
243 Gershon Bacon, "Poland: Poland from 1795 to 1939," in *YIVO Encyclopedia of Jews in Eastern Europe*, 14 March 2011, <http://www.yivoencyclopedia.org/article.aspx/Poland/Poland_from_1795_to_1939> (accessed 29 June 2011).
244 To learn more about Galicia, see Larry Wolf, *The Idea of Galicia: History and Fantasy in Habsburg Political Culture* (Palo Alto, CA: Stanford University Press 2010).
245 Michael C. Steinlauf, "Józio Grojeszyk: A Jewish City Slicker on the Warsaw Popular Stage," in *Jewish Theatre: A Global View*, ed. Edna Nahshon (Lieden, Boston: Brill 2009), 70.
246 Anna Kuligowska-Korzeniowska, "The Polish Shulamis: Jewish Drama on the Polish Stage in the Late 19th–Early 20th centuries," in *Jewish Theatre: A Global View*, ed. Edna Nahshon (Lieden, Boston: Brill 2009), 81.
247 Larry Wolf, *The Idea of Galicia: History and Fantasy in Habsburg Political Culture.* (Palo Alto, CA: Stanford University Press, 2010), 33–35.
248 Steinlauf, "Józio Grojeszyk: A Jewish City Slicker on the Warsaw Popular Stage," 71.
249 Ibid.
250 To learn more about the history of Jews in Galicia during World War I, see Marsha Rozenblit, *Reconstructing a National Identity: The Jews of Habsburg Austria during World War I* (New York: Oxford University Press 2004).
251 Sandauer, *On the Situation of the Polish Writer of Jewish Descent*, 19.
252 Ibid.
253 Ibid.
254 Ibid., 23.
255 For more information on the Jewish politics in interwar Poland, see Ezra Mendelsohn, *Zionism in Poland: The Formative Years, 1915–1926* (New Haven, CT: Yale University Press 1981) and *The Jews of East Central Europe between the World Wars* (Bloomington, IN: Indiana University Press 1983).
256 Sandauer, *On the Situation of the Polish Writer of Jewish Descent*, 24.
257 Jan Błoński, "The Poor Poles Look at the Ghetto," in *Four Decades of Polish Essays*, ed. Jan Kott (Evanston, IL: Northwestern University Press 1990), 222–35, at 222. Originally published in *Tygodnik Powszechny* in 1987.
258 Tadeusz Kantor, quoted in Krzysztof Pleśniarowicz, *The Dead Memory Machine: Tadeusz Kantor's "Theatre of Death"* (Cracow: Cricoteka 1994), 9.
259 Chone Shmeruk, "Hebrew-Yiddish-Polish: A Trilingual Jewish Culture," in *The Jews of Poland Between Two World Wars* (Boston: Brandeis University Press 1989), 285–6.
260 Ibid., 286.
261 Ibid.
262 Ibid., 287.
263 Ibid., 311.
264 Tadeusz Kantor, quoted in Krzysztof Pleśniarowicz, *The Dead Memory Machine: Tadeusz Kantor's "Theatre of Death"* (Cracow: Cricoteka 1994), 9.
265 Lichten, "Some Aspects of Polish–Jewish Relations," 155, 160.

266 Błoński, "The Poor Poles Look at the Ghetto," 222.
267 Lichten, "Some Aspects of Polish–Jewish Relations," 159.
268 Ibid., 168.
269 See Jozef Garlinski, *Fighting Auschwitz: The Resistance Movement in the Concentration Camp* (Robbinsdale, MI: Fawcett Publications 1975), 191–7; Michael Richard Daniell Foot, "Witold Pilecki," in *Six Faces of Courage: Secret Agents against Nazi Tyranny* (Barnsley, South Yorkshire, UK: Leo Cooper 2003); Konstanty R. Piekarski, *Escaping Hell: The Story of a Polish Underground Officer in Auschwitz and Buchenwald* (Toronto, ON: Dundurn Press Ltd 1990); and Kamil Tchorek, "Double Life of Witold Pilecki, the Auschwitz Volunteer Who Uncovered Holocaust Secrets," *Times* (London), 12 March 2009, <http://www.timesonline.co.uk/tol/news/world/europe/article5891132.ece> (accessed 16 March 2009).
270 "Witold Pilecki," Jewish Virtual Library, <http://www.jewishvirtuallibrary.org/jsource/biography/Witold_Pilecki.html> (accessed 1 August 2001). In 2006, the Polish director Ryszard Bugajski made the movie *Death of Captain Pilecki*, which narrates the story of Pilecki's tortures and murder.
271 Movies like Jon Avnet's 2001 *Uprising*, about the Warsaw Ghetto Uprising, is just one of many examples. In Avnet's movie, all of the Polish underground fighters are cruel and materialistic anti-Semites. Roman Polanski's 2002 *The Pianist*, a film that chronicles the tale of a Polish-Jewish musician, revered in pre- and postwar Poland as the first global mainstream movie, "allowed that a modicum of Polish decency outlasted the war," as the *New York Times* noted. In the same 2009 article, the *New York Times* wrote that the pattern of representing Polish resistance fighters as anti-Semitic is so prevalent that when *Defiance*, the 2008 Hollywood action flick about the two Jewish brothers Bielski, fighting Nazis in a Belarusian forest, was released, it prompted "[m]ovie critics in Poland [to wonder] whether Hollywood would ever get around to showing Polish partisans as heroes, as opposed to anti-Semites" (Kimmelman, "Poland Searches Its Own Soul").

Likewise, for a number of years, many Poles felt very bitter about movies such as *Schindler's List*, for example, which glorify the one good German, while no Hollywood movie ever narrativized the quiet and humble life of Irena Sendler, the heroic Polish social worker who risked her own life many times rescuing 2,500 Jewish children from the Warsaw Ghetto, carrying some of them in suitcases and bags. After the war, like Pilecki, Sendler was persecuted by the communist government for collaborating with the Polish Home Army. Following Stalin's death, Sendler's courage and heroism were finally recognized, earning her iconic status in Polish society; she was revered and awarded numerous prizes, including the Jan Karski award for "Courage and Heart." She died in 2008, to the great dismay of the Polish public. In 2011, a documentary about Sendler was finally made thanks to the Taube and Koret Foundation. The movie, *Irena Sendler: In the Name of Their Mothers*, was broadcast on PBS, and it profiled both Sendler and the children, now adults, whom she rescued. The documentary, seen as long overdue, was widely promoted by the Polish-American media and organizations.

Another example is that of the Polish hero Doctor Janusz Korczak, who twice was offered and refused to save himself, sacrificing his own life and dying with the orphaned Jewish children in his care only so that the children would not be frightened. Szpilman, in his book *The Pianist*, movingly tells the story of Korczak's children:

> The evacuation of the Jewish orphanage run by Janusz Korczak had been ordered for that morning. The children were to have been taken away alone. He had the chance to save himself, and it was only with difficulty that he persuaded the Germans to take him too. He had spent long years of his life with children and now, on this last journey, he could not leave them alone. He wanted to ease things for them. He told the orphans they were going out in to the country, so they ought to be cheerful. At last they would be able to exchange the horrible suffocating city walls for meadows

of flowers, streams where they could bathe, woods full of berries and mushrooms. He told them to wear their best clothes, and so they came out into the yard, two by two, nicely dressed and in a happy mood. The little column was led by an SS man who loved children, as Germans do, even those he was about to see on their way into the next world. He took a special liking to a boy of twelve, a violinist who had his instrument under his arm. The SS man told him to go to the head of the procession of children and play – and so they set off. When I met them in Gęsia Street, the smiling children were singing in chorus, the little violinist was playing for them and Korczak was carrying two of the smallest infants, who were beaming too, and telling them some amusing story. I am sure that even in the gas chamber, as the Zyklon B gas was stifling childish throats and striking terror instead of hope into the orphans' hearts, the Old Doctor must have whispered with one last effort, "it's all right, children, it will be all right." So that at least he could spare his little charges the fear of passing from life to death. (Władysław Szpilman, *The Pianist*, trans. Anthea Bell (New York: Picador; 8th edition 1999), 95–6)

Korczak's story is well-known to every child in a middle-class Polish family, and Andrzej Wajda's 1990 black and white movie (released three years before *Schindler's List*) *Korczak* is a masterpiece, yet Korczak's name is barely known in the United States, and Wajda's movie is not included in Plunka's book.

272 Lichten, "Some Aspects of Polish–Jewish Relations," 155.
273 Ibid., 166.
274 Ibid.
275 Teresa Prekerowa, a Polish-Jewish historian, calculated statistically "the extent of Polish wartime help to the Jews. Based on her research, she concludes that between 80,000 and 120,000 Jews were in hiding during the occupation, of which about 40,000 to 60,000 survived the war. According to Prekerowa, support to these fugitives was provided by between 160,000 to 360,000 Poles, who constituted only about 1 to 2.5 percent of the 15 million Poles who could have helped. Her figures are considerably lower than those provided by other scholars. In his 1971 monograph *He Who Saves One Life*, Kazimierz Iranek-Osmecki estimated that 1 million righteous Poles were involved in hiding Jews in occupied Poland." (John A. Drobnicki, "A Touch of Controversy," *Polish-American Journal*, February 1991, <http://www.york.cuny.edu/~drobnick/polonsky.html> (accessed 20 June 2011).
276 Lichten, "Some Aspects of Polish–Jewish Relations," 165–6.
277 Katyń has a particular place in Polish martyrology. In April–May 1940, the Soviet Secret Police, the NKVD, carried out the mass execution of 22,000 Poles. Of these, 8,000 were Polish officers, and the rest constituted Polish intelligentsia: doctors, lawyers, university professors (15,000 of the victims were POWs). The massacre took place in Katyń Forest, and it came to be referred to as the Katyń Massacre. The mass graves were discovered by Nazis in 1943. The Soviet regime denied responsibility for the massacre until 1990, when it acknowledged that the NKVD was responsible for the massacre, but still refused to classify it as genocide or as a war crime. During the Soviet regime, it was forbidden to even mention Katyń, and the families of the victims never had a chance to officially mourn or even bury their dead. In 2010, the Russian State Duma finally acknowledged that Stalin had ordered the murders. During World War II, at a time when the official Polish government resided in London, demanding an investigation, the Katyń Massacre became a point of contention in Polish–Soviet–British–US relations. Eventually, as it became increasingly clear that the Allies needed Soviet support to fight the Germans and the Japanese, both Great Britain and the USA decided to side with Stalin, halt the investigation, and suppress talk of the massacre. For years, Poles remained bitter about what they perceived to have been a betrayal by the Allies. The Katyń Massacre continues to inspire strong emotions in

Poland. To read more about the Katyń Massacre, see Allen Paul's *Katyń: Stalin's Massacre and the Triumph of Truth* (DeKalb: Northern Illinois University Press 2010).
278 Kramer, "Memo from Warsaw: 'Origins' of the RRC," 8.
279 Lichten, "Some Aspects of Polish–Jewish Relations," 155.
280 Ibid.
281 Grzegorz Niziołek, "Zawsze nie w porę. Teatr polski a Zagłada" [It's Never the Right Time: Polish Theatre and the Holocaust], interview with Joanna Wichowska, *Dwutygodnik: Strona Kultury* 20 (29 December 2009), <http://www.dwutygodnik.com.pl/artykul/759-zawsze-nie-w-pore-polski-teatr-i-zaglada.html> (accessed 20 February 2010).
282 In another essay, Jan Błoński notices that, paradoxically, following World War II at a time when Poland was no longer the epicenter of the Jewish world, and when anti-Semitic sentiments infiltrated Polish culture and politics, a group of Polish-Jewish writers emerged, which Błoński calls the "Jewish School of Polish Literature," including writers such as Julian Stryjkowski, Adolf Rudnicki, Stanisław Wygodzki, and the most well known, Hanna Krall, author of *Shielding the Flame*, a biography of Marek Edelman, founder of the Jewish Combat Organization and one of the leaders of the Warsaw Ghetto Uprising (Karen Auerback and Antony Polonsky, "Insiders/Ousiders: Poles and Jews in Recent Polish Jewish Fiction and Autobiography," in *Insiders and Outsiders: Dilemmas of East European Jewry*, ed. Richard J. Cohen, Jonathan Frankel, and Stefani Hoffman (Oxford: Littman Library of Jewish Civilization 2010), 70).
283 Błoński, "The Poor Poles Look at the Ghetto," 222.
284 To read more on the subject of the controversy that Błoński's essay evoked, see John A. Drobnicki's "A Touch of Controversy," *Polish-American Journal*, February 1991, 13; and Antony Polonsky's *My Brother's Keeper? Recent Polish Debates on the Holocaust* (New York: Routledge 1990).
285 Kolata, Pieta, and Stup, "Never Again? Contemporary Anti-Semitism and Representations of Jews in Modern Poland."
286 Steinlauf, "Józio Grojeszyk: A Jewish City Slicker on the Warsaw Popular Stage," 66.
287 Niziołek, "Zawsze nie w porę. Teatr polski a Zagłada" [It's Never the Right Time: Polish Theatre and the Holocaust].
288 Adorno, *Aesthetic Theory*, 6.
289 Harries, *Forgetting Lot's Wife*, 19.
290 Niziołek, "Zawsze nie w porę. Teatr polski a Zagłada" [It's Never the Right Time: Polish Theatre and the Holocaust].
291 Gordon Parson, "Fringe Benefits: Review of 'Dead Class' at Edinburgh Fringe Festival," *Morning Star*, 11 September 1976, 4.
292 Richard Eder, "Avant-Gardist from Poland at La Mama," *New York Times*, 13 February 1979, C7.
293 "Awards," *Plays and Players* (1976). Cricoteka Archives.
294 Tadeusz Kantor, quoted in Miklaszewski, *Tadeusz Kantor: Między śmietnikiem a wiecznością* [Tadeusz Kantor: Between Garbage and Eternity], 182.
295 Richard Schechner, "Want to Watch? Or Act?" *New York Times*, 12 January 1969, D1.
296 Some have accused Gross of distorting historical facts by questioning, for example, the fact of the death penalty for any gentile who helped Jews in any way (Poland was the only country in Europe where Nazis punished such help with death). Particularly vocal were children of the Jewish survivors and Poles, whose parents, the Righteous Among the Nations, risked their lives while saving their Jewish friends and neighbors.
297 For more on the subject, consult Robert Blobaum's *Antisemitism and Its Opponents in Modern Poland* (Ithaca, NY: Cornell University Press 2005); Jan Tomasz Gross and Irena Grudzińska-Gross, *Golden Harvests. Events at the Periphery of the Holocaust* (Oxford University Press 2012) [English translation of *Złote żniwa. Rzecz o tym, co się udało na obrzeżach zagłady Żydów* (Cracow: Editions Znak 2011)]; Jan Grabowski's *Judenjagd. Polowanie na Żydów 1942–1945. Studium*

dziejów pewnego powiatu [Judenjagd. Jew Hunt 1942–1945. Studies on the history of a county] (Warsaw: Stowarzyszenie Centrum Badań nad Zagładą Żydów 2011); Barbara Engelking's *Jest taki piękny słoneczny dzień… Losy Żydow szukających ratunku na wsi polskiej 1942–1945* [The weather is so nice today. The fate of Jews looking for help in the Polish countryside, 1942–1945] (Warsaw: Stowarzyszenie Centrum Badań nad Zagładą Żydów 2011).

298 As I write this, Władysław Pasikowski, one of Poland's leading film directors, is making a movie, *Pokłosie*, about the events in Jedwabne, where 300 Polish Jews were burned alive by their Polish neighbors right after World War II. In 2010, Tadeusz Słobodzianek's play, *Our Class*, based on Jan Gross' book *Neighbors: The Destruction of the Jewish Community in Jedwabne, Poland*, Anna Bikont's *My z Jedwabnego* [*We From Jedwabne*] (2004) and Agnieszka Arnold's documentary *Sąsiedzi* (*Neighbors*; 2001), was staged in Poland. It was the first Polish drama to be given the country's prestigious Nike Literary Prize. The play initially premiered at the National Theatre in London. The US premiere was directed by Blanka Zizka at the Wilma Theater in Philadelphia, in November, 2011. (See the excellent review by Kathleen Cioffi, "The Ghosts of Memory," *Theater*, 13 November 2011, <http://theatermagazine.yale.edu/our-class> (accessed 13 December 2011)).

299 For example, in December 2011, the Jewish Historical Institute in Warsaw, the German Historical Institute in Warsaw, and the Nordost-Institut Lüneburg at the University of Hamburg organized the joint conference "To Stay or Go? Jews in Europe in the Immediate Aftermath of the Holocaust."

300 Frustrated, the Polish government in 2006 filed a formal request with UNESCO to change the official name of Auschwitz from "Auschwitz Concentration Camp" to "former Nazi German concentration camp Auschwitz-Birkenau" to make sure that it was clear that the camps were built and run by Nazis. The request was supported by the American Jewish Committee, and in 2007 it was approved, but this didn't stop the American and German media from continuing to refer to the camps as "Polish." In May 2011, the Polish Consul General in New York wrote yet another letter to American editors and broadcasters, imploring them to stop using the term:

> I address all those members of the media who have used this inaccurate and offensive term when I say simply and unambiguously, there were no Polish concentration or death camps during WWII. All those terrible places of profound human tragedy were built, operated and administered by the German Nazis. The only death camps were German Nazi death camps, some of which were located in German-occupied Poland. If Poland is to be referenced in any report, it should only be mentioned with this descriptive phrase: "Nazi German-occupied Poland." I strongly recommend that members of the news media follow in the footsteps of the *San Francisco Chronicle*, the *Wall Street Journal* and most recently the *New York Times*. These outlets have changed their respective stylebooks to disallow the use of the erroneous term, "Polish death camp." I implore you to make necessary corrections now and to refrain from journalistic sloppiness in the future. (Ewa Junczyk-Ziomecka, Consul General of Poland in New York, letter to American press, 13 May 2011, <http://www.polishconsulateny.org/en/m.43.Consular_Announcements.html?agid=124> (accessed 4 June 2011))

301 One example: in 2011, during his visit to Israel, Polish foreign minister Radoslaw Sikorski said,

> We feel solidarity with both people of the Holy Land who have a right to live in secure borders, but above all it was also the fact that because the Polish state was too weak in 1939 to stand up to Nazi Germany and to protect all of its citizens and Nazi Germany carried out the Holocaust on our own soil, against our will but in front of our eyes. (Adar Primor, "Polish Foreign Minister: The Holocaust Was Perpetrated Against Our Will," *Haaretz.com*, 25 February 2011, <http://www.haaretz.com/

print-edition/news/polish-foreign-minister-the-holocaust-was-perpetrated-against-our-will-1.345542> (accessed 29 May 2011))

302 Connolly, "Museum to Mark Jewish Life in Poland," 16.
303 In her essay "Unquiet Places," Erica Lehrer points out that many American-Jewish tourists are ambivalent about the Polish attempts to revive Polish-Jewish culture: "Many Jews express understandable ambivalence on encountering a celebration when they were anticipating a cemetery. As one young Jewish tourist told me, 'I don't like all this business. I don't think a Jewish concert is good for anyone. I want to see the synagogue in ruins. I have to see the ruins because that's what I came to find here – ruins of a culture. I just don't like to have so much life here.'" Lehner suggests that in Poland, "symbols and spaces of Jewishness have been inherited by default. They have been renewed largely by non-Jews, some of whom have grown into their new roles as keepers of memory with a sense of profound obligation." Many non-Jewish Poles feel a sense of obligation to preserve the memory of a people and history that were once a part of their own. To quote one Polish craftsman, "it is my aim not to let the traces of this ancient culture sink into oblivion." Similarly, a non-Jewish shopkeeper at a Jewish bookshop asks philosophically, "What's the matter who's doing this? To keep tradition, to try to save the memory of the people who lived here for [hundreds of] years. That's part of Polish history." The recent revival of Jewish culture in Poland resembles at times a desperate attempt to piece together a picture of a deceased, close family member that one never knew and was forbidden for years to talk about; a singular photo or family story, evoking both the good and the bad, is important because it helps to reconstruct the image and preserve a memory. As Lehrer concludes, Natalia, a Polish student, "relates that she feels a profound connection to Jewish life as part of her Polish history. She laments the loss of Polish Jewish culture and the pre-war Jewish community, explaining that 'It's a profound sense of loss that I want to do something to repair.'

"Natalia, and others in Kazimierz, and elsewhere, regard themselves as having become the non-Jewish caretakers of Poland's Jewish tradition." (Erika Lehrer, "Unquiet Places: A second look at Jewish Poland today," *Pakn Treger: The Magazine of the Yiddish Book Center* 56 (Spring 2008), <http://www.yiddishbookcenter.org/pakn-treger/12-09/unquiet-places-a-second-look-at-jewish-poland-today> (accessed 30 July 2011).)
304 Kimmelman, "Poland Searches Its Own Soul."
305 Lehner, "Unquiet Places: A second look at Jewish Poland today."
306 Błoński, quoted in Karen Auerback and Antony Polonsky, "Insiders/Ousiders: Poles and Jews in Recent Polish Jewish Fiction and Autobiography," in *Insiders and Outsiders: Dilemmas of East European Jewry*, ed. Richard J. Cohen, Jonathan Frankel, and Stefani Hoffman (Oxford: Littman Library of Jewish Civilization 2010), 70.
307 Robert L. Nelson's *Germans, Poland, and Colonial Expansion to the East: 1850 through the Present* (New York: Palgrave Macmillan 2009) and Shelley Baranowski's *Nazi Empire: German Colonialism and Imperialism from Bismarck to Hitler* (Cambridge: Cambridge University Press 2010) are just two examples of such an approach. See also: Claire Cavanagh, "Postcolonial Poland," *Common Knowledge* 10, no. 1 (Winter 2004): 82–92; Walter Kolarz, *Communism and Colonialism*, ed. George Gretton (London: Palgrave Macmillan 1964); Izabela Surynt, *Postęp, kultura i kolonializm. Polska a niemiecki projekt europejskiego Wschodu w dyskursach publicznych XIX wieku* [Progress, Culture and Colonialism: Poland and German Project of European East in the 19th Century Political Discourse] (Wrocław: Wydawnictwo "Atut" 2006); Ewa M. Thompson, *Imperial Knowledge: Russian Literature and Colonialism* (London, UK; Westport, CT: Greenwood Press 2000); Janusz Korek, "Central and Eastern Europe from a Postcolonial Perspective," *Postcolonial Europe*, <http://www.postcolonial-europe.eu/index.php/en/essays/60--central-and-eastern-europe-from-a-postcolonial-perspective> (accessed 1 August 2011).
308 See, for example, Dariusz Skorczewski, "Modern Polish Literature Through a Postcolonial Lens," *The Sarmatian Review* 26, no. 3 (2006): 1229–33, <http://www.postcolonial-europe.

eu/index.php/en/essays/91-modern-polish-literature-through-a-postcolonial-lens-> (accessed 1 August 2011).

309 Filipowicz, "Mickiewicz: 'East' and 'West,'" 609.

310 See for example, Krzysztof Jasiewicz, "Niepogrzebani ludzie, umarłe miasteczka," *Świat Niepożegnany, Żydzi na dawnych ziemiach wschodnich Rzeczypospolitej w XVIII–XX wieku* [*A World We Bade No Farewell: Jews in Eastern Poland in the 18th–20th Centuries*] (Warsaw/London: Wydawnictwo Rytm 2004), 39–41.

311 For example, the 2008 documentary *The Soviet Story*, based on ten years of archival research and recently discovered documents, brings to light the previously unknown – and unimaginable – scale of genocides instigated by Stalin before and during World War II, including the mass murder of Russian Jews. Although in pure numbers Stalin's genocides (including Jewish genocides) outnumber Hitler's (and are widely estimated to be in the neighborhood of 20 million – three times as many as Hitler, though some scholars estimate that the numbers can be as high as 61 million, with Stalin himself personally responsible for 43 million deaths, including those of 13 million Russian Jews), due to the historical circumstances (the Yalta conference, etc.), many American scholars of the Holocaust outside of history and Slavic departments still tend to overlook Stalin's atrocities (<http://www.sovietstory.com>).

312 Edward Lucas, "Russia's Reset and Central Europe," *Diplomaatia* 92 (April 2011), <http://www.diplomaatia.ee/index.php?id=242&L=1&tx_ttnews[tt_news]=1254&tx_ttnews[backPid]=577&cHash=1d2a1a24dc> (accessed 4 May 2011).

313 A. A. Fatouros, "Sartre on Colonialism," *World Politics* 17, no. 4 (July 1965): 703–19, at 703.

314 Kolata, Pieta, and Stup, "Never Again? Contemporary Anti-Semitism and Representations of Jews in Modern Poland."

315 Adorno, "Trying to Understand *Endgame*," 273.

316 Anne Whitehead, *Trauma Fiction* (Edinburgh: Edinburgh University Press 2004), 4.

317 Cathy Caruth, *Trauma: Explorations in Memory* (Baltimore: John Hopkins University Press 1995), 4.

318 In extreme circumstances, the function of memory is tied to survival. The body remembers violence and learns to avoid it. Post-traumatic stress disorder (PTSD), with its panoply of symptoms that are essentially expressions of the inability to forget, such as flashbacks or nightmares, can be then thought of as the mind's survival strategy: to remember means to avoid, and to avoid means to survive. To quote Roberta Culbertson:

> [S]uch slivered memories [of traumatic events] take on various lives of their own, perhaps altering behavior, working out as templates for response to current life circumstances. Violence is about survival, and the body is designed to take the lessons of violence seriously. To do so, it need not, perhaps best not, recall the violence itself, but rather must merely arrange to avoid it in the future, using whatever cues can be stored and maintained from before. This is not memory to be told, not memory to be analyzed, but memory to be used for purposes of survival. (Roberta Culbertson, "Embodied Memory, Transcendence, and Telling: Trauma, Re-Establishing the Self," *New Literary History* 26, no. 1 (Winter 1995): 169–95, at 175)

319 Culbertson, "Embodied Memory, Transcendence, and Telling," 169.

320 Dori Laub, "Bearing Witness, or the Vicissitudes or Listening," in *Testimony: Crisis of Witnessing in Literature, Psychoanalysis, and History*, ed. Shoshana Felman and Dori Laub (New York: Routledge 1992), 69.

321 Caruth, *Trauma: Explorations in Memory*, vii.

322 Ibid., 5.

323 Bernhard Giesen, "The Trauma of Perpetrators: The Holocaust as the Traumatic Reference of German National Identity," in *Cultural Trauma and Collective Identity*, ed. Jeffrey

Alexander, Ron Eyerman, Bernhard Giesen, Neil J. Smelser, and Piotr Sztompka (Berkeley: University of California Press 2004), 113.
324 Arthur G. Neal, *National Trauma and Collective Memory: Major Events in the American Century* (Armonk, NY: M. E. Sharpe 1998), ix.
325 Jeffrey Alexander, "Toward a Theory of Cultural Trauma," in *Cultural Trauma and Collective Identity*, ed. Jeffrey Alexander, Ron Eyerman, Bernhard Giesen, Neil J. Smelser, and Piotr Sztompka (Berkeley: University of California Press 2004), 14.
326 Ibid., 1.
327 Harries, *Forgetting Lot's Wife*, 18.
328 John Simon, "Vaulting Pole," *New York Theatre*, 1 December 1969, 58.
329 Anna Boska, "Umarła klasa" [Dead Class], *Kobieta i Życie* 8 (20 February 1977), <http://www.e-teatr.pl/pl/artykuly/11898.html> (accessed 23 February 2011).
330 Jan Skotnicki, "Ukradzione poranki" [Stolen Mornings], *Scena* 9 (November 1983): 21.
331 Józef Szczawiński, "Tadeusz Kantor – epitafium dla epoki" [Tadeusz Kantor – Epitaph for the Epoch], *Słowo Powszechne*, 11 March 1976. Cricoteka Archives: 000546.
332 Roman Szydłowski, "Bez Teatru Rzeczypospolitej" [Without the Theatre of the People's Republic], *Życie Literackie* 25 (19 June 1983).
333 Barba, *Land of Ashes and Diamonds*, 32–3.
334 Hans-Ties Lehman, *Postdramatic Theatre* (New York: Routledge 2006), 59.
335 Niziołek, "Zawsze nie w porę. Teatr polski a Zagłada" [It's Never the Right Time: Polish Theatre and the Holocaust].
336 Alexander, "Toward a Theory of Cultural Trauma," 1.

Part I Our Auschwitz: Grotowski's *Akropolis*

1 Kathleen Cioffi, *Alternative Theatre in Poland 1954–1989* (London and New York: Routledge 1996), 86.
2 Romana Konieczna, "Przed premierą 'Pechowców.' Rozmowa z reżyserem" [Before the Opening of the "Jinxed": Conversation with the Director], *Trybuna Opolska* 265 (1958): 4.
3 Ibid.
4 Jerzy Grotowski, "Co to jest teatr?" [What Is Theatre?], *Dziennik Polski* 200 (23–24 August 1959). Grotowski Institute Archives.
5 Richard Schechner, "Want to Watch? Or Act?" *New York Times*, 12 January 1969, D1.
6 "Kordian do gory nogami" [Kordian with Legs Upside Down], *Słowo Polskie*, 24 May 1962. Reprinted in *Akropolis*, program notes, October 1962. Grotowski Institute Archives.
7 Roger Planchon, quoted in "Planchon o Grotowskim" [Planchon about Grotowski: An Interview with Planchon for *Cité Panorama*], *Kierunki* 5 (29 January 1967). Grotowski Institute Archives.
8 Hovhannes I. Pilikian, "Grotowski: Seen from Poland," *Drama: The Quarterly Theatre Review* 95 (Winter 1969): 61–3, at 63.
9 Tymon Terlecki, "A Critical Appraisal of Mickiewicz's Lecture about Theatre," in *Studies in Polish Civilization*, ed. Damian Wandycz (New York: Institute on East Central Europe, Columbia University and The Polish Institute of Arts & Sciences in America 1966), 276.
10 Jan Kłossowicz, "Grotowski in Poland," *Le Théâtre en Pologne / Theatre in Poland* 5 (1971): 7. Special issue devoted to Jerzy Grotowski.
11 Daniel C. Gerould, "Jerzy Grotowski's Theatrical and Paratheatrical Activities as Cosmic Drama: Roots and Continuities in the Polish Romantic Tradition," *World Literature Today* 54, no. 3 (Summer 1980): 381.
12 Adam Mickiewicz, quoted in Halina Filipowicz, "Performing Bodies, Performing Mickiewicz: Drama as Problem in Performance Studies," *Slavic and East European Journal* 43, no. 1 (Spring 1999): 1–18, at 15.

13 Halina Filipowicz argues that, despite the political circumstances, the Romantic dramas were being perfomed; however, these performances were sporadic, fragmentary and under the radar. (See Halina Filipowicz, "Mickiewicz: 'East' and 'West,'" *Slavic and East European Journal* 45, no. 4 (Winter 2001): 605–731.)
14 Jan Kott, *Theatre Notebook: 1947–1967*, trans. Boleslaw Taborski (Garden City, NY: Doubleday 1968), 259.
15 Kathleen Cioffi, "From the Great Reform to the Post-Dramatic: Adaptation in the Polish Postwar Theatre," *Canadian Slavonic Papers* 52 (2010): 413–30, at 416.
16 Ibid.
17 "In the early postwar era, Mieczysław Kotlarczyk's influential Rhapsodic Theatre also produced adaptations of many classic works of prose and epic poetry." (Ibid.)
18 Ibid.
19 Kazimierz Braun, "Theater Training in Poland," in *Performer Training: Developments across Cultures*, ed. Ian Watson Amsterdam (Amsterdam: Harwood 2001), 28.
20 Konstantyn Puzyna, "Grotowski and Polish Romantic Drama," trans. Jacob Conrad, *Theatre Three* 4 (Spring 1988): 44–50, at 45.
21 Raymonde Temkine, *Grotowski*, trans. Alex Szogyi (New York: Avon Books 1972), 17.
22 Quoted in Tom Sellar, "Poland's Old and New Masters," *Theater* 33, no. 3 (Fall 2003): 2–19, at 5.
23 Igor Krenz, quoted in Przemysław Kwiek, Igor Krenz, and Jarosław Kozłowski, "Grotowski: hosztapler czy inspirator?" [Grotowski: Conman or Visionary?], *Dziennik* 80 (13 March 2009), <http://www.dziennik.pl/kultura/teatr/article340537/Jerzy_Grotowski_hochsztapler_czy_inspirator_.html> (accessed 3 July 2010).
24 Jerzy Grotowski, "Wokół Teatru Przyszłości" [About the Theatre of the Future], *Ekran* 21 (24 May 1959). Grotowski Institute Archives.
25 Temkine, *Grotowski*, 14.
26 Jan Paweł Gawlik, "Sztuka Skromności" [The Art of Humility], *Życie Literackie* 40 (4 October 1959). Grotowski Institute Archives.
27 Poland's most revered and influential movies – Andrzej Wajda's *Canal* (1957) and *Ashes and Diamonds* (1958), Andrzej Munk's *Eroica* (1957) and Roman Polanski's *Knife in the Water* (1960) – are main examples of the Polish School. Eugenio Barba confessed that Wajda's *Ashes and Diamonds* was what originally drove him to Poland and what eventually inspired the title of his book *Land of Ashes and Diamonds: My Apprenticeship in Poland*. As Barba put it: Wajda's *Ashes and Diamonds*

> hit me like a punch in the stomach and I went back to see it again and again, three, five, maybe ten times. The images that flashed onto the screen were of a civil war, of a desperate passion, of a sense of honour and a contempt for life, of a tenderness for the madness and the weakness of human beings crushed by the ferocity of history. The protagonist Zbigniew Cybulski, had a virile yet vulnerable expression which I was to find again years later in the face of Grotowski's actor Ryszard Cieślak. (Eugenio Barba, *Land of Ashes and Diamonds: My Apprenticeship in Poland* (Aberystwyth, UK: Black Mountain Press 1999), 15)

28 Robert Findlay and Halina Filipowicz, "Grotowski's Laboratory Theatre: Dissolution and Diaspora," *TDR: The Drama Review* 30, no. 3 (T111) (Fall 1986): 207.
29 In 1962, Tadeusz Kudliński praised the move:

> I wrote once that Cracow does not respect people who take chances and who are creative. I repeat this again here because a talented group of people escaped from Cracow to Opole. As the only one of them, Flaszen – like Gulliver among the Liliputs – stands with one leg in Opole and one in Cracow. (Tadeusz Kudliński, "Ofensywa Grotowskiego'" [Grotowski's Offensive], *Dziennik Polski*, 5 April 1962; reprinted in *Akropolis*, program notes, October 1962. Grotowski Institute Archives)

30 Teresa Kudyba, "Opole było odpowiednią pustelnią" [Opole Was a Perfect Hermitage: Conversation with Ludwik Flaszen], *Gazeta Wyborcza*, 28 March 2009, 4.
31 Collages of different texts, including some from drama, poetry, prose and film.
32 "Autorowi udało się urzeczywistnić postulat nowoczesnej homiletyki, gardzącej przesadną barokową retoryką, zmierzając do osiągnięcia możliwie oszczędnymi środkami jak największej prostoty, bezpośredniości i szczerości wyrazu. Do urzeczywistnienia tej koncepcji bardzo się nadaje godny wyróżnienia styl operujący krótkimi zdaniami, układającymi się jednak w pewną rytmiczną całość, styl będący przeciwstawieniem patosu i frazeologii. Bierze za serce piękna polszczyzna" (Józef Maria Święcicki, review of the sermons by Władysław Mirski, *Tygodnik Powszechny*, 26 March 1950).
33 Joanna Targoń, "Don Kichot w okularach dla krótkowidzów" [Don Quixote in Glasses for the Nearsighted], *Gazeta Wyborcza*, 20 March 2009, 10.
34 Jan Kott, "Why Should I Take Part in the Sacred Dance?" *TDR: The Drama Review* 14, no. 2 (T46) (Winter 1970): 200. Reprinted in *Theatre of Essence* (Evanston, IL: Northwestern University Press 1984) 139–45, and in *The Grotowski Sourcebook*, ed. Richard Schechner and Lisa Wolford (New York: Routledge 1997), 134–40.
35 Some critics have argued that the state-owned national theatres were comparatively "rich," and that Grotowski's drive towards "poor" theatre was a reaction to their "richness."
36 Peter Brook, preface to Jerzy Grotowski's *Towards a Poor Theatre* (London: Methuen 1968), 11.
37 Richard Gilman, "What Not to Do in the Theater," *New York Times*, 8 February 1970, 263.
38 Roman Pawłowski, "Ewangelia nowego teatru" [The Gospel of a New Theatre], *Gazeta Wyborcza*, 13 February 2007, <http://www.teatry.art.pl/!inne/grotowski/ente.htm> (accessed 15 June 2012).
39 Findlay and Filipowicz, "Grotowski's Laboratory Theatre: Dissolution and Diaspora," 209.
40 Irving Wardle, "Big Catch from Poland," *Times*, 24 August 1968, 18.
41 Ibid.
42 Oleg Kerensky, "Jerzy Grotowski's Laboratory," *Stage and Television Today*, 25 September 1969, 15.
43 Clive Barnes, "Theatre: Grotowski's View of Reality," *New York Times*, 18 October 1969, 36.
44 Allan Lewis, "Too Few Can Attend," *New Haven Register*, 2 November 1969, 1.
45 Ellen Steward, "Uninformed," *New York Times*, 23 February 1969, D21.
46 Gilman, "What Not to Do in the Theater," 263.
47 Barnes, "Theatre: Grotowski's View of Reality," 36.
48 Ronald Bryden, review of *Constant Prince*, by Juliusz Słowacki, directed by Jerzy Grotowski, Polish Laboratory Theatre, Washington Square Methodist Church, New York, "A Myth in Stepney," *Observer*, 28 September 1969, 27.
49 Kłossowicz, "Grotowski in Poland," 10.
50 Kott, "Why Should I Take Part in the Sacred Dance?" 199.
51 Witold Filler, "Z Wrocławia w świat" [From Wrocław into the World], *Kultura* 8 (23 February 1969). Grotowski Institute Archives.
52 Ibid.
53 Wisz, "Grotowski i inni" [Grotowski and Others], *Trybuna Robotnicza* 51 (1–2 March 1969). Grotowski Institute Archives.
54 "Poland Begins to Appreciate Grotowski," *Times*, 16 August 1965. Grotowski Institute Archives.
55 Pilikian, "Grotowski: Seen from Poland," 62.
56 Krzysztof Jędrysek, quoted in Beata Guczalska, "Polskie środowisko teatralne wobec Grotowskiego" [Polish Theatre Community's Relationship towards Grotowski], *Didaskalia. Gazeta Teatralna* (June 2009): 21. (Originally published in *Dialog* 6 (1999): 135.)
57 The Grotowski Institute, "The Grotowski Year, 2009." <http://www.grotowski-institute.art.pl/index.php?option=com_content&task=view&id=146&lang=en> (accessed 5 March 2012).

58 Guczalska, "Polskie środowisko teatralne wobec Grotowskiego" [Polish Theatre Community's Relationship towards Grotowski], 21.
59 Joanna Wichowska, "'Akropolis': duchy i ludzie" ["Akropolis": Ghosts and People], *Dwutygodnik: Strona Kultury* 20 (24 December 2009), <http://www.dwutygodnik.com.pl/artykul/738-akropolis-duchy-i-ludzie.html> (accessed 2 March 2011).
60 Guczalska, "Polskie środowisko teatralne wobec Grotowskiego" [Polish Theatre Community's Relationship towards Grotowski], 21.
61 Joanna Derkaczew, "Grotowski po raz pierwszy" [Grotowski for the First Time], *Gazeta Wyborcza*, 18 December 2009, 17.
62 In her memoir, Marrianne Ahrne writes as her alter ego about her relationship with Grotowski. Following an injury during a rehearsal, where she worked herself to the point of exhaustion, she confesses that "She would have gladly died the day before, if that had been his wish" (Marianne Ahrne, "The Man in Her Dream," in *Grotowski's Empty Room*, ed. Paul Allain (London: Seagull Books 2010), 13). One can't help wondering how healthy a relationship between a director and his actress is when the actress wants to die at the "whistling" of the director. There is something deeply disturbing and masochistic in Ahrne's confessions, particularly when considering the gendered nature of their relationship.
63 Gustaw Holoubek, quoted in Guczalska, "Polskie środowisko teatralne wobec Grotowskiego" [Polish Theatre Community's Relationship towards Grotowski], 23.
64 Ewa Lubowiecka, quoted in Dorota Wodecka, "Grotowski zawsze był sam" [Grotowski Was Always Alone: A Conversation with Ewa Lubowiecka], *Gazeta Wyborcza*, 16 January 2009, 6.
65 Wodecka, "Grotowski zawsze był sam" [Grotowski Was Always Alone: A Conversation with Ewa Lubowiecka], 6.
66 Krystian Lupa, "Fałszywy mag świątyni teatru" [The False Prophet of the Theatrical Temple], interview by Łukasz Drewniak, *Dziennik* 80 (4–5 April 2009), <http://www.dziennik.pl/magazyn-dziennika/article354424.ece> (accessed 15 February 2010).
67 Stanisław Rosiek, *Grotowski powtórzony* [Grotowski Repeated] (Gdańsk: Słowo/Obraz Terytoria 2009), 38.
68 Guczalska, "Polskie środowisko teatralne wobec Grotowskiego" [Polish Theatre Community's Relationship towards Grotowski], 21–4.
69 Wodecka, "Grotowski zawsze był sam" [Grotowski Was Always Alone: A Conversation with Ewa Lubowiecka], 6.
70 Perhaps nowhere is the ambivalence towards Grotowski more noticeable than in Opole. In 2004, to commemorate the fifth anniversary of his death, a monument to Grotowski was erected in front of Collegium Maius. The university awarded Grotowski an honorary doctorate in 1999; however, the artist died before the ceremony, so the monument was erected as a postmortem tribute instead. Regardless, to this day in Opole, despite Grotowski's international reputation, there is not a single street or building named after him. Tellingly, only a lone parking lot in front of the symphony hall carries his name (Magdalena Mach, "Nie oszczędzajmy na Grotowskim" [Let's Not Be Cheap on Grotowski], *Gazeta Wyborcza*, 3 April 2009, 2). "In May 2008, to celebrate Grotowki's connection with Opole, 13 actors wearing cast masks made from Grotowski's monument, and a few others dressed in black (since Grotowski also used to dress in black), marched through the streets of Opole to remind the inhabitants about Grotowski's connection to the city" (Izabella Żbikowska, "Grotowski zapomniany" [Grotowski Forgotten], *Gazeta Wyborcza*, 9 May 2008, 2).
71 Irving Wardle, "Grotowski the Evangelist," *Times*, 4 October 1969, IIIc.
72 "Writing into the desk drawer" – "pisanie do szuflady" – is an idiomatic expression meaning that one's writing, if one were to be true to oneself, would be considered too dangerous for the regime. Such writing was most likely never intended to be published, unless by the underground illegal press.

73 On his end, in *The Captive Mind*, Miłosz considers an attitude of "writing into the desk drawer" hypocritical, labeling it "Ketman," a term he borrows from Arthur de Gobineau's *Religions and Philosophies of Central Asia*. Travelling through Asia, Gobineau noticed the Persian practice of hiding one's true feelings and opinions behind a mask of false identity. Quoting Gobineau, Miłosz writes:

> The people of the Mussulman East believe that "He who is in possession of truth must not expose his person, his relatives or his reputation to the blindness, the folly, the perversity of those whom it has pleased God to place and maintain in error." One must, therefore, keep silent about one's true convictions if possible. "Nevertheless," says Gobineau, "There are occasions when silence no longer suffices, when it may pass as an avowal. Then one must not hesitate. Not only must one deny one's true opinion, but one is commanded to resort to all ruses in order to deceive one's adversary. One makes all the protestations of faith that can please him, one performs all the rites one recognizes to be the most vain, one falsifies one's own books, one exhausts all possible means of deceit. Thus one acquires the multiple satisfactions and merits of having placed oneself and one's relative under cover, of not having exposed a venerable faith to the horrible contact of the infidel, and finally of having, in cheating the latter and confirming him in his error, imposed on him the shame and spiritual misery that he deserves." (*The Captive Mind*)

According to Miłosz, under the Soviet regime, most Polish intellectuals developed multiple personalities, believing wholeheartedly that by writing for the desk drawer they had preserved their inner freedom. The secret writing "brings comfort, fostering dreams of what might be, and even the enclosing fence affords the solace of reverie […] Fear of the indifference with which the economic system of the West treats its artists and scholars is widespread among Eastern intellectuals. They say it is better to deal with an intelligent devil than with a good-natured idiot." The secret writers solve the contradiction between their public proclaimations and private lives

> by becoming actors. It is hard to define the type of relationship that prevails between people in the East otherwise than as acting, with the exception that one does not perform on a theater stage but in the street, office, factory, meeting hall, or even the room one lives in. Such acting is a highly developed craft that places a premium upon mental alertness. Before it leaves the lips, every word must be evaluated as to its consequences. A smile that appears at the wrong moment, a glance that is not all it should be even occasion dangerous suspicions and accusations. Even one's gestures, tone of voice, or preference for certain kinds of neckties are interpreted as signs of one's political tendencies. (*The Captive Mind*)

74 In his 1987 play *Hunting Cockroaches*, Janusz Głowacki perfectly captures the absurdity of that phenomenon. The main characters, Anka and Janek, two Polish intellectuals, an actress and a writer, try to adjust to their new life in America. Not surprisingly, they struggle with the dilemma of how to fit their own experience of America *vis-à-vis* communism within the New York political environment. Głowacki takes not-too-subtle jabs at the gentle, spoiled hypocrisy of upper-class liberals. Since Janek's career depends on the couple's acceptance in the New York art circle, they try to figure out how to talk about socialism without antagonizing anyone. "What did I ask you to do?" – asks Anka after one such encounter. "To keep my mouth shut and not to say anything bad about socialism, Jaruzelski, Gorbachev, and the Soviet Union" – Janek replies. "If you say bad things about it, they'll say you're a classic example of paranoia affecting émigrés" – Anka asserts. "If I say good things about them, they'll ask me why I left Poland" – Janek retorts, pointing out the absurd, catch-22 logic. On the other end, the Thompsons, the upper-class liberal couple who come to visit

Anka and Janek, have a similar conversation: "And please, dear, don't say good things about socialism in their presence" – Mr. Thompson asks of his wife. Mrs. Thomson, astonished, answers "But socialism is a noble idea!" – to which Mr. Thomson replies: "I know, dear, I know. But they've suffered a lot over there. And if they say something good about Reagan, don't be upset" (Janusz Głowacki, *Hunting Cockroaches and Other Plays* (Chicago: Northwestern University Press 1990), 118). Those two short exchanges poignantly reveal a huge divide in political consciousness. The Thompsons, who know socialism only from books, are suspicious of the actual accounts of life under socialism; they dismiss Anka and Janek's experiences as exaggerated. Anka and Janek, knowing viscerally what socialism means, force themselves to humor the liberal New York couple; there is no point trying to convince them otherwise.

75 Eugenio Barba, *Land of Ashes and Diamonds: My Apprenticeship in Poland* (Aberystwyth, UK: Black Mountain Press 1999), 22.
76 Adam Hanuszkiewicz, quoted in Pilikian, "Grotowski: Seen from Poland," 63.
77 Jerzy Tymicki and Andrzej Niezgoda, "New Dignity: The Polish Theatre 1970–1985," *TDR: The Drama Review* 30, no. 3 (Autumn 1986): 13–46, at 19–22.
78 Barba, *Land of Ashes and Diamonds*, 24–5.
79 Ibid., 23–4.
80 Ibid., 24.
81 Ibid., 24–5.
82 Jerzy Grotowski, "Szkoła szczerości" [The School of Honesty], *Echo Tygodnia* 9 (26 February 1955). Grotowski Institute Archives.
83 Ibid.
84 Jerzy Grotowski, "Marzenie o teatrze: Głos Młodego Aktora" [Dreaming about Theatre: Voice of a Young Actor], *Dziennik Polski* 46 (1955). Grotowski Institute Archives.
85 Jerzy Grotowski, "Jakie dostrzegłem zmiany w życiu kulturalnym ZSRR" [What Changes I Noticed in the Cultural Life of the SSSR], *Dziennik Polski* 216 (9–10 October 1956). Grotowski Institute Archives.
86 Jerzy Grotowski, "Cywilizacja i wolność – nie ma innego socjalizmu" [Civilization and Freedom – There Is No Other Socialism], *Walka Młodych* 6 (1957). Grotowski Institute Archives.
87 Jerzy Grotowski, quoted in Dariusz Kosiński, *Grotowski: Przewodnik* [Grotowski: A Handbook] (Wrocław: Instytut Im. Jerzego Grotowskiego 2009), 51.
88 Kosiński, *Grotowski: Przewodnik* [Grotowski: A Handbook], 51.
89 Ludwik Wittgenstein, *Culture and Value*, trans. Peter Winch, ed. G. H. von Wright and Heikki Nyman (Chicago: University of Chicago Press 1980), 78e.
90 Umberto Eco and V. V. Ivanhoe, *Carnival! (Approaches to Semiotics)* (Berlin and New York: Mouton de Gruyter 1984), 3.
91 Peter Sloterdijk, *Critique of Cynical Reason*, trans. Michael Eldred (Minneapolis: University of Minnesota 1987), 103.
92 One only needs to have followed the last few American presidential elections to notice that having a sense of humor and being able to laugh at oneself is as much a requirement for the American presidency as is knowledge of foreign policy. One candidate after the next, from Clinton to Bush, to Kerry, to McCain, to Obama, had to pass the *Saturday Night Live* test: to be deemed worthy of the highest office in the nation, a politician needs not only to withstand mockery, but to join in the fun of mocking him- or herself. A sense of distance from oneself, a nonchalant self-awareness of one's faults and limitations, is an essential quality in a leader of a democratic country. Americans almost intuitively understand the curious, though little-analyzed, phenomenon: totalitarian leaders and dictators are unable to make fun of themselves.
93 Slavoj Žižek, *The Sublime Object of Ideology* (London: Verso 1989), 28.
94 Sloterdijk, *Critique of Cynical Reason*, 101–33.

95 Ibid.
96 One of Poles' most beloved figures is Stańczyk, a wise jester, employed by three kings: Alexander, Sigmund the Old, and Sigmund Augustus. Stańczyk is known as a highly intelligent political philosopher who often spoke truth to power. In the most famous portrait of Stańczyk, by Jan Matejko, the jester, with his head hanging low, is the only person at the court concerned about the news of Russians capturing Smolensk in 1514. In Polish literature, Stańczyk is often perceived as the symbolic conscience of the nation. He is a Shakespearean character in terms of the depth and breadth of his knowledge (like the Jester from *Twelfth Night*). The most well-known representation of Stańczyk is in Wyspiański's play *The Wedding*. Here, Stańczyk's ghost appears to a journalist, scolding him for his political passivity. Under communism, the figure of Stańczyk became a model for a number of Polish actors, particularly those involved in political stand-up comedy.
97 It can be argued that the term "political theatre" in a free society is an oxymoron. In a free society, which upholds freedom-of-speech protections, political dissent is absorbed into the election process. Even the most extreme elements, though often labeled as "fringe," have an opportunity to secure their place in the national debate. In other words, in a free society, there is no need for kynicism.
98 Konrad Swinarski, quoted in Guczalska, "Polskie środowisko teatralne wobec Grotowskiego" [Polish Theatre Community's Relationship towards Grotowski], 22.
99 Jan Kreczmar, one of the few living Polish actors trained before World War II, shared Swinarski's assessment:

> Both our theatres and our schools teach us to be overly careful, fearful, protectionists. We are so horribly afraid to offend the rules of good taste, culture, emotional restraint, that our stages are full of boredom, polished mediocrity. (Jan Kreczmar, quoted in Guczalska, "Polskie środowisko teatralne wobec Grotowskiego" [Polish Theatre Community's Relationship towards Grotowski], 22)

100 Gustaw Holoubek, quoted in Guczalska, "Polskie środowisko teatralne wobec Grotowskiego" [Polish Theatre Community's Relationship towards Grotowski], 23.
101 Ibid.
102 Adam Hanuszkiewicz, quoted in Pilikian, "Grotowski: Seen from Poland," 63.
103 Juliusz Tyszka, *Widowiska Nowojorskie* [New York Spectacles] (Poznań: Wydawnictwo ARS NOVA, 1994), 198.
104 Marina Vaizey, quoted in "Critics Forum," BBC Radio 3, 16 October 1976.
105 Jerzy Grotowski, *Towards a Poor Theatre*, ed. Eugenio Barba (New York: Routledge 2002), 40. Hereafter *Towards a Poor Theatre*.
106 Zbigniew Osiński, "Grotowski and the Reduta Tradition," in *Grotowski's Empty Room*, ed. Paul Allain (London: Seagull Books 2010), 22. Juliusz Osterwa founded Reduta Theatre in 1919 in Warsaw. He spent some time in Russia working with Stanislavky and incorporated his methods upon his return to Poland. Grotowski was very much influenced by Osterwa. Osiński even argues that "For Grotowski, the Reduta was the only true sacral theatre of its time, in Europe and in the West" (22).
107 Jerzy Grotowski, "I Said Yes to the Past," interview by Margaret Croyden, *Village Voice* 23 (January 1969): 41–2; reprinted in *The Grotowski Sourcebook*, ed. Richard Schechner and Lisa Wolford (New York: Routledge 1997), 41. Hereafter *The Grotowski Sourcebook*.
108 Peter Brook, *The Empty Space* (Austin, TX: Touchstone 1995), 59.
109 Ibid.
110 Osiński, "Grotowski and the Reduta Tradition," 37.
111 Grotowski's relationship with the institution of the Polish Catholic Church was quite interesting. On the one hand, the Cardinal of Poland, Stefan Wyszyński, publically denounced Grotowski's work during a Mass in 1976, calling *Apocalypsis cum Figuris* disgusting. On the

other hand, in 1998 Grotowski was awarded the prize Il Beato Fra Angelico, sponsored by Pope John Paul II (Michał Masłowski, "Od obrzędu żałobnego do świeckiej mszy" [From Funeral Rite to Secular Mass], *Performer* 1 (2009) <http://www.grotowski.net/performer/performer-1/od-obrzedu-zalobnego-do-swieckiej-mszy> (accessed 3 January 2010)).

112 Writing about *Apocalypsis*, Eric Schorter of the *Daily Telegraph* mocked the religious-like piety of Grotowki's production:

> When it was over we filed out dumbly. We had attended at the shrine of Grotowski and the experience as in a piece about Auschwitz at Edinburgh last year had been distinctly chilling. I felt tempted to joke, as at a funeral, but the faces round me forbade it. Especially the face of Mr. Grotowski himself behind those mysterious dark glasses. (Eric Schorter, "Revelation by Avant-Garde Company," *Daily Telegraph*, 18 October 1969; Grotowski Institute Archives)

113 Adam Hanuszkiewicz, quoted in Pilikian, "Grotowski: Seen from Poland," 63.
114 The only American critic who even mentioned the issue of laughter (or its lack) in Grotowski's work was John Simon, who in *New York Theatre* wrote: "There is also laughter, but this is the cruelest, most bestial sound of all, serving only to cow and humiliate a victim" (John Simon, "Vaulting Pole," *New York Theatre*, 1 December 1969, 58).
115 Jan Kott, "Koniec teatru niemożliwego" [The End of the Impossible Theatre], *Dialog* (1980); reprinted in Jan Kott, *Pisma wybrane* [Selected Texts], ed. Tadeusz Nyczek (Warsaw: Wydawnictwo Krąg 1991), 339.
116 Leszek Kolankiewicz, *Wielki mały wóz. Teatr jako wehikuł* [The Big Small Dipper: Theatre as a Vehicle] (Gdańsk: Słowo/Obraz Terytoria 2001), 290.
117 Lech Raczak, "Para-ra-ra," *Dialog* 7 (1980): 134, 137.
118 Krystian Lupa, "Fałszywy mag świątyni teatru" [The False Prophet of the Theatrical Temple].
119 Igor Krenz, of the young, contemporary Polish artists, bluntly sums up his generation's view of Grotowski: "Grotowski represents the depressing, dismal, and pompous trend in expressive art" (Przemysław Kwiek, Igor Krenz and Jarosław Kozłowski, "Grotowski: hosztapler czy inspirator?" [Grotowski: Conman or Visionary?] *Dziennik* 80 (13 March 2009), <http://www.e-teatr.pl/pl/artykuly/69339.html?josso_assertion_id=3F9F727F7395B065> (accessed 15 June 2012).
120 Pilikian, "Grotowski: Seen from Poland," 62.
121 Andrzej Seweryn, quoted in Guczalska, "Polskie środowisko teatralne wobec Grotowskiego" [Polish Theatre Community's Relationship towards Grotowski], 25.
122 Służba Bezpieczeństwa, secret Security Bureau governed by the Soviet NKWD (НКВД - Народный комиссариат внутренних дел).
123 Kott, "Why Should I Take Part in the Sacred Dance?" 201–3.
124 Ibid., 203.
125 Ross Wetzsteon, "Theatre: Two by Grotowski," *Village Voice*, 27 October 1969, 46.
126 The only American critic who echoed Hanuszkiewicz's sentiments about Grotowski was John Simon, who mercilessly wrote:

> For whom is the Polish Laboratory Theatre designed? For frightened people who, having lost the crutch of religion, seek a new Messianism; for anti- or pseudo-intellectuals who can revel in the mindless or arcane hocus-pocus of this theatre; and for snobs, who relish the one-upmanship of having spent an hour [...] at a shrine accessible to only 40 to 90 of the elect per evening. As for me, I deplore this in-, anti-, and non-human theatre. (John Simon, "Vaulting Pole," *New York Theatre*, 1 December 1969, 58)

127 Andre Gregory, interview by Andrzej Bonarski (1975); reprinted in *Ziarno* (Warsaw: Czytelnik 1979), 46–61, at 52.

128 Schechner, "Want to Watch? Or Act?" 7.
129 Richard Schechner, "Exoduction: Shape-Shifter, Shaman, Trickster, Artist, Adept, Director, Leader, Grotowski," in *The Grotowski Sourcebook*, 458–92, at 473.
130 Richard Schechner, "Grotowski and the Grotowskian," *TDR: The Drama Review* 52, no. 2, (Summer 2008): 7–13. Special issue titled "Re-Reading Grotowski."
131 Allen Kuharski, "Jerzy Grotowski: Ascetic and Smuggler," *Theater* 29, no. 2 (1999): 10–15, at 10.
132 Richard Gilman, quoted in John Simon, "Grotowski's Grotesqueries," *Hudson Review* 23, no. 3 (Autumn 1970): 510–21, at 516.
133 Ibid., 518–19.
134 Thirty years later, in 1999, on the occasion of Grotowski's death, Gilman soberly admitted that he had lost "sight of [Grotowski], and lost interest in his ideas when he became cultish and prematurely New Agish" (quoted in Holger Teschke, "Jerzy Grotowski, 1933–1999," *Theater* 29, no. 2 (1999): 4–15, at 9).
135 In the USA, responding to Gilman, John Simon sarcastically notes: "Pure at what? And all this from a critic who does not even speak Polish, a language of which Grotowski occasionally does make some sort of use" (Simon, "Grotowski's Grotesqueries," 519–20).
136 Martin Harries, *Forgetting Lot's Wife: On Destructive Spectatorship* (New York: Fordham University Press 2007), 24.
137 Michał Masłowski, "Od obrzędu żałobnego do świeckiej mszy" [From Funeral Rite to Secular Mass], *Performer* 1 (2009) <http://www.grotowski.net/performer/performer-1/od-obrzedu-zalobnego-do-swieckiej-mszy> (accessed 3 January 2010).
138 Puzyna, "Grotowski and Polish Romantic Drama," 44–50, at 46.
139 Ibid., 47.
140 Kosiński, *Grotowski: Przewodnik* [Grotowski: A Handbook], 142.
141 Konstantyn Puzyna, "Grotowski and Polish Romantic Drama," trans. Jacob Conrad, *Theatre Three* 4 (Spring 1988): 44–50, at 47.
142 Ciotka Agnieszka, "List do p. Falkowskiego" [Letter to Mr. Falkowski], *Trybuna Opolska*, 28 October 1962. Grotowski Institute Archives.
143 Ibid.
144 From notes found in the Grotowski Institute Archives.
145 Zbigniew Osiński, *Teatr Dionizosa. Romantyzm w polskim teatrze wpółczesnym* [Dionysian Theatre: Romanticism in Polish Contemporary Theatre] (Cracow: Wydawnictwo Literackie 1972), 181.
146 From notes found in the Grotowski Institute Archives.
147 Quoted in Temkine, *Grotowski*, 27.
148 C. van Hoboken, "Is Jerzy Grotowsky a Genie or a Charlatan?" *Trouw. Amsterdam*, 30 June 1967. Grotowski Institute Archives.
149 Ludwik Flaszen, "Teatr Laboratorium za granicą" [The Laboratory Theatre Abroad], *Odra* 2 (1969). Grotowski Institute Archives.
150 Temkine, *Grotowski*, 33.
151 Louis Calta, "Polish Theater Is Coming Here: Jerzy Grotowski Troupe's U.S. Debut Due in October," *New York Times*, 10 September 1969, 36.
152 Sam Zolotow, "Protest Over Ban by U.S.," *New York Times*, 14 September 1968, 34. Others who signed the letter include Anthony Abeson, Robert Anderson, Joseph Anthony, James Baldwin, Richard Barr, Julian Beck, Herbert Berghof, Kermit Bloomgarden, Robert Brustein, Joseph Chaikin, Harold Clurman, Toby Cole, Christine Conrad, Francis Fergusson, Zelda Fichhandler, H. William Fitelson, Gene Frankel, Rosamond Gilder, Richard Gillman, Martin Gottfried, Saul Gottleib, T. Edward Hambleton, Lillian Hellman, Theodore Hoffman, John Houseman, Kim Hunter, Fred Jordan, Allan Kaprow, Ninon Tallon Karlweis, Arthur Kober, Paul Liban, Judith Malina, Theodore Mann, Sanford

Meisner, David Merrick, Arthur Miller, W. Kelly Morris, Rosemary Murphy, Mike Nichols, John O'Neal, Paul Osborne, Stuart Oster, Joseph Papp, Harold Prince, Ellis Rabb, Oliver Rea, Larry Rivers, Jerome Robbins, Gordon Rogoff, Dore Schary, Richard Schechner, Alan Schneider, Neil Simon, Oliver Smith, Susan Sontag, Ellen Stewart, Megan Terry, Jean Claude van Itallie, Martha Wadsworth, Gerald Weales, Robert Whitehead, and Donald Windham (I thank my colleague Kermit Dunkelberg for sharing this list with me).

153 Mark Shivaslondon, "'I Propose Poverty in the Theater,'" *New York Times*, 22 December 1968, D5.
154 There is also an anecdotal story about a bootlegged copy of the *Constant Prince*. First, someone secretly filmed the video and then, two years later, someone else recorded the sound. The two versions matched identically, a fact that regardless of his disagreement over the recording, Grotowski was very proud of, as it proved the clockwork precision of his productions (Joanna Targoń, "O Grotowskim wielokrotnie" [About Grotowski in Many Ways], *Gazeta Wyborcza*, 14 March 2009, 6).
155 Ibid.
156 Jerzy Grotowski, quoted in Shivaslondon, "'I Propose Poverty in the Theater,'" D5.
157 Ibid.
158 Shivaslondon, "'I Propose Poverty in the Theater,'" D5.
159 *Akropolis*, stage dir. Jerzy Grotowski, film dir. James MacTaggart, prod. Lewis Freedman (New York: Arthur Cantor Films 1968). See Jack Gould's review "TV: P.B.L. Presents Polish Experimental Theater: Grotowski's 'Akropolis' Poses Challenges. Auschwitz Set Against Bible and Homer," *New York Times*, 14 January 1969, 91; John Simon's review "Does Genuine Art Require Special Pleading?" *New York Times*, 26 January 1969, D21; and the rejoinder by William Kinsolving, "Was Grotowski Too Lightly Dismissed?" *New York Times*, 23 February 1969, D21.
160 Shivaslondon, "'I Propose Poverty in the Theater,'" D5.
161 Leo Mishkin, "TV Had Something Else Besides Football Sunday," *Morning Telegraph*, 14 January 1969, 3.
162 Jack Gould, "TV: P.B.L. Presents Polish Experimental Theater: Grotowski's 'Akropolis' Poses Challenges. Auschwitz Set Against Bible and Homer," *New York Times*, 14 January 1969, 91.
163 Stanley Kauffmann, "Grotowski's Theater," *Persons of the Drama: Theater Criticism and Comment* (New York: Harper & Row 1976), 63–72, at 67–8.
164 Wetzsteon, "Theatre: Two by Grotowski," 46.
165 John Simon, "Does Genuine Art Require Special Pleading?" *New York Times*, 26 January 1969, D21.
166 John Simon, "Vaulting Pole," *New York Theatre*, 1 December 1969, 58.
167 Ibid.
168 Kinsolving, "Was Grotowski Too Lightly Dismissed?" *New York Times*, 23 February 1969, D21.
169 Ibid.
170 Ibid.
171 Many of these American artists found in Grotowski's work not just a source of inspiration but a recipe for life. This is quite ironic in light of Grotowski's own statement: "There is no art, or activity that would give one a recipe for life" ("Obok teatru" [Next to Theatre], conversation with Jerzy Grotowski and Konstantyn Puzyna on 19 December 1972, *Dialog* 7 (1973): 102).
172 Joseph Chaikin, interview with Andrzej Bonarski, in *Ziarno* (Warsaw: Czytelnik 1979), 62–83, at 82.
173 Ibid.
174 Stuart Little, "Grotowski: An Unsettled American Theatre Replies," *Saturday Review*, 7 February 1970, 31.

175 Eugenio Barba, "Dr. Faustus in Poland," *Tulane Drama Review* [later known as *The Drama Review*] 8, no. 4, Marlowe issue (Summer 1964): 120–33.
176 Henry Popkins, "Theatre in Eastern Europe," *Tulane Drama Review* [later known as *The Drama Review*] 11, no. 3 (Spring 1967): 23–51.
177 After Grotowski's tour, *TDR* also published "A Series of Critiques" and Konstanty Puzyna's description of *Apocalypsis cum Figuris*, and number of other articles.
178 Schechner, "Want to Watch? Or Act?" D1.
179 Ibid., 7.
180 Ibid.
181 Ibid.
182 Kolankiewicz, *Wielki mały wóz* [The Big Small Dipper], 290.
183 Ibid., 299.
184 Ibid. Following his death, Grotowski's friends received a letter from him, in which Grotowski decisively corrects Schechner's rather loose treatment of facts regarding his life and family, singling out *The Grotowski Sourcebook* for criticism. According to Schechner, Grotowski was compliant with the communist regime because his brother, a nuclear physicist, was "sensitive" and "exposed." Grotowski's letter was written specifically to Grotowski's Polish friends, trying to clear up what he perceived to be misrepresentations of his family and his own political viewpoints (his brother, in fact, participated in the Solidarity movement). When Grotowski's letter was published in the Polish magazine *Dialog*, Schechner asked the journal to remove what he saw as compromising passages. Leszek Kolankiewicz suggests that Schechner's misrepresentation touched Grotowski deeply because it involved his own country, and could be construed as subtly suggesting Grotowski's open collaboration with the regime. Grotowski felt compelled to denounce it even after his death. Why did Grotowski, in his last words, made that postmortem gesture towards his homeland? (Ibid., 251).
185 Schechner, "Grotowski and the Grotowskian," 7–13.
186 Kott, "Koniec teatru niemożliwego" [The End of the Impossible Theatre], 339–40.
187 The production itself, however, didn't match in ignorance some of the statements that Schechner made about Grotowski based on his "knowledge" of Poland:

> Even with Grotowski in Poland, where circumstances make direct political involvement impossible, a special kind of social mysticism has emerged – a sharp turning toward the mechanics of personal confrontation. When Grotowski tells a performer to confront himself in his role, to reject all that means nothing to him while playing out his contradictory reactions to what remains, Grotowski is introjecting the structure of confrontation politics into the interior situation of the performer. (Schechner, "Want to Watch? Or Act?" 7)

And another bit about socialism:

> The bomb, the Nuremberg and Eichmann trials, participatory democracy, and socialism (as a goal, not as it is practiced in any country today) have made salutary marks on performers. (Ibid.)

188 Robert Brustein, "New Theatre, New Politics?" *New York Times*, 25 August 1968, D1.
189 Elenore Lester, "...Or the Wave of the Future?" *New York Times*, 30 June 1968, D1.
190 Harold Clurman, quoted in Schechner, *The Grotowski Sourcebook*, 162.
191 Robert Brustein, "New Fads, Ancient Truths," *New York Times*, 17 August 1969, D1–3.
192 Mel Gussow, "Grotowski, 88 Pounds Lighter, Explains His 'Method,'" *New York Times*, 14 December 1970, 60.
193 Margaret Croyden, "The Most Avant-Garde of Them All," *New York Times*, 5 October 1969, D1.

194 Walter Benjamin, "The Work of Art in the Age of Mechanical Reproduction" (1935); reprinted in *Illuminations*, trans. Harry Zohn (New York: Random House 1988), 211.
195 Ibid.
196 Ibid., 223–4.
197 Ibid., 229.
198 *Variety*, 29 October 1969.
199 Barnes, "Theatre: Grotowski's View of Reality," 36.
200 "Polish Group Shifts Opening to Church," *New York Times*, 15 October 1969, 36.
201 Robert Findlay, "Grotowski's *Akropolis*: A Retrospective View," *Modern Drama* 27, no. 1 (March 1984): 1–20, at 1.
202 Reviewing the play for the *Los Angeles Times*, Sandra Schmidt describes a similar experience: "All the pews are gone and the audience, the 75 or 80 of us, are on benches, on high scaffolds, resting our chins on the chin-level railing and staring down into a wooden-sided pit, like a very-much-shrunken rectangular bull ring (or, as the program says, a circus arena or an operating room)." (Sandra Schmidt, "Polish Theatre Lab in American Debut," *Los Angeles Times*, 20 October 1969, C23)
203 Little, "Grotowski: An Unsettled American Theatre Replies," 30.
204 Barnes, "Theatre: Grotowski's View of Reality," 36.
205 Eric Bentley, "Dear Grotowski: An Open Letter from Eric Bentley," *New York Times*, 30 November 1969, D1.
206 Simon, "Grotowski's Grotesqueries," 520.
207 Leonard Lyons, "The Lyons Den," *New York Post*, 23 October 1969, 51.
208 Richard Coe, "Either a Cruel Game or a Surgical Operation," *Washington Post*, 2 November 1969, E3.
209 Bentley, "Dear Grotowski," D1.
210 Coe, "Either a Cruel Game or a Surgical Operation," E3.
211 Croyden, "The Most Avant-Garde of Them All," D1.
212 James Roose-Evans, quoted in Simon, "Grotowski's Grotesqueries," 520.
213 Simon, "Grotowski's Grotesqueries," 521.
214 Simon, "Vauling Pole," 58.
215 Little, "Grotowski: An Unsettled American Theatre Replies," 30–31.
216 Barnes, "Theatre: Grotowski's View of Reality," 36.
217 Ibid.
218 Ibid.
219 Grotowski, *Towards a Poor Theatre*, 40.
220 In the *Playboy Bunny Manual*, we read: "Men are very excited about being in the company of Elizabeth Taylor, but they know they can't paw or proposition her. The moment they felt they could become familiar with her, she would not have the aura of glamour that now surrounds her. The same must be true for our Bunnies" (Quoted in Gloria Steinem, *Outrageous Acts and Everyday Rebellion* (New York: Holt, Rinehart and Winston 1983), 40). The bunny had to be inaccessible to everyone with the exception of a select group of men, the so-called Number One Keyholders (per Steinem's report, a bunny could be fired if she refused to date the Number One Keyholder). Hefner played on both Benjamin's notion of "aura," and what Girard calls a "mimetic desire": by identification, men desire only that which they think is desired by other men. The nature of desire is structured and produced by the mechanisms of envy and accessibility. The limited accessibility was meant to raise the Bunny's market value. By making her inaccessible, Playboy made her desirable. The more desired she was by others, the greater her value as a commodity for those whom she was allowed to date.
221 Martin Gottfried, "The Polish Laboratory Theatre 'genius,'" *Vogue*, December 1969, 136.
222 Quoted in Findlay, "Grotowski's *Akropolis*: A Retrospective View," 1–20, at 1. Brook is quoted as saying: "Grotowski is unique. Why? Because no one else in the world, to my

knowledge, no one since Stanislavski, has investigated the nature of acting, its phenomenon, its meaning, the nature and science of its mental-physical-emotional processes as deeply and completely as Grotowski" (Peter Brook, *With Grotowski, Theatre Is Just a Form* (Wrocław: Grotowski Institute 2009), 9).
223 Findlay, "Grotowski's *Akropolis*: A Retrospective View," 18.
224 Martin Gottfried, "Acropolis," *Women's Wear Daily*, 5 November 1969, 63.
225 Thomas Quinn Curtiss, "Polish Theater Group Impressive in Paris," *International Herald Tribune*, 3 October 1968.
226 Findlay, "Grotowski's *Akropolis*: A Retrospective View," 2.
227 Quoted in Brook, *With Grotowski, Theatre Is Just a Form*, 14.
228 Gould, "TV: P.B.L. Presents Polish Experimental Theater," 91.
229 Gottfried, "Acropolis," 63.
230 Barnes, "Theatre: Grotowski's View of Reality," 36.
231 Clive Barnes, "Jerzy Grotowski's 'Acropolis'; 1904 Drama Is Adapted for Polish Group," *New York Times*, 5 November 1969, 40.
232 Ibid.
233 Irving Wardle, "Polish Avant-Garde Stages 'Acropolis' at Edinburgh Fete," *New York Times*, 24 August 1968, 24.
234 Harold Clurman, "Jerzy Grotowski," in *The Grotowski Sourcebook*, ed. Richard Schechner and Lisa Wolford (1997; reprint New York: Routledge 2001): 161–4, at 162. (Originally published as a chapter in Harold Clurman, *The Divine Pastime* (New York: Macmillan 1974), 221–6.
235 Stefan Brecht, "The Laboratory Theatre in New York, 1969: A Set of Critiques," *TDR: The Drama Review* 14, no. 2 (T46) (Winter 1970): 185.
236 Edith Oliver, "Off-Broadway: Grotowski," *New Yorker*, 25 October 1969, 139.
237 Filler, "Z Wrocławia w świat" [From Wrocław into the World]. Grotowski Institute Archives.
238 Bohdan Drozdowski, "Wester, Grotowski i inni" [Wester, Grotowski and the Others], *Kultura* 4 (26 January 1969). Grotowski Institute Archives.
239 Ibid.
240 Wolfe Kauffman, "Unhappy Week for Drama Critic," *Herald Tribune*, 25–26 June 1966. Grotowski Institute Archives.
241 Wardle, "Big Catch from Poland," 18.
242 Harry Harris, "PBL Offers US Premiere of Polish Director's 'Akropolis,'" *Philadelphia Inquirer*, 13 January 1969, 14.
243 Bryden, review of *Constant Prince*, by Juliusz Słowacki, directed by Jerzy Grotowski, Polish Laboratory Theatre, Washington Square Methodist Church, New York, "A Myth in Stepney," 27.
244 Sandra Schmidt, "Polish Theatre Lab in American Debut," *Los Angeles Times*, 20 October 1969, C23.
245 Lewis, "Too Few Can Attend," 7.
246 Henry Hewes, review of *Apocalypsis cum Figuris*, written and directed by Jerzy Grotowski, Polish Laboratory Theatre, Washington Square Methodist Church, New York, "A Mass Not for the Masses," *Saturday Review*, 6 December 1969, 72.
247 Harries, *Forgetting Lot's Wife*, 9.
248 Jan Kott admits that both "*Akropolis* and *The Constant Prince*, which I saw years ago in Poland, seemed to me contrived and very distant. *Apocalypsis cum figures*, which I saw in New York, struck me at once with its Polishness" (Kott, "Why Should I Take Part in the Sacred Dance?" 200).
249 Findlay, "Grotowski's *Akropolis*: A Retrospective View," 2.
250 Frank Marcus, "More than Essentials," *Sunday Telegraph*, 5 October 1969, 16.

251 Joseph Papp, quoted in Little, "Grotowski: An Unsettled American Theatre Replies," 31.
252 Michael Kustow, "*Ludens Mysterium Tremendum et Fascinosum*," *Encore*, October 1963, 11.
253 Ibid., 13.
254 Margaret Croyden, "Images that Recall the Polish Past," *New York Times*, 9 May 1982, D4.
255 Jan Wiktor, foreword to *Listy do Stanisława Lacka* [Letters to Stanisław Lack], by Stanisław Wyspiański (Cracow: Wydawnictwo Literackie 1957), 3–10, at 8.
256 Ewa Miodońska-Brookes, *Wawel – 'Akropolis.' Studium o dramacie Stanisława Wyspiańskiego* [Wawel – *Akropolis*: A Study of Wyspiański's Drama] (Cracow: Wydawnictwo Literackie 1980), 8.
257 Tomasz Raczek, "I stał się moment wielki czaru" [And the Great Moment of Magic Came], *Kultura* 14 (1978): 11.
258 Władysław Prokesch, "'Akropolis' St. Wyspiańskiego" [Stanisław Wyspiański's "Akropolis"], *Biesiada Literacka* (Warsaw) 17 (1904): 325–6, at 325.
259 Antoni Mazanowski, "Z poetyckiej niwy, re: St. Wyspiański's *Akropolis*" [From the Poetic Perspective, Re: Stanisław Wyspiański's *Akropolis*], *Przegląd Powszechny* (Cracow) 86 (1904): 79–81, at 80.
260 Ibid.
261 Miodońska-Brookes, *Wawel – 'Akropolis.' Studium o dramacie Stanisława Wyspiańskiego* [Wawel – *Akropolis*: A Study of Wyspiański's Drama], 221.
262 The story goes that in February 1905, Wyspiański applied for the position of Artistic Director of Słowacki Theatre, for which he competed with Kotarbinski, who eventually, under public pressure, withdrew his candidacy. The direction of the theatre eventually went to Solski, who received 31 votes. Wyspiański received only 2. The election sparked public outrage among Cracow's theatregoing intelligentsia, but the decision stayed in force. Under the direction of Solski, so it seems, the conflict continued, with Solski refusing any suggestions about Wyspiański's leadership role and offering him only playwriting credits, the same that were offered to other playwrights. That's Wyspiański's version, at least. Solski's account is different, though; he argues that Wyspiański was simply too sick at that time to assume any managerial position (see Jan Wiktor's foreword to *Listy do Stanisława Lacka* [Letters to Stanisław Lack]). Whatever the true story, the conflict influenced how Kotarbinski and Solski each viewed Wyspiański's new dramas.
263 See Leon Płoszewski, "Korespondencja teatralna Wyspiańskiego z mecenasem Józefem Skąpskim" [Theatrical Correspondence between Wyspiański and Józef Skąpski], *Teatr* 1 (1969).
264 Krystyna Zbijewska, "*Akropolis* po pół wieku" [*Akropolis* after Half a Century], *Dziennik Polski*, 4–5 February 1978, 7.
265 Miodońska-Brookes, *Wawel – 'Akropolis.' Studium o dramacie Stanisława Wyspiańskiego* [Wawel – *Akropolis*: A Study of Wyspiański's Drama], 223.
266 *Akropolis, Pomysł zabudowania Wawelu. Obmyśleli Stanisław Wyspiański i Władysław Ekielski w latach 1904–1907* [Akropolis: The Idea for the Reconstruction of Wawel. Designed by Stanisław Wyspiański and Władysław Ekielski in 1904–1907] (Cracow: Drukarnia Uniw. Jagielońskiego 1908).
267 Maria Prussak, *Stanisław Wyspiański w labiryncie teatru* [Stanisław Wyspiański in the Labyrinth of Theatre] (Cracow: Wydawnictwo Literackie 2005), 104; Andrzej Gaczoł, "Wawelu Wyspiański nie dostał" [Wyspiański Didn't Get Wawel], *Echo Krakowa* 104 (10–11 May 1980): 4.
268 Franciszek Pułaski, "S. Wyspiański, W. Ekielski," *Piśmiennictwo, Biblioteka Warszawska* 4 (1908): 386–8, at 388.
269 Quoted in Prussak, *Stanisław Wyspiański w labiryncie teatru* [Stanisław Wyspiański in the Labyrinth of Theatre], 103.

270 Wojciech Bałus, "Ożywianie posągów. Głosa do 'Akropolis" [Resurrecting the Statues: The Voice of *Akropolis*], in *Stanisław Wyspiański – studium artysty* [Stanisław Wyspiański – Study of an Artist], ed. Ewa Miodońska-Brookes (Cracow: Wydawnictwo Universitas 1996), 169–80, at 170.
271 Jan Nowakowski, *Wyspiański: Studia o dramatach* [Wyspiański: Study of His Dramas] (Cracow: Wydawnictwo Literackie 1972), 13.
272 Miodońska-Brookes, *Wawel - 'Akropolis.' Studium o dramacie Stanisława Wyspiańskiego* [Wawel – *Akropolis*: A Study of Wyspiański's Drama], 104.
273 Józef Mączyński, quoted in Miodońska-Brookes, *Wawel – 'Akropolis.' Studium o dramacie Stanisława Wyspiańskiego* [Wawel – *Akropolis*: A Study of Wyspiański's Drama], 18.
274 Kazimierz Kosiński, "Wawel w ideologii Wyspiańskiego. Na 30-lecie 'Akropolis' 1904–1934" [Wawel in Wyspiański's Ideology: 30th Anniversary of "Akropolis" 1904–1934], *Droga* (Warsaw, 1934): 357.
275 Wawel Royal Castle, <http://www.wawel.krakow.pl/en/> (accessed 15 January 2011).
276 Kosiński, "Wawel w ideologii Wyspiańskiego" [Wawel in Wyspiański's Ideology], 359.
277 Prussak, *Stanisław Wyspiański w labiryncie teatru* [Stanisław Wyspiański in the Labyrinth of Theatre], 105.
278 Ibid.
279 Jan Błoński, "Grotowski and His Laboratory Theatre," *Dialog* 15 (1970): 142–50, at 144. Special issue.
280 Gerould, "Jerzy Grotowski's Theatrical and Paratheatrical Activities," 381.
281 Tymon Terlecki, *Stanisław Wyspiański* (Boston: Twayne 1983), 109.
282 Aniela Łempicka, *Wyspiański pisarz dramatyczny. Idee i formy* [Wyspiański the Dramatist: Ideas and Forms] (Cracow: Wydawnictwo Literackie 1973).
283 Miodońska-Brookes, *Wawel – 'Akropolis.' Studium o dramacie Stanisława Wyspiańskiego* [Wawel – *Akropolis*: A Study of Wyspiański's Drama], 7.
284 Mazanowski, "Z poetyckiej niwy, re: St. Wyspiański's *Akropolis*" [From the Poetic Perspective, Re: Stanisław Wyspiański's *Akropolis*], 79–81, at 81.
285 Ibid., 79.
286 Ibid., 81.
287 Elżbieta Kalemba-Kasprzak, "Akropolis – dwie teatralne wizje Europy" [Akropolis: Two Theatrical Visions of Europe], in *Studia o dramacie i teatrze Stanisława Wyspiańskiego* [Study of the Drama and Theatre of Stanisław Wyspiański], ed. Jan Błoński and Jacek Popiela (Cracow: Wydawnictwo Baran i Suszczyński 1994), 209–26, at 212–13.
288 Jan Stena, quoted in Miodońska-Brookes, *Wawel – 'Akropolis.' Studium o dramacie Stanisława Wyspiańskiego* [Wawel – *Akropolis*: A Study of Wyspiański's Drama], 80.
289 Karol Homolacs, "Wyspiański Plastyk-Poeta" [Wyspiański: Painter-Poet], *Gazeta Literacka* (Cracow) 3 (1932–33): 41.
290 Wacław J. Tkaczuk, "Wyspiański w blasku i cieniu. Rozmowa z Wojciechem Natansonem" [Wyspiański in the Light and Shadows: Conversation with Wojciech Natanson], *Za i Przeciw* 14 (6 April 1969). Grotowski Institute Archives.
291 Puzyna, "Grotowski and Polish Romantic Drama," 46.
292 Terlecki, *Stanisław Wyspiański*, 115.
293 Ibid.
294 Nina Taylor, "Stanisław Wyspiański and Symbolist Drama: The Work of Art as 'dramatis persona,'" *Slavonic and East European Review* 66, no. 2 (April 1988): 198–209, at 198.
295 Tymon Terlecki, "Stanisław Wyspiański and the Poetics of Symbolist Drama," *Polish Review* 15, no. 4 (Autumn 1970): 55–63, at 56–7.
296 Likewise, Kantor's own concept of the "autonomous work of art" derives as much from Wyspiański as it does from Gordon Craig. *Dead Class*, in fact, was an autonomous work of art par excellence and was often subtitled as such.

297 Miodońska-Brookes, *Wawel – 'Akropolis.' Studium o dramacie Stanisława Wyspiańskiego* [Wawel – Akropolis: A Study of Wyspiański's Drama], 13.
298 Ibid., 13.
299 Kosiński, "Wawel w ideologii Wyspiańskiego" [Wawel in Wyspiański's Ideology], 348.
300 Findlay, "Grotowski's *Akropolis*: A Retrospective View," 1–20, at 2.
301 Kosiński, "Wawel w ideologii Wyspiańskiego" [Wawel in Wyspiański's Ideology], 349.
302 Taylor, "Stanisław Wyspiański and Symbolist Drama," 204.
303 Stanisław Wyspiański, *Akropolis* (Cracow: Jagiellonian University Press, Skład w księgarni Gebethnera 1904), act 1, lines 1–19.
304 Ibid., act 1, lines 110–18.
305 Taylor, "Stanisław Wyspiański and Symbolist Drama," 204.
306 Wyspiańki, *Akropolis*, act 1, lines 220–25.
307 Kalemba-Kasprzak, "Akropolis – dwie teatralne wizje Europy" [Akropolis: Two Theatrical Visions of Europe], 209–26, at 215.
308 Lu Ter, "Na marginesie inscenizacji krakowskiej: S. Wyspiański: Akropolis" [On the Margins of Cracow's Production of St. Wyspiański's "Akropolis"], *Comoedia* (Warsaw) 2 (1927).
309 Terlecki, *Stanisław Wyspiański*, 112.
310 Ibid.
311 Taylor, "Stanisław Wyspiański and Symbolist Drama," 205.
312 Terlecki, *Stanisław Wyspiański*, 112.
313 Ludwik Flaszen, "Wyspianski's *Akropolis*," in *The Grotowski Sourcebook*, 64–72, at 64. (Originally published as Ludwik Flaszen, "A Theatre of Magic and Sacrilege," *TDR: The Drama Review* 9, no. 3 (1965): 172–89.)
314 Raczek, "I stał się moment wielki czaru" [And the Great Moment of Magic Came], 11.
315 Wyspiańki, *Akropolis*, act 1, lines 606–13.
316 Halina Filipkowska, *Wśród Bogów i Bohaterów* [Among the Gods and Heroes] (Warsaw: Państwowy Instytut Wydawniczy 1973), 41.
317 Juliusz Kleiner, "Tragizm dwoistego oblicza czynu w 'Edypie królu'" [The Tragedy of the Dual Nature of One's Act in "Oedipus Rex"], in *W kręgu Mickiewicza i Goethego*, ed. Juliusz Kleiner (Warsaw: Wydawnictwo Rój 1938), 162.
318 Stanisław Brzozowski, quoted in Elżbieta Morawiec, "Nasze 'Akropolis'" [Our *Akropolis*], *Życie Literackie* 12 (1978): 7.
319 Bałus, "Ożywianie posągów" [Resurrecting the Statues], 169–80, at 179.
320 Wyspiański, *Akropolis*, act 2, scene 4, page 75.
321 Terlecki, *Stanisław Wyspiański*, 112.
322 Mazanowski, "Z poetyckiej niwy, re: St. Wyspiański's *Akropolis*" [From the Poetic Perspective, Re: Stanisław Wyspiański's *Akropolis*], 79.
323 Władysław Zawistowski, "Stanisław Wyspiański poetą naszego pokolenia" [Stanisław Wyspiański: Poet of Our Generation], in *Wyspiańskiemu Teatr Krakowski* [For Wyspiański from Cracow's Theatre] (Cracow: Zakłady Graficzne "Styl" 1932), 7–11, at 10.
324 Terlecki, *Stanisław Wyspiański*, 113.
325 Kalemba-Kasprzak, "Akropolis – dwie teatralne wizje Europy" [Akropolis: Two Theatrical Visions of Europe], 214.
326 Tadeusz Sinko, "O greckich tragedjach Wyspiańskiego" [About Wyspiański's Greek Tragedies], in *Wyspiańskiemu Teatr Krakowski* [For Wyspiański from Cracow's Theatre] (Cracow: Zakłady Graficzne "Styl" 1932), 40–44, at 40–42.
327 Józef Kretz-Mirski, *Akropolis, jako dramat świadomości narodowej* ["Akropolis" as the Drama of National Consciousness] (Krosno: W. Lenik 1910).
328 Józef Kretz-Mirski, "'Akropolis' Wyspiańskiego a Biblia" [Wyspiański's "Akropolis" *vis-à-vis* the Bible], *Przegląd Warszawski* 4, no. 33 (1924): 413–14.

329 Terlecki, *Stanisław Wyspiański*, 113.
330 Maria Stobrecka, *Trzy dramaty Wyspiańskiego. Wesele – Wyzwolenie – Akropolis* [Three Plays of Wyspiański: *The Wedding, Liberation, Akropolis*], unpublished manuscript at Wojewódzka i Miejska Biblioteka Publiczna in Cracow, 29.
331 Miodońska-Brookes, *Wawel – 'Akropolis.' Studium o dramacie Stanisława Wyspiańskiego* [Wawel – Akropolis: A Study of Wyspiański's Drama], 8.
332 Mazanowski, "Z poetyckiej niwy, re: St. Wyspiański's *Akropolis*" [From the Poetic Perspective, Re: Stanisław Wyspiański's *Akropolis*], 80.
333 Jozef Rachwał, *Akropolis Stanisława Wyspiańskiego: źródła i ideologia* [Stanisław Wyspiański's *Akropolis*: Origins and Ideology] (Tarnów: Nakładem Księgarni Zygmunta Jelenia 1926), 24.
334 Bałus, "Ożywianie posągów" [Resurrecting the Statues], 171.
335 Ibid., 217.
336 Wyspiański, *Akropolis*, act 4, pages 159–60.
337 Terlecki, *Stanisław Wyspiański*, 111.
338 Ibid.
339 Rachwał, *Akropolis Stanisława Wyspiańskiego* [Stanisław Wyspiański's "Akropolis"], 44.
340 Władysław Prokesch, "'Akropolis' St. Wyspiańskiego" [Stanisław Wyspiański's "Akropolis"], *Biesiada Literacka* (Warsaw) 17 (1904): 325–6, at 326.
341 Elżbieta Morawiec, "Nasze 'Akropolis'" [Our *Akropolis*], *Życie Literackie* 12 (1978): 7.
342 Jerzy Bober, "Inny Wyspiański" [Another Wyspiański], *Gazeta Południowa*, 18–19 February 1978, 6.
343 Maciej Szybist, "Akropolis," *Echo Krakowa* 45 (24 February 1978): 2.
344 Marta Fik, "Wizje na Wawelu" [Visions at the Wawel], *Polityka* 9 (1978): 23.
345 Krzysztof Pleśniarowicz, "W kręgu pewnej przypowieści" [In the Realm of a Story], *Dziennik Polski*, 24–25 March 1978, 6.
346 Roman Taborski, *Dramaty Stanisława Wyspiańskiego na scenie do 1939 roku* [Stanisław Wyspiański's Dramas on the Stage to 1939] (Warsaw: Semper 1994), 121.
347 Miodońska-Brookes, *Wawel – 'Akropolis.' Studium o dramacie Stanisława Wyspiańskiego* [Wawel – Akropolis: A Study of Wyspiański's Drama], 219.
348 Ibid., 230.
349 Leon Schiller, quoted in Jan Paweł Gawlik, "'Akropolis' 1962," in *Mysterium zgrozy i urzeczenia: Przedstawienia Jerzego Grotowskiego i Teatru Laboratorium* [Mysterium of Horror and Allure: Productions of Jerzy Grotowski and Teatr Laboratorium], ed. Janusz Degler and Grzegorz Ziółkowski (Wrocław: Ośrodek Badań Twórczości Jerzego Grotowskiego i Poszukiwań Teatralno-Kulturowych 2006), 167–70, at 168. "'Akropolis' 1962" was originally published in 1962.
350 Miodońska-Brookes, *Wawel – 'Akropolis.' Studium o dramacie Stanisława Wyspiańskiego* [Wawel – Akropolis: A Study of Wyspiański's Drama], 239.
351 Zbigniew Osiński, "'Akropolis' w Teatrze Laboratorium" [*Akropolis* at the Teatr Laboratorium], in *Mysterium zgrozy i urzeczenia: Przedstawienia Jerzego Grotowskiego i Teatru Laboratorium* [Mysterium of Horror and Allure: Productions of Jerzy Grotowski and Teatr Laboratorium], 300–34, at 301.
352 Taborski, *Dramaty Stanisława Wyspiańskiego na scenie do 1939 roku* [Stanisław Wyspiański's Dramas on the Stage to 1939], 124.
353 Kalemba-Kasprzak, "Akropolis – dwie teatralne wizje Europy" [Akropolis: Two Theatrical Visions of Europe], 209–26, at 210.
354 It is interesting that in the production notes to Kotlarczyk's production, under the history of the production, there is no mention of Grotowski's 1962 version. See Osiński, "'Akropolis' w Teatrze Laboratorium," 302.
355 Ibid.
356 Bober, "Inny Wyspiański" [Another Wyspiański], 6.

357 For the full history of the staging of *Akropolis*, see Stanisław Dąbrowski's *Sceniczne dzieje 'Akropolis,' 'Nasza Scena'* [Production History: *Akropolis*, Our Stage] (Łódź: Teatr Nowy, No. 4 1960).
358 Richard Schechner, introduction to *The Grotowski Sourcebook*, 23–7, at 25.
359 Józef Kelera, *Grotowski wielokrotnie* [Grotowski Many Times] (Wrocław: Ośrodek Badań Twórczości Jerzego Grotowskiego i Poszukiwań Teatralno-Kulturowych 1999), 92.
360 Osiński, "'Akropolis' w Teatrze Laboratorium" [*Akropolis* at the Teatr Laboratorium], 301.
361 Dariusz Kosiński cites an anecdote about the apparently random evolution of the show, often veiled in elaborate theoretical divagations: "In the first version, Rachel and Helen were played by Ewa Lubowiecka, later by Maja Komorowska (the only one of Grotowski's actresses who eventually had commercial success). When in 1962 Maja Komorowska left the troupe for a few months, her part was played by Maciej Prus. Hence the love dialogue between Paris and Helen was now taking place between two male actors. Many years later Prus joked that Grotowski would add a theoretical and exotic explanation for this scene, which was accidental" (Kosiński, *Grotowski: Przewodnik* [Grotowski: A Handbook], 152).
362 Puzyna, "Grotowski and Polish Romantic Drama," 49.
363 Zbijewska, "'Akropolis' po pół wieku" ["Akropolis" after Half a Century], 7.
364 Ludwik Flaszen, "*Akropolis*. Komentarz do przedstawienia" [*Akropolis*: Program Notes], in *Mysterium zgrozy i urzeczenia: Przedstawienia Jerzego Grotowskiego i Teatru Laboratorium* [Mysterium of Horror and Enchantment: Productions of Jerzy Grotowski and Teatr Laboratorium], 51. Flaszen's program notes were originally published in 1962.
365 Konstantyn Puzyna, *Półmrok* [Twilight] (Warsaw: Wydawnictwo PAN 1982), 135.
366 Tadeusz Kudliński, "Ofensywa Grotowskiego'" [Grotowski's Offensive], *Dziennik Polski*, 5 April 1962; reprinted in *Akropolis*, program notes, October 1962. Grotowski Institute Archives.
367 Findlay, "Grotowski's *Akropolis*: A Retrospective View," 1–20, at 4–5.
368 Croyden, "The Most Avant-Garde of Them All," D1.
369 Ludwik Flaszen, "Po awangardzie" [After Avant-Garde], *Odra* 4 (1967): 39–42.
370 Masłowski, "Od obrzędu żałobnego do świeckiej mszy" [From Funeral Rite to Secular Mass].
371 Mateusz Lipko, "Całkowitość doświadczenia według Jerzego Grotowskiego. Problem ujęty w kotekście idei samozbawienia" [Total Act According to Jerzy Grotowki, Analyzed in the Context of the Self-Salvation], lecture at Jagiellonian University conference "*Via Negativa*. Wobec Grotowskiego – krytyczne interpretacje" [*Via Negativa*: Vis-à-vis Grotowski – Critical Interpretations], Cracow, 2009.
372 Miodońska-Brookes, *Wawel – 'Akropolis.' Studium o dramacie Stanisława Wyspiańskiego* [Wawel – *Akropolis*: A Study of Wyspiański's Drama], 251.
373 Konstantyn Puzyna, *Syntezy za trzy grosze* [Three-Penny Synthesis] (Warsaw: Wydawnictwo PAN 1974), 185–6.
374 Jan Paweł Gawlik, "'Akropolis' 1961" (1962), reprinted in *Mysterium zgrozy i urzeczenia: Przedstawienia Jerzego Grotowskiego i Teatru Laboratorium* [Mysterium of Horror and Allure: Productions of Jerzy Grotowski and Teatr Laboratorium], 167.
375 M. Jagorzewski, "Wyspiański w 'Teatrze 13 Rzędów'" [Wyspiański at the Theatre of 13 Rows], *Dziennik Łódzki*, 20 February 1963. Grotowski Institute Archives.
376 Jerzy Grotowski, quoted in Richard Schechner and Theodore Hoffman, "Interview with Grotowski," in *The Grotowski Sourcebook*, 38–55, at 49.
377 Ibid.
378 Mark Fortier, *Theory/Theatre: An Introduction* (London: Routledge 1997), 77.
379 Jean Améry, *At the Mind's Limits: Contemplations by a Survivor on Auschwitz and Its Realities* (Bloomington: Indiana University Press 1980), vii.

380 Jerzy Grotowski, quoted in "'If I Said Yes to the Past': An Interview with Grotowski," 41–2.
381 Temkine, *Grotowski*, 35.
382 Jerzy Panasewicz, "7 dni w teatrze" [Seven Days in Theatre], *Express Ilustrowany*, 2–3 March 1963. Grotowski Institute Archives.
383 Wodecka, "Grotowski zawsze był sam" [Grotowski Was Always Alone: A Conversation with Ewa Lubowiecka], 6.
384 Grotowski considered his adaptation of *Studium* a failed project, and he did not include it in his list of accomplishments (Eugenio Barba, *Ziemia popiołu i diamentów* [*The Land of Ashes and Diamonds*] (Wrocław: Ośrodek Badań Twórczości Jerzego Grotowskiego i Poszukiwań Teatralno-Kulturowych 2001), 108.
385 Zygmunt Molik, quoted in Agnieszka Wójtowicz, "Próba leczenia postawy romantycznej za pomocą postawy romantycznej (Grotowski i narodowe mity)" [An Attempt to Cure Romantic Attitude with Romantic Attitude (Grotowski and the National Myths)], in Dariusz Kosiński, *Tradycja romantyczna w teatrze polskim* [Romantic Tradition in Polish Theatre] (Cracow: Towarzystwo Naukowe Societas Vistulana 2007), 192.
386 Wójtowicz, "Próba leczenia postawy romantycznej za pomocą postawy romantycznej" [An Attempt to Cure Romantic Attitude With Romantic Attitude], 192.
387 Zbigniew Osiński and Tadeusz Burzyński, *Laboratorium Grotowskiego* [Grotowski's Laboratory] (Warsaw: Wydawnictwo Interpress 1978), 25.
388 Andrzej Wirth, "A Discovery of Tragedy: The Incomplete Account of Tadeusz Borowski," *Polish Review* 12, no. 3 (Summer 1976): 43–52, at 43.
389 Tadeusz Borowski, "Pieśń" [Song], in *Wspomnienia, Wiersze, Opowiadania* [Essays, Poems, Short Stories], 4th ed. (Warsaw: Państwowy Instytut Wydawniczy 1981), 25–6.
390 For more information, see Marcel Cornis-Pope and John Neubauer, *History of the Literary Cultures of East-Central Europe* (Amsterdam: John Benjamins 2004).
391 In 1970, Janusz Morgenstern directed a TV series of the same title, for which Bratny wrote the screenplay. The series, starring all the greatest actors of Polish film of that time, was a great success.
392 The best example of Soviet propaganda is the Auschwitz museum. Starting in 1949, the camp was used as a propaganda tool in the Soviet fight for peace and against Anglo-American imperialism.
393 See Eric L. Santner, *Stranded Objects: Mourning, Memory, and Film in Postwar Germany* (Ithaca, NY: Cornell University Press 1990).
394 Wodecka, "Grotowski zawsze był sam" [Grotowski Was Always Alone: A Conversation with Ewa Lubowiecka], 6.
395 Jerzy Grotowski, quoted in Schechner and Hoffman, "Interview with Grotowski," 38–55, at 53.
396 Ibid., 54.
397 Harold Clurman, "Jerzy Grotowski," *The Grotowski Sourcebook*, 159–4, at 160. (Originally published as a chapter titled "Jerzy Grotowski" in *The Divine Pastime* by Harold Clurman (New York: Macmillam 1974), 221–6.)
398 Temkine, *Grotowski*, 35.
399 Bogdan Bąk, "'Akropolis' z laboratorium" ["Akropolis" from the Laboratory], *Słowo Polskie* 277 (1963): 3.
400 Holger Teschke, "Jerzy Grotowski, 1933–1999," *Theater* 29, no. 2 (1999): 4–15, at 4.
401 Tadeusz Borowski, *U nas w Auschwitzu* [At Our Auschwitz] (Warsaw: Państwowy Instytut Wydawniczy PIW 1971), 83–4. English version: Tadeusz Borowski, *This Way for the Gas, Ladies and Gentlemen*, ed. and trans. Barbara Vedder (New York: Penguin 1992), 131–2.
402 Ibid., 55. In a letter to a friend, Borowski wrote something very similar:

> Do you remember how I used to like Plato? Today I know he was lying. Earthly matters do not reflect ideals. It was us who build the pyramids, tore down the marble

for churches and cathedrals, stones for the imperial roads; it was us who rowed at the galleys and pulled the ploughs, while they wrote dialogues and dramas, justified their intrigues, fought for democracy and borders. We were dirty and dying for real. They were the aesthetes who led make-believe discussions. (Quoted in Bogdan Wojdowski, "Borowski haftling," *Współczesność* 13, no. 119 (1–15 July 1961): 3)

403 Ibid., 116. DAW is the abbreviation for Deutsche Ausrüstungswerke (German Equipment Works), the Auschwitz-based company that used prison labor. It was divided into metalworking and woodworking shops, where a reported 600 prisoners in 1942 worked to make wood and metal products for Auschwitz-Birkenau and the SS staff. FKL is the abbreviation for the Das Frauenkonzentrationslager (women's concentration camp).
404 Ibid., 112.
405 Others that set the conceptual framework for Grotowski's plays include Borowski's *Kamienny Świat* [The World Made of Stone] and *Pożegnanie z Marią* [Farewell to Maria], translated into French by Laurence Dyèvre and Eric Veaux as *Le Monde de pierre* and *L'Adieu à Maria*, which were both first published in 1964 (reprinted by Christian Bourgois in 2002). Veaux visited Teatr 13 Rzędów in 1963, when Grotowski was working on *Akropolis*, and it was this experience that inspired him to translate Borowski's stories.
406 Jerzy Grotowski, quoted in Schechner and Hoffman, "Interview with Grotowski," 50.
407 Hołuj's *Puste pole* [Empty Field] was first staged at Teatr Polski (Polish Theatre) in Warsaw in 1948, as *Dom pod Oświęcimiem* [The House near Auschwitz].
408 August Grodzicki, *Reżyserzy polskiego teatru* [Polish Theatre Directors] (Warsaw: Wydawnictwo Interpress 1979), 159.
409 Ibid., 155.
410 Zbigniew Osiński, *Jerzy Grotowski: Źródła, inspiracje, konteksty* [Jerzy Grotowski: Origins, Inspirations, Contexts] (Gdańsk: Słowo/Obraz Terytoria 1998), 135.
411 Józef Szajna, "List do Redakcji. Grotowski: Teatr Laboratorium" [Letter to the Editor: Grotowski: Laboratory Theatre], *Polityka* 7 (1968): 1.
412 Temkine, *Grotowski*, 125.
413 Gawlik, "'Akropolis' 1961," 168. The Polish edition of Borowski's *This Way for the Gas, Ladies and Gentlemen* had a detail from *Bird's Hell*, a work by the German expressionist painter Max Beckmann, on its cover.
414 Émile Copermann, "Une métaphysique obscure" [An Obscure Metaphysics], *Les Lettres Francaises*, 9 October 1968, 17. In 1968, Émile Copermann wrote a long review of the play, which was shown in Paris by pure accident. Grotowski with his Teatr 13 Rzędów was on his way to America when Russian tanks entered Czechoslovakia. The group was refused American visas, and French manager Antoine Bourseiller, who was planning to organize a few performances of the group at a later time, decided to add a few additional shows at L'Epée de Bois theatre. So, *Lettres Francaises* concludes, "thanks to the invasion of Czechoslovakia, Paris was able to discover Grotowski's *Akropolis*" (ibid., 20).
415 Osiński, *Teatr Dionizosa* [Dionysian Theatre], 181.
416 Raymonde Temkine, *Grotowski*, translated from French by Alex Szogyi (New York: Avon Books 1972), 125.
417 Harold Clurman, quoted in *The Grotowski Sourcebook*, ed. Richard Schechner and Lisa Wolford (1997; reprint New York: Routledge 2001): 161–4, at 163.
418 Croyden, "The Most Avant-Garde of Them All," D1.
419 Jerzy Grotowski, quoted in Schechner and Hoffman, "Interview with Grotowski," 51.
420 In contemporary drama, the structure that most closely parallels Grotowski's approach is Peter Weiss' 1964 *Marat/Sade*, in which the prisoners of the 1808 mental hospital in Charenton near Paris reenact the assassination of Marat, one of the French Revolution's bloodiest leaders. The play within the play is written by the Marquis de Sade, who at

that time was one of the inmates at Charenton. Perhaps it is no coincidence that *Marat/Sade* was first performed in West Berlin in 1964 under the direction of Konrad Swinarski (1929–1975), a Polish theatre director who worked and studied at Brecht's Berliner Ensemble during the years 1955–7.
421 Jerzy Grotowski, quoted in Schechner and Hoffman, "Interview with Grotowski," 50.
422 Borowski, *This Way for the Gas, Ladies and Gentlemen*, 31–2.
423 In *Dead Class*, Kantor's actors too break into Hebrew prayers and wailings. The pile of dusty books (prayers books?) is moved from one side to the other like a useless pile of junk.
424 Bruno Bettelheim, "Individual and Mass Behavior in Extreme Situations," *Journal of Abnormal and Social Psychology* 38 (1943): 446.
425 Ibid., 422.
426 Panasewicz, "7 dni w teatrze" [Seven Days in Theatre].
427 Kalemba-Kasprzak, "Akropolis – dwie teatralne wizje Europy" [Akropolis: Two Theatrical Visions of Europe], 209–26, at 214–15.
428 Lisa Wolford, *Grotowski's Objective Drama Research* (Jackson: University Press of Mississippi 1996), 198.
429 Ludwik Flaszen, quoted in Jennifer Kumiega, *The Theatre of Grotowski* (London: Methuen 1985), 59.
430 Kalemba-Kasprzak, "Akropolis – dwie teatralne wizje Europy" [Akropolis: Two Theatrical Visions of Europe], 221–2. Lisa Wolford points out that "a feminist critic might construct an interesting analysis of *Akropolis*, in which female characters were represented by male actors and inanimate objects (the biblical Rachel signified by a stovepipe), but male characters were consistently embodied by men" (Wolford, *Grotowski's Objective Drama Research*, 198–9).
431 Fortier, *Theory/Theatre: An Introduction*, 77.
432 Jerzy Grotowski, quoted in Schechner and Hoffman, "Interview with Grotowski," 49–50.
433 Bettelheim, "Individual and Mass Behavior in Extreme Situations," 429.
434 Czesław Miłosz, *Zniewolony umysł* [*The Captive Mind*] (1953; Warsaw: Logos 1981).
435 Adolf Rudnicki describes Borowski's change of heart:

> [Borowski] goes to Berlin as a friend of the West and an enemy of socialist realism and everything that is happening in Poland. Two years later he returns a confirmed supporter of social realism and an enemy of the West […] his instinctive love of contradiction was revised the moment he came in contact with a different political system. In attacking what he found to be the pattern of life in the West, he rediscovered the meaning of all the things in Poland which before he could not stomach and had regarded as perverse. In the days when broadcasts from the West were estimating the numbers of people going over to the West in tens of thousands, Borowski returned home and urged the necessity of subordinating literature to the nobler things then coming into being. Moreover, to all appearances, he seemed to be acting according to his conscience, and then that sudden death! Death or suicide? (Quoted in Wirth, "A Discovery of Tragedy: The Incomplete Account of Tadeusz Borowski," 43–52, at 44)

436 Bogdan Wojdowski, "Borowski häftling," *Współczesność* 13, no. 119 (1–15 July 1961): 3.
437 Perhaps closest in style to Borowski is Jean Améry, who in his own memoir famously wrote: "…one was hardly concerned with whether, or *that*, one had to die, but only with *how* it would happen. Inmates carried on conversations about how long it probably takes for the gas in the gas chamber to do its job" (Améry, *At the Mind's Limits*, 17).
438 Temkine, *Grotowski*, 123.
439 Wirth, "A Discovery of Tragedy: The Incomplete Account of Tadeusz Borowski," 49.
440 Wojdowski, "Borowski häftling," 3.
441 Ibid., 44.

442 Wirth, "A Discovery of Tragedy: The Incomplete Account of Tadeusz Borowski," 44.
443 Ibid., 49.
444 Tadeusz Borowski, "Alicja w Krainie Czarów" [Alice in Wonderland], *Pokolenie* 1 (12 January 1947): 9, quote reprinted in Jan Kott's "Introduction" to Borowski, *This Way for the Gas, Ladies and Gentlemen*, introduction trans. by Michael Kandel, 11–28, at 22.
445 In one of the short stories, "January Offensive," Borowski writes:

> [I]n this war morality, national solidarity, patriotism and the ideals of freedom, justice and human dignity had all slid off man like a rotten rag. We said that there is no crime that a man will not commit in order to save himself. And having saved himself, he will commit crimes for increasingly trivial reasons; he will commit them first out of duty, then from habit, and finally – for pleasure. […] The world is ruled by neither justice nor morality; crime is not punished nor virtue rewarded, one is forgotten as quickly as the other. The world is ruled by power and power is obtained with money. To work is senseless, because money cannot be obtained through work but through exploitation of others. (Tadeusz Borowski, "January Offensive," in *This Way for the Gas, Ladies and Gentlemen*, 167–73, at 168)

446 Wirth, "A Discovery of Tragedy: The Incomplete Account of Tadeusz Borowski," 50.
447 Ibid.
448 Irving Howe, "Writing and the Holocaust," *New Republic*, 27 October 1986, 27–39, at 27.
449 Ibid.
450 Jan Kott, introduction to *This Way for the Gas, Ladies and Gentlemen*, by Tadeusz Borowski, introduction trans. Michael Kandel, 24.
451 Wirth, "A Discovery of Tragedy: The Incomplete Account of Tadeusz Borowski," 49.
452 Wojdowski, "Borowski häftling," 3.
453 Wirth, "A Discovery of Tragedy: The Incomplete Account of Tadeusz Borowski," 45.
454 Jerzy Grotowski, quoted in "I Said Yes to the Past," 41–2.
455 Theodore W. Adorno, "Cultural Criticism and Society," in *Prisms*, trans. Samuel and Shierry Weber (Cambridge, MA: MIT Press 1967), 17–34, at 19.
456 Améry, *At the Mind's Limits*, 16.
457 Hayden White, "Historical Emplotment and the Problem of Truth," in *Probing the Limits of Representation: Nazism and the "Final Solution,"* ed. Saul Friedlander (Cambridge, MA: Harvard University Press 1992), 37–53, at 43.
458 Claude Lanzmann, "The Obscenity of Understanding: An Evening with Claude Lanzmann," in *Trauma, Explorations in Memory*, ed. Cathy Caruth (Baltimore: John Hopkins University Press 1995), 200–20, at 204.
459 Michael Andre Bernstein, *Foregone Conclusions: Against Apocalyptic History* (Berkeley: University of California Press 1994), 89–94.
460 Ibid.
461 During the years following World War II, there was a big public debate in the Polish press about what to do with the site. Jerzy Putrament, a communist author and active Party member (portrayed as "Gamma" in Miłosz's *Captive Mind*), proposed that the place be leveled. Though never seriously considered, Putrament's idea gained some support from those who wanted to forget the Holocaust and start anew.
462 Jerzy Grotowski, quoted in Schechner and Hoffman, "Interview with Grotowski," 38–55, at 49.
463 Ibid.
464 Ibid.
465 Findlay, "Grotowski's *Akropolis*: A Retrospective View," 1–20, at 5.
466 Peter Brook's introduction to *Akropolis*, stage dir. Jerzy Grotowski, film dir. James MacTaggart, prod. Lewis Freedman (New York: Arthur Cantor Films 1968).
467 Barnes, "Jerzy Grotowski's 'Acropolis'; 1904 Drama Is Adapted for Polish Group," 40.

468 Ludwik Flaszen, "'Dziady,' 'Kordian,' i 'Akropolis' w Teatrze 13 Rzędów," *Pamiętnik Teatralny*, 3 (1964): 229. Quoted from Jozef Kelera's *Grotowski wielokrotnie* [Grotowski Many Times] (Wrocław: Ośrodek Badań Twórczości Jerzego Grotowskiego i Poszukiwań Teatralno-Kulturowych 1999), 93–4.
469 For a detailed history of the Auschwitz site and the history of its commemoration, see Jonathan Huener's award-winning book *Auschwitz, Poland, and the Politics of Commemoration, 1945–1979* (Athens: Ohio University Press 2003).
470 Grzegorz Niziołek, "Auschwitz – Wawel – Akropolis: niewczesny montaż" [Auschwitz – Wawel – Akropolis: Untimely Montage], *Didaskalia. Gazeta Teatralna*, June 2009, 27.
471 For more information about the history of Auschwitz, see Huener, *Auschwitz, Poland, and the Politics of Commemoration, 1945–1979*; Michael C. Steinlauf, *Bondage to the Dead: Poland and the Memory of the Holocaust (Modern Jewish History)* (Syracuse, NY: Syracuse University Press 1997); and Marek Kucia, *Auschwitz jako fakt społeczny. Historia, współczesność i świadomość społeczna KL Auschwitz w Polsce* [Auschwitz as a Social Fact: History, Modernity and Social Awareness of Auschwitz in Poland] (Cracow: Universitas 2005).
472 For an extensive study of the way that the Holocaust became commercialized, see Tom Cole, *Selling the Holocaust: From Auschwitz to Schindler; How History is Bought, Packaged and Sold* (New York: Routledge 2000). Reviewing the book, Zalewski (1999) wrote:

> In 1997, the Bee Gees toured Anne Frank's house in Amsterdam, along with 700,000 other bubble-gum chewing, minicam-clutching voyeurs. A man was spotted at Auschwitz wearing, with supreme irony, a Megadeth T-shirt. Gifted with a sensitive understanding of the Holocaust, Cole, history professor at the University of Bristol, sets out to parse the shifting myths created from the historical event of the Holocaust, especially its morphing into a ubiquitous, feel-good affirmation of America's core values. In seeking to understand the subtle implications of marketing remembrance, Cole focuses on three figures: Anne Frank, Adolph Eichmann and Oskar Schindler; and three sites: Auschwitz, Yad Vashem (Israel's Holocaust museum in Jerusalem) and the United States Holocaust Memorial Museum in Washington, D.C. What does it mean when *Schindler's List* becomes a de facto primary historical text, or when the United States Holocaust Memorial Museum (where Cole is a visiting fellow) is just one more item on an itinerary that includes the peep show thrills of the Texas Book Depository and Graceland? At a time when tourists flock to the Spielberg film location rather than to the actual ghetto, argues Cole, the Holocaust has been turned into a sort of virtual history. (Jeff Zalewski and Paul Gediman, review of Tim Cole's *Selling the Holocaust: From Auschwitz to Schindler, How History is Bought, Sold and Packaged*, *Publishers Weekly* 246, no. 31 (1999): 65)

473 Tadeusz Różewicz, *Proza* [Prose], vol. 1 (Cracow: Wydawnictwo Literackie 1990), 184.
474 Roman Polanski's *Knife in the Water*, a 1963 short, black-and-white film about a love triangle, was the first postwar Polish film that didn't deal at all with World War II, or any other national issue, for that matter.
475 Marta Wróbel, "'Ostatni Etap' Wandy Jakubowskiej jako pierwszy etap polskiego kina ideologicznego" [Wanda Jakubowska's "The Last Stage" as the First Stage of Polish Ideological Cinema], *Kwartalnik Filmowy* 43 (2003): 6–7.
476 Wanda Jakubowska, quoted in ibid., 6–11.
477 J. Karnaś (1948), quoted in ibid., 8.
478 Ryszard Bibr (1948), quoted in ibid., 8.
479 Wanda Jakubowska, quoted in ibid., 12.
480 Wojciech Roszewski (1980), quoted in ibid., 12.
481 Another good example of this trend is "a monument commemorating the Warsaw Ghetto uprising, which emphasizes the massive and heroic figures of the fighters. The relief showing a crowd destined for the gas chambers is placed in the back and can be seen

only from the side street" (Niziołek, "Auschwitz – Wawel – Akropolis: niewczesny montaż" [Auschwitz – Wawel – Akropolis: Untimely Montage], 28).
482 Aleksander Ford, quoted in *Ulica graniczna* [*Border Street*], <http://www.filmpolski.pl/fp/index.php/122529> (accessed 1 March 2010).
483 Grzegorz Niziołek, "Zawsze nie w porę. Teatr polski a Zagłada" [It's Never the Right Time: Polish Theatre and the Holocaust], interview by Joanna Wichowska, *Dwutygodnik: Strona Kultury* 20 (29 December 2009), <http://www.dwutygodnik.com.pl/artykul/759-zawsze-nie-w-pore-polski-teatr-i-zaglada.html> (accessed 2 April 2011).
484 Améry, *At the Mind's Limits*, 6.
485 Michael Bernard-Donals and Richard Glejzer, *Between Witness and Testimony: The Holocaust and the Limits of Representation* (New York: State University of New York Press 2001), 89.
486 Dori Laub, "Bearing Witness, or the Vicissitudes or Listening," in *Testimony: Crisis of Witnessing in Literature, Psychoanalysis, and History*, ed. Shoshana Felman and Dori Laub (New York: Routledge 1992), 61–75, at 69.
487 Wojdowski, "Borowski häftling," 1.
488 Ibid., 3.
489 The spelling of the word varies from German to Anglified: *Muselmann* (pl. *Muselmänner*), *Mussulman, Muselman, Musselman*.
490 Wolfgang Sofsky, *The Order or Terror*, trans. William Templer (Princeton: Princeton University Press 1997), 199.
491 Améry, *At the Mind's Limits*, 9.
492 Aldo Capri, *Diaro di Gusen* (Turin: Einaudi 1993), quoted in Giorgio Agamben's *Remnants of Auschwitz: The Witness and the Archive* (New York: Zone Books 2002), 41.
493 Sofsky, *The Order or Terror*, 329n5.
494 Zdzisław Ryn and Stanisław Kłodziński, "Na granicy życia i śmierci. Studium obozowego muzułmaństwa" [At the Border Between Life and Death: A Study of the Appearance of 'Musselman' in Concentration Camps], *Przegląd Lekarski* [Polish Journal "Medical Review"] 1, no. 40 (1983): 27–73 (quoted in Agamben, *Remnants of Auschwitz*, 42–3).
495 Agamben, *Remnants of Auschwitz*, 45.
496 Eugen Kogon, *The Theory and Practice of Hell: The German Concentration Camps and the System Behind Them*, trans. Heinz Norden (New York: Octagon Books 1979), 284.
497 Ryn and Kłodziński, "Na granicy życia i śmierci" [At the Border Between Life and Death], 94 (quoted in Agamben, *Remnants of Auschwitz*, 42–3).
498 Sofsky, *The Order or Terror*, 199.
499 Ibid., 200.
500 Ibid., 201.
501 Bettelheim, "Individual and Mass Behavior in Extreme Situations," 418.
502 Ibid., 445.
503 Ibid., 434.
504 Agamben, *Remnants of Auschwitz*, 65.
505 Ibid., 46–7.
506 Ibid., 48.
507 Ibid., 63.
508 Bruno Bettelheim (1960; 157), quoted in Agamben, *Remnants of Auschwitz*, 56.
509 Sofsky, *The Order or Terror*, 203.
510 Ibid., 204.
511 Agamben, *Remnants of Auschwitz*, 51.
512 Sofsky, *The Order or Terror*, 200.
513 *Przegląd Lekarski* 1 (1961).
514 Wojdowski, "Borowski häftling," 1.
515 Ibid., 1; 3.

516 Niziołek, "Auschwitz – Wawel – Akropolis: niewczesny montaż" [Auschwitz – Wawel – Akropolis: Untimely Montage], 26–31, at 28.
517 Antoni Kępiński, "KZ-syndrom. Próba syntezy" [KZ-Syndrome: An Attempt at Synthesis], *Przegląd Lekarski* 1 (1970); reprinted in Antoni Kępiński, *Refleksje oświęcimskie* [Reflections on Auschwitz] (Cracow: Wydawnictwo Literackie 2005).
518 Kępiński, *Refleksje oświęcimskie* [Reflections on Auschwitz], 108.
519 Ibid., 101.
520 Niziołek, "Auschwitz – Wawel – Akropolis: niewczesny montaż" [Auschwitz – Wawel – Akropolis: Untimely Montage], 30.
521 Ibid.
522 Jerzy Grotowski, "I Said Yes to the Past," 41–2.
523 Grotowski, *Towards a Poor Theatre*, 128.
524 Jennifer Levy, "Theoretical Foundations of Grotowski's Total Act, Via Negativa, and Conjunctio Oppositorum," *Journal of Religion and Theatre* 4, no. 2 (2005): 180.
525 Eugenio Barba, *Land of Ashes and Diamonds: My Apprenticeship in Poland* (Aberystwyth, UK: Black Mountain Press 1999), 49.
526 Jerzy Grotowski, *Teksty z lat 1965–1969* [Texts from 1965–1969] (Wrocław: Drukarnia Uniwestytetu Wrocławskiego 1990), 82.
527 Bentley, "Dear Grotowski," D1.
528 Simon, "Grotowski's Grotesqueries," 513.
529 Theodor W. Adorno, *Aesthetic Theory*, trans. Robert Hullot-Kentor (Minneapolis: University of Minnesota Press 1998), 6.
530 Susan D. Gubar, *Poetry After Auschwitz: Remembering What One Never Knew* (Indianapolis: Indiana University Press 2003), 27.
531 Grotowski, *Towards a Poor Theatre*, 15.
532 Walter Kerr, "Is Grotowski Right – Did the Word Come Last?" *New York Times*, 30 November 1969, D1.
533 Jerzy Grotowski, quoted in "I Said Yes to the Past," 42.
534 Flaszen, "'Dziady,' 'Kordian,' i 'Akropolis' w Teatrze 13 Rzędów," 229. Quoted in Kelera, *Grotowski wielokrotnie* [Grotowski Many Times], 93–4.
535 When he was 16, Grotowski caught scarlet fever and suffered kidney complications. He spent a year in Cracow's hospital, mostly spending his time reading. He left the hospital on his own orders, but his doctor predicted that he wouldn't live to see 30. For the rest of his life, Grotowski constantly felt as if he was living on borrowed time. In a recent interview published in a Polish newspaper, Grotowski's brother Kazimierz spoke about the issue openly: "From very early on, he lived in the constant shadow of death. Only his loved ones knew about it. This vision of death hung over him, driving him to action. He believed his days were numbered" (Kazimierz Grotowki, quoted in Targoń, "Don Kichot w okularach dla krótkowidzów" [Don Quixote in Glasses for the Nearsighted], 10). Was the distance between the living and the dead that Grotowski insisted on in *Acropolis* somewhat inspired by his own sense of alienation, being one of the living dead amongst the living?
536 Ludwik Flaszen, quoted in Kumiega, *The Theatre of Grotowski*, 61.
537 Grotowski, *Teksty z lat 1965–1969* [Texts from 1965–1969], 68.
538 Jerzy Grotowski, quoted in Schechner and Hoffman, "Interview with Grotowski," 38–55, at 50.
539 Findlay, "Grotowski's *Akropolis*: A Retrospective View," 8.
540 Kumiega, *The Theatre of Grotowski*, 61.
541 Ibid.
542 Osiński, *Teatr Dionizosa* [Dionysian Theatre], 178.
543 Temkine, *Grotowski*, 126.
544 Oliver, "Off-Broadway: Grotowski," 139.
545 Wetzsteon, "Theatre: Two by Grotowski," 46.

546 Jerzy Grotowski, quoted in Jerzy Falkowski, "Z Jerzym Grotowskim o teatrze" [With Jerzy Grotowski about Theatre], *Współczesność* 30 (1–30 December 1958): 8.
547 Grotowski, *Towards a Poor Theatre*, 22–3.
548 Gottfried, "Acropolis," 63.
549 Ludwik Flaszen, quoted in Osiński, "'Akropolis' w Teatrze Laboratorium" [Akropolis at the Teatr Laboratorium], 311.
550 Jerzy Grotowki, quoted in Schechner and Hoffman, "Interview with Grotowski," 50.
551 Kerr, "Is Grotowski Right – Did the Word Come Last?" D1.
552 Jerzy Grotowski, "Aktor ogołocony" [The Actor Uncovered], *Teatr* 17 (1–15 September 1965). Grotowski Institute Archives.
553 Thomas Richards, *At Work with Grotowski on Physical Actions* (London and New York: Routledge 1995), 25–6.
554 Grotowski, *Teksty z lat 1965–1969* [Texts from 1965–1969], 97–8.
555 Barba, *Ziemia popiołu i diamentów* [*The Land of Ashes and Diamonds*] (Wrocław: Ośrodek Badań Twórczości Jerzego Grotowskiego i Poszukiwań Teatralno-Kulturowych 2001), 73.
556 Barnes, "Jerzy Grotowski's 'Acropolis': 1904 Drama Is Adapted for Polish Group," 40.
557 In this approach, Grotowski was influenced very much by Osterwa, a prewar Polish director. Grotowski spoke extensively about his relationship to Osterwa's work:

> Osterwa treated acting as a human experience that exists not *for* the public, but vis-à-vis the public. It's from him that I borrowed the word "publico-tropism": The orientation of that actor who wants to play to the public, be accepted by the public and who, as a result, is always imprisoned and degraded as a human being. […] if you create a sort of osmosis in space between the actors and spectators, the spectator feels himself much more alienated in a psychological sense. There is a sort of iron curtain between the spectator and the actor… There are exceptions… But I have found that this is the direct consequence of osmosis. And that's why when we sought to have a gap between the actors and spectators, we mixed the actors and spectators. As in *Akropolis* […]. On the other hand, the possibility of direct emotional participation is much stronger if you create conditions in which the spectator really feels himself cut off from the actors: He can see them but there is a literal abyss between the actor and the spectator. (Jerzy Grotowski, quoted in Anna Kisselgoff, "Grotowski Stresses Need for System," *New York Times*, 25 November 1969, 54)

558 Oliver, "Off-Broadway: Grotowski," 140.
559 Thomas Quinn Curtiss, "Polish Theater Group Impressive in Paris." Grotowski Institute Archives. Reviewing the performance of *Constant Prince* for the *Wall Street Journal*, George Oppenheimer evoked similar emotions: "At times I had the feeling of being witness to an Eleusinian mystery. I had a strange mixture of wonder and discomfort, bewitchment and alienation. There were other moments when I felt I was at a Passion Play, such as had never been performed before" (George Oppenheimer, "Polish Play Opens in City Church," *Wall Street Journal*, 17 October 1969, Grotowski Institute Archives).
560 Ludwik Flaszen, "'Akropolis': Treatment of the Text," in Grotowski, *Towards a Poor Theatre*, 64–73.
561 Jerzy Grotowski, "For a Total Interpretation," *World Theatre* 15, no. 1 (1966): 22.
562 Karen Underhill, "Ecstasy and Heresy: Martin Buber, Bruno Schulz, and Jewish Modernity," in *(Un)masking Bruno Schulz: New Combinations, Further Fragmentations, Ultimate Reintegrations*, ed. Dieter De Bruyn and Kris van Heuckelom (Amsterdam: Rodopi 2009), 27–46, at 32; 38.
563 Rosiek, *Grotowski powtórzony* [Grotowski Repeated], 38.
564 Niziołek, "Auschwitz – Wawel – Akropolis: niewczesny montaż" [Auschwitz – Wawel – Akropolis: Untimely Montage], 27.

565 Agnieszka Wojtowicz, "Oby ci się, dziecko, jakos żyło w tym sierocińcu" [Have a good life, my child, in that orphanage], conversation with Ewa Lubowiecka, *Notatkik Teatralny* 20–21 (2000): 93.
566 Seth L. Schlein, "The Cassandra Scene in Aeschylus' 'Agamemnon,'" *Greece and Rome* 21, no. 1 (April 1982): 12.
567 Niziołek, "Auschwitz – Wawel – Akropolis: niewczesny montaż" [Auschwitz – Wawel – Akropolis: Untimely Montage], 29.
568 For more about the *Sonderkommando*, see Gideon Grief's *We Wept Without Tears: Testimonies of Jewish Sonderkommando from Auschwitz* (New Haven, CT: Yale University Press 2005).
569 Wirth, "A Discovery of Tragedy: The Incomplete Account of Tadeusz Borowski," 43–52, at 46.
570 Ibid., 46–7.
571 Harold Clurman, "Jerzy Grotowski," in *The Grotowski Sourcebook*, ed. Richard Schechner and Lisa Wolford (1997; reprint New York: Routledge 2001): 161–4, at 160–61.
572 Flaszen, "'Akropolis': Treatment of the Text," 63.
573 Wardle, "Big Catch from Poland," 18.
574 Findlay, "Grotowski's *Akropolis*: A Retrospective View," 5.
575 Barnes, "Jerzy Grotowski's 'Acropolis'; 1904 Drama Is Adapted for Polish Group," 40.
576 Kalemba-Kasprzak, "Akropolis – dwie teatralne wizje Europy" [Akropolis: Two Theatrical Visions of Europe], 209–26, at 224.
577 Peter Brook's introduction to *Akropolis*, stage dir. Jerzy Grotowski, film dir. James MacTaggart, prod. Lewis Freedman (New York: Arthur Cantor Films 1968).
578 Jerzy Grotowski, quoted in Schechner and Hoffman, "Interview with Grotowski," 38–55, at 49.
579 Flaszen, "'Akropolis': Treatment of the Text," 73.
580 Jean Améry describes a similar experience:

> Death was omnipresent. The selection for the gas chambers took place at regular intervals. For a trifle prisoners were hanged on the roll call grounds, and to the beat of light march music their comrades had to file past the bodies – Eyes right! – that dangled from the gallows. Prisoners died by the score, at the work site, in the infirmary, in the bunker, within the block. I recall times when I climbed heedlessly over piled-up corpses and all of us were too weak or too indifferent even to drag the dead out of the barracks into the open. (Améry, *At the Mind's Limits*, 15)

581 Findlay, "Grotowski's *Akropolis*: A Retrospective View," 13.
582 Flaszen, "'Akropolis': Treatment of the Text," 73.
583 Ibid., 12.
584 Croyden, "I Said Yes to the Past," interview with Jerzy Grotowski, 41.
585 Carol Delaney, *Abraham on Trial: The Social Legacy of Biblical Myth* (Princeton, NJ: Princeton University Press 1998), 21.
586 "Is done" (German).
587 Borowski, *This Way for the Gas, Ladies and Gentlemen*, 142.
588 Jerzy Grotowski, quoted in Schechner and Hoffman, "Interview with Grotowski," 38–55, at 49.
589 Kalemba-Kasprzak, "Akropolis – dwie teatralne wizje Europy" [Akropolis: Two Theatrical Visions of Europe], 209–26, at 221.
590 Bettelheim, "Individual and Mass Behavior in Extreme Situations," 436.
591 Kalemba-Kasprzak, "Akropolis – dwie teatralne wizje Europy" [Akropolis: Two Theatrical Visions of Europe], 221.
592 Flaszen, "'Akropolis': Treatment of the Text," 63.
593 Jerzy Gurawski, quoted in Osiński, *Jerzy Grotowski: Źrodła, inspiracje, konteksty* [Jerzy Grotowski: Origins, Inspirations, Contexts], 135.

594 Panasewicz, "7 dni w teatrze" [Seven Days in Theatre].
595 Ciotka Agnieszka, "Deficytowy artykuł" [The Deficit Article], *Trybuna Opolska*, 18 October 1962. Grotowski Institute Archives.
596 Agnieszka, "List do p. Falkowskiego" [Letter to Mr. Falkowski].
597 Findlay, "Grotowski's *Akropolis*: A Retrospective View," 16.
598 Peter Brook's introduction to *Akropolis*, stage dir. Jerzy Grotowski, film dir. James MacTaggart, prod. Lewis Freedman (New York: Arthur Cantor Films 1968).
599 Gould, "TV: P.B.L. Presents Polish Experimental Theater," 91.
600 Findlay, "Grotowski's *Akropolis*: A Retrospective View," 17.
601 Osiński, *Teatr Dionizosa* [Dionysian Theatre], 175.
602 Osiński, "'Akropolis' w Teatrze Laboratorium" [*Akropolis* at the Teatr Laboratorium], 300–34, at 306.
603 Grotowski, *Teksty z lat 1965–1969* [Texts from 1965–1969], 97–8.
604 Grotowski, *Towards a Poor Theatre*, 57.
605 Ludwik Flaszen, quoted in Kumiega, *The Theatre of Grotowski*, 60.
606 Findlay, "Grotowski's *Akropolis*: A Retrospective View," 6.
607 Flaszen, 62.
608 Wyspiański's letter, quoted in Osiński, "'Akropolis' w Teatrze Laboratorium" [*Akropolis* at the Teatr Laboratorium], 300–34, at 309.
609 Zenon Parvi, "U Wyspiańskiego" [At Wyspiański], *Kurier Codzienny*, 19 February 1904, 52.
610 Kalemba-Kasprzak, "Akropolis – dwie teatralne wizje Europy" [Akropolis: Two Theatrical Visions of Europe], 209–26, at 212.
611 Thomas Quinn Curtiss, "Polish Theater Group Impressive in Paris."
612 Overall it was seen by 1,600 people, with an average attendance of 44.19 percent during the first season and 27 percent during the second season. I would like to thank Paweł Płoski, a literary manager at the National Theatre, for providing this data.
613 Roman Pawłowski, "Podręczny Mesjanism: 'Akropolis' Wyspiańskiego w Teatrze Narodowym" [Handy Mesjanism: 'Akropolis' at the National Theatre], *Gazeta Wyborcza*, 14 May 2001, 17.
614 Ibid.
615 Ibid.
616 Ibid.
617 Ibid.
618 Kermit Dunkelberg, "Confrontation, Simulation, Admiration: The Wooster Group's *Poor Theater*," *TDR: The Drama Review* 49, no. 3 (T187) (2005): 43–56.
619 Richard Schechner, "There's Something Happenin' Here…," *TDR: The Drama Review* 54, no. 2, (T 206) (Summer 2010): 12–17, at 15.
620 Wichowska, "'Akropolis': duchy i ludzie" ["'Akropolis': Ghosts and People].
621 Joanna Targoń, "Zrób to sam" [Do It Yourself], *Dwutygodnik: Strona Kultury* 2 (17 April 2009), <http://www.dwutygodnik.com/artykul/56-zrob-to-sam.html> (accessed 2 March 2011).
622 Michael Marmarinos, quoted in an interview with Leszek Pułka, "Doskonałość jest przeciwieństwem życia. Dziś 'Akropolis. Rekonstrukcja.' We Wrocławskim Teatrze Współczesnym" [Perfection is an Antithesis of Life: Today "Akropolis: The Reconstruction" at the Wrocław's Teatr Współczesny], *Dziennik Gazeta Prawna* 242 (11 December 2009), <http://www.e-teatr.pl/pl/artykuly/84316.html> (accessed 3 April 2010).
623 "*Akropolis*. Reconstruction," press release, Teatr Współczesny, Wrocław, <http://www.wteatrw.pl/przedstawienie.xml?id=114> (accessed 11 February 2011).
624 Wojciech Sitarz, "Optymistyczna wersja 'Akropolis' – recenzja sztuki" [The Optimistic Version of "Akropolis." Review] (2009) <http://pik.wroclaw.pl/pressroom/Optymistycznawersja-Akropolis-recenzja--n743.html> (accessed 3 March 2011).
625 Ibid.

626 Michael Marmarinos, quoted in Grzegorz Chojnacki, "Akropolis, czyli pamięć" [Akropolis, or Memory], interview with Michael Marmarinos, *Gazeta Wyborcza*, 9 December 2009, "Kultura," 6.
627 Sitarz, "Optymistyczna wersja 'Akropolis' – recenzja sztuki" [The Optimistic Version of "Akropolis": Review].
628 Krzysztof Kucharski, "Po premierze 'Akropolis.' Reconstrukcja. We Wrocławskim Teatrze Współczesnym" [After the Opening of "Akropolis": Reconstruction at the Wrocław's Teatr Współczesny], *Gazeta Wrocławska*, 14 December 2009, <http://www.gazetawroclawska.pl/kultura/198072,po-premierze-akropolis-rekonstrukcja-we-wroclawskim-teatrze,id,t.html#material_1> (accessed 5 April 2011).
629 Kucharski, "Po premierze 'Akropolis'" [After the Opening of "Akropolis"].
630 Pułka, "Doskonałość jest przeciwieństwem życia" [Perfection is an Antithesis of Life].
631 Sitarz, "Optymistyczna wersja 'Akropolis' – recenzja sztuki" [The Optimistic Version of "Akropolis": Review].
632 Ibid.
633 Targoń, "Zrób to sam" [Do It Yourself].
634 Michael Marmarinos, quoted in an interview with Pułka, "Doskonałość jest przeciwieństwem życia" [Perfection is an Antithesis of Life].
635 Derkaczew, "Grotowski po raz pierwszy" [Grotowski for the First Time], 17.
636 Katarzyna Kamińska, "Zagubieni w pamięci" [Lost in Memory], *Gazeta Wyborcza*, 17 December 2009, 6.

Part II Our Memory: Kantor's *Dead Class*

1 Tadeusz Kantor, quoted in Krzysztof Pleśniarowicz, *The Dead Memory Machine: Tadeusz Kantor's Theatre of Death* (Cracow: Cricoteka 1994), 9.
2 Ibid.
3 Hans-Ties Lehman, *Postdramatic Theatre* (New York: Routledge 2006), 71.
4 Daniel C. Gerould, "A Visual Artist Works Magic on the Polish Stage," *Performing Arts Journal* 4, no. 3 (1980): 29.
5 Tadeusz Kantor, quoted in Krzysztof Pleśniarowicz, *Powrót Odysa. Podziemny Teatr Niezależny, 1944* [*The Return of Odysseus*: The Clandestine Independent Theatre, 1944] (Cracow: Cricoteka 1994), 23; 28.
6 Tadeusz Kantor, *Partytura Powrotu Odysa* [Partitura of *The Return of Odysseus*] (director's notes, 1944. Unpublished manuscript in the Cricoteka collection).
7 Tadeusz Kantor, quoted in Michal Kobialka, "Let the Artists Die? An Interview with Tadeusz Kantor," *The Drama Review: TDR* 30, no. 3 (Autumn 1986): 177–83.
8 Pleśniarowicz, *Powrót Odysa* [*The Return of Odysseus*], 60.
9 Kantor, "Partytura *Powrotu Odysa*" [Partitura of *The Return of Odysseus*] (director's notes).
10 Kantor, quoted in Plesniarewicz, *The Dead Memory Machine*, 23.
11 Tadeusz Kantor, quoted in Pleśniarowicz, *Powrót Odysa* [*The Return of Odysseus*], 56.
12 Tadeusz Kantor, "Illusion and Concrete Reality: Autonomous Theatre Notes," (trans. William Brand, Unpublished manuscript in the Cricoteka Collection, 1963).
13 Kantor, "Partytura *Powrotu Odysa*" [Partitura of *The Return of Odysseus*], (director's notes).
14 Jacek Stokłosa, quoted in Krzysztof Miklaszewski, *Tadeusz Kantor: Między śmietnikiem a wiecznością* [Tadeusz Kantor: Between Garbage and Eternity] (Warsaw: Państwowy Instytut Wydawniczy 2007), 96.
15 Christine Olga Kiebuzinska, *Intertextual Loops in Modern Drama* (Madison, NJ: Fairleigh Dickinson University Press; London: Associated University Presses 2001), 48.
16 Klaudiusz Święcicki, *Historia w teatrze Tadeusza Kantora* [History in the Theatre of Tadeusz Kantor] (Poznań: Wydawnictwo Poznańskie 2007), 245.

17. Kantor, quoted in Gerould, "A Visual Artist Works Magic on the Polish Stage," 29.
18. Charles Edelman, "'The Dead Class' by Tadeusz Kantor" [review], *Educational Theatre Journal* 30, no. 4 (December 1978): 546.
19. Gerould, "A Visual Artist Works Magic on the Polish Stage," 31.
20. Michal Kobialka, *A Journey Through Other Spaces: Essays and Manifestos, 1944–1990* (Berkeley: University of California Press 1993), 282.
21. Agata Miklaszewska, "Kantora teatr informel" [Kantor's Informel Theatre], *Dialog* 7 (1978): 126–7.
22. Gerould, "A Visual Artist Works Magic on the Polish Stage," 33.
23. Ibid., 28.
24. Pleśniarowicz, *The Dead Memory Machine*, 23.
25. Tadeusz Kantor (1957), "Emballages 1957–65," in Kobialka, *A Journey Through Other Spaces*, 154.
26. Kantor, quoted in Pleśniarowicz, *The Dead Memory Machine*, 23.
27. Tadeusz Kantor, "Cricot 2 and The Theatre of Death," in *Theatre Papers The Second Series, 1979–80*, ed. Peter Hulton (Exeter: Arts Documentation Unit, Exeter University 2004), 24.
28. Ibid.
29. Gerould, "A Visual Artist Works Magic on the Polish Stage," 36.
30. Grzegorz Niziołek, "Zawsze nie w porę. Teatr polski a Zagłada" [It's Never the Right Time: Polish Theatre and the Holocaust], interview with Joanna Wichowska, *Dwutygodnik. Strona kultury*, 29 December 2009, http://www.dwutygodnik.com.pl/artykul/759-zawsze-nie-w-pore-polski-teatr-i-zaglada.html (accessed 20 January 2011).
31. Ibid.
32. Artur Sandauer, "Sztuka po końcu sztuki" [Art After the End of Art], *Dialog* 3 (1981): 111–12.
33. Kantor, quoted in Barbara Natkaniec, "Przed premierą 'Cricot 2'" [Before the Opening of Cricot 2], *Echo Cracowa*, 15 November 1975, <http://www.e-teatr.pl/pl/artykuly/48260.html> (accessed 22 January 2011).
34. Kantor, "Cricot 2 and The Theatre of Death," 21.
35. Zuzanna Jastrzębska, "Umarła klasa" [Dead Class], *Filipinka* 3 (30 January 1977), <http://www.e-teatr.pl/pl/artykuly/11893.html> (accessed 3 February 2011).
36. Kantor, "Cricot 2 and The Theatre of Death," 28.
37. Pleśniarowicz dates the beginning of rehearsals to 1974 (Krzysztof Pleśniarowicz, *Kantor* (Wrocław: Wydawnictwo Dolnośląskie 1997), 214), and Święcicki dates it to 1975 (Święcicki, *Historia w teatrze Tadeusza Kantora* [The History in the Theatre of Tadeusz Kantor], 243).
38. Pleśniarowicz, *Kantor*, 215.
39. That same year, the retrospective of Kantor's emballages took place at the Museum of Art in Łódź. The retrospective was then exhibited in Kulturhuset in Stockholm.
40. Adam Ciesielski, "Teatr czeka na wizjonerów" [Theatre Waits for the Visionaries], *Kultura i Życie* [addendum to *Życie Warszawy*], 26 June 1991, <http://www.e-teatr.pl/pl/artykuly/11897.html> (accessed 3 June 2010).
41. Ibid.
42. Pleśniarowicz, *Kantor*, 215.
43. Andrzej Wajda, quoted in Jota, "Kantor miał dar widzenia" [Kantor Had a Vision], *Gazeta Wyborcza*, 16 November 2005, 2.
44. Andrzej Wajda, quoted in Barbara Kazimierczyk, "'Umarła klasa' w tearze i na taśmie" ['Dead Class' in the Theatre and on Film], *Kierunki*, 5 June 1977, <http://www.e-teatr.pl/pl/artykuly/48267.html> (accessed 3 June 2010).
45. Andrzej Wajda, quoted in "Rozmowa o Umarłej Klasie: Konstanty Puzyna, Tadeusz Różewicz, and Andrzej Wajda" [Conversation about 'Dead Class': Konstanty Puzyna, Tadeusz Różewicz, and Andrzej Wajda], *Dialog* 2 (1977): 135–42, at 137.

46 Kazimierczyk, "'Umarła klasa' w tearze i na taśmie" ['Dead Class' in the Theatre and on Film].
47 Jastrzębska, "Umarła klasa" [Dead Class].
48 Krzysztof Miklaszewski, *Zatracenie się w Schulzu: historia pewnej fascynacji* [Losing Oneself in Schulz: A Story of One Fascination] (Warsaw: Państwowy Instytut Wydawniczy 2009), 71.
49 Wajda, quoted in "Rozmowa o Umarłej Klasie" [Conversation about 'Dead Class'], 139.
50 Miklaszewski, *Tadeusz Kantor: Między śmietnikiem a wiecznością* [Tadeusz Kantor: Between Garbage and Eternity], 106.
51 Ibid.
52 Frank Rich, "Tadeusz Kantor's Intimations of God and Death", review *Dead Class* by Tadeusz Kantor, directed by Tadeusz Kantor, Cricot 2 Theatre,, *New York Times*, 16 June 1988, C21.
53 Pleśniarowicz, *Kantor*, 223–4.
54 Urszula Rzewiczok and Katarzyna M. Gliwa, *Drodzy Nieobecni Tadeusza Kantora: Wspomnienie o Tadeuszu Kantorze, Marianie Kantorze-Mirskim i Józefie Kantor* [Dear Departed of Tadeusz Kantor: Recollections about Tadeusz Kantor, Marian Kantor-Mirski and Józef Kantor] (Katowice: Muzeum Historii Katowic 2002), 21.
55 Jacek Cieślak, "Niecały umarł, choć odszedł jego świat" [Not All of Him Died, Though His World Is Gone], *Rzeczypospolita*, 8 December 2005, available at *Polish Theatre Portal*, <http://www.e-teatr.pl/pl/artykuly/19356.html> (accessed 3 April 2011).
56 Pleśniarowicz, *The Dead Memory Machine*, 45.
57 Roman Szydłowski, "Bez Teatru Rzeczypospolitej" [Without the Theatre of the People's Republic], *Życie Literackie* (Cracow), 19 June 1983, 4.
58 Olgierd Jędrzejczyk, "Znak i znaczenie w teatrze Tadeusza Kantor czyli spektakl 'Umarłej klasy' w sali dawnego 'Sokoła'" [Signs and Significance in the Theatre of Tadeusz Kantor, or The Dead Class in the Former Space of Sokół], *Gazeta Krakowska*, 22 June 1981, 1–2, at 1. Cricoteka Archives: CRC III/000619.
59 Magdalena Hniedziewicz, "Teatr. Czas przeszły, czas żywy teatru Kantora" [Theatre: Time Gone, Time Alive in Kantor's Theatre], *Kultura* 72 (21 March 1976). Cricoteka Archives CRC III/004802.
60 Krzysztof Pleśniarowicz, "Symbolizm 'Umarłej klasy'" [The Symbolism of 'Dead Class'], *Dziennik Polski*, 14 December 1978, 4.
61 Tadeusz Burzyński, "Festiwal który zwodzi i zawodzi" [Festival which Disillusions and Disappoints], *Scena* 9 (November 1976): 2–5, at 4.
62 Zygmunt Greń, "Nie pogrzebani" [The Unburied Ones], *Życie Literackie*, 26 June 1977, available at *Polish Theatre Portal*, <http://www.e-teatr.pl/pl/artykuly/48338.html> (accessed 21 June 2011).
63 Henryk Bieniewski, "Krok naprzód" [Step Forward], *Teatr*, 22 August 1976, 12–13, at 13.
64 Marta Fik, "Kantora Teatr Śmierci" [Kantor's Theatre of Death], *Polityka*, 14 August 1976. Cricoteka Archives: III/004811.
65 Konstanty Puzyna, quoted in "Rozmowa o Umarłej Klasie" [Conversation about 'Dead Class'], 135–42, at 135.
66 Tadeusz Różewicz, quoted in "Rozmowa o Umarłej Klasie" [Conversation about 'Dead Class'], 139.
67 Andrzej Wajda, quoted in "Rozmowa o Umarłej Klasie" [Conversation about 'Dead Class'], 135.
68 Ibid.
69 Ibid., 136.
70 Konstanty Puzyna, "My, Umarli" [We, the Dead Ones], in *Półmrok, Felietony teatralne i szkice* (Warsaw: Państwowy Instytut Wydawniczy 1982), 102–114, at 102.

71 Józef Kelera, "Postać jaskrawa i niemal cyrkowna" [A Bright and Almost Circus-like Figure], *Odra* 9 (September 1976): 87–90.
72 Maciej Szybist, "Umarła Klasa" [Dead Class], *Echo Cracowa*, 18 November 1975. Cricoteka Archives: CRC III/005913, III/000539, III/004792.
73 Jan Kłossowicz, "Galwanizacja Teatru" [Galvanizing Theatre], *Literatura* 24, no. 226 (10 June 1976): 13. Cricoteka Archives: CRC III/000552.
74 Wiesław Borowski, "Umarła Klasa" [Dead Class], *Literatura* (22 April 1976): 33B.
75 Andrzej Górny, "Bez końca powtórka" [Repetition Without End], *Nurt* 4 (1976): 30–32, at 32.
76 Krystian Lupa, "Fałszywy mag świątyni teatru" [The False Prophet of the Theatrical Temple], interview by Łukasz Drewniak, *Dziennik* 80 (4–5 April 2009), <http://www.dziennik.pl/magazyn-dziennika/article354424.ece> (accessed 1 March 2011). On more than one occasion, Lupa spoke candidly about his fascination with *Dead Class*:

> I felt it was a masterpiece, that everything that Kantor has done so far was a prelude to this masterwork. I left *Dead Class* in shock. If I have ever experienced catharsis, it was then. I was going to see this show many times, like one goes to the water fountain. I couldn't live without it. Later on, I watched it change, its actors change, for worse, in my opinion. I couldn't accept any change in something that shook me up so much. (Krystian Lupa, "Kantor żywy" [Kantor Alive], trans. Renata Kopyto, *Gazeta Wyborcza*, 6 January 2006, 12)

77 Kłossowicz, "Galwanizacja Teatru" [Galvanizing Theatre], 13. Cricoteka Archives: CRC III/000552.
78 Jerzy Tymicki and Andrzej Niezgoda, "New Dignity: The Polish Theatre 1970–1985," *The Drama Review: TDR* 30, no. 3 (Autumn 1986): 13–46, at 19.
79 Tadeusz Kantor, *Klasa szkolna. Dzieło Zamknięte, 1983* [Classroom. Closed Work], catalog for the exhibit, ed. Krzysztof Pleśniarowicz (Cracow: Cricoteka 1995), 6. Also quoted in Święcicki, *Historia w teatrze Tadeusza Kantora* [The History in the Theatre of Tadeusz Kantor], 250.
80 Krzysztof Miklaszewski, *Encounters with Tadeusz Kantor*, trans. George M. Hyde (New York: Routledge 2002), 42.
81 Ibid., 34.
82 Roman Szydłowski, "Czarno na białym. 'Umarła klasa' po latach" [In Black and White: 'Dead Class' After All Those Years], *Rzeczypospolita*, 15 June 1983, 4.
83 Wacław Janicki, "Dramaturg Kantor," interview by Roman Pawłowski, *Gazeta Wyborcza*, 29 October 2001, 16.
84 Elżbieta Morawiec, "Apokalipsa według Tadeusza Kantora" [Apocalypse According to Tadeusz Kantor], *Życie Literackie* 51/52 (21–28 December 1975). Cricoteka Archives: CRC III/004797, III/000541.
85 Szybist, "Umarła Klasa" [Dead Class]. Cricoteka Archives: CRC III/005913, III/000539, III/004792.
86 In March 1998 an exhibit, *Tadeusz Kantor – Memory plates*, opened in Copenhagen. *Le Théâtre en Pologne: The Theatre in Poland* (International Theatre Institute. Polish Centre, Authors Agency 1998), 79.
87 Bogdan Gieraczyński, "Na przykład 'Cricot 2'" [For Example Cricot 2], *Tygodnik Demokratyczny* 38 (18 September 1976): 16.
88 "Po szwajcarskim turnee 'Cricot 2,'" *Dziennik Polski* (Cracow), 11 June 1981. Cricoteka Archives: CRCIII/000616.
89 D. Brian Barron, "Atelier '76 at 61 High St. 'The Dead Class,'" [review], by Tadeusz Kantor, directed by Tadeusz Kantor, Cricot 2 Theatre, Edinburgh, *Festival Times*, 25 August 1976, 5.

90 Gordon Parson, "Fringe Benefits: Review of 'Dead Class' at Edinburgh Fringe Festival," [review], by Tadeusz Kantor, directed by Tadeusz Kantor, Cricot 2 Theatre, Edinburgh, *Morning Star*, 11 September 1976, 4.
91 W. B., "Cricot 2 in Great Britain," *The Theatre in Poland/ Le Theatre en Pologne* 3, no. 223 (1977): 27.
92 Richard Calvoressi, "Edinburgh Festival: Tadeusz Kantor: Cricot 2 Theatre," [review], directed by Tadeusz Kantor, Edinburgh *Studio International* 193, no. 985 (February 1977): 45.
93 W. B., "Cricot 2 in Great Britain," 27.
94 A. W., "A Painting Comes Alive," *Glasgow Herald*, 23 August 1976, 5.
95 W. B., "Cricot 2 in Great Britain," 27.
96 "'Cricot 2' ratuje londyńską placówkę przed plajtą. Kolejne wojaże teatru Kantora" [Cricot 2 Saves London's Studio from Bankrupcy. Kantor's Next Voyage], *Dziennik Polski*, 13 December 1982.
97 Ibid.
98 "Invitation Only," *Evening Standard* (London), 13 September 1976, 6.
99 Ann McFerran, review of *Dead Class*, *Time Out*, 10–16 September 1976, 16.
100 Ibid.
101 Michael Billington, "Fringe on Top," *Guardian*, 30 August 1976. Cricoteka Archives: CRC III/000187.
102 W. B. "Cricot 2 in Great Britain," 27.
103 G. S., Theatre column in *Politique Hebdomidaire*, 12–23 October 1977, quoted in Miklaszewski, *Encounters with Tadeusz Kantor*, 53.
104 Hubert Gignoux, "Nancy 77," *Théâtre/Publique* 16–17 (1977), quoted in Miklaszewski, *Encounters with Tadeusz Kantor*, 54.
105 Raymonde Temkine, "Theatre Review," *Europe* (October 1977): 201–2.
106 Ellen Stewart, quoted in Zbigniew Basara, "Kantor wrócił do Nowego Jorku" [Kantor Returned to New York], *Gazeta Wyborcza*, 13 November 2008, 21.
107 Richard Eder, "Stage: Avant-Gardists From Poland at La Mama," *New York Times*, 13 February 1979, C7.
108 Tish Dace, "The Class of the Living Death," *Soho Weekly News*, 15 February 1979. Cricoteka Archives: CRC III/000487.
109 Marilyn Stasio, "Tadeusz Kantor's *The Dead Class*" [review], *New York Post*, 21 February 1979. Cricoteka Archives: CRC III/000491.
110 Merle Ginsberg, "Poland's Incomparable 'Theatre of the Dead': A Matter of Death and Life," *Villager*, 19 February 1979, 13.
111 Ibid.
112 I wasn't able to confirm Pleśniarowicz's claim with *Newsweek*, but both Pleśniarowicz and Miklaszewski mention the note (Krzysztof Pleśniarowicz, *Kantor* (Wrocław: Wydawnictwo Dolnośląskie 1997), 222; Krzysztof Miklaszewski, *Encounters with Tadeusz Kantor*. Trans. George M. Hyde (New York: Routledge 2002), 59).
113 Peter Brook, quoted in Marcin Fybes, "Śmierć jest nieodwołalnym zamknięciem dzwi" [Death is the Final Closure], *Gazeta Wyborcza*, 12 December 1990, 9.
114 Margaret Croyden, "Images that Recall the Polish Past," *New York Times*, 9 May 1982, D4.
115 Michael Boue, "La classe du maître Kantor," *L'Humanité Dimanche* 88 (5–11 October 1977): 4.
116 Mathilde La Bardonnie, "Tadeusz Kantor: Le Maître," *Le Monde*, 14 October 1977, 28.
117 Henri Chapier, *Le Quotidien de Paris*, 11 October 1977, 13.
118 A. W., "A Painting Comes Alive," 5.
119 Rosalind Carne, "'The Dead Class'/ Riverside Studios," *Financial Times*, 18 November 1982. Cricoteka Archives: CRC III/000653.
120 "Masterpiece at Edinburgh Festival," *National Herald Tribune*, 7 September 1976, 7.

121 Julia Elwall, "Puppets in the String of Life," *Echo*, 9 September 1976. Cricoteka Archives: CRCIII/000196.
122 Martin Esslin, "The Dead Class," *Plays and Players* (October 1976). Cricoteka Archives: CRCIII/000205.
123 Reynolds, quoted in "Critics' Forum," *BBC Radio 3*, 16 October 1976.
124 Christopher Hudson, "How Death Is Brought to Life," *Standard*, 18 November 1982, 17.
125 Eileen Fisher, "*The Dead Class* by Tadeusz Kantor" [review], *Theatre Journal* 31, no. 3 (October 1979): 417.
126 Glenn Loney, "Kantor and *The Dead Class*," *Other Stages*, 8 February 1979, 11.
127 Harold Clurman, "*The Dead Class* by Tadeusz Kantor" [review], directed by Tadeusz Kantor, *The Nation*, 3 March 1979, 252. Clurman jokingly begins his review: "Foreign languages of which I am ignorant comprise the verbal matter of two theater events I recently attended. I much preferred them to a Broadway hit in dialogue I grasp all too well" (251).
128 In 1991, Mel Gussow repeated the same mantra, this time in his review of *Let the Artists Die*: "Performed in Polish, the play is less concerned with words than with signposts of behavior" (Mel Gussow, "Tadeusz Kantor's Troupe Carries On," *New York Times*, 20 October 1985, C15).
129 M. A. M., "The Dead Class," *Stage and Television Today*, 23 September 1976, 12.
130 Not surprisingly, other Kantor spectacles later evoked similar critical responses. Writing years later about *Wielopole, Wielopole*, Margaret Croyden concluded that, as in *Dead Class*, "The story and the spoken Polish, however, are less important than the symbols and metaphors, and the montages of physical images that crystallize the work" (Croyden, "Images that Recall the Polish Past," D4). And in 1985, Mel Gussow wrote something strikingly similar about *Let the Artists Die*: "Performed in Polish, the play is less concerned with words than with signposts of behavior" (Mel Gussow, "Polish Experimentalist Examines Man and History," *New York Times*, 20 October 1985, C15).
131 Dace, "The Class of the Living Death." Cricoteka Archives: CRC III/000487.
132 Ibid.
133 Eileen Blumenthal, "Haunted by History," *Village Voice*, 26 February 1979, 77.
134 Ginsberg, "Poland's Incomparable 'Theatre of the Dead,'" 13.
135 Stasio, "Tadeusz Kantor's *The Dead Class*," [review]. Cricoteka Archives: CRC III/000491.
136 Eder, "Stage: Avant-Gardists From Poland at La Mama," C7.
137 Cordelia Oliver, "Cricot Theatre," *Guardian*, 23 August 1976, 10. Cricoteka Archives: CRCIII/000181.
138 Nicholas de Jongh, "The Dead Class," *Guardian*, 18 November 1982. Cricoteka Archives: CRC III/000652.
139 Barron, "Atelier '76 at 61 High St. 'The Dead Class,'" 5.
140 John Thaxter, "Drama Wherever You Look at Riverside," *Richmond and Twickenham Times*, 19 November 1982. Cricoteka Archives: CRC III/000654.
141 Eder, "Stage: Avant-Gardists From Poland at La Mama," C7.
142 Carne, "'The Dead Class'/ Riverside Studios." Cricoteka Archives: CRC III/000653.
143 Mel Gussow, "Tadeusz Kantor's Troupe Carries On," *New York Times*, 14 June 1991, C15.
144 Edelman, "*The Dead Class* by Tadeusz Kantor" [review], 546.
145 Ibid.
146 Michael Billington, "The Dead Class," *Arts Guardian*, 13 September 1976, 8.
147 "Tadeusz Kantor," *Chambers Biographical Dictionary* (London: Chambers Harrap Publishers Ltd 2007), <http://www.credoreference.com/entry/chambbd/kantor_tadeusz> (accessed 3 June 2011).
148 Ann Barry, "Arts and Leisure Guide: Theater," *New York Times*, 11 March 1979, D35.
149 Clurman, "*The Dead Class* by Tadeusz Kantor" [review], 251–2, at 252.
150 "Masterpiece at Edinburgh Festival," 7.

151 Billington, "Fringe on Top." Cricoteka Archives: CRC III/000187.
152 Gussow, "Tadeusz Kantor's Troupe Carries On," C15.
153 Paul Overy, "Surrealism without Surfeit," *Times*, 31 August 1976. Cricoteka Archives: CRC III/000189.
154 Gignoux, "Nancy 77."
155 Ginsberg, "Poland's Incomparable 'Theatre of the Dead,'" 13.
156 Eder, "Stage: Avant-Gardists From Poland at La Mama," C7.
157 Esslin, "The Dead Class." Cricoteka Archives: CRCIII/000205.
158 Stasio, "Tadeusz Kantor's *The Dead Class*" [review]. Cricoteka Archives: CRC III/000491.
159 Frank Marcus, "Foreign Bodies," *Sunday Telegraph*, 19 September 1976. Cricoteka Archives: CRC III/000202.
160 Billington, "Fringe on Top." Cricoteka Archives: CRC III/000187.
161 Noel Witts, *Tadeusz Kantor* (London: Routledge 2010), 28.
162 Parson, "Fringe Benefits: Review of 'Dead Class' at Edinburgh Fringe Festival," 4.
163 Urszula Czartoryska, "Kantor: New Propositions," *Projekt* 4 (1976): 58–63, at 62. Cricoteka Archives: CRC III/004812.
164 John Barber, "Digging Up Our Buried Years," *Daily Telegraph*, 6 September 1976. Cricoteka Archives: CRC III/000192.
165 *Plays and Players*, 1976 Awards. Cricoteka Archives.
166 William Harris, "Tadeusz Kantor: Exploring the Dead Theater," *Soho Weekly News*, 22 February 1979, 27.
167 "The Dead Class Review," *West London Observer*, 24 November 1982. Cricoteka Archives: CRC III/000659.
168 Ibid.
169 "Cricot-2 at Riverside Studios," *Financial Times*, 8 September 1976. Cricoteka Archives: CRC III/000195.
170 Parson, "Fringe Benefits: Review of 'Dead Class' at Edinburgh Fringe Festival," 4.
171 Jasia Reichardt, "Kantor's Tragic Theatre," *Architectural Design* 46 (November 1976): 692–3, at 693.
172 Parson, "Fringe Benefits: Review of 'Dead Class' at Edinburgh Fringe Festival," 4.
173 Blumenthal, "Haunted by History," 77.
174 Ibid.
175 Święcicki, *Historia w teatrze Tadeusza Kantora* [History in the Theatre of Tadeusz Kantor], 251.
176 Temkine, "Theatre review," 201–2.
177 Jean-Pierre Leonardini, "L'ecureuil sur la roué. Le Polonaise Kantor gère l'économie de la mort," *L'Humanité*, 18 October 1977. Cricoteka Archives: CRC III/000311.
178 Nella Bielski, "L'emotion immediate," *Le Matin*, 17 October 1977. Cricoteka Archives: CRC III/000310.
179 Mitchell, quoted in "Critics' Forum."
180 Ascherson, "The Artist as Traitor." Cricoteka Archives: CRC III/000184.
181 Oliver, "Cricot Theatre," 10.
182 Blumenthal, "Haunted by History," 77.
183 Carne, "'The Dead Class'/ Riverside Studios." Cricoteka Archives: CRC III/000653.
184 Vaizey, quoted in "Critics' Forum."
185 Rich, "Tadeusz Kantor's Intimations of God and Death" [review], C21. Many years later, Margaret Croyden made a similar point about Kantor's *Wielopole, Wielopole*, as a metaphor for Western man's loss of his humanity:

> Polish writers since the 19th century, regardless of political persuasion, have presented Poles as a persecuted people on the one hand, and as a people relentlessly sacrificing themselves on the other. But Mr. Kantor's *Wielopole, Wielopole* goes beyond the fate of

the Poles to depict at the same time Western man condemned to ritualized cruelty in a world where humanism has lost its meaning. […] *Wielopole, Wielopole* is both an homage and a dirge to Kantor's past, a recollection of his family and childhood experiences which, as they unfold, evoke the essential Polish experience, a world of suffering and sacrifice, of mass murder and wars, a provincial Poland dominated by Church and Army whose presence lead inexorably to destruction and death. (Croyden, "Images that Recall the Polish Past," D4)

186 Reynolds, quoted in "Critics' Forum."
187 Yosunari Takahashi, *Yomiuri Shimbun*, 6 August 1982, quoted in Miklaszewski, *Encounters with Tadeusz Kantor*, 67.
188 Clurman, "*The Dead Class* by Tadeusz Kantor" [review], 251–2, at 252.
189 Mitchell, quoted in "Critics' Forum."
190 Vaizey, quoted in "Critics' Forum."
191 Julia Pascal, "'The Dead Class' by Tadeusz Kantor (Riverside)," *City Limits*, 26 November–2 December 1982. Cricoteka Archives: CRCIII/000662.
192 Jean-Pierre Leonardini of *L'Humanite* notes that "it is an irony – like those explored in his Theatre of Death, that Kantor exists in the valley of shadows at the time when his home country just elected a new president who promises that, starting tomorrow, there'll be a chicken in every pot" (Marcin Fybes, "Śmierć jest nieodwołalnym zamknięciem dzwi" [Death Is the Final Closure], *Gazeta Wyborcza*, 12 December 1990, 9).
193 Dace, "The Class of the Living Death." Cricoteka Archives: CRC III/000487.
194 Rich, "Tadeusz Kantor's Intimations of God and Death," C21.
195 It took more than 40 years for New York circles to recognize *Dead Class* as a work primarily focused on the Holocaust. Ironically, it was the art world – not the theatre community – that did so first. In 2008, the Jewish Museum in New York's exhibit "Theatres of Memory: Art and Holocaust" showcased Kantor's installation *The Desk*, which features a lone mannequin of a boy sitting on a school bench. Next to him is a simple black cross resembling a grave marker. *The Desk* references *Dead Class*; in a description of the installation, the museum curator writes:

In [*Dead Class*], live actors carried effigies of their younger selves, an evocation of the tragic history Kantor lived through during World War II. Kantor proclaimed through his *Theaters of Death* an existential despair in the face of political conflict and senseless annihilation. (Anne Edgar, "Theaters of Memory: Art and the Holocaust Opens at the Jewish Museum on November 9, 2008," [press release] (New York: The Jewish Museum in New York, 31 October 2008) <http://www.thejewishmuseum.org/site/pages/page.php?id=1111> (accessed 20 January 2010))

196 Marek Jodłowski, "Seans Kantora" [Kantor's Séance], *Opole*, 14 September 1976, available at *Polish Theatre Portal*, <http://www.e-teatr.pl/pl/artykuly/48396.html> (accessed 4 April 2011).
197 Barron, "Atelier '76 at 61 High St. 'The Dead Class,'" 5.
198 Krzysztof Pleśniarewicz, *Teatr nie-ludzkiej formy* [The Theatre of the Un-Human Form] (Cracow: Jagiellonian University 1994), 25.
199 Blumenthal, "Haunted by History," 77.
200 Krzysztof Miklaszewski, "*Dead Class*, or a New Treatise on Mannequins" [Conversation with Tadeusz Kantor, October 1975], in *Encounters with Tadeusz Kantor*, 34.
201 Kantor, quoted in Barbara Natkaniec, "Przed premierą 'Cricot 2'" [Before the Opening of Cricot 2], *Echo Cracowa*, 15 November 1975, available at *Polish Theatre Portal*, <http://www.e-teatr.pl/pl/artykuly/48260.html> (accessed 20 November 2011).
202 Katarzyna Fazan, *Projekt intymnego teatru śmierci: Wyspiański, Leśmian, Kantor* [The Project of the Intimate Theatre of Death: Wyspiański, Leśmian, Kantor] (Cracow: Wydawnictwo Uniwersytetu Jagiellonskiego 2009), 263.

203 Greń, "Nie pogrzebani" [The Unburied Ones].
204 Marek Bartelik, *Early Polish Modern Art: Unity in Multiplicity* (Manchester, UK: Manchester University Press 2005), 204.
205 All titles follow Daniel Gerould's established translations.
206 Kiebuzinska, *Intertextual Loops in Modern Drama*, 48.
207 Jan Kott and Martin Esslin, *The Theatre of Essence, and Other Essays* (Evanston, IL: Northwestern University Press 1984), 62.
208 Ibid., 74.
209 Jan Błoński, *Stanisław Ignacy Witkiewicz jako dramaturg* [Stanisław Ignacy Witkiewicz as Playwright] (Cracow: Państwowe Wydawnictwo Naukowe 1973), 243.
210 Tadeusz Boy-Żeleński, "Witkiewicz. Tumor Mózgowicz," in *Flirt z Melpomeną, wieczór trzeci* (Cracow: Krakowska Spółka Wydawnicza 1922), 68–76, at 70.
211 Kott and Esslin, *The Theatre of Essence, and Other Essays*, 66.
212 Ibid., 78.
213 Jan Błoński, *Witkacy na zawsze* [Witkacy Forever] (Cracow: Wydawninctwo Literackie 2003), 245.
214 Kott and Esslin, *The Theatre of Essence, and Other Essays*, 75.
215 Jan Kott, *Theatre Notebook, 1947–1967* (New York: Doubleday 1968), 25.
216 Ewa Szkudlarek, "An Anxiety of Existence in the Dramas of Stanisław Ignacy Witkiewicz," in *Witkacy w Polsce na na świecie*, ed. Marta Skwara (Szczecin: Wydawn. Naukowe Uniwersytetu Szczecińskiego 2001), 414.
217 Kott and Esslin, *The Theatre of Essence, and Other Essays*, 72.
218 Ibid.
219 Szkudlarek, "An Anxiety of Existence in the Dramas," 414.
220 Boy-Żeleński, "Witkiewicz. Tumor Mózgowicz," 69.
221 Ibid.
222 Kott and Esslin, *The Theatre of Essence, and Other Essays*, 74.
223 Witkacy [Stanisław Ignacy Witkiewicz], "O nowym typie sztuki teatralnej" [About a New Type of Theatrical Play], in *Czysta Forma w teatrze* (Warsaw: Wydawnictwo Artystyczne i Filmowe 1977), 74–8.
224 Boy-Żeleński, "Witkiewicz. Tumor Mózgowicz," 68.
225 Andrzej Wirth, "Gertruda Stein i Stanisław Ignacy Witkiewicz" [Gertrude Stein and Stanisław Ignacy Witkiewicz], in *Witkacy w Polsce na na świecie*, ed. Marta Skwara (Szczecin: Uniwestytet Szczeciński 2001), 25–36.
226 To be precise, the first literary essay on Witkiewicz was written by Czesław Miłosz in 1943. An essay, titled "The Limits of Art: Stanisław Ignacy Witkiewicz from the Perspective of Post-War Changes," argued that Witkiewicz should be evaluated foremost as a thinker, and his work as a commentary on his epoch, not as a body of literature per se. The essay, however, due to Miłosz's dissident position, was simply ignored.
227 Alina Grabowska, "O dramaturgi Witkiewicza" [About Witkiewicz's Dramaturgy], *Dialog* 1 (January 1957): 195; reprinted in Alina Grabowska, *Polska w komentarzach*, vol. 1 [Poland in Commentaries] (London: Polska Fundacja Kulturalna 1999), 139–41.
228 Janusz Degler, "Witkiewicz on the Polish Stage: 1921–1984," in *Witkacy – teatr, dokumentacja: inscenizacje sztuk Witkacego na scenach polskich, 1921–1985: katalog wystawy*, ed. Agnieszka Koecher-Hensel (Warsaw: CSS 1985).
229 Ibid.
230 Konstanty Puzyna, *Witkacy* (Warsaw: Oficyna Wydawnicza Errata 1999), 133.
231 Jacek Sieradzki, quoted in ibid., 135.
232 Witkacy [Stanisław Ignacy Witkiewicz], "Tumor Mózgowicz: Wstęp teoretyczny" [Tumor Brainiowicz: Theoretical Preface], in *Dzieła zebrane*, ed. Anna Micińska, Janusz Degler, and Lech Sokół (Warsaw: Państwowy Instytut Wydawniczy 1992), 213.

233 Witkacy [Stanisław Ignacy Witkiewicz], "Zwierzenia osobiste na temat 'Tumora Mózgowicza' i teorii Czystej Formy na scene" [Personal Confessions About 'Tumor Brainowicz' and Theory of Pure Form on the Stage], in *Czysta Forma w teatrze* (Warsaw: Wydawnictwo Artystyczne i Filmowe 1977), 207.
234 Quoted in Jacek Popiel, "Witkacy a antyiluzjonizm w teatrze" [Witkacy and Anti-Illusion in Theatre], in *Dramat a teatr polski dwudziestolecia międzywojennego* (Cracow: Wydawnictwo Universitas 1995), 125–32, at 125–6.
235 Kiebuzinska, *Intertextual Loops in Modern Drama*, 56.
236 Degler, "Witkiewicz on the Polish Stage: 1921–1984."
237 Emil Haecker, "Z teatru. Ofensywa futuryzmu przeciw sztuce" [From Theatre: Futurist Offensive Against Art], *Naprzód* 145 (1921).
238 Marian Szyjkowski, "Z teatru im. Jul. Słowackiego, 'Tumor Mózgowicz.' Dramat w 3 aktach z prologiem Stanisława Ignacego Witkiewicza" [From Słowacki Theatre, "Tumor Brainowicz"], *Ilustrowany Kurier Codzienny* 177 (1921); quoted in Janusz Degler, "Witkacego teaoria teatru" [Witkacy's Theory of Theatre], in *Czysta Forma w teatrze* (Warsaw: Wydawnictwo Artystyczne i Filmowe 1977), 7.
239 Szyjkowski, "Z teatru im. Jul. Słowackiego, 'Tumor Mózgowicz'" [From Słowacki Theatre, "Tumor Brainowicz"].
240 Wilhelm Fallek, "Z teatru im. Juliusza Słowackiego, Tumor Mózgowicz. Dramat w 3 aktach z prologiem Stanisława Ignacego Witkiewicza," *Nowy Dziennik* 170 (1921).
241 Skoczylas, quoted in Diana Poskuta-Włodek, "Dżuma w teatrze?! (1918–1926)" [Plague in the Theatre], in *Co dzień powtarza się gra... Teatr im. Juliusza Słowackiego w Cracowie 1893–1993* (Warsaw: Wydawnictwo Arta 1993), 92–112, at 107.
242 Janusz Degler, "Witkacego teoria teatru" [Witkacy's Theory of Theatre] In *Czysta Forma w teatrze* [Pure Form in Theatre]. (Warsaw: Wydawnictwo Artystyczne i Filmowe 1977), 8.
243 Boy-Żeleński, "Witkiewicz. Tumor Mózgowicz," 70.
244 Ibid.
245 Anatol Stern, "Manekiny naturalizmu" [Mannequins of Naturalism], in *Myśl teatralna polskiej awangardy 1919–1939*, ed. S. Marczak-Oborski (Warsaw: Wyd. Artystyczne i Filmowe 1973), 99–114, at 111.
246 Ibid., 112.
247 Ibid., 114.
248 Witkacy, "Zwierzenia osobiste na temat 'Tumora Mózgowicza' i teorii Czystej Formy na scene," [Personal Confessions About 'Tumor Brainowicz' and Theory of Pure Form on the Stage], 207.
249 Witkacy [Stanisław Ignacy Witkiewicz], "Odpowiedź Fallkowi na jego krytykę 'Tumora Mózgowicza'" [The Rebuttal to Fallek's Review of 'Tumor Brainowicz'], in *Czysta Forma w teatrze* (Warsaw: Wydawnictwo Artystyczne i Filmowe 1977), 213.
250 Degler, "Witkacego teoria teatru" [Witkacy's Theory of Theatre], 8.
251 Krzysztof Piech, "Tumor Mózgowicz: Kabaret matematyczny. Kabaret metamatematyczny" [Tumor Brainowicz: Mathemathical Cabaret, Metamathematical Cabaret], *Gazeta Wielkopolska*, 9 March 2000, <http://www.teatry.art.pl/!recenzje/tumormkmno/kabaret.htm> (accessed 3 June 2011).
252 Kott and Esslin, *The Theatre of Essence, and Other Essays*, 76.
253 Ibid.
254 Witkacy [Stanisław Ignacy Witkiewicz], "Tumor Mózgowicz," in *Dramaty*, vol. 1, ed. Konstanty Puzyna (Warsaw: Państwowy Instytut Wydawniczy 1972), 178.
255 Clurman, "*The Dead Class* by Tadeusz Kantor" [review], 251–2, at 252.
256 Daniel Gerould, foreword to *Witkiewicz: Seven Plays*, by Witkacy [Stanisław Ignacy Witkiewicz], ed. and trans. Daniel Gerould (New York: Martin E. Segal Theatre Center 2004), xix.
257 Ibid.

258 Jędrzejczyk, "Znak i znaczenie w teatrze Tadeusza Kantora'" [Signs and Significance in Theatre of Tadeusz Kantor], 1–2, at 1.
259 Ryszard Smożewski, "Uczestniczył w seansie dramatycznym Tadeusza Kantora" [Participated in Tadeusz Kantor's Dramatic Séance], *Szpilki* 3 (18 January 1976): 18.
260 Kiebuzinska, *Intertextual Loops in Modern Drama*, 48.
261 Wojciech Owczarski, *Miejsca wspólne, miejsca własne. O wyobraźni Leśmiana, Schulza i Kantora* [Common Spaces, Private Spaces. About the Imagination of Leśmian, Schulz and Kantor] (Gdańsk: Słowo/Obraz Terytoria 2006), 340.
262 Jan Kłossowicz, "Próba zapisu" [Trying to Record It], *Dialog* 2 (1 February 1977): 118–34, at 118.
263 Święcicki, *Historia w teatrze Tadeusza Kantora* [History in the Theatre of Tadeusz Kantor], 254.
264 Kantor, quoted in Wiesław Borowski, *Tadeusz Kantor* (Warsaw: Wydawnictwo Artystyczne i Filmowe 1982), 51.
265 Kazimierczyk, "'Umarła klasa' w tearze i na taśmie" ['Dead Class' in the Theatre and on Film].
266 Kantor, quoted in Barbara Natkaniec, "Przed premierą 'Cricot 2.'" [Before the Opening of Cricot 2], *Echo Cracowa*, 15 November 1975, <http://www.e-teatr.pl/pl/artykuly/48260.html> (accessed 28 June 2011).
267 Miklaszewski, "*Dead Class*, or a New Treatise on Mannequins" [Conversation with Tadeusz Kantor, October 1975], in *Encounters with Tadeusz Kantor*, 34.
268 Rzewiczok and Gliwa, *Drodzy Nieobecni Tadeusza Kantora* [Dear Departed of Tadeusz Kantor], 26.
269 Tadeusz Kantor, "Postacie 'Umarłej klasy'" [Characters from *Dead Class*], *Dialog* 2 (1 February 1977).
270 Hniedziewicz, "Teatr. Czas przeszły, czas żywy teatru Kantora" [Theatre: Time Gone, Time Alive in Kantor's Theatre], 13.
271 Kantor, "Postacie 'Umarłej klasy'" [Characters from *Dead Class*] *Dialog* 2 (1 February 1977).
272 Kantor, quoted in Puzyna, "My, Umarli" [We, the Dead Ones], 102–114, at 107.
273 Puzyna, "My, Umarli," 105.
274 Kantor, "The Dead Class," program from Theatre Cricot 2 Performance at LaMaMa ETC, New York, June 1991.
275 Witkacy [Stanisław Ignacy Witkiewicz], "Tumor Brainowicz," in *Witkiewicz: Seven Plays*, ed. and trans. Daniel Gerould (New York: Martin E. Segal Theatre Center 2004).
276 Kazimierczyk, "'Umarła klasa' w tearze i na taśmie" ['Dead Class' in the Theatre and on Film].
277 Jodłowski, "Seans Kantora" [Kantor's Séance].
278 Lehman, *Postdramatic Theatre*, 71.
279 Jodłowski, "Seans Kantora" [Kantor's Séance].
280 Kantor, quoted in Jastrzębska, "Umarła klasa" [Dead Class].
281 Anna Hoffman, "Witkiewicz i teatr Tadeusza Kantora" [Witkiewicz and Theatre of Tadeusz Kantor], *Dziennik Polski*, 6 September 1976. Cricoteka Archives: CRC III/004817.
282 Miklaszewski, *Encounters with Tadeusz Kantor*, 46.
283 Łukasz Maciejewski, "Nigdy tu już nie powrócę" [I Shall Never Return], *Dziennik* 3 (4 January 2008), available at *Polish Theatre Portal*, <http://www.e-teatr.pl/pl/artykuly/49465.html> (accessed 1 December 2011).
284 Marcus, "Foreign Bodies."
285 Święcicki, *Historia w teatrze Tadeusza Kantora* [History in the Theatre of Tadeusz Kantor], 247.
286 Krzysztof Miklaszewski, "Zapis wypowiedzi dla *Kroniki Krakowskiej*" [Transcript of the Interview for *Kronika Krakowska*], manuscript, 15 November 1975. Cricoteka Archives: CRC III/000538–III/1/2/324, III/004798–III/1/2/327.

287 Święcicki, *Historia w teatrze Tadeusza Kantora* [History in the Theatre of Tadeusz Kantor], 250.
288 Harold Clurman rightly notes the Brechtian maneuver of historical displacement: "*The Dead Class* alludes to Poland before and at the outbreak of World War I. For this reason, the current Polish Government cannot now reasonably object to it. But the specific historic circumstances referred to are a mask which might just as well apply to present-day constrictions and bitterness" (Clurman, "*The Dead Class* by Tadeusz Kantor" [review], 252).
289 Tadeusz Kantor, quoted in Miklaszewski, *Zatracenie się w Schulzu* [Losing Oneself in Schulz], 31.
290 Miklaszewski, *Zatracenie się w Schulzu* [Losing Oneself in Schulz], 31.
291 Bronisław Mamoń, "Republika marzeń" [The Republic of Dreams], *Tygodnik Powszechny* 46 (1987): 7.
292 *The Hour-Glass Sanatorium*, adapted and directed by Wojciech J. Has, music by Jerzy Maksymiuk, set by Jerzy Skarżyński (Poland: Film Polski 1973). Adapted from Bruno Schulz's *Sanatorium Under the Sign of the Hourglass*.
293 Puzyna, quoted in "Rozmowa o Umarłej Klasie" [Conversation about 'Dead Class'], 135–42, at 136.
294 Witold Kieracz, "'Sanatorium pod klepsydrą' – proza Schulza i wizje Hasa" ['Sanatorium Under the Sign of Hourglass' – Schulz's prose and Has' vision], in *Studia o prozie Brunona Schulza*, ed. Kazimiera Czaplowa (Katowice: Uniwersytet Śląski 1976), 136.
295 Miklaszewski, "Zapis wypowiedzi dla *Kroniki Krakowskiej*" [Transcript of the Interview for Kronika Krakowska].
296 Sandauer, "Sztuka po końcu sztuki" [Art After the End of Art], 111–12, at 111.
297 Puzyna, "My, Umarli" [We, the Dead Ones], 102–114, at 107.
298 Puzyna, quoted in "Rozmowa o Umarłej Klasie" [Conversation about 'Dead Class'], 136.
299 Nina Király, "Schulz i Kantor" [Schulz and Kantor], in *Teatr pamięci Brunona Schulza*, ed. Jan Ciechowicz and Halina Kasjaniuk (Gdynia: Teatr Miejski w Gdyni 1993), 132–42, at 134.
300 Ibid., 136–7.
301 Puzyna, "My, Umarli" [We, the Dead Ones], 107.
302 The letter has been reprinted in English in Jerzy Ficowski, *Regions of the Great Heresy*, trans. and ed. Teodosia Robertson (New York: W. W. Norton & Company 2003), 189.
303 Bruno Schulz, "Sanatorium Under the Sign of the Hourglass," in *The Complete Fiction of Bruno Schulz*, trans. Celina Wieniewska (New York: Walker and Company 1989), 298.
304 Ibid., 300; 301; 301; 303.
305 Russell E. Brown, *Myths and Relatives: Seven Essays on Bruno Schulz* (Munich: Verlag Otto Sagner 1991), 113.
306 Schulz, "Sanatorium Under the Sign of the Hourglass," 307.
307 Ibid.
308 Wojciech Wyskiel, *Inna twarz Hioba: problematyka alienacyjna w dziele Brunona Schulza* [Hiob's Other Face: Alienation in the Works of Bruno Schulz] (Cracow: Wydawnictwo literackie 1980), 134.
309 Jerzy Ficowski, *Regions of the Great Heresy: Bruno Schulz, A Biographical Portrait*, trans. and ed. Theodosia Robertson (New York: W. W. Norton 2003), 72.
310 Ibid.,73.
311 Ibid., 76.
312 "To, co Pan mówi o naszym sztucznie przedłużonym dzieciństwie – o niedojrzałości – dezorientuje mnie trochę. Gdyż zdaje mi sie, że ten rodzaj sztuki, jaki mi leży na sercu, jest właśnie regresją, jest powrotem dzieciństwa. Gdyby można było uwstecznić rozwój, osiągnąć jakąś okrężną drogą powtórnie dzieciństwo, jeszcze raz miec pełnie i bezmiar – to byłoby to ziszczeniem 'genialnej epoki,' 'czasów mesjaszowych,' które nam są przyrzeczone i zaprzysiężone. Moim ideałem jest 'dojrzeć' do dziecinstwa. To by dopiero była prawdziwa dojrzałość" (Bruno Schulz, *Opowiadania. Wybór esejów i listów* [Short Stories, Essays and

Letters], ed. Jerzy Jarzębski (Wrocław: Ossolineum 1989), 424. The letter has been reprinted in English in Ficowski, *Regions of the Great Heresy*, 186).
313 Bruno Schulz, "List do S.I. Witkiewicza" [Letter to S. I. Witkiewicz], in *Pisarze awangardy dwudziestolecia międzywojennego: autokomentarze: Leśmian – Witkacy – Schulz – Gombrowicz*, ed. Tomasz Wójcik (Warsaw: Państwowe Wydawnictwo Naukowe 1995), 152.
314 Quoted in Ficowski, *Regions of the Great Heresy*, 77.
315 Ibid., 72.
316 Miklaszewski, *Tadeusz Kantor: Między śmietnikiem a wiecznością* [Tadeusz Kantor: Between Garbage and Eternity], 79–80.
317 Naomi Norsworthy and Mary Theodora Whitley, *The Psychology of Childhood* (New York: Macmillan 1918), 150.
318 Józef Zbigniew Białek, *Literatura dziecięca okresu międzywojennego na tle ówczesnych kierunków pedagogicznych* (Cracow: Rocznik Naukowo – Dydaktyczny WSP 1962), 12.
319 Czesław Karkowski, "System kultury Brunona Schulza" [Bruno Schulz's Cultural System], in *Studia o prozie Brunona Schulza*, ed. Kazimiera Czaplowa (Katowice: Uniwersytet Śląski 1976), 31–48, at 39.
320 Ginsberg, "Poland's Incomparable 'Theatre of the Dead,'" 13.
321 Borowski, "Umarła Klasa" [Dead Class], 33B.
322 Święcicki, *Historia w teatrze Tadeusza Kantora* [History in the Theatre of Tadeusz Kantor], 250.
323 Tadeusz Kantor, director's notes, 1974, quoted in Lech Stangret, *Tadeusz Kantor. Fantomy Realności* [Tadeusz Kantor: Phantoms of Reality], catalog for the exhibit of Tadeusz Kantor's theatrical constumes, (Cracow: Cricoteka 1996), 73.
324 Gerould, "A Visual Artist Works Magic on the Polish Stage," 28–36, at 36.
325 Fisher, "*The Dead Class* by Tadeusz Kantor" [review], 417–18, at 417.
326 McFerran, review of *Dead Class*, 16.
327 Rzewiczok and Gliwa, *Drodzy Nieobecni Tadeusza Kantora* [Dear Departed of Tadeusz Kantor], 27.
328 Kantor, "Cricot 2 and The Theatre of Death."
329 Evgeni Zamyatin, "On Literature, Revolution, and Entropy," in *Literary Modernism*, ed. Irving Howe (New York: Fawcett 1976), 176.
330 Michal Kobialka, "Let the Artists Die? An Interview with Tadeusz Kantor," *The Drama Review: TDR* 30, no. 3 (Autumn 1986): 177–83.
331 Gerould, "A Visual Artist Works Magic on the Polish Stage," 36.
332 M. A. M., "The Dead Class," 12.
333 Hudson, "How Death Is Brought to Life," 17.
334 Kantor, "Cricot 2 and The Theatre of Death," 39.
335 Ibid.
336 Tadeusz Kantor, *Cricot 2 Theatre 1955–1988*, ed. Teresa Bazarnik (Cracow: Cricoteka 1988).
337 Kantor, quoted in Krzysztof Pleśniarewicz, *Teatr Śmierci Tadeusza Kantora* [Tadeusz Kantor's Theatre of Death] (Chotomow: VERBA 1990).
338 Kantor, "Notes about the Informel Theatre," trans. William Brand. Unpublished manuscript in the Cricoteka collection, 1960.
339 Kantor, quoted in Pleśniarewicz, *Teatr Śmierci Tadeusza Kantora*, page number.
340 Barron, "Atelier '76 at 61 High St. 'The Dead Class,'" 5.
341 Jastrzębska, "Umarła klasa" [Dead Class].
342 Rolando Perez, *Bruno Schulz: Literary Kabbalist of the Holocaust* (New York: Hunter College of the City University of New York 2002), 3–4.
343 Calvoressi, "Edinburgh Festival: Tadeusz Kantor: Cricot 2 Theatre," 45.
344 Krzysztof Pleśniarowicz, *Teatr Śmierci Tadeusza Kantora* [Tadeusz Kantor's Theatre of Death] (Chotomów: VERBA 1990), 107.

345 Jan Bończa-Szabłowski, "Korowód starych dzieci" [Pageant of the Old Children], *Rzeczpospolita*, 20 January 2009, available at *Polish Theatre Portal*, <http://www.e-teatr.pl/pl/artykuly/81526.html> (accessed 20 November 2011).
346 Bettina Knapp and Witold Gombrowicz, "Gombrowicz: An Interview," *The Drama Review* 14, no. 1 (Autumn 1969): 84–94, at 84.
347 Gombrowicz, quoted in ibid., 85.
348 Jan Lorentowicz, review of *Ferdydurke*, *Nowa książka 1934–1939*, zeszyt 1 ed. Stanisław Lem (Warsaw 1938), 28.
349 The scene that Lorentowicz criticized, "Going 'na parobka," is now considered to clearly have homoerotic undertones. Although in 1938 Lorentowicz didn't dare write openly about what his problem was with the scene, he was nonetheless displeased by it.
350 J. E. Skiwski, "Kurza pierś" [Chicken Breast], *Kronika Polski i Świata* 2 (1938): 9.
351 Bruno Schulz, review of "Ferdydurke," *Skalamander* 96/98 (1938): 183–9.
352 Alfred Łaszowski, "Szkoła Gombrowicza," *Myśl Polska* 22, no. 44 (15–30 November 1937): 5.
353 Gustaw Herling-Grudziński, "Zabawa w 'Ferdydurke'" [Playing the Game of Ferdydurke], *Orka* 2 (1938): 6.
354 *Drang nach Osten* (German for "yearning for the East," "drive toward the East"): a nineteenth-century expression describing the German desire for expansion into the Slavic territories. In the late nineteenth century, it became a motto of the German nationalist movement.
355 Natalia Wiśniewska, "Literatura w malignie" [Literature in Delirium], *Epoka* (Warsaw), 25 November 1938, 11.
356 Stanisław Baczyński, *Rzeczywistość i fikcja (Współczesna powieść polska)* [Reality and Fiction: The Contemporary Polish Novel] (Warsaw: Nowa Biblioteka Społeczna 1939), 290–91.
357 Rochelle H. Ross, "Witold Gombrowicz: An Experimental Novelist," *South Central Bulletin* (Winter 1971): 214–16, at 214.
358 Ibid., 215.
359 Mieczysław Inglot, *Romantyczne konteksty twórczości Witolda Gombrowicza* (Katowice: Wyższa Szkoła Zarządzania Marketingowego i Języków Obcych 2006), 148.
360 Witold Gombrowicz, "Foreword to *Ferdydurke*," reprinted in *Pisma zebrane* [Collected Works], quoted in Łukasz Garbal, *Ferdydurke: biografia powieści* [Ferdydurke: The Story of a Novel] (Cracow: Tow 2010), 602.
361 Witold Gombrowicz, *Ferdydurke*, trans. Danuta Borchardt (New Haven, CT: Yale University Press 2000), 3.
362 Ibid., 19.
363 Konstanty Jelenski, "Witold Gombrowicz," *Tri-Quarterly* 9 (1967): 37–41, at 38.
364 Gombrowicz, *Ferdydurke*, 10.
365 Lorentowicz, review of *Ferdydurke*, 28.
366 Robert Boyers, "Gombrowicz and Ferdydurke: The Tyranny of Form," *Centennial Review*, no. 14 (1970): 284–312, at 290.
367 Jelenski, "Witold Gombrowicz," 38.
368 Garbal, *Ferdydurke: biografia powieści*, 157.
369 Vaizey, quoted in "Critics' Forum."
370 Gombrowicz, *Ferdydurke*, 17.
371 Brown, *Myths and Relatives*, 113.
372 Gombrowicz, *Ferdydurke*, 15.
373 Czesław Miłosz, *Ziemia Ulro* [Urlo's Earth] (Paris: Institute Literacki 1977), 54.
374 Marian Sienkiewicz, "Demiurg z Cricot 2," *Przekrój* 1601 (1975): 9.
375 Święcicki, *Historia w teatrze Tadeusza Kantora* [History in the Theatre of Tadeusz Kantor], 254.

376 Tadeusz Kantor, "Umarła Klasa, Partytura," [Dead Class, Script], in Tadeusz Kantor, *Teatr Śmierci. Teksty z lat 1975–1984. Tom drugi pism* [The Theatre of Death: Tests from 1975–1984, Volume II] (Wrocław: Ossolineum 2005), 82. Also cited in Święcicki, *Historia w teatrze Tadeusza Kantora* [History in the Theatre of Tadeusz Kantor], 254.

377 Marek Jodłowski notes that "Next to the 'normal' lesson (like the one led by Gombrowicz's Pimko), there is the 'night' lesson. It is made up of the night promenades of the Old Man with the Bicycle, the walks of the Somnambulist Prostitute, the adventures of the Old Man in the Toilet" (Jodłowski, "Seans Kantora" [Kantor's Séance]), 20.

378 Tomasz Bocheński, *Czarny humor w twórczości Witkacego, Gombrowicza, Schulza – Lata trzydzieste* [Black Humor in the Works of Witkacy, Gombrowicz, Schulz – 1930s] (Cracow: Towarzystwo Autorów i Wydawców Prac Naukowych UNIVERSITAS 2005), 7.

379 Borowski, "Umarła Klasa" [Dead Class], 33B.

380 Barron, "Atelier '76 at 61 High St. 'The Dead Class,'" 5.

381 Loney, "Kantor and *The Dead Class*" 11.

382 Wojciech Owczarski tells a poignant anecdote from his experience teaching *Dead Class*:

> Tadeusz Kantor used to say that you can't enter the theatre with impunity. One day, I got a taste of what he meant. I was a young assistant professor, teaching an evening class. Back then, the average student taking evening classes was about fifty years old. One evening, I decided to show *Dead Class* to a group of older ladies (some of whom were already retired). Because I had seen it many times before, I left the class for a few minutes. When I returned, I was horrified. You need to know that the characters of *Dead Class* are old people returning to their childhood. Morbidly pale, senile, and stiff like mannequins, they sit in school benches, raising their hands, or freezing in 'memory plates' as if unable to accept the merciless fate of approaching death. My students, who were also not so young, were sitting as if hypnotized. They were still, with their jaws dropped, staring at the screen, seeing there – as I immediately realized – their own image. There was something incredible in this symmetry; over there, dead pupils, and here, in my classroom, older ladies frozen in fear and horror. I understood my error, but it was too late. The atmosphere was getting heavier and heavier; my students were getting paler and paler. In my mind's eye, I saw the ER, chaotic CPRs, obituaries, and myself behind bars. Kantor sitting in the first row of the court benches, smiling at me ironically, shrugging his shoulders as if wanting to say: "I told you so." (Owczarski, "Umarła klasa" [*Dead Class*], *Gazeta Wyborcza*, 30 March 2006, 9)

383 Sandauer, "Sztuka po końcu sztuki" [Art After the End of Art], 101–12, at 102–3.

384 Marcel Cornis-Pope and John Neubauer, *History of the Literary Cultures of East-Central Europe: Junctures and Disjunctures in the 19th and 20th Centuries* (The Netherlands: John Benjamins 2004), 426.

385 Ibid., 427.

386 Norbert Zmijewski explains the trend:

> Popular nationalist Catholicism has often been taken to represent pre-war Catholicism. For example, J. Zawieyski, one of the members of *Znak*, saw pre-war Catholicism as hostile to the progressive social movement, anti-intellectual and sentimental. He wrote: 'When I read Turowicz's utterances about Odrodzenie…I ask my dear friend: where was it, when was it; in Poland, or on some other planet?' Odrodzenie was an elitist group operating mainly in universities and was not popular or well-known enough to balance the nationalist image of Catholicism. This popular image often caused a rejection of Catholicism as the narrow-minded and sentimental religion of nationalists. (Zmijewski, "Vicissitudes of Political Realism in Poland: Tygodnik Powszechny and Znak," *Soviet Studies* 43, no. 1 (1991): 83–106)

387 Kathleen Cioffi, "Review of *Ferdydurke,*" *Theatre Journal* 54, no. 2 (May 2002): 301–3, at 303.
388 Cioffi, "Review of *Ferdydurke,*" 303.
389 Pleśniarowicz, *The Dead Memory Machine*, 10.
390 Kantor, quoted in Miklaszewski, *Tadeusz Kantor: Między śmietnikiem a wiecznością* [Tadeusz Kantor: Between Garbage and Eternity], 92.
391 Ibid., 93.
392 Overy, "Surrealism without Surfeit."
393 Harris, "Tadeusz Kantor: Exploring the Dead Theater," 27.
394 Tomasz Bocheński, "Czarny humor w twórczości Brunona Schulza" [Black Humor in the Work of Bruno Schulz], in *W ułamkach zwierciadła – Bruno Schulz w 110 rocznicę urodzin i 60 rocznicę śmierci*, ed. Małgorzata Kitowska-Łysiak and Władysław Panas (Lublin: Towarzystwo Naukowe KUL 2003), 211–28, at 214.
395 Bruno Schulz, "Letters," in *Bruno Schulz: New Documents and Interpretations*, ed. Czesław Z. Prokopczyk (New York: Peter Lang 1999), 24.
396 Dorota Głowacka, "Sublime Trash and the Simulactrum: Bruno Schulz in the Postmodern Neighborhood," in *Bruno Schulz: New Documents and Interpretations*, ed. Czesław Z. Prokopczyk (New York: Peter Lang 1999), 79–122, at 81.
397 Modris Eksteins, *Rites of Spring: The Great War and the Birth of the Modern Age* (New York: Mariner Books 2000), 248.
398 Bogusław Gryszkiewicz, "Bruno Schulz a tradycja czarnego humoru" [Bruno Schulz and the Tradition of Black Humor], in *W ułamkach zwierciadła – Bruno Schulz w 110 rocznicę urodzin i 60 rocznicę śmierci*, ed. Małgorzata Kitowska-Łysiak and Władysław Panas (Lublin: Towarzystwo Naukowe KUL 2003), 229–48, at 235.
399 Bruno Schulz, "Wędrówki sceptyka" [Skeptic's Travels], *Tygodnik Ilustrowany* 6 (19 January 1936): 44.
400 Theodor Adorno and Max Horkheimer, "The Culture Industry: Enlightenment as Mass Deception," in *The Cultural Studies Reader*, ed. Simon During (New York: Routledge 1993), 31–41, at 36.
401 Ofra Nevo and Jacob Levine, "Jewish Humor Strikes Again: The Outburst of Humor in Israel during the Gulf War," *Western Folklore* 53, no. 2 (April 1994): 125–45, at 126.
402 Elliot Oring, "The People of the Joke: On the Conceptualization of a Jewish Humor," *Western Folklore* 42, no. 4 (October 1983): 261–327, at 268.
403 Czartoryska, "Kantor: New Propositions," 58–63, at 62.
404 Oliver, "Cricot Theatre," 10.
405 Jerzy Jarzębski, "'Umarła klasa' po 30 latach" [*Dead Class* after 30 Years], *Gazeta Wyborcza*, 15 November 2005, available at *Polish Theatre Portal*, <http://www.e-teatr.pl/pl/artykuly/18345.html> (accessed 24 April 2011).
406 Kantor, "Postacie 'Umarlej klasy'" [Characters from *Dead Class*].
407 Barbara Kirshenblatt-Gimblett, "'Contraband': Text and Analysis of a 'Purim-Shpil,'" *The Drama Review: TDR* 24, no. 3, (September 1980): 5. Jewish Theatre Issue.
408 Ahuva Belkin, "Ritual Space as Theatrical Space in Jewish Folk Theatre," in *Jewish Theatre: A Global View*, ed. Edna Nahshon (Lieden, Boston: Brill 2009), 15.
409 Lehman, *Postdramatic Theatre*, 71–2.
410 Miklaszewski, *Tadeusz Kantor: Między śmietnikiem a wiecznością* [Tadeusz Kantor: Between Garbage and Eternity], 202.
411 Hoffman, "Witkiewicz i teatr Tadeusza Kantora" [Witkiewicz and Theatre of Tadeusz Kantor]. Cricoteka Archives: CRC III/004817.
412 Billington, "The Dead Class," 8.
413 Kantor, "Postacie 'Umarłej klasy'" [Characters from *Dead Class*].
414 Ibid.

415 Greń, "Nie pogrzebani" [The Unburied Ones].
416 Gussow, "Tadeusz Kantor's Troupe Carries On," C15.
417 Leszek Kolankiewicz, *Wielki mały wóz. Teatr jako wehikuł* [The Big Small Dipper: Theatre as a Vehicle] (Gdańsk: Słowo/Obraz Terytoria 2001), 227.
418 Ibid.
419 Emilia Zimnica-Kuziola, "Tadeusz Kantor," *Gazeta Wyborcza*, 2 August 2005, 9.
420 John Elsom, "Décor by Babel," *Listener*, 2 September 1976. Cricoteka Archives: CRC III/000190.
421 Ibid.
422 Vaizey, quoted in "Critics' Forum."
423 Barker, quoted in "Critics' Forum."
424 Mitchell, quoted in "Critics' Forum."
425 Katarzyna Boruń-Jagodzińska, "Franz Kafka Superstar," *Gazeta Wyborcza*, 7 September 1992, 9.
426 B. A. Young, "Picking at the Fringe," *Financial Times*, 31 August 1976, 10.
427 Barker, quoted in "Critics' Forum."
428 Tamara Karren, "'Umarła Klasa' Kantora" [Kantor's 'Dead Class'], *Tydzień Polski*, 9 October 1976, 7.
429 Dace, "The Class of the Living Death." Cricoteka Archives: CRC III/000487.
430 Miklaszewski, "*Dead Class*, or a New Treatise on Mannequins" [Conversation with Tadeusz Kantor, October 1975], in *Encounters with Tadeusz Kantor*, 34.
431 Miklaszewski, *Encounters with Tadeusz Kantor*, 45.
432 Bessel A. van der Kolk, "The Compulson to Repeat the Trauma: Re-enactment, Revictimization, and Masochism," *Psychiatric Clinics of North America* 12, no. 2 (June 1989): 386–411, at 386.
433 Sigmund Freud, "Beyond the Pleasure Principle" (1920), in *Complete Psychological Works*, Standard Edition, vol. 3., trans. and ed. J. Strachey (London: Hogarth Press 1954), 18.
434 Eder, "Stage: Avant-Gardists From Poland at La Mama," C7.
435 Loney, "Kantor and *The Dead Class*," 11.
436 Cathy Caruth, *Trauma: Explorations in Memory* (Baltimore, MD: John Hopkins University Press 1995), 5.
437 Geoffrey H. Hartman, "On Traumatic Knowledge and Literary Studies," *New Literary History* 26, no. 3 (Summer 1995): 542.
438 I owe this phrase to one of my students, A. D. Spunt.
439 Fisher, "*The Dead Class* by Tadeusz Kantor" [review], 417–18, at 417.
440 William Faulkner, *Requiem for a Nun* (New York: Library of America 1952), 92.
441 Szydłowski, "Czarno na białym. 'Umarła klasa' po latach" [In Black and White: 'Dead Class' After All Those Years], 4.
442 Anna Boska, "Umarła klasa" [Dead Class], *Kobieta i Życie*, 20 February 1977, available at *Polish Theatre Portal*, <http://www.e-teatr.pl/pl/artykuly/11898.html> (accessed 24 April 2011).
443 Jan Skotnicki, "Ukradzione poranki" [Stolen Mornings], *Scena* 9 (November 1983): 21.
444 Dace, "The Class of the Living Death." Cricoteka Archives: CRC III/000487.
445 Mel Gussow, "Polish Experimentalist Examines Man and History," *New York Times*, 20 October 1985, <http://www.nytimes.com/1985/10/20/theater/stage-view-polish-experimentalist-examines-man-and-history.html> (accessed 24 April 2011).
446 Jan Kott, *Kadysz. Strony o Tadeuszu Kantorze* [Kaddish: Pages About Tadeusz Kantor] (Gdańsk: Słowo/Obraz Terytoria 1997), 16.
447 Kott and Esslin, *The Theatre of Essence, and Other Essays*, 71–2.
448 Sandauer, "Sztuka po końcu sztuki" [Art After the End of Art], 111–12.
449 Brown, *Myths and Relatives*, 39.

450 Shanon Lindenbaum, "'Sanatorium pod klepsydrą' – Hades czy sanatorium?" ["Sanatorium Under the Sign of the Hourglass" – Hades or Sanatorium?], in *W ułamkach zwierciadła – Bruno Schulz w 110 rocznicę urodzin i 60 rocznicę śmierci*, ed. Małgorzata Kitowska-Łysiak and Władysław Panas (Lublin: Towarzystwo Naukowe KUL 2003), 47–74, at 49.
451 Schulz, "Sanatorium Under the Sign of the Hourglass," 115.
452 Brown, *Myths and Relatives*, 43.
453 Emanuel Tov, *Textual Criticism of the Hebrew Bible* (Minneapolis, MN: Fortress Press 2012), 60.
454 Giorgio Agamben, *Language and Death: The Place of Negativity* (Minneapolis, MN: University of Minnesota Press 1991), 30.
455 Jacques Derrida, "Difference," in *Margins of Philosophy* (Chicago: University of Chicago Press 1982), 9–11.
456 Kiebuzinska, *Intertextual Loops in Modern Drama*, 50.
457 Miklaszewski, *Zatracenie się w Schulzu* [Losing Oneself in Schulz], 99.
458 Kantor, quoted in Krzysztof Pleśniarowicz, *Kantor* (Wrocław: Wydawnictwo Dolnośląskie 1997), 7.
459 Pascal, "'The Dead Class' by Tadeusz Kantor (Riverside)."
460 Anne Edgar, "Theatre of Memory: Art and Holocaust," press release, the Jewish Museum, New York, 31 October 2008, <http://www.thejewishmuseum.org/site/pages/page.php?id=1111> (accessed 24 April 2011).
461 Pleśniarowicz, *Kantor*, 7, 15.
462 Morawiec, quoted in Zimnica-Kuziola, "Tadeusz Kantor," 9.
463 Pleśniarowicz, *Teatr Śmierci Tadeusza Kantora* [Tadeusz Kantor's Theatre of Death], 107, 152.
464 Blumenthal, "Haunted by History," 77.
465 Karen Underhill, "Ecstasy and Heresy: Martin Buber, Bruno Schulz, and Jewish Modernity," in *(Un)masking Bruno Schulz: New Combinations, Further Fragmentations, Ultimate Reintegrations*, ed. Dieter De Bruyn and Kris van Heuckelom (Amsterdam: Rodopi 2009), 27–46, at 27–8.
466 Ibid. 30; 46.
467 Tadeusz Kantor, quoted in Miklaszewski, *Zatracenie się w Schulzu* [Losing Oneself in Schulz], 31.
468 Perez, *Bruno Schulz: Literary Kabbalist of the Holocaust*, 5.
469 Greń, "Nie pogrzebani" [The Unburied Ones].
470 Święcicki, *Historia w teatrze Tadeusza Kantora* [History in the Theatre of Tadeusz Kantor], 255.
471 Anna Madeyska-Pawlikowska, "Na pograniczu dwóch światów" [On the Borderline of Two Worlds], introduction to *Dybuk. Na pograniczu dwóch światów: przypowieść w czterech aktach według hebrajskiej wersji dramatu Chaima Nachmana Bialika* [Dybbuk. On the Borderline of Two Worlds: Story in Four Acts, According to the Hebrew Version of the Drama by Chaim Nachman Bialik], edited and translated by Awiszaj Hadari (Cracow: Wydawnictwo Austeria 2007), 19.
472 Kantor, "Cricot 2 and The Theatre of Death."
473 Greń, "Nie pogrzebani" [The Unburied Ones].
474 Quoted in Pleśniarowicz, *Teatr nie-ludzkiej formy* [The Theatre of the Un-Human Form], 25.
475 Dominick LaCapra, "Trauma, Absence, Loss," *Critical Inquiry* 25, no. 4 (Summer 1999): 698.
476 Greń, "Nie pogrzebani" [The Unburied Ones].
477 Kantor, quoted in Miklaszewski, *Tadeusz Kantor: Między śmietnikiem a wiecznością* [Tadeusz Kantor: Between Garbage and Eternity], 182.
478 Ibid.
479 Święcicki, *Historia w teatrze Tadeusza Kantora* [History in the Theatre of Tadeusz Kantor], 252.

480 Robert E. Helbing, *The Major Works of Heinrich von Kleist* (New York: New Direction Books 1975), 36.
481 Ibid.
482 The concept of the marionette was explored by other German expressionists of that time as well, particularly those connected with Bauhaus. Schreyer claimed that he and Oskar Schlemmer were the first to come up with the notion of the "Uber-marionette, as our form was called, not by us, but by others" (David F. Kuhns, *German Expressionist Theatre: The Actor and the Stage* (Cambridge: Cambridge University Press 1997), 161). Bauhaus designers were foremost interested in the geometry of the human body and the ways in which marionettes could potentially replace it; and, vice versa, the ways in which the human body could potentially replicate the grace and perfection of a marionette.
483 Ibid., 66.
484 Edward Gordon Craig, "The Actor and the Uber-Marionette," in *On The Art of the Theatre*, ed. and intro. Franc Chamberlain (New York: Routledge 2009), 28.
485 Ibid., 40.
486 Ibid., 39.
487 Ibid., 36.
488 Ibid., 45.
489 Bruno Schulz, *The Street of Crocodiles*, in *The Complete Fiction of Bruno Schulz*, trans. Celina Wieniewska (New York: Walker and Company 1989), 33.
490 Ibid., 31.
491 Ibid., 34–5.
492 Wiesław Borowski, *Tadeusz Kantor*,
493 Bocheński, *Czarny humor w twórczości Witkacego, Gombrowicza, Schulza* [Black Humor in the Works of Witkacy, Gombrowicz, Schulz], 203.
494 Schulz, *The Street of Crocodiles*, 39.
495 Perez, *Bruno Schulz: Literary Kabbalist of the Holocaust*, 9.
496 Bozena Shallcross, *The Holocaust Object in Polish and Polish-Jewish Culture* (Bloomington, IN: Indiana University Press 2011), 1–2.
497 Ibid., 4.
498 Tadeusz Różewicz, quoted in Jodłowski, "Seans Kantora" [Kantor's Séance], 2.
499 Kantor, quoted in Kobialka, *A Journey Through Other Spaces*, 112.
500 Kantor, quoted in Miklaszewski, *Encounters with Tadeusz Kantor*, 39.
501 Ibid.
502 Kantor, quoted in Pleśniarewicz, *Teatr Śmierci Tadeusza Kantora* [Tadeusz Kantor's Theatre of Death], 55.
503 Neal Ascherson, "*Class* of Cantor," *Observer*, 14 November 1982, 31.
504 Irving Wardle, "'The Dead Class.' College of Art," *Times*, 30 August 1976. Cricoteka Archives: CRC III/000186.
505 Richard Cork, "Enter the Hollow Men," *Evening Standard*, London Art Review, 29 September 1976, 26.
506 Vaizey, quoted in "Critics' Forum."
507 Lehman, *Postdramatic Theatre*, 73.
508 Gussow, "Polish Experimentalist Examines Man and History."
509 Fisher, "*The Dead Class* by Tadeusz Kantor" [review], 417–18, at 417.
510 Kantor, quoted in Rosette C. Lamont, "Builder of Bridges Between the Living and the Dead," *New York Times*, 6 October 1985, <http://theater.nytimes.com/mem/theater/treview.html?res=9C0DEEDA1239F935A35753C1A963948260&scp=1&sq=die%20mannequin&st=cse> (accessed 21 January 2011).
511 Dace, "The Class of the Living Death." Cricoteka Archives: CRC III/000487.
512 Calvoressi, "Edinburgh Festival: Tadeusz Kantor: Cricot 2 Theatre," 46.

513 Tadeusz Kantor, *Further Development: The Object*, trans. William Brand. In *Annexing the Impossible: The Writings of Tadeusz Kantor*, ed. Daniel F. Simpson (unpublished manuscript in the Cricoteka collection, 1987), 493.
514 Kobialka, *A Journey Through Other Spaces*, 391.
515 Kantor, quoted in ibid., 110.
516 Kobialka, *A Journey Through Other Spaces*, 290.
517 Tadeusz Kantor, *The Play – The World of Fiction, Its Place in the BIO-OBJECT*, trans. William Brand. In *Annexing the Impossible: The Writings of Tadeusz Kantor*, ed. Daniel F. Simpson (unpublished manuscript in the Cricoteka collection, 1987), 494.
518 Kantor, quoted in Pleśniarewicz, *The Dead Memory Machine*.
519 Ibid., 36.
520 Ibid.
521 Tadeusz Kantor, *Teatr Cricot 2. Teatr Autonomiczny* (Cracow: Galeria Krszysztofory 1963). Cricoteka Archives.
522 Kantor (1988), quoted in Kobialka, *A Journey Through Other Spaces*, 101.
523 Aldona Skiba-Lickel, *Aktor według Kantora* (Wrocław: Zakład Narodowy im. Ossolinskich – Wydawnictwo 1995).
524 Tadeusz Kantor, notes to *Balladyna* (1942), trans. William Brand. Unpublished manuscript in the Cricoteka collection.
525 Pleśniarewicz, *The Dead Memory Machine*, 55.
526 Ibid., 68.
527 Connecting actor and object, Kantor was partially influenced by early twentieth-century avant-garde theatre, particularly that of the Bauhaus directors Oskar Schlemmer and Lothar Schreyer. For Schlemmer, confrontation between actor and objectifying space led to "an intensification of their peculiar natures." Entrapped by objectifying space, man's subjective existence demands recognition. As Schlemmer put it, "Man, the human organism, stands in the cubical, abstract space of the stage […] Each has different laws of order. Whose shall prevail? […] Either abstract space is adapted […] to the natural man and transformed back to nature […] or natural man… is recast to fit its mold" (Oskar Schlemmer, "Man and Art: Figure," in *The Theatre of the Bauhaus*, ed. Walter Gropius (Baltimore: John Hopkins University Press 1996), 22).
528 David F. Kuhns, *German Expressionist Theatre: The Actor and The Stage* (Cambridge: Cambridge University Press 1997), 161.
529 Tadeusz Kantor, "Space, Notes" (1948). Unpublished manuscript in the Cricoteka collection.
530 Plesniarewicz, *The Dead Memory Machine*, 152.
531 Ibid., 94.
532 Pleśniarowicz, *Teatr Śmierci Tadeusza Kantora* [Tadeusz Kantor's Theatre of Death].
533 Ibid.
534 Pleśniarowicz, *The Dead Memory Machine*, 67.
535 Kantor, "Cricot 2 and The Theatre of Death," 41.
536 Plesniarewicz, *The Dead Memory Machine*.
537 Lehman, *Postdramatic Theatre*, 73.
538 Kantor, "Cricot 2 and The Theatre of Death," 44.
539 Ibid., 38.
540 Tadeusz Kantor, quoted in Anna Halczak, *Tadeusz Kantor. Epoka chłopca* [Tadeusz Kantor: Boyhood Epoch], catalog for the exhibit, (Cracow: Cricoteka 2008), 12.
541 Plesniarewicz, *The Dead Memory Machine*, 76.
542 Miklaszewski, *Encounters with Tadeusz Kantor*, 42.
543 Edvard Braun, *Meyerhold on Theatre* (New York: Hill and Wang 1969), 199.
544 Gerould, "A Visual Artist Works Magic on the Polish Stage," 28–36, at 36.
545 Tadeusz Kantor, "To Save from Oblivion" (1988), in Kobialka, *A Journey Through Other Spaces*, 482.
546 Ibid., 27.

547 Quoted in J. M. Bates, "Dziady," reprinted in *Censorship: A World Encyclopedia*, ed. Derek Jones (London: Fitzroy Dearborn Publishers 2000), <http://www.arts.gla.ac.uk/Slavonic/Dziady.html> (accessed 21 June 2012).
548 Ibid.
549 Halina Filipowicz, "Performing Bodies, Performing Mickiewicz: Drama as Problem in Performance Studies," *Slavic and East European Journal* 43, no. 1 (Spring 1999): 1–18, at 15.
550 Kazimierz Braun, *A History of Polish Theatre, 1939–1989: Spheres of Captivity and Freedom* (Westport, CT: Greenwood Press 1996), 74.
551 Ibid.
552 Ibid.
553 Ibid.
554 Ibid., 75.
555 Quoted in Bates, "Dziady."
556 For the contemporary production history of *Forefathers' Eve*, see Braun, *A History of Polish Theatre, 1939–1989: Spheres of Captivity and Freedom*.
557 Quoted in Bates, "Dziady."
558 Agnieszka Fryz-Więcek, "Utoczyć twochę krwi" [To Draw Some Blood], conversation with Jan Nowicki, *Didaskalia. Gazeta Teatralna* (Cracow) 13–14 (June–August 1996): 48.
559 Stephen Moeller-Sally, *Gogol's Afterlife: The Evolution of a Classic in Imperial and Soviet Russia* (Evanston, IL: Northwestern University Press 2002), 180.
560 Halina Filipowicz, "Mickiewicz: 'East' and 'West,'" *Slavic and East European Journal* 45, no. 4 (Winter 2001): 605–731, at 606.
561 Ibid., 607.
562 Artur Sandauer, *On the Situation of the Polish Writer of Jewish Descent in the Twentieth Century* (Jerusalem: Hebrew University, Magnes Press 2005).
563 Ibid., 12.
564 Jadwiga Mauer, *"Z matki obcej-": Szkice o powiązaniach Mickiewicza ze światem Żydów* ["Of a Foreign Mother": Essays about Mickiewicz's Connections with the Jewish World] (Polska Fundacja Kulturalna 1990).
565 Stuart Goldberg, "Konrad and Jacob: A Hypothetical Kabbalistic Subtext in Adam Mickiewicz's *The Forefathers' Eve*, Part III," *Slavic and East European Journal* 45, no. 4 (Winter 2001): 695–715.
566 Pleśniarowicz, *The Dead Memory Machine*, 10.
567 Kantor, quoted in Miklaszewski, *Tadeusz Kantor: Między śmietnikiem a wiecznością* [Tadeusz Kantor: Between Garbage and Eternity], 32.
568 Helen N. Fagin, "Adam Mickiewicz: Poland's National Romantic Poet," *South Atlantic Bulletin* 42, no. 4 (November 1977): 103–13, at 103.
569 Adam Mickiewicz, "Dziady, Part I," in *Dziady*, ed. Maria Cieśla-Korytowska (Cracow: Towarzystwo Autorów i Wydawców Prac Naukowych UNIVERSITAS 1998), 95.
570 "Bo kto nie doznał goryczy ni razu,/ Ten nie dozna słodyczy w niebie." (Ibid., 101)
571 "Bo kto nie był ni razu człowiekiem,/ Temu człowiek nic nic pomoże." (Ibid., 107)
572 Ibid., 111.
573 Leszek Kolankiewicz, *Dziady. Teatr święta zmarłych* [Dziady: Theatre of *The Forefathers' Eve*] (Gdańsk: Słowo/Obraz Terytoria 1999), 407.
574 Sandauer, "Sztuka po końcu sztuki" [Art After the End of Art], 111–12.
575 Święcicki, *Historia w teatrze Tadeusza Kantora* [History in the Theatre of Tadeusz Kantor], 253.
576 Wojciech Szulczynski, "Review: *The Forefathers' Eve: Twelve Improvisations*," *Theatre Journal* 48, no. 4, Eastern European Transitions (December 1996): 499–503, at 503.
577 Gussow, "Tadeusz Kantor's Troupe Carries On," C15.
578 Roman Pawłowski, "Żywa martwa klasa" [Living *Dead Class*], *Gazeta Wyborcza*, 26 October 2001, 21.

579 Ibid.
580 Ibid.
581 Wacław Janicki, quoted in "Dramaturg Kantor," interview by Roman Pawłowski, *Gazeta Wyborcza*, 29 October 2001, 16.
582 Ibid., 5.
583 Włodzimierz Staniewski, quoted in Grzegorz Józefczuk, "Kantor, ale inaczej" [Kantor, But Differently], *Gazeta Wyborcza*, 15 January 2002, 5.
584 Józefczuk, "Kantor, ale inaczej" [Kantor, But Differently], 5.
585 Ibid., 5.
586 Wacław Janicki, quoted in Pawłowski, "Dramaturg Kantor," 16.
587 Ibid.
588 Cieślak, "Niecały umarł, choć odszedł jego świat," [Not All of Him Died, Though His World Is Gone].
589 Katarzyna Bik, "Żywe pomnik, umarła klasa" [Living Monuments, Dead Class], *Gazeta Wyborcza*, 8 December 2004, 7.

Postscript

1 Karen Jürs-Munby, "Introduction" to Hans-Ties Lehman, *Postdramatic Theatre* (New York: Routledge 2006), 2.
2 Ibid., 13.
3 Hans-Ties Lehman, *Postdramatic Theatre* (New York: Routledge 2006), 183.
4 Jacques Derrida, *Of Grammatology*, trans. by Gayatri Chakravorty Spivak (Baltimore: Johns Hopkins University Press 1998), 110.
5 Ibid., 112.

BIBLIOGRAPHY

Adorno, Theodor W. and Max Horkheimer. "The Culture Industry: Enlightenment as Mass Deception." *The Cultural Studies Reader*. Ed. Simon During. New York: Routledge, 1993. 31–41.
Adorno, Theodor W. *Aesthetic Theory*. Trans. Robert Hullot-Kentor. Minneapolis: University of Minnesota Press, [1970] 1998.
_____. "Cultural Criticism and Society." *Prisms*. Trans. Samuel and Shierry Weber. Cambridge, MA: MIT Press, 1967. 17–34.
_____. "Trying to Understand *Endgame*." *Notes to Literature: Volume 1*. Ed. Rolf Tiedemann, trans. Shierry Weber Nicholson. New York: Columbia University, 1958.
Agamben, Giorgio. *Language and Death: The Place of Negativity*. Minneapolis: University of Minnesota Press, 1991.
_____. *Homo Sacer: Sovereign Power and Bare Life*. Stanford, CA: Stanford University Press 1998.
_____. *Remnants of Auschwitz: The Witness and the Archive*. New York: Zone Books, 2002.
Ahrne, Marianne. "The Man in Her Dream." *Grotowski's Empty Room*. Ed. Paul Allain. London: Seagull Books, 2010. 7–18.
A. K. "The Grotowski Theatre in USA." *Le Théâtre en Pologne/Theatre in Poland* 6–7 (1970): 29–31.
Alexander, Jeffrey. "Toward a Theory of Cultural Trauma." *Cultural Trauma and Collective Identity*. Ed. Jeffrey Alexander, Ron Eyerman, Bernhard Giesen, Neil J. Smelser and Piotr Sztompka. Berkeley: University of California Press, 2004.
Améry, Jean. *At the Mind's Limits: Contemplations by a Survivor on Auschwitz and Its Realities*. Bloomington: Indiana University Press, 1980.
Anderson, Benedict. *Imagined Communities: Reflections on the Origin and Spread of Nationalism*. London: Verso, 1983.
Ariel, David S. *Kabbalah: The Mystic Quest in Judaism*. Lanham, MD: Rowman & Littlefield Publishers, 2005.
Ascherson, Neal. "The Artist as Traitor." *Scotsman*, 28 August 1976. Cricoteka Archives: CRC III/000184.
_____. "Class of Cantor." *Observer*, 14 November 1982, 31.
_____. *The Struggles for Poland*. New York: Random House, 1988.
Auerback, Karen and Antony Polonsky. "Insiders/Outsiders: Poles and Jews in Recent Polish Jewish Fiction and Autobiography." *Insiders and Outsiders: Dilemmas of East European Jewry*. Ed. Richard J. Cohen, Jonathan Frankel and Stefani Hoffman. Oxford: The Littman Library of Jewish Civilization, 2010. 70–102.
A.W. "A Painting Comes Alive." *Glasgow Herald*, 23 August 1976, 5.
Bacon, Gershon. "Poland: Poland from 1795 to 1939." *YIVO Encyclopedia of Jews in Eastern Europe* (2011). <http://www.yivoencyclopedia.org/article.aspx/Poland/Poland_from_1795_to_1939> (accessed 29 June 2011).
Baczyński, Stanisław. *Rzeczywistość i fikcja (Współczesna powieść polska)* [Reality and Fiction: The Contemporary Polish Novel]. Warsaw: Nowa Biblioteka Społeczna 1939. 290–91.
Bąk, Bogdan. "*Akropolis* z laboratorium" ['Akropolis' from the Laboratory]. *Słowo Polskie* 277 (1963): 3.

Bałus, Wojciech. "Ożywianie posągów. Głosa do'Akropolis" [Resurrecting the Statue. Voice to "Akropolis"]. *Wawel – 'Akropolis.' Studium o dramacie Stanisława Wyspiańskiego* [Wawel – 'Akropolis'. Studium about Wyspiański's Drama]. Ed. Ewa Miodońska-Brookes. Cracow: Wydawnictwo Literackie, 1980. 169–80.

Barba, Eugenio. *Land of Ashes and Diamonds: My Apprenticeship in Poland*. Aberystwyth, UK: Black Mountain Press, 1999.

_____. *Ziemia popiołu i diamentów* [The Land of Ashes and Diamonds]. Wrocław: Ośrodek Badań Twórczości Jerzego Grotowskiego i Poszukiwań Teatralno-Kulturowych, 2001.

Barba, Eugenio, Ludwik Flaszen and Simone Sanzenbach. "The Theatre of Magic and Sacrilege." *Tulane Drama Review* 9, no. 3 (1965): 166–89.

Barber, John. "Digging Up Our Buried Years." *Daily Telegraph*, 6 September 1976. Cricoteka Archives: CRC III/000192.

Bardonnie, Mathilde La. "Tadeusz Kantor: Le Maître." *Le Monde*, 14 October 1977, 28.

Barnes, Clive. "Jerzy Grotowski's 'Acropolis': 1904 Drama Is Adapted for Polish Group" *New York Times*, 5 November 1969, 40.

_____. "Theatre: Grotowski's View of Reality." *New York Times*, 18 October 1969, 36.

Barranger, Milly S. *Theatre: Ways of Seeing*. Belmont, CA: Thomson Wadsworth Publishing, 2005.

Barron, D. Brian "Atelier '76 at 61 High St. 'The Dead Class.'" *Festival Times*, 25 August 1976, 5. Cricoteka Archives: CRC III/000183.

Barry, Ann. "Arts and Leisure Guide; Theater." *New York Times*, 11 March 1979, D35.

Bartelik, Marek. *Early Polish Modern Art: Unity in Multiplicity*. Manchester: Manchester University Press, 2005.

Basara, Zbigniew. "Kantor wrócił do Nowego Jorku" [Kantor Returns to New York]. *Gazeta Wyborcza*, 13 November 2008, 21.

Bates, J. M. "Dziady." *Censorship: A World Encyclopedia*. Ed. Derek Jones. London: Fitzroy Dearborn Publishers, 2000.

Bauman, Zygmunt. *Modernity and Ambivalence*. Ithaca, NY: Cornell University Press, 1991.

_____. *Modernity and the Holocaust*. Ithaca, NY: Cornell University Press, 1989.

BBC Radio 3. "Critics Forum." 16 October 1976, 4.

Bean, Heidi R. "'Professing Performance: Theatre in the Academy from Philology to Performativity' (review)." *Cultural Critique* 71 (Winter 2009): 151–4.

Belkin, Ahuva. "Ritual Space a Theatrical Space in Jewish Theatre." *Jewish Theatre: A Global View*. Ed. Edna Nahshon. Lieden, Boston: Brill, 2009.

Benjamin, Walter. "The Work of Art in the Age of Mechanical Reproduction" (1935) *Illuminations*. Trans. Harry Zohn. Random House: New York, 1998. 217–52.

Bentley, Eric. "Dear Grotowski: An Open Letter From Eric Bentley." *New York Times*, 30 November 1969, D1.

Berger, James. *After the End: Representations of Post-Apocalypse*. Minneapolis: University of Minnesota Press, 1999.

Bernard-Donals, Michael and Richard Glejzer. *Between Witness and Testimony: The Holocaust and the Limits of Representation*. New York: State University of New York Press, 2001.

Bernstein, Michael Andre. *Foregone Conclusions: Against Apocalyptic History*. Berkeley, CA: University of California Press, 1994.

Bettelheim, Bruno. "Individual and Mass Behavior in Extreme Situations." *Journal of Abnormal and Social Psychology* 38 (1943): 417–52.

Białek, Józef Zbigiew. *Literatura dziecięca okresu międzywojennego na tle ówczesnych kierunków pedagogicznych*. Cracow: Rocznik Naukowo – Dydaktyczny WSP, 1962.

Bielski, Nella. "L'emotion immediate." *Le Matin*, 17 October 1977. Cricoteka Archives: CRC III/000310.

Bieniewski, Henryk. "Krok naprzód" [Step Forward]. *Teatr*, 22 August 1976, 12–13.

Bik, Katarzyna. "Żywe pomnik, umarła klasa" [Living Monuments, Dead Class]. *Gazeta Wyborcza*, 8 December 2004, 7.
Biliński, Tadeusz. "Święto Wielkiej Poezji w Krakowie. 'Akropolis' Wyspiańskiego w Teatrze im. Słowackiego" [Celebrating Great Poetry in Cracow. Wyspiański's 'Akropolis' at the Słowacki Theatre]. *Comoedia* (1927): 2.
Billington, Michael. "The Dead Class." *Arts Guardian*, 13 September 1976, 8.
———. "Fringe on Top." *Guardian*, 30 August 1976. Cricoteka Archives: CRC III/000187.
Blobaum, Robert. *Antisemitism and its Opponents in Modern Poland*. Ithaca, NY: Cornell University Press, 2005.
Błoński, Jan. "Grotowski and His Laboratory Theatre." *Dialog* 15 (1970): 142–50. Special issue.
———. "The Poor Poles Look at the Ghetto." *Four Decates of Polish Essays*. Ed. Jan Kott. Evanston, IL: Northwestern University Press, 1990. 222–35.
———. *Stanisław Ignacy Witkiewicz jako dramaturg* [Stanisław Ignacy Witkiewicz as Playwright]. Cracow: PWN, 1973.
———. *Witkacy na zawsze* [Witkacy Forever]. Cracow: Wydawnictwo Literackie, 2003.
Blumenthal, Eileen. "Haunted by History." *Village Voice*, 26 February 1973, 77.
Boak, Sharon. "The Reflection of the Napoleonic Legend in Adam Mickiewicz's Pan Tadeusz." *Slovo* 20, no. 2 (2008): 107–18.
Bober, Jerzy. "Inny Wyspiański" [Another Wyspiański]. *Gazeta Południowa*, 18–19 February 1978, 6.
Bocheński, Tomasz. "Czarny humor w twórczości Brunona Schulza" [Black Humor in the Work of Bruno Schulz]. *W ułamkach zwierciadła– Bruno Schulz w 110 rocznicę urodzin i 60 rocznicę śmierci*. Ed. Małgorzata Kitowska-Łysiak and Władysław Panas. Lublin: Towarzystwo Naukowe KUL, 2003. 211–28.
———. *Czarny humor w twórczości Witkacego, Gombrowicza, Schulza – Lata trzydzieste* [Black Humor in the Works of Witkacy, Gombrowicz, Schulz – 1930s]. Cracow: Towarzystwo Autorów i Wydawców Prac Naukowych UNIVERSITAS, 2005.
Bodnar, Izabela. "Edynburg – Arena Najlepszych" [Edinburgh – The Stage of the Best]. *Przekrój*, 10 October 1976, 140.
Bodnicki, Władysław. *Między niebem a piekłem* [Between Heaven and Hell]. Łódź: Wydawnictwo Łódzkie, 1973.
Bonarski, Andrzej. *Ziarno*. Warsaw: Czytelnik, 1979.
Bończa-Szabłowski, Jan. "Korowód starych dzieci" [Pageant of the Old Children]. *Rzeczpospolita*, 20 January 2009. Available at *Polish Theatre Portal*. <http://www.e-teatr.pl/pl/artykuly/81526.html> (accessed 29 November 2011).
Bordwell, David. *Making Meaning: Inference and Rhetoric in the Interpretation of Cinema*. Cambridge, MA: Harvard University Press, 1996.
Borowski, Tadeusz. *Alicja w Krainie Czarów* [Alice in Wonderland]. *Pokolenie* 1, no. 7 (12 January 1947): 9.
———. *This Way for the Gas, Ladies and Gentlemen*. Ed. Trans. Barbara Vedder. New York: Penguin, 1992.
———. *U nas w Auschwitzu* [At Our Auschwitz]. Warsaw: Państwowy Instytut Wydawniczy PIW, 1971.
———. *Wspomnienia, Wiersze, Opowiadania* [Essays, Poems, Short Stories]. Fourth Edition. Warsaw: Państwowy Instytut Wydawniczy, 1981.
Borowski, Wiesław. *Kantor*. Warsaw: Wydawnictwo Artystyczne i Filmowe, 1982.
———. "Umarła Klasa" [Dead Class]. *Literatura*, 22 April 1976, 33B.
Boruń-Jagodzińska, Katarzyna. "Franz Kafka Superstar." *Gazeta Wyborcza*, 7 October 1992, 9.
Boska, Anna. "Umarła klasa" [Dead Class]. *Kobieta i Życie*, 20 February 1977. Available at *Polish Theatre Portal*. <http://www.e- teatr.pl/pl/artykuly/11898.html> (accessed 24 April 2011).
Boue, Michael. "La classe du maître Kantor." *L'Humanité Dimanche* 88 (5–11 October 1977): 4.

Boy-Żeleński, Tadeusz. "Witkiewicz. Tumor Mózgowicz." *Flirt z Melpomeną, wieczór trzeci.* Cracow: Krakowska Spółka Wydawnicza, 1992. 68–76.
Boyers, Robert. "Gombrowicz and Ferdydurke: The Tyranny of Form." *Centennial Review* 14 (1970): 284–312.
Braun, Edvard. *Meyerhold on Theatre.* New York: Hill and Wang, 1969.
Braun, Kazimierz. *A History of Polish Theatre, 1939–1989: Spheres of Captivity and Freedom.* Westport, CT: Greenwood Press, 1996.
_____. "Theater Training in Poland." *Performer Training: Developments Across Cultures.* Ed. Ian Watson. Amsterdam: Harwood, 2001.
Brecht, Stefan. "On Grotowski: A Series of Critiques." *TDR: A Journal of Performance Studies* 14, no. 2 (T46) (Winter 1970): 178–211.
Brook, Peter. *The Empty Space.* Austin, TX: Touchstone, 1995.
_____. "Preface" to Jerzy Grotowski's *Towards a Poor Theatre.* London: Methuen, 1968.
_____. *With Grotowski, Theatre is Just a Form.* Wrocław: The Grotowski Institute, 2009.
Brown, Russell E. *Myths and relatives: seven essays on Bruno Schulz.* München: Verlag Otto Sagner, 1991.
Brumer, Wiktor. *Teatr Wyspiańskiego* [Wypiański's Theatre]. Warsaw: Drukarnia. Wł. Łazarskiego, 1933.
Brustein, Robert. "New Fads, Ancient Truths." *New York Times,* 17 August 1969, D1.
_____. "New Theatre, New Politics?" *New York Times,* 25 August 1968, D1.
Bryden, Ronald. "A Myth in Stepney." *Observer,* 28 September 1969, 27.
Burleigh, Michael. *Ethics and Extermination: Reflections on Nazi Genocide.* Cambridge: Cambridge University Press, 1997.
Burzyński, Tadeusz. "Festiwal który zwodzi i zawodzi" [Festival which Disillusions and Disappoints]. *Scena* 9 (November 1976): 2–5.
_____. *Mój Grotowski* [My Grotowski]. Wrocław: Ośrodek Badań Twórczości Jerzego Grotowskiego i Poszukiwań Teatralno-Kulturowych, 2006.
Calta, Louis. "Polish Theater is Coming Here: Jerzy Grotowski Troupe's U.S. Debut Due in October." *New York Times,* 10 September 1969, 36.
Calvoressi, Richard. "Edinburgh Festival: Tadeusz Kantor: Cricot 2 Theatre." *Studio International* 193, no. 985 (February 1977): 45.
Carne, Rosalind. "'The Dead Class'/Riverside Studios." *Financial Times,* 18 November 1982. Cricoteka Archives: CRC III/000653.
Caruth, Cathy. *Trauma: Explorations in Memory.* Baltimore: The Johns Hopkins University Press, 1995.
Cavanagh, Claire. "Postcolonial Poland." *Common Knowledge* 10, no. 1 (Winter 2004): 82–92.
Chambers Biographical Dictionary. "Tadeusz Kantor." Chambers Harrap Publishers Ltd (2007). <http://www.credoreference.com/entry/chambbd/kantor_tadeusz> (accessed 3 June 2011).
Chambers, Colin. "Experiments in the Polish Experience." *Morning Star,* 20 September 1976. Cricoteka Archives: CRC III/000203.
Chapier, Henri. *Le Quotidien de Paris,* 11 October 1977, 13.
Chojnacki, Grzegorz. "'Akropolis,' czyli pamięć" ['Akropolis,' or Memory], interview with Michael Marmarinos. *Gazeta Wyborcza,* 9 December 2009, 6.
Ciesielski, Adam. "Teatr czeka na wizjonerów" [Theatre Waits for the Visionaries]. *Kultura i Życie,* 29 June 1991 [addendum to *Życie Warszawy*]. Available at *Polish Theatre Portal.* <http://www.e-teatr.pl/pl/artykuly/11897.html> (accessed 3 June 2011).
Cieślak, Jacek. "Niecały umarł, choć odszedł jego świat" [Not All of Him Died, Though His World Is Gone], *Rzeczypospolita,* 8 December 2005. Available at *Polish Theatre Portal.* <http://www.e-teatr.pl/pl/artykuly/19356.html> (accessed 3 April 2011).
Cioffi, Kathleen. *Alternative Theatre in Poland 1954–1989.* London and New York: Routledge, 1996.
_____. "From the Great Reform to the Post-Dramatic: Adaptation in the Polish Postwar Theatre." *Canadian Slavonic Papers* 52 (2010): 413–30.

_____. "Review of *Ferdydurke*." *Theatre Journal* 54, no. 2 (May 2002): 301–3.

_____. "The Ghosts of Memory. Review of *Our Class*." *Theater*, 13 November 2011. <http://theatermagazine.yale.edu/our-class> (accessed 13 December 2011).

Ciotka Agnieszka. "Deficytowy artykuł" [The Deficit Article]. *Trybuna Opolska*, 18 October 1962. The Grotowski Institute Archives.

_____. "List do p. Falkowskiego" [Letter to Mr. Falkowski]. *Trybuna Opolska*, 28 October 1962. The Grotowski Institute Archives.

Clurman, Harold. "Jerzy Grotowski." *The Grotowski Sourcebook*. Ed. Richard Schechner and Lisa Wolford. New York: Routledge, 1997. 161–3. Originally published as a chapter titled "Jerzy Grotowski" in *The Divine Pastime* by Harold Clurman. New York: Macmillan, 1974. 221–6.

_____. "*The Dead Class* by Tadeusz Kantor." Review. *The Nation*, 3 March 1979, 251–2.

Coe, Richard. "Either a Cruel Game or a Surgical Operation." *Washington Post*, 2 November 1969, E3.

Cohen, Roger. "The Glory of Poland." *New York Times*, 13 April 2010. <http://www.nytimes.com/2010/04/13/opinion/13iht-edcohen.html?_r=1&emc=eta1> (accessed 10 August 2011).

Connolly, Kate. "Museum to mark Jewish life in Poland: Director says million-pound site in Warsaw will show Poland is 'more than just the world's largest Jewish graveyard.'" *Guardian* (London), 18 July 2002, 16.

Cork, Richard. "Enter the Hollow Men." *Evening Standard*, London Art Review, 29 September 1976, 26.

Cornis-Pope, Marcel and John Neubauer. *History of the Literary Cultures of East-Central Europe: Junctures and Disjunctures in the 19th and 20th Centuries*. The Netherlands: John Benjamins, 2004.

Copermann, Émile. "Une métaphysique obscure." *Lettres Francaises*, 9 October 1968, 17.

Croyden, Margaret. "Images that Recall the Polish Past." *New York Times*, 9 May 1982, D4.

_____. "The Most Avant-Garde of Them All." *New York Times*, 5 October 1969, D1.

Culbertson, Roberta. "Embodied Memory, Transcendence, and Telling: Trauma, Re-Establishing the Self." *New Literary History* 26, no. 1 (Winter 1995): 169–95.

Curtiss, Thomas Quinn. "Polish Theater Group Impressive in Paris." *International Herald Tribune*, 3 October 1968.

Czaplowa, Kazimiera, ed. *Studia o prozie Brunona Schulza*. Katowice: Uniwersytet Śląski, 1976.

Czartoryska, Urszula. "Kantor: New Propositions." *Projekt* 4 (1976). Cricoteka Archives: CRC III/004812, 58–63.

Dąbrowski, Stanisław (1960) *Sceniczne dzieje 'Akropolis', 'Nasza Scena'* [Production History: 'Akropolis', Our Stage]. Łódź: Teatr Nowy, No. 4.

Dace, Tish. "The Class of the Living Death." *Soho Weekly News*, 15 February 1979. Cricoteka Archives: CRC III/000487.

Davis, Norman. *God's Playground: History of Poland*. New York: Columbia University Press, 2005.

De Bruyn, Dieter and Kris van Heuckelom, eds. *(Un)masking Bruno Schulz: New Combinations, Further Fragmentations, Ultimate Reintegrations*. Amsterdam: Rodopi, 2009.

Degler, Janusz. "Witkacego teoria teatru" [Witkacy's Theory of Theatre]. *Czysta Forma w teatrze*. Warsaw: Wydawnictwo Artystyczne i Filmowe, 1977.

_____. "Witkiewicz on the Polish Stage: 1921–1984." *Witkacy – teatr, dokumentacja: inscenizacje sztuk Witkacego na scenach polskich, 1921–1985: katalog wystawy*. Ed. Agnieszka Koecher-Hensel. Warsaw: CSS, 1985.

de Jongh, Nicholas. "'The Dead Class.'" *Guardian*, 18 November 1982. Cricoteka Archives: CRC III/000652.

Delaney, Carol. *Abraham on Trial: The Social Legacy of Biblical Myth*. Princeton, NJ: Princeton University Press, 1998.

DeMan, Paul. "Semiology and Rhetoric." *Diacritics* (Fall 1973): 29

Derkaczew, Joanna. "Grotowski po raz pierwszy" [Grotowski For the First Time]. *Gazeta Wyborcza*, 18 December 2009, 17.
Derrida, Jacques. "Difference." *Margins of Philosophy*. Trans. Alan Bass. Chicago: University of Chicago Press, [1972] 1985. 11–15.
———. *Of Grammatology*. Trans. Gayatri Chakvavorty Spivak, Baltimore: The John Hopkins University Press, [1967] 1998.
Dialog. "Rozmowa o Umarłej Klasie: Konstanty Puzyna, Tadeusz Różewicz, and Andrzej Wajda" [Conversation about 'Dead Class': Konstanty Puzyna, Tadeusz Różewicz, and Andrzej Wajda]. *Dialog* 2 (1977): 135–42.
Drobnicki, John A. "A Touch of Controversy." *The Polish-American Journal* (February 1991). <http://www.york.cuny.edu/~drobnick/polonsky.html> (accessed 20 June 2011).
Drozdowski, Bohdan. "Wester, Grotowski i inni" [Wester, Grotowski and the Others]. *Kultura* 4 (26 January 1969). The Grotowski Institute Archives.
Duker, Abraham G. "Some Cabbalist and Frankist Elements in Adam Mickiewicz's 'Dziady.'" *Studies in Polish Civilization*. Ed. Damian Wandycz. New York: Institute on East Central Europe, Columbia University and The Polish Institute of Arts & Sciences in America, 1966. 213–35.
Dunkelberg, Kermit. "Confrontation, Simulation, Admiration: The Wooster Group's *Poor Theater*." *TDR: The Drama Review* 49, no. 3 (T187) (2005): 43–56.
Dziennik Polski. "Cricot 2' ratuje londyńską placówkę przed plajtą. Kolejne wojaże teatru Kantora." [Cricot 2 Saves London's Studio from Bankrupcy. Kantor's Next Voyage]. 13 December 1982.
———. "Po szwajcarskim turnee 'Cricot 2'" [After the Swedish Tournee of Cricot 2]. (Cracow), 11 June 1981. Cricoteka Archives: CRCIII/000616.
Dziewulska, Małgorzata. *Artyści i pielgrzymi* [Artists and Pilgrims]. Wrocław: Wydawnictwo Dolnośląskie, 1995.
———. "Ogniokrad" [Fire Stealer]. *Teatr* 47, no. 3 (1992): 12–21.
Eco, Umberto. *Carnival! (Approaches to Semiotics)*. Berlin and New York: Mouton de Gruyter, 1984.
Edelman, Charles. "'The Dead Class' by Tadeusz Kantor." Review. *Educational Theatre Journal* 30, no. 4 (December 1978): 546–8.
Eder, Richard. "Stage: Avant-Gardists From Poland at La Mama." *New York Times*, 13 February 1979, C7.
Edgar, Anne. "Theaters of Memory: Art and the Holocaust Opens at the Jewish Museum on November 9, 2008." The Jewish Museum in New York. Press release, 31 October 2008. <http://www.thejewishmuseum.org/site/pages/page.php?id=1111> (accessed 20 January 2010).
Eksteins, Modris. *Rites of Spring: The Great War and the Birth of the Modern Age*. New York: Mariner Books, 2000.
Elsom, John. "Décor by Babel." *Listener*, 2 September 1976. Cricoteka Archives: CRC III/000190.
Elwall, Julia. "Puppets in the String of Life." *Echo*, 9 September 1976. Cricoteka Archives: CRCIII/000196.
Esslin, Martin. "'The Dead Class.'" *Plays and Players* (October 1976). Cricoteka Archives: CRCIII/000205.
Evening Standard. "Invitation Only." (London), 13 September 1976, 6.
Fagin, Helen N. "Adam Mickiewicz: Poland's National Romantic Poet." *South Atlantic Bulletin* 42, no. 4 (November 1977): 103–13.
Falkowski, Jerzy. "Z Jerzym Grotowskim o teatrze" [With Jerzy Grotowski About Theatre]. *Współczesność* 30 (1–30 December 1958): 8.
Fallek, Wilhelm. "Z teatru im. Juliusza Słowackiego, 'Tumor Mózgowicz.' Dramat w 3 aktach z prologiem Stanisława Ignacego Witkiewicza." *Nowy Dziennik* 170 (1921).
Fatouros, A. A. "Sartre on Colonialism." *World Politics* 17, no. 4 (July 1965): 703–19
Faulkner, William. *Requiem for a Nun*. New York: Library of America, 1952.

Fazan, Katarzyna. *Projekt intymnego teatru śmierci: Wyspiański, Leśmian, Kantor* [The Project of the Intimate Theatre of Death: Wyspiański, Leśmian, Kantor]. Cracow: Wydawnictwo Uniwersytetu Jagielonskiego, 2009.

Ficowski, Jerzy. *Regions of the Great Heresy: Bruno Schulz A Biographical Portrait*. Trans. and ed. by Theodosia Robertson. New York: W. W. Norton, 2003.

Fik, Marta. "Kantora Teatr Śmierci" [Kantor's Theatre of Death]. *Polityka*, 14 August 1976. Cricoteka Archives: III/004811.

———. "Wizje na Wawelu" [Visions at the Wawel]. *Polityka* 9 (1978): 23.

Filipowicz, Halina. "Demythologizing Polish Theatre." *TDR: The Drama Review* 39, no. 1 (Spring 1995): 122–9.

———. "Mickiewicz: 'East' and 'West.'" *Slavic and East European Journal* 45, no. 4 (2001): 605–731.

———. "Performing Bodies, Performing Mickiewicz: Drama as Problem in Performance Studies." *The Slavic and East European Journal* 43, no. 1 (Spring 1999): 1–18.

———. "Where Is 'Gurutowski'?" *TDR: The Drama Review* 35, no. 1 (Spring 1999): 181–6.

———. *Wśród Bogów i Bohaterów* [Among the Gods and Heroes]. Warsaw: Państwowy Instytut Wydawniczy, 1973.

Filler, Witold. "Z Wrocławia w świat" [From Wrocław Into the World]. *Kultura* 8 (23 February 1969). The Grotowski Institute Archives.

Financial Times. "Cricot-2 at Riverside Studios." 8 September 1976. Cricoteka Archives: CRC III/000195.

Findlay, Robert. "Grotowski's 'Akropolis': A Retrospective." *Modern Drama* 27, no. 1 (March 1984): 1–20.

Findlay, Robert and Halina Filipowicz. "Grotowski's Laboratory Theatre: Dissolution and Diaspora." *TDR: The Drama Review* 30, no. 3 (T111) (Fall 1986): 201–25. Reprinted in an abridged (by Lisa Wolford) and supplemented version, signed by Robert Findlay, in *The Grotowski Sourcebook*. Ed. Richard Schechner and Lisa Wolford. New York: Routledge, 1997.

Fisher, Eileen. "*The Dead Class* by Tadeusz Kantor." Review. *Theatre Journal* 31, no. 3 (October 1979): 417–18.

Flaszen, Ludwik. "'Akropolis.' Komentarz do przedstawienia" ['Akropolis.' Program Notes] (1962). Reprinted in *Mysterium zgrozy i urzeczenia: Przedstawienia Jerzego Grotowskiego i Teatru Laboratorium* [Mysterium of Horror and Allure: Productions of Jerzy Grotowski and Teatr Laboratorium]. Ed. Janusz Degler and Grzegorz Ziółkowski. Ośrodek Badań Twórczości Jerzego Grotowskiego i Poszukiwań Teatralno-Kulturowych: Wrocław, 2006. 51–2.

———. "'Akropolis': Treatment of the Text." In Jerzy Grotowski's *Towards a Poor Theatre*. New York Routledge, 2002. 61–77. Originally published in *Pamiętnik Teatralny* (Warsaw, 3, 1964) *Alla Ricerca del Teatro Perduto* (Padova: Marsillio Editori, 1965), and *Tulane Drama Review* (New Orleans, Y 27, 1965).

———. "Po Awangardzie" [After Avant-Garde]. *Odra* 4 (1967): 39–42.

———. "Teatr Laboratorium za granicą" [The Laboratory Theatre Abroad]. *Odra* 2 (1969). The Grotowski Institute Archives.

———. "Wyspiański's 'Acropolis.'" *The Grotowski Sourcebook*. Ed. Richard Schechner and Lisa Wolford. New York: Routledge, 1997. 64–72. Originally published under the title "A Theatre of Magic and Sacrilege." *TDR: The Drama Review* 9, no. 3 (1965): 172–89.

Ford, Aleksander. *Ulica graniczna* [*Border Street*] (1948). <http://www.filmpolski.pl/fp/index.php/122529> (accessed 1 March 2010).

Fortier, Mark. *Theory/Theatre: An Introduction*. London and New York: Routledge, 1997.

Foucault, Michel. *Language, Counter-Memory, Practice*, new ed. Ithaca, NY: Cornell University Press, 1980.

Freud, Sigmund. "Beyond the Pleasure Principle" (1920). *Complete Psychological Works*, Standard Edition, vol. 3. Trans. and ed. by J. Strachey. London: Hogarth Press, 1954.

Fryz-Więcek Agnieszka. "Utoczyć trochę krwi" [To Draw Some Blood]. Conversation with Jan Nowicki. *Didaskalia. Gazeta Teatralna* 13–14 (June–August 1996): 48.

Fybes, Marcin. "Śmierć jest nieodwołalnym zamknięciem drzwi" [Death is the Final Closure]. *Gazeta Wyborcza*, 12 December 1990, 9.

Gaczoł, Andrzej. "Wawelu Wyspiański nie dostał" [Wyspiański Didn't Get Wawel]. *Echo Krakowa* 104 (10–11 May 1980): 4.

Garbal, Łukasz. *Ferdydurke: biografia powieści*. Cracow: Tow, 2010.

Garlinski, Jozef. *Fighting Auschwitz: The Resistance Movement in the Concentration Camp*. Robbinsdale, MI: Fawcett, 1975.

Gawlik, Jan Paweł. "'Akropolis' 1961" (1962). Reprinted in *Mysterium zgrozy i urzeczenia: Przedstawienia Jerzego Grotowskiego i Teatru Laboratorium* [Mysterium of Horror and Allure: Productions of Jerzy Grotowski and Teatr Laboratorium]. Ed. Janusz Degler and Grzegorz Ziółkowski. Wrocław: Ośrodek Badań Twórczości Jerzego Grotowskiego i Poszukiwań Teatralno-Kulturowych, 2006. 167–70.

———. "Sztuka Skromności" [The Art of Humility]. *Życie Literackie* 40 (4 October 1959). The Grotowski Institute Archives.

Gazeta Olsztyńska. "Tadeusz Kantor i jego 'Cricot 2.'" 2–4 October 1981.

Gerould, Daniel C. "Foreword." *Witkiewicz: Seven Plays*. Ed. and trans. Daniel Gerould. New York: Martin E. Segal Theatre Center, 2004.

———. "Jerzy Grotowski's Theatrical and Paratheatrical Activities as Cosmic Drama: Roots and Continuities in the Polish Romantic Tradition." *World Literature Today* 54, no. 3 (Summer 1980): 381–3.

———. "A Visual Artist Works Magic on the Polish Stage." *Performing Arts Journal* 4, no. 3 (1980): 28–36.

Gerould Daniel and L. Ploszewski. "Introduction: From Adam Mickiewicz's 'Lectures on Slavic Literature' Given at the Collège de France." *The Drama Review: TDR* 30, no. 3 (Autumn 1986): 91–7.

Gieraczyński, Bogdan. "Na przykład 'Cricot 2'" [For Example Cricot 2]. *Tygodnik Demokratyczny* 38 (18 September 1976): 16.

Giesen, Bernhard. "The Trauma of Perpetrators: The Holocaust as the Traumatic Reference of German National Identity." *Cultural Trauma and Collective Identity*. Ed. Jeffrey Alexander, Ron Eyerman, Bernhard Giesen, Neil J. Smelser and Piotr Sztompka. Berkeley: University of California Press, 2004.

Gignoux, Hubert. "Nancy 77." *Théâtre/Publique* 16–17 (1997).

Gilman, Richard. "What Not to Do in the Theater." *New York Times*, 8 February 1970, 263.

Ginsberg, Merle. "Poland's Incomparable 'Theatre of the Dead': A Matter of Death and Life." *Villager*, 19 February 1979, 13.

Glenn, Susan A. and Naomi B. Sokoloff, eds. *Boundaries of Jewish Identity*. Seattle: University of Washington Press, 2010.

Głowacki, Janusz. *Hunting Cacroaches and Other Plays*. Chicago: Northwestern University Press, 1990.

Goldberg, Stuart. "Konrad and Jacob: A Hypothetical Kabbalistic Subtext in Adam Mickiewicz's *The Forefathers' Eve, Part III*." *Slavic and East European Journal* 45, no. 4 (2001): 695–715.

Gombrowicz, Witold. *Ferdydurke*. Trans. Danuta Borchardt. New Haven: Yale University Press, 2000.

Górny, Andrzej. "Bez końca powtórka" [Repetition Without End]. *Nurt* 4, no. 132 (1976): 30–32. Cricoteka Archives: CRC III/004806, III/000548.

Gordon Craig, Edward. *On the Art of the Theatre*. Ed. and introduced by Franc Chamberlain. New York: Routledge, 2009.

Gottfried, Martin. "Acropolis." *Women's Wear Daily*, 5 November 1969, 63.

———. "The Polish Laboratory Theatre 'genius.'" *Vogue*, December 1969, 136.

Gould, Jack. "TV: P.B.L. Presents Polish Experimental Theater: Grotowski's 'Akropolis' Poses Challenges Auschwitz Set Against Bible and Homer." *New York Times*, 14 January 1969

(1857–current file), 91. Retrieved 26 August 2009 from ProQuest Historical Newspapers the *New York Times* (1851–2006). Document ID: 77431378.

Grabowska, Alina. *Polska w komentarzach, Vol. 1* [Poland in Commentaries]. London: Polska Fundacja Kulturalna, 1999.

Greń, Zygmunt. "Nie pogrzebani" [The Unburied Ones]. *Życie Literackie*, 26 June 1977. Available at *Polish Theatre Portal*. <http://www.e-teatr.pl/pl/artykuly/48338.html> (accessed 21 June 2011).

Grief, Gideon. *We Wept Without Tears: Testimonies of Jewish Sonderkommando from Auschwitz.* New Haven: Yale University Press, 2005.

Grodzicki, August. *Reżyserzy polskiego teatru* [Polish Theatre Directors]. Warsaw: Wydawnictwo Interpress, 1979.

Grotowski, Jerzy. "Aktor ogołocony" [The Actor Uncovered]. *Teatr* 17 (1–15 September 1965). The Grotowski Institute Archives.

_____. "Co to jest teatr?" [What is Theatre?] *Dziennik Polski* 200 (23–24 August 1959). The Grotowski Institute Archives.

_____. "Cywilizacja i wolność – nie ma innego socjalizmu" [Civilization and Freedom – There Is No Other Socialism]. *Walka Młodych* 6 (1957). The Grotowski Institute Archives.

_____. "'Dziady' jako model teatru nowoczesnego. Rozmowa z dyrektorem Teatru 13 Rzędów w Opolu Jerzym Grotowskim, rozmawiał Jerzy Falkowski" ['Forefathers' Eve' as a Model for Modern Theatre: A Conversation with Jerzy Grotowski, Jerzy Falkowski]. *Współczesność* 21, no. 101 (1–15 November 1961): 8.

_____. "Jakie dostrzegłem zmiany w życiu kulturalnym ZSRR" [What Changes I Noticed in the Cultural Life of SSSR]. *Dziennik Polski* 216 (9–10 October 1956). The Grotowski Institute Archives.

_____. "Marzenie o teatrze: Głos Młodego Aktora" [Dreaming About Theatre: Voice of a Young Actor]. *Dziennik Polski* 46 (1955). The Grotowski Institute Archives.

_____. "Obok teatru" [Next to Theatre]. Conversation with Jery Grotowski and Konstantyn Puzyna on 19 December 1972, recorded for *Dialog* 7 (1973): 102.

_____. "Szkoła szczerości" [School of Honesty]. *Echo Tygodnia* 9 (26 February 1955). The Grotowski Institute Archives.

_____. "Wokół Teatru Przyszłości" [About the Theatre of the Future]. *Ekran* 21 (24 May 1951). The Grotowski Institute Archives.

_____. "Teatr a rytuał" [Theatre Versus Ritual]. *Dialog* 8 (1969).

_____. *Teksty z lat 1965–1969* [Texts from 1965–1969]. Wrocław: Drukarnia Uniwestytetu Wrocławskiego, 1990.

_____. *Towards a Poor Theatre*. Ed. Eugenio Barba. New York: Routledge, 2002.

_____. "Z Jerzym Grotowskim o teatrze" [With Jerzy Grotowski about Theatre], interview conducted by Jerzy Falkowski. *Współczesność* 30 (1–30 December 1958): 8.

Gryszkiewicz, Bogusław. "Bruno Schulz a tradycja czarnego humoru" [Bruno Schulz and the Tradition of Black Humor]. *W ułamkach zwierciadła– Bruno Schulz w 110 rocznicę urodzin i 60 rocznicę śmierci*. Ed. Małgorzata Kitowska-Łysiak and Władysław Panas, Lublin: Towarzystwo Naukowe KUL, 2003. 229–48.

G. S. Theatre column in *Politique Hebdomadaire*, 12–23 October 1977.

Guczalska, Beata. "Polskie środowisko teatralne wobec Grotowskiego" [Polish Theatre Community's Relationship Towards Grotowski]. *Didaskalia. Gazeta Teatralna* (June 2009): 21–6. Originally published in *Dialog* 6 (1999): 135.

Gussow, Mel. "Grotowski, 88 Pounds Lighter, Explains His 'Method.'" *New York Times*, 14 December 1970, 60.

_____. "Polish Experimentalist Examines Man and History." *New York Times*, 20 October 1985. <http://www.nytimes.com/1985/10/20/theater/stage-view-polish-experimentalist-examines-man-and-history.html> (accessed 24 April 2011).

_____. "Tadeusz Kantor's Troupe Carries On." *New York Times*, 20 October 1985, C15.

Haecker, Emil. "*Z teatru. Ofensywa futuryzmu przeciw sztuce*" [From Theatre. Futurist Offensive Against Art]. *Naprzód* 145 (1921).
Halczak, Anna. *Tadeusz Kantor. Epoka chłopca* [Tadeusz Kantor: Boyhood Epoch]. Catalog of the exhibit. Cracow: Cricoteka Archives, 2008.
Halecki, Oscar. "Poland's Place in Europe 966–1966." *Studies in Polish Civilization*. Ed. Damian Wandycz. New York: Institute on East Central Europe, Columbia University and The Polish Institute of Arts & Sciences in America, 1966. 15–22.
Harries, Martin. *Forgetting Lot's Wife: On Destructive Spectatorship*. New York: Fordham University Press, 2007.
Harris, Harry. "PBL Offers US Premiere of Polish Director's 'Akropolis.'" *Philadelphia Inquirer*, 13 January 1969, 14.
Harris, William. "Tadeusz Kantor: Exploring the Dead Theater." *Soho Weekly News*, 22 February 1979, 27.
Hartman, Geoffrey H. "On Traumatic Knowledge and Literary Studies." *New Literary History* 26, no. 3 (Summer 1995): 537–63.
Hausner, Gideon. *Justice in Jerusalem*. New York: Herzl Press, 1978.
Helbing, Robert E. *The Major Works of Heinrich von Kleist*. New York: New Direction Books, 1975.
Henkel, Barbara. "Niezależna rzeczywistość" [Independent Reality]. *Sztandar Młodych*, 9 December 1976. Cricoteka Archives: KWZ124/2005/88.
Herling-Grudziński, Gustaw. "Zabawa w 'Ferdydurke'" [Playing the Game of 'Ferdydurke']. *Orka* 2 (1938): 6.
Hewes, Henry. "A Mass Not for the Masses." *Saturday Review*, 6 December 1969, 72.
Hniedziewicz, Magdalena. "Teatr. Czas przeszły, czas żywy teatru Kantora" [Theatre. Time Gone, Time Alive in Kantor's Theatre]. *Kultura* 72 (21 March 1976): 13. Cricoteka Achives: CRC III/004802.
Hoffman, Anna. "Witkiewicz i teatr Tadeusza Kantora" [Witkiewicz and the Theatre of Tadeusz Kantor]. *Dziennik Polski*, 6 September 1976. Cricoteka Archives: CRC III/004817.
Holden, Stephen. "Tadeusz Kantor's Last Self-Portrait." Review. *New York Times*, 20 June 1991, C16.
Holmberg, Arthur. "A Conversation with Robert Wilson and Heiner Müller." *Modern Drama* 31 (1988): 453–8.
Homolacs, Karol "Wyspiański Plastyk-Poeta" [Wyspiański: Painter-Poet]. *Gazeta Literacka* (Cracow) 3 (1932/33): 41.
Honegger, Gita. "Lost in Translation, or 'Rather than bury Zadek, I come to praise him!'" *Theater* 40, no. 3 (2010): 116–27.
Howe, Irving. "Writing and the Holocaust." *New Republic*, 27 October 1986, 27.
Hudson, Christopher. "How Death Is Brought to Life." *Standard*, 18 November 1982, 17. Cricoteka Archives: CRC III/000650.
Huener, Jonathan. *Auschwitz, Poland and the Politics of Commemoration, 1945–1979*. Athens, OH: Ohio University Press.
Inglot, Mieczysław. *Romantyczne konteksty twórczości Witolda Gombrowicza*. Katowice: Wyższa Szkoła Zarządzania Marketingowego i Języków Obcych, 2006.
Jackson Shannon. *Professing Performance: Theatre in the Academy from Philology to Performativity*. New York: Cambridge University Press, 2004.
Jagorzewski, M. "Wyspiański w 'Teatrze 13 Rzędów'" [Wyspiański at the Theatre of 13 Rows]. *Dziennik Łódzki*, 20 February 1963. The Grotowski Institute Archives.
Jarzębski, Jerzy. "Nie ma Kantora bez Kantora: 'Umarła klasa' po 30 latach" [There is no Kantor without Kantor: 'Dead Class' after 30 Years]. *Gazeta Wyborcza*, 15 November 2005, 2.
Jasiewicz, Krzysztof. "Niepogrzebani ludzie, umarłe miasteczka." *Świat Niepożegnany, Żydzi na dawnych ziemiach wschodnich Rzeczypospolitej w XVIII–XX wieku* [The World Left Without Farewell.

Jews in Eastern Poland in 18th–20th Centuries]. Warsaw and London: Wydawnictwo Rytm, 2004.
Jasińska, Zofia. "XII Warszawskie Spotkania Teatralne" [Eighth Warsaw Theatre Gatherings]. *Tygodnik Powszechny* 5 (30 January 1977). Cricoteka Archives: KWZ124/2005/69.
Jastrzębska, Zuzanna. "Umarła klasa" [Dead Class]. *Filipinka* 3 (30 January 1977). Available at *Polish Theatre Portal*. <http://www.e-teatr.pl/pl/artykuly/11893.html> (accessed 3 February 2011).
Jędrzejczyk, Olgierd. "Znak i znaczenie w teatrze Tadeusza Kantora czyli spektakl 'Umarłej klasy' w sali dawnego 'Sokoła'" [Signs and Significance in Theatre of Tadeusz Kantor, or The Dead Class in the Former Space of Sokół]. *Gazeta Krakowska*, 22 June 1981, 1–2. Cricoteka Archives: CRC III/000619.
Jelenski, Konstanty. "Witold Gombrowicz." *Tri-Quarterly* 9 (1967): 37–41.
Jodłowski, Marek. "Seans Kantora" [Kantor's Séance]. *Opole* (September 1976): 20.
Jota. "Kantor miał dar widzenia" [Kantor Had a Vision]. *Gazeta Wyborcza*, 16 November 2005, 2.
_____. "'Umarła klasa' po 30 latach" ['Dead Class' after 30 Years]. *Gazeta Wyborcza*, 15 November 2005. Available at *Polish Theatre Portal*. <http://www.e-teatr.pl/pl/artykuly/18345.html> (accessed 24 April 2011).
Józefczuk, Grzegorz. "Kantor, ale inaczej" [Kantor, But Differently]. *Gazeta Wyborcza*, 15 January 2001, 5.
Kalemba-Kasprzak, Elżbieta. "Akropolis – dwie teatralne wizje Europy" [Akropolis – Two Theatrical Visions of Europe]. *Studia o dramacie i teatrze Stanisława Wyspiańskiego* [Study of the Drama and Theatre of Stanisław Wyspiański]. Ed. Jan Błoński and Jacek Popiela. Cracow: Wydawnictwo Baran i Suszczyński, 1994. 209–26.
Kamińska, Katarzyna. "Zagubieni w pamięci" [Lost in Memory]. *Gazeta Wyborcza*, 17 December 2009, 6.
Kantor, Tadeusz. "Cricot 2 and The Theatre of Death." *Theatre Papers The Second Series, 1979–80*. Ed. Peter Hulton. Exeter: Arts Documentation Unit, Exeter University 2004.
_____. *Cricot 2 theatre 1955–1988*. Ed. Teresa Bazarnik. Cracow: Cricoteka, 1988.
_____. "The Dead Class." Program from Theatre Cricot 2 Performance at LaMaMa ETC, New York (June 1991).
_____. *Further Development: The Object*. Trans. William Brand. Unpublished manuscript in the Cricoteka collection.
_____. *Illusion and Concrete Reality. Autonomous Theatre Notes* (1963). Trans. William Brand. Unpublished manuscript in the Cricoteka Collection.
_____. *Klasa szkolna. Dzieło Zamknięte* [Classroom. Closed Work] (1995). Catalog of the exhibit, edited by Krzysztof Pleśniarewicz, Cracow.
_____. "A Meeting with the Rhinoceros of Durer, Notes." Trans. William Brand. Unpublished manuscript in the Cricoteka collection.
_____. Notes to *Balladyna* (1942). Trans. William Brand. Unpublished manuscript in the Cricoteka collection.
_____. Notes about the Informel Theatre (1960). Trans. William Brand. Unpublished manuscript in the Cricoteka collection.
_____. *O powinnościach artysty* [About the Responsibilities of an Artist, Conversation with Tadeusz Kantor, Krzysztof Miklaszewski]. Cracow: TVP, 1985.
_____. *Partytura Powrotu Odysa* [Partitura of *The Return of Odysseus*] (1944). Unpublished manuscript in the Cricoteka collection.
_____. *The Play – The World of Fiction, Its Place in the BIO-OBJECT*. Trans. William Brand. Unpublished manuscript in the Cricoteka collection.
_____. "Postacie 'Umarłej klasy'" [Characters from Dead Class]. *Dialog* 2 (1 February 1977).
_____. "Space, Notes" (1948). Unpublished manuscript in the Cricoteka collection.
_____. *Teatr Cricot 2. Teatr Autonomiczny*. Cracow: Galeria Krzysztofory, 1963.

———. "Umarła Klasa, Partytura" [Dead Class. Script] ([1975] 2000). In Tadeusz Kantor's *Teatr Śmierci. Teksty z lat 1975–1984. Tom drugi pism* [The Theatre of Death: Tests from 1975–1984, Volume II]. Wrocław: Ossolineum, 2005.

Karkowski, Czesław. "System kultury Brunona Schulza" [Bruno Schulz' Cultural System]. *Studia o prozie Brunona Schulza*. Ed. Kazimiera Czaplowa. Katowice: Uniwersytet Śląski, 1976. 31–48.

Karren, Tamara. "'Umarła Klasa' Kantora" [Kantor's 'Dead Class']. *Tydzień Polski*, 9 October 1976, 7. Cricoteka Archives: CRC III/004818.

Kauffmann, Stanley. "Grotowski's Theater." *Persons of the Drama: Theater Criticism and Comment*, New York, Hagerstown, San Francisco, London: Harper & Row, 1976. 63–72.

Kauffman, Wolfe. "Unhappy Week for Drama Critic." *Herald Tribune*, 25–26 June 1969.

Kazimierczyk, Barbara. "Umarła klasa w tearze i na taśmie" ['Dead Class' in the Theatre and On Film]. *Kierunki*, 5 June 1977. Available at *Polish Theatre Portal*. <http://www.e-teatr.pl/pl/artykuly/48267.html> (accessed 3 June 2010).

Kelera, Józef. *Grotowski wielokrotnie* [Grotowski Many Times]. Wrocław: Ośrodek Badań Twórczości Jerzego Grotowskiego i Poszukiwań Teatralno-Kulturowych, 1999.

———. "Postać jaskrawa i niemal cyrkowna" [Figure Bright and Almost Circus-like]. *Odra* 9 (September 1976): 87–90. Cricoteka Archives: CRC III/000556.

Kępiński, Antoni. "KZ-syndrom. Próba syntezy" [KZ-Syndrome: An Attempt at Synthesis]. *Przegląd Lekarski* 1 (1970). Reprinted in Antoni Kępiński, *Refleksje oświęcimskie* [Reflections on Auschwitz]. Cracow: Wydawnictwo Literackie, 2005.

Kępinski, Zdzisław. "Stanisław Wyspiański – Malarz i Myśliciel" [Stanisław Wyspiański – Painter and Thinker]. *Sztuka* 6 (1977): 11–13.

Kerensky, Oleg. "Jerzy Grotowski's Laboratory." *Stage and Television Today*, 25 September 1969, 15.

Kerr, Walter. "Is Grotowski Right – Did the Word Came Last?" *New York Times*, 30 November 1969, D1.

Kiebuzinska, Christine Olga. *Intertextual Loops in Modern Drama*. Madison, NJ: Fairleigh Dickinson University Press; London: Associated University Presses, 2001.

Kieracz, Witold. "'Sanatorium pod klepsydrą' – proza Schulza I wizje Hasa" ['Sanatorium Under the Sign of Hourglass' – Schulz' prose and Has' vision]. *Studia o prozie Brunona Schulza*. Ed. Kazimiera Czaplowa. Katowice: Uniwersytet Śląski, 1976. 135–45.

Kimmelman, Michael. "Poland Searches Its Own Soul." *New York Times*, 8 April 2009. <http://www.nytimes.com/2009/04/09/movies/09abro.html?_r=2> (accessed 21 March 2011).

King, Robert L. *The Ethos of Drama: Rhetorical Theory and Dramatic Worth*. Washington, DC: The Catholic University of America Press, 2010.

Kinsolving, William. "Was Grotowski Too Lightly Dismissed?" *New York Times*, 23 February 1969, D21.

Király, Nina. "Schulz i Kantor" [Schulz and Kantor]. *Teatr pamieci Brunona Schulza*. Ed. Jana Ciechowicza and Haliny Kasjaniuk. Gdynia: Teatr Miejski w Gdyni, 1993. 132–42.

Kirshenblatt-Gimblett, Barbara. "'Contraband': Text and Analysis of a 'Purim-Shpil.'" *The Drama Review: TDR* 24, no. 3, Jewish Theatre Issue (September 1980): 5–16.

Kisselgoff, Anna. "Grotowski Stresses Need for System." *New York Times*, 25 November 1969, 54.

Kitowska-Łysiak, Małgorzata and Władysław Panas, eds. *W ułamkach zwierciadła– Bruno Schulz w 110 rocznicę urodzin i 60 rocznicę śmierci*. Lublin: Towarzystwo Naukowe KUL. 47–74.

Kleiner, Juliusz. *Tragizm dwoistego oblicza czynu w 'Edypie królu'* [The Tragedy of the Dual Nature of One's Act in "Oedipus Rex"]. *W kręgu Mickiewicza i Goethego*. Warsaw: Towarzystwo Wydawnicze Rój, 1938.

Kłossowicz, Jan. "Galwanizacja Teatru" [Galvanizing Theatre]. *Literatura* 24, no. 226 (10 June 1976): 13. Cricoteka Archives: CRC III/000552.

———. "Grotowski in Poland." *Le Théâtre en Pologne/Theatre in Poland* 5 (1971): 3–10. Special issue devoted to Jerzy Grotowski.

_____. "Próba zapisu" [Trying to Record It]. *Dialog* 2 (1 February 1977): 118–34.
Knapp, Bettina and Witold Gombrowicz. "Gombrowicz: An Interview." *The Drama Review* 14, no. 1 (Autumn 1969): 84–5.
Kobialka, Michal. *A Journey Through Other Spaces: Essays and Manifestos, 1944–1990*. Berkeley: University of California Press, 1993.
_____. *Further On: Nothing: Tadeusz Kantor's Theatre*. Minneapolis, MN: University of Minnesota Press, 2009.
Kobialka, Michal and Tadeusz Kantor. "Let the Artists Die? An Interview with Tadeusz Kantor." *The Drama Review: TDR* 30, no. 3 (Autumn 1986): 177–83.
Kogon, Eugen. *The Theory and Practice of Hell: The German Concentration Camps and the System Behind Them*. Trans. Heinz Norden. New York: Octagon Books, 1979.
Kolaczkowski, Stefan. *Stanisław Wyspiański: Rzecz o Tragediach i tragizmie* [Stanisław Wyspiański: About Tragedy and the Tragic]. Poznań: Fiszer i Majewski, 1992.
Kolakowski, Leszek. "The Poor Poles Look at the Ghetto." *Four Decates of Polish Essays*. Ed. Jan Kott. Evanston, IL: Nortwestern University Press, 1990. 291–303.
Kolankiewicz, Leszek. *Dziady. Teatr święta zmarłych* [*The Forefathers' Eve*: Theatre of the *The Forefathers' Eve*]. Gdańsk: Słowo/Obraz Terytoria, 1999.
_____. *Na drodze do kultury czynnej: O działalności instytutu Grotowskiego Teatr Laboratorium w latach 1970–1977* [On the Way to the Active Culture: About Grotowski's Laboratory Theatre 1970–1977]. Wrocław: Instytut Aktora, 1978.
_____. *Wielki mały wóz. Teatr jako wehikuł* [The Big Small Dipper: Theatre as a Vehicle]. Gdańsk: Słowo/Obraz Terytoria, 2001.
Kolarz, Walter. *Communism and Colonialism*. London: Palgrave Macmillan, 1964.
Kolata, Kamil, Barbara Pieta and Ira Stup. "Never Again? Contemporary Anti-Semitism and Representations of Jews in Modern Poland." *Humanity in Action*. <http://www.humanityinaction.org/knowledgebase/63-never-again-contemporary-anti-semitism-and-representations-of-jews-in-modern-poland> (accessed 14 November 2011).
Konieczna, R. "Przed premierą 'Pechowców'. Rozmowa z reżyserem." [Before the Opening of the 'Jinxed Family': Conversation with the Director]. *Trybuna Opolska* 265 (1958): 4.
"Kordian do gory nogami" [Kordian With Legs Upside Down]. *Słowo Polskie*, 24 May 1962. Reprinted in *Akropolis*, program notes, October 1962. The Grotowski Institute Archives.
Koropeckyj, Roman. *Adam Mickiewicz: The Life of a Romantic*. Ithaca, NY: Cornell University Press, 2008.
Kosiński, Dariusz. *Grotowski: Przewodnik* [Grotowski: A Handbook]. Wrocław: Grotowski Institute, 2009.
_____. *Polski teatr przemiany* [Polish Theatre of Transformation]. Wrocław: Instytut im. Jerzego Grotowskiego, 2007.
_____. *Teatra Polskie: historie* [History of Polish Theatre]. Warsaw: Wydawnictwo Naukowe PWN, Instytut Teatralny, 2010.
_____. *Tradycia romantyczna w teatrze polskim* [Romantic Tradition in Polish Theatre]. Cracow: Towarzystwo Naukowe Societas Vistulana, 2007.
Kosiński, Dariusz and Emil Orzechowski. *Teatr polski poza krajem* [Polish Theatre Abroad]. Poznań: Fundacja Uniw. Im. A. Mickiewicza, 1992.
Kosiński, Kazimierz. "Wawel w ideologii Wyspiańskiego. Na 30-lecie 'Akropolis' 1904–1934" [Wawel in Wyspiański's Ideology: 30th Anniversary of 'Akropolis' 1904–1934]. *Droga* (Warsaw) (1934): 348–60, 479–88.
Korek, Janusz. "Central and Eastern Europe from a Postcolonial Perspective." *Postcolonial Europe* (2009). <http://www.postcolonial-europe.eu/index.php/en/essays/60--central-and-eastern-europe-from-a-postcolonial-perspective> (accessed 1 August 2011).
Kott, Jan. "Czemu mam tańczyć w tym tragicznym chórze..." [Why Should I Dance in That Tragic Chorus]. *Kamienny Potok. Eseje*. London: Aneks, 1986. 109–10.

———. "Introduction" to Tadeusz Borowski's *This Way for the Gas, Ladies and Gentlemen*. Introduction trans. Michael Kandel. Ed. and trans. Barbara Vedder. New York: Penguin, 1992. 11–28.

———. *Kadysz. Strony o Tadeuszu Kantorze* [Kaddish. Pages About Tadeusz Kantor]. Gdańsk: Słowo/Obraz Terytoria, [1997] 2006.

———. "Koniec teatru niemożliwego" [The End of the Impossible Theatre]. *Pisma Wybrane*. Ed. Tadeusz Nyczek. Warsaw: Wydawnictwo Krąg, 339–40. Reprinted in "After Grotowski: The End of the Impossible Theater," trans. Krystyna Bittenek, in Jan Kott, *The Theatre of Essence and Other Essays*, with an introduction by Martin Esslin, Evanston: Northwestern University Press, 1980. 139–45, 147–58.

———. *Theatre Notebook: 1947–1967*. Trans. Boleslaw Taborski. Garden City, NY: Doubleday, 1968.

———. *The Theatre of Essence, and Other Essays*. Evanston, IL: Northwestern University Press, 1984.

———. "Why Should I Take Part in the Sacred Dance." Trans. Edward J. Czerwinski. First published in *TDR: The Drama Review* 14, no. 2 (T46) (Winter 1970): 199–203.

Kramer, Mark. "Memo from Warsaw: 'Origins' of the RRC." *Novosti* 16, no. 1 (Fall 2010): 7–8.

Kretz-Mirski, Józef. *Akropolis, jako dramat świadomości narodej* ['Akropolis' as Drama of the National Consciousness]. Krosno: W. Lenik 1910.

———. "'Akropolis' Wyspiańskiego a Biblia" [Wyspiański's 'Akropolis' *vis-à-vis* the Bible]. *Przegląd Warszawski* 4, no. 33 (1924): 413–14.

Kridl, Manfred. *An Anthology of Polish Literature*. New York: Columbia University Press, 1957.

———. *The Democratic Heritage of Poland*. London: G. Allen & Unwin Ltd, 1944.

———. *A Survey of Polish Literature and Culture*. New York: Columbia University Press 1967.

Kucharski, Krzysztof. "Po premierze 'Akropolis.' Reconstrukcja. We Wrocławskim Teatrze Współczesnym" [After the Opening of 'Akropolis'. Reconstruction at the Wrocław's Teatr Współczesny]. *Gazeta Wrocławska*, 14 December 2009. <http://www.gazetawroclawska.pl/kultura/198072,po-premierze-akropolis-rekonstrukcja-we-wroclawskim-teatrze,id,t.html#material_1> (accessed 5 April 2011).

Kudyba, Teresa. "Opole było odpowiednią pustelnią" [Opole Was a Perfect Hermitage: Conversation with Ludwik Flaszen]. *Gazeta Wyborcza*, 28 March 2009, 4.

Kudliński, Tadeusz. "Ofensywa Grotowskiego'" [Grotowski's Offensive]. *Dziennik Polski*, 5 April 1962. Reprinted in *Akropolis*, program notes, October 1962. The Grotowski Institute Archives.

Kuharski, Allen. "Jerzy Grotowski: Ascetic and Smuggler." *Theater* 29, no. 2 (1999): 10–15.

Kuhns, David F. *German Expressionist Theatre: The Actor and the Stage*. Cambridge: Cambridge University Press, 1997.

Kuligowska-Korzeniowska, Anna. "The Polish Shulamis: Jewish Drama on the Polish Stage in the Late 19th–Early 20th Centuries." *Jewish Theatre: A Global View*. Ed. Edna Nahshon. Lieden, Boston: Brill, 2009.

Kumiega, Jennifer. *The Theatre of Grotowski*. London: Methuen, 1985.

Kundera, Milan. *Encounter*. New York: HarperCollins, 2010.

———. "The tragedy of Central Europe." *New York Review of Books*, 26 April 1984, 33–8. Initially published in French under the title "Un Occident kidnappe ou la tragedie de l'Europe centrale." *Le Débat* 27 (November 1983).

———. *Vanek Plays*. Vancouver: University of British Columbia Press, 1987.

Kuraś, Bartłomiej. "Bo Tadeusz Kantor to przeciętność" [Tadeusz Kantor is a Mediocrity]. *Gazeta Wyborcza*, 10 July 2009, 5.

Kustow, Michael. "*Ludens Mysterium Tremendum et Fascinosum.*" *Encore* (October 1963): 9–14.

Kwiek, Przemysław, Igor Krenz and Jarosław Kozłowski. "Grotowski: hosztapler czy inspirator?" [Grotowski: Conman or Visionary?] *Dziennik* 80 (13 March 2009). <http://www.dziennik.

pl/kultura/teatr/article340537/Jerzy_Grotowski_hochsztapler_czy_inspirator_.html> (accessed 3 July 2010).
LaCapra, Dominick. "Trauma, Absence, Loss." *Critical Inquiry* 25, no. 4 (Summer 1999): 696–727.
Lamont, Rosette C. "Builder of Bridges between the Living and the Dead." *New York Times*, 6 October 1985. <http://theater.nytimes.com/mem/theater/treview.html?res=9C0DEEDA 1239F935A35753C1A963948260&scp=1&sq=die%20mannequin&st=cse> (accessed 21 January 2011).
Lanzmann, Claude. "The Obscenity of Understanding: An Evening With Claude Lanzmann." *Trauma, Explorations in Memory*. Ed.Cathy Caruth. Baltimore: The John Hopkins University Press, 1995. 200–20.
Łaszowski, Alfred. "Szkoła Gombrowicza" [The School of Gombrowicz]. *Myśl Polska* 22, no. 44 (15–30 November 1937): 5.
Laub, Dori. "Bearing Witness, or the Vicissitudes or Listening." *Testimony: Crisis of Witnessing in Literature, Psychoanalysis, and History*. Ed. Shoshana Felman and Dori Laub. New York: Routledge, 1992. 61–75.
Lavy, Jennifer. "Theoretical Foundations of Grotowski's Total Act, Via Negativa, and Conjunctio Oppositorum." *Journal of Religion and Theatre* 4, no. 2 (2005): 175–88.
Lehman, Hans-Thies. *Postdramatic Theatre*. Routledge: New York, 2006.
Lehrer, Erika. "Unquiet Places: A second look at Jewish Poland today." *PaknTreger: The Magazine of the Yiddish Book Center* 56 (Spring 2008). <http://www.yiddishbookcenter.org/pakn-treger/12-09/unquiet-places-a-second-look-at-jewish-poland-today> (accessed 30 July 2011).
Łempicka, Aniela. *Wyspiański pisarz dramatyczny. Idee i formy* [Wyspiański the Dramatists: Ideas and Forms]. Cracow: Wydawnictwo Literackie, 1973.
Leonardini, Jean-Pierre. "L'ecureuil sur la roué. Le Polonaise Kantor gère l'économie de la mort." *L'Humanité*, 18 October 1977. Cricoteka Archives: CRC III/000311.
Lester, Elenore. "…Or the Wave Of the Future?" *New York Times*, 30 June 1968, D1.
Lewis, Allan. "Too Few Can Attend." *New York Haven Register*, 2 November 1969, 1, 7.
Lichten, Joseph L. "Some Aspects of Polish-Jewish Relations During the Nazi Occupation." *Studies in Polish Civilization*. Ed. Damian Wandycz. New York: Institute on East Central Europe, Columbia University and The Polish Institute of Arts & Sciences in America, 1966. 154–75.
Lindenbaum, Shanon. "'Sanatorium pod klepsydrą' – Hades czy sanatorium?" [Sanatorium Under the Sign of the Hourglass – Hades or Sanatorium?] *W ułamkach zwierciadła– Bruno Schulz w 110 rocznicę urodzin i 60 rocznicę śmierci*. Ed. Małgorzata Kitowska-Łysiak and Władysław Panas. Lublin: Towarzystwo Naukowe KUL, 2003. 47–74.
Lipko, Mateusz. "Całkowitość doświadczenia według Jerzego Grotowskiego. Problem ujęty w kotekście idei samozbawienia" [Total Act According to Jerzy Grotowki, Analyzed in the Context of the Self-Salvation]. Lecture given at Jagiellonian University conference *"Via Negativa. Wobec Grotowskiego – krytyczne interpretacje"* [*Via Negativa. Vis-à-vis* Grotowski – Critical Interpretations], Cracow, 2009.
Little, Stuart. "Grotowski: An Unsettled American Theatre Replies." *Saturday Review*, 7 February 1970, 30–31.
Loney, Glenn. "Kantor and the 'Dead Class.'" *Other Stages*, 8 February 1979, 11.
Lorentowicz, Jan. Review of *Ferdydurke. Nowa książka 1934–1939*, zeszyt 1 ed. Stanisław Lem (Warsaw 1938). 28–9.
Lu Ter. "Na marginesie inscenizacji krakowskiej: S. Wyspiański: 'Akropolis'" [On the Margins of Cracow's Production of St. Wyspiański's Akropolis']. *Comoedia* (Warsaw) 2 (1927).
Lupa, Krystian. "Fałszywy mag świątyni teatru" [The False Prophet of Theatrical Temple]. Interview with Krysian Lupa, Łukasz Drewniak. *Dziennik* 80 (4–5 April 2009). <http://www.dziennik.pl/magazyn-dziennika/article354424.ece> (accessed 15 February 2010).

———. "Kantor żywy" [Kantor Alive]. Trans. Renata Kopyto. *Gazeta Wyborcza*, 6 January 2006, 12.
Lyons, Leonard. "The Lyons Den." *New York Post*, 23 October 1969.
Mach, Magdalena. "Nie oszczędzajmy na Grotowkim" [Let's Not Be Cheap on Grotowski]. *Gazeta Wyborcza*, 3 April 2009, 2.
Maciejewski, Łukasz. "Nigdy tu już nie powrócę" [I Shall Never Return]. *Dziennik* 3 (4 January 2008). Available at *Polish Theatre Portal*. <http://www.e-teatr.pl/pl/artykuly/49465.html> (accessed 26 October 2011).
Madeyska-Pawlikowska, Anna. "Na pograniczu dwóch światów" [On the Bordeline of Two Worlds]. Introduction to *On the Borderline of Two Worlds: Dybbuk*. Cracow: Wydawnictwo Austeria, 2007.
M.A.M. "The Dead Class." *Stage and Television Today*, 23 September 1976, 12.
Mamoń, Bronisław. "Republika marzeń" [The Republic of Dreams]. *Tygodnik Powszechny* 46 (1987): 7.
Marcus, Frank. "Foreign Bodies." *Sunday Telegraph*, 19 September 1976. Cricoteka Archives: CRC III/000202.
———. "More than Essentials." *Sunday Telegraph*, 5 October 1969, 16.
Masłowski, Michał. "Od obrzędu żałobnego do świeckiej mszy" [From Funeral Rite to Secular Mass]. *Performer* 1 (2009). <http://www.grotowski.net/performer/performer-1/od- obrzedu-zalobnego-do-swieckiej-mszy> (accessed 10 August 2011).
Mauer, Jadwiga. *"Z matki obcej-": Szkice o powiązaniach Mickiewicza ze światem Żydów* ["Of a Foreign Mother": Essays about Mickiewicz's Connections with the Jewish World]. London: Polska Fundacja Kulturalna, 1999.
Mazanowski, Antoni. "Z poetyckiej niwy, re: St. Wyspiański's *Akropolis*" [From Poetic Perspective: Re: Stanisław Wyspiański's *Akropolis*]. *Przegląd Powszechny* (Cracow) 86 (1904): 79–81.
McFerran, Ann. Review of *Dead Class*. *Time Out*, 10–16 September 1976, 16.
McQuillen, Colleen. "The Myths and Meta-theatricality of Resurrection in Akropolis (or Apollo-Christ at the Polish Acropolis: A Mettheatrical Moment of Incarnation)." Panel: "Dreaming the Life of the Nation: The Monumental Vision of Stanisław Wyspiański (1869–1907): A panel in honor of the Wyspiański centennial: 1907–2007." Modern Language Association conference, Chicago, IL, 2007.
Mickiewicz, Adam. "Dziady, Part I." *Dziady*. Ed. Maria Cieśla-Korytowska. Cracow: Towarzystwo Autorów i Wydawców Prac Naukowych UNIVERSITAS, 1998.
Miklaszewska, Agata. "Kantora teatr informel" [Kantor's Informel Theatre]. *Dialog* 7 (1978): 126–30.
Miklaszewski, Krzysztof. *Encounters with Tadeusz Kantor*. Trans. George M. Hyde. New York: Routledge, 2002.
———. *Kantor od Kuchni* [Kantor from the Kitchen]. Warsaw: Wydawnictwo Książkowe Twój Styl, 2003.
———. *Tadeusz Kantor: Między śmietnikiem a wiecznością* [Tadeusz Kantor: Between Garbage and Eternity]. Warsaw: Państwowy Instytut Wydawniczy, 2003.
———. "Zapis wypowiedzi dla *Kroniki Krakowskiej*" [Transcript of the Interview for *Kronika Krakowska*], 15 November 1975. Manuscript. Cricoteka Archives: CRC III/000538 – III/1/2/324, III/004798 – III/1/2/327.
———. *Zatracenie się w Schulzu: historia pewnej fascynacji* [Losing Oneself in Schulz: A Story of One Fascination]. Warsaw: Państwowy Instytut Wydawniczy, 2009.
Miłosz, Czesław. *Ziemia Ulro* [Urlo's Earth]. Paris: Institute Literacki, 1977.
———. *Zniewolony umysł* [Captive Mind]. Warsaw: Logos, [1953] 1981.
Miodońska-Brookes, Ewa. *Wawel – 'Akropolis.' Studium o dramacie Stanisława Wyspiańskiego* [Wawel – 'Akropolis'. Studium about Wyspiański's Drama]. Cracow: Wydawnictwo Literackie, 1980.

Mishkin, Leo. "TV Had Something Else Besides Football Sunday." *Morning Telegraph*, 14 January 1969, 3.
Moeller-Sally, Stephen. *Gogol's Afterlife: The Evolution of a Classic in Imperial and Soviet Russia*. Evanston, IL: Northwestern University Press, 2002.
Morawiec, Elżbieta. "Apokalipsa według Tadeusza Kantora" [Apocalypse According to Tadeusz Kantor]. *Życie Literackie* 51/52 (21–28 December 1975). Cricoteka Archives: CRC III/004797, III/000541.
———. "Nasze 'Akropolis'" [Our 'Akropolis']. *Życie Literackie* 12 (1978): 7.
National Herald Tribune. "Masterpiece at Edinburgh Festival." 7 September 1976, 7.
Natkaniec, Barbara. "Przed premierą 'Cricot 2'" [Before the Opening of Cricot 2]. *Echo Krakowa*, 15 November 1975. Available at *Polish Theatre Portal*. <http://www.e-teatr.pl/pl/artykuly/48260.html> (accessed 28 June 2011).
Neal, Arthur G. *National Trauma and Collective Memory: Major Events in the American Century*. Armonk, NY: M. E. Sharpe, 1998.
Nelson Robert L. *Germans, Poland, and Colonial Expansion to the East: 1850 through the Present*. New York: Palgrave Macmillan, 2009.
Nevo, Ofra and Jacob Levine. "Jewish Humor Strikes Again: The Outburst of Humor in Israel during the Gulf War." *Western Folklore* 53, no. 2 (April 1994): 125–45.
New York Times. "Polish Group Shifts Opening to Church." 15 October 1969, 36.
Nightingale, Benedict. "Proper Stuff." *New Statesman*, 3 September 1976. Cricoteka Archives: CRC III/000191.
Niziołek, Grzegorz. "Auschwitz – Wawel – Akropolis: niewczesny montaż" [Auschwitz – Wawel – Akropolis: Untimely Montage]. *Didaskalia. Gazeta Teatralna* (June 2009): 26–31.
———. "Zawsze nie w porę. Teatr polski a Zagłada" [It's Never the Right Time: Polish Theatre and the Holocaust]. Interview with Joanna Wichowska. *Dwutygodnik: Strona Kultury* 20 (29 December 2009) <http://www.dwutygodnik.com.pl/artykul/759-zawsze-nie-w-pore-polski-teatr-i-zaglada.html> (accessed 2 April 2011).
Norsworthy, Naomi and Mary Theodora Whitley. *The Psychology of Childhood*. New York: Macmillan, 1918.
Novick, Peter. *The Holocaust in American Life*. New York: Houghton Mifflin, 1999.
Nowakowski, Jan. *Wyspiański: Studia o dramatach* [Wyspiański: Study of His Dramas]. Cracow: Wydawnictwo Literackie, 1972.
Oliver, Cordelia. "Cricot Theatre." *Guardian*, 23 August 1976, 10. Cricoteka Archives: CRCIII/000181.
Oliver, Edith. "Off-Broadway: Grotowski." *New Yorker*, 25 October 1969, 139.
Oppenheimer, George. "Polish Play Opens in City Church." *Wall Street Journal*, 17 October 1969.
Oring, Elliot. "The People of the Joke: On the Conceptualization of a Jewish Humor." *Western Folklore* 42, no. 4 (October 1983): 261–327.
Ortwin, Ostap. *O Wyspiańskim i dramacie* [About Wyspiański and Drama]. Warsaw: Państwowy Instytut Wydawniczy, 1969.
Osiński, Zbigniew. "'Akropolis' w Teatrze Laboratorium" [Akropolis at the Teatr Laboratorium]. Reprinted in *Mysterium zgrozy i urzeczenia: Przedstawienia Jerzego Grotowskiego i Teatru Laboratorium* [Mysterium of Horror and Allure: Productions of Jerzy Grotowski and Teatr Laboratorium]. Ed. Janusz Degler and Grzegorz Ziółkowski. Wrocław: Ośrodek Badań Twórczości Jerzego Grotowskiego i Poszukiwań Teatralno-Kulturowych, 2006.
———. *Grotowski and His Laboratory*. New York: PAJ Publications, 1986.
———. "Grotowski and The Reduta Tradition." *Grotowski's Empty Room*. Ed. Paul Allain. London: Seagull Books, 2010. 19–54.
———. *Grotowski wytycza trasy* [Grotowski Paves the Ways]. Warsaw: Wydawnictwo Pusty Obłok, 1993.

———. *Jerzy Grotowski: Źródła, inspiracje, konteksty* [Jerzy Grotowski: Origins, Inspirations, Contexts]. Gdańsk: Słowo/Obraz Terytoria, 1998.

———. *Nazywał nas bratnim teatrem* [He Called Us Brotherly Theatre]. Gdańsk: Słowo/Obraz Terytoria, 2005.

———. "Tadeusz Kantor i Jerzy Grotowski Wobec Romantyzmu" [Tadeusz Kantor and Jerzy Grotowski vs. Polish Romanticism]. In Dariusz Kosiński, *Tradycia romantyczna w teatrze polskim* [Romantic Tradition in Polish Theatre]. Cracow: Towarzystwo Naukowe Societas Vistulana, 2007.

———. *Teatr Dionizosa. Romantyzm w polskim teatrze wpołczesnym* [Dionysian Theatre: Romanticism in Polish Contemporary Theatre]. Cracow: Wydawnictwo Literackie, 1972.

Osiński, Zbigniew and Tadeusz Burzyński. *Laboratorium Grotowskiego* [Grotowski's Laboratory]. Warsaw: Wydawnictwo Interpress, 1978.

Overy, Paul. "Surrealism Without Surfeit." *Times*, 31 August 1976. Cricoteka Archives: CRC III/000189.

Owczarski, Wojciech. *Miejsca wspólne, miejsca własne. O wyobraźni Leśmiana, Schulza i Kantora* [Common Spaces, Private Spaces. About Imagination of Leśmian, Schulz and Kantor]. Gdańsk: Słowo/Obraz Terytoria, 2006.

———. "Umarła klasa" [Dead Class]. *Gazeta Wyborcza*, 30 March 2006, 9.

Panasewicz, Jerzy. "7 dni w teatrze" [Seven Days in Theatre]. *Express Ilustrowany*, 2–3 March 1963. The Grotowski Institute Archives.

Parson, Gordon. "Fringe Benefits: Review of 'Dead Class' at Edinburgh Fringe Festival." *Morning Star*, 11 September 1976, 4. Cricoteka Archives: CRC III/000199.

Parvi, Zenon. "U Wyspiańskiego" [At Wyspiański's]. *Kurier Codzienny*, 19 February 1904, 52.

Pascal, Blaise. *Pensées*. Trans. W. T. Trotter. Oxford: Benediction Classics, 2011.

Pascal, Julia. "'The Dead Class' by Tadeusz Kantor (Riverside)." *City Limits*, 26 November–2 December 1986. Cricoteka Archives: CRCIII/000662.

Pavis, Patrice. "The State of Current Theatre Research." *Applied Semiotics/Sémiotique appliqué* 1, no. 3 (1997): 203–30.

———. *Languages of the Stage: Essays in the Semiology of Theatre*. New York: Methuen, 1992.

Pavis, Patrice and Christine Shantz. *Dictionary Of The Theatre: Terms, Concepts, and Analysis*. Toronto: University of Toronto Press, 1999.

Pawełczyk, Joanna. "Grotowskologia en français" [Grotowskology in French]. *Dwutygodnik: Strona Kultury* 43 (13 November 2010) <http://www.dwutygodnik.com.pl/artykul/579> (accessed 4 March 2011).

Pawłowski, Roman. "Dramaturg Kantor." Interview with Wacław Janicki, *Gazeta Wyborcza*, 29 October 2001, 16.

———. "Ewangelia nowego teatru" [The Gospel of a New Theatre]. *Gazeta Wyborcza*, 13 February 2007. <http://www.teatry.art.pl/!inne/grotowski/ente.htm> (accessed 15 June 2012).

———. "Podręczny mesjanizm: 'Akropolis' Wyspiańskiego w Teatrze Narodowym" [Handy Mesjanism: Wyspiański's 'Akropolis at the National Theatre]. *Gazeta Wyborcza*, 14 May 2001, 17.

———. "Żywa martwa klasa" [Living Dead Class]. *Gazeta Wyborcza*, 26 October 2001, 21.

Perez, Rolando. *Bruno Schulz: Literary Kabbalist of the Holocaust*. New York: Hunter College of the City University of New York, 2002.

Piech, Krzysztof. "Tumor Mózgowicz: Kabaret matematyczyny. Kabaret metamatematyczny" [Tumor Brainiowicz. Mathematical Cabaret. Metamathematical Cabaret]. *Gazeta Wielkopolska*, 9 March 2000. <http://www.teatry.art.pl/!recenzje/tumormkmno/kabaret.htm> (accessed 3 June 2011).

Pilikian, Hovhannes I. "Grotowski: Seen From Poland." *Drama: The Quarterly Theatre Review* 95 (Winter 1969): 61–3.

Pleśniarewicz, Krzysztof. *The Dead Memory Machine: Tadeusz Kantor's "Theatre of Death."* Cracow: Cricoteka, 1994.
_____. *Kantor.* Wrocław: Wydawnictwo Dolnośląskie, 1997.
_____. "Kantor–Grotowski: między maglem a wiecznością." [Kantor–Grotowski: Between the Calender and Eternity]. *PERFORMER* 2 (2011). <http://www.grotowski.net/performer/performer-2/kantor-grotowski-miedzy-maglem-wiecznoscia#footnote3_w8f1j6n>
_____. *Powrót Odysa. Podziemny Teatr Niezależny, 1944* [*The Return of Odysseus*: The Clandestine Independent Theatre, 1944]. Cracow: Cricoteka, 1994.
_____. "Symbolizm 'Umarłej klasy'" [The Symbolism of the Dead Class]. *Dziennik Polski*, 14 December 1978, 4.
_____. *Teatr nie-ludzkiej formy* [The Theatre of the Un-Human Form]. Cracow: Jagiellonian University, 1994.
_____. *Teatr Śmierci Tadeusza Kantora* [Tadeusz Kantor's Theatre of Death]. Chotomow: VERBA, 1990.
_____. "W kręgu pewnej przypowieści" [In the Realm of a Story]. *Dziennik Polski*, 24–25 1978, 6.
Popiel, Jacek. "Witkacy a antyiluzjonizm w teatrze" [Witkacy and Anti-Illusion in Theatre]. *Dramat a teatr polski dwudziestolecia międzywojennego*. Cracow: Wydawnictwo Universitas, 1995. 125–32.
Poskuta-Włodek, Diana. "Dżuma w teatrze?! (1918–1926)" [Plaque in The Theatre]. *Co dzień powtarza się gra...Teatr im. Juliusza Słowackiego w Krakowie 1893–1993.* Warsaw: Wydawnictwo Arta, 1993. 92–112.
Primor, Adar. "Polish Foreign Minister: The Holocaust Was Perpetrated Against Our Will." Haaretz.com, 29 May 2011. <http://www.haaretz.com/print-edition/news/polish-foreign-minister-the-holocaust-was-perpetrated-against-our-will-1.345542> (accessed 29 May 2011).
Prokesch Władysław. "'Akropolis' St. Wyspiańskiego" [Stanisław Wyspiański's 'Akropolis']. *Biesiada Literacka* (Warsaw) 17 (1904): 325–6.
Prokopczyk, Czesław Z., ed. *Bruno Schulz: New Documents and Interpretations.* New York: Peter Lang, 1999.
Prusak, Maria. "Pieśń o Wawelu." *Stanisław Wyspiański w labiryncie teatru* [Stanisław Wyspiański in the Labyrinth of Theatre]. Cracow: Wydawnictwo Literackie, 2005.
_____. *Po ogniu szum wiatru cichego – Wyspiański i mesjanizm* [Silent Wind After the Fire: Wyspiański and Mesjanism]. Cracow: Wydawnictwo Literackie, 1993.
Puławski, Franciszek. "S. Wyspiański, W. Ekielski." *Piśmiennictwo, Biblioteka Warszawska* 4 (1908): 386–8.
Pułka, Leszek. "Doskonałość jest przeciwieństwem życia. Dziś 'Akropolis. Rekonstrukcja.' We Wrocławskim Teatrze Współczesnym" [Perfection is an Antithesis of Life. Today 'Akropolis. The Reconstruction' at the Wrocław's Teatr Współczesny]. *Dziennik Gazeta Prawna*, 11 December 2009. <http://www.e-teatr.pl/pl/artykuly/84316.html> (accessed 3 April 2010).
Puzyna, Konstantyn. "Grotowski and Polish Romantic Drama." Trans. Jacob Conrad. *Theatre Three* 4 (Spring 1988): 44–50.
_____. "Grotowski i dramat romantyczny" [Grotowski and Romantic Drama]. *Półmrok, Felietony teatralne i szkice.* Warsaw: Państwowy Instytut Wydawniczy, 1982. 132–40.
_____. "My, Umarli" [We, the Dead Ones]. *Półmrok, Felietony teatralne i szkice.* Warsaw: Państwowy Instytut Wydawniczy, 1982. 102–14, at 102.
_____. *Półmrok* [Twilight]. Warsaw: Wydawnictwo PAN, 1982.
_____. *Półmrok, Felietony teatralne i szkice.* Warsaw: Państwowy Instytut Wydawniczy, 1982.
_____. "Polska tradycja i dramat współczesny" [Polish Tradition and Modern Drama]. *Półmrok, Felietony teatralne i szkice.* Warsaw: Państwowy Instytut Wydawniczy, 1982. 97–101.
_____. *Syntezy za trzy grosze* [Three-Penny Syntheses]. Warsaw: Wydawnictwo PAN, 1974.
_____. *Witkacy.* Warsaw: Oficyna Wydawnicza Errata, 1999.

Rachwał, Józef. *'Akropolis' Stanisława Wyspiańskiego: źródła i ideologia* [Stanisław Wyspiański's 'Akropolis': Origins and Ideology]. Tarnów: Nakładem Księgarni Zygmunta Jelenia, 1926.
Raczak, Lech. "Para-ra-ra." *Dialog* 7 (1980) 132–7.
Raczek, Tomasz. "I stał się moment wielki czaru" [And the Great Moment of Magic Came]. *Kultura* 14 (1978): 11.
Reichardt, Jasia. "Kantor's Tragic Theatre." *Architectural Design* 46 (November 1976): 692–3.
Rich, Frank. "Tadeusz Kantor's Intimations of God and Death." *New York Times*, 16 June 1988, C21.
Richards, Thomas. *At Work with Grotowski on Physical Actions*, London and New York: Routledge, 1995.
Rosiek, Stanisław. *Grotowski powtórzony* [Grotowski Repeated]. Gdańsk: Słowo/Obraz Terytoria, 2009.
Rosman, M. "Poland: Poland before 1795" *YIVO Encyclopedia of Jews in Eastern Europe*, 14 March 2011. <http://www.yivoencyclopedia.org/article.aspx/Poland/Poland_before_1795> (accessed 29 June 2011).
Ross, Rochelle H. "Witold Gombrowicz: An Experimental Novelist." *South Central Bulletin* (Winter 1971): 214–16.
Ryn, Zdzisław and Stanisław Kłodziński. "Na granicy życia i śmierci. Studium obozowego muzułmaństwa" [At the Border Between Life and Death. A Study of the Appearance of 'musselman' in concentration camps]. *Przegląd Lekarski* [Polish Journal "Medical Review"] 1, no. 40 (1983): 27–73.
Rzewiczok, Urszula and Katarzyna M. Gliwa. *Drodzy Nieobecni Tadeusza Kantora: Wspomnienie o Tadeuszu Kantorze, Marianie Kantorze-Mirskim i Józefie Kantor* [Dear Departed of Tadeusz Kantor: Recollections about Tadeusz Kantor, Marian Kantor-Mirski and Józef Kantor). Katowice: Muzeum Historii Katowic, 2002.
Sandauer, Artur. *On the Situation of the Polish Writer of Jewish Descent in the Twentieth Century*. Jerusalem: Hebrew University, Magnes Press, 2005.
_____. "Sztuka po końcu sztuki" [Art After the End of Art]. *Dialog* 3 (1981): 101–12.
Santner, Eric L. *Stranded Objects: Mourning, Memory, and Film in Postwar Germany*. Ithaca, NY: Cornell University Press, 1990.
Schechner, Richard. "Grotowski and the Grotowskian." *TDR: The Drama Review* 52, no. 2, Re-Reading Grotowski (Summer 2008): 7–13.
_____. *The Grotowski Sourcebook*. Ed. Richard Schechner and Lisa Wolford. New York: Routledge, 1997.
_____. "There's Something Happenin' Here…" *TDR: The Drama Review* 54, no. 2 (T 206) (Summer 2010): 12–17.
_____. "Want to Watch? Or Act?" *New York Times*, 12 January 1969, D1.
Schlein, Seth L. "The Cassandra Scene in Aeschylus' Agamemnon." *Greece and Rome* 21, no. 1 (April 1989): 11–16.
Schlemmer, Oscar. "Man and Art: Figure." *The Theatre of the Bauhaus*. Ed. Walter Gropius. Baltimore: John Hopkins University Press, 1996.
Schmidt, Sandra. "Polish Theatre Lab in American Debut." *Los Angeles Times*, 20 October 1969, C23.
Schorter, Eric. "Revelation by Avant-Garde Company." *Daily Telegraph*, 18 October 1969. The Grotowski Institute Archives.
Schulz, Bruno. "Sanatorium Under the Sign of the Hourglass." *The Complete Fiction of Bruno Schulz*. With an afterword by Jerzy Ficowski. Trans. Celina Wieniewska. New York: Walker and Company, 1989.
_____. Review of "Ferdydurke." *Skalamander* 96/98 (1938): 183–9.
_____. "Wędrówki sceptyka" [Skeptic's Travels]. *Tygodnik Ilustrowany* 6 (1936).
Segel, Harold B. *Polish Romantic Drama: Three Plays in English Translation*. Ithaca, NY: Cornell University Press, 1977.

Sellar, Tom. "Poland's Old and New Masters." *Theater* 33, no. 3 (Fall 2003): 2–19.
Shallcross, Bozena. *The Holocaust Object in Polish and Polish-Jewish Culture*. Bloomington: Indiana University Press, 2011.
Sheridan, Mark, ed. *Genesis*. Downers Grove, IL: InterVarsity Press, 2002.
Shivaslondon, Mark. "'I Propose Poverty in the Theater.'" *New York Times*, 22 December 1968, D5.
Shmeruk, Chone. "Hebrew-Yiddish-Polish: A Trilingual Jewish Culture." *The Jews of Poland Between Two World Wars*. Boston, MA: Brandeis University Press, 1989.
Sienkiewicz, Marian. "Demiurg z Cricot 2" [Demiurg from Cricot 2]. *Przekrój* 1601 (1975): 9. Cricoteka Archives: CRC III/005918.
Simon, John. "Does Genuine Art Require Special Pleading?" *New York Times*, 26 January 1969, D21.
_____. "Grotowski's Grotesqueries." *Hudson Review* 23, no. 3 (Autumn 1970): 510–21.
_____. "Vaulting Pole." *New York Theatre*, 1 December 1969, 58.
Sinko, Tadeusz. "O greckich tradedjach Wyspiańskiego" [About Wyspiański's Greek Tragedies]. *Wyspiańskiemu Teatr Krakowski* [For Wyspiański from Cracow's Theatre – publication celebrating 25th anniversary of Wyspiański's death]. Cracow: Zakłady Graficzne "Styl," 1932. 40–44.
Sitarz, Wojciech. "Optymistyczna wersja 'Akropolis' – recenzja sztuki" [The Optimistic Version of Akropolis] (2009). <http://pik.wroclaw.pl/pressroom/Optymistyczna-wersja-Akropolis-recenzja--n743.html> (accessed 3 March 2011).
Skiba-Lickel, Aldona. *Aktor według Kantora*. Wrocław: Zakład Narodowy im. Ossolinskich – Wydawnictwo, 1995.
Skiwski, J. E. "Kurza pierś" [Chicken Breast]. *Kronika Polski i Świata* 2 1938): 9.
Skorczewski, Dariusz. "Modern Polish Literature Through a Postcolonial Lens," *The Sarmatian Review* 26, no. 3 (2006): 1229–33. <http://www.postcolonial-europe.eu/index.php/en/essays/91-modern-polish-literature-through-a-postcolonial-lens> (accessed 1 August 2011).
Skotnicki, Jan. "Ukradzione poranki" [Stolen Mornings]. *Scena* 9 (November 1983): 21.
Sloterdijk, Peter. *Critique of Cynical Reason*. Trans. Michael Eldred. Minneapolis: University of Minnesota, 1987.
Slowacki, Juliusz. *Poland's Angry Romantic: Two Poems and a Play by Juliusz Slowacki*. Ed. and trans. Peter Cochran et al. Cambridge: Cambridge Scholars, 2009.
Slowiak, James. *Jerzy Grotowski*. London: Routledge, 2007.
Slowiak, James and Jairo Cuesta. *Jerzy Grotowski*. London and New York: Routledge, 2007.
Smożewski, Ryszard. "Uczestniczył w seansie dramatycznym Tadeusza Kantora" [Participated in Tadeusz Kantor's Dramatic Séance]. *Szpilki* 3 (18 January 1976): 18.
Sofsky, Wolfgang. *The Order or Terror*. Trans. William Templer. Princeton, NJ: Princeton University Press, 1997.
Sontag, Susan. *Against Interpretation, and Other Essays*. New York: Picador, 1966.
Spivak, Gayatri Chakravorty. *A Critique of Postcolonial Reason: Toward a History of the Vanishing Present*. Cambridge, MA: Harvard University Press, 1999.
Stasio, Marilyn. "Tadeusz Kantor's *The Dead Class*." *New York Post*, 21 February 1979. Cricoteka Archives: CRC III/00049.
Stangret, Lech. *Tadeusz Kantor. Fantomy Realności* [Tadeusz Kantor: Phantoms of Reality]. Cracow: Cricoteka, 1996.
Steinem, Gloria. *Outrageous Acts and Everyday Rebellion*. New York: Holt, Rinehart and Winston, 1983.
Steinlauf, Michael C. "Józio Grojeszyk: A Jewish City Slicker on the Warsaw Popular Stage." *Jewish Theatre: A Global View*. Ed. Edna Nahshon. Lieden, Boston: Brill, 2009.
Stern, Anatol. "Manekiny naturalizmu" [Mannequins of Naturalism]. *Myśl teatralna polskiej awangardy 1919–1939*. Ed. S. Marczak-Oborski's. Warsaw: Wyd. Artystyczne i Filmowe, 1921. 99–114.
Steward, Ellen. "Uninformed." *New York Times*, 23 February 1969, D21.

Stobrecka, Maria. *Trzy dramaty Wyspiańskiego. Wesele – Wyzwolenie – Akropolis* [Three Plays of Wyspiański: Marriage, Liberation, Akropolis]. Manuscript stored at Wojewódzka i Miejska Biblioteka Publiczna in Cracow.

Surynt, Izabela. *Postęp, kultura i kolonializm. Polska a niemiecki projekt europejskiego Wschodu w dyskursach publicznych XIX wieku* [Progress, Culture and Colonialism. Poland and German Project of European East in the 19th Century Political Discourse]. Wrocław: Wydawnictwo "Atut," 2006.

Szczawiński, Józef. "Tadeusz Kantor – epitafium dla epoki" [Epitaph For the Epoch]. *Słowo Powszechne*, 11 March 1976. Cricoteka Archives: CRC III/000546.

Szkudlarek, Ewa. "An Anxiety of Existence in the Dramas of Stanisław Ignacy Witkiewicz." *Witkacy w Polsce na na świecie*. Ed. Marta Skwara. Szczecin: Wydawn. Naukowe Uniwersytetu Szczecińskiego, 2001. 414.

Szulczynski, Wojciech. "Review: *The Forefathers' Eve: Twelve Improvisations*." *Theatre Journal* 48, no. 4, Eastern European Transitions (December 1996): 499–503.

Szybist, Maciej. "Akropolis." *Echo Krakowa* 45 (24 February 1978): 2.

_____. "Umarła Klasa" [Dead Class]. *Echo Krakowa*, 18 November 1975. Cricoteka Archives: CRC III/005913, III/000539, III/004792.

Szydłowski, Roman. "Bez Teatru Rzeczypospolitej" [Without the Theatre of People's Republic]. *Życie Literackie* 25 (19 June 1983).

_____. "Czarno na białym. 'Umarła klasa' po latach" [In Black and White: 'Dead Class' After All Those Years]. *Rzeczypospolita*, 15 June 1983, 4.

Szyjkowski, Marian. "Z teatru im. Jul. Słowackiego, 'Tumor Mózgowicz.' Dramat w 3 aktach z prologiem Stanisława Ignacego Witkiewicza" [From Slowacki Theatre, Tumor Brainiowicz]. *Ilustrowany Kurier Codzienny* 177 (1921).

Święcicki, Jan Maria. Review of the sermons by Władysław Mirski. *Tygodnik Powszechny*, 26 March 1950.

Święcicki, Klaudiusz. *Historia w teatrze Tadeusza Kantora* [History in the Theatre of Tadeusz Kantor]. Poznań: Wydawnictwo Poznańskie, 2007.

Taborski, Roman. *Dramaty Stanisława Wyspiańskiego na scenie do 1939 roku* [Stanisław Wyspiański's Dramas on the Stage until 1939]. Warsaw: Semper, 1994.

Targoń, Joanna. "Don Kichot w okularach dla krótkowidzów" [Don Kichote in Glasses for Nearsighted]. *Gazeta Wyborcza*, 20 March 2009, 10.

_____. "O Grotowskim wielokrotnie" [About Grotowski in Many Ways]. *Gazeta Wyborcza*, 14 March 2009, 6.

_____. "Zrób to sam" [Do It Yourself]. *Dwutygodnik: Strona Kultury* 2 (17 April 2009). <http://www.dwutygodnik.com.pl/artykul/56-zrob-to-sam.html> (accessed 2 March 2011).

Taylor, Nina. "Stanisław Wyspiański and Symbolist Drama: The Work of Art as 'dramatis persona.'" *Slavonic and East European Review* 66, no. 2 (April 1988): 198–209.

TEM. "Planchon o Grotowskim" [Planchon About Grotowski: An Interview With Planchon for *Cité Panorama*]. *Kierunki* 5 (29 January 1967). The Grotowski Institute Archives.

Temkine, Raymonde. *Grotowski*. Trans. Alex Szogyi. New York: Avon Books, 1972. First published in French by La Cite in 1968.

_____. Theatre review. *Europe* (October 1977): 201–2.

Terlecki, Tymon. "A Critical Appraisal of Mickiewicz's Lecture About Theatre." *Studies in Polish Civilization*. Ed. Damian Wandycz. Institute on East Central Europe, Columbia University and The Polish Institute of Arts & Sciences in America, 1966. 275–9.

_____. *Stanisław Wyspiański*. Boston: Twayne Publishers, 1983.

_____. "Stanisław Wyspiański and the Poetics of Symbolist Drama." *Polish Review* 15, no. 4 (Autumn 1970): 55–63.

Teschke, Holger. "Jerzy Grotowski, 1933–1999." *Theater* 29, no. 2 (1999): 4–15.

Thaxter, John. "Drama wherever you look at Riverside" *Richmond and Twickenham Times*, 19 November 1982. Cricoteka Archives: CRC III/000654.

Thompson, Ewa M. *Imperial Knowledge. Russian Literature and Colonialism*. Westport, CT and London: Greenwood Press, 2000.
Times. "Poland Begins to Appreciate Grotowski." 16 August 1965. The Grotowski Institute Archives.
Tkaczuk, Wacław J. "Wyspiański w blasku i cieniu. Rozmowa z Wojciechem Natansonem" [Wyspiański In the Light and Shadows: Conversation with Wojciech Natanson]. *Za i Przeciw* 14 (6 April 1969). The Grotowski Institute Archives.
Trojanowska, Tamara. "Many Happy Returns: Janusz Glowacki and His Exilic Experience." *Living In Translation: Polish Writers in America*. Ed. Halina Stephan. New York: Radopi, 2003.
Truszkowska, Teresa. "Umarła Klasa" [Dead Class]. *Dziennik Polski*, 30–31 October 1976, 6.
Turner, Jane. *Eugenio Barba*. London and New York: Routledge, 2005.
Tymicki Jerzy and Andrzej Niezgoda. "New Dignity: The Polish Theatre 1970–1985." *The Drama Review: TDR* 30, no. 3 (Autumn 1986): 13–46.
Tyszka, Juliusz. *Widowiska Nowojorskie* [New York Spectacles]. Poznań: Wydawnictwo ARS NOVA, 1994.
Underhill, Karen. "Ecstasy and Heresy: Martin Buber, Bruno Schulz, and Jewish Modernity." *(Un)masking Bruno Schulz: new combinations, further fragmentations, ultimate reintegrations*. Ed. Dieter De Bruyn and Kris van Heuckelom. Amsterdam: Rodopi, 2009. 27–46.
Van der Kolk, Bessel A. "The Compulson to Repeat the Trauma: Re-enactment, Revictimization, and Masochism." *Psychiatric Clinics of North America* 12, no. 2 (1989): 386–411.
Van Hoboken, C. "Is Jerzy Grotowsky a Genie or a Charlatan?" *Trouw. Amsterdam*, 30 June 1967. The Grotowski Institute Archives.
Walicki, Andrzej. *Philosophy and Romantic Nationalism: The Case of Poland*. Oxford: Clarendon Press 1982.
Wardle, Irving. "Big Catch from Poland." *Times*, 24 August 1968, 18.
_____. "'The Dead Class.' Collage of Art." *Times*, 30 August 1976. Cricoteka Archives: CRC III/000186.
_____. "Grotowski the Evangelist." *Times*, 4 October 1969, IIIc.
_____. "Haunted Visions of Museum of Memory." *Times*, 18 November 1982, 8.
_____. "Polish Avant-Garde Stages 'Acropolis' at Edinburgh Fete." *New York Times*, 24 August 1968, 24.
Wawel Royal Castle website <http://www.wawel.krakow.pl/en/> (accessed 15 January 2011).
W.B. "Cricot 2 in Great Britain." *The Theatre in Poland / Le Theatre en Pologne* 3, no. 223 (1977): 27.
Weintraub, Wiktor. *Literature as Prophecy: Scholarship and Martinist Poetics in Mickiewicz's Parisian Lectures*. The Hague: Mouton & Co. Publishers, 1956.
Wełminski, Andrzej. *Trumpf, trumpf… Lalki, manekiny i przedmioty ze spektaklu "Umarła klasa" Tadeusza Kantora* [Triumph, triumph… Dolls, Mannequins and Objects from Tadeusz Kantor's Dead Class]. Introduction by Lech Stangret. Nadarzyn: Green Gallery, 2005.
West London Observer. "The Dead Class Review." 24 November 1982. Cricoteka Archives: CRC III/000659.
Wetzsteon, Ross. "Theatre: Two by Grotowski." *Village Voice*, 27 October 1969, 46.
White, Hayden. "Historical Emplotment and the Problem of Truth." *Probing the Limits of Representation: Nazism and the "Final Solution."* Ed. Saul Friedlander. Cambridge, MA: Harvard University Press, 1992. 37–53.
Whitehead, Anne. *Trauma Fiction*. Edinburgh: Edinburgh University Press, 2004.
Wichowska, Joanna. "Akropolis: Duchy i ludzie" [Akropolis: Ghosts and People]. *Dwutygodnik: Strona Kultury* 20 (24 December 2009). <http://www.dwutygodnik.com.pl/artykul/738-akropolis-duchy-i-ludzie.html> (accessed 2 March 2011).
Wiktor, Jan. "Foreword." *Listy do Stanisława Lacka* [Letters to Stanisław Lack]. Cracow: Wydawnictwo Literackie, 1957.

Wirth, Andrzej. "A Discovery of Tragedy: The Incomplete Account of Tadeusz Borowski." *Polish Review* 12, no. 3 (Summer 1976): 43–52.
———. "Gertruda Stein i Stanisław Ignacy Witkiewicz" [Gertrude Stein and Stanisław Ignacy Witkiewicz]. *Witkacy w Polsce na na świecie*. Ed. Marta Skwara. Szczecin: Wydawn. Naukowe Uniwersytetu Szczecińskiego, 2001. 25–36.
Wiśniewska, Natalia. "Literatura w malignie" [Literature in Delirium]. *Epoka* (Warsaw), 25 November 1938, 11.
Wisz. "Grotowski i inni" [Grotowski and Others]. *Trybuna Robotnicza* 51 (1–2 March 1969). The Grotowski Institute Archives.
Witkiewicz, Stanisław Ignacy. *Czysta Forma w teatrze* [Pure Form in Theatre]. Ed. J. Degler. Warsaw: Wydawnictwa Artystyczne i Filmowe, 1977.
———. "Tumor Brainowicz." *Witkiewicz: Seven Plays*. Ed. and trans. Daniel Gerould. New York: Martin E. Segal Theatre Center, 2004.
———. "Tumor Mózgowicz" [Tumor Brainiowicz]. *Dzieła zebrane*. Ed. Anna Micińska, Janusz Degler and Lech Sokół. Warsaw: Państwowy Instytut Wydawniczy, 1992.
"Witold Pilecki." *Jewish Virtual Library*. <http://www.jewishvirtuallibrary.org/jsource/biography/Witold_Pilecki.html> (accessed 1 August 2001).
Wittgenstein, Ludwig. *Culture and Value*. Trans. Peter Winch. Ed. G. H. von Wright and Heikki Nyman. Chicago: University of Chicago Press, 1980.
Witts, Noel. *Tadeusz Kantor*. London: Routledge, 2010.
Wodecka, Dorota. "Grotowski zawsze był sam" [Grotowski Was Always Alone. A conversation with Ewa Lubowiecka. *Gazeta Wyborcza*, 16 January 2009, 6.
Wolf, Larry. *The Idea of Galicia: History and Fantasy in Habsburg Political Culture*. Palo Alto, CA: Stanford University Press, 2010.
Wójcik, Tomasz, ed. *Pisarze awangardy dwudziestolecia międzywojennego: autokomentarze: Leśmian – Witkacy – Schulz – Gombrowicz*. Warsaw: Wydawnictwo Naukowe, 1995.
Wojdowski, Bogdan. "Borowski häftling." *Współczesność* 13, no. 119 (1–15 July 1961): 1, 3.
Wojtowicz, Agnieszka. "Oby Ci się, dziecko, jakos żyło w tym sierocińcu" ["Have a good life, my child, in that orphanage." A conversation with Ewa Lubowiecka]. *Notatnik Teatralny* 20–21 (2000): 93.
———. "Próba leczenia postawy romantycznej za pomocą postawy romantycznej (Grotowski i narodowe mity)" [An Attempt to Cure Romantic Attitude With Romantic Attitude (Grotowski and the National Myths)]. *Tradycia romantyczna w teatrze polskim* [Romantic Tradition in Polish Theatre]. Ed. Dariusz Kosiński. Cracow: Towarzystwo Naukowe Societas Vistulana, 2007.
Wolford, Lisa. *Grotowski's Objective Drama Research*. Jackson: University Press of Mississippi, 1996.
Woolf, Virginia "On Not Knowing Greek" (1925). *The Common Reader*. New York: Harcourt, 1984. 23–37.
Worthen, W. B. "Disciplines of the Text/Sites of Performance." *The Drama Review* 39, no. 1 (1995): 13–28
Wróbel, Marta. "'Ostatni Etap' Wandy Jakubowskiej jako pierwszy etap polskiego kina ideologicznego" [Wanda Jakubowska 'The Last Stage' as the First Stage of Polish Ideological Cinema]. *Kwartalnik Filmowy* 43 (2003): 6–11.
Wyka, Anna. *Gęba polska, czyli, Mistrz Gombrowicz* [Polish Face, or The Master Gombrowicz]. Łomża: Oficyna Wydawnicza Stopka, 2006.
Wysińska, Elżbieta. "Teatr od 'Wesela' do Umarłej Klasy" [Theatre, from the 'Marriage' to the 'Dead Class']. *Kultura*, 9 January 1977. Cricoteka Archives: CRCIII/000569.
Wyskiel, Wojciech. *Inna twarz Hioba: problematyka alienacyjna w dziele Brunona Schulza* [Hiob's Other Face: Alienation in the Works of Bruno Schulz]. Cracow: Wydawnictwo literackie, 1980.
Wyspiański i Teatr 1907–1957 [Wyspiański and Theatre 1907–1957]. Cracow: Praca zbiorowa wydana przez teatr im. J. Słowackiego, 1957.

Wyspiański, Stanisław. *Akropolis*. Cracow: Jagiellonian University Press, Skład w księgarni Gebethnera, 1904.

———. *Akropolis*. Ed. Ewa Miodońska-Brookes. Redakcja Biblioteki Narodowej. Wrocław: Zakład Narodowy im. Ossolinskich, 1985.

———. *Letters to Stanisław Lack* [Listy do Stanisława Lacka]. Cracow: Wydawnictwo Literackie, 1957.

Wyspiańskiemu Teatr Krakowski [For Wyspiański from Cracow's Theatre – publication celebrating 25th anniversary of Wyspiański's death]. Cracow: Zakłady Graficzne "Styl," 1932.

Young, B. A. "Picking at the Fringe." *Financial Times*, 31 August 1976, 10. Cricoteka Archives: CRC III/000188.

Zalewski, Jeff and Paul Gediman. Review of Tim Cole's "Selling the Holocaust: From Auschwitz to Schindler, How History is Bought, Sold and Packaged." *Publishers Weekly* 246, no. 31 (2 August 1999): 65.

Zamyatin, Evgeni. "On Literature, Revolution, and Entropy." *Literary Modernism*. Ed. Irving Howe. New York: Fawcett, 1976.

Zawistowski, Władysław (1932) "Stanisław Wyspiański poetą naszego pokolenia" [Stanisław Wyspiański: Poet of Our Generation]. *Wyspiańskiemu Teatr Krakowski* (For Wyspiański from Cracow's Theatre. Cracow: Zakłady Graficzne "Styl." 7–11.

Zbijewska, Krystyna. "'Akropolis' po pół wieku" ['Akropolis' after Half a Century]. *Dziennik Polski*, 4–5 February 1978, 7.

Żbikowska, Izabella. "Grotowski zapomniany" [Grotowski Forgotten]. *Gazeta Wyborcza*, 9 May 2008, 2.

Zimnica-Kuziola, Emilia. "Tadeusz Kantor." *Gazeta Wyborcza*, 2 August 2005, 9.

Zmijewski, Norbert. "Vicissitudes of Political Realism in Poland: Tygodnik Powszechny and Znak." *Soviet Studies* 43, no. 1 (1991): 83–106.

Ziomek, Jerzy. "Epoki i formacje w dziejach literatury polskiej." *Pamiętnik literacki* 77, no. 4 (1986): 23–54.

Žižek, Slavoj. *The Sublime Object of Ideology*. London: Verso, 1989.

INDEX

40 Mandelbaums, The (Kantor) 190

A

Abdoh, Reza 6
Abraham 102, 145
Abramek (*This Way for the Gas, Ladies and Gentlemen*) 145–6
"About the Marionette Theater" (Kleist) 262
Absent Old Man 193, 234, 253
absolute act 133–4
Academie Calarossi 90
Achilles 92, 101
"Actor and the Über-Marionette, The" (Gordon Craig) 262
Adorno, Theodor W. 1–2, 4, 26, 28, 40, 46, 122, 133, 135
Aesthetic Theory (Adorno) 28
"Against Interpretation" (Sontag) 3
Agamben, Giorgio 129, 131–2, 135, 256
Ajax 100
Akropolis (Grotowski's production) 5–9, 14–16, 20, 22–4, 26–31, 39–40, 44–6, 57, 60, 73–9, 83–4, 86–90, 105–18, 121, 123–4, 132–9, 141–4, 146–8, 150–55, 197, 204, 210, 224, 279
Akropolis (Wyspiański's drama) 8, 22, 56, 65, 73, 90–92, 94–101, 103–5, 113, 116, 148, 151–2, 155, 245, 277
Akropolis, According to Stanisław Wyspiański (Grotowski) 7, 54
Akropolis from the Epoch of the Ovens (Bąk) 113
Akropolis. Reconstruction 153
Albee, Edward 74
Alexander, Jeffrey 44
Allah 129
Allain, Paul 8
American Committee of the Laboratory Theatre 82–3
Amery, Jean 109, 122, 129
An Anthology of Polish Literature (Kridl) 19

Anatomy Lesson Based on Rembrandt (Kantor) 190
Anderson, Benedict 16
Andromache 98, 100
Ankwicz, Andrzej 97
Annihilation Machine 192
Ansky (Shloyme Zanvl Rappoport) 9, 46, 260–61
Apocalypsis cum Figuris (Grotowski) 56, 65, 70, 75, 83, 89
Apollo 91, 101, 103, 142
Apollo-Salvatore 104–5
Arendt, Hannah 117
Aristotle 3
Artaud, Antonin 57, 70, 79, 218, 227
Ascherson, Neal 10, 17
Aeschylus 99
At Our Auschwitz (Borowski) 113
Augustynowicz, Anna 5
Aunt Agnieszka 73
Auschwitz 17, 22–3, 26, 28–31, 36–9, 72, 76, 98, 108–9, 111–24, 126–9, 132–4, 139, 141–2, 144–7, 151, 155, 191–2, 224, 249, 252, 261, 264, 279
  prisoners 142, 145
    Jewish prisoners 142
  survivors 115, 118
  trauma of 155
Auschwitz Volunteer: Beyond Bravery, The (Pilecki) 37

B

Bablet, Denis 56, 195
Bacchae, The (Euripides) 80
Bagatela Theatre in Cracow 193, 195, 260
Bajewski, Tomasz 222
Bald Soprano, The (Ionesco) 218
Balladyna (Słowacki) 262
Bałus, Wojciech 92, 102–3
Banu, Georges 8, 282

Barba, Eugenio 7–8, 29, 45, 56, 58, 63, 65, 73, 78, 134
Barber, John 202, 210
Barca, Pedro Calderon de la 17, 52
Bardini, Aleksander 275
Bardonnie, Mathilde La 204
Barker 250–51
Barnes, Clive 57, 84–5, 87, 124, 144
Barranger, Milly 8
Barrault, Jean-Louis 88
Barron, Brian 201, 207, 215, 243
Barry, Anne 209
Bąk, Bogdan 113
Beadle in Past Perfect 193
Beckett, Samuel 1, 9, 54, 208, 212, 219, 243, 247, 283
Bednarczyk, Zbigniew 193
Belkin, Ahuva 23
Benjamin, Walter 82
Bentley, Eric 83, 134–5
Bernard, Michael 128
Berstein, Michael 122–3
Beta (*The Captive Mind*) 119
Bettelheim, Bruno 117, 130–31, 147
Białoszewski, Miron 62
Bible 22, 55, 101, 145, 215
  Book of Genesis 101
  Book of Esther 246
  Creation in Bible 145
  New Testament 141
  Old Testament 20, 22, 32, 116, 144, 215, 257
Bielska, Urszula 61
Bielski, Nella 212
Bieniewicz, Henryk 197
Bildungsroman 229, 233
Billington, Michael 202, 208–10, 248
Binczycki, Jerzy 222
bio-objects 12, 191, 267–72
Blumenthal, Eileen 206, 211, 213, 215, 258
Błoński, Jan 34–6, 38, 94, 217–18
Bober, Jerzy 104–5
Bocheński, Tomasz 14, 243, 245, 263
Bogusławski, Wojciech 222
Bończa, Leonard 104
Bończa-Szabłowski, Jan 238
Book of Letters (Schulz) 229
Border Street (Ford) 127
Bordwell, David 3, 5
Borie, Monique 45, 247
Borowski, Tadeusz 8, 46, 111–14, 116–21, 123, 126–9, 132–3, 137, 142–6, 149, 263

Borowski and Maria 119
Borowski, Wiesław 198, 224, 234
Boruń-Jagodzińska, Katarzyna 250
Bosch, Hieronymus 74, 115, 210
Boska, Anna 44, 254
Boue, Michael 204
Boundaries of Jewish Identity (Glenn, Sokoloff) 32
Boyers, Robert 240
Boy-Żeleński, Tadeusz 218–19, 221
Brandhuber, Jerzy Adam 115
Brandys, Kazimierz 17
Bratny, Roman 111
Braun, Kazimierz 19, 51, 275
Brecht, Stefan 87, 101, 218, 236, 250
Breughel, Pieter 115
Brockett, Oscar G. 19
Broniewski, Władysław 61
Brook, Peter 6, 8, 55–7, 68, 75–6, 124, 144, 148, 204, 248
Brooklyn Academy of Music 82
Brown, Russell 241, 255
Brunstein, Robert 80
Brutus 27
Bryden, Ronald 57, 88
Brzozowski, Stanisław 99
Buber, Martin 31, 60, 141, 258
Buñuel, Luis 194
Buchdrama 50
Byron, George 54
Byrski, Irena 61
Byrski, Tadeusz 61
Bzdyl, Leszek 153

C

Caesar, Julius 27
Cain (Byron) 54
Calvoressi, Richard 201, 267
Capri, Aldo 129
Captive Mind (Miłosz) 62
Caravaggio, Michelangelo Merisi da 115
Carne, Rosalind 205, 207, 213
Carnival! (Eco) 67
Carlson, Marvin 1
Caruth, Cathy 44, 253
Cassandra 100, 105, 137, 142
Catharsis 107
Chagall, Marc 115, 210, 227
Chambers Biographical Dictionary 208
Chanel, Coco 83
Chava (*Fiddler on the Roof*) 33
Chaikin, Joseph 6, 77
Charlady-Death 200

Chien Andalou, La (Buñuel) 194
Chmiel, Adam 151
Cracow Academy of Fine Arts 185
Cranach Lucas 210
Chairs, The (Ionesco) 50
Christ 13–14, 98, 100, 103
Christ-Salvatore 102–3
Christian mysticism 185
Cieślak, Ryszard 11, 106
Cinnamon Shops (Schulz) 229
Cioffi, Kathleen 13, 51, 244
Cleaning Lady 193, 248, 250
Cleopatra 27, 242
Clurman, Harold 23, 80, 87, 115, 143, 206, 209, 214
Cockroaches (Witkacy) 216
Cocteau, Jean 52, 54
Coe, Richard 83
Cohen, Roger 16
Columbuses, Generation of 111–12, 119
Commedia dell'arte 250, 252
Comte, Auguste 241
coincidentia oppositorum 149
Constant Prince, The (Grotowski) 30, 56, 58, 65, 79, 83
Conrad, Joseph 223
Copermann, Émile 115
Cork, Richard 265
Cosmos (Gombrowicz) 238
Country House (Kantor's play) 189
Country House (Witkacy's drama) 188–9, 216
Cricot 2 (Theatre) 6, 11, 187–9, 201–2, 215, 223, 280
Cricotage (Kantor) 189
cricotages 189, 193
Cricoteka 281–2
Croyden, Margaret 84, 90, 107, 116, 121, 204
Cuesta, Jairo 8
Culbertson, Roberta 44
Curse, The (Wyspiański) 91
Curtiss, Thomas Quinn 86, 139, 151
Cuttlefish, The (Witkacy) 188, 216, 219, 223, 267
Cynkutis, Zbigniew 105, 115, 145
Czerniaków, Adam 30

D

Dace, Tish 203, 206, 214, 252, 254, 267
Dainty Shapes and Hairy Apes (Kantor) 190
Dainty Shapes and Hairy Apes (Witkacy) 188, 190, 192

Dance of Death 237
Dance of the Vampires (Polanski) 243
danse macabre 97
Dante, Alighieri 74, 255
David, King 152
Davis, Norman 17
Dead Class (Kantor) 5–6, 8–10, 14–16, 20, 22–4, 26–31, 39–40, 44–6, 187, 190–216, 223–8, 230–31, 234–8, 242–8, 250, 252–4, 256–63, 265, 267, 270–72, 278–82
Dear Brother Death (Hesse) 122
Death in Venice (Mann) 122
Death of Tintagiles (Maeterlinck) 185
Degler, Janusz 219
"Degraded Reality" 258–9
Dejmek, Kazimierz 105, 275
Demarco, Richard 201
Democratic Heritage of Poland, The (Kridl) 19
Derrida, Jacques 2, 12, 256, 283–4
Devil Made a Woman, The (Merimee) 49
Dialectic of Enlightenment (Adorno) 28
Dine, Jim 212
Dionysus in 69 (Performance Group's) 79–80
Discreet Charm of Bourgeoisie (Buñuel) 194
Dividing Line, The (Kantor) 189
Divine Comedy (Dante) 255
Doctor Mengele 210
Dom pod Oświęcimiem (Hołuj) 332n407
Don Juan 92
Dostoyevsky, Fyodor 56
Dr. Faustus (Grotowski) 79
"Dr. Faustus in Poland" (Barba) 78
Drozdowski, Bohdan 87–8
Dubowski, Grzegorz 222
Duchamp, Marcel 267
Duker, Abraham 20
dybbuk 260–61
Dybbuk or Between Two Words (Ansky) 215, 260–61
Dyevre, Laurence 8
Dziukeb, Piotr 153

E

Eco, Umberto 67
Encounters with Tadeusz Kantor (Miklaszewski) 9
Edelman, Charles 188, 207–8
Eder, Richard 207, 210, 253
Eisenstein, Sergei 52
Ekielski, Władysław 92
Eksteins, Modris 245

Eliot, T. S. 56
Elsom, John 202, 250
Elwal, Julie 205
Empty Fields (Holuj) 114–15, 123
   Józef Szajna's adaptation 123
Endgame (Beckett) 1
End of the Impossible Theatre, The (Kott) 69
Engelking, Barbara 40
Esau 98, 101–2, 105, 145
Essay on Cultural Criticism and Society
   (Adorno) 122
Esslin, Martin 205, 210
Eternal Wanderers 19, 191, 257, 282
Euripides 80

F

Fagin, Hellen 16
Fallek, Wilhelm 220
False Prophets (Buber) 60
Fantazy (Słowacki) 18
Farewell to Autumn (Witkacy) 216
Farewell to Maria (Borowski) 8
Faulkner, William 253
Faustus (Goethe) 255
Fazan, Katarzyna 215
Fear: Anti-Semitism in Poland after Auschwitz; An
   Essay in Historical Interpretation (Gross) 41
Fellini, Federico 249
Ferdydurke (Gombrowicz) 215, 238–45, 249
Ficowski, Jerzy 232
Fiddler on the Roof 33, 84
Fik, Marta 104, 197
Filipowicz, Halina 6, 16, 18, 42, 276
Filler, Witold 39, 58, 87
Findlay, Robert 7–8, 26, 83, 86, 89, 107,
   137, 144–5, 148, 150
Fisher, Eileen 205, 253, 266
Flaszen, Ludwik 6–8, 10–12, 15, 53–5,
   58–9, 78, 84, 87, 107, 115, 118, 125,
   136, 139, 143, 145, 148, 150
Ford, Aleksander 127
Ford Foundation 74
Forefathers' Eve (Mickiewicz) 15–16, 18,
   20–24, 54, 65, 72, 152, 214–15, 274–9
Foreman, Richard 6, 8, 204
Forgotten Earth (Brandhuber) 115
Fortier, Mark 7–8, 108
Foucault, Michel 2
Frank, Jacob 20
Fredro, Aleksander 219
Freedman, Lewis 74, 86, 152–3

Fret, Jarosław 55
Freud, Sigmund 70, 233, 253
Further on, Nothing: Tadeusz Kantor's Theatre
   (Kobialka) 9
Fyedka (*Fiddler on the Roof*) 33

G

Gajewski, Jarosław 222
Gall, Halina 61
Gall, Iwo 105
Garbal, Łukasz 240
Gardzienice Theatre 5, 280
Garliński, Jarek 37
Gawlik, Jan Paweł 53, 108, 115
Germans (Kruczkowski) 123
Gerould, Daniel 17–19, 21, 50, 94, 186,
   188–90, 223, 226, 234, 236, 273
Gesamtkunstwerk (Wagner) 21, 96
Gieraczyński, Bogdan 12, 201
Giesen, Bernhard 44
Gignaux, Hubert 202, 210
Gilgul 260
Gilgamesh 255
Gilman, Richard 55, 71
Ginsberg, Merle 203, 206, 210
Glenn, Susan A. 32
Głowacka, Dorota 263
Głowiński, Michał 42
Goat Ceremony 278
God 13, 22–3, 102–3, 108–9, 118, 145, 214,
   256, 260, 274, 277
God's Playground (Davis) 17
Gods of Rain (Grotowski) 49
Goering, Hermann 110
Goethe, Johann Wolfgang von 255
Gog and Magog (Buber) 141
Gogol, Nikołaj 276
Goldberg, Stuart 277
Gombrowicz, Witold 12–13, 46, 54, 120,
   211, 215–16, 224, 227, 238–45, 249
Gomułka, Władysław 29, 54, 74, 275
Gordon Craig, Edward 51, 96, 262–3
Górecka, Maria 193
Górny, Andrzej 198
Gostomski, Zbigniew 193
Gothard, David 201
Gottfried, Martin 26, 85–7, 138
Gould, Jack 76, 148
Grabowska, Alina 219
Grabowski, Jan 40
Grammar Lesson, The (Kantor) 190

Great Theatrical Reform 96
Greek mythology 101, 142, 215, 242
Greek chorus 205
Gregory, Andre 70, 77
Greń, Zygmunt 259, 261
Gross, Jan T. 40–41
Grosz, George 210
Grotowski's Akropolis: A Retrospective (Flaszen) 7
Grotowski & Company (Flaszen) 8
Grotowski: A Handbook 66
Grotowski and His Laboratory (Osiński) 7
Grotowski's Empty Room: A Challenge to the Theatre (Allain) 8
Grotowski Institute 8, 10, 55, 58–9
Grotowski, Jerzy 4–8, 10–16, 18–26, 28, 30, 39–40, 42–3, 45–6, 49–50, 52–90, 93–4, 98–9, 105–18, 121, 123–5, 132–55, 188–9, 197–8, 203–4, 215, 224, 243–5, 278–80, 283–4
Grotowski's Objective Drama Research (Wolford) 7
Grotowski: Sourcebook 7–8, 71, 79
Grunwald, Matthias 115
Grynberg, Henryk 42
Gryszkiewicz, Bogusław 245
Grzegorzewski, Jerzy 279
Grzybowicz, Bogdan 193
Grzymała-Siedlecki, Adam 104
Guczalska, Beata 59–60
Gurawski, Jerzy 115, 148
Gussow, Mel 207, 210, 249, 266, 280
Gustaw (*Forefathers' Eve*) 274

H

Haecker, Emil 220
Halbwach, Maurice 28
Halpern, Romna 231
Hamlet (Shakespeare) 49, 94, 110
Hamletian dilemma 152
Hanuszkiewicz, Adam 50, 63–4, 68–9
Haran 102
Harries, Martin 28, 40, 44, 71, 89
Harris, Harry 88
Harris, William 9, 12, 210, 245
Has, Wojciech J. 230
Hartman, Jan 253
Havel, Vaclav 213
Heart of Darkness (Conrad) 223
"Hebrew-Yiddish-Polish: A Trilingual Jewish Culture" (Shmeruk) 34
Hector 92, 98, 100–102, 105, 152
Helena (*Iliad*) 100

Helena Modrzejewska Old Theatre in Cracow 187
Hell (Bosch) 115
Hellman, Martin 74
Helpless Man with a Table 191
Hepburn, Katharine 83
Herbert, Zbigniew 62–3
Herling-Grudziński, Gustaw 239
Hernani (Hugo) 18, 277
Hesse, Herman 122
Hewes, Henry 89
Himmler, Heinrich 110
Hiroshima 283
History of Polish Literature, The (Miłosz) 19
History of Polish Theatre, 1939–1989: Spheres of Captivity and Freedom, A (Braun) 19
History of Theatre (Brockett) 19
Hitler, Adolf 70, 110, 264
Hłasko, Marek 240
Hniedziewicz, Magdalena 196
Hoboken, C. van 74
Hoffman, Anna 227, 248
Holocaust 8–9, 22, 26, 29–31, 35, 37–41, 45, 68, 90, 110, 122–3, 127, 134, 143, 146, 151, 153, 190, 200, 210–11, 214, 247, 249–50, 252, 256–7, 259, 261, 264, 279, 283
Holocaust (NBC miniseries) 31
Holocaust Drama (Plunka) 31
Holoubek, Gustaw 60, 68, 275
Hołuj, Tadeusz 114
Homer 22, 99, 116, 152
  Homeric hero 186
  Homeric ode 186
Homolacs, Karol 96
Honegger, Gitta 1, 4
Howe, Irving 120
Hrabal, Bohumil 229
Hudson, Christopher 205
Hugo, Victor Marie 18
Human Nature Preserve 191
Hyde, George M. 9
Hymn at Sunset (Słowacki) 19

I

I and Thou (Buber) 141
Ides of March (Roman holiday) 27
Ides of March, The (Wilder) 27
Iliad (Homer) 99, 152
Individual and Mass Behavior in Extreme Situations (Bettelheim) 130

Insatiability (Witkacy) 216
Ionesco, Eugene 49, 54, 218–19
Iron Curtain 4, 6, 24, 40, 62
Isaac 102, 106, 145
I Shall Never Return (Kantor) 193
Iwona, Princess of Burgundy (Gombrowicz) 238
Izydor Brainowicz (*Tumor Brainowicz*) 223

J

Jackson, Shannon 4, 6
Jacob 98–9, 102, 106, 118, 142, 144–5, 152, 277
   Jacob/Priam 142
Jagiellonian University 90, 107
Jaholkowski, Antoni 106
Jakubowska, Wanda 126–7
Jeleński, Konstanty 240
Jan Karol Maciej Hellcat (Witkacy) 216
Janowski, Mieczysław 106
Janicki, Wacław 200, 281
Jarry, Alfred 17, 90
Jarząbski, Jerzy 246
Jastrzębska, Zuzanna 191, 194, 237
Jerzy Grotowski (Cuesta, Slowiak) 8
Jewish eschatology 145
Jewish martyology 142
Jewish mysticism 20, 185, 256, 260
Jewish mythology 142
Jędrysek, Krzysztof 59
Jędrzejczyk, Olgierd 196, 223
Jinxed Family, A (Krzyształ) 49
Joey-Józio (*Ferdydurke*) 239, 240–41
Jodłowski, Marek 215, 226
Jongh, Nicholas de 207
Joselewicz, Berek 33
Journey Through Other Spaces: Essays and Manifestos, 1944–1990, A (Kobialka) 9
Joyce, James 92, 233
Julius Caesar (Shakespeare) 27
Jurs-Munby, Karen 283

K

Kabbalah 15–16, 20–21, 42, 260, 277
Kaddish 23, 195, 247, 249, 256, 259
Kafka, Franz 258
Kalemba-Kasprzak, Elżbieta 95, 98, 101, 117, 144, 147, 151
Kalidasa 52, 54
Kalińska, Zofia 193
Kaminska, Ida 30

Kamińska, Katarzyna 154
Kantor, Tadeusz 4–6, 8–16, 18–30, 34, 39–40, 42–3 45–6, 54, 185–216, 218–19, 222–31, 234–8, 242–62, 264–74, 277–84
Kanters, Robert 25–6
Karasiński, Adam 227
Karlweis, Ninon Tallon 74, 82
Karren, Tamara 12
Karski, Jan 41
Kathakali 79
Katyń massacre/tragedy 16, 38, 43, 113
Kaufman, Moisés 6
Kauffmann, Stanley 76
Kauffman, Wolfe 88
Kazimierczyk, Barbara 194, 224, 226
Kelera, Józef 106
Keer, Walter 136, 139
Kelera, Józef 197
Kępiński, Antoni 132–3
Khrushchev, Nikita 53–4
Kiebuzinska, Olga 217
Kieślowski, Krzysztof 63
King, Robert 11
Kinsolving, William 77–8
Király, Nina 230
Kis, Danilo 229
Klata, Jan 5
Kleiner, Juliusz 99
Kleist, Henrich von 262–3
Kłodziński 130
Kłossowicz, Jan 9, 24–5, 50, 57, 198–9, 224
Kobialka, Michal 9, 235, 268
Kochanowski, Jan 53, 222
Kogon 129
Kolankiewicz, Leszek 10, 15, 23, 69, 79, 249
Konrad (*Forefathers' Eve*) 20, 152, 274, 277
Konrad Wallenrod (Mickiewicz) 79
Kordian (Grotowski) 50
Kordian (Słowacki) 54, 65, 72
Kosiński, Dariusz 21, 23, 66, 73
Kosiński, Kazimierz 93, 96
Kotarbiński, Józef 91–2
Kotlarczyk, Mieczysław 105
Kott, Jan 13, 51, 55, 57, 69–70, 80, 120, 214, 217–19, 222, 254, 256, 266
Korcelli 51
Koropeckyj, Roman 19
Krasicka, Lika 193
Krasiński, Zygmunt 18, 51, 94, 97, 99
Krassowski, Feliks 221

INDEX 395

Kremer, Józef 92
Krentz, Igor 52
Kretz-Mirski, Józef 101
Kridl, Manfred 18
Kruczkowski, Leon 123
Krygier, Waldemar 60, 108
Krzysztoń, Jerzy 49
Książek, Jan 193
Kucharski, Krzysztof 154
Kudewicz, Bolesław 105
Kudliński, Tadeusz 107
Kuharski, Allen 30, 71
Kumiega, Jennifer 7–8, 137
Kundera, Milan 14, 16
Kunstlerroman 229, 233
Kustow, Michael 89
"KZ-Syndrome" (Kępiński) 132

L

Laban 102, 118, 145
Laboratory Theatre 5–7, 11, 56–60, 68, 71, 73, 75–6, 78, 83, 85–6, 88, 116, 155
LaCapra, Dominick 261
lagered 145–6
La haine de la musique (Quignard) 142
La MaMa Experimental Theatre 11, 203, 222, 280
Landau, Felix 229
Land of Ashes and Diamonds: My Apprenticeship in Poland (Barba) 7
Lanzmann, Claude 30–31, 122, 128
Last Stage, The (Jakubowska) 126
Lautremont, Comte de 277
Lawrence, D. H. 138
Leah 102
Legion (Wyspiański) 91
Lehman, Hans-Thies 45, 185, 226, 247, 265, 271, 283–4
Lelewel, Joachim 274
Lenin, Vladimir 70
Leonardini, Jean-Pierre 212
Lesedrama 50
Lester, Elenore 80
Letter, The (Kantor) 189
Let the Artist Die (Kantor) 193
Lewis, Allan 89
Levy, Jennifer 134
Liberation (Wyspiański) 91, 96, 105, 152, 244
Lichten, Joseph 29, 35, 37–8
Lichtenstein, Harvey 84–5

Life and Death in the Works of Wyspiański (Brzozowski) 99
Life Is a Dream (Barca) 17
Limanowski, Mieczysław 5
Lindenbaum, Shalom 255
Lipko, Mateusz 108
Little, Stuart W. 83–4
Living Theatre 6, 57, 64, 77, 136
Loney, Glenn 206, 243, 253
Lorentowicz, Jan 239
Lubowiecka, Ewa 60–61, 110, 112, 141
Lucas, Edward 43
Lunacharsky Institute of Theatre Arts (GITIS) 49
Lupa, Krystian 5, 9, 60, 69, 198, 204
Luther, Martin 83
Lyons, Leonard 83

Ł

Łaszowski, Alfred 239
Ławski, Eugeniusz 53
Łempicka, Tamara 95
Łodyński, Wojciech 193
Łomnicki, Tadeusz 61
Łopuszański, Stanisław 53

M

Macbeth (Shakespeare) 82
Machine of Love and Death (Kantor) 193
MacTaggart, James 74–5, 123
Madman and the Nun (Kantor) 189, 192
Madman and the Nun (Witkacy) 188–9, 216
Maeterlinck, Maurice 9, 185
Magic Mountain (Mann) 255
Magritte, Rene 210
Majchrowski, Zbigniew 278
Making Meaning (Bordwell) 3
Malinowski, Bronisław 216
Malinowski, Seweryn 275
Mallarme, Stephane 50
Mamoń, Bronisław 230
Man, Paul de 12
Mandelbaums 190
Manifesto of the Theatre of Death (Kantor) 265
Mann, Theodore 83
Mann, Thomas 122, 255
Man of Marble (Wajda) 193–4
Man Passing Obituaries 193
Man with His Door 191

Man with a Sack and Its Unknown
	Contents 191
Man with a Suitcase 191
Man with the Bicycle 193, 236, 237, 272
Man with Two Bicycle Wheels Grown into
	His Legs 268
Marat/Sade (Swinarski) 61
Marc Antony 27
Marcus, Frank 89, 202, 210, 227
Marecka, Rena 106
Marianowicz, Antoni 42
Marlowe, Christopher 78
Marmarinos, Michael 153–5
Marx, Karl 70
Marxist critique 211
Masłowski, Michał 15, 72, 108
Marecka, Irena 142
Maurer, Jadwiga 277
Mayakovski, Vladimir 54
Mazowski, Antoni 91, 95, 101
Mączyński, Józef 93
Mądzik, Leszek 5
McFerran, Ann 202
Meisel, Dov Berush 33
Meleager (Wyspiański) 91
Mérimée, Prosper 49
Messiah, The (Schulz) 229
Messiah of Stockholm, The (Ozick) 229
Metaphysics of a Two-Headed Calf (Witkacy)
	216, 222
Meyerhold, Vsevolod 12, 49, 272
Mickiewicz, Adam 9, 12, 15, 18–22, 31–2,
	46, 51–2, 54, 65, 72, 79, 87, 94, 96,
	102, 141, 152, 214–15, 241, 274,
	276–9
Miklaszewska, Agata 189
Miklaszewski, Krzysztof 9, 40, 193, 195,
	227, 230, 233, 248, 252, 257, 261,
	272, 280–82
Mikulski, Kazimierz 193
Mikulski, Marek 222
Miller, Herman 74
Miłosz, Czesław 19, 38, 62–3, 119, 242
Minty-Miętus (*Ferdydurke*) 241
Mirski, Władysław 55
Mister (Schulz) 227
Miszkin, Leo 76
Moczar, Mieczysław 29
Moeller-Sally, Stephen 276
Molière (Jean-Baptiste Poquelin)
	249–50, 276

Molik, Zygmunt 106, 110, 142
Moniuszko, Stanisław 276
Mostowicz, Arnold 42
Morawiec, Elżbieta 104, 200, 257
Mrożek, Sławomir 54, 219
Muller, Heiner 247, 283
Munch, Edvard 210, 251
Munk, Andrzej 54
Muselmann/Muselmänner (Muslims) 120,
	129–35, 139, 145
Mystery Buffo (Mayakovski) 54
mysterium tremendum 94, 226

N

Natanson, Wojciech 96
National Theatre in Warsaw 105
Neal, Arthur 44
*Neighbors: The Destruction of the Jewish
	Community in Jedwabne, Poland* (Gross) 41
New Deliverance, The (Witkacy) 216
*New Forms in Painting and Misconceptions Around
	Them* (Witkacy) 216
Niezgoda, Andrzej 5, 64–5
Niziołek, Grzegorz 39, 45, 127, 132–3,
	141, 190
Norsworthy, Naomi 233
Norwid, Cyprian Kamil 33
Noskowski, Witold 91
Notes from the Warsaw Ghetto (Ringelblum) 38
Notes on Aesthetics (Witkacy) 216
Novalis 122
November Night (Wyspiański) 91
Nowakowski, Zygmunt 105
Nowara, Jan 222
Nowicki, Jan 276

O

Obama, Barack 41
objet trouvé 12, 225
O'Brien, Mathilda 201
Ochman, Agata 222
Odrzywolski, Sławomir 92
Odysseus 185–6, 255
Oedipus Rex (Sophocles) 99
O'Harra, Brookes 222
Old Charwoman 243
Old Man Exhibitionist 193
Old Man in the Toilet 193, 227, 272
Old Man Pederast 193, 200
Old Man with a Bicycle 200, 271–2

Old Man from the Lavatory 200, 237
Old Theatre in Cracow 50, 279
Oliver, Cordelia 207, 212, 246
Oliver, Edith 87, 138–9
Olszowka, Iwona 222
"On Not Knowing Greek" (Woolf) 2
Open Theatre 6
Orling, Elliot 246
Orpheus 255
Orpheus (Cocteau) 54
Osiński, Zbigniew 7, 10, 14, 22–3, 28, 105–6, 111, 137, 148–9
Osterwa, Julius 5, 61, 68
Owczarski, Wojciech 224
Ozick, Cynthia 229

P

Paleone-Bladaczka, Professor (*Ferdydurke*) 241
Pan Tadeusz (Mickiewicz) 19
Panasiewicz, Jerzy 109, 117, 148
Panoramic Sea Happening (Kantor) 189
Panthei Mythos 261
Papp, Joseph 89
"Para-ra-ra" (Raczak) 69
Paris (*Iliad*) 100–101, 106
Parson ,Gordon 201, 211
Pascal, Blaise 27
Pawłowski, Roman 152, 280, 281
Pavis, Patrice 4,
Pensées (Pascal) 27
Perez, Rolando 237, 259, 264
Performance Group 6
Peryt, Ryszard 105, 152
Petersburg, Jerzy 142
Picasso, Pablo 220
Piech, Krzysztof 222
Pietrusińska, Zofia 222
Pilecki, Witold 36–7
Pilikian, Hovhannes I. 59
Piłsudski, Józef 242
Pimko, Professor (*Ferdydurke*) 240–41
Plato 50
Planchon, Roger 50
Pleśniarowicz, Krzysztof 10, 104, 186, 196, 203, 232, 257, 269–70, 281
Plunka, Gene 31
Poetics (Aristotle) 3
Poirot-Delpech, Bertrand 74
Poland's Angry Romantic: Two Poems and a Play by Juliusz Słowacki (2009) 18
Polanski, Roman 4, 54, 63, 243

Polish martyrology 121
Polish messianism 14
Polkowski, Ignacy 100
Pomerantz-Meltzer, Roza 34
poor theatre/ *teatr biedny*/ *teatr ubogi* 12, 28, 39, 55, 243, 259
Poor Theatre: a series of simulacra, The (Wooster Group) 152–3
Popkin, Henry 78
Pornography (Gombrowicz) 238
Postdramatic Theatre (Lehmann) 45, 226, 247, 283
post-traumatic stress disorder (PTSD) 43–5, 253
Pragmatists (Witkacy) 216
Priam 100, 142
Professing Performance (Jackson) 4
Prokesch, Władysław 91, 104
Prometheus 242
Pronaszko, Andrzej 277
Protestilas and Laodamia (Wyspiański) 91
Proszanek, Andrzej 104
Proszanek, Zbigniew 104
Proust, Marcel 233
Prus, Maciej 60
Psychology of Childhood, The (Norsworthy, Whitley) 233
Public Broadcast Laboratory 74
Puławski, Franciszek 92
Pułka, Leszek 154
Pure Form 221
Purim 23, 247
Puzyna, Konstanty 11, 13–14, 52, 72–3, 96, 107–8, 194, 197, 225, 230–31

Q

Quay Brothers 6
Quignard, Pascal 142

R

Rachel 118, 145
Rachwał, Józef 102–3
Raczak, Lech 69
Raczyński, Bolesław 104
rat trap machine 192
Reality of the Lowest Rank 195, 258–9, 264, 267
Rebecca 102, 106, 142
Rebecca/Cassandra 142
Reduta 5, 61

Reichardt, Jasia 211
Regular Old Man 193, 195
Rembrandt, Harmenszoon van Rinn 115
Replica (also *Requiem*) (Szajna) 114
Retired, The (also as *Old Age Pensioner, The*) (Schulz) 227
Return of Odysseus (Kantor's play) 186–7, 269
Return of Odysseus (Wyspiański's text) 91, 185–6
Reynolds, Paul 205, 213
Ribera, Jusepe de 115
Rich, Frank 195, 213–14
Richards, Thomas 139
Rilke, Rainer Maria 122
Ringelblum, Emanuel 37–8
Robbins, Tim 74
Roman mythology 215, 242
Romantic martyrology 13
Romantic poetry 107, 241
Romantic tradition 12–14, 18, 94–5, 107, 239
Roose-Evans, James 84
Rosenzweig, Franz 258
Ross, Rochelle H. 239
Roszewski, Wojciech 127
Różewicz, Tadeusz 54, 62, 126, 194, 264
Rozhulantyna (*Tumor Brainowicz*) 223, 225, 227
Rühle, Günther 2
Rychlicka, Mira 193
Rychlicki, Stanisław 193
Ryn, Zdzisław 130
Rzewiczok, Urszula 235

S

Sanatorium Under the Sign of The Hourglass (Schulz) 215, 229, 231, 255
  Wojciech J. Has adaptation 230
Sandauer, Adam 32, 34, 215, 244, 254, 276, 277, 279
Santner, Eric 112
Sartre, Jean-Paul, 43
Save From Oblivion, To (Kantor) 273
Scenes from Dead Class (Miklaszewski) 280
Schechner, Richard 3, 6, 7 25–6, 56, 71, 77–80, 153
Schiller, Leon 51–2, 91, 105, 107, 277
Schindler's List (Spielberg) 31
Schmidt, Sandra 88
Scholem, Gershom 258
Schopenhauer, Arthur 122

Schossburg, Gavri'el ben Yehoshu'a 32
Schreyer, Alfred 265
Schudrich, Michael 37
Schulz, Bruno 9, 46, 120, 196, 211, 215–16, 224, 227, 229–34, 236–9, 241, 243, 245–6, 254–5, 258–9, 263–5, 267, 280
Segel, Harold B. 17–18
Shallcross, Bożena 264
Shakespeare, Our Contemporary (Kott) 217
Shakespeare, William 9, 27, 49, 276
Shakuntala (Kalidasa) 54
Shepherd 186
Shivaslondon, Mark 75
Shmeruk, Chone 34–5
Shoah 122–3, 259
Shoah (Lanzmann) 30–31
Shoemakers (Kantor) 261
Shoemakers (Witkacy) 216
Sienkiewicz, Marian 242
Sieradzki, Jacek 219
Simon, John 44, 76–8, 83–4, 134–5, 231
Sina, Tadeusz 91
Sings and Significations in the Theatre of Tadeusz Kantor (Jędrzejczyk) 196
Sinko, Tadeusz 101
Sitarz, Wojciech 154
Siwulak, Roman 193
Sketch of the Modern Erotic (Różewicz) 264
Skiba-Lickel, Aldona 269
Skiwski, J. W. 239
Skoczylas, Władysław 220
Skotnicki, Jan 44, 254
Skotnicki, Stanisław 97
Skuszanka, Krystyna 5, 104–5
Sloterdijk, Peter 67
Slowiak, James 8
Słowacki, Juliusz 12, 18–20, 31, 51–2, 54, 56, 72, 91, 94, 97, 262
Słowacki Theatre in Cracow 91, 98, 104
Small Rock, A (Wyspiański) 91
Smożewski, Ryszard 223
Sofsky, Wolfgang 129
Sokoloff, Naomi B. 32
Solomon 242
Solski, Leon 91, 95
Sołtyk, Roman 97
Somnambulist Prostitute 193, 200, 236
Sonderkommando 142–3, 145
Sontag, Susan 3
Sophocles 99
Sosnowski, Józef 105

Spielberg, Steven 31
Spivak, Gayatri 25, 43
Spring (Schulz) 233
Stalin, Joseph 53–4, 66, 68, 70, 126–7, 275
Stangret-Kantor, Maria 193
Stangret, Leszek 193
Staniewski, Włodzimierz 280–81
Stanisław, Saint 93, 97, 103
Stanislavski, Konstantin Sergeyevich 5,
    11–12, 49, 55, 63, 68, 139, 272
Starewicz, Artur 201
Starowiejska, Ewa 152
Stasio, Marilyn 203, 206, 210
State School of Theatre in Cracow 59
Stein, Gertrude 219
Stein, Peter 2
Steinlauf, Michael C. 39
Stena, Jan 95
Seniuk, Anna 222
Stern, Anatol 221
Steward, Ellen 11, 74, 203
Stobrecka, Maria 102
Stokłosa, Jacek 187
Stoss, Veit 113
Stranger, the 193
Street- and Sleep-Walker 237, 271
Street of Crocodiles (Schulz) 215, 229
Strugglers for Poland (Ascherson) 17
Study of Hamlet, A (Grotowski's play) 55, 110
Study of Hamlet, A (Wyspiański's text) 55,
    94, 110
Survey of Polish Literature and Culture, A
    (Kridl) 19
Święcicki, Jan Maria 12, 55, 188, 212,
    224, 261
Święcicki, Klaudiusz 279
Swinarski, Konrad 5, 61, 67–8
Szajna, Józef 5, 106, 114–15, 135
Szczawiński, Józef 45
Szkudlarek, Ewa 218
Szułczyński, Wojciech 6, 279
Szybist, Maciej 104, 197, 200
Szydłowski, Roman 45, 196, 200, 253
Szyjkowski, Marian 220
Szymborska, Wisława 17, 62

T

Taborski, Bolesław 62
tabulae rasae 28
Tadeusz Kantor (Witts) 9
Tadeusz Kantor – Theatre (Klossowicz) 9

Tairov, Alexander 50
Takahashi, Yosunari 213
Tanakh (Hebrew Bible) 99
Targoń, Joanna 153–4
Tatzer, John 207
Taylor, Nina 97–8
Teatr Miejski (in Lwów) 104
Teatr Ósmego Dnia 5
Teatr Polski (in Poznań) 105
Teatr Rapsodyczny (in Cracow) 105
Teatr Zar 5
Temkine, Raymonde 8, 25–6, 52, 58, 62,
    73–4, 109, 115, 119, 137, 202, 212
Tango Milonga 142
Terlecki, Tymon 19, 21, 50, 95–6, 98,
    100–103
Teschke, Holger 113
Tęcza, Ewa 105
The Drama Review (*TDR*) 6, 78
"Theater Place, The" (Kantor) 267
Theatre (Witkacy) 216
Theatre as a Vehicle (Kolankiewicz) 79
Theatre: A Way to Seeing (Barranger) 8
Theatre of a Two-Headed Calf 222
Theatre of Death 12, 14, 22, 39, 200, 257,
    265, 281
Theatre of Grotowski, The (Kumiega) 7
Theatre of the Absurd 212, 219, 227, 238
Theatre School in Cracow 49
Theatre/Theatre (Fortier) 7
Theatre/Theory/Theatre (Gerould) 19
Theatre Versus Ritual (Grotowski) 134
Theory of Pure Form (Witkacy) 216–17, 219,
    221, 227
Thirteen Row Theatre in Opole 8, 53,
    59, 137
This Way for the Gas, Ladies and Gentlemen
    (Borowski) 111
Three Thoughts of Henryk Ligenza (Krasiński)
    97, 99
Titans (*Tumor Brainowicz*) 222
Today Is My Birthday (Kantor) 193
Toller, Ernst 250
Torah 15, 32
torture machine 192
Toulouse-Lautrec, Henri de 210
Towards a Poor Theatre (Grotowski) 6, 55–6,
    62, 75, 78, 138, 150
*Tragic Fate of Doctor Faust, According to
    Christopher Marlowe, The* (Grotowski)
    54–5

Trans-Atlantic (Gombrowicz) 238
Treatise on Mannequins (Schulz) 227, 263
Trip to the Museum (Borowski) 126
Tropical Madness (Witkacy) 216
Trzciński, Teofil 104
Tulane Drama Review 57
Tumor (*Tumor Brainiowicz*) 222–3, 227
Tumor Brainiowicz (Witkacy) 9, 215, 219–28, 237
Turner, Victor 3
Tymicki, Jerzy 5, 64–5, 199
Tyszka, Juliusz 24–5, 78
Tzara, Tristan 218

U

Ubu Roi (Jarry) 17, 90, 223
Ulysses (Joyce) 92
"Unburied Ones, The" (Greń) 261
Un-Divine Comedy, The (Krasiński) 18
Underhill, Karen 258
Updike, John 229

V

Vaizey, Marina 213–14, 250, 265
Vakhtangov, Evgeny Bagrationovich 49, 260
Valse Français (Grandma's Waltz) 227, 235
Van der Kolk, Bessel A. 252
Varsovian Anthem (Wyspiański) 91
Veaux, Eric 8

W

Wagner, Richard 21, 96, 122
Wajda, Andrzej 54, 63, 193–5, 197
Walaciński, Adam 105
Walenrodyzm 79
Walicki, Andrzej 13
Wardle, Irving 6, 62, 87–8, 144, 265
Water Hen, The (Kantor's play) 191–2, 262
Water Hen, The (Witkacy's drama) 188
Warsaw Theatre Rampa 280
Wąsowicz, Tadeusz 123
Wedding, The (Wyspiański) 91, 96, 105, 154
Wedekind, Frank 250
Weil, Simone 56
Weiss, Marta (*The Last Stage*) 127
Wełmiński, Andrzej 193
Wetzsteon, Rose 70, 76–7, 138
Wgrzdągiel, Józef 248
Where Are the Snows of Yesterday (Kantor) 193
Whitley, Mary Theodora 233

Wichowska, Joanna 59, 153
Wielopole, Wielopole (Kantor) 193, 199, 204, 247, 279
Wiesel, Elie 119
Wierciak, Zygmunt 104
Wilder, Thornton 27
Wilson, Robert 6, 8, 204
Wiśniewska, Natalia 239
With Grotowski, Theatre Is Just a Form (Allain, Ban, Ziółkowski) 8
Witkacy's Tumor (Dubowski) 222
Witkiewicz, Ignacy Stanisław (Witkacy) 9, 46, 54, 187–90, 192, 211, 215–28, 232, 237–8, 243–5, 267, 282
Witkiewicz, Stanisław 12–13, 216
Witlin, Józef 16
Wirth, Andrzej 119–20, 143, 219
Wittgenstein, Ludwig 66
Witts, Noel 9, 210
Własta, Andrzej 142
Wojdowski, Bogdan 120, 128, 132
Wojtowicz, Agnieszka 23, 108, 110
Wolf, Wolfgang 132
Wolford, Lisa 7, 117
Woman Behind the Window 193, 200, 225, 237, 271
Woman Drowned in a Bathtub 191
Woman with a Mechanical Cradle 193, 195, 200, 225, 227, 237, 248–9, 271–2
Woolf, Virginia 2,
Wooster Group 6, 152–3
"Work of Art in the Age of Mechanical Reproduction, The" (Benjamin) 82
World Made of Stone, The (Borowski) 8
World War I 13, 26, 33–4, 104, 199, 200, 211, 213, 216, 239, 242, 245, 257, 276, 281, 283
World War II 5, 13, 29–30, 32, 35–6, 38, 41–2, 45, 52, 54, 62, 68, 72, 105, 109, 112, 126, 187, 191, 200, 210–11, 213, 219, 229, 237, 239, 241, 244, 256, 259, 275–6, 281, 283
  Ghetto Uprising 36, 41
  Home Army (Armia Krajowa, AK) 36–7, 54, 111
  Warsaw Uprising 17, 36–8, 41, 111
Woszczerowicz, Jacek 61
Wrocławski's Modern Theatre 153
Wróbel, Marta 126
Wyczółkowski, Leon 105

Wyspiański's Akropolis (Flaszen) 6
Wyspiański, Stanisław 6, 7, 12, 19, 21–3,
    46, 55–6, 65, 73, 79, 86–7, 90–105,
    107–10, 112–13, 116, 118, 121, 133,
    141–2, 147–8, 150–55, 185–6, 244–5,
    275, 277

Y

yoga 58, 69
Young, B. A. 251
Young Polishness 244

Z

Zakrzewski, Janusz 222
Zamyatin, Evgeni 235
Zarycki, Andrzej 222
Zavadsky, Yiru 65
Zawistowski, Władysław 101
Zienkowicz, Leon 92
Zimnica-Kuziola, Emilia 250
Ziółkowski, Grzegorz 8, 55
Ziomek, Jerzy 16
Zygmunt August (Wyspiański) 91

www.ingramcontent.com/pod-product-compliance
Lightning Source LLC
Chambersburg PA
CBHW021814300426
44114CB00009BA/178